The Course of
American
Democratic Thought

RALPH HENRY GABRIEL
STERLING PROFESSOR OF HISTORY
YALE UNIVERSITY

SECOND EDITION

THE RONALD PRESS COMPANY · NEW YORK

Library of Congress Catalog Card Number: 56–6263

This book is for C. D. G.

FOREWORD

In the middle years of the twentieth century, Americans were attempting to adjust their thinking to the possession of vast power and to the responsibilities that went with it. They had carried the battle in a global war. They had then guarded and aided ancient nations, wounded and endangered by a rampant communist totalitarianism. In World War II and in the years immediately following it Americans, with the aid of their allies, had preserved for the time being the principles of human freedom and dignity whose formulation had been the greatest consummation of Western civilization. Scarcely more than three centuries before these momentous events the first Englishmen had built at Jamestown their habitations and a church. In the twentieth century the center of power in Western civilization had moved across the Atlantic to rest with a people who had so recently originated in an outthrust of Europe.

No one can grasp the full power and meaning of this new America, so suddenly come into being. The story of the rise of the United States and of the evolution of the American variant of Western civilization resembles a tall tale of the frontier. Perhaps for this reason, perhaps because of the conditions and contingencies of an age of revolution and violence, mid-twentieth-century Americans have more and more looked backward for understanding to the origins of their institutions.

Every civilization rests on a body of knowledge and changes as that knowledge grows. American history began in that seventeenth century in which Western men first mastered the method of science. The story of American culture has paced with that of science. The trench of the archeologist cuts through two, sometimes three or more culture levels, each distinguishable by its artifacts. The historian finds something analogous to culture levels in the evolving civilization of the United States. The eighteenth-century scythe and spinning wheel suggest a culture in the handicraft stage. The millstones lying in creek beds below broken masonry dams imply the crude nineteenth-century beginnings of modern industrialism. The assembly line characterized the first half of the twentieth century as the nuclear reactor does its second half. These changing artifacts express in material form the course of evolution in the continuing struggle to maintain life.

But scientific knowledge has bounds, even though its frontiers move out swiftly and far. There are problems which it can illuminate but for which it can give no final answers. Every person faces as a condition of conscious life two questions: first, what is the desirable relation of the individual to the society of which he is a part; second, what is his relation to the mystery that envelops him. The two questions cannot be dissociated. The second query leads to philosophical and religious attempts to explain the meaning and significance of life. These hypotheses and beliefs have an intimate bearing on those political and social theories, those proposed or accepted patterns of the good life, that spring from attempts to discover the nature of a man's relation to his fellows.

The historian finds culture levels also in the deposit of ideas left by time. In New England the bottom culture level in ideas is to be found in seventeenth-century Puritanism. In Pennsylvania it is Quakerism. In the Southern colonies the investigator discovers a transplanted gentility together with Anglicanism shaping the lives of the upper classes. Above this level lie the remains left by the eighteenth-century Enlightenment. Still above this is a confused stratum showing evidence of tension and conflict among an old Puritanism, a declining Deism, a new Unitarianism, a radical Transcendentalism, and a simple evangelical Protestantism. The present inquiry begins with this last stratum.

This book attempts a study of the social beliefs that emerged among Americans to serve as guides for action, as standards by which to judge the quality of social life, and as goals to inspire humane living. The roots of these beliefs run far back in the tradition of the West. They began to assume their particular American emphases as soon as Englishmen, transplanted across the Atlantic, established permanent settlements between the sea and the forest. In the two hundred eight years between 1607 and 1815, when the Second War of Independence came to an end, Americans evolved a system of beliefs and values that was to condition all their later history. The present book takes up the record of that system at the time when Americans, freed for the first time from European involvements, turned their primary attention to North American tasks.

Americans by 1815 had formulated three major beliefs, each a complex of ideas. The first tenet assumed the dignity of human personality and asserted the conviction that that dignity could be realized only when the individual was free to express himself and to participate in decisions of vital import to him. The second tenet assumed that principles of universal validity underlie the common life of men in society, the application of which to affairs makes possible the realization of freedom and dignity. The third tenet asserted that the nation created in 1776 exists as a corporate entity not only to further the peace and security of its citizens but to aid—at home and, by example, abroad—the cause of freedom and humane living. These three tenets, either singly or together, have been lauded, criticized, doubted, denied, and often allowed to fall into neglect. They have undergone evolution in a changing America and a changing world. Their history after 1815 provides the theme of this book.

The writer originally concluded his exploration of these themes in 1940, when this book was published in its first form. The background of the time was significant. In 1940 France fell before the armed forces of a momentarily triumphant totalitarianism. The Royal Air Force fought and won the Battle of Britain. Americans, irresolute and divided on the policy of neutrality, faced an uncertain future. It was a dark time in which swift change blurred perspective. The events of the fifteen following years have clarified the prospect somewhat, though uncertainties and anxieties persist. In this present attempt to trace the course of American democratic thought the writer has carefully scanned the original work. The analysis and exposition of the basic themes set forth in Chapter 2 have been revised and expanded. New knowledge derived from the vastly productive American scholarship of these fifteen years has made possible revision of the discussion of particular individuals, especially Melville, Thoreau, Calhoun, Henry George, and Edward Bellamy. Beginning with William James at the turn of the century, the account has been largely rewritten and greatly enlarged, as required by a dynamic and swiftly moving age.

But the objective of the new work is the same as that of the old. It is to achieve such insights as may be gained in a study of the past to illumine partially a present, that, like all presents, is obscured by shadows. "History," Thomas Mann remarked in *Joseph and his Brothers*, "is that which has happened and that which goes on happening in time. But it is also the stratified record upon which we set our feet, the ground beneath us; and the deeper the roots of our be-

ing go down into the layers that lie below and beyond the . . . confines of our ego, yet at the same time feed and condition it, . . . the
heavier is our life with thought, and the weightier is the soul of
our flesh."

Ralph Henry Gabriel

New Haven
   February, 1956

ACKNOWLEDGMENTS

THE AUTHOR IS GRATEFUL to the following publishing houses for permission to make quotations from books published by them: to the Central Book Company for quotations from Oliver Wendell Holmes, *His Book Notices and Uncollected Papers;* to the Harvard University Press for quotations from *Walt Whitman's Workshop* by C. J. Furness, from *Fugitive Essays* by Josiah Royce, from *The Fifth Amendment Today* by E. N. Griswold, from Charles Saunders Peirce, *Collected Works;* to G. P. Putnam's Sons for quotations from *Recollections and Impressions* by Octavius Brooks Frothingham, from *Young Ward's Diary* by B. J. Stern, from *The Plantation Negro as a Freeman* by P. A. Bruce, from *Glimpses of the Cosmos* by L. F. Ward, from *Social Facts and Forces* by Washington Gladden; to the Viking Press for quotations from *Kamongo* by Homer W. Smith; to Charles Scribner's Sons for quotations from Theodore Roosevelt's *Works*, from *The Southerner's Problem* by Thomas Nelson Page, from *The Challenge to Liberty* by Herbert Hoover, from *Philosophies at War* by Fulton J. Sheen; to The Round Table Press for quotations from *Statesmanship and Religion* by Henry Wallace; to Little, Brown and Company for quotations from *The Thought and Character of William James* by R. B. Perry, from *The Good Society* by Walter Lippmann; to Henry Holt and Company for quotations from *The Frontier in American History* by F. J. Turner; to the University of Wisconsin Press for quotations from *Early Writings of Frederick Jackson Turner* by Fulmer Mood; to Longmans, Green and Company for a quotation from *Varieties of Religious Experience* by William James; to Appleton-Century-Crofts for quotations from *The Labor Movement in the United States, 1660–1895* by Norman J. Ware, from *The Strenuous Life* by Theodore Roosevelt; to Harcourt, Brace and Company for quotations from *God's Gold* by John T. Flynn, from *The Autobiography of Lincoln Steffens*, from *America's Strategy in World Politics* by Nicholas Spykman, from *Catholicism in America;* to E. P. Dutton and Company for quotations from *Labor and the Common Welfare* by Samuel Gompers; to Harper & Brothers for quotations from *Acres of Diamonds* by R. H. Conwell, from *Armaments and Arbitration* by A. T. Mahan, from *American Socialism: its Aims and Practical Program* by Harry W. Laidler, from *The End of Illusion* by H. W. Smith; to The Macmillan Company for quotations from *The New Basis of Civilization* by Simon Patten, from *The Ground Under our Feet* by R. T. Ely, from *Mount Vernon on the Potomac* by G. King, from *The Open Door at Home* by Charles A. Beard, from *Law and the Lawyers* by E. S. Robinson, from *Walden Two* by B. F. Skinner, from *Science and Human Behaviour* by B. F. Skinner; to the Yale University Press for quotations from *Symbols of Government* by Thurman Arnold, from *The Folklore of Capitalism* by Thurman Arnold, from *Essays of William Graham Sumner*, ed. by A. G. Keller and M. Davie, from *Psychoanalysis and Religion* by Erich Fromm; to Houghton Mifflin Company for quotations from *The Education of Henry Adams*, from *Fifty Years* by William Lawrence; to Doubleday, Doran and Company for quotations from *The New Freedom* by Woodrow Wilson, from *The Life of Andrew Carnegie* by B. J. Hendrick; to Ginn and Company for quotations from *Folkways* by W. G. Sumner; to the Paulist Fathers for quotations from *The Life of Father Hecker* by W. Elliott; to Alfred A. Knopf for quotations from *Characteristically American* by R. B. Perry; to the Duke University Press for a quotation from *Melville's Use of the Bible* by N. Wright; to the John Day Company for a quotation from *Can the Schools Create a New Society* by G. S. Counts; to The Free Press, Glencoe, Ill., for quotations from *American Thought* by M. R. Cohen; to American Book Company for a quotation from *Introduction to Sociology* by Kimball Young; to W. W. Norton & Company for a quotation from *Sovereign Reason* by E. Nagel.

The author also wishes to note his obligation and to express his thanks to the following: to Thomas R. Drake of Haverford College for the assistance in the study of Comte's influence in the United States and of the Lincoln myth; to Norman Pearson, Yale University, for important suggestions; to Hajo Holborn, Yale University, for suggestions concerning German economic thought; to Arthur Bestor, University of Illinois, for contributions to the study of the religion of humanity; to C. Howard Hopkins, Stetson University, for aid in the study of the social gospel; to Frontis Johnson of Davidson College for contributions concerning the evolution of the planning state; to Edgar Robinson, Stanford University, for discussions of the nature of American democracy; to the late E. S. Robinson and the late Underhill Moore, both of Yale, for assistance in gaining an understanding of the naturalistic approach to law; to

Stanley T. Williams, Yale University, long a colleague in a course in American intellectual history, for aid in understanding the literary history of the United States; to John Farrell, Catholic University, and to the late Richard Purcell, Catholic University, for help in the investigation of Isaac Thomas Hecker; to Robert C. L. Scott, Williams College, for assistance in the study of the cult of the Constitution; to Peter Murdock, Yale University, for aid in studying the work of mid-twentieth century anthropology; to Erwin Goodenough, Yale University, for aid in understanding the Greek concept of Natural Law; to H. R. Warfell, University of Florida, for criticism of the first manuscript; to Harold H. Saunders of the Yale Graduate School for help derived from his doctoral dissertation that deals with changing ideas in the early twentieth century of the individual and his relation to society; to Keith Melder of the Yale Graduate School for his study of mid-twentieth century literature on culture and personality. The author wishes also to express appreciation for the cooperation of the staff of the Yale University Library.

CONTENTS

I

The doctrines of the American democratic faith examined and set against the social and intellectual background of the Middle Period

II

The American democratic faith passes safely through the fires of sectional controversy

III

After Appomattox the democratic faith is modified and developed, an attempt to bring it into harmony with the new naturalism of Darwinian evolution and to make it useful in a society undergoing industrial revolution

xiii

IV

American democratic thought is conditioned by the coming of a new intellectual age

V

The American democratic faith survives in a time of revolution and violence

I

THE DOCTRINES OF THE AMERICAN DEMOCRATIC
FAITH EXAMINED AND SET AGAINST THE SOCIAL
AND INTELLECTUAL BACKGROUND OF THE
MIDDLE PERIOD

Chapter 1

MID-NINETEENTH-CENTURY
PATTERNS OF INDIVIDUALISM

On a winter day in the 1850's, according to a tradition of the West, a party of mountain men, fleeing a band of hostile Sioux, sought refuge in an isolated canyon whose entrance was concealed by a growth of cedar. To their astonishment they saw in a clearing beneath a cliff a starving horse, facing a numbing wind. One of the party recognized the mustang as Nez Perce, the mount of the lonely trapper, Bill Williams. Not far away they found the body of the old hunter, reclining against a tree, the feet stretched toward some charred pine logs half buried in snow. Bill Williams had died, as he had lived, alone. His fellows among the fraternity of free trappers normally went in small companies into the wilderness for mutual assistance against the dangers of nature and of the Indians. Williams' success in meeting single-handed the hazards of the mountains made his name a legend. His exploits and his death became part of the oral literature of the West. A peak in Arizona was named in his honor. Bill Williams personified the ideal of the American frontier. He was the individualist who never surrendered his independence.

In the western mountains the prospector followed the trapper. First in California and then in the broken country to the eastward mining towns appeared. Silver City in the high Sierras reached in the 1850's a population of some ten thousand in a few weeks after the first news of the strike. For months it was a center of feverish activity. Then it vanished and its name was added to a long and growing list of mountain ghost-towns. Silver City illustrates a contrast between Europe and America. In the upland hamlets of Switzerland the same families have lived for generations. There individual men are born and die, but the community goes on through decades

3

and centuries. On the mining frontier it was normal for the individual to outlast the community. Camps formed and dissolved while the miner still lived. Those towns which, surviving the first months, persisted for a decade or more displayed again and again the same cycle of development: the high hopes of those first on the ground, the swift creation of a camp without form and without standards, the plunge into anarchy, the profits of parasitic individuals, mob violence, lynch law, and the final development of social controls. One wonders what effect a sojourn in Silver City would have had upon the social philosophy of Thomas Hobbes, of John Locke, or of Jean Jacques Rousseau. Did this unintended social experiment demonstrate the soundness of the Hobbes contention that the natural condition of men is liberty, equality, and war? Would the history of Silver City have suggested to Locke that the rights of men are derived from nature and are guaranteed by a social contract? Or would this mining community have persuaded Rousseau that human nature is fundamentally good? All of these philosophies had been brought across the Atlantic and were part of the culture of eastern Americans. But they seemed remote from the realities of Silver City. On the frontier, civilization was always moving from the simpler to the more complex. Out of such a social background came not the elaborate rationalizations of a Hobbes or a Locke but two convictions so fundamental to the thinking of the frontiersman as scarcely to be recognized for the basic postulates they were. The first was that human affairs should be thought of in terms of the individual; the second was that progress is normal and that the future promises more than has been realized in the present.

∽

The simplified patterns of individualism of the western mountain region became more complex in the agricultural communities of the continental interior. Some of these, as in Kansas, were only beginning to take form in the 1850's. Others, in Illinois, in Ohio, or in western New York had decades of history behind them. These American communities displayed one striking contrast to the typical peasant villages of France or Germany. The compact little towns of European husbandmen stood often at the base of a hill once dominated by a castle. The hazards of life in the feudal period had caused men to draw close together, like a herd of bison, for protection against their enemies, and social inertia had caused the retention of the old pattern. Seventeenth-century farmers in New England, facing Indians not yet demoralized by the advance of the whites, had built their homes in villages protected by a blockhouse or a stockade. But in the middle decades of the nineteenth century, fear of invasion by foreign enemies was nonexistent among the citizens of the United States, and apprehension of Indian depredations was limited to a few localities where the tepees of the red men were close to the fields of the farmers. As a result, husbandmen could scatter and could establish isolated homesteads. The compact New England village did not become important west of the Appalachians. One of the chief conditioning factors not only for agricultural communities but for all American civilization in this period was a sense of military security.

Even the physical characteristics of the agricultural community in the Upper Mississippi Valley expressed its dominant mood and ideas. The center of the community was the county seat, a village of from one to three or four thousand people. Here the courthouse, built usually in the monumental style of the Greek Revival, symbolized the dignity of the Law in a society governed by its own citizens. Near by on the main street clustered the mercantile and financial establishments of those more ambitious entrepreneurs who aspired to patronage from the entire county. Above the show windows of the stores were others on which were printed the names of hopeful lawyers who, for a consideration, would assist individuals in their disputes with their fellows. The village skyline was dominated by the steeples of Protestant churches in which, each Sunday, ministers preached that the salvation of society could only be achieved by the saving of individual souls. From the unpaved streets of such a local metropolis radiated highways covered with dust in summer and transformed into bottomless sloughs in the spring. These country roads had something to do with rural individualism, for they made travel slow and difficult. They emphasized that factor of isolation which was so important in compelling the husbandman to think in terms of self-dependence. At occasional highway intersections were hamlets in which a general store with a post office on the counter, a church or two, a school house, and a blacksmith shop were the center of a cluster of houses. About these were scattered farmsteads separated from one another by distances ranging from a quarter to a half mile. In rural New York the county seats averaged some twenty miles apart; in some more sparsely settled grasslands of the western half of the Mississippi Valley the distances were greater. Travel beyond the boundaries of his own community was for the farmer a relatively rare occurrence.

In such an environment the pattern of rural individualism took form. Because small farmers dominated the life of most northern states west of the Appalachian Mountains in the middle decade of the nineteenth century, this pattern was of great importance in American civilization. The personality of the typical husbandman of the '50's was not warped by the routine of a narrow specialty or dwarfed by slavery to a machine. The farmer was a rounded man: a producer of crops and a breeder of animals, a mechanic who could mend a wagon or shoe a horse, an entrepreneur who understood that the conditions of survival compelled him to develop the shrewdness of the trader and the foresight of the wise investor. He was an empiricist whose common-sense materialism was for many softened by Christian idealism. Life for him was a compound of struggle against nature, contacts with his animals, and personal relationships with his family and neighbors. He met and gossiped with the latter in one of his three clubs, the church, the saloon, or the circle about the stove in the general store. Inevitably he was an individualist. His thinking was cast in the mold of the problems and relations of individuals. His social view was atomistic. He was only vaguely aware of that abstraction, the State, which bound the atoms together. In his community the State was not symbolized, as in Europe, by soldiers or a uniformed police. He saw the State engaged in no collectivist activity beyond the carrying of mail. Even the building and care of the roads which he traveled was the responsibility of the local community, and in many regions the farmer by custom and law gave each year a fixed amount of labor in working on the highways.

Aside from the distant State and an occasional unimportant Owenite or Fourieristic communistic experiment the only collectivism known to the mid-nineteenth-century husbandman was that of the home. The fundamental economic and social unit of the rural community was the family, a partnership in which the farmer and his sons performed the heavier outdoor tasks while his wife and daughters not only cared for the house but made the butter, preserved the fruit and vegetables, and fabricated at least part of the clothing. Outside of the church, the general store, and the saloon the only social life was in the home. There were the parties and there the weddings and the funerals. The home was the basic economic and social unit of rural America.

One of the principal reasons for the tremendous success of Harriet Beecher Stowe's antislavery tract, *Uncle Tom's Cabin*, was the fact that she made the tragedy of Uncle Tom that of the broken home. Again and again the Kentucky slave, sold down the river, seemed on the point of being able to reunite his family, but in the end he failed. The tragedy of the defeated slave was heightened by the subplot in which Eliza's home was reconstituted in Canada. Mrs. Stowe spoke a language which the common man could understand. The implication of her story was that, if the arrangements of American society were changed for the Negroes so that they could found homes free from the fear of forcible disruption, the nation would be on the way to that better day forecast by the native philosophy of progress.

The emphasis upon the family in this individualistic culture of the mid-nineteenth century was also suggested by the number and popularity of the "home" songs of the period. Stephen Foster, whose *Old Folks at Home* first swept the nation in the same year in which Mrs. Stowe's novel appeared, was the greatest of these song writers. Foster sensed that the individualism of the common people was supported by a simple religious faith which promised rest for the weary and compensation for the suffering. The thought structure of this faith was built up in terms of the home. In *Old Black Joe*, written on the eve of secession, Foster gave perfect expression to the mood and the faith of the religion which satisfied rural individualism and sanctified the rural home. The vague and unreal Negro of the song was none other than the man who had faced the buffets of life standing on his own feet and who now, weary and worn out, was thankfully making his way to the peace and security of that final and larger home beyond the skies.

〜

Among the papers left at death by Ulrich Bonnell Phillips, one of the best of the students of the plantation of the Old South, was found the following fragment. "[The children of the imported Negro captives of the eighteenth and of the early nineteenth centuries] and their children's children, having no memory of African scenes or tribal ways or Negro languages, cheerfully made the plantation life their own, for the most part accepting slavery as a matter of course and adopting their masters much as a child appropriates his parents or a pupil his teacher. This mutuality was the swifter and stronger in growth because white children had black nurses and playmates; and when grown to maturity they could never look upon 'their' Negroes as mere chattels, whatever the law might say. A plantation, in fact, was a home of very diverse human beings, brought up in an isolated group with a prospect of lifelong relationship one with another, each with all. It was a small and closely knit community, each member knowing the traits and habits of every other, and each more or less conscious that his own peace and comfort would depend upon the good will and esteem, or at least the tolerance, of the rest. This pattern of life did not permit the masters to remain mere Englishmen or Frenchmen, any more than it permitted Negroes to remain Africans. It put a new impress upon all and sundry, producing new types and the rudiments of new philosophies. The blacks were in a degree civilized and Christianized whether they would or no; the whites found their servants often engagingly responsive and found themselves vested with all the responsibility which goes with power over subordinates. As one of the many paradoxes of history, many a slave acquired pride and self-respect and many a master and mistress was mellowed by the very harshness of the law which gave them privilege. The slaves in their service must be fed, clothed and sheltered, sanitated at all times, nursed when ill, cheered when down-hearted, spurred when indolent, disciplined when unruly. The gamut of administrative concern was endless, and the need of attention constant. The scheme of life was a steady challenge to resourcefulness, moderation, and wisdom. It was a school of responsibility, which as a settled order bred a code of morals, a set of manners, a sense of dignity blended with patronage and good humor."[1] In short, the plantation rounded and developed the planter and made of him such an individualist as Jefferson Davis or George Washington.

The plantation was a collectivistic enterprise developing a sense of the group and requiring, even on the part of the planter, a certain surrender of individual desire to group interest. Another of the paradoxes of history is the fact that the most important and most successful of American experiments in collectivism before Sumter fell was the plantation in which two diverse races were bound together in the common task of the husbandman. Success depended, however, upon personal contact. Therefore, when absenteeism appeared, failure soon followed.

The plantation system produced social gradations among the white people of the agricultural South which were almost unknown in the rural communities of the Upper Mississippi Valley. On the plantation itself were whites in subordinate station. The smith, the overseer, and the tutor were hired men. Throughout the Cotton Kingdom small farmers were more numerous than the great planters. As the plantations spread over the rich bottom lands, the lesser husbandmen were driven into the sandy, often submarginal regions or were held isolated in the mountains. The life and the outlook of these crackers and sand-hillers were not unlike those of the small farmer north of the Ohio and the Missouri, save in one all-important particular. The Northern independent husbandman met only equals on the highway, as he drove to town; the man from the sand hills was conscious of a difference in status and in power between himself and his planter neighbor whose carriage passed his cabin. Not until after the disintegration of the plantation system did the lesser white man begin to assert his political power and aspire to a rôle in the affairs of his state and of the nation. But the jealousy of the humbler man was blunted by the thought, supported by evidence on every hand, that individuals of his class could by their own efforts lift themselves into the ruling group. While the frontier still existed and enterprising men could reclaim cotton land from the wilderness, individualism, after the model of the plantation, dominated the civilization of the expanding South.

～

On Sunday morning, November 18, 1847, the highways leading north from Springfield, Massachusetts, along the Connecticut River were filled with carriages hurrying to the rapids where the city of Holyoke now stands. Small crowds of sight-seers gathered on either bank of New England's largest stream. All eyes were on the river. There, stretching from side to side, was a wooden dam whose lip was protected by iron plates. Through its open gates the river ran quietly. Conspicuous near the structure was a little group of men clad in the long coats, the stocks, and the tall hats of the period. They gave last-minute instructions and at intervals talked nervously together. Curious persons in the crowd pointed them out as the rich men from Boston and from Springfield who had organized the company which had undertaken to harness the Connecticut, the most daring engineering enterprise yet undertaken within the United States. When all was ready, the gates were lowered. A hush fell over the crowd as the giant timbers slid into their stations squarely across the main current. Steadily the water rose. Cheers filled the air when, finally, the river plunged in a mighty waterfall over the iron lip. But, at the very moment of success, an abutment began to crumble. A cracking sound was heard in midstream. Suddenly the dam disintegrated, and a man-made flood swept downstream toward Long Island Sound.

The group of financiers was reorganized and strengthened. Before winter had set in, work on a second dam was under way. When the gates of the new structure were closed in 1849, the dam held; the river had been conquered. Already the Boston men were planning and building a city in a region where before a scattered rural population had labored through the recurring seasons. They called it Holyoke. It became in time an important manufacturing center.

All the elements of New England capitalism were epitomized in the series of events which brought the city of Holyoke into being. There was the group of entrepreneurs who risked their private capital in an enterprise which their combined judgments said was logically sound but the outcome of which was not assured, until it was put to the pragmatic test. Their financial power, when managed with initiative, foresight, and courage, had created a dam and a city. Neither Massachusetts nor the United States had any plan for the Connecticut River. Nor did the Commonwealth exercise any control over the building of the new city of Holyoke. The Boston capitalists asked nothing of Massachusetts, save the protection of their property, or of the United States, save a tariff to aid the new textile mills which were being built. A private dam across the mighty Connecticut was a typical product of an age of individualism and of *laissez faire*.

The family lines of many of the Boston capitalists ran back to Puritan ancestors. These had listened, in the seventeenth century, to John Cotton or Richard Mather expound the wonderful and inscrutable ways of the Calvinist God who interfered for His own purposes in the humblest affairs of men. The capitalists of 1847 still, for the most part, sincerely believed in God. They did not, however, pray to Him to point out to them their offense which had caused Him to wash away their dam. Instead, with some heat they asked the luckless engineers to explain the error which had sent so much hard Boston money down the Connecticut River. The behavior of both entrepreneurs and engineers expressed a wholly rationalistic and materialistic philosophy. The founders of Holyoke were empiricists.

Unlike the planters of the South, they lived in a society in which the relationships between men were the result of contract rather than of inherited status. They were not overawed by a hereditary aristocracy, as were their contemporary industrialists in England. They were leaders in a community in which social ties were contractual ties. In theory all contracts, capable of standing the test of the courts, were made by free men acting intelligently in their own interests. It was a tacit but sometimes expressed assumption of this society that the general good is best served when free men pursue, each in an enlightened manner, their self-interest. There were slums, it is true, in Boston; and Wendell Phillips, fearless reformer, even while the Holyoke dam was building, was asking the Boston capitalists what was the origin of such poverty and what was to be done about it. The answer was not only easy, but old. Poverty, suggested the men of power, is the result of individual failure, the consequence of sloth, stupidity, thriftlessness, vice, or perhaps sometimes of regrettable misfortune. Its cure lies with the individual, not the State.

But Americans were not preoccupied with the problem of poverty when the first Holyoke dam was built. The Panic of 1837 was a memory now a decade old. The communistic communities, formed on the model of Charles Fourier, which had followed in the wake of that depression were already passing. The best answer which New England industrialists could give to Wendell Phillips, when he asked what was to be done about poverty, was the dam across the Connecticut, and new jobs so numerous that the men who held them filled a city. Here was opportunity for the individual not only to earn subsistence, but to win wealth and power. Nor was the dream illusory, for many of the masters of Holyoke at the end of the nineteenth century were men who had first come to the city as mill hands. Industrial advance stood in the United States in 1849, when the second Holyoke dam was built and when California was being peopled by the gold rush, in much the same relative position as that of the frontier advance in 1783 when the Revolution was over and the Appalachian barrier had been surmounted. Before the westward-trekking pioneer in 1783, and before the industrial pioneer in 1849, lay periods of expansion too great for the imagination to encompass. The American individualism of the middle of the nineteenth century was the product of the advance of the frontier and of the expansion of industry in a country which not only was vast, but which enjoyed almost complete military security.

Chapter 2

THE DOCTRINES
OF THE AMERICAN
DEMOCRATIC FAITH

THE GROUP OF ANXIOUS MEN who assembled at Philadelphia in 1787 to frame a constitution for the new United States
had almost universally that confidence in human reason which
stemmed from Newton's scientific achievements and those of other
scientists of the century before. Barring the Quakers, there was no
social or religious mysticism in their thought. True to the Enlightenment, of which they were in fact a part, their social philosophy
emphasized atomism. They centered their interest on the individual
man. Democracy is the appropriate political expression of the atomistic social emphasis, yet many of the Founding Fathers had a
healthy skepticism of democracy. To some it suggested the triumph
of mediocrity, to others the substitution of the rule of passion for
that of reason. But the United States was committed to the principle of democracy by the logic of the Revolution and, as a consequence, the delegates at Philadelphia founded their government, in
frank Lockean style, upon the consent of the governed. But because they saw outside the windows of the convention hall the
disturbing specter of the possible tyrant seizing power and enslav-
ing the people, the framers hedged about and balked political power,
by whomever exercised, with their famous system of checks and
balances. In the drawing up of their great document they were
both rationalists and empiricists. When they had finished, they
properly looked upon themselves as initiating a great experiment in
popular government.

A half century elapsed. When Americans of the new generation met to celebrate the fiftieth anniversary of the Constitution, they remarked—as it turned out, prematurely—that the experimental period had passed. For them the demonstration of the efficacy of popular sovereignty under the Constitution had been made. The young United States had become an important nation. The fears of the Fathers concerning democracy had not been justified by later events. With Andrew Jackson the common man had come to power to the advantage rather than the detriment of the nation.

Americans of the decades after the close of the War of 1812 lived in an intellectual climate considerably different from that of the period of the Founding Fathers. The religion of nature whose American prophet was Tom Paine had been charged with causing the excesses of the French Revolution and as a consequence had lost its former prestige. Paine, returning to the United States an old man, had found the doors of respectability closed and had gone to a lonely death. Evangelical Protestantism was spreading over the land, a phase of Christianity that emphasized emotion more than reason. Almost universally this generation believed that morality rests on religion, as, in turn, religion rests on faith. "We were born believing," remarked Emerson on one occasion. "A man bears beliefs as a tree bears apples."[1] In 1840 an inconspicuous citizen named George Sidney Camp wrote a small volume which he called *Democracy*, and which Harper & Brothers thought to express so well the mood of the age that they published it in their Family Library and later brought out a second edition. "Faith," said Camp, "is as necessary to the republican as to the Christian, and the fundamental characteristic of both."[2] Faith is the clue to the understanding of the democracy of the Middle Period, an age that seemed far removed from that decade when the Founding Fathers had created the Constitution. "The ideal of a static society having been put away," wrote Vernon Parrington a century later, "progress was assumed to be the first law of nature, and innovation was accepted as the sign and seal of progress. It was our first great period of exploitation, and from it emerged, as naturally as the cock from the mother egg, the spirit of romance, gross and tawdry in vulgar minds, dainty and refined in the more cultivated. But always romance. The days of realism were past, and it was quietly laid away with the wig and smallclothes of an outgrown generation."[3]

Parrington exaggerated the decline of realism. Among Americans of the Middle Period the word *democracy* took on two different but related connotations; it had both a realistic and a romantic meaning. Realistic democracy was a behavior pattern that included caucuses and log-rolling, the struggle for office among individuals, and the sparring for advantage among the sections of the nation. Martin Van Buren, chief architect of the Democratic Party that elected Jackson president, personified the realism of the political professional. Romantic democracy consisted of a cluster of ideas and ideals that, taken together, made up a national faith which, although unrecognized as such, had the power of a state religion. Some of the ideas were as old as classical Greece and others as new as the American nation. But, though most of the ideas were old and had been handed down by tradition, the configuration of the cluster was unique. Taken together they comprised quite literally an American democratic faith.

◇

Nineteenth-century Americans affirmed, as the primary doctrine of their democratic faith, that beneath society, its customs and institutions, a law exists that men did not make. This law outlines the patterns of both individual and social life. For the individual it establishes the principles on which to found a beneficent and constructive life. For society it institutes an order within which persons may grow in understanding and in virtue. The idea of the fundamental law as it existed in the thought of early nineteenth-century America had two different origins and, as a consequence, two different emphases. It came, on the one hand, from the idea of natural law as first formulated by Plato in ancient Athens and, on the other hand, from that belief in a moral law that had been carried down from the time of Moses by the Judeo–Christian tradition.

Nature, Plato insisted, is not chaos governed by chance. The regular movements of the sun and stars demonstrated to him a basic order, a harmony at the center of reality. Since life, reason, and intelligence are part of nature they presumed—in the thought of the great Athenian—a First Cause characterized by life, reason, and intelligence. Plato thought of the human soul as part of nature. Like the body, it might be healthy or unhealthy. He described the healthy soul as one in which reason by means of the will constrains and governs impulses and desire. The healthy soul is the one in which the triumph and supremacy of reason has put an end to internal conflict with desire that leads to evil and disorder. Such a soul expresses itself in acts that are lawful and just. Plato thought of the natural law as an urge toward justice. For him the natural law was a principle; it was not a code. Unlike the Commandments that Moses brought down from Sinai, Plato's natural law did not particularize that behavior which is good and that which is bad. Plato assumed that justice in society is the counterpart of order in nature. From nature itself through a natural law comes that strain toward justice which, when made the guide of life, becomes the health of the soul.

Plato's concept of order and his emphasis on the strain toward justice as an essential aspect of the order of nature lay back of the thinking of the Enlightenment. Aristotle in his treatment of ethics departed from the position of Plato and advanced what he considered a more realistic position. Thomas Aquinas in the thirteenth century followed Aristotle and mortised into his ideas of the natural law the theology of the Medieval Church. The Enlightenment rejected this theology. Plato's concept of order in nature was supported in the later age with what seemed to be finality by Newton's laws of motion and celestial mechanics. Plato's emphasis on the strain in nature and in the human heart toward justice provided the ultimate background for the Enlightenment idea of the natural law. From the idea of justice and also from the Enlightenment assumption of the reasonableness of the Author of Nature grew the idea of natural rights of John Locke and of the eighteenth century. Logically the Creator who brought forth man must have endowed him with the right to life and to liberty. For the Author of Nature to have denied these rights to his creature would have been cruel injustice. The idea of natural rights was general among Americans of the pre-Revolutionary years.[4] Thomas Jefferson wrote into the Declaration of Independence a doctrine to which virtually all his contemporaries assented.

Jefferson's formulation of the natural rights theory varied significantly, however, in one particular from that of Locke. The change reflected a difference between civilization as it was evolving in America and as it existed in Europe. Newton's philosopher friend Locke had affirmed the natural right of the individual to life, liberty, and property. By property Locke meant the clothing, habitations, and tools that make life possible. Jefferson substituted for property the natural right of the individual to the pursuit of happiness.

This new idea did not originate by accident. It came out of a new society, one in which feudalism had never been important and whose last vestiges were soon to be swept away by the changes that followed 1776. In American communities, two with a history of more than a century and a half, an open class system was emerging that contrasted with the fixed and rigid class hierarchies of European nations. The rise of Benjamin Franklin (a member with Jefferson of the committee to draw up the Declaration) from humble beginnings to the highest status and to international fame was but the most striking among a multitude of illustrations of what by 1776 had become a primary characteristic of life in the English-speaking New World. Here, west of the Atlantic, men had originated and put into common practice a new idea concerning the relation of the individual to society. Instead of being confined within the stratum of his class, as in Europe, a man in the New World might achieve in accordance with his abilities and, what was more important, could enjoy acceptance by his fellows on the basis of his character and his accomplishments. For the American, "this new man," as the eighteenth-century Crèvecoeur called him, there was no social level to which he could not aspire. The idea and reality of the open class system is perhaps the most important single contribution of Americans to the social thinking of Western civilization. Jefferson gave this American practice a formulation in theory when he declared in the Declaration the natural right of the individual to the pursuit of happiness.

In the years that followed 1776 the Declaration, with its affirmation of the natural rights to life, liberty, and the pursuit of happiness became in a manner of speaking the conscience of the American people, reminding them of standards by which to judge the conduct of their national life. It spurred men to action in the matter of the slave and later of minorities oppressed by unequal treatment at the hands of their fellow men. These illustrations of efforts to give reality in specific instances to the ideal of liberty suggest how deeply the idea of justice was embedded in the doctrine of natural rights. This natural rights philosophy, an aspect of the theory of natural law, was half of the more inclusive doctrine of the fundamental law.

The other half, differing more in theology than in substance, came from the Judeo–Christian tradition. "There are principles of abstract justice which the Creator of all things has impressed on the mind of his creature man," said John Marshall in 1823 in an opinion from the bench, "and which are admitted to regulate, in great degree, the rights of civilized nations."[5] "In ascending to the great principles upon which all society rests," added Justice Joseph Story in 1828, "it must be admitted that there are some which are of eternal obligation, and arise from our common dependence upon our Creator. Among these are the duty to do justice, to love mercy, and to walk humbly before God."[6] "There is a higher law," proclaimed William Ellery Channing long before Seward's famous speech in the Senate, "even Virtue, Rectitude, the voice of Conscience, the Will of God."[7] "The moral law," said Emerson in 1836, "lies at the center of nature and radiates to the circumference."[8] The ancient expression of this divinely given law was the Decalogue to which had been added the New Testament law of love.

For Christians the moral law was the will of God. For the intellectual descendents of the Enlightenment it was the natural law of the eighteenth-century philosophers. Justice Story in his *Commentaries on the Constitution* succeeded in phrasing the doctrine of the fundamental law in terms that would be acceptable both to those who found their guide in reason and to those who looked for direction to the Scriptures. "The rights of conscience," he said, "are, indeed, beyond the just reach of human power. They are given by God and cannot be encroached upon by human authority, without criminal disobedience of the precepts of natural as well as revealed religion."[9] Actually the fundamental law of the Middle Period, as it was accepted by a people little trained in philosophy, consisted of a blend of two familiar things, the doctrine of natural rights of the Declaration of Independence and the eternal will of a just and loving God about which the minister preached in church.

Out of the moral and the natural law came, in the opinion of the theorists of the 1830's, the "law" in the lawyer's sense of a body of authoritative rules enforceable by the courts. "The law, as a science," said Chancellor Kent of the New York bench in 1836 addressing the Law Association of the City of New York, "is only a collection of general principles, founded on the moral law, and in the common sense of mankind, and applied to particular cases as they arise, by the diligence of the bar and the erudition of the courts."[10] Equity, declared Justice Story, becomes necessary when the rules of law become "rigid, severe, and uncompromising" and when, as a consequence, it becomes necessary for the courts "to administer justice with reference to the principles of universal and natural justice."[11] Story, addressing the bar of Suffolk County in

Massachusetts in 1829, was particularly impressive when he described the lawyer's role in contemporary civilization. "What indeed can tend more to exalt and purify the mind," he asked, "than speculations required of those who profess the law upon the origins and extent of moral obligations; upon the great truths and dictates of natural law; and upon the immutable principles, that regulate right and wrong in social and private life. . . ."[12] For the purpose of the present discussion the importance of Kent and Story does not so much lie in the fact that they were eminent jurists as in the fact that they wrote commentaries on the law of the land that became the virtually universal textbooks of the young men reading for the lawyer's profession.

Here, then, was the mid-nineteenth-century concept of the fundamental law. Made up of both the moral and the natural law, it was looked upon as absolute and immutable. Out of it came ultimately the law which governed the lives of men, in particular the famous common law built up by the courts of England and extended to the United States. The common law was always changing and developing to meet expanding human needs. But its foundations, the basic principles on which it rested, remained changeless and eternal.

It was therefore certain. It could be depended upon. It created a sense of security. This sense of security for the individual was the peculiar and all-important value that men found in a legal theory and structure that Chancellor Kent described as a "government of laws, and not of men." Such a government was, in the opinion of mid-nineteenth-century Americans, a most important distinguishing characteristic of the United States. American government rested on constitutionalism and differed in essence from tyrannies abroad where law was the will of the man in power.

The universal acceptance of the doctrine of the fundamental law suggests that it had uses in the culture of the time. American skies were darkened during the Middle Period by a storm which gathered momentum and increased in intensity with the passing years. The controversy over human slavery divided the nation. Northerners and Southerners alike defended their positions by reference to the law of nature and of God as they understood and interpreted both. Garrison in the North and Yancey in the South early advocated breaking the ties which bound the sections together. Americans turned to the Constitution whose foundations rested on the fundamental law to find those common agreements between the contending parties without which debate is impossible. But this instrument seemed to fail them. Instead of resolving the dispute, the Constitution became the very center of controversy as the sections divided on the question of its origin and its nature. Webster for the North affirmed that the document drawn up at Philadelphia was the supreme law of the land; Calhoun for the South replied that it was no more than a compact among sovereign states. The positions were at opposite poles and were irreconcilable; yet faith in constitutionalism was not shaken. Even after the final break the Confederacy did not abandon constitutionalism. It drew up a constitution that differed only in details, though these were important, from that of 1787.

The event suggests that the American faith in constitutionalism did not have its ultimate origin in the Constitution which established it. Emerson, in 1854, suggested an origin that may help to explain the paradox. "Whenever a man," he said, "has come to this state of mind, that there is no church for him but his believing prayer; no Constitution but his dealing well and justly with his neighbor; no liberty but his invincible will to do right,—then certain aids and allies will promptly appear: for the constitution of the Universe is on his side."[13] Though Emerson was not a scientist, but rather the prophet of a mystical faith, his thought grew out of the basic assumptions of his age concerning the cosmos. This was the cosmos of Newton whose parts were arranged in order. The motions of these parts could be predicted after Newton had discovered the secret of the celestial mechanics by which they were governed. These laws of motion were part of what Emerson called "the constitution of the Universe." He was convinced that the moral law was another aspect. Constitutionalism as a foundation for political institutions reflected the belief in that cosmic order that was the essence of the concept of the fundamental law.

∽

The second doctrine of the democratic faith of the Middle Period was that of the free and responsible individual. The social thinking of the time focused on the individual as Jefferson had done in the Declaration of Independence. The men of the Middle Period thought of society as an aggregation of discrete individuals, as their eighteenth-century predecessors had done. In the United States free individuals were the ultimate governors of the nation. Government implies power and the instrument of power for the individual was the ballot. The strength and importance of the doctrine of liberty in the first half of the nineteenth century was demonstrated by the successful drive after 1815 to bring about universal white suffrage. The age of the common man began in the United States in Andrew Jackson's time—nearly a century before its appearance in Europe.

Power, of necessity, implied responsibility; responsibility suggested something above the individual to which he must be responsible. The aphorism, liberty under law, stated in political terms the doctrine of the free individual.

The doctrine of the free individual, like that of the law enforceable in the courts, ultimately grew out of and was related to the doctrine of the fundamental law. The path that led from the one to the other was a philosophy of progress. This philosophy affirmed that the advance of civilization is measured by the progress of men in apprehending and translating into individual and social action the eternal principles of right and justice. The men of the time of Kent and Story thought of the advance of civilization as the progress of virtue. "Nothing can be plainer," remarked William C. Jarvis, counsellor-at-law, in 1820, "than that the barbarian of the desert requires the restraint of a more powerful arm than the individual, whose passions and propensities are under the internal restraint of moral and religious sentiments."[14] "Civilization," added Frederick Grimke thirty-six years later, "is that state in which the higher part of our nature is made to predominate over the lower."[15] Out of this idea that civilized man is the virtuous man and this hopeful philosophy that mankind is on the march toward a better world came the eighteenth- and nineteenth-century theory of liberty. As men gained deeper understanding of the fundamental law and succeeded in making it the monitor of their lives, they needed less the external control of man-made laws. "Hence," insisted Emerson—following Jefferson—"the less government we have the better. . . . The antidote to this abuse of formal government is the influence of private character, the growth of the Individual. . . . To educate the wise man the State exists, and with the appearance of the wise man the State expires."[16] Henry Thoreau, Emerson's Concord friend, carried this reasoning to its logical conclusion. The man who has achieved moral maturity, he thought, should reject imperfect laws and decisions made by compromising majorities and should hold fast to the higher law disclosed by his conscience as the sole guide and regulator of his life. In particular he should practice civil disobedience when the State embarks upon an immoral policy.

Before Thoreau built his hut at Walden Pond, James Fenimore

Cooper had personalized the early nineteenth-century doctrine of the free and responsible individual in the idealized character, Leatherstocking. Cooper presented him against the background of many frontiers and gave him different names, such as Deerslayer or Hawkeye. In Leatherstocking Cooper drew the portrait of the natural democrat who lived in the freedom of the wilderness beyond the restraints of man-made laws. In *The Deerslayer*, published in 1841, four years before Andrew Jackson's death, the novelist described Leatherstocking's opposite in the character, Hurry Harry, the lawless and barbarous forest giant. Deerslayer, Cooper went on, "was a very different person in appearance, as well as in character. In stature, he stood about six feet in his moccasins, but his frame was comparatively slight and slender. . . . His face would have little to recommend it except youth, were it not for an expression that seldom failed to win upon those who had leisure to examine it, and to yield to the feeling of confidence it created. This expression was simply that of guileless truth, sustained by an earnestness of purpose, and a sincerity of feeling, that rendered it remarkable." Cooper did not leave to inference the foundation of Deerslayer's character. The story-teller disclosed its cornerstone in a rebuke Deerslayer gave to the licentious Hurry Harry. "I know we live in the woods, Hurry," Cooper made Leatherstocking say, "and are thought to be beyond human laws—and perhaps we are so, in fact, whatever it may be in right—but there is a law, and a law maker, that rule across the whole continent. He that flies in the face of either, need not call me friend."[17] Cooper's Leatherstocking Tales enjoyed a vast popularity in the Middle Period, suggesting, perhaps, a widespread approval of his ideal of the natural democrat consciously guided by the fundamental law. Cooper's frank and discerning criticisms of the realities of American life at the time did not meet with equal favor. His essays on American democracy in the 1830's subjected him to abuse. But he did not permit an understanding of realities to undermine idealism. Like Deerslayer, he saw in the ideals of the fundamental law the standards by which citizens could judge and improve the reality.

It has commonly been said that the exaltation of the individual and the apotheosis of individual liberty of the mid-nineteenth century was the natural result of certain economic factors. A relatively small population was scattered over a vast area. Capitalistic enterprise had not developed beyond the stage in which its most important figure was the individual entrepreneur. Inevitably in such a social scene the focus of attention must be upon the individual. Moreover, the conquest of the West and the attempt to establish a new industrialism in the East put a premium upon individual initiative and hence on individual liberty. There can be no doubt that such an economic and social situation stimulated greatly the development of the doctrine of the free individual. Jefferson's theory that the free and independent husbandman, master of a family-size farm, must be the ultimate bulwark of democracy suggests the importance of American economic and social conditions.

But conditions of a different sort reinforced the urge toward individual liberty. Down to the eve of the fall of Sumter, Americans of the Middle Period enjoyed a sense of security rarely duplicated in modern history. Not only were there no dangerous political enemies beyond the national frontiers holding the threat of invasion over the citizens of the Republic, but instead Americans marched in triumph into the capital of Mexico and dictated terms of peace. An ocean guarded the eastern cities against attack from Europe, and in international affairs an outlook akin to that of an island people developed among the citizens of the Republic. At home the opportunities of the frontier offered to every able-bodied man the possibility of economic security in a world of accelerating change. The American philosophy of liberty had first taken shape in the eighteenth century in a protest against imperial domination and had been established amidst the ebb and flow of a long and desperate war. In the Middle Period the doctrine of the free individual matured in an age of security, its maturity symbolized by the establishment of universal male citizen suffrage and the opening in America of the age of the common man.

∽

The third doctrine of the democratic faith was that of the mission of America. It was a mid-nineteenth-century version of those myths of unique origin and of unique destiny so common in tribal traditions. Liberty, according to a widely accepted version of American mythology of the early nineteenth century, had been established by Deity in an empty western continent so that, freed from the burden of European tradition, it might flourish and become an inspiration to the world.

> O God, beneath thy guiding hand
> Our exiled fathers crossed the sea. . . .

sang Leonard Bacon in 1833.[18] George Bancroft, historian, saw the hand of the Omnipotent in the founding and in the history of the Republic. As late as 1866, Samuel Kirkland Lothrop, addressing a great Boston meeting on the anniversary of the Declaration of Independence, proclaimed again the supernaturalistic interpretation of the origin of American democracy. "If ever civil and religious liberty,—that boon which every man craves for himself and every noble man would accord to others,—if ever that great intelligent, responsible freedom, which through the gospel and the spirit of the Lord, comes to the soul of man, is to prevail over the earth, if it is ever to maintain a strong foothold among the nations, it will be because at the hour of its utmost need, God gave it an opportunity to plant itself on this new continent, and strike its roots so deep that no despotic power could tear them up, no storm of passion and folly blight its blossoms, or destroy the fruit of the tree."[19]

The doctrine of mission was merely an extension of that of origin. Thomas Jefferson put it into words in 1826 in his reply to a committee of citizens of Washington who had invited him to come to the capital to be present at the celebration of the fiftieth anniversary of the Declaration. "Respected Sir," wrote the aged Jefferson who was to die on that anniversary day, ". . . I should, indeed, with peculiar delight, have met and exchanged there congratulations, personally, with the small band, the remnant of that host of worthies who joined with us on that day, in the bold and doubtful election we were to make, for our country, between submission and the sword; and to have enjoyed with them the consolatory fact that our fellow citizens, after half a century of experience and prosperity, continue to approve the choice we made. May it be to the world, what I believe it will be, (to some parts sooner, to others later, but finally to all) the signal of arousing men to burst the chains, under which monkish ignorance and superstition had persuaded them to bind themselves, and to assume the blessings and security of self-government . . ."[20] "We stand the latest, and, if we fail, probably the last experiment of self-government by the people," said Justice Story in that same anniversary year. "Already," he added, "the age has caught the spirit of our institutions."[21]

On July 4, 1843, George Robertson, Chief Justice of the Kentucky Court of Appeals, rose at Camp Madison near Frankfort to lead the community in the annual American ceremony of homage to the nation. He expressed the sentiments and the conviction of his generation when he bracketed Christianity and democracy. Each had a role in the saving of men. Each was destined to achieve a world victory. In the rounded periods that come so easily to the Southern orator he repeated the doctrine of mission and asserted the conviction of the age of the ultimate triumph of Christianity and democracy. "The seminal principles of sound philosophy, true liberty, pure religion," said the judge, "were imported by our pilgrim ancestors to a land which seems to have been prepared by Providence for their successful development. . . . The temperate zone of North America already exhibits many signs that it is the promised land of civil liberty, and institutions destined to liberate and exalt the human race. . . . Christianity, rational philosophy, and constitutional liberty, like an ocean of light, are rolling their united and resistless tide over the earth. . . . Doubtless there may be partial revulsions. But the great movement will . . . be progressive, until the millennial sun shall rise in all the effulgence of Universal day."[22]

July 4, 1852, fell on Sunday. In New Orleans, although it was the gayest port in America, all cannon salutes, military parades, and dinners were omitted in deference to religion. On this day an editorial in the New Orleans *Picayune* took the place of the conventional oration. Anxiety hung over the city. The editor sought neither to exaggerate nor to minimize the fact that the practice of self-government in the United States was threatened by dissensions and mounting passions that divided the North and South. The editor was appalled when he tried to visualize the magnitude of the calamity involved in the breakdown of American democracy. But he looked beyond the national boundaries to the peoples of the world for whom Americans had a peculiar responsibility. "We may be enabled to purify and redeem ourselves at last, if the rule of reason should give way to a war between the sections," wrote the editor, "but, in the mean-time, humanity will suffer dreadful penalties for our transgressions and nations everywhere give themselves up, unresistingly to the power of despotism, from which there is no escape."

Eight years passed. On February 22, 1861, President-elect Lincoln paused a few hours in Philadelphia on his way to his inauguration. Secession had begun and Southerners had organized the Confederate States of America. Lincoln tried to recreate a sense of union among a divided people. "I have never had a feeling politically," he said, "that did not spring from the Declaration of Independence. . . . I have often inquired of myself what great principle it was that kept this confederacy so long together. It was not the mere matter of separation of the colonies from the motherland, but something in that declaration giving liberty, not alone to the people of this country, but hope for the world for all future time. It was that which gave promise that in due time the weights should be lifted from the shoulders of all men, that all should have an equal chance. This was the sentiment embodied in the Declaration of Independence. . . . I would rather be assassinated on the spot than surrender it."

It was a moving scene, this confession of faith by an inexperienced man suddenly called upon to lead his people in the greatest crisis of their history. In his statement of belief that democracy will bring life to the oppressed and suffering peoples of the world he gave classic expression to the doctrine that it is the mission of America to cherish and to hold steadfastly before the nations the ideal of the free and self-governing individual.

What was the significance of this doctrine of origin and of destiny? Ideas arise out of social situations and persist because they have utility. The idea of the mission of America gave a sense of superiority to a people who smarted frequently under the condescensions and criticisms of Europeans who, after a journey to the United States, wrote books about them. Early nineteenth-century Americans held up to view their free institutions when foreign critics commented on the feebleness of their development in the arts. As an expression of American tribal ethnocentrism the doctrine assisted in that subtle osmosis by which a federation of particularist states was transformed into a united nation. In this connection the evidence of the editorial in the New Orleans *Picayune* has particular significance. The doctrine of mission, furthermore, provided for American democracy, with its emphasis on freedom and diversity of opinion, a philosophy of unity. And, finally, the conviction of the destiny of America held up before the humble democrat, whose drab world rarely extended beyond the main street of his village, a romantic vision in which he could see his inconspicuous performance of civic duties invested with a world significance.

Chapter 3

CHRISTIANITY
AND THE DEMOCRATIC FAITH

KARL MARX IN ENGLAND and Lewis Henry Morgan in America brought out independently in the middle years of the nineteenth century the theory of economic determinism. Both asserted that economic institutions are of fundamental importance in any culture, and both taught that shifts in the substratum of economics create stresses which cause readjustments throughout the social superstructure. Social beliefs grow out of social institutions and change with them. But social beliefs are affected by other forces than economic change. If man on earth must eat, so also must he adjust his life and thought to the mystery surrounding him. His explanation of the unknown may lead him to people with spirits the darkness encircling the campfire which lights his village. Or his attitude may be that of an astronomer exploring remote space, intent not upon the mystery of interplanetary space but upon the task of accumulating knowledge. The principal purpose of cosmic philosophies, whether they be supernaturalistic or naturalistic, is to give orientation to human life and to evaluate its significance. For this reason the reigning cosmic philosophy is as fundamental to a particular climate of opinion as are its economic foundations to a selected social scene. The social beliefs of a given place and time adjust themselves to the ruling ideas concerning the cosmos in essentially the same manner in which the social institutions of that place and time adapt themselves to their economic substructure. As cosmic philosophies change, social beliefs change with them.

The romantic democratic faith in the Middle Period took form among a vigorous people who were not merely overrunning an

26

empty continent but who, in wooden sailing ships, were also seeking profits on the seven seas. The core of American life was activism; citizens of the United States had little time or training for contemplation. Christian supernaturalism, part of the tradition their ancestors had brought from Europe, pervaded their climate of opinion.

Naturalism was also part of the tradition from Europe. By the middle of the nineteenth century, natural philosophy held a secure place in American thought. The prestige of science, moreover, was high, not only in the older institutions of the Atlantic seaboard but also in the newer colleges which Protestant denominations were founding and maintaining in Trans-Appalachia. In 1837, the year in which Emerson, at Harvard, proclaimed the American declaration of intellectual independence, James Dwight Dana published a pioneer treatise on mineralogy which established the permanent framework of that branch of science. Dana's book, promptly accepted in Europe, fulfilled Emerson's hope that his fellow countrymen would cease being mere borrowers and would begin to think their own thoughts. It marked the end of American intellectual provincialism in one area of knowledge.

Yet the growth of science in the middle period of the nineteenth century did not shake the hold of Christianity upon the people of the United States. The experience of the eighteenth century had been different. The American Revolution had been fought and the Constitution had been drawn up in the decades in which deistic philosophy reached its zenith west of the Atlantic. After 1800, however, Timothy Dwight, the Puritan president of Yale, fought Deism and encouraged science with equal enthusiasm. By so doing he piloted the New Haven college into the main current of American thought, for early nineteenth-century Americans witnessed the paradoxical phenomenon of the synchronous decline of Deism and advance of science. When in 1818 Benjamin Silliman founded *The American Journal of Science and Arts,* Deism, as such, was almost forgotten; the editor's personal life was guided by an unobtrusive, conventional yet resolute Christian faith.

The harmony between science and Protestant orthodoxy in the Middle Period arose chiefly from the fact that the mechanistic concept of the universe derived from Newton's celestial mechanics did not deny any important specific assertions in the Scriptures. Newton, a devout Christian, had left voluminous writings on theological and biblical matters and had given to his discoveries a religious interpretation. Natural philosophers of the early nineteenth century could and did, like Newton, accept the prevailing supernaturalistic interpretation of the cosmos. Premonitory rumblings of future battle, however, disturbed the Middle Period when geologists began to reconstruct the earth's history from the record of the rocks. Their story of creation differed considerably from that of Genesis. To Protestantism, dependent for its authority upon Holy Writ, any undermining of the doctrine of literal interpretation of the Bible was dangerous.

In spite of the occasional discharge of ecclesiastical muskets at geological theory the issue did not become important before 1861, partly because geology was still a young science, partly because the slavery controversy absorbed the attention of the churches, and partly because the evangelical Protestantism dominating America during the Middle Period emphasized the New rather than the Old Testament. As a result, the Gettysburg of science and theology in America was postponed until Darwin denied the Christian doctrine of man as a special creation of God. After 1865, when the controversy over Darwinism raged in American religious and intellectual circles, James Dwight Dana, defending orthodox Christian theology, fought the English biologist's hypothesis. By Dana's side battled the Harvard naturalist, Louis Agassiz, whose popular influence vastly surpassed that of the New Haven mineralogist. "All these facts in their natural connection," Agassiz had written in 1857 in his famous *Essay on Classification*, "proclaim aloud the One God, whom man may know, adore, and love; and Natural History must, in good time, become the analysis of the thoughts of the Creator of the Universe, as manifested in the animal and vegetable kingdoms."[1] Agassiz denied that Darwin had discovered the processes of God.

In an age when Christian supernaturalism still influenced scientific thought, inevitably social beliefs were profoundly influenced by the same religious formulas. In the United States the democratic faith and evangelical Protestantism grew up side by side. Unique American factors conditioned both. To understand the relation between them it is necessary to recall some significant elements in the history of Protestantism in the New World.

∽

The Protestant revolt occurred, of course, in the Old World. The initial battles of the great schism produced a new doctrine of the Kingdom of God; in the transformations of history, this altered conception became the foundation for the intellectual structure of the American democratic faith. The Medieval Church, with Gothic cathedrals symbolizing its faith, emphasized God as the eternal perfection of truth, goodness, and beauty. "The end of ends for an intelligent man," said Thomas Aquinas, "is to see God as He essentially is."[2] A man must pause from time to time in the business of living, counseled the churchmen of the Middle Ages; one must withdraw to the chapel or perhaps even to the monastic cell to contemplate the dazzling mystery of God. Theology was the highest branch of learning in the universities. The Medieval Church had also its theory of society. God had organized all living creatures on the earth into a harmony of gradations. According to the divine plan, those in higher station governed the lower, as the feudal lord ruled his vassal. The Church, as the chief earthly representative of its divine Founder and as the agency of His grace, was the ultimate governor of men in matters of faith and morals. This theory of a planned society contained the principle of Plato's *Republic*. But God, not man, was the author of the plan. It had become known to men through reason and through revelation. Its execution in the world had been left by Deity to those who shared in the necessary divine wisdom. Aquinas, repudiating the doctrine that God interferes at first hand in the affairs of his human children, affirmed: "As to the design of government, God governs all things immediately; whereas in its execution, he governs some things by means of others."[3] This doctrine was the cornerstone of ecclesiastical supremacy.

Against such supremacy the Reformation prophets revolted. They found the necessary formula to support their rebellion in a revision of the old Christian doctrine of the kingdom of God. All men, according to the rebels, are earthly citizens of the divine kingdom and are subjects immediately responsible to its Monarch. Before the heavenly King all men are equal in the sense that He deals directly with them and not through the intervention of a mediator of superior spiritual status. Yet in this great kingdom men are not free. Even their lives are not their own. God does not exist for the benefit of man, but rather man lives for the glory of God. "We are not our own," warned John Calvin of Geneva; "therefore neither our reason nor our will should predominate in our deliberations and actions. We are not our own; therefore let us not presuppose it as our end to seek what may be expedient to us according to the flesh. . . . We are God's; toward him, therefore, as our only legitimate end, let every part of our lives be directed."[4] Out of the Protestant revolt came the concept of the immediate and absolute kingdom of God ruled by the divine will, to obey which all men are equally responsible. This theory provided the theological background for that doctrine of the moral order and of the fundamental law which was the first postulate of the romantic democratic faith of mid-nineteenth-century America. Calvin, it should be added, rejected, in the passage quoted, the alternative of law founded upon that philosophy of expediency so attractive to the twentieth century.

Because of its importance in opposing the rule of priests, the doctrine of the kingdom of God was universal throughout early Protestantism. It was to the Protestant rebellion against the Holy See what John Locke's theory of natural rights was to the revolt of the English against James II. When the rebels against Rome turned, however, from opposition to the positive task of reconstructing society, unanimity ceased. Three types of constructive Protestantism appeared.

The first was Pietism, the name for the social outlook of Lutheranism. Luther, militant mystic, emphasized the inner life: only God can rule the human spirit; only the spirit is important. Pietism led its followers to focus their attention upon reforming the world's sinful institutions.

The second type of constructive Protestantism was Calvinism. The brilliant Genevan, although often represented as a pessimist, was optimist enough to believe that all areas of human life, all institutions of society, could be redeemed. He was unwilling to abandon to Satan even politics and economics. As he looked out upon his sixteenth-century European world, a sense of crisis filled him. Calvin saw the hearts of the sons of Adam full of sin, the institutions which they had created to make life possible hastening them to destruction, and evil triumphant and threatening the world. Evil in 1536, when young Calvin hurried his *Institutes of the Christian Religion* to the press of Thomas Platter and Balthasar Lasius at Basle, was personified by France's political rulers who had compelled the prophet of reform to flee his native land to save his life. The purpose of God and the duty of man, thought Calvin, is to restrain Satan, ranging over the earth like a beast seeking his prey. Both Church and State must share in the all-important task of checking the corrupt passions of men. American constitutionalism, which seeks by means of a written document to restrain individuals, majorities, and even governments from wrong doing, owes a heavy debt to that young

Frenchman who, in the summer of 1536, made his home in Geneva and began to expound the epistles of St. Paul.

The Separatists formulated the third approach to the problem of constructive Protestantism. Like some disillusioned citizens of the twentieth century, the Separatists were convinced that politicians as a breed are beyond the possibility of saving. Because of the close alliance of Church and State in their day, these radicals grouped bishops and ministers of state in that company of human rebels whom a despairing God had marked for destruction. The Separatists urged the faithful to withdraw themselves from a corrupt world. They were the anarchists of their day. They felt that the time was near at hand when the present sinful order would pass away and when the kingdom of God would take on its final perfection. Of all the early Protestants the Separatists, alone, emphasized the millennial hope.

Lutheranism, Calvinism, and Separatism challenged in Europe powerful ecclesiastical, social, and political traditions. It required more than the strength of Martin Luther and of John Calvin to overthrow the Church of Rome, mighty champions though these prophets were. Strife in the Old World sent religious refugees scurrying to the New. In America Protestants turned from their war against Rome to a battle with the wilderness. The Church of England became the official religious establishment in the Southern colonies. Elsewhere more radical types of Protestantism prevailed. Calvinism became the frame for New England thought, and in the settlements of the back country it was influential as far south as Georgia. From its principal centers in Philadelphia, and from the lesser communities, the influence of Quakerism spread out to all Colonial America. In the continental English colonies, including the Catholic refuge Maryland, Protestantism was supreme; the God most worshipped in America was the Deity to whom John Calvin prayed with such intensity of devotion and singularity of purpose.

The uncompromising Genevan system was well adapted to pioneers struggling against a wilderness. Beginning at the edge of the clearings beyond the village palisade, the untamed forest stretched endlessly westward into the unknown. The hard conditions of life required labor; the system of John Calvin sanctified work. It urged men to be prodigal in the expenditure of constructive effort, but saving of the gains they won. When the tension of the frontier struggle relaxed and life became easier, certain defects of Calvinism became increasingly evident. Its theology was as harsh as the social conditions in the sixteenth-century European cities in which it had had its origin. The doctrine of an avenging Deity who flings multitudes of His creatures into the eternal torment of the burning lake was out of harmony with the warm sympathies expressing themselves in the humanitarian movements of the nineteenth century. The time came when Calvin's portrait of God seemed an immoral caricature. The dour determinism essential in the Calvinist doctrine of foreordination fitted ill with the mood of post-Yorktown Americans, jubilant over their successful defiance of the world's most powerful empire. The generation which created the American Republic was not pleased to be told from the pulpit that man could do nothing to save himself and that his every act was ordained from the alpha of time. Unitarianism and transcendentalism rose to deny the Genevan system. In 1856, Oliver Wendell Holmes, Cambridge physician, celebrated his conviction that Calvinism was no more. For Holmes, John Calvin's brilliant logical creation was only the Deacon's "one-hoss shay."

> All at once the horse stood still,
> Close by the meet'n'-house on the hill.
> First a shiver, and then a thrill,
> Then something decidedly like a spill,
> And the parson was sitting upon a rock,
> At half-past nine by the meet'n'-house clock,
> Just the hour of the Earthquake shock!
> What do you think the parson found,
> When he got up and stared around?
> The poor old chaise in a heap or mound,
> As if it had been to the mill and ground!
> You see, of course, if you're not a dunce,
> How it went to pieces all at once,
> All at once and nothing first,
> End of the wonderful one-hoss shay.
> Logic is logic. That's all I say.

The first form of the American rebellion against Calvinism was evangelical Protestantism. Evangelism came to New England in Calvinist guise when Jonathan Edwards in the eighteenth century lighted the fire of the Great Awakening in the Connecticut Valley. It swept the back country of the southern colonies when the magic words of George Whitefield, Methodist evangelist, called thousands of simple frontiersmen into the fold. Then, at the close of the eighteenth century the frontier, which for a century and a half had been inching westward from the Atlantic shoreline toward the Appalachians, suddenly began an advance that, in scarcely more than fifty years, carried it across the continent to distant Oregon and to the Golden Gate. Organized Puritanism and Quakerism stood helpless before the unchurched west. Beyond the wooded Appalachians the prophets of a new evangelicalism, hard-riding Methodist circuit riders and vehement Baptist preachers, deployed on the thin battle lines of the Lord. The camp meeting, that unique American contribution to Christianity, evolved as the only practicable solution of the problem of carrying the Gospel to the cabin population of a sparsely settled border. Lonely clearings became suddenly filled with homespun crowds through which at times swept mass-hysteria with tornado violence. Sinners answered the warnings of exhorters with shouted prayers for mercy from on high. Women swooned and men were flung about by uncontrollable paroxysms. To the repentant, who crowded the mourner's bench, such physical manifestations seemed proof that God was in their very midst, that he was putting his finger on human hearts to cleanse them of evil. Burned out in one community, emotionalism appeared in others, as evangelists hastened from settlement to settlement. Protestant sects broke into fragments which coalesced into new and often strange denominations as earnest men, unrestrained by the conservatism of a State Church, sought diligently to discover the one true way leading to Paradise. But evangelical Protestantism was more than revivalism, more than denominationalism. It knit and held sober men and women in the enduring unity of their local churches. It brought forth laymen and preachers whose lives were filled with a prophetic zeal akin to that of the humble company who once carried to Palestine and to the world the message of their Leader. The frontier was crude, turbulent, and godless. Evangelical Protestantism, more than any other single force, tamed it.

The central appeal of the movement was the winning by the individual of freedom from bondage. The simple theory of the evangelist was that before conversion a man was held in the shackles of sin which were broken when he knelt before the Mercy Seat. Evangelical Protestantism shifted the emphasis of American Christianity from John Calvin's preoccupation with a monarch-God to Horace Bushnell's emphasis upon Jesus, the divine man. "The way the Spirit of God works with me," said Henry Ward Beecher, pastor of Brooklyn's Plymouth Church and most famous of the mid-nineteenth-century evangelicals, "makes it necessary that I should have something that I can clasp, and to me the Father is vague. I believe in a Father, but the definition of Him in my vision, is not to me what the portraiture of Christ is. . . . I cannot pray to the Father except through Christ. I pray to Christ. I must."[5] Such a faith has been called the "religion of the Savior." A better name would be Romantic Christianity. Its emphasis upon the individual and his emotions, its central vision of the perfect man in remote antiquity, its gospel of love which cleanses the world—all reflected that romantic mood so important in Europe and in America in the first half of the nineteenth century. For Calvin's ideals of justice and of duty, the evangelicals substituted sentiment. In place of his grim insistence upon law, they preached the pleasant doctrine of liberty for men who have incorporated the law into their lives. The central theme of romantic, evangelical Christianity was the teaching that liberty comes to the man from whose limbs the fetters of sin have fallen. The central theme of the romantic, democratic faith was the doctrine of the free individual. Its view of civilization was that of the progress of men away from the necessity of external restraint by man-made laws and toward individual liberty founded upon self-control. So great is the similarity that the doctrine of liberty seems but a secular version of its counterpart in evangelical Protestantism.

More striking even than the parallels in Protestantism for those doctrines of the democratic faith of the fundamental moral order and of the free individual were the religious counterparts of the doctrine of the mission of democratic America. There developed in the eighteenth, and particularly in the nineteenth, century an emphasis in American Protestantism upon the millennial hope which set off that faith in the United States from that of the Protestant churches of Europe. The difference was one of degree only, however, for millenarianism is as old as Christianity. The essence of millenarianism is that Christ shall come again to earth and reign for a thousand years; during this time Satan shall be chained in the abyss. Then shall come the final judgment and the end of earthly things.

This tenet had been transformed by medieval Catholicism, following Augustine, into a doctrine which affirmed that the thousand-year reign of Christ had already begun and that his kingdom on earth was the Church. According to the authority of the *City of God* the old enemy, Satan, is confined, not in some shadowy nether region, but in an abyss of "the countless multitude of the wicked, whose hearts are unfathomably deep in malignity against the church of God."[6]

Early Protestantism naturally rejected this version of the millennial doctrine, because it supported ecclesiastical authority. But the prophets of the Reformation made little effort to formulate a revised doctrine of the New Jerusalem. This hope received its first important impetus in America from the Great Awakening led by Edwards. When the Northampton minister beheld with amazement the unexpected power of his words, he cast about for an explanation. It was characteristic of this humble-minded worker in the vineyard that he should put away vainglory and should give the credit to God. "It is the work of a new creation," he said excitedly, forgetting the smallness of the Connecticut Valley, "which is infinitely more glorious than the old. The New Jerusalem . . . has begun to come down from heaven."[7] Yet the Great Awakening was a backyard bonfire in comparison with the religious conflagration lighted by the Revival of 1800. Among thousands of American Christians not only of Trans-Appalachia but of the older states, the millennial hope became almost a certainty. Through the dissolving mists of the future these eager disciples saw the shining walls of the heavenly city only a little way off. "When will the Millennium commence?" Joseph Emerson, Massachusetts minister, schoolmaster, and cousin to the Concord transcendentalist asked in 1818. "The signs of the times," he answered, "proclaim that the Millennial day is approaching."[8] "The day draws near," declared in 1849 Seth Williston, an aging preacher of western New York, "when according to Scripture prophesy Satan is to be cast out, and not permitted to deceive the nations any more for a thousand years."[9]

Between 1818 and 1849 two movements founded upon millenarianism emerged from obscurity and drew to themselves for a moment the attention of the nation. The first was Mormonism. The handful of Latter-Day Saints who in the early 1830's gathered about their prophet, Joseph Smith, at Kirkland, Ohio, grew steadily in number. They sought larger opportunities on the Missouri frontier, but were driven out by borderers enraged by their beliefs and practices. In spite of persecution they multiplied. It was a large company that followed in the later 1840's the new leader, Brigham Young, across the plains to safety within the protecting rim of the Great Central Basin. The Latter-Day Saints in Utah defied the desert. They had sufficient hands with which to establish irrigation works and an ecclesiastical organization which, directing the life of the community, made their labor effective. The power of early Mormonism was the millennial hope, the vision of Zion soon to arise upon the earth. "For I am God," said the Lord through the Mormon scriptures, "and mine arm is not shortened and I will show miracles, signs and wonders, unto all those who believe on my name . . . and the time speedily cometh, that great things are to be shown forth unto the children of men. . . . Wherefore, I have called upon the weak things of the world, those who are unlearned and despised, to thresh the nations by the power of my Spirit; And their arm shall be mine arm, and I will be their shield and their buckler, and I will gird up their loins, and they shall fight manfully for me . . . and I will cause the heavens to shake for your good: and Satan shall tremble; and Zion shall rejoice upon the hills, and flourish. . . . Fear not little flock, the kingdom is yours until I come, Behold I come quickly; even so: Amen."[10]

In 1836, William Miller, like Joseph Smith a product of the New York frontier, in a volume of calculations based upon the biblical prophecies declared that the end of the present world would come about the year 1843. Beginning, as did Mormonism, with a tiny company of believers, Millerism swiftly developed into the most spectacular evangelistic crusade of the Middle Period. As exhorters in scores of camp meetings pleaded with sinners to repent before it was too late, the heavens displayed a sign as though to magnify the power of their words. In the fateful year of 1843 a great comet swung so near the earth that the tail was visible in daylight. It lay across the sky at noonday like a sword poised above a guilty world. From East to West men and women stampeded into conversion. The Millerite episode suggests a reason why evangelical Protestantism drifted toward millenarianism. Christianity has produced no doctrine more effective in shepherding sinners into the protecting fold. "Surely no other subject," wrote Joseph Emerson in the quiet of his study in Beverly, Massachusetts, "is better suited to rouse benevolent souls to action."[11]

The achievements of Mormonism and of Millerism are evidence of the hold upon popular American thought of the dream of a coming new world. Nor was this vision limited to the ignorant or the illiterate. "Sooner or later, in one way or another," said Mark Hopkins, president of Williams College, "the time must come, when the evils which now provoke the vengeance of heaven and curse humanity shall come to an end." He was addressing in Boston the American Board of Commissioners of Foreign Missions. The year was 1845, when thousands of disappointed Millerites were painfully adjusting themselves to the necessity of continuing to live upon the earth. "Wars, and intemperance, and licentiousness, and fraud, and slavery, and all oppression shall cease," Hopkins added, ". . . through the transforming influence of Christianity; there shall be a society as perfect as we can conceive of in the present state when the Kingdom of God shall be set up, and his will shall be done on earth."[12] The president of Williams represented the conservative strain in the philosophy of the coming perfection; William Miller and Joseph Smith were radicals. Yet the agreements between Hopkins and Miller were more important than their differences. Both believed in progress on the earth. Both faced the future with confident hope. Miller expected a divine revolution; Hopkins a gradual improvement. Miller appealed primarily to the ignorant; Hopkins spoke the mind of thoughtful Protestant America.

Beside the Protestant philosophy of progress, as expressed in radical or conservative millenarianism, should be placed the doctrine of the democratic faith which affirmed it to be the duty and the destiny of the United States to assist in the creation of a better world by keeping lighted the beacon of democracy. "Christianity, rational philosophy, and constitutional liberty," said Justice George Robertson in Kentucky on July 4, 1843, "like an ocean of light are rolling their resistless tide over the earth. . . . Doubtless there may be partial revulsions. But the great movement will . . . be progressive, till the millennial sun shall rise in all the effulgence of universal day."[13] The vision of the world saved by democracy was the secular version of the Protestant millennial hope.

Not only was there similarity between the religious and the nonreligious visions of the golden future, but the same signs were used to nourish both hopes. Throughout the Middle Period the prophets of religion and of democracy pointed to the developing humanitarian crusade as evidence that a new day was at hand. The parallels were made complete when one enthusiastic advocate of the approach of the New Jerusalem pointed to the Revolution of 1776 for proof that the advent of Christ was not far off. "Without it," he argued in the rhetoric of the public orator on Independence Day, "Europe would have remained in a state of comparative darkness and barbarity, and the cause of the Redeemer, which is the cause of liberty, could never have been developed."[14] The New Jerusalem was impossible without American democracy.

∽

The parallels between the doctrine of the democratic faith and Protestant Christianity number five. The doctrine of the fundamental moral law is related to that of the law of the divine monarch in the early Protestant version of the Kingdom of God. American constitutionalism owes a debt to John Calvin's insistence upon the restraint of evil, whether it results from the activities of individuals or of governments. The doctrine of the free individual, postulating the gradual escape of men from external political control, as they learned to obey the moral law, had its counterpart in the emphasis of the Evangelicals upon the freedom of the regenerated man from the terrors of that Old Testament code framed for the curbing of unruly and sinful generations. The philosophy of progress was similar to the Utopian hopes of the millenarians. The mission of American democracy to save the world from the oppression of autocrats was a secular version of the destiny of Christianity to save the world from the governance of Satan.

These parallels become more significant when it is recalled that certain disparities between religious and social beliefs tended to disappear in the nineteenth century. The harsh Calvinistic doctrine of man as a being corrupt by nature, incapable of saving himself, and dependent for his salvation wholly upon the grace of God, was modified by the emphasis of the evangelicals upon good works. These nineteenth-century prophets pictured man as capable of practicing virtue and so of developing character. The Unitarians at a more intellectual level emphasized the same hopeful doctrine. Both realistic and romantic democracy were postulated upon faith in the intelligence and rectitude of the common man. This faith developed slowly at first in the United States; its symbol, the right of all men to vote, was not generally accepted until the Jacksonian period. Because the Calvinist doctrine of the corrupt individual was an impediment to faith in man, Calvinism declined in significance. Because Calvinistic determinism was incompatible with the democratic theory of man-made progress, it gave way in evangelical Protestantism to a reassertion of the old Catholic doctrine of the freedom of the will, without which the democratic doctrine of the free individual was impossible.

Common influences were obviously at work modifying both religious and social beliefs. Both evangelical Protestantism and the democratic faith took form among generations whose fortune it was to live in a fruitful land, rich in undeveloped possibilities; these vigorous generations carried the boundaries of the United States westward to the Pacific in one of the most remarkable national outward thrusts in modern history. Within the United States, whether in

New England with its developing industry, or in the Old South with its expanding cotton plantations, or on the frontier on the edge of the wilderness, community life was characterized by swift change from simpler to more complex conditions. Americans of the Middle Period were conditioned from their cradles to think in terms of change and to fix their minds upon the future. Inevitably they saw civilization upon the march. The faith which had come out of Palestine was of necessity modified to fit conditions such as neither Europe nor the Near East had ever experienced. Inevitably, also, there grew up social beliefs which not only were adjusted to American conditions but which had functional significance in New World society.

The democratic faith, as has been pointed out, was a formulation of a religion of nationalism. In the twentieth century, State worship has, at times, become the aggressive rival of the Christian worship of God. Nowhere in the Western world, however, did State worship challenge in the nineteenth century the traditional religion. Such a challenge was unthinkable in the America of the Middle Period, because nationalism, beset by the obstacles of rapid expansion and of sectionalism, was struggling for supremacy over local loyalties. Protestant Christianity had not yet been weakened by its later head-on collision with naturalistic philosophies. Supernaturalism remained dominant in the American climate of opinion; as a result, during the Middle Period, the secular faith of democracy and the religious faith of a changing Protestantism were not only closely interrelated but were mutually interdependent. They complemented one another. There was no suggestion of rivalry between them. Together they provided the American with a theory of the cosmos which gave significance and direction to human life, and with a theory of society which gave a meaning not only to the relation of the individual to the group, but of the United States to the congregation of nations.

Chapter 4

EMERSON AND THOREAU

IN THE MIDDLE PERIOD of the nineteenth century the village of Concord in the Commonwealth of Massachusetts stirred with new life. Here Hawthorne wrote polished studies of damaged souls; here Bronson Alcott turned from schoolmastering to philosophy. Here Emerson, during summer days, walked often along the town's main street past stores where farmers' families came to trade, and continued on the thoroughfare after it had become a dusty country road winding into the surrounding hills. At the northern edge of the village, the Concord River was crossed by a bridge where in 1775 the opening battle of the Revolution had been fought. The patriots of Concord proudly recalled that first blow struck for American liberty by Concord men. Their bridge was becoming a shrine to which pilgrims came to venerate the spot where Americans first died for the ideal of constitutional democracy. In 1837 Concord erected a battle monument beside the bridge. Concord, therefore, was no ordinary village metropolis of a rural area. It had a past. It was old—several times as old as contemporary villages of equal size in the Upper Mississippi Valley. Many of its houses were, according to American standards, venerable. The mood of Puritanism, which had dominated its thought in the seventeenth century, still clung to it like wisps of fog that the morning sun has not yet driven from the fields. In its periodic town meetings its quiet life was governed by the methods of a well-tried democracy. To these gatherings went Emerson, to discuss with his neighbors the problems of highway upkeep and the management of the Common.

Citizen Emerson was one of the atoms that made up the Concord community. So was his young friend, Henry Thoreau, who, by the 1850's, had acquired a reputation for being a little strange.

There was mild neighborhood curiosity in 1845 concerning his lonely sojourn in a hut at Walden Pond not far away. In 1848 the villagers of Concord sometimes saw Thoreau working in Emerson's garden when the latter was in Europe. After the philosopher's return, the townspeople often watched the older and the younger man stride off together on a hike across the neighboring fields. There was some shaking of heads on the part of the church-goers. The proper business of a man, according to Puritan ethics, was work. To spend a week day alone or with a friend, as both Emerson and Thoreau frequently did, loitering about Walden Pond without even the excuse of hunting or fishing, was little short of a sin. To the scandal of the neighborhood, moreover, Thoreau refused to attend religious worship; Emerson, who had quit the ministry for what seemed to be no good cause, was only a little better. Emerson, however, was easily forgiven. He was a true son of Concord who, on the Fourth of July, 1837, had disposed of the pretensions of the rival patriots of Lexington when he had written his "Concord Hymn" to be read beside the new battle monument:

> By the rude bridge that arched the flood,
>   Their flag to April's breeze unfurled,
> Here once the embattled farmers stood
> And fired the shot heard round the world.

Concord in the Middle Period was the scene of another battle. Like the tiff of April 19, 1775, this was also a fight for liberty. There were no shock troops engaged, however, for Emerson believed neither in numbers nor in disciples. He put his faith in battalions of one or two. Only such minorities, he thought, could accomplish concrete social advances. In Concord in the 1840's and 1850's, Emerson and Thoreau marched out, like the minute men of old, to fight for new ideals. The older man was not the originator of the democratic faith, for that cluster of social beliefs rose spontaneously among the Americans of his generation, but he was its greatest prophet. Emerson sensed the individualism of his rural America. He believed in it wholeheartedly, yet he felt that the emerging faith of democracy, in spite of its momentary victories, was imprisoned within a militant and advancing evangelical Christianity. Protestantism, he thought, was a lost cause. The problem of the hour for him was the rescue, from entangling Christian superstitions, of the great doctrines of the fundamental law, of progress, and of the free individual. When Harvard, his Alma

Mater, refused to let him again speak to the student body after his address in 1838 to the Divinity School, he anticipated no quarter from his theological adversaries. As for Thoreau, he thought conventional Christianity little better than the medicine bundle carried by the Indian brave for protection.

$\sim$

In his later years Emerson, become famous, put shutters outside the lower half of his study windows to protect himself from the world. But in the two decades before the Civil War he traveled on lecture tours for thousands of miles in the crowded promiscuity of river steamboats and railroad trains. He knew the *genus Americanus* from first-hand contact. Emerson, like the commercial drummer, made his living by traveling, and the Concord philosopher was extraordinarily successful in vending his intellectual wares. His success creates a problem for the historian.

Emerson, who lectured quietly on the lyceum platform, was the antithesis of that familiar American type, the camp-meeting evangelist. No contrast could be more complete than that between the serenity of the scholar from Concord and the excited emotionalism of the exhorter. Nor was the difference limited to manner. Emerson's lectures were full of subtleties; their intellectual level was high; they usually contained passages which were over the heads of audiences untrained in philosophical thinking. By contrast, the preachers of evangelical Protestantism dispensed a simple theology. They did not normally tax the minds of their hearers; the clergy appealed from the head to the heart. The phenomenon of Emerson, ex-Unitarian minister from New England, making a success of lecturing in the Trans-Appalachian stronghold of evangelical Protestantism in the middle decades of the nineteenth century is one of the more significant episodes of the age.

Emerson's success was not due to his preaching of a mystical pantheistic transcendentalism. He talked to practical men for most of whom mysticism was, in all probability, incomprehensible. That particular type of religious experience has never been important in American culture. Emerson impressed the common folk of his generation because he preached a philosophy of individualism that not only seemed to set men free, but to provide them with dynamic, creative energy. He gave the doctrine of the free individual sharpness of definition, causing it to emerge, with the clarity of an etching, from the cloudy background of half-formulated ideas.

Throughout his early years Emerson struggled almost constantly with problems raised by the varieties of Christianity which were prevalent in the United States of his day. He never went through a Calvinist stage, so he did not have to formulate an answer to the problem of how to reconcile democracy's trust in the common man with Calvin's doctrine of the complete corruptness of human nature. Nor was Emerson compelled to undertake to harmonize Calvinistic determinism with the idea that in a democracy free men create and rule the government under which they live. For the early Emerson, Protestantism meant Unitarianism; one of the familiar stories in American history is the narrative of Emerson's growing discontent with the "pale negations" of this system, and his final decision to abandon the security of a comfortable pastorate for the hazards of independent lecturing and writing. Unitarianism, in Emerson's opinion, did not provide the dynamics which are necessary for individual creation. Unitarianism freed men from old superstitions but, when these had been thrown off, its power was spent.

Emerson, traveling over America, was aware of the forces released by evangelical Protestantism. He knew the power of that experience called conversion. He understood the evangelical concept of the free individual. But he had no use for the theology which lay behind the conversion, for it rested upon the authority of a literally inspired Scripture. For Emerson the Bible was no more inspired than some other great books. At best it recorded the experience with living of other men in other days. The poet-philosopher was willing to learn from the past, but he sought final sanctions in his own experience in the present. Man, thought Emerson, is a creature of nature. From nature he derives his individuality and his freedom. He must find in nature, rather than in the Bible, that ultimate authority which makes his freedom possible.

To Emerson the popular American version of the doctrine of the free individual was the beginning, rather than the end, of social philosophy. In American communities of the period, individualism meant the independence of the shopkeeper or of the husbandman, each man managing his affairs according to his lights and his tastes. Popular individualism emphasized social atoms; the one closely knit group which was universally recognized and approved was the family. To Emerson a man appeared to be part of something; Emerson's taste was for wholes rather than for parts. He rejected atomism, whether it appeared in social or in scientific thought. As an undergraduate at Harvard, he had studied natural philosophy only to find the scientists preoccupied with the parts of nature. Following the path of scientists since the days of Galileo and Newton, they broke down matter into molecules and molecules into atoms. But Emerson basically had as little sympathy for test tube seers as for crystal gazers. The philosophies of both were, in his opinion, destined to come to a bad end. The curse of science was its sole dependence upon the intellect. "Pure intellect," remarked Emerson, paying his respects to the eighteenth-century Enlightenment, "is the pure devil when you have got off all the masks of Mephistopheles."[1] Reason, he observed, when men depend solely upon it, leads only to science. Feeling, to him, was as important as intellectual analyses in the apprehension of nature, and, significant though science is, nature can teach man more than Newton's materialism. Scientific naturalism in Emerson's day emphasized the parts, the atoms which were thought to be the ultimate units of matter. It pictured the universe as a vast cosmic machine whose wheels within wheels fitted and worked together with infinite nicety. The incompleteness of the atom and of the individual man left Emerson dissatisfied; it outraged his aesthetic sense as did a musical discord. "To a sound judgment," he remarked, "the most abstract truth is the most practical."[2] He put behind him all systems which emphasized the many; he turned his thought—and his feelings—to the discovery of a philosophy of the one. By so doing he set his face against the prevailing winds of social and scientific thought in nineteenth-century America. "Whoso would be a man must be a nonconformist,"[3] he explained quietly as he bested his way forward.

"We walked this afternoon to Edmund Hosmer's and Walden Pond," Emerson recorded in his journal on April 9, 1842. "The south wind blew and filled with bland and warm light the dry and sunny woods. The last year's leaves blew like birds through the air. As I sat on the bank of the Drop, or God's Pond, and saw the amplitude of the little water, what space, what verge, the little scudding fleets of ripples found to scatter and spread from side to side and take so much time to cross the pond, and saw how the water seemed made for the wind and the wind for the water, dear playfellows for each other,—I said to my companion, I declare this world is so beautiful that I can hardly believe it exists."[4] Emerson did not see nature in one of its grander aspects as he walked that afternoon beside Walden Pond. Men stand in awe on the rim of the canyon of the Colorado or beneath El Capitan towering above the Merced. Emerson saw only a simple New England landscape, a commonplace composition which included water, a strip of sand and rocks, and the encircling woods. Any scientist could analyze it into its component parts. The farmers who tilled the fields lying on the flanks of the hills could do that and more. They knew where the muskrats built their tunnels and where, in the autumn, the farm dog was likely to tree a raccoon. The lore of the particular had no interest for Emerson that day at Walden. The aspect of the scene which impressed him was that "the water seemed made for the wind and the wind for the water." And the feeling came to him that he, an individual man, was made for both and both were made for him. The essence of the scene was the unity which bound the parts together and which fused the observer with the observed. In such fusion Emerson experienced the exaltation of a mystic. "The world is so beautiful," he said half in pain, "that I can hardly believe it exists." He made this unity his god. "We see the world by piece," he remarked at another time, "as the sun, the moon, the animal, the tree; but the whole, of which these are the shining parts, is the soul."[5] Emerson came to an understanding of the nature and power of that vast impersonal spirit, that Over-Soul, which is the ultimate reality of nature. "Standing on the bare ground,—my head bathed in the blithe air, and uplifted into infinite space,—all mean egotism vanishes. I become a transparent eyeball; I am nothing; I see all; the currents of the Universal Being circulate through me; I am part or parcel of God."[6]

So Emerson penetrated, as he thought, the material husks of reality to its core. Looking out from here, as from the center of a sphere, the poet saw nature and man taking on new meanings. Nature "is a great shadow pointing always to the sun behind us." A man laboring for a brief day on the earth strives for food to eat and for protection against the elements. He has the body and some of the ways of an animal. He is a transient phenomenon important today, forgotten tomorrow. His petty, untutored egotism, like that of some self-important ant, causes him to listen wistfully to the preacher who asserts that man will live forever—in another world. What a picture, thought Emerson—the Christian preacher trying with a bellows of egotism to fan into flame that divine spark, the human soul. What is man? He is a conduit through which flows moral energy, the very essence of the Over-Soul. He is a part of God; his body is an instrument to work out the purposes of God.

"Within man is the soul of the whole; the wise silence; the universal beauty, to which every part and particle is equally related; the eternal One."[7] And what of eternity? Emerson knew eternity that day at Walden Pond, when the breeze disturbed the leaves of other summers, for eternity is the realization of the unity between the transient individual and the everlasting One.

In this concept of the individual and of his relation to God may be found the key to Emerson's social philosophy. Society, he thought, is an aggregation of cohering individuals. The centrifugal forces tending to disrupt it are all too evident. They were clear enough in Emerson's day when section was muttering against section, and when the rich mill owner was too often ruthlessly exploiting the wage earner, his wife, and his child. The poor men of the East and of the West were asserting the power of their mass strength and, putting Andrew Jackson in the presidency, were smashing that symbol of financial autocracy, the great bank of the United States. Why did not democratic America, filled with greed and strife, collapse into futile chaos? Because within and behind all men was the eternal, stabilizing, unifying Over-Soul, God. The stresses in American society might seem alarming to little minds devoid of faith. They would not, however, prove fatal. Emerson welcomed even an increase of American heterogeneity. Let the immigrants come. "The energy of Irish, Germans, Swedes, Poles, and Cossacks, and all the European tribes,—and of the Africans, and of the Polynesians,—will construct a new race, a new religion, a new state, a new literature, which will be as vigorous as the new Europe which came out of the smelting-pot of the Dark Ages . . ."[8] Here was a robust optimism born of faith.

Emerson had, however, few illusions concerning the breed of American politicians, local or national. He once remarked that, if he were ever in danger of loving life unduly, he would attend a caucus of the followers of Andrew Jackson, and, "I doubt not the unmixed malignity, the withering selfishness, the impudent vulgarity, that mark those meetings would speedily cure me of my appetite for longevity."[9] Yet his faith was invincible. Within each of these slattern democrats was the spirit of the One. The mechanic plying his trade or the farmer breaking the prairie held in his hand, if he could only be made to understand it, the lightning of Jove. One such Kansas husbandman, born of the common herd, sensed his power. He struck a blow for righteousness; America quaked from Cape Cod to the Rockies. Then John Brown of Osawatomie made "the gallows glorious like the cross."

To Emerson, Brown was merely another proof of the power and importance of the free individual. The philosopher himself was such a minority of one. He sought no disciples; he formed no cult. Emerson emphasized to enthusiastic admirers that no man could follow him step by step and be a disciple. All men are different; each expresses in his own peculiar way the Over-Soul within him. To attempt to superimpose upon dissimilar men an intellectual stereotype or a fixed pattern of action was for Emerson the unforgivable sin. Regimentation, he thought, destroyed the souls of men.

When Emerson was preparing the lectures published as *Essays, First Series*, the collectivist philosophy of Charles Fourier was much discussed in America. Albert Brisbane and Horace Greeley were its New World prophets. The decade of the 1840's was a time of ferment as America slowly recovered from the depression of 1837–1842. American mores were not fixed; the desire for experiment was in the air. The famous Brook Farm Community near Concord did not at first accept the Fourierist pattern, but tried out the collectivist ideas of the Concord transcendentalists. Emerson's attitude toward the Brook Farm venture illustrates the quality of his thought. He, the philosopher of individualism, did not dismiss collectivism with sarcasm. He attended the preliminary conferences which created the Farm. Here was a social experiment to be honestly undertaken. It might demonstrate that collectivism is the handmaid of individualism; it might prove that the soul of the individual man can develop more readily and express itself more freely in a communal than in a competitive social pattern. Emerson listened to the plans of the eager founders. On October 17, 1840, he set down his conclusions in his *Journal*. "Yesterday George and Sophia Ripley, Margaret Fuller and Alcott discussed here the Social Plans [Brook Farm]. I wished to be convinced, to be thawed, to be made nobly mad by the kindling before my eye of a new dawn of human piety. But this scheme was arithmetic and comfort; this was a hint borrowed from Tremont House and the United States Hotel; a rage in our poverty and politics to live rich and gentlemanlike, an anchor to leeward against a change of weather; a prudent forecast on the probable issue of the great questions of Pauperism and Poverty. And not once could I be inflamed, but sat aloof and thoughtless; my voice faltered and fell. It was not the cave of persecution which is the palace of spiritual power, but only a room in the Astor House hired for the Transcendentalists. I do not wish to remove from my present prison to a prison a little larger. I wish to break all prisons. I have not yet conquered my own house. It irks me and repents me.

Shall I raise the siege of this hencoop, and march baffled away to a pretended siege of Babylon? It seems to me that to do so were to dodge the problem I am set to solve, and to hide my impotency in the thick of a crowd. I can see too, afar,—that I should not find myself more than now,—no, not so much, in that select, but not by me selected, fraternity. Moreover, to join this body would be to traverse all my long-trumpeted theory, and the instinct which spoke from it, that one man is a counterpoise to a city,—that a man is stronger than a city, that his solitude is more prevalent and beneficent than the concert of crowds."[10]

So Emerson rejected the experimental collectivism of his day. It is the individual man in whose heart the Over-Soul, the Universal Mind, finds a dwelling place who is all important, Emerson concluded, in spite of Brook Farm. Standing on the frontier between the past, with its social heritage, and the future, with its promises, he fashions his own history and with it that of nations and of the world. Too long the dogmas of an outworn Christianity have kept man from understanding the power that lies within him. In the United States where the democratic faith provides the ideals by which to measure conduct, men are beginning to discover the individual, but their vision of what constitutes a man is blurred by old theologies. Teach these sons to know themselves and the nation will be on the march toward an empire of the spirit. Such an America, rising on the western shore of the Atlantic, must become a flaming beacon, lighting for all the world the path of human destiny.

⌢

"I spoke of friendship," wrote Emerson in his *Journal* in 1848, "but my friends and I are fishes in our habit. As for taking Thoreau's arm, I should as soon take the arm of an elm tree."[11] "Henry is military," he added five years later. "He seems stubborn and implacable; always manly and wise, but rarely sweet. One would say that, as Webster could never speak without an antagonist, so Henry does not feel himself except in opposition. He wants a fallacy to expose, a blunder to pillory, requires a little sense of victory, a roll of the drums, to call his powers into full exercise."[12] Emerson was, perhaps, a bit unfair to his young friend, who had been a member of his household, and who, after some schoolmastering and a little surveying, was in 1845 retiring from society to his hut on Walden Pond. *Walden*, which Thoreau distilled from that experiment, was more affirmation than rejection. Even so, to the end of his days the celibate pencil-maker remained an adversary of American civilization, a stiff-backed solitary soldier who tramped stubbornly in the opposite direction from the army's line of march.

Thoreau's New England was bustling with industrial enterprise. The Holyoke dam first successfully held back the Connecticut in 1849, the year in which Thoreau published *Civil Disobedience*. Almost every New England stream was turning the wheels of some mill or factory. Boston was the rendezvous of entrepreneurs great and small, men skilled in the strategems and tactics, the deceptive retreats and surprise attacks essential to the art of pecuniary competition. Thoreau was shocked at the thought of a man spending his years at such an occupation when nature had given so short a time to live. In 1843 he read with growing anger in an English pamphlet of that economy of plenty which would result from the harnessing of the powers of nature and making them serve men through machines. "Fellowmen!" exclaimed the enthusiastic innovator, J. A. Etzler, "I promise to show the means of creating a paradise within ten years, where everything desirable for human life may be had by every man in superabundance, without labor, and without pay."[13] For Thoreau machines were gadgets which made life so complicated that they made living difficult; they were burdens which men carried on their backs; they blighted alike the lives of the children who tended them in factories and of the entrepreneurs who had them built. Thoreau never compromised with the machine; he never ceased to despise—and to pity—those men whose days were filled with business and whose goal was wealth. Fortunes, like machines, increased the difficulty of living. Thoreau lived for many months in his hut at Walden to prove to himself and to whomsoever might be interested that nature is sufficient, that the machine confines rather than frees the spirit. The machine, he thought, was becoming a menace to the free individual.

What made the machine, and the economic system of which it was a part, evil in Thoreau's eyes was a philosophy of life, a system of ethics. Puritanism still possessed sufficient power in his day to cast what Thoreau looked upon as a blight over New England. Puritanism had sanctified work and the Puritans had developed the principle that man serves God by working into a worldly asceticism. Work became a prime symbol of the good life. Thoreau objected. Work, he thought, is not in itself noble. It is, however, necessary. Thoreau earned his livelihood; he had neither patron nor inherited wealth. By the material standards of the day he remained always a poor man. Thoreau rejected the Puritan ethic of work because so often and so persuasively it betrayed men into sacrificing their lives in the struggle for material success. Thoreau once suggested that the goods of the market place be priced in terms of the amount of living that had been given up to produce them. Such an amount was considerable in Thoreau's time, when the twelve-hour day was normal for the wage-earners in factory and shop.

To be free to enjoy the companionship of men and of nature; to know the beauty of the woods and of the stars and to be able to appreciate it; to sense the reality of that Divine Spirit that moves in all living things and to feel the thrill that comes from that awareness; that is living. Like Emerson, Thoreau sought the transcendentalist's god in nature. Not the disciplined and domesticated nature of the husbandman and the gardener which Bronson Alcott glorified, but nature in its wild state. The creation of national parks in the twentieth century and especially the setting aside of wilderness areas express an urge that Thoreau, a century earlier, made articulate. Thoreau found in nature a solution for his own personal desire to simplify his life so that he might live. Other men might find other ways. The quality of human life, more than the achievements of a man, interested the Concord pencil-maker.

As for the State, in spite of its potential capacity to assist its citizens in finding life, it compromised with evil. It sanctioned the materialism that warped and stunted human lives. More important, Massachusetts compromised with that greatest of all evils, chattel slavery. When the Federal government called for soldiers from 1846 to 1848 in the war against Mexico whose purpose James Russell Lowell declared was "to lug new slave states in," Massachusetts responded. Thoreau, aged thirty-two, wrote *Civil Disobedience*.

Thoreau's argument assumed that the individual comes into the world to live and not necessarily to make it better. This particular and separate personality has a conscience enabling him to know, and directing him to obey, the "higher law" of his nature. The citizen must not "resign his conscience to the legislator." He cannot accept the principle of majority rule; "any man more right than his neighbors constitutes a majority of one already." Majorities, in deciding what is expedient, rule by force. They make the law; the State is their instrument for its enforcement. "Laws never made a man a whit more just." The men who serve the government too often forget conscience and obey force; the State robs them of their manhood. "Visit the Navy-yard," said Thoreau, "and behold a marine, such a man as an American government can make, or such as it can make a man with its black arts,—a mere shadow and reminiscence of humanity, a man laid out alive and standing, and already, as one may say buried under arms." To Thoreau the professional soldier personified the negation of individual freedom.

If, perchance, the State be just, added the militant Thoreau, let the citizen share in its virtue. But if it be unjust, and such is the common characteristic of government, let him remember that "all men recognize the right of revolution; that is, the right to refuse allegiance to, and to resist the government, when its tyranny or its inefficiency are great and unendurable." Thoreau made no distinction between federal and local power; because Massachusetts did not refuse completely to cooperate in the war of spoliation against Mexico, he called her "a drab of state, a cloth-o'-silver slut." And it was a Massachusetts tax which he refused to pay. He advocated and practiced passive resistance.

Before his mind rose a vision of a better world, not the Paradise of the Christians, nor the communal Utopia of the Fourierists, but one dominated by the individual, free in all things save in the right to violate his conscience. "There will never be a really free and enlightened State until the State comes to recognize the individual as a higher and independent power, from which all its own power and authority are derived, and treats him accordingly. I please myself with imagining a State at last which can afford to be just to all men, and to treat the individual with respect as a neighbor; which even would not think it inconsistent with its own repose if a few were to live aloof from it, not meddling with it, nor embraced by it, who fulfilled all the duties of neighbors and fellow-men. A State which bore this kind of fruit, and suffered it to drop off as fast as it ripened, would prepare the way for a still more perfect and glorious State, which also I have imagined, but not yet anywhere seen."[14] Disclaim it though he did, Thoreau was a crusader for a better world.

Emerson was often puzzled by the words and the doings of his brilliant friend. In spite of their mutual sympathy and of their common transcendentalism, they were, in some respects, far apart. The older man shook his head over the Walden experiment. "Henry Thoreau," he remarked, "is like the wood-god who solicits the wandering poet and draws him into antres vast and deserts idle, and bereaves him of his memory, and leaves him naked, plaiting vines and with twigs in his hand."[15] Thoreau's rebellion seemed to

Emerson too much a matter of denials. So it was, for the naturalist was not given time to work his way through to the affirmations concerning the conduct of life which he wished one day to make, and which he hoped to find in a study of nature. Fate overruled him. One day in the spring of the year 1862, when McClellan in Virginia was preparing his assault upon Richmond, Emerson wrote sadly in his *Journal:* "Sam Staples yesterday had been to see Henry Thoreau. 'Never spent an hour with more satisfaction. Never saw a man dying with so much pleasure and peace.' " On May 6 Thoreau passed, content with his denials and to leave the affirmations to other men.

Thoreau did not change the trends of his age. The state continued unaltered. The tempo of industrial development increased. Within two decades after Thoreau's death the name Horatio Alger became a household word. But Americans did not forget the man who refused to compromise his principles. Today the pile of stones, placed by pilgrims on the spot where Thoreau built his Walden hut, grows higher each year.

∾

Emerson and Thoreau lived in that epoch in which the American frontier was sweeping westward to the Pacific. On the edge of the wilderness, individualism was the normal and inevitable way of life. Here men, like Bill Williams, were free. Out of the frontier came American insistence upon personal liberty. But the freedom of Williams was that of escape. He abandoned a society whose growing complexity increased the problem of living. In the older communities, increase in numbers multiplied the restraints upon the individual man. The institutions which men established put them in shackles. The strong preyed upon the weak. For such problems the frontier, save only as it kept alive the ideal of the free individual, had no solution. It was a transient moment. And when it passed, the tasks of the East would become those of the West.

Emerson and Thoreau remained in New England in an environment in which, already, wealth was passing into the hands of the few. The rough equalitarianism of the frontier had long since disappeared. These two friends faced the issues of their day in the region where solutions were hardest to find. Both were dissenters. Their significance lay in the fact that they served as spokesmen for an emerging democratic faith and, in so doing, gave comfort to men groping for enlightenment in an era in which society was closing in upon the individual. Emerson taught the individual the nobility of himself, the divinity of the average human. Thoreau insisted that the individual was right in his dissatisfaction with organized society, whether it was the college, the bank, the railroad, the Church, or the State. For both men the central problem was one of ethics, and the task of the moment was to make moral energy effective upon the earth. Both began with the doctrine of the fundamental law and interpreted it in ethical terms. Each insisted that human freedom is only achieved when men express, in their lives, that moral sentiment which permeates nature from the center of the cosmos to its circumference. Both were hopeful that the ideals of the democratic faith could be made to triumph over the materialism of American business and politics. Emerson expressed the mood of these two Concord rebels, who were carrying on the fight which had been started by the farmers at the bridge. "We are not minors and invalids," said the poet speaking for all Americans who venerated the idealism of democracy, "not cowards fleeing before a revolution, but guides, redeemers, benefactors, obeying the Almighty effort and advancing on Chaos and the Dark."[16]

Chapter 5

DEMOCRACY AND CATHOLICISM
IN THE MIDDLE PERIOD

A NATIONAL FAITH NEEDS AN ADVERSARY. It thrives best, as Emerson remarked, when its prophets have a fallacy to expose, a blunder to pillory. The faithful require a little sense of victory, a roll of the drums, to call their powers into full exercise. What the capitalist was to Lenin in 1917 and the Jew to Hitler in 1935, the Catholic was to the American democrat in the middle of the nineteenth century. The ogre of American democracy was the Scarlet Woman of Babylon. The shadow of the Reformation still lay across America.

Catholics were a small minority in the Middle Period. Some were descended from seventeenth-century refugees from England, and others from French and Spanish colonists in communities such as New Orleans and in the Upper Mississippi Valley which had become parts of the United States. More recently they were immigrants from Ireland and Germany. Catholicism in pre-Sumter America, when the Church was still weak, was, for the democrats, an enemy close at hand. It could be attacked with impunity, a great advantage when a bellicose mood was to be created. The chief utility for the democratic faith of the Catholic "menace" was the transference of the crusade of democracy from the level of intellectual combat, where only a few champions could participate, to that of practical politics and physical violence, where every son of liberty could strike his blow for righteousness. During the 1830's and the 1840's, mobs in widely separated parts of the United States terrorized and oppressed at times the Catholic minority. When, in 1834, Massachusetts democrats burned the Ursuline Convent in

Charlestown, they not only gave expression to their native pugnacity, but they achieved a victory which, however specious, was of a type they could understand.

On January 11, 1830, respectable citizens of Connecticut, that land of steady habits where Congregationalists predominated, drew close to their fires to read their conservative newspaper, *The Connecticut Observer*. It was a dull journal, on the whole, and much given to the dissemination of religious news; yet on this day the editor exploded a bomb. "It has more than once been stated," he wrote, "that the crowned heads of Europe would make almost any sacrifice to bring this country under a similar form of government. So long as the example of the United States is held out before the world, the subjects of monarchical governments will have a hankering after the liberty enjoyed by republicans. And it has been suggested that the monarchs of Europe would hope, by the introduction of the Roman Catholic religion into this country, to effect their object. One thing appears certain. The king of Bavaria, a Roman Catholic empire, is preparing to pour out her treasures for the same purpose.—And Catholic France unites in the project. Let infidelity succeed in checking the associations among us for disseminating the truth, and the way will be opened for the success of these schemes, which we are informed on the authority of Roman Catholics themselves, are forming against us in more than one country in Europe." Four years later S. F. B. Morse, tinkerer with electrical impulses and portrait painter to America's elite, returned from Europe to write a book proving the truth of the theory of a foreign Catholic plot against American democracy. He published his astonishing assertions in the same year the Charlestown convent was gutted.

Anti-Catholicism became a nation-wide movement. Secret organizations sprang up under such names as the Sons of the Sires, the United Sons of America, and the Supreme Order of the Star-Spangled Banner. These societies coalesced into the Native American party, known in the early 1850's as the Know-Nothing party because of the secrecy enshrouding its membership and its activities. The stream of immigrants, most of whom were Catholics, increasing to a veritable flood after 1848, created a sense of crisis in the minds of thousands of Americans. Members of the in-group resented, sometimes violently, the intrusion of outlanders. In the South where foreigners were scarce, politicians sometimes ranted against "Catholic control" in the cities of the North and East. To them Catholicism seemed to threaten the civilization of America. Patriots, breathing fire, stamped into nativism.

One of these was William G. Brownlow of Knoxville, Tennessee. For Parson Brownlow the way of life was completely illumined by evangelical Protestantism and by the democratic faith. He had been brought up, a poor boy, in the hill country of eastern Tennessee. Denied any but a rudimentary education, he became a carpenter and later an itinerant Methodist preacher. Standing in the pulpit six feet tall and booming out his periods in a powerful voice, he was a man to make sinners quail. For ten years after 1826 he battled on the circuit for the Lord. Then that almost universal interest of mid-nineteenth-century Americans claimed him. He went into politics and became an editor for the Whigs. During two turbulent pre-Sumter decades he fought unceasingly and effectively for nationalism. His Knoxville *Whig* became the most influential paper before the war in that section of the state. Through its columns he assailed secession unceasingly until, at the order of the Confederate government, his journal was suppressed in October, 1861. Through the stresses of the Civil War period, Brownlow held fast to his nationalist faith. After Appomattox he followed Andrew Johnson as reconstruction governor of Tennessee.

A militant Know-Nothing in the 1850's, Brownlow gave the perfect expression to the mood of the nativist crusade to save American democracy from Catholicism. "Mental light and personal independence, constitutional union, national supremacy, submission to law and rules of order, homogeneous population, and instinctive patriotism, are all vital elements of American liberty, nationality, and upward and onward progress," he proclaimed in 1856. "Foreign immigration, foreign Catholic influence, and sectional factions nourished by them—and breeding demagogues in the name of *Democracy*, by a prostitution of the elective franchise—have already corrupted our nationality, degraded our councils, both State and National, weakened the bonds of union, disturbed our country's peace, and awakened apprehensions of insecurity and *progressive deterioration*, threatening ultimate ruin!"[1]

When Brownlow wrote, however, Know-Nothingism was already in decline. The issue of slavery had torn the party asunder at its national convention in 1855. Americans were moving toward 1861. When John Brown was hanged in 1859, nativism as a significant movement had disappeared. The foe within the gates took precedence over the enemy without. In 1862 a brigade of Irish Catholics stormed Marye's Heights at Fredericksburg, fighting shoulder to shoulder with ex-nativists for "liberty" and "union."

◇

"The Roman Catholic religion . . . is necessary to sustain popular liberty," wrote Orestes Brownson in 1852 when nativism was at flood tide, "because popular liberty can be sustained only by a religion free from popular control, above the people, speaking from above and able to command them,—and such a religion is the Roman Catholic. It acknowledges no master but God, and depends only on the divine will in respect to what it shall teach, what it shall ordain, what it shall insist upon as truth, piety, moral and social virtue. It was made not by the people, but for them; is administered not by the people, but for them; is accountable not to the people, but to God."[2] What gave sting to Brownson's words was the fact that he was not a foreigner, but had been born and reared a Protestant among the granite hills of Vermont.

The weakness of Protestantism in the Middle Period was its sectarianism. To some Americans, Protestant preachers in urging their exclusive brands of Christianity seemed like the barkers for rival attractions at the county fair. Denominationalism impaired the prestige of Protestantism. When Methodists, Baptists, Presbyterians, and Campbellites all claimed the Bible as authority for their varying beliefs, some individuals became bewildered. They lost that sense of intellectual security which is the end product of religion. Inevitably some anxious souls sought the reassurance of an authoritarian Church. Two such organizations played minor rôles in the United States during the Middle Period. One, the Catholic Church, was old; the other, the Church of Jesus Christ of the Latter-Day Saints, was new. The latter was indigenous. Its creed and its theology were under debt to a wide variety of American folk beliefs. In spite of its Americanisms, however, it attracted in the nineteenth century only a handful of followers. Mormonism became a local phenomenon, practically limited to the western mountains. Catholicism, however, thanks to the immigrant flood which did not end until 1914, grew in time to be a nation-wide organization. In twentieth-century America the Catholic Church, overtopping even the largest Protestant denominations, has become a power of unmeasurable importance. For this reason, if for no other, the efforts in the Middle Period of

Orestes Brownson and of Isaac Hecker to harmonize Catholic doctrine and the American democratic faith are matters of significance.

◇

Orestes Brownson was a product of American religious liberty.
He belonged to a type which that keen and genial observer of
things American, Hector St. John de Crèvecoeur, had noticed as
early as the eighteenth century. The author of *The Letters of an
American Farmer* had described an acquaintance who passed in
rapid succession from Presbyterianism to the brotherhood of the
Baptists, to schism, and finally to a church in which he was both
shepherd and flock. Brownson was such an intellectual wanderer.
His mother, left a destitute widow when he was four, entrusted the
child to an elderly Vermont farm family. With them Orestes attended the Congregational meeting house where he heard the
doctrines of Jonathan Edwards. As he grew older, disillusion sapped
his faith, for the church seemed but an association of men without
knowledge or authority. Brownson longed for security; Congrega-
tionalism did not offer it. He joined the Presbyterians, only to find
his developing humanitarianism jolted by a Calvinism still insisting
that God desired the eternal damnation of some men. Brownson fled
to Universalism. By this time he was grown to manhood and had to
think of earning a living. He became a Universalist preacher and
the editor of their periodical, *The Gospel Advocate*. For a time,
satisfied with the doctrine of universal salvation, he sought to make
everybody happy. But his joy faded when one day he asked himself
and then his irritated co-religionists why, if all men are to be saved,
any man should be good. Brownson gave up Universalism and
Christianity to be a "World Reformer." He fell in with the re-
formism and the socialism of Fanny Wright and of Robert Owen.
He grieved over the hard lot of the wage earner. In 1829, after
Owen's New Harmony community had collapsed when its patron
refused longer to meet its deficit, Brownson assisted in the founding
of a secret society for the purpose of de-Christianizing the United
States by establishing a system of schools from which God would
be excluded. "The whole country was to be organized," remarked
Brownson later, "somewhat on the plan of the carbonari of Italy, or
as were the revolutionists throughout Europe by Bazard preparatory
to the revolutions of 1820 and 1830."[3] The carbonari phase of
Brownson's life lasted about a year. He found that he could not live
in a Godless world. Continuing his search for security, he allied

himself with the liberal Unitarians and again became a preacher. He read the philosophy of Benjamin Constant and Victor Cousin. He resigned his pastorate to support a growing family by editing in Boston what he called the *Democratic Review*. Because he was a vigorous writer, forthright, and always controversial, his magazine became a success, with enthusiastic subscribers as far away as South Carolina. He knew most of the literary men of New England and discussed their writings. Theology, philosophy, and politics were his staples. Yet the editor was still dissatisfied. Finding in Unitarianism no security, he pursued this phantom with the determination of a hound on the track of a fox, baying the while. All New England knew by the noisy *Review* whither led Brownson's trail. In 1844 he joined the Catholic Church, a few months before Oxford's Newman and about a year after his young friend, Isaac Hecker.

At once the indefatigable Brownson set out to convert his fellow countrymen to Catholicism with all the ardor with which he had once sought to bring them into the happy fold of the Universalists. His new friends among the bishops did not share his optimism, but they organized a cheering section when he turned the editorial guns of the *Review* upon the Know-Nothings. In Brownson they had a native American to pit against the Native Americans. Editor Brownson brought such patriots as Parson Brownlow to the verge of apoplexy when the *Democratic Review* proclaimed that only the Pope could make America safe for democracy.

Brownson's argument has already been suggested. The democratic faith, whether preached by the Protestants or by the transcendentalists, implied the fundamental goodness of human nature. If human nature were not sound at core, how could men be trusted to govern themselves. "It is a beautiful theory," said Brownson, "and would work admirably, if it were not for one little difficulty, namely,—the people are fallible, both individually and collectively, and governed by their passions and interests, which not unfrequently lead them far astray, and produce much mischief. The government must necessarily follow their will; and whenever that will happens to be blinded by passion, or misled by ignorance or interest, the government must inevitably go wrong; and government can never go wrong without doing injustice. The government may be provided for; the people may take care of that; but who or what is to take care of the people, and assure us that they will always wield the government so as to promote justice and equality, or maintain order, and the equal rights of all, of all classes and interests? Do not answer by referring us to the virtue and intelligence of the people. We are writing seriously, and have no leisure to enjoy a joke, even if it be a good one."[4]

The people, Brownson went on, are subjects of God and in duty bound to obey his law. Their wills are free, and they may be disobedient if they choose. And many choose this way. But in the end they pay the price, because God is just. The most important part of the democratic faith in Brownson's opinion was its first doctrine, that of a fundamental moral law. Beside this tenet, the doctrine of the free individual seemed to him of small importance. "We have heard enough of liberty and the rights of man," snorted Brownson; "it is high time to hear something of the duties of men and the rights of authority."[5] Two questions demanded answer. They had to do with the precise content of the moral law and with the discovery of what authority on earth is charged with ultimate responsibility for enforcing that law. Brownson thought the answers to these questions so simple as to be found in a child's catechism.

The Founder of Christianity, before he left the earth, passed on his authority to Peter and through Peter to the one true Church. God works through this Church in the world. Because it is inspired, its knowledge of the will of God is infallible. "We say, then," Brownson went on, "if democracy commits the government to the people to be taken care of, religion is to take care that they take proper care of the government, rightly direct and wisely administer it. But what religion? It must be a religion which is above the people and controls them, or it will not answer the purpose . . . It cannot be Protestantism. . . . The people must have a master. . . . The religion which is to answer our purpose must be above the people and able to command them. We know the force of the word, and we mean it. The first lesson of the child is, obey. . . . The Roman Catholic religion, then, is necessary to sustain popular liberty, because popular liberty can be sustained only by a religion free from popular control, above the people, speaking from above and able to command them."[6]

Parson Brownlow boiled over. "Protestants!" he shouted, "do you hear. . . . The price of liberty is eternal vigilance. We apply the remark to civil as well as religious liberty. All we ask of the people is to be vigilant."[7]

The usual retort to Brownson was to call him a weathervane who shifted with the changing winds. What faith, asked the scoffers, will he espouse tomorrow? But Brownson disappointed them. After years of intellectual wandering he had found security. He cast his lot with a persecuted minority and openly defended them. He faced calmly, almost indifferently, jibes and abuse. "I have never been a slave to my own past," he said in 1866 in the preface of his last important book, "and truth has always been dearer to me than my own opinions." Brownson at the time was aging. His full beard was white, as was also the hair which he brushed back from a high, sloping forehead. His eyes looked out through small, gold-rimmed spectacles. "It is no discredit to a man in the United States at the present day to be a firm, sincere, and devout Catholic," he added. "The old sectarian prejudice may remain with a few, 'whose eyes,' as Emerson says, 'are in their hind-head, not in their fore-head': but the American people are not at heart sectarian, and the nothingarianism so prevalent among them only marks their state of transition from sectarian opinions to postive Catholic faith."[8] This dream of a golden age when American democracy would be settled firmly upon the foundation of Catholicity dominated the adult life of Isaac Thomas Hecker.

꙳

Hecker was born in New York City in 1819, the birth year of Herman Melville and of Walt Whitman. His Protestant parents were thrifty German immigrants, substantial people who, when they had no money to give their son a college education, apprenticed him to a baker. Hecker, a precocious boy, apparently inherited from his devout mother his tendency to preoccupation with religious matters. When scarcely in his teens he espoused the communistic ideals of the Workingman's party in his native city. His activities brought him into contact with Orestes Brownson, sixteen years his senior and then a vigorous humanitarian. The boy accepted the perfectionism of Brownson's social philosophy with uncritical admiration.

Isaac was what his companions would call an odd boy. Born to a life of seriousness and from his early years given to lonely brooding, he had a feeling of being sent into the world to accomplish a mission. What the mission was he did not know, but its discovery he accepted as his first duty. Within him at times raged emotional storms which originated in the mysterious shadows of his inner life. Their passing left him limp and sometimes ill. There were times when the adolescent doubted himself. Yet he never lost sight of the perfectionist dream acquired from Brownson.

At the latter's suggestion young Hecker, who had became a good baker, propped Immanuel Kant's *Critique of Pure Reason* beside his kneading board. A little later, again following Brownson's advice, much as his contemporaries went to college, he went to Brook Farm. In spite of a seriousness which kept him aloof from such gaieties as the Farm afforded, he seems to have been liked by the transcendentalists. No doubt his popularity was due in part to the good bread he made; an experienced baker was a godsend to the visionary "Farmers." Yet he was liked for himself. He attended Ripley's lectures on Kant and Spinoza. He journeyed to the village of West Roxbury to hear that great humanitarian, Theodore Parker, and to Concord to talk with Emerson. After Hecker had left the Farm, Ripley wrote: "When will you come back to Brook Farm? Can you do without us? Can we do without you? But do not come as an amateur, a self-perfectionizer, an aesthetic self-seeker, willing to suck the orange of Association dry and throw away the peel."[9] The overtones of the last sentence suggest Hecker's preoccupation with his personal problems even in the midst of "Association." His closest friend at the Farm, George William Curtis, dubbed him "Ernest the Seeker," after the title of a story of unrest from the pen of William Henry Channing which was being published at the moment in the *Dial*. Isaac came to Brook Farm to find his mission; at the end of six months he admitted that his quest had failed. The transcendentalism of the "Farmers" did not stir his soul.

He left the Farm with regret; he liked its friendliness and the interest of its people in things of the mind and spirit. It was a welcome escape from the materialism of New York City. But Hecker was not seeking escape. The riddle of his mission drew him on. "I am called with a stronger voice," he noted a little sadly in his diary on July 7, 1843; "I go to Mr. Alcott's at Fruitlands next Tuesday."[10] So Hecker gave transcendentalism one last chance. Five days later, after the plates had been pushed away at the end of his first breakfast at Fruitlands, he participated in a community discussion on "Friendship and its laws and conditions. Mr. Alcott placed Innocence first; Larned, Thoughtfulness; I, Seriousness; Lane, Fidelity."[11] No conversation could have better disclosed the men; the unbelievable innocence of Bronson Alcott in a hard-boiled world, the super-seriousness of Hecker, and the faithfulness of Charles Lane who had come from England to put his few shillings into the purchase of Fruitlands for Alcott's experiment. After the philosophical discussion, the community turned to the day's work on the land. On the following morning Alcott led the conversation on "The Highest Aim." The schoolmaster declared it to be integrity; Hecker, rising to philosophic heights, propounded as the answer "Harmonic Being." What he meant he apparently did not know, for, four days later, he admitted to his journal that "being is incomprehensible." He added: "I cannot understand what it is that leads me, or what I am after."[12] Whatever it was, it led Hecker out of Fruitlands in exactly two weeks. He returned to New York.

"Hecker has flunked out," Alcott remarked to Lane. Scarcely four months later Lane wrote pathetically to Hecker: "As all my cash has been expended in buying and keeping up the affair, I am left in a precarious position, out of which I do not see the way without some loveful aid, and to you I venture freely to submit my feelings."[13]

In the following summer when young Isaac was on the threshold of the Catholic Church, he summed up his conclusions concerning transcendentalism: "A transcendentalist," he noted in his dairy, "is one who has keen sight but little warmth of heart; who has fine conceits but is destitute of the rich glow of love. . . . He is all nerve and no blood—colorless. He talks of self-reliance, but fears to trust himself to love. . . . Behold him sitting on a chair; he is not sitting, but braced upon its angles, as if his bones were of iron and his nerves steel; every nerve is drawn, his hands are closed like a miser's—it is his lips and head that speak, not his tongue and heart. . . . Nature is his church, and he is his own god."[14] There was some rationalization here—and some forgetting. Breaking away from transcendentalism was a hard wrench for Isaac, the Seeker, and it was aided by calling the old faith hard names.

The spring of 1844 found Hecker in Concord studying Greek and Latin with a famous teacher, George P. Bradford, and still trying to solve, if possible, the mystery of his mission. He found lodgings at the home of Cynthia Thoreau, Henry's mother. "All that is needed for my comfort is here," he wrote his family, "a good straw bed, a large table, carpet, washstand, book-case, stove, chairs, looking-glass—all, all that is needful. And this for seventy-five cents a week, including lights; wood is extra pay. . . . The lady of the house, Mrs. Thoreau, *is a woman*. The only fear I have about her is that she is too much like dear mother—she will take too much care of me. She has told me how she used to sit up nights, waiting for a young man whom she had taken to board, to come home. He was a stranger to her, but still she insists that she must treat all as she would her own, and even with greater care."[15]

Mrs. Thoreau, who loved the out-of-doors almost as much as her brilliant son, must have shaken her head more than once when she discovered that her tenant, save for a brief hour with his tutor, stayed in his room from morning till night. She would have been more worried if she had been aware that heavenly messages, coming in dreams and in reveries in the solitude of his study, were pulling young Hecker toward the Catholic Church. One day he went off to Boston. When he returned, he let it be known that he had become a Catholic. Henry Thoreau, who had recently returned from Staten Island and was beginning to plan the Walden experiment, listened to Hecker's announcement with mingled astonishment and contempt. "What's the use of your joining the Catholic Church?" he asked. "Can't you get along without hanging to her skirts?"[16] The attitude was typical of Thoreau, upstanding and self-contained, who looked upon Christianity as a sheaf of superstitions. He did not know that Hecker's lonely quest for his mission had ended in a religious experience of an intensity which in frontier camp meetings sent men and women into convulsions. The day after the doors of the Church opened and Hecker first received the Sacrament, he poured out his heart to his diary: "My soul is clothed in brightness; its youth is restored. O blessed, ever-blessed, unfathomable, divine faith! O faith of apostles, martyrs, confessors and saints! Holy Mother of Jesus, thou art my mother."[17] Isaac Hecker could not say such things in the presence of Henry Thoreau.

Thoreau told Emerson of the conversation. The Sage of Concord was disturbed. Hecker's was the first defection from the ranks of the transcendentalists. Emerson invited Isaac to tea and in the talk led up again and again to the subject, only to find his guest skillful in avoiding his stratagem. On the next day Emerson asked the young ex-transcendentalist to go with him to their mutual friends, the Shakers, at Harvard, some fifteen miles from Concord. They stayed all night. During the two long drives the older man earnestly sought the reasons for Hecker's decision, with the purpose of trying to dissuade him. Then Alcott and Emerson arranged matters in such a way as to corner the convert in an interview which ended abruptly when Hecker, becoming angry, said: "Mr. Alcott, I deny your inquisitorial right in this matter." Emerson made one last effort. He overtook Hecker on the road one day, when each was out for a walk. "Mr. Hecker," he remarked as they swung into stride, "I suppose it was the art, the architecture, and so on in the Catholic Church which led you to her?" "No," replied the Seeker, "but it was what caused all that."[18] Hecker saw Emerson only once after that day.

The first years in the new life into which Isaac Hecker had entered were crammed with experiences. He went to Europe to study Catholicism with the Redemptorists. He became a member of that order and returned to America as a Redemptorist missionary. As the months passed, however, the order seemed so rooted in tradition as to be ineffective for his purpose in the United States. After many years, Isaac Hecker had found his mission. It was nothing less than to save American democracy by converting Americans to Catholicism. The perfectionism which he had learned from Brownson, the World Reformer, and from his Brook Farm associates, still dominated his thought. He dreamed of a golden age in America when men would be made perfect through the union of democratic liberty with Catholic spirituality; he felt himself called of God to bring this vision to realization. His Redemptorist brothers did not understand. Difficulties arose. Hecker went to Rome where he confessed his hopes and dreams to Pius IX, who listened eagerly. The Pope released Brother Hecker from his Redemptorist vows and commissioned him to found a new order, to be called significantly, the Paulists.

As Paul had been the missionary to the Gentiles, so Hecker would become the missionary to America. He gathered a small but intensely earnest group of American Catholics. They took no vows, for Hecker, true to his mid-nineteenth-century American background, emphasized individualism. They conducted missions in Catholic churches where the flame of religion was burning low. They were, in fact, the Catholic counterpart of the Protestant revivalists, but, unlike so many of these exhorters, the Paulists were carefully selected and were highly trained. Their organization, moreover, increased the effectiveness of each one. They remained small in numbers, yet their influence in American Catholicism was beyond the possibility of measurement. It was a Paulist missionary who, in New Orleans, discovered and turned toward the priesthood that son of poverty who ultimately became Cardinal Gibbons.

But Hecker was not content. His objective was the capture of America. After Sumter he turned to lecturing to non-Catholic audiences. He founded the first daily paper of his Church in America, *The Catholic World*. In the press and on the platform he presented the formula which he had developed and which he believed would bring the victory he sought.

Unlike Brownson, Hecker emphasized the second doctrine of the democratic faith, that of the free individual. He began with Jefferson, who had put into the Declaration of Independence the fundamental democratic tenet that men possess the natural rights of life, liberty, and the pursuit of happiness. This affirmation, declared Hecker, is sound. Jefferson reached his conclusions by following reason. Reason, thought Hecker, when properly guarded, is the Holy Spirit working in the individual. Was it not reason which had taken Isaac Hecker out of transcendentalism and into the Catholic Church? Reason had brought Jefferson to that great truth, the importance of individual liberty. "Man is by nature in possession of his free will," said Hecker, "and therefore freedom is his birthright, and he holds it in trust for his creator as the source of his happiness."[19] So the American Paulist was wont to begin his discourse to the Protestants who, after Appomattox, crowded night after night into his lecture halls. "Man has lost none of his original faculties," Hecker went on, "and has forfeited none of his natural rights by Adam's fall, and therefore is by nature in possession of his natural rights, and it is rightly said: 'Among these are life, liberty, and the pursuit of happiness.' 'God has created all men equal' in regard to these rights, and therefore no man has the natural right to govern another; and all political authority in individuals is justly said to be derived, under God, from the consent of the collective people who are governed. The people, under God, associated in a body politic, are the source of the sovereign political power of the civil state."[20] American Protestants were amazed to hear a Catholic thus preach to them their democratic doctrine. Their astonishment grew when he added: "With the light of these statements, which are in conformity with her authoritative teaching, the connection of the Catholic Church with the American republic can easily be understood."[21]

Here was the nub of the Hecker argument. Good Catholic that he was, he pictured Creation as divided into two realms, the natural and supernatural. The Declaration of Independence, the fabrication of human reason, was a product of the natural order, as were also those social virtues, honesty, loyalty to law, and justice, which Americans held to be of such importance. Jefferson and the democratic idealists who were his disciples, in affirming natural rights and emphasizing natural virtues, had advanced half way toward the solution of the problem of human perfection. Through reason, the light of God in the soul, they had come thus far. To transform the ideals of the Declaration into human realities required but one further step. The Church, which God has created as his instrument in the world, must lead Americans beyond the natural into the supernatural realm, and must teach them the importance of the supernatural virtues of penitence, prayer, and regard for the sacraments. It must instruct them in the precise meaning of the moral law when applied to the affairs of men and societies. Why would not Protestantism suffice? With the vehemence of a Parson Brownlow, Hecker reminded his Protestant hearers of John Calvin's picture of the human soul corrupt from birth, of Calvin's man, a slave whose every act is foreordained. What can a man do to be saved? Nothing, answered Calvin. The Paulist reminded his hearers of Jonathan Edwards' argument against the freedom of the will. Does Calvin's man have the natural right to life, liberty, and the pursuit of happiness? asked Hecker. Calvinism, he answered, outrages the dignity of human nature; it denies the efficacy of human effort. The Paulist asked how such a philosophy of degradation and of death could be reconciled with the democratic faith. Democracy is founded upon belief, not only in the essential goodness of men but also in their power to act for themselves. There can be no compromise, he pointed out, between democracy and determinism.

The great American delusion, taught Hecker, is the belief that democracy springs from Protestantism. Indeed, he said, democracy is the denial of the fundamental tenets of Luther and of Calvin. Democracy, tied to Protestantism, is bound to a dying system. Hecker sought to relieve the democratic faith of the burden of the death it bore. His effort was the same as that of his old friends, Emerson and Thoreau. They too sought to rid democracy of the incubus of Protestantism. Here the parallelism ceased. Emerson put his trust in the individual whose soul was but a manifestation of that Over-Soul which permeates nature. Hecker put his faith in the Catholic Church, infallible representative of God on earth, commissioned to teach men their duty to one another and to the All-Highest. Implicit in his lectures was all that Brownson had said. The divine Church has the truth, and God himself had laid upon it the responsibility of making this truth known to the people. For its task it has been given from on high adequate authority. Hecker saw in his vision the golden age when American democrats should manage their civil State under the moral and spiritual guidance of the Catholic Church. He would save democracy through the agency of an authoritarian church whose hierarchical ecclesiastical structure was originally patterned on the political structure of Imperial Rome. He would make the Church the final interpreter of the fundamental law.

During the war, Father Hecker gave such a lecture one Sunday evening in Concord. As he looked out over his Yankee audience, he saw the familiar face of Bronson Alcott, lined with years and with disappointments. Emerson was not there. A few days later Hecker, in walking the familiar streets, chanced upon the aging transcendentalist; as of old, the two fell into conversation. But they were strangers. More than years had intervened since the two had met. Emerson was little changed. He was still the philosopher—still searching for the truth. Hecker had the truth. He knew all the right answers to the questions men have asked about the Mystery and its meaning. The flow of talk dried up. Emerson still believed that the doctrine of the free individual meant that the individual should search on his own for the answer to the great questions as to what should be the relation of the individual to society and to the cosmos. He was still convinced that no final answer could be found and that each advance toward understanding only provided a starting point for a new campaign. Even the memories of old associations could not thaw the cold Emerson. He turned away. Hecker did not understand. "None of these men are comfortable in conversation with an intelligent Catholic," he explained complacently. "He avoided my square look, and actually kept turning to avoid my eyes until he had quite turned round! Such men, confronted with actual, certain convictions, are exceedingly uncomfortable. They feel in subjection to you. They cannot bear the steadfast glance of a man of certain principles any better than a dog can the look of his master. Like a dog, they turn away the head and show signs of uneasiness."[22] The story of Ernest the Seeker had long since ended.

∽

When Emerson on that day at Concord had literally turned his back on Father Hecker, he symbolized the rejection by the American people of the Paulist's argument. The golden day when the American democratic faith should for all Americans rest squarely upon Catholic theology did not dawn. Yet Hecker did not work in vain. If he failed to convert American democrats to Catholicism, he succeeded in converting an immigrant Catholic Church to New World democracy.

Archbishop Ireland, after the Paulist's death, summed up his importance for American Catholicism. "The circumstances of Catholics have been peculiar in the United States," said Ireland in 1894, "and we have unavoidably suffered on this account. Catholics in largest numbers were Europeans, and so were their priests, many of whom—by no means all—remained in heart and mind and mode of action as alien to America as if they had never been removed from the Shannon, the Loire, or the Rhine. No one need remind me that immigration has brought us inestimable blessings, or that without it the Church in America would be of small stature. The remembrance of a precious fact is not put aside, if I recall an accidental evil attaching to it. Priests foreign in disposition and work were not fitted to make favorable impressions upon the non-Catholic American population, and the American-born children of Catholic immigrants were likely to escape their action. . . . Even priests of American ancestry, ministering to immigrants, not unfrequently fell into the lines of those around them, and did but little to make the Church in America throb with American life. Not so Isaac Thomas Hecker. Whether consciously or unconsciously I do not know, and it matters not, he looked on America as the fairest conquest for divine truth, and he girded himself with arms shaped and tempered to the American pattern. I think that it may be said that the American current, so plain in the last quarter of a century in the flow of Catholic affairs, is, largely at least, to be traced back to Father Hecker and his early co-workers. It used to be said of them in reproach that they were the 'Yankee' Catholic Church; the reproach was their praise."[23]

Chapter 6

MELVILLE, CRITIC OF MID-NINETEENTH-CENTURY BELIEFS

In 1846, when Emerson's star was high, a comet swept into the American literary firmament. In that year a romance by an unknown named Herman Melville went on sale in the book shops. The book was called *Typee*. It described with rich and frank detail the life of a cannibal tribe on one of the Marquesas Islands and told what purported to be the story of the author's captivity and his escape. The book sold well and Herman Melville, aged twenty-seven, became for the moment a celebrity. He had written much autobiography into the book but had supplemented his own knowledge by reading about the islands and had blended all into a semi-fictitious tale.

Melville had in fact shipped on a whaler, the *Acushnet*, in 1841. After eighteen months he had escaped to the Typees. He made off from the island on an Australian whaler which took him to Tahiti. There he worked for a time as a field laborer and observed the ways of the natives in a British dependency. Perhaps homesickness or perhaps fear of the law (the captain of the *Acushnet* had filed papers in Honolulu dealing with the deserter) led Melville, who by this time had turned up in the Hawaiian Islands, to enlist as able-bodied seaman on the frigate *United States*. The warship sailed into Boston harbor on October 3, 1844. With the rest of the crew Melville got his discharge.

The success of *Typee* was prelude to an outpouring of books from the pen of the young traveler. *Omoo*, a light-hearted tale about

Tahiti, appeared in 1847. Two years later came *Mardi* and *Redburn*. The latter narrative grew out of Melville's earlier experience as seaman on a merchant ship from New York to Liverpool. The former shifted from more conventional writing to allegory in which Taji, the central figure, made his way from island to island in the archipelago of Mardi and thence into the open sea. *Omoo* and *Redburn* did reasonably well, but mid-nineteenth-century Americans found *Mardi* both dull and hard to understand. In 1850 Melville gave his readers *White Jacket*, the materials for which came in part from his naval experience. *Moby Dick* followed in 1851, to get a disappointing reception at the hands of the critics and to be largely ignored by the public. *Pierre* went on sale in the following year and proved a complete failure. Melville had lost his public.

He turned out other books and a collection of stories, but his income from writing could not support his family. After failing to get a consulship, as his one-time friend Hawthorne had managed to do, Melville became a customs inspector on a New York City wharf—a strange fate for a one-time literary lion and the son of a proud, old family. In spite of a sheaf of verses dealing with the Civil War called *Battle Pieces* and a long narrative poem, *Clarel*, Melville was forgotten by his fellow Americans. After nineteen years on the pier a small legacy freed a man now grown old from the daily grind. From his memoirs and from his studies in naval lore he wrote a little book dedicated to Jack Chase, captain of the main top men of the *United States* who, under the name of Billy Budd, was its hero. Melville died in 1891 leaving *Billy Budd* unpublished.

Americans in the 1920's, with some British help, discovered Melville. As they began to read his long-neglected volumes, he seemed unexpectedly contemporary. *Moby Dick,* now looked upon as one of the great literary achievements of the nineteenth century, went into new and sometimes sumptuous editions. *Billy Budd* appeared for the first time. In mid-century it became a play in the United States and an opera in England. At the same time the corpus of critical and scholarly writing about Melville grew to extended proportions, a phenomenon partly accounted for by the need for subjects of Ph.D. candidates in American literature. By 1950 the author of *Moby Dick* and *Billy Budd* had attained a secure position among the greatest of those writing in English in the nineteenth century. For the present inquiry, however, Melville becomes important not so much for his contribution to the development of the American democratic faith as for the perspective for the study of that system

of beliefs provided by his rejection in his own century and his acceptance in the twentieth.

◇

Of all the assignments on the whaler *Acushnet*, Herman Melville,
twenty-two, liked best that of lookout in the crow's-nest. The
members of the crew manned in turn from sunup to sundown each
of three lofty posts. Young Melville amused himself with the fancy
that he and his mates were striding across the Pacific on giant stilts.
For eighteen months Melville lived and worked as a member of a
crew drawn from the waterfront in the heyday of American whaling when a lucky voyage brought high rewards. But, if the young
whaler shipped because he needed a job and money, he, according
to his own account, proved a poor lookout, never discovering the
spouting that identified a whale. The artist within him, yet unreal-
ized, was stirred by the sea stretching away to the horizon's circle.
In later years when his ideas and his art had matured, he set down
thoughts that, no doubt, first dimly came to him on board the
smelly *Acushnet*. Describing the mood of a character with whom
for the moment he seemed to have identified himself he spoke of
the lookout: "Lulled into such an opium-like listlessness of vacant,
unconscious reverie is this absent-minded youth by the blending
cadence of waves with thoughts, that at last he loses his identity;
takes the mystic ocean at his feet for the visible image of that deep,
blue, bottomless soul, pervading mankind and nature; and every
strange, half-seen, gliding, beautiful thing that eludes him; every
dimly-discovered, uprising fin of some undiscernible form, seems
to him the embodiment of those elusive thoughts that only people
the soul by flitting through it."[1] But Melville apprehended more
than mystery in the sea. Action, at intervals, interrupted listlessness.
No matter if the seas ran high, the crew hustled to their stations
when the lookout spotted a whale. Pulling an oar in a whale boat
in which men not only braved the sea but the monster in it, Melville
looked with pleasure at the green mountains about him. "It was a
sight full of quick wonder and awe!" he recalled in later years.
"The vast swells of the omnipotent sea; the surging, hollow roar
they made, as they rolled along . . . the gunwales . . . the brief suspended agony of the boat, as it would tip for an instant on the
knife-like edge of the sharper waves, that seemed almost threatening
to cut it in two; the sudden profound dip into the watery glens and
hollows; the keen spurrings and goadings to gain the top of the
opposite hill; the head-long, sled-like slide down its other side:—all

this was thrilling."[2] In addition to mystery the sea emphasized action, insecurity, the hazard of the small boat battling the rollers. The time came when Melville looked upon the sea as a symbol of that violence that he believed to be an essential condition of life. In his Agatha letter to Hawthorne he spoke of "the malignity of the sea" and suggested a story in which her sea-lover would come to Agatha in a storm.

∽

"Until I was twenty-five," Melville wrote to Hawthorne, "I had no development at all. From my twenty-fifth year I date my life."[3] He was twenty-five when the *United States* docked at Boston. Melville left the sea and plunged into the writing of the romance *Typee*. He also had to re-orient himself in an America he had not seen for some three years. In the year of Melville's discharge from the Navy American voters elected the expansionist, Polk, to the presidency. *Typee* came off the press in 1846, not many months from the time General Zachary Taylor led an army southward across the Rio Grande. In the same year General Stephen Kearny in a bloodless campaign conquered Santa Fé, became military governor of the Spanish-speaking population of this northern Mexican state, and at the point of the bayonet forced upon them a constitution complete with a proper bill of rights. The vigorous Kearny translated the old slogans of Manifest Destiny into action. In his romance Melville described Typee warriors staggering into their village carrying the carcasses of their conquered Happar enemies. In 1848 Melville read in the newspapers that President Polk had sent to the Senate the Treaty of Guadaloupe Hidalgo, bringing within the national boundaries the immense and rich territory of the Southwest. Melville had come home to his country at a time when Americans were making the greatest outward thrust in their history. Save for an angry minority that looked upon the Mexican War as an undertaking to open up new territory for slavery, citizens of the Republic found justification for expansion in the mission of America to extend the principles and practices of democracy, as Kearny had so promptly done, into the virtually empty Western wilderness.

Expansion not only forecast but also manifested progress. Enlargement of territory further confirmed Americans in that hopeful outlook, that future-mindedness which had long been a basic characteristic of the American temper. The returning Melville brought back to a nation on the march a perspective gained from contact with cultures vastly different from that of the United States. He described two of these as entities important in and for themselves. His experience had given him the rudiments of the cross-cultural approach to the observation of society that was to become basic to twentieth-century anthropology. In *Omoo* and *Mardi*, in particular, the results of the enlarged perspective appeared. At a time when Americans generally took progress for granted, almost as an axiom of history, Melville in *Omoo* described with sympathy the decline of an ancient culture. It came about as a result of diseases introduced by white men, of the efforts of missionaries to substitute for old religious sanctions those of a foreign moral code and of an inept colonialism. He quoted a mournful chant in which Polynesians sang of their ultimate extinction. The immediate attacks upon a book that so emphatically ran counter to prevailing preconceptions, particularly those by religious spokesmen, illumined the narrow and provincial outlook of a generation which believed that its brand of Christianity and democracy were destined one day to save the world.

In *Mardi*, published in the year of the California gold rush, Melville, now thirty, ventured some direct comments on the Republic and the beliefs of its citizens. He recalled the belief in the moral progress of civilization that had become increasingly important in an age of humanitarian reform. Melville did not think that mankind was advancing toward any moral Utopia. "There are many who erstwhile believed that the age of pikes and javelins was passed"; he remarked, "that after a heady and blustering youth, . . . [the world] was at last settling down into a serene old age; and that the Indian summer, first discovered in your land [of America], sovereign kings! was the hazy vapour emitted from its tranquil pipe. But it has not so proved. [The world's] peaces are but truces. Long absent, at last the red comets have returned. And return they must though their periods be ages. And should . . . [the world] endure till mountain melt into mountain, and all the isles form one tableland; yet it would but expand the old battle plain."[4] Melville's gloomy forecast antedated by nearly a century some assumptions concerning international politics current in the United States before and after World War II and also the discovery by Protestantism's neo-orthodoxy of the stubborn persistence of evil in the world. In the middle of the nineteenth century Melville's pessimism made no imprint on a generation that assumed international peace to be normal and wars (always unexpected by Americans) to be met and won by citizen volunteers called from the plow and the counter.

As for the mission of America, Melville suggested that the fate of the Republic might be the same as that of its Roman predecessor. His observation must be read in the light of the rampant materialism of which the rush to gain wealth in California was momentarily the most conspicuous manifestation. It must also be read against the background of the power in national councils of the representatives of the section whose economy was built on slavery and who were determined at all costs to preserve the peculiar institution.

"You are free, partly, because you are young," said Melville speaking of the United States in *Mardi*. "Your nation is like a fine, florid youth, full of fiery impulses, and hard to restrain. . . . The oppressor he defies to his beard; the high walls of old opinions he scales with a bound. . . . But years elapse, and this bold boy is transformed. His eyes open not as of yore; his heart is shut up as a vice. He yields not a groat; and seeking no more acquisitions, is only bent on preserving his hoard. . . . And he who hated oppressors is become an oppressor himself. Thus, often, with men; thus, often, with nations." The democracy of which mid-nineteenth-century Americans boasted, thought Melville, might not endure. As for the assumption that it was destined to triumph in the world Melville commented: "Each age thinks its own eternal."[5]

Whether Melville as the years passed continued to hold to the same gloomy forecast for the United States as that implied in *Mardi* may be doubted. When he had virtually given up the profession of writing, the Civil War, breaking out in 1861, stirred him deeply. He rejoiced in Northern victories because he believed right to be on the side of the Union. Yet he had sympathy for the Southern leaders whom he considered to be misguided. In this fratricidal struggle the fate of the common soldier seems to have touched him most.

> There is glory for the brave
> Who lead, and nobly save,
> But no knowledge in the grave
> Where the nameless followers sleep.

In 1866 Melville joined the ranks of the nameless among the civil servants of the United States as he reported for duty on the pier at the foot of Gansevoort Street.

⌒

Melville's significance for the student of the American democratic faith as it took form in the first half of the nineteenth century does not lie in any contribution he made to its pattern of ideas. His one attempt, in *Omoo*, served only to rouse opposition; the lumbering, wordy *Mardi* found few readers. The same fate, however, befell the masterpiece *Moby Dick*, a commentary on the time that needs no amplification. The mid-nineteenth-century democratic faith possessed two characteristics that insured its popular acceptance and support. It was a simple pattern of ideas that to the men of the times seemed adequate. It provided effective material for orations on the Fourth of July. In addition to the quality of simplicity it set forth a formula for intellectual security. In partnership with Christianity (primarily Protestant Christianity at the time) it explained the meaning of human life and the destiny not only of America but of all men. To the Christian doctrine of a loving God who is close at hand and cares for those who trust Him it added the social belief in a universal fundamental law sufficient for the government of free men who apprehend and follow it. The constitution of the universe was on the side of such men. Melville, however, could find no security in religious or in social beliefs. He could not be persuaded by the either-or philosophy of his contemporaries: his questions could not be answered so easily. In his writing, as some have suggested, perhaps his primary purpose was to develop and follow an artistic method. But it seems clear that he hoped to gain through and beyond art some partial insights into the mysterious unknown.

Perhaps from his experience on the *Acushnet*, when he took his turn in the crow's-nest, he got the first faint suggestion of what became the symbol basic to his art and thought. For the lookout, high above the deck, the horizon circumscribed a circle.[6] It had no beginning and no end. Each particular sector, each pair of opposite sides, was united to and part of all the rest. Beyond the horizon lay the unknown, into which Taji, the traveler through the Archipelago of Mardi, pushed out as the narrative ended. Within the circle for the lookout lay the malignant, terrifying sea, through which swim mysterious and frightening creatures. Melville's experience with life impressed on him first of all a sense of the mystery of life and of the universe in which he had his being. He was convinced that truth lay partly in the unseen, unknown universe beyond the limits of pedestrian reason. He had a vision of a world where "matter and mind . . . unite"; in which "fact and fancy, half-way meeting, interpenetrate and form one seamless whole."

He sought things "infinite in the finite; and dualities in unities." The circle or the sphere were the best expressions of unity.

The theme of dualities in unities runs through most of his writings. His method was to state problems through juxtaposing opposites with the understanding that the opposites were somehow, as part of the same circle, one. In *Redburn* the narrator sets a description of a beautiful English countryside against a picture of rotting tenements in Liverpool in which he saw a mother and her babes dying of starvation. In *Typee* the glorious Faway moved near a pile of bones left from a cannibal feast. In *Omoo* the missionaries worked with noble purpose and wrecked an ancient culture. Moby Dick had a white skin yet within lived the "incarnation of all those malicious agencies which some deep men feel eating in them, till they are left living on with half a heart and half a lung." If the method did not lead on to attempts to provide systematic answers to the questions raised, it emphasized the complexity of problems of life and conduct. If Melville hoped, as he said, for insights by intuition, he found some in *White Jacket* in his description of the denial and degradation of human dignity involved in the flogging he so vividly described. A duality that he did not intend seems to have arisen here. In *Pierre* he satirized the fanatical, single-minded reformers who infested the age, but in *White Jacket* two years before he had himself become a reformer. There can be little doubt that Melville's book hastened the Navy's abolition—which occurred within a year after its publication—of the old barbarism.

Amid the endless ambiguities, dilemmas, and dualities that Melville found, what became the doctrine of the fundamental law? One of the most common particularizations of that law in Melville's day was the Puritan ethical code that after 1800 had been carried far and wide by the evangelical denominations such as the Methodists and Baptists. It was a catalogue of don'ts. Don't dance; don't play cards; don't attend the theater (above all don't enter the actor's profession); don't work or play on the Sabbath; don't indulge in prideful display of finery; don't blaspheme. Behind the code, so categorical and specific, lay the assurance of those—who used it to force village life into patterns they approved—that they knew what was right and what was wrong, that they had the truth. Melville had no such assurance.

It was an age in which the Bible, an almost universal book, exercised a surpassing influence in the thought and in the speech of Americans. Melville also studied the Bible diligently. He marked verses and phrases that suggested deeper problems than those dealt with by the popular version of the Puritan ethic. In Isaiah he read: "I form the light, and create darkness: I make peace, and create evil: I the Lord do all these things." Many were the passages that Melville marked in his Bible "illustrating the unequalled and often curiously demonstrated power of Jehovah: his use of Necho the Egyptian to slay Josiah and of Assyria to destroy Samaria. Many were the verses he checked describing Jehovah's darker designs: '. . . for who can make straight, which he hath made crooked?' '. . . for it must needs be that offences come; but woe to the man by whom the offence cometh!' 'He made darkness his secret place; his pavilion round about him were dark waters and thick clouds of the skies.' "[7] The checked passages suggest how far Melville had moved from the simple precepts that currently passed for the moral law. They also suggest, however, how close Melville was to the ethical preoccupations of the age. But for Melville the search for the fundamental law ended in mystery.

What is man, what is the free individual? Freedom, thought Melville, is circumscribed. Melville called Ahab, in mad pursuit of Moby Dick, Fate's lieutenant. Fate and freedom were also parts of a duality within the uniting circle. As for the soul of man— Melville described it at one time as vast beyond measure in its out-reaches and at another time as an emptiness in the heart of a pyramid. "Pierre saw," said Melville, "that human life doth truly come from that which all men are agreed to call by the name of *God;* and that it partakes of the unravellable inscrutableness of God."[8] What, then, asked the Christian critics of Melville's philosophy, is the purpose and significance of human life? "That," he replied, "is the last mystery which underlieth all the rest."[9]

∽

Certainly Melville made no important impression on the thought of nineteenth-century America. He rejected the optimistic belief in progress. He insisted that evil is permanent. Philosophies of security seemed to him illusions. He believed hazard to be the primary condition of life. He found reality ultimately lost in mystery and seemed almost to have made acceptance of and wonder at mystery his religion. Even so, his basic outlook was positive, not negative. He was no nihilist or futilitarian.

Because Melville was an artist rather than a philosopher it fell his lot to express his affirmations most clearly in his life. When his artistic method failed him in the 1850's and when the readers of the time refused to buy enough of his books to enable him to make a living, he took his defeat. He accepted a humble job and supported his family. Perhaps some times he recalled the last words of Ahab, master of the *Pequod*: "O lonely death in lonely life." He carried on. He gave up none of his old convictions and abandoned none of his old aspirations. When fate freed him from the daily routine, he wrote his second great book. In it appeared the dualities of evil and good in the persons of Claggert and Budd, both part of the unity of the ship. The story unfolded the dilemma of the good law that condemned an innocent man to death. It developed the tragedy of Captain Vere who would be free but whom fate required to silence the noble impulses of his heart and enforce the law. And the book contained beyond these more obvious situations an overplus of meanings within this cosmos of the ship that lead the questioning reader out into mystery.

If Melville could not accept the simple doctrines of the free individual and the moral law that nineteenth-century men found adequate, his career illustrates one form that individualism could take in a matrix of insecurity.

Chapter 7

NATIONALISM, DETERMINISM, AND THE DEMOCRATIC FAITH

DEMOCRACY, LIKE MONARCHY, is always an aspect of a particular culture. What is called democracy in Great Britain varies from that in the United States, because democratic practices and ideas are conditioned by the culture of which they are a part. Democracy has little meaning when divorced from a particular nationality; it is a culture trait which distinguishes from others the national group which professes it.

The culminating doctrine of the American democratic faith was that of mission. The tenet was an expression of nationalistic consciousness. It did not achieve developed form until after the Treaty of Ghent had put an end to the secessionist movement in New England, and Waterloo had terminated the danger of further embroilment in Europe. As Americans faced the West and centered their energies in the building of a nation, Monroe announced in 1821 his famous doctrine of aloofness. Sixteen years later Emerson in his Phi Beta Kappa address held up the ideal of national intellectual independence. He affirmed with his contemporaries that the American democratic principles were the nation's most important contribution to the civilization of the world.

On the surface the democratic faith of the Middle Period appeared to be a consistent pattern of harmonious doctrines. Hidden within it, however, were some of the oldest issues of human thinking. How free is the free individual? Calvin had answered the question with his theistic determinism, a reply which mid-nineteenth-century American democrats had instinctively rejected. Melville, when he called Ahab Fate's lieutenant, had affirmed a naturalistic determinism. Melville was exiled to the customs house. But the

80

issue would not down. The question of determinism appeared a third time when American economists brought from England the theories of the classical school of economics. So long as the doctrines of Malthus, Ricardo, and Mill did not get outside the textbooks they were of little importance in American culture. But when they were used as weapons to prevent the establishment of a protective tariff, the issue of determinism rocked the nation. The tariff was an effort at national economic planning. In the pre-Sumter battles over protection, the importance of determinism and of nationalism for the doctrine of the free individual was brought into the open.

Economic nationalism, however, was only one aspect of a growing national consciousness. This new national sentiment was, in part, the product of the War of 1812. That conflict had been precipitated by the War Hawks, young nationalists who came out of the West. Henry Clay of Kentucky not only resented the humiliations inflicted by England in the impressment of American seamen, but saw an imperialist vision of Canada added to the United States. During the years from 1807 to 1815 when American buyers were cut off from British factories, entrepreneurs in the eastern and northern states in an effort to achieve national economic independence threw dams across creeks and rivers and built crude mills above wooden water wheels. In New England the population began to move from the older villages on the hilltops to the new towns in the valley bottoms. The change in the economic foundation of the northeastern section was destined to effect a revolution, but it did not come with sufficient swiftness to modify New England sentiment during the second war with England. Representatives of the commercial interests sat in the seats of power and opposed Mr. Madison's war. The sentiment of nationalism waned in the northeastern states as New England Federalists put loyalty to section ahead of that to the nation. In 1814 the western Republic stood on the brink of the abyss. The dread word, secession, was heard in the taverns and on the street corners of the northern coast towns. A war which had begun with a fanfare of nationalistic trumpets seemed about to end in humiliation and disintegration.

After two years of inconclusive fighting in North America the enemy, triumphant over Napoleon in Europe, began in 1814 a vigorous prosecution of the conflict west of the Atlantic. The British navy tightened and extended its blockade of American ports. A detachment of troops began what was expected to be the permanent occupation of Maine. Britain hoped to rectify the boundary between the United States and Canada. Another landing party in August marched into Washington, whence the harried and discredited Madison had fled, and put the torch to the Capitol. Two British armies of invasion were formed, one to take New Orleans and the other, under General Prevost, to advance into the Hudson Valley by Burgoyne's old route along the west shore of Lake Champlain. The attack upon New Orleans was slow in getting under way, with the result that the decisive operations were those initiated by Prevost. Before he began his southward march the American high command, with an ineptitude which amounted almost to genius, removed to Sackett's Harbor on Lake Ontario most of the force which should have opposed the invader. When Prevost faced the earthworks at Plattsburg, the decisive moment in the history of the Republic had come.

Fortune, as the event turned out, favored the United States. The blundering Prevost forced Captain Downie, his flotilla commander, to fight the defending American warships on terms which the Americans dictated. McDonough's brilliance in taking advantage of the opportunities his enemy gave him stopped the most formidable foreign invasion which has threatened the United States since the achieving of independence. The battle of Plattsburg Bay probably saved the United States from dissolution. Prevost was put down for court martial, but death saved him the humiliation of standing trial.

Localism, reaching its New England apogee in 1814, found expression in that convention of bitter opponents of the Madison party which met at Hartford and demanded a radical revision of the Constitution. Disaster, however, was avoided. McDonough's victory prepared the way for that return to the *status quo ante bellum* which was called the Treaty of Ghent.

The sentiment of nationalism, like character, is strengthened by adversity. In that calamitous year of 1814 Mathew Carey, head of the leading publishing house in Philadelphia, read with a sinking heart the sentiments which a northern Federalist published in the New York *Evening Post*. "What would be the value of peace," asked the disaffected writer, "if not attended with a change of those rulers who are driving the country headlong to ruin? A peace, if such be its effects, would be the heaviest of curses."[1] "The National vessel," remarked Carey sadly, "is on rocks and quicksand, and in danger of shipwreck. . . . This, I am fearful, will be our fate. It may be prevented. All that is necessary is for a few influential men to step forward. . . . One hundred individuals throughout the union setting the example, would have sufficient efficacy to accomplish the blessed object of saving their country."[2] Carey himself was the first to step forward. He wrote and distributed an appeal to patriotism which he called *The Olive Branch or Facts on Both Sides, Federal and Democratic.* "This book," he noted, "(as a mark of gratitude for inestimable blessings enjoyed, in liberty of person, and liberty of opinions, to a degree never exceeded in the world,) is respectfully dedicated to a beloved and bleeding country, torn in pieces by desperate and convulsive struggles for power."[3] Mathew Carey spoke from the heart. His *Olive Branch* was the effort of a refugee of the struggle for Irish liberty to make a return to the nation for the freedom and opportunity which it had given to a penniless fugitive.

Americans relaxed in 1815 when the war ended with what was called, not unjustly, an honorable peace. But Mathew Carey had only begun to fight. Looking across the Atlantic he still saw England as an enemy menacing the Republic. The United States was a country of husbandmen, shopkeepers, and sailormen. The sprawling nation produced raw materials which British factories fabricated into goods to be sold in the American market. To Carey the situation suggested economic servitude; the United States was in an economic sense an outlying province dominated by the industrial lords of Manchester and Birmingham. Carey dreamed of economic independence for his adopted land.

∽

The Treaty of Ghent was a signal to English manufacturers that the American market, closed since 1807, was again open. From bulging warehouses they filled the holds of square-rigged packet ships. The flood of British goods, offered for sale at almost any price, threatened the new mills which had sprung up in the United States. The American government countered with the Tariff of 1816, but the relief proved ineffective. In 1819 American economic life collapsed in a postwar depression.

During the years of economic insecurity which followed Ghent, Henry Clay, ex-war hawk, perfected the blueprint of a national policy which he called the American System. He proposed a rudimentary economic nationalism that looked backward toward mercantilism and at the same time marked a first step toward patterns of the twentieth century. He urged that the United States erect a tariff wall to protect against ruinous competition the war-born manufacturing establishments. Clay pointed out that growing mill towns would provide an expanding market for the produce of American farms. He advocated the improvement of transportation facilities in order that the producer and consumer might be brought closer together.

Mathew Carey, after 1815, gave unsparingly of his time, talents, and substance to further the Clay plan. His activities gave him a place with the Kentuckian as co-author of the American System. Carey, however, pointed out that Alexander Hamilton was the true founder of the policy. Washington's Secretary of the Treasury had suggested to Congress in his "Report on Manufactures" that Americans were building their nation upon an unbalanced economic foundation. Agriculture and commerce were, in Hamilton's opinion, overemphasized when compared with the primitive development of the manufacturing industries. But Hamilton's advice that a policy of protection would bring about a balanced economy had come to little. After 1815 Clay and Carey took up the work which he had left. The two were an effective team. Clay was the politician, skilled in parliamentary maneuver; Carey was the scholar who accumulated data—he was also an organizer and publicist. He was indefatigable in his efforts to indoctrinate his generation with the gospel of economic nationalism. Carey's moment of triumph came in 1828 when he toured the Ohio Valley to be feted for his part in the protectionist victory of that year. Back home in Pennsylvania he was toasted by the citizens of Montgomery County as "a pillar of adamant to the American system; a hedge of thorns to British agents."[4]

∽

Carey, in his crusade for the protective system, was not primarily interested in swelling the profits of American manufacturers. His thought ranged further than the cash drawer. Like Emerson, Thoreau, and Melville, Carey had a philosophy of Individualism. He saw a direct relation between protection and the democratic doctrine of the free individual. Carey defined freedom in terms of economic opportunity. To Carey that young man was free who, as he chose his life work, found many possible roads opening before him. Measuring freedom by such a rod, Carey felt that the youth he saw about him were not free. The farmer's boy had little choice but to be a farmer and the planter's son a planter. In the towns and cities young men could choose among mercantile establishments or, perhaps, could go to sea. The defect of America, Carey thought, was the simplicity of its civilization. The United States was, in reality, an undeveloped province producing only staples. The economic power of England prevented the maturing of American economic life. The British manufacturers led the world in technical equipment and in financial power. Free trade, by giving them access to the American market, prevented the development of industry in the United States and condemned the Republic to a civilization founded on agriculture and commerce. The inevitable consequence of such enforced simplicity must be the restriction of opportunity for ambitious and adventurous individuals. "It is a disheartening truth," remarked Carey in 1824, "that in a country capable of maintaining one hundred times its present population, there are too many of almost every class—too many farmers—too many planters—too many merchants—too many lawyers—too many doctors—too many of nearly every kind of manufacturers and mechanics. Hence there is no encouragement whatever to immigration. This arises from our citizens being wholly precluded by foreign supplies, from so many branches of business and so many various occupations, that all those which are not thus closed to them, are crowded. There can be no truth more clear than this, that the greater the variety of occupations in a community, the greater the scope for ingenuity and talent, the reward for industry, and the higher the grade of individual and general prosperity."[5]

Carey saw the limitations of the agricultural communities of the United States. He wished America to advance from simplicity to complexity. He hoped to multiply many times the number of callings open to young men of America. Only in such a mature and complex society could the democratic ideal of the free individual be realized. But such economic maturity could only be achieved by an effort of the national will. The United States must break the shackles which bound it to English economy. The nation must become independent in an economic as well as in a political sense. Until such independence had become a reality, Americans could not call themselves free men. The instrument which would enable the citizens of the Republic to create the new society was the protective tariff.

Powerful interests in the United States opposed the American System. Calhoun suggested to the intransigents of South Carolina the theory of nullification. The opponents of the tariff borrowed from English economists some of their most persuasive arguments. The theories of Malthus, Ricardo, and Mill dominated the economic thinking of the civilized world. They taught that economic enterprise is governed by natural laws with which man interferes at his peril. The wise policy for the nation is *laissez faire*. Free trade is nature's plan. Carey found that he had not only to meet the practical arguments of the cotton planters but the theoretical arguments of the English philosophers. He gave battle on both fronts.

Malthus, Ricardo, and James Mill were determinists. They taught that the fundamental law which underlies society includes the Malthusian law of population. Malthus declared that population increases by a geometric ratio to the limit of the supporting power of the environment and that, because the food supply increases only at an arithmetic ratio, numbers of the people must always live on the brink of starvation. The mass of humanity seemed to Malthus doomed by nature to hunger as it fought its losing battle against the law of diminishing returns and the iron law of wages. Nature's remedy for overpopulation is famine, pestilence, and war.

Such doctrines seemed to Carey the essence of evil. They outraged his moral sense. The Philadelphia publisher was a humanitarian deeply interested in the weak and helpless. He was outstanding in his generation in his appreciation of the hard lot of the poor. He sought to make his contemporaries charity-minded. He appealed particularly to women to come to the aid of their sisters whose lives were dwarfed by too long hours and by inadequate wages. Carey believed that social justice is the flower of the humane actions of socially minded individuals. For the achievement of social justice he depended, with Thoreau, upon the fundamental moral law made effective in society through the consciences of individual men and women. "Every principle of honor, justice, and generosity," said Carey, "forbids the employer to take advantage of the distress and wretchedness of those he employs, and cut down their wages below the minimum necessary to procure a sufficiency of plain food and of clothes to guard against inclemency of weather. Whoever passes this line of demarcation, is guilty of the heinous offence of 'grinding the faces of the poor.' "[6] Carey was himself a considerate employer and a man of many charities. On the day of his funeral in 1839 the United States *Gazette* reported that "thousands followed Mr. Carey to the grave . . . but more mourned, in unobtrusive silence, their friend and benefactor."[7]

Opposed to Carey's warm humanism was the cold determinism

of Malthus. In his efforts to make his contemporaries socially minded, Carey encountered the Puritan argument that poverty is the result of indolence, or the Malthusian argument that nature decrees that many men must always be about to starve. Carey looked upon the determinism of the classical economists as an attempt "to dry up the sources of charity and benevolence." He called such economics "an unholy and ungodly employment." Henry Carey, Mathew's son, carried on his father's war against the determinism of English economics. He also was a protectionist. The younger Carey had greater capacity in the formulation of theory. In elaborating the half-formed ideas of his father into a logical system, he became the first American economist.

Henry Carey founded his thought upon the postulate that the basic fact in nature is the unity of law. The laws of economics must harmonize with those of the moral order. Carey turned fiercely on the Malthus theory that nature's remedy for inevitable overpopulation is famine, pestilence, and war. "Can it be," he asked in 1859, "that the Creator has thus been inconsistent with himself? . . . Can it be then that after having given man all the faculties required for assuming the mastery over nature, it has been part of His design to subject him to absolute and irreversible laws, in virtue of which he must inevitably become nature's slave?" The fatal error in the English system, Carey thought, lay in the conception of the "economic man," that dehumanized automaton who was the sport of nature. "Security against the disease of over-population," declared Henry Carey, "is to be found in the development of the real MAN, as distinguished from the human animal treated of in the Ricardo-Malthusian books—a being that eats, drinks, and procreates, and has but the form of a man."[8] The mythical "economic man," the slave of nature, knew nothing of the moral law; the supreme task of the "real man" is to discover the basic harmonies which exist in the heart of nature and which unify natural and moral law. Carey believed that he had made the basic discovery in what he called the "principle of association."

Carey's principle of association would be called in the twentieth century national planning. He took over his father's idea of the importance of a balanced economy. He repeated his father's arguments concerning the importance of providing a multiplicity of opportunities for the free individual. Carey advocated a protective tariff and what was in essence a managed currency. He opposed with all the force he could muster the internationalism of the British economists. The American economist believed that classical economic theory was a device to ensure the continuance of the industrial supremacy of England. The island kingdom had pioneered in the industrial revolution. So great was the start of the British manufacturer over any possible rival that world free trade would make the survival of that rival impossible. Economic internationalism, therefore would, in Carey's opinion, retard the development of all the world and would concentrate in London overwhelming economic power. Human energy would be wasted in transporting to England from the far corners of the earth the raw materials which, when fabricated, would have to be carried back to the place whence the raw materials came. Because of this waste in energy and because of its checking of world-wide economic development, economic internationalism, Carey argued, makes for "pauperism, depopulation, and barbarism." It "looks toward universal war." National economic planning in the form of a protective tariff and a managed currency would, on the other hand, enable the outlying provinces of the world to match England's achievements. They would become developed powers. Economic nationalism, declared Carey, makes for "increasing wealth, comfort, intelligence, combination of action, and civilization." It looks "toward universal peace."[9]

Carey's principle of association, when applied to international affairs, required that each nation permit and encourage the fullest possible economic evolution on the part of its neighbors. Economic well-being is the foundation of moral advance. Carey looked forward toward Utopia. Economic national planning, he said, "we may be proud to call the American system, for it is the only one ever devised, the tendency of which was the elevating while equalizing the condition of man throughout the world. Such is the true mission of the United States . . . to prove that among the people of the world, whether agriculturists, manufacturers, or merchants, there is perfect harmony of interests, and that the happiness of individuals, as well as the grandeur of nations, is to be promoted by that greatest of all commands, 'Do unto others as ye would that others should do unto you,' [and to demonstrate that this happiness and this grandeur] is the object and will be the result of that mission."[10]

∾

The American democratic faith of the Middle Period was a formulation of humanism. Its central affirmation was that the free individual is, in the end, the master of his own destiny. In the same decades in which American Christians were abandoning the theistic determinism of Calvin the two Careys were combatting the naturalistic determinism of Malthus and Ricardo. The Careys went beyond mere denial. They proposed that the State be used as an instrument for the creation of a better society. When measured by the standards of the twentieth century, their ideas of national planning were crude and immature. But they grasped the principle and introduced it into the American thought stream. They were the first in America to formulate the theory of the positive State.

Before Sumter, therefore, Americans faced that fundamental question of the relation of the individual to the State. Emerson declared that the task of the State is to produce wise and virtuous men and that, when such men have come into being, the State should disappear. Emerson thought of the State primarily as a policeman, giving the good a chance to develop by restraining evil. Henry Carey went further. He would use the State to create a new and more complex economic order. When all nations of the world had achieved maturity and a rough equality, Carey thought, economic nationalism would have served its purpose and world-wide free trade would be the appropriate international arrangement. Carey, like Emerson, looked toward the time when the State should decline in importance. Into this pre-Sumter discussion of political theory, Henry Thoreau introduced another concept. He reaffirmed the traditional American conviction that the State, because it wields power, may and frequently does become malevolent. In such an event the free individual must obey his conscience and oppose passive resistance to evil expressing itself in governmental action. The men of the Middle Period sensed the contradiction between the concepts of the malevolent and the benevolent State; but they did not resolve the dilemma.

∽

In 1825 German reactionaries drove Friedrich List, economist, from Württemberg into exile in the United States. Before he left Germany, List had been a disciple of Malthus and Ricardo. The same forces which shaped the thought of Hamilton, Clay, and the two Careys forced List, in America, to abandon the orthodox determinist position. He plunged into American life. At different times he was a farmer, an editor of a German paper, and a promoter. He became associated with the Philadelphia Society for the Encouragement of Manufactures of which Mathew Carey was the leading figure. List, in fact, had read some of the elder Carey's writings before coming to the United States. In America he appropriated many of Mathew Carey's ideas. He was also under obligation to Henry Carey. But the chief source of his thought was America itself. "When afterwards I visited the United States," he once reminisced, "I cast all books aside—they would only have tended to mislead one. The best book on Political Economy which one can read in that modern land is actual life. There one may see wilderness grow into rich and mighty states; progress which requires centuries in Europe goes on before one's eyes. That book of actual life I have earnestly and diligently studied and compared with the results of my previous studies, experience, and reflections . . . and the result has been (as I hope) the preparing of a system which . . . is not founded on bottomless cosmopolitanism but on the nature of things, the lessons of history, and the requirements of nations."[11]

List published in 1827 an *Outline of American Political Economy*. He brought out in 1841 his developed theories under the title *Das Nationale System der Politischen Oekonomie*. List transplanted to his native land the principles which underlay the American system. He initiated a rebellion among German economists against the English masters and prepared the way for German historical economics. He was the pioneer intellectual who started Germans on the road to economic nationalism. After Appomattox, although List was dead, his influence became a mighty force in the United States.

Chapter 8

THE PRE-SUMTER SYMBOLISM
OF THE DEMOCRATIC FAITH

A NATION IS AN IN-GROUP whose members cooperate to achieve certain ends. Yet the citizens compete with one another for the prizes of life. The need to cooperate is a frustrating factor in their lives. It leads inevitably to aggressions which tend to disrupt the group. Patriotism, national consciousness, group feeling (all are synonyms) is a force operating mostly at the level of the emotions to counteract the disruptive tendencies which, if unchecked, sometimes destroy group cohesion. The democratic faith appeared in American culture as one of the principal forces making for what Whitman used to call adhesiveness. The ultimate appeal of the formula was to the feelings. If it were to have utility in the culture, it must be able to evoke an emotional response. To stir the sentiments of the people the faith must express itself in symbols.

∾

Symbolism, in the form of effigies, personifications, or ritual is most developed in the religious aspects of culture. The Medieval Church lit candles and built cathedrals. It held processions. Its priests performed the dramatic ritual of the Mass. The Church elevated the Cross; the faith for which the Cross stood was personified in the Savior and the Virgin. All were symbols. Every doctrine of this complex religion was expressed in one or more symbols. A theology is a mosaic of abstract ideas. Symbols give these concreteness and make it possible for common people to grasp them. A religion is a cluster of beliefs capable of stirring the emotions. A cult may arouse its members to action; it may make them resigned to their

91

fate. In either event its symbolic expression must evoke appropriate responses.

The concept of nation is necessarily abstract. The nationals and the officers of government are concrete, but the ideas of nationality or of the State are abstractions. They require symbolic expression.

From the beginning of the history of the developed State, men seem to have turned for their political symbolism to religion. In classical antiquity, kingship was associated with divinity. Emperor worship was an important part of the State religion of Rome. The emperor of Japan is the descendant through scores of generations of the Sun Goddess. When feudalism was at its height in Nippon and government was decentralized among many nobles, the emperor was devoid of temporal power. But his divinity prevented the complete extinguishment of this central symbol. Significantly in 1868 when the modern Japanese nation began with the Meiji restoration, emperor worship was revived and became the center of an elaborate national religion. No practice in the State symbolism of the West equaled, in emotional power, the ritual when the newly elevated emperor of Japan, in the midst of elaborate ceremony, approached a small Shinto shrine and informed the spirits of his ancestors that he had ascended the throne. Then, appearing in robes whose color was the first orange of the rising sun, the head of the State heard from the prime minister the proclamation to the people of his accession. In this ceremony in which the visible and the unseen worlds became one, the people were reminded of the continued solicitude of the Sun Goddess for the nation over whose destinies another of her sons was about to preside. The history of the emperor symbol in Japan suggests a need that appeared in the United States as soon as the new nation took form.

As feudalism gave way to nationalism in Europe, the new kingship was closely associated with religious beliefs and practices. In England, after the break with Rome, the crown became head of the State Church. The early Stuarts insisted upon the doctrine of the divine right of kings. For centuries the association between kingship and divinity in Europe was expressed in the popular belief that the king's touch had curative powers. Even after the Revolution of 1688 had established the supremacy of Parliament and after John Locke had rationalized the change with the philosophy that the authority of the State is derived from the people, the Crown continued to be set against a religious background. The climax of the English coronation ceremony is reached when the new monarch partakes of communion. The ritual suggests harmony between the mundane and the spiritual kingdoms and the subordination of the former kingdom to the latter.

One of the chief functions of a king or emperor is to personify the nation. In England, after 1688, this became the monarch's primary rôle. Where the king is, there is Britain; a toast to the king is a toast to England. In both England and Japan the fact that the monarch has virtually no political power has added vastly to his utility for symbolic purposes.

As nationalism has developed in the culture of the modern world, the military has become increasingly important as an adjunct to religion in providing the political symbolism required by the State. In the English coronation ceremony the armed forces of the realm participate conspicuously as a kind of background for the religious rites appropriate to monarchy performed by the Archbishop of Canterbury. Nazi Germany in the 1930's, giving State worship precedence over Christianity, depended primarily upon the military for its symbolism. Both Nazi Germany and Soviet Russia achieved tremendous dramatic effects on ceremonial occasions from the massing of soldiers and of the banners which the armies carry.

This modern variation makes clear that the purpose of political symbolism is to suggest power. It may come from on high or from the sword. No State can exist without authority. Above all else the symbols of the State must express strength.

∽

The circumstances which surrounded the beginnings of the American nation were responsible for an unusual poverty in symbolism on the part of the early Republic. The United States was an offspring of rebellion. The thirteen colonies were settled primarily by Protestants who had thrown off papal authority. Many provinces, particularly in New England and Pennsylvania, were dominated by nonconformist religious groups that either sought to "purify" the ritual of the Church of England or rejected outright the authority of that institution. One of the characteristics of Protestant denominations, other than the Anglican Church, was the meagerness of their ritual. They symbolized their separation from Rome by rejection as far as possible of all symbols and rituals. In the normal non-Anglican Protestant service in eighteenth-century America, the sermon was the center of the service of worship. In many congregations not even singing was permitted. When Americans began to develop a ritual for the sentiment of nationalism, such Protestant services offered the only religious guide which would be universally acceptable.

But the American Republic was also the product of rebellion against monarchy. The fear among eighteenth-century Americans that the president might become a king made it difficult for Washington to establish an official etiquette that would be sufficiently formal to be appropriate for an independent nation. Late eighteenth-century republicans symbolized their rejection of monarchy by attempting to purge American institutions of every suggestion of monarchical ritual.

They were stopped, moreover, from turning to the military forces. The American rebels were afraid of a standing army even while the Revolution was in progress. To the patriots of 1776 and of 1789 such an establishment suggested tyranny, a government not of laws but of men. If soldiers were to be used for ceremonial purposes, they must be militiamen, citizen soldiers who bore arms only in times of emergency.

◇

One of the more extraordinary political events of the eighteenth century was the coalescing of thirteen rebelling provinces into a stable political unit. The nation in 1783, when distances are measured in time, was larger than the United States of the twentieth century. Each state represented an in-group with particular traditions which, in some cases, included antagonism to other states. The war emergency compelled these former colonies to cooperate, and the events of the struggle for independence gave, to all, common experiences and memories. The conflict, moreover, gave them in the rebel general, Washington, a living personification of the idea of unity. Where Washington established his headquarters, there was the heart of the Revolution.

Washington's generation gave to him the title of "Father of His Country." It is difficult to overestimate his significance in the founding of the nation. He was a product of the culture of his age and he exemplified so well qualities which his generation admired that his person became the rallying point of the rebellion. He combined devotion to the cause, personal integrity, physical courage, a sound judgment of men, and considerable military ability. During the conflict the stature of Congress declined, while that of the general-in-chief increased. After Yorktown, Washington's prestige was greater than that of the government of the United States. The general increased it still further by three acts: he refused the crown suggested by a group who wished to establish a strong State; he persuaded his discontented officers at Newburgh not to use the sword to compel an impotent Congress to give them their pay; and after the signing of the peace treaty he resigned his commission, in a conspicuous ceremony, and returned to private life. The advocates of reform who finally succeeded in bringing about the Constitutional Convention took pains to secure the support of Washington at the outset of their movement, for they well knew that without the support of his prestige their effort would be futile. Even after the Philadelphia instrument was ratified, Americans called upon him to take the lead in organizing the new government.

In a country in which James Madison said that he knew as little of the affairs of Georgia as he did of Kamchatka, the surprising thing is that, after the menace of the common enemy had been removed, two or three nations did not come into being. One of the most important of the factors which prevented such an outcome was the existence of a leader who not only personified national unity but in his behavior conformed to the ideals for which the rebellion had been fought. The importance of this personification is suggested by the reference to Washington, still living but no longer president, in the first of the patriotic songs of the new United States. Robert Treat Paine published in 1798 "Adams and Liberty" which was sung to the old tune which Francis Scott Key later used for the "Star-Spangled Banner":

> Should the tempest of war overshadow our land
> Its bolts could ne'er rend Freedom's temple asunder;
> For, unmoved, at its portal would Washington stand
> And repulse with his breast the assaults of his thunder.

Eighteenth-century American republicans, establishing a new nation, first turned for their symbolism to the greatest republic they knew, Rome. They called the upper house of Congress a Senate. Led by the imaginative Jefferson they used Roman architectural forms in the building of their first national Capitol and of the White House. These Classical Revival buildings were acceptable because they were not far removed from the Georgian structures with which Americans were familiar. The domed Capitol with its Roman columns expressed so well the dignity of the new nation that the type has become virtually indigenous to the United States.

When classicism was carried beyond architecture, it failed. The goddess of liberty which appeared on the coins had no emotional value for Americans and persisted only because there was nothing available with which to replace the figure. Classicism degenerated into absurdity in the giant seated statue of the first President done by Horatio Greenough and placed in 1843 before the Capitol building at Washington. The patriotic sculptor stripped the toga-clad Washington to the waist and seated him in a Roman chair. The figure became the joke of the city of hotels and boarding houses sprawling beside the Potomac. Greenough's carving suggests an almost wistful groping after national symbols on the part of the Americans of the Middle Period.

As a result of the poverty in symbolism, the flag became the chief representation of the nation. During the War of 1812, Key's verses began their rise to the ultimate status of national anthem. It is no accident that the two great patriotic songs of the English-speaking peoples, "God Save the King" and "The Star-Spangled Banner," refer to a living symbolic person and to a material symbolic object. The peculiar importance of the national banner in American political symbolism was a result of the rejection of monarchy. The American President who replaced the king was so important a political officer that his value as a symbol was negligible.

A material object can never express an idea or an emotion so effectively as can an individual who in some manner has come to personify it. The worship of the saints in the Catholic Church suggests the importance of associating certain virtues or attitudes with definite personalities. The life of the saint becomes a vehicle for the instruction of the people in what would otherwise be abstract ideas. A flag can never escape abstractness. Americans of the Middle Period, lacking a living symbol, turned for the personification of the idea of the nation and of the principles upon which it was founded to the leader of the Revolution. Greenough's Washington suggested that the apotheosis of a dead hero had been already long in process of development.

Parson Weems in his best-selling biography referred to the father of his country as early as 1800 as a "Demigod." Reverence for the memory of Washington early became a standard American attitude, although it was impaired somewhat during the period of the Virginia dynasty by memories of the first President's Federalist leanings. As the slavery issue became a growing threat to the Union, citizens in both North and South sought to strengthen the symbols of nationality by making the memory of a great name a living force. In 1848, amid impressive ceremonies, the cornerstone of the great obelisk on the bank of the Potomac was laid. Slowly, during the succeeding years, the tiers of stones, contributed for the most part by popular subscription, grew higher. Then Anna Pamela Cunningham of Charleston, South Carolina, sent out her first call in 1853 to the women of the South to rescue Mount Vernon, which had long been falling into dilapidation, from threatened commercial exploitation. "A descendant of Virginia," she wrote, "and now a daughter of South Carolina, moved by feelings of reverence for departed greatness and goodness,—by patriotism and a sense of national and, above all, of Southern honor,—ventures to appeal to you in behalf of the home and grave of Washington!"[1] Five years later the triumphant Charleston lady, who during the entire period of her crusade had been aided by Edward Everett in the North, received the keys of Washington's house, and Mount Vernon became the property of the American people. Equally significant of the same trend were the lines of Oliver Wendell Holmes's "Ode to Washington," written in 1856 when both North and South were roused to anger by bloodshed in Kansas:

> Vain is Empire's mad temptation!
> Not for him an earthly crown!
> He whose sword hath freed a nation
> Strikes the offered sceptre down.
> See the throneless conqueror seated,
> Ruler by a people's choice;
> See the Patriot's task completed;
> Hear the Father's dying voice;
> "By the name that you inherit
> By the suffering you recall,
> Cherish the fraternal spirit;
> Love your country first of all!
> Listen not to idle questions
> If its bands may be untied;
> Doubt the patriot whose suggestions
> Strive a nation to divide!"

Before 1861, Washington had come to occupy in American civilization a place similar to that of the culture hero in simpler societies. Like the culture hero his memory was associated with those institutions and customs upon which the people put the highest value. He personified more than the idea of nationality. His biography, as suggested in Holmes's stanzas, seemed to mid-nineteenth-century

Americans to dramatize one after another the articles of the democratic faith. He had led to success the people's army in the war for liberty. Instead of taking advantage of his personal power, he had championed the cause of constitutionalism, the philosophy of a government of laws. He was a figure to whom Americans could point and say: This is the type of leader democracy can produce.

～

The apotheosis of a departed hero did not, however, meet fully the American need for national symbols. This demand was supplied most adequately by the recurring ceremonies on the anniversary of independence. The Fourth of July, in the Middle Period, was both a gala day and a national sabbath. The celebration of "the Glorious Fourth" manifested in some aspects the boisterous extravagances of the camp meetings of evangelical Protestantism and in others the austere dignity of a Calvinist service of worship. Alexis de Tocqueville, stopping at Albany, New York, on July 4, 1831, listened to the public reading of the Declaration of Independence and pronounced it one of the more thrilling experiences of his life. But the parade of citizen soldiers which preceded the reading seemed to him a ludicrous imitation of European pageantry. For the oration which was the climax of the ceremony his contempt was without bounds. Yet the oration was the important thing.

The middle decades of the nineteenth century were pre-eminently in America the age of the orator and of the actor. Edwin Forrest, the greatest of the stars on the American stage, was winning triumphs in J. A. Stone's *Metamora* and R. M. Bird's *The Gladiator*. In his part as Metamora, the last of the Wampanoags, and as Spartacus, the leader of an uprising among the Roman gladiators, the muscular and emotional Forrest brought hundreds of audiences in widely separated American cities cheering to their feet. What Forrest was to the theater, Webster was to the platform. His great orations, particularly those in the Senate, became national events. Americans could most easily be moved by the spoken word. Even Emerson in the 1840's was better known as a lyceum lecturer than as a man of letters. In such an age, the Fourth of July oration became inevitably the principal American ceremonial expression of homage to the nation. It was a ritual performance. Though the words differed, the pattern was always the same. It was an affirmation of the doctrines of the American democratic faith. It had no sectional variations. Novelty in essential form would have been as unwelcome as a revision of the Bethlehem story. The oration at the center of the Fourth of July celebration was the counterpart in nationalistic ritual of the emphasis in the Protestant service upon the sermon.

The Declaration of Independence was for ceremonial purposes vastly more important than the Constitution. There was no celebration of a Constitution Day. A few liberals were, in fact, beginning to complain that the younger generation was growing up without adequate knowledge of that great document because its text was to be found in few school books. As a result, enterprising publishers began, with appropriate sales propaganda, to make this "palladium of our liberties" available to the youth of the land. Another difficulty that impaired the value of the Constitution as a ceremonial document was the disagreement as to its interpretation between the school of Webster and that of Calhoun. Was the Constitution a palladium of liberty because it was the supreme law of a nation or because it was a compact among sovereign states? Cogent arguments supported either position. Until this question was settled, the Constitution could not become an effective symbol. The Declaration, on the contrary, created no problems and roused no controversies. The Declaration was not law but rather rhetoric, brilliant rhetoric. For decades the famous phrases that all men are created equal and are endowed by nature with the right to life, liberty, and the pursuit of happiness provided the text for patriotic homilies. When, however, it became possible in the 1850's to charge Americans who took their stand upon the Declaration with proposing equality and even intermarriage between the races, all national symbolism was failing and crisis was near.

∽

A description of a "Fourth" in the Middle Period helps to suggest the mood of American national ritual in the Middle Period. The citizens of Charleston, South Carolina, were awakened at dawn on July 4, 1843, by the pealing of the bells of St. Michael's, a handsome Georgian church built by eighteenth-century wealth. In its pews on Sundays sat the aristocracy of that ante-bellum heyday of the Cotton Kingdom. On this holiday morning, however, the bells of St. Michael's called to worship not only its own congregation, but all citizens in the little city between the Ashley and the Cooper Rivers. Families stirred in houses of brick and stucco huddled together in the friendly gregariousness of a European town. As the clangor of the bells died away, cannon on the battery boomed a salute across the sleepy harbor. Gradually the sidewalks filled with spectators.

Men, women, and children walked across gardens still wet with dew and passed through iron gates, often beautifully wrought, to flag-bedecked streets. The Charleston Light Dragoons paraded down the avenues toward the waterfront; the Sixteenth and the Seventeenth Regiments of infantry and the battalion of artillery followed. Near the reviewing stand at the Battery were assembled a crowd of men in tall hats and of ladies in hoop skirts. When the last marching four had passed and the military units were drawn up at attention on the edge of the harbor, the United States cutter *Van Buren*, riding at anchor not far from Fort Sumter, fired a salute. The artillery battalion replied impressively from the shore. The infantry regiments raised their muskets to conclude this part of the day's long ritual with a *feu de joie*.

Back home from the ceremonies on the Battery, Charlestonians sat on their porches to enjoy the coolness which followed the breaking of a heat wave and to read with approval the editorial of the *Courier*. "Year after year rolls on," wrote the editor, "and finds us unabated in our devotion to the principles of the revolution; determined to keep burning for ever the vestal fire of liberty, kindled by our fathers in the temple of union, and rejoicing in the success of our glorious experiment of popular self-government. We have had our reverses and our trials; but, under the blessings of Providence, not only has nothing transpired to shake our confidence in the stability and permanence of our systems, but on the contrary, the experience of the past only brightens the hope of the future, that our career will continue to realize its full promise of individual happiness and national glory."[2]

Already new processions were forming in the city. The Society of the Cincinnati and the Association of 1776 moved together slowly, as befitted old men who remembered the days when Washington commanded the armies of the United States. In the First Baptist Church the marchers listened to a prayer and then to an oration delivered by a member of the '76. Meanwhile the Washington Society had marched in procession to St. Mary's where the ritual consisted of prayer, the reading of the Declaration, and an address. Note the similarity to the normal Protestant service—prayer, scripture reading, and sermon.

A third procession suggested, more even than the other two, the importance of July Fourth. If a struggling cause could associate itself with the ritual of the day, it might hope with some confidence for a favorable hearing. Early in the 1840's the spreading temperance movement had reached Charleston. Its local leaders seized upon the Fourth of July, 1843, as the best occasion to present their arguments. A procession of temperance societies from the city and from the Neck wound through several streets to the New Theatre; here, after a prayer and anthem, Albert Rhett, Esq., addressed what the *Courier* described as "a numerous, brilliant and gratified audience of both sexes." Orator Rhett, after "a brief allusion to the grateful and hallowed occasion," proceeded to take "the boldest and highest ground in favor of total abstinence."

In the afternoon another parade, following the technique of the temperance people, suggested, again indirectly, the importance of the anniversary of independence. The new institution of the Sunday School was also struggling for a place in American culture. The parade of the Charleston children began at four. Preceded by ministers, teachers, and "a Band of Music," thirteen hundred "young immortals" marched to the shady Mall in front of the Second Presbyterian Church. Here the exercises consisted of a prayer, a "religious parody of the Declaration of Independence" delivered by one of the boys, a poem for the occasion, recited by another boy, and "an oration in which the blessings of liberty and the yet higher blessings of Sabbath School influences were glowingly portrayed" by a third youth. "These performances were interspersed," according to the *Courier*, "with the singing of appropriate anthems by a musical choir of ladies." Charleston's first "Sabbath School Pic Nic" was concluded with box lunches and games. In the evening fireworks illuminated Tivoli Garden. The Charleston celebration exemplified national ceremonialism at its best. It illustrated the relation between religious and national symbolism.

∽

The symbols and rituals of the Middle Period were not limited to the idea of nationalism. Some gave concrete expression to the abstract doctrines of the American democratic faith. The national symbolism was new because the nation was young. Beside it in American civilization were two older symbols, brought by tradition from the Old World.

When a traveler in the days of President Pierce entered any of the hundreds of county towns in the United States, the objects which first drew his eye were the churches and the courthouse. The architecture of a people frequently reflects its hierarchy of values. There were points of similarity between the churches and the courthouses. Both stood, often on little greens, apart from the jostling intimacy of the stores, the banks, and the blacksmith's shops on Main Street. Both displayed evidence of builder's desire to achieve dignity. This was usually accomplished in the Middle Period by the plain porticoes and the white columns of the Greek Revival style. The churches and the courthouses which dominated the county towns of mid-nineteenth-century America were material symbols of the fundamental law. Associated with them and giving them meaning were certain stereotyped behavior patterns which amounted to social rituals.

On the Sabbath, villagers put aside their work-day attire and passed down the aisles of the meeting-house to their pews. The flame of religious zeal burned with significant brightness only in the hearts of a minority; Americans were a practical people, preoccupied with the problems of making a living and little given to mysticism. But by inheritance from their Puritan ancestors they were uncompromising Sabbatarians. The practices of respite from work on Sunday, of church attendance, and of church support were deeply imbedded in the American mores of the village and rural communities. And these communities before 1861 contained a very large proportion of the American population. Behind the Sabbath customs was the almost universal conviction that religion maintained the morals of society, and that, if America were to be suddenly bereft of its churches, moral collapse would result. The old war between good and evil stood clearly revealed in every village community. At opposite ends of the American Main Street, the saloon and the church faced each other. The most elementary American symbols were those of the steeple, pointing heavenward, and of the swinging door, concealing iniquity within. The man who stood for respectability went to church, because, no matter how small a part Christianity might play in his personal life, in his heart he believed that morals and good order rest upon religion. Was not the Church dedicated to the task of reminding sinners that they are rebels against the law of God, and that punishment awaits those who refuse to repent? The church building, the services within it, and all the self-denying Sabbath customs were symbolic expressions of a folk belief in an eternal and changeless moral order upon which society rests. Of all the symbolisms in mid-nineteenth-century America these were the most powerful.

Along Illinois roads in the days of President Pierce a lawyer named Abraham Lincoln rode sometimes. Making the circuit with him were other attorneys and the judge. When stopping at an inn in the county town, they spent the evening swapping stories in the friendly intimacy of democratic equals. Next day in the court the scene was different. Court week was a time of unusual stir in the community. The central figures in the cases were personally known to many people; the public seats were normally filled with curious or anxious spectators. The jury of the defendant's peers took their places; farmers and villagers, called from their routine tasks, enjoyed for the moment the conspicuous responsibility of a citizen's duty. Lawyers and court attendants busied themselves with last-minute preparations. The judge entered. At command all persons in the courtroom rose and stood until he took his seat behind the bench. The lawyers, who perhaps the night before had called him by his first name, now addressed him as "Your Honor." The dignity of the Greek columns before the courthouse door was duplicated by the formalized courtesy within. One after another the cases were tried according to the rules of an elaborately ritualistic procedure. The purpose of the procedural rules was not to embarrass unskilled attorneys, as some unsuccessful litigants suspected, but rather to make the accomplishment of justice more certain. From the beginning of the proceedings to the sentencing of the convicted criminal, the behavior of all who had to do with the case was governed by purposeful ritual. The courthouse was the center of the most elaborate symbolic behavior known to American culture. This ritual was not a sudden creation but was the growth of centuries. Its long history suggests its important uses in civilization. One of the greatest was its symbolic representation of the American folk belief in the certainty of the law and of that allied belief that, in the words of Hicks, "the destruction of certitude as a mass attitude toward law would result in the destruction of law itself."

The churches emphasized the moral law; the courts the secular law. But Chancellor Kent had pointed out that the two were, in reality, one. "The law as a science," he had said, "is only a collection of general principles founded on the moral law, and in the common sense of mankind." This union was also expressed in the almost universal American concept of God as a just judge before whose great assize every individual must come on the Last Day.

∽

Americans of the Middle Period, while they groped for symbols to express ideas and to evoke emotions, had little understanding of the importance of symbolism in a culture. Such knowledge is the fruit of modern anthropological and psychological research. In the twentieth century symbols have become instruments of power often consciously manipulated by individuals, organizations, or governments to further definite ends. Early American symbolism was a folk product. As such it is of prime importance in any investigation of popular thought. The symbols which had meaning for the people reveal, as nothing else does, the ideas and attitudes of the inarticulate masses. The symbolism of the Middle Period suggests the hold upon the common man of that pattern of social beliefs which made up the American democratic faith.

II

*THE AMERICAN DEMOCRATIC FAITH PASSES
SAFELY THROUGH THE FIRES OF SECTIONAL
CONTROVERSY*

II

Chapter 9

A FOOTNOTE
ON JOHN C. CALHOUN

CALHOUN DIED IN 1850 as Melville was rising to his greatest heights. As a brilliant youngster in the arena of Washington politics, Calhoun, like Clay, was a nationalist, ardent in the defense of American honor against British insults. After the War of 1812, his wide-ranging imagination visioned a union of far-separated sovereign states through a system of military roads constructed by the central government. Long before his death, however, he became to both North and South the principal leader of a section. As an old man he seemed to his enemies to personify sectional intransigence. He forged in the busy smithy of his mind the intellectual weapons with which the champions of the Cotton Kingdom sought to defeat the democratic principle of majority rule. Before Robert E. Lee rose to fame, Calhoun was the greatest of the sectionalists, the most brilliant among the champions of a cause which was ultimately lost. In Washington a few weeks after Appomattox, Walt Whitman overheard a conversation of two Union soldiers discussing a monument to Calhoun in the South. One man remarked that the true monuments to the South Carolinian were to be found scattered over the Confederacy in wasted farms, in broken railroads, in destroyed shops, and in the gaunt chimneys which marked the places where families once had made their homes. This soldier expressed a harsh judgment. But his generation in the victorious North was in a mood to agree with him.

Since 1865 Calhoun's thought almost always has been studied by Americans only against the background of sectional conflict. Among the conventions in the teaching of American history in the schools is one which assigns Calhoun and his theory of nullification irrevocably to the past. Washington, Hamilton, and Jefferson, through their beliefs and admonitions, still speak to the present. The issues which they debated still live. The same is not true of Calhoun. Unlike his contemporaries Webster and Marshall, his words are seldom used by moderns to point an argument. Political scientists have charted his theories, have pronounced them brilliant, and then have tossed them into the scrap-heap of discarded ideas. Perhaps the scholars have been too preoccupied with his political devices to consider fully the ideas lying behind them. When his philosophy is analyzed in terms of the American democratic faith, some new insights are achieved both concerning that faith and in the understanding of his thought. The simplest approach is to interrogate the dead Calhoun with respect to the ruling ideas of those decades when he was the champion of the South.

What was his stand on the tenet of the fundamental law? This concept included both the natural law of the Enlightenment and the moral law of the Christians. Emerson in his transcendentalism had united the two in his theory that the moral sense pervaded nature from the center of the cosmos to its circumference. Calhoun, unlike Melville, did not reject such absolutism. The opening sentences of his *Disquisition on Government*, published in the year after his death, state his position: "In order to have a clear and just conception of the nature and object of government, it is indispensable to understand correctly what the constitution or law of our nature is, in which government originates; or, to express it more fully and accurately,—that law, without which government would not, and with which, it must necessarily exist. Without this, it is as impossible to lay any solid foundation for the science of government as it would be to lay one for that of astronomy, without a like understanding of that constitution or law of the material world, according to which several bodies composing the solar system mutually act on each other, and by which they are kept in their respective spheres."

In these somewhat ponderous phrases Calhoun repeated the doctrine of the fundamental law. Whence comes this unwritten constitution or law ultimately governing human life? Calhoun answered simply that the fundamental law of human nature compels men to live in society, and that existence in society requires a government. But of the two, thought Calhoun, society is the more important. "Both are, however," he added, "necessary to the existence and well-being of our race, and equally of Divine ordination."[1] The fundamental law comes of God. Calhoun accepted also the concept of the moral law. In the Senate on February 13, 1840, in discussing the right of petition, he elaborated an argument that if they are to be protected at all, rights must be defended at the first challenge. The individual or group that gives way when a moral issue is raised is, therefore, irreparably weakened in its efforts to maintain the justice of its cause. "The moral is like the physical world," he said, employing an unusual metaphor, "Nature has incrusted the exterior of all organic life, for its safety. Let that be broken through, and it is all weakness within. So in the moral and political world. It is at the extreme limits of right that all wrong and encroachments are the most sensibly felt and easily resisted."[2]

One must understand the application of these generalizations in the affairs of everyday life to comprehend their meaning for the man who during Jackson's administration became the acknowledged and militant leader of a section. Calhoun concurred in the general assumption of Southerners concerning the relation between chattel slavery and the fundamental law. "Negroes are not free," said Calhoun's contemporary George Fitzhugh, "because God and nature, and the general good, and their own good, intended them for slaves."[3] Nature, thought Fitzhugh, had created the races unequal and slavery was the institution through which civilized man gave to the African that share in civilization of which he was capable of making use. Slave owners, moreover, found in Holy Writ divine sanction for the institution. This premise must be read into all Calhoun's statements concerning the fundamental law and concerning liberty.

What was his stand on the doctrine of the free individual? Calhoun felt himself to be more sensitive than his age to the problems of liberty. "We have had so many years of prosperity," he said in 1848 as the Mexican War was closing, "we have passed through so many difficulties and dangers without loss of liberty—that we begin to think that we hold it by divine right from heaven itself." "It is harder to preserve than to obtain liberty," he added. "After years of prosperity, the tenure by which it is held is but too often forgotten; and, I fear, Senators, that such is the case with us. There is no solicitude now about liberty. It was not so in the early days of the Republic."[4]

The threat of tyranny which Calhoun saw close at hand was that of a numerical majority within the nation seeking to use the power of the central government to build up an agricultural, commercial, and industrial economy based on free labor to the disadvantage of an agrarian economy resting on the institution of slavery. After 1831, the year of the Nat Turner uprising in Virginia and the first issue of William Lloyd Garrison's *Emancipator* in Massachusetts, Southerners became a "conscious minority" within the nation. Until his death in 1850 Calhoun remained the chief spokesman in Washington for that minority. For him liberty meant freedom for the Southern people to carry on their lives and to develop their institutions in ways that seemed best to them. He saw in the rising anti-slavery movement in the North a threat that must be faced and countered. He embodied his proposals in the theories of nullification and of the concurrent majority.

Calhoun proclaimed and insisted upon the rights of the states, thirteen of which were older as independent sovereignties than the Constitution. He described this instrument as a compact among sovereign states to set up a central government to perform certain general functions as an agent of the states. In the midst of Jackson's administration, when the protective tariff became an issue, Calhoun developed the theory of nullification. This theory stated, in brief, that when one of the principals (one of the states) believed that the agent had exceeded the authority given it by the compact, the state might nullify the act. South Carolina took such action in 1832 in the matter of a protective tariff. Only South Carolina, however, actively supported so drastic a measure as nullification. This device in Calhoun's mind was merely an aspect of a larger theory, namely, that of the "concurrent majority." Phrased simply, the idea of the concurrent majority meant that each of the major interests—agriculture, commerce, manufacturing—and each of the great sections—North, South, West—should have the power to prevent or halt national actions deemed adverse to its vital interests. On the questions of high policy unanimous consent among major interests must replace decisions by mere majorities. Calhoun devoted the two final decades of his life to the building up of a set of principles which, if accepted throughout the nation, would protect the Southern minority and permit it to carry on without external coercion its chosen way of life. Calhoun supported his theory with an analysis of the doctrine of the free individual and of the sentiment of nationalism unrivaled in his generation.

Calhoun, in his assumptions concerning human nature, was under an unconscious, but nonetheless heavy, debt to Calvin. Man, thought the South Carolinian, was created to live in society but, paradoxically, his egoistic tendencies outweigh the altruism in his nature. Because of this fact government is necessary to prevent self-seeking individuals from overreaching and exploiting their fellows. The purpose of the State is to enable society to function. Government is the policeman of society. "But government," Calhoun went on, "although intended to protect and preserve society, has a strong tendency to disorder and abuse of its powers, as all experience and almost every page of history testify. The cause is to be found in the same constitution of our nature which makes government indispensable. The powers which it is necessary for government to possess, in order to repress violence and preserve order, cannot execute themselves. They must be administered by men in whom, like others, the individual are stronger than the social feelings. And hence, the powers vested in them to prevent injustice and oppression on the part of others, will, if left unguarded, be by them converted into instruments to oppress the rest of the community. That, by which this is prevented, is what is meant by CONSTITUTION, in its most comprehensive sense, when applied to GOVERNMENT."[5]

Calhoun had Calvin's low opinion of human nature. The lawyers expressed the same attitude in the maxim *caveat emptor*. Upon such assumptions of human fallibility American politics had been founded. It was this skepticism which held in check, in the politics of the United States, the tendencies toward doctrinaire extremism found in the constitutions written during the French Revolution. Calhoun's words were those of the scholar and the theorist, but his thought was that of the run-of-the-mill American democrat. A realism harvested from a life spent in the practice of the political art prevented Calhoun from putting faith in the power of words, even if written on parchment, to restrain the activities of government officials. For him, in spite of the Constitution, the federal Republic was governed by men. The Constitution could not enforce itself. What power it had to restrain public officials must come from its use as an instrument of protection by free citizens. "Power can only be resisted by power,—and tendency by tendency," said Calhoun. "Those who exercise power and those subject to its exercise,—the rulers and the ruled,—stand in antagonistic relations to each other. The same constitution of our nature which leads rulers to oppress the ruled,—regardless of the object for which government is ordained,—will, with equal strength, lead the ruled to resist, when possessed of the means of making peaceable and effective resistance."[6]

Calhoun's was not exactly the doctrine of the malevolent State. It was rather the doctrine that no public official can be trusted unless he knows that he is being watched by citizens who have the power to check usurpations. But, for all his realism, the South Carolinian was an idealist. He believed that he had discovered a political device which, by making constitutional democracy work, would guarantee liberty. Human liberty, the dream of the free individual, was the vision that beckoned him and urged him on. "With me," he said in 1848, two years before his death, "the liberty of the country is all in all. If this be preserved, every thing will be preserved; but if lost, all will be lost."[7]

It is difficult to picture Calhoun outside that small semicircular Senate chamber in the old Capitol which the Supreme Court later occupied for more than half a century. In this almost intimate room he presided in the prime of life as Vice-President. Here, as Senator, he grew old. In this chamber one day, when his failing strength was proclaimed by his pinched features and his sunken cheeks, he spoke of the destiny of America. He had never been more impressive. "It has been lately urged in a very respectable quarter," he said, "that it is the mission of this country to spread civil and religious liberty over all the globe, and especially over this continent—even by force, if necessary. It is a sad delusion. . . . To preserve . . . liberty it is indispensable to adopt a course of moderation and justice toward all nations; to avoid war whenever it can be avoided; to let those great causes which are now at work, and by which the mere operation of time will raise our country to an elevation and influence which no country has ever heretofore attained, continue to work. By pursuing such a course, we may succeed in combining greatness and liberty—the highest possible greatness with the largest measure of liberty—and do more to extend liberty by our example over this continent and the world generally, than would be done by a thousand victories."[8] In such a mood the author of the theory of nullification approached that last doctrine of the democratic faith, that doctrine of destiny which was the essence of the spirit of American nationalism.

Nationalism is a sentiment. It is a thing which is less of the mind than of the emotions. It is a consciousness of the group, a feeling in the heart of the individual that his fate is inextricably bound up with those of his people. It is enhanced by external danger. It deteriorates when the population spreads over an area so wide that communication across the nation becomes difficult. During the decades in which Calhoun urged the adoption of his device of nullification, the American people, with the exception of a brief threat of war with England in 1837, felt secure from attack by foreigners. They did not fear the Mexicans. The civil liberty enjoyed by American citizens was founded upon this sense of security. This liberty, greater than that possessed by any other people in the mid-nineteenth-century world, became the boast of American nationalism. It was the trait which was pointed out to distinguish the civilization of the United States from that of other nations.

Calhoun looked deeper than the superficialities of Independence Day orations. As he felt that liberty was a boon easily lost, so also he was convinced that the sentiment of nationalism might under certain circumstances disappear and leave the citizens of the Republic confounded. Almost alone among his contemporaries, Calhoun saw that nationalism in the United States also depends upon security. The loyalty of the individual or of the local community to the national group is primarily the product of the conviction, often unrecognized, that safety lies in merging the life of the locality with that of the nation. As the middle of the century approached, the growing anti-slavery movement in the North threatened the civilization of the South with disruption. The people of the Cotton Kingdom believed that they had accomplished a practicable solution of that most difficult of all social puzzles, the problem of getting two unlike races to live and work together with a minimum of disorder and a reasonable amount of mutual profit. The solution was the ancient institution of slavery. In communities where Negroes outnumbered the white population by two or three to one, it was impossible in the middle decades of the century for the dominant race to see how civilization could be preserved, if the discipline of slavery were relaxed. The appearance in the North of a vociferous and determined movement to bring African servitude to an end filled the South with apprehension. Calhoun foresaw, what ultimately turned out to be the fact, that this sense of insecurity would erode the sentiment of nationalism until, if measures were not taken to protect the South, the old group loyalty would disappear and the nation would fall apart.

Calhoun saw that the numerical majority offered no security to endangered Southern civilization. A majority is made up of men; and, according to the Calhoun theory of human nature, men in the mass can be as selfish and as tyrannical as they are as individuals. He proposed, therefore, the political doctrine of the concurrent majority. Calhoun thought that the sentiment of nationalism can live only so long as the vital interests of all groups within the nation are equally protected. Guarantee such security to all men, to all interests, and to all sections, argued the South Carolinian, and the sentiment of nationalism will flourish as a garden in the warmth of the summer sun. "The concurrent majority . . . ," he said, "tends to unite the most opposite and conflicting interests, and to blend the whole into one common attachment to the country. By giving to each interest, or portion, the power of self-protection, all strife and struggle between them for ascendency is prevented. . . . Under the combined influence of these causes, the interests of each would be merged in the common interests of the whole; and thus, the community would become a unit, by becoming a common centre of attachment of all its parts. And hence, instead of faction, strife, and struggle for party ascendency, there would be patriotism, nationality, harmony, and a struggle only for supremacy in promoting the common good of the whole."[9] Calhoun defined nationalism in terms of a satisfied and happy minority. He was a nationalist in the sense that he preferred that the Union be preserved. But he made the principle of the concurrent majority the condition of union. Give the South autonomy in matters it deemed vital and "patriotism, nationality, and harmony" would follow.

Chapter 10

THE CIVIL WAR AND THE
AMERICAN DEMOCRATIC FAITH

THE ROAR OF THE BATTERIES beside Charleston Harbor opening fire on Fort Sumter on the morning of April 12, 1861, announced the defeat of American political democracy. If political democracy be defined as government by the consent of the governed, the shells over Sumter made clear that a large minority among the American people had withdrawn their consent from the existing federal institutions. If the definition be that democracy is government by discussion among free men, the arguments of statesmen were silenced by those of the cannon. If democracy is merely government by the majority, the American majority in 1861 was seeking to enforce, at the point of the bayonet, its will upon a recalcitrant and determined minority. By any definition, political democracy had, for the time being, lapsed. The Republic, whose citizens had boasted for decades of their ability to govern themselves, became in 1861 the scene of a war so fierce and so bloody as to shock the civilized world. When Beauregard's batteries ceased firing, the breached and crumbling walls of Sumter perfectly symbolized American political democracy when Americans appealed from reason to force.

Responsibility for the disaster rested with the American people. No outside nation was involved. No foreign ideologies played any part in causing the tragedy. If to walk out of the council chamber and begin to fight is a fault, only Americans were guilty of such wrongdoing.

The tragedy is enhanced in the view of later generations when it is recalled that the machinery of peace was at hand. The national Congress was a forum for the discussion and the settlement of po-

115

litical disagreements. There was in that body an old and honorable tradition of compromise. The Supreme Court of the United States was a tribunal for the settlement of justiciable disputes. The sections, moreover, were disarmed. The military establishment of the United States, consisting of about thirteen thousand men scattered mostly over the frontier, did not menace the South. Americans spoke a common language. The North and South were tied together by bonds of sentiment—memories of national exploits and of sacrifices in which all sections shared. To many a thoughtful man in those trying months from November, 1860, to April, 1861, the notion that this people could relapse into such savagery as that of Bloody Angle at Spotsylvania in 1864 seemed fantastic. "There must be no war," said the Niles, Michigan, *Republican* on February 9, 1861. "Let us have peace meetings," urged the Detroit *Free Press* on April 17, 1861, "and let them demand that the national difficulties shall be settled in accordance with the civilization of this age and not in accordance with the barbarism of the Dark Ages. Let them demand that the people of the North and the South —brethren and kindred—shall not be transformed into wild beasts and set upon each other." The tide, however, was running toward war. The editors who urged peace in that fateful April could as easily have prevented with a dam of shingles a wave from sweeping in from the sea.

This is not the place to recount again the familiar story of sectional rivalry. For the present purposes only a few points need be recalled. The central issue was security. Two economic systems took form in the United States in the first half of the nineteenth century. One was staple crop agriculture founded on slavery. The other was industrial capitalism based on the wage system. Slavery was so old that its origins were lost in that shadowy past before the time of written records. It was a strange fate which made the vigorous young Republic of the West the last important stronghold in the civilized world of this ancient institution. Industrial capitalism was new. Once planted in the United States, it grew prodigiously. The natural resources which it required were abundant. The prestige of the industrialists was not subordinated to that of a hereditary aristocracy or a military caste. The United States was a place where the forces and tendencies loosed by the Industrial Revolution expressed themselves with a freedom unequalled elsewhere in the world.

In time the two economic systems collided. Each became identified with a section. Between these sections a contest for power was waged in the arena of national politics. For some years compromises maintained peace, but the task became increasingly difficult. Calhoun announced as early as the 1830's that on some points the South could not compromise. In the middle years of the nineteenth century the institution of slavery had a rigidity which had not yet fixed the capitalism of the North. Slavery was more than the solution of the economic problem of finding a supply of laborers. It was also the solution of a race problem. It was a social discipline which enabled two unlike races to live together. Because the Negro population was large and because in many places it outnumbered that of the whites, social discipline seemed to be the first need of the people. Without it the white man feared either that his civilization would fall into slow decay or that it would be consumed in the holocaust of a race war. Calhoun, clearly aware of the dangers, demanded that his section be given power to defend itself against that numerical majority which drew its strength from small farms and from industrial and commercial towns of the North. When the constitutional weapon of nullification was denied the South, its leaders increased their efforts to strengthen their section by carving out a slave empire within the national domain.

A sense of insecurity goaded the South to what were finally desperate efforts to increase its political power by westward expansion. By 1850, however, the leaders of the section recognized that the contest was unequal. Talk of secession grew ominous in the couthouse yards of the Cotton Kingdom. The appearance of the idea of secession signified that in the South the sentiment of loyalty to the national group was undergoing erosion. It was being worn away by the growing conviction that the Northern majority was a threat to Southern civilization. The sentiment of nationalism, as Calhoun had seen, is a product of the belief of the citizens that the nation is united in the protection of the vital interests of all the people composing it. The group as a whole, if it would survive, must guarantee, in so far as it is able, the security of its parts. Human sentiments are unstable things, yet nations must be built upon them. Loyalty can never be taken for granted; it must in the end be deserved by its object. When an appreciable number of Southerners became convinced that their families and their civilization were no longer safe within the political framework of the United States, they began to dream of a new nation which with their own hands they could shape into a shield and buckler. Few men can exist without some loyalties. If loyalty is withdrawn from one object or cause, it is transferred to another. Such a transfer occurred among the Confederates in 1860–1861. Armed invasion, validating old apprehensions, made the Confederacy a spiritual as well as political reality.

The threat of secession impaired the sense of security in the North. If the nation should begin to disintegrate, no one could foresee where the process might end or what it would mean for the economic and social arrangements of Northern civilization. In their turn Northerners became frightened.

In both sections fear bred anger. Mutual recriminations became louder. Minor aggressions of partisans on either side multiplied. Blood flowed in Kansas on the frontier where the struggle for power was keenest. Blood was spilled again in the abortive raid of John Brown, and a thrill of fear ran through the plantation country at the thought of what might have happened had the abolitionist fanatic succeeded in arming a considerable number of slaves. In 1860 a sectional party elected a president on a platform demanding that slavery be put in the way of ultimate extinction. Then it was that anger, born of fear, burned so intensely that reason gave way to emotion. Peaceful democratic discussion became impossible as citizens of the Republic reached for swords and muskets. The smoking ruins of Sumter were the melancholy verification of the soundness of Calhoun's foresight.

∽

This is not the place to discuss the validity of the hypothesis implied in the phrase, "irrepressible conflict." The answer to that question must rest, in part, upon speculation. The present task is a humbler one. It is merely to inquire as to what happened to the American democratic faith during the years between 1861 and 1865. Paradoxically, the general outlines of the thought-patterns of Northern and Southern leaders were the same.

Numberless partisans on either side accepted without question, as they had for decades, the first doctrine of the democratic faith, that of the fundamental law. Abraham Lincoln referred to it in his first inaugural. "I hold," he said, "that in contemplation of universal law and of the Constitution the Union of these States is perpetual."[1] Robert Toombs, speaking after the war was over to a prostrate people suffering under the oppression of the conqueror, repeated again the old doctrine. "The laws of nations," he said at Atlanta in midsummer, 1868, "though wanting in the certainty of municipal laws by reason of the want of authoritative interpretation, are still laws; they are the laws of nations and of God, divine laws; the rock of ages is their corner-stone and the golden rule is their standard and exponent. They decide upon the rights of peace and war, fix limits to the rights of conquest, and establish rules for the government of the conquered beyond which he cannot pass without placing himself outside of their protection."[2]

Partisans on both sides, moreover, looked upon the war as a battle for the doctrine of the free individual, a war for liberty. Here, however, the details of the patterns diverged.

Abolitionists had for years affirmed that human slavery was an offense against the fundamental moral law. It was a denial, they asserted, of the right of every unoffending individual to be free. Anti-slavery agitation constructed out of the institution a symbol, and they made that symbol visual with a picture of the auction block where a young woman was put up for sale and where children were torn from their parents. Slavery was pointed out as a system which made a mockery of that great doctrine of the mission of the United States to support freedom and to advance the cause of liberty throughout the world. Anti-slavery sentiment was sufficiently powerful to persuade the leaders of the Republican party to write into the platform of 1860 that the new political organization would oppose the further extension of an institution so fraught with evil for the nation and for its citizens. When the Southern states seceded, their act appeared, therefore, to anti-slavery men to be not merely an effort to destroy the Republic, but to overthrow the principles upon which it was founded. Secessionists seemed to be upholding the principle of slavery against that of freedom. If the partisans of slavery should succeed and America should fail, the one great hope of the world for the establishment of liberty would be lost. From platform and from pulpit, from the coast of Maine to the forests of Minnesota thundered the message: This is a holy war. In the midst of the war Horace Bushnell, liberal Congregational theologian, stood in the pulpit of the South Church in Hartford, Connecticut, upon the occasion of a national thanksgiving. "No people of the world were ever sheltered under institutions as genial and benign as ours," he said. "They have yielded us blessings of freedom and security hitherto, which no nation of mankind has ever enjoyed in the same degree . . . law is . . . grounded in right, right is a moral idea, at whose summit stands God, as the everlasting vindicator of right. . . . Our cause, we love to think, is specially God's . . . every drum-beat is a hymn, the cannon thunder God, the electric silence, darting victory along the wires, is the inaudible greeting of God's favoring word and purpose. . . . We associate God and religion with all we are fighting for, and we are not satisfied with any mere human atheistic way of speaking as to means, or measures, or battles, or victories, or the great deeds to win them."[3]

But Southern Americans believed also in the doctrine of the free individual. That the docrtine did not extend to the colored men and women who were held as bond servants was not the result of the volition of the master. The inferior status of the Negro was written, said the Southern philosophers, in the fundamental law of nature and of God. By this law the races are unequal. Alexander H. Stephens reflected a universal Southern sentiment when he spoke of the "great barrier . . . which the Creator has placed between this, our inferior class, and ourselves."[4]

From this premise followed inevitably the arguments and the institutions of the South. Slavery was an adjustment to a fact of nature; it was an institution constructed in obedience to a law of God. In spite of its manifest evils it was not founded upon mere exploitation. Slavery laid burdens upon the master as well as conferring benefits upon him. It provided for the security of the laboring masses. At its best it expressed the principle of stewardship. George Fitzhugh had pointed out this fact in 1856 in a biting little book which he called *Cannibals All;* he reminded his fellow countrymen of the North of that liberty to freeze and to starve which was the right of the industrial laborer when his acquisitive employer had no further use for his services.

When Southern leaders beheld the triumph at the polls of a party whose declared objective was to destroy slavery, they brought about the secession of the plantation states. They declared that their fundamental rights as free men had been invaded. They returned to the philosophy of 1776. "Whatever may be said of the loyalty or disloyalty of any, in the late most lamentable conflict of arms," remarked Stephens sadly after the guns had been silenced, "I think I may venture safely to say, that there was, on the part of the great mass of people . . . of the entire South, no *disloyalty* to the principles of the Constitution of the United States. To that system of representative Government; of delegated and limited powers; that establishment in a new phase, on this continent, of all the essentials of England's *Magna Charta*, for the protection and security of life, liberty and property, with the additional recognition of the principle of a fundamental truth, that all political power resides in the people. With us it was simply a question as to where our allegiance was due in the maintenance of these principles—which authority was paramount in the last resort—State or Federal. To [the maintenance of these principles of self-government] my whole soul was ever enlisted, and to this end my whole life has heretofore been devoted, and will continue to be the rest of my days—God willing."[5]

The reasoning of Jefferson Davis ran in a similar groove when, on January 10, 1861, he discussed in the Senate of the United States the President's message concerning the secession of South Carolina. "I do not regard the failure of our constitutional Union," said the Senator from Mississippi, "as very many do, to be the failure of self-government, to be conclusive in all future time of the unfitness of man to govern himself. . . . Representative liberty may remain in the States after they are separated. . . . If we accept the argument of today in favor of coercion as the theory of our government, its only effect will be to precipitate men who have pride and self-reliance into the assertion of the freedom and independence to which they were born!" Davis turned to the Republican Senators from the North. "You aggress upon our rights and homes," he said quietly, "and under the will of God, we will defend them."[6]

As President of the new Southern nation, Jefferson Davis never ceased to insist that the Confederates were the true disciples of the American democratic faith against a tyrannical Northern majority. "Our present political position has been achieved in a manner unprecedented in the history of nations," he said in his inaugural as President of the Provisional Government. "It illustrates the American idea that governments rest on the consent of the governed, and that it is the right of the people to alter or abolish them at will whenever they become destructive of the ends for which they were established. The declared purpose of the compact of the Union from which we have withdrawn was to 'establish justice, insure domestic tranquility, provide for the common defence, promote the general welfare, and secure the blessings of liberty to ourselves and our posterity'; and when in the judgment of the sovereign states composing this Confederacy, it has been perverted from the purposes for which it was ordained, and ceased to answer the ends for which it was established, a peaceful appeal to the ballot box declared that, so far as they are concerned, the Government created by that compact should cease to exist. In this they merely asserted the right which the Declaration of Independence of July 4, 1776, defined as 'inalienable'!"[7] A few months later Davis journeyed from Montgomery to Richmond to establish the capital of the Confederacy in the principal city of the Old Dominion. Arriving in the afternoon of May 30, he went to the New Fair Grounds to address the people. "I look upon you," said the President, as his eye ran over the massed throng among whom were many men in uniform, "as the last best hope of liberty; and in our liberty alone is our Constitutional Government to be preserved."[8]

Three years of war went by. The Confederacy passed from the Chancellorsville triumph to the Atlanta defeat. Sherman was marching through Georgia when, on November 29, 1864, Gustavus A. Henry of Tennessee rose in the Senate of the Confederate States to speak to his resolution reaffirming the determination of the Confederate Congress and people to prosecute the war until their independence should be acknowledged. "In 1776 . . . ," said Henry, "the common ancestors of the parties to the present conflict of arms, in Congress assembled, proclaimed to the world the Declaration of American Independence, in which these great political truths . . . were submitted to the candid judgment of mankind." The Senator repeated the familiar phrases setting forth the doctrines of natural rights, of government by the consent of the governed, and of the right of revolution. "On these same principles," he continued, "we have staked our all. . . . We stand where our fathers stood in defense of the same rights. The United States occupy the ground of George the Third, and are re-enacting his despotism. . . . The contest about our domestic institutions, the right of the States to legalize, destroy or perpetuate them, as an attribute of their sovereignty, are all embraced under the general idea, and purely an American one, the right of the people to self-government. . . . It was not until . . . Lincoln had made his proclamation for seventy-five thousand men to subjugate these States, that the people began to prepare for war. . . . It is emphatically the people's war. . . . Stonewall Jackson, Polk, Stuart, Rodes, Morgan, Preston Smith [are dead]. . . . Their spirits walk abroad, and stir the hearts of living men to do or die in the cause of liberty."[9]

Davis and Henry argued that the doctrine of the free individual implied inevitably another tenet, namely, the right of revolution. Henry Thoreau had affirmed as much. The argument was as old as

Locke. It was almost universally accepted in the North. President Lincoln mentioned it in his first inaugural. "This country," said Lincoln, "with its institutions, belongs to the people who inhabit it. Whenever they shall grow weary of the existing Government, they can exercise their *constitutional* right of amending it or their *revolutionary* right to dismember or overthrow it."[10] Why not, then, let the seceded states go in peace? Northern editors from East to West had been discussing the right of revolution since before the secession of South Carolina. Consistency with American tradition compelled them to admit such a right. The right of secession was a problem of constitutional law about which there was wide disagreement among Northern editors. But they found it difficult to repudiate the Declaration of Independence.

Abraham Lincoln, indefatigable reader of the press, must have been familiar, when he delivered his inaugural, with the resolution in the North of the logical dilemma. It ran as follows: it is one thing, declared the Northern editors, to revolt against such manifest "tyranny" as that of England in the fateful 1770's, but quite a different thing to rebel against that nation which was created to be a witness for human liberty before the world. To attempt to strike down "the most beneficent government the world has ever seen," the argument continued, was so fantastic an action that even the most stupid could understand that the effort was conceived in wickedness and was born in iniquity.[11]

The point to note is that the expressed premises of Lincoln and of Davis were identical in so far as they made use of the doctrine of the free individual. Both North and South, then, made war to defend the tenets of an established American faith. Both fought for liberty. Each party to the conflict justified its position by reference to an eternal and absolute law which transcends the laws of men. The democratic faith, which had aided in postponing the sectional conflict, manifested, then, after Sumter fell, a new utility. To both the Blue and the Gray it provided those ideals for which men are willing to die. It laid the spiritual foundation for a prolonged and desperate war. It gave a new and terrible connotation to those place names which had once suggested peace and contentment: Antietam, Fredericksburg, Cold Harbor. When Lee surrendered at Appomattox, slavery had been abolished and a civilization had been destroyed, but the American democratic faith remained unimpaired. It had, in fact, won a double triumph. It had, at the same time, conquered in battle and had suffered martyrdom. One of the paradoxes

of the war may be found in the strange fact that, though the sentiment of nationalism in the old sense failed, the doctrine of the
destiny of America to stand before the world as a witness for democratic liberty was unimpaired. Both North and South believed that
theirs was the true witness. At the level of ideas and of ideals the
separation of the sections was similar to a religious schism. Each
side felt that it alone was faithful to the old truths and to the
ancient faith.

～

But the American democratic faith was of more significance in
the Civil War than merely to provide the ideals which caused men
to enlist in volunteer armies and women to endure privation and
hardship at home. The faith had importance in that tangled story
called the constitutional history of the war.

The problems of constitutional interpretation began with the
secession of South Carolina. They became urgent after the fall of
Sumter. That event created more than a crisis. When Anderson
hauled down his flag, he lowered at the same time the pride of a
great nation. For Americans the event was an earthquake shock.
The old stability of their institutions disappeared. The future was
dark and uncertain. In the crisis confronting the nation loyal citizens
looked to the leader in Washington.

Lincoln saw clearly the implications of the events of April, 1861.
For more than half a century Americans had been developing and
managing a clumsy, lumbering national government. Its duties were
relatively simple and its servants, by modern standards, few. Alexis
de Tocqueville, traveling in the United States in the 1830's, had
remarked, that, though he had searched diligently, he had had difficulty to find the government. He saw neither soldiers nor bureau-
crats. The American democrat before 1861 came into contact with
that distant abstraction, the federal government, seldom more often
than on the quadrennial occasions of the presidential election. The
crisis of civil war revolutionized the rôle of the Washington Government. Lincoln saw that this government must be transformed as
swiftly as possible into an instrument which the loyal citizens could
use effectively to preserve the integrity of the nation. The federal
government must have power and efficiency. It must be capable of
quick decision and of rapid action. Lincoln was the first war President to sense fully the change of function which a national emergency must bring to the office of the Presidency. He saw that the
Chief Executive must exercise almost dictatorial powers.

The ex-lawyer of the prairies moved swiftly after Anderson's surrender. He developed the actual powers of the central government and particularly of his office far beyond their normal peace-time constitutional limits. Wherever possible, Lincoln used as his guide the clauses of the written Constitution. But he found the document of 1787 inadequate and even at times an obstacle. He did not hesitate, when in his judgment it seemed wise and necessary, to transgress the letter of the supreme law. He suspended, by executive order, the writ of *habeas corpus* when the Constitution gave that power only to Congress. He declared martial law in communities far removed from the active fighting and in which the civil courts were open and functioning. Soon after Sumter, he increased by Executive order the military forces of the nation. Nor did he limit his call to the summoning of recruits to a temporary volunteer force; he enlarged the permanent military establishment of the United States. Americans, influenced by a tradition which had come to the New World from England, had long feared a standing army as an instrument of tyranny. The framers of the Constitution had specifically given to Congress the power to raise armies, and fearful lest the military arm should become more powerful than the civil State, had denied Congress the power to make appropriations for the army which would run beyond two years. Against such a background the President who, without Congressional authorization, enlarged the regular army of the United States took giant strides toward dictatorship as conceived by democratic philosophy. It is true that some of Lincoln's acts were legalized by *ex post facto* Congressional legislation. But the fact remains that Lincoln became a president incomparably more powerful than any of his predecessors and that in acquiring this power he sometimes defied the express provisions of the supreme law of the land. The extent of his power is suggested by his most audacious act. By an order issued as Commander-in-Chief of the Army he freed the slaves of those citizens who on January 1, 1863 were still in rebellion against the government of the United States. By so doing he not only decided with finality a question which had perplexed for a generation the statesmen of the nation, but he struck the foundation from under an old civilization.

Lincoln became powerful in order that he might protect and defend a supreme law which was no longer supreme. It was defied in the entire area of the Confederacy. A paradox resulted. The President became the preserver of the law by which he, along with the humblest citizen, was supposed to be governed. When, in his opinion, the limits which that law set to his activities seemed unwise, he ignored them. The essence of constitutionalism is the theory that the public official is restrained by a law whose status is superior to his. Lincoln, on the occasions in which he specifically violated the Constitution, took a position above the law. Yet he believed in the principle of constitutionalism. He did not become a dictator; he accepted freely and completely the restraint of what was for him the ultimate law. He found it, unwritten, in the doctrines of the American democratic faith.

For Lincoln the controlling tenet of this faith was the doctrine of the mission of America. This, as has already been suggested, was the belief that American nationality exists not as an end in itself, but as a means to the larger end of furthering the ideal of human freedom. Lincoln shared the conviction of a majority of his generation that the nation existed that men might be free. "Fourscore and seven years ago our fathers brought forth on this continent," he said at Gettysburg, "a new nation, conceived in liberty, and dedicated to the proposition that all men are created equal. . . . Now we are engaged in a great civil war, testing whether that nation, or any nation so conceived and so dedicated, can long endure." The belief that the freedom of the individual was inseparably bound to American nationalism was the greatest single coercive force behind the formulation of his policy as President. "I would save the Union," he said to Horace Greeley. "I would save it the shortest way under the Constitution. . . . My paramount object in this struggle is to save the Union and not either to save or to destroy slavery."

Lincoln, then, conceived of the federal government as an instrument in the hands of the people which they could use for the protection of the ideal of the free individual. He assumed power as president to further this same ideal. His use of his power was limited and controlled by the ends he sought. But these ends were not wholly contained in the doctrine of the free individual or of the mission of America.

As already suggested, Lincoln believed in a universal and fundamental law not made by men. A basic postulate of his thought was the existence of an absolute and authoritarian moral law. His concept of the requirements of this law controlled also his use of the power which he wielded. His ideas of justice dictated his policy of a magnanimous peace. He disclosed the fountainhead of his thinking in that famous concluding paragraph of the second inaugural:

"With malice toward none; with charity for all; with firmness in the right, as God gives us to see the right, let us strive to finish the work we are in; to bind up the nation's wounds; to care for him who shall have borne the battle, and for his widow, and his orphan —to do all which may achieve a just and lasting peace among ourselves, and with all nations."

Before 1861 the American democratic faith had provided those common agreements which made democratic debate possible when the Constitution became an object of controversy. From 1861 to 1865 this same cluster of social beliefs, variously interpreted, provided the idealism of both antagonists in a mighty war. During those same years it set the limits which governed the policy of the President, when he pioneered in the exploration of that vague constitutional domain known as the war powers. In his meticulous adherence to these self-imposed limits when he was possessed of overwhelming authority, Lincoln personified the American ideal of the autonomous, self-determined, free individual.

Chapter 11

WHITMAN AND THE CIVIL WAR

THE SIGNIFICANCE OF THE CIVIL WAR for the history of the American democratic faith is suggested by the evolution of the thought of one man. Walt Whitman was no ordinary citizen. He looked upon himself—correctly—as both seer and poet. He understood the ruling ideals of mid-nineteenth-century America; he made its dominant moods his own. He developed with the American people but he was no mere follower. When Whitman shifted his emphasis, he was usually in the van. From 1855 until 1873, when he was stricken with paralysis, his was an authentic American voice. What the war did to Whitman's thought concerning the democratic faith, it did also to that of his articulate fellow countrymen of the North and West and ultimately of the South.

Whitman was one of the first to coin the phrase "democratic faith." He used it in an editorial in the Brooklyn *Eagle* on November 7, 1846, when a young journalist of twenty-seven years. His early editorial writings reflect the exuberant and bombastic creed of the age when Manifest Destiny was at flood tide. "Let us not think," he wrote in the *Eagle* on July 28, 1848, "that because we are ahead of the tyrannical system of the Old World that *we* of the New have no advance to make. Every season, indeed, witnesses a great onward movement, even now. . . . The old and moth-eaten systems of Europe have had their day. . . . *Here,* we have planted the standard of freedom, and here we will test the capacities of men for self-government."[1] Whitman in 1847 belonged with those American republicans whom Melville satirized so mercilessly two years later in *Mardi.*

In 1855 the journalist sent to Ralph Waldo Emerson a small sheaf of poems gathered under the title, *Leaves of Grass.* Emerson was intrigued by the strange cadences of the lines, stirred at their expression of the American faith. He wrote to the unknown poet: "I greet you at the beginning of a great career." Whitman by 1855 had tamed the somewhat bumptious mood of 1846. He had translated bombast into song. The result was a handful of powerful pieces. Throwing reserve to the winds yet compelling his verse to an iron discipline, Whitman in 1855 celebrated the glory of the individual man, the glory of a nation of pioneers tramping to the conquest of a wilderness, and, above all, the glory of the democratic faith. Whitman was in high spirits when he received Emerson's letter.

The next year, however, found the clouds drifting across his sky. It was the year of that quadrennial climax in American political democracy, the presidential election. The term of the unhappy Franklin Pierce was ending. His party had put forward James Buchanan. Another faction had written the name of Millard Fillmore upon its banner. Here were two little men, thought Whitman, dwarfs beside the great Emerson, and yet they were candidates for the highest office in the Republic. Whitman considered them political time-servers. He looked upon Buchanan, in particular, as the tool of the Southern slaveocracy. Whitman in 1856 was disillusioned He composed under the title, "The Eighteenth Presidency," one of the bitterest diatribes against the practices of realistic democracy to be found in literature of American politics. He hoped for a publisher of the piece but failed. "Neither in the Presidency, nor in Congress, nor in foreign ambassadorships," said Whitman, "nor in the governorships of The States, nor in legislatures, nor in the mayoralties of cities, nor the aldermanships, nor among the police, nor on the benches of judges, do I observe a single bold muscular, young, well-informed, well-beloved, resolute American man, bound to do a man's duty, aloof from all parties, and with a manly scorn of all parties. Instead of that, every trustee of the people is a traitor, looking only to his own gain, and to boost up his party. The berths, the Presidency included, are bought, sold, electioneered for, prostituted, and filled with prostitutes."[2] Whitman laid upon "politics" responsibility for the crisis which threatened the nation as the American people chose their eighteenth President. He saw in the North and East, swarms of "dough-faces, office-vermin, kept-editors," and in the South, no end of "blusterers, braggarts, windy, melodramatic, . . . altogether the most impudent persons that have yet appeared in the history of lands, . . . having pistol'd, bludgeoned, yelled and threatened America, the past twenty years into one long train of cowardly concessions."[3]

Disillusionment with realistic democracy did not cause Whitman to despair of the democratic faith. He thought he saw a new generation rising which would rid itself of factions and of parties. He spoke of the possibility of the appearance of a President of a new type out of the common people of the West. "Whenever the day comes for him to appear," wrote Whitman, "the man who shall be the Redeemer President of These States, is to be one that fullest realizes the rights of individuals, signified by the impregnable rights of The States, the substratum of the Union."[4] In other words the great President-to-be would make the ideals of the democratic faith realities in the life of the nation. As the months ran on and the crisis deepened, Whitman's spirit soared. He came to believe in the possibility of the triumph of the democratic faith in that day, perhaps so near at hand, when the common people would throw off the yoke of the politician and declare that freedom must not perish in America. Whitman welcomed the struggle which lay ahead. He expressed his belief in lines which he did not publish but which served as the background later for his "O Captain, My Captain."

> Blow mad winds!
> Rage, boil, vex, yawn wide, yeasty waves,
> Crash away—
> Tug at the planks—make them groan—fall around, black clouds,—
>   clouds of death
> Ship of the world,—ship of Humanity—Ship of the ages
> Ship that circlest the world
> Ship of the hope of the world—Ship of Promise
> Welcome the storm—welcome the trial
> Why now I shall see what the old ship is made of
> Anybody can sail with a fair wind, or a smooth sea

> *   *   *

> I welcome this menace—I welcome thee with joy
> Why now I shall know whether there is any thing in you,
>   Libertad,
> I shall see how much you can stand
> Perhaps I shall see the crash—is all lost?[5]

During these anxious months when Americans, North and South, were moving toward Sumter, Whitman was adding new pieces to *Leaves of Grass*. Their mood was vigorous optimism. Much as he distrusted and disliked politicians, Whitman did not fear the results of secession. Nor did most of his fellow countrymen of both North and South. In 1860 both sections suffered under delusions as to their respective abilities to defeat the other side in a short campaign. Whitman, however, looked beyond combat to reunion. He seems to have felt that in the conflict to come the ideals of the democratic faith would emerge triumphant in all of "These States" and would create that unity foreshadowed in the 1860 edition of the *Leaves*.

> I will make the continent indissoluble,
> I will make the most splendid race the sun ever shone upon
> I will make divine magnetic lands,
>   With the love of comrades
>   With the life-long love of comrades.[6]

Within a twelvemonth after Whitman wrote these lines, war was sweeping, like a hurricane, through the "union of these States." It tumbled him, like many other drifting Americans, into Washington. He became a clerk in a government office and a volunteer worker in the military hospitals of the capital. As he made his daily rounds, the stream of wounded from the battlefields swelled to a flood. Whitman in his poems had glorified physical well-being. Health and strength were part of his religion. The sight of the maimed and dying brought him an anguish of which few men were capable. Yet he persisted in his self-appointed work of cheering and aiding the suffering. He brought little presents; he read aloud; sitting beside hospital cots, he wrote, at dictation, last letters home; and sometimes he merely sat in silence, for hours, to bring what comfort he could until death came. The flood of wounded continued, rising and falling like the tide, as campaigns were pressed or slackened. Whitman went south to work in the open-air camps of the wounded behind the firing lines, where "the odor of blood, mixed with the fresh scent of the night, the grass, the trees—that slaughter-house! . . . Amid the woods, that scene of flitting souls—amid the crack and crash and yelling sounds—the impalpable perfume of the woods—and yet the pungent, stifling smoke—the radiance of the moon, looking from heaven at intervals so placid . . . the melancholy, draperied night above, around. And there, upon the roads, the fields, and in those woods, that contest, never one more desperate in any age or land—both parties now in force—masses—no fancy battles, no semi-play, but fierce and savage demons fighting there—courage and scorn of death the rule, exceptions almost none."[7]

War was more dreadful than Whitman had imagined. It wrecked the dream world of his youth. It begot doubts which haunted him like specters in the night. It challenged his democratic faith. He paused one day between visits to bedsides to give voice to the conflict within him.

> Year that trembled and reel'd beneath me!
> Your summer wind was warm enough, yet the air I breathed froze me,
> A thick gloom fell through the sunshine and darken'd me,
> Must I change my triumphant songs? said I to myself,
> Must I learn to chant the cold dirges of the baffled
> And sullen hymns of defeat?[8]

Whitman, however, did not yield to despair. He ministered to the wounded until the war hospitals ceased to exist. He made no distinction between Gray and Blue. As crowded months raced by, the conviction grew upon him that he was in immediate and intimate contact with the thoughts and feelings of the inarticulate common men of America. He was seeing America as he never had before. When the ordeal had passed, he tried to analyze his experience. "It arous'd and brought out," he said, "and decided un-dream'd-of depths of emotion. It has given me my most fervent views of the true *ensemble* and extent of the States."[9] The war gave to Whitman meaning and a connotation for his own prewar phrase, "the substratum of the Union."

Appomattox opened the door upon a new and unlovely America. In an atmosphere of corroding hatred, Whitman lifted American poetry to perhaps its greatest heights in his two poems to the dead Lincoln, the redeemer President, of whose coming he had once spoken.

Whitman grew old. Looking back upon the receding war in whose suffering he had shared so intimately, he pronounced it a good war. It was good, he thought, not so much because it had freed the slave nor even because it had saved the Union, but because it had provided for him and for his countrymen that proof which was needed to make the democratic faith invincible. "The movements of the late secession war and their results," he wrote in 1872, ". . . show that popular democracy, whatever its faults and danger, practically justifies itself beyond the proudest claims and the wildest dreams of its enthusiasts. Probably no future age can know, but I well know, how the gist of this fiercest and most resolute of the world's warlike contentions resided exclusively in the unnamed, unknown rank and file; how the brunt of its labor of death, to all essential purposes, was volunteered. The People, of their own choice, fighting, dying for their own idea." With this sentiment the vast majority of Americans in both North and South agreed.

Whitman was no builder of philosophical systems. He had no logical theory of democracy. Yet what he called "Democracy" absorbed his thought and stirred his emotions throughout his adult life. For him it was an ideal, or better, a cluster of ideals. And it was certainly a faith. Clifton J. Furness in his volume, *Walt Whitman's Workshop*, has gathered from random scraps of memoranda in the papers of the poet a collection which he has presented under the title, "Notes for Lectures on Democracy and 'Adhesiveness.'" Most of the ideas found here were presented by Whitman in more finished form in his published verse and prose. His thought, however, is best revealed in this informal raw material out of which he constructed his books.

Whitman was an undiscouraged believer in two things: the essential goodness of human nature and the power of ideals to enable that innate goodness to express itself. He did not close his eyes to the political skulduggery which followed Appomattox. "I perceive all the corruption," he said. "I observe shallow men are put in the greatest offices, even in the Presidency—and yet with all that . . . I know that underneath all this putridity of Presidents and Congressmen that has risen at the top, lie pure waters a thousand fathoms deep. They make the real ocean, whatever the scum may be on its surface."[10] Belief in the efficacy of political democracy as a practicable institution assumes a faith in the ultimate soundness of human nature as expressed in the common man.

Whitman, realist, did not dodge this implication. He boldly affirmed such a faith. But he did so with his eyes open. Whitman knew the common men of the age as did few of his contemporaries. "About this business of Democracy and human rights, etc.," he went on, "often comes the query—as one sees the shallowness and miserable selfism of these crowds of men, with all their minds so blank of high humanity and aspiration—then comes the terrible query, and will not be denied, Is not Democracy of human rights humbug after all—Are these flippant people with hearts of rags and souls of chalk, are these worth preaching for and dying for upon the cross? May be not—may be it is indeed a dream—yet one thing sure remains—but the exercise of Democracy, equality, to him who, believing, preaches, and to the people who work it out—*this* is not a dream—to work for Democracy is good, the exercise is good—strength it makes and lessons it teaches—gods it makes, at any rate, though it crucifies them often."[11] Whitman clearly thought that one such human divinity was Abraham Lincoln.

Whitman's formulation of the specific ideals which he included within the broad word "Democracy" followed the pattern of his age. In all the literature of American folk philosophy there is no better expression of the doctrine of the fundamental law than that of the first citizen of Camden, New Jersey, written near the end of his life. "The whole Universe is absolute Law," he said. "Freedom only opens entire activity and license *under the law*. . . . Great—unspeakably great—is the Will! the free Soul of man! At its greatest, understanding and obeying the laws, it can then, and then only, maintain true liberty. For there is to the highest, that law as absolute as any—more absolute than any—the Law of Liberty. The shallow, as intimated, consider liberty a release from all law, from every constraint. The wise see in it, on the contrary, the potent Law of Laws, namely, the fusion and combination of the conscious will, or partial individual law, with those universal, eternal, unconscious ones, which run through all Time, pervade history, prove immortality, give moral purpose to the entire objective world, and the last dignity to human life."[12] From the doctrine of the fundamental law, Whitman inferred not determinism but humanism.

The formulation of the concept of the fundamental law includes some of his ideas of the free individual. But others must be mentioned to complete Whitman's portrait of the democrat. Whitman emphasized, more than his age, equality. He went beyond the mere affirmation of equality of rights derived from the fundamental law. He looked forward to a hoped-for equality of virtue. Going back to the Quaker tradition in which he was reared, he reaffirmed an old ideal of that sect. "I want no more of these deferences to authority—this taking off of hats and saying Sir—I want to encourage in the young men the spirit that does not know what it is to feel that it stands in the presence of superiors."[13]

Whitman had long dreamed of "a race of perfect men, women, and children, grandly developt in body, emotions, heroism and intellect—not a select class so developt but the general population."[14] To equality Whitman added fraternity, which he called "adhesiveness." He thought of the free individual as an isolated person and yet at the same time as one who was bound to his fellows by the strongest of ties. "The final meaning of Democracy," he wrote in 1864, "in the most terrible year of the Civil War, "is to press on through all ridicules, arguments, and ostensible failures to put in practice the idea of the sovereignty, license, sacredness of the individual. This idea isolates, for reasons, each separate man and woman in the world:—while the idea of Love fuses and combines the whole. Out of the fusing of these twain, opposite as they are, I seek to make a homogeneous Song."[15] In this emphasis upon brotherhood Whitman looked forward from the atomistic individualism of the frontier to new concepts of cooperation which were to take form after Appomattox.

But Whitman, in spite of his emphasis upon brotherhood, emphasized with his age in America the solitary individual. For the poet the most important thing in the cosmos was the great soul. He saw everything in the universe making way for the progress of souls. He declared that all governments, arts, and religions are but instruments which the individual soul, the solitary personality, uses in living. He did not think that the average among American individuals measured up to his grand vision of the soul. He searched tirelessly among the common people for companions who would approximate the great soul. He counted close friends among cab drivers, streetcar conductors, ferrymen, farmers, and fishermen.

He discovered in his generation one great soul. He saw Lincoln more than once, but he did not know him personally. Yet the poet's estimate of the President has proved more acceptable to posterity than that of the majority of the men of the 1860's. For them Lincoln was an intimate and very human hero. For Whitman he was a cosmic figure, a personification of the great soul brought to earth. The author of the *Leaves* wrote two poems in honor of the martyred statesman. The first, "O Captain, My Captain," was a lament at the departure of the leader. The Great Soul had vanished; disaster had befallen democracy. But Whitman reconsidered. In his second poem, "When Lilacs Last in the Dooryard Bloomed," he fitted his particular doctrine of the free individual into that cosmic outlook which he had derived from Emerson's transcendentalism. Whitman sang of the love of comrades and mourned the death of "a great companion," "the sweetest and wisest soul of all my days and lands." In it Whitman seemed to say, with Emerson, that it is the Over-Soul, or God, dwelling in the heart which makes possible the great soul. The final triumph of life, then, is for the body to return to the earth and the soul to the infinite spirit.

> . . . I glorify thee above all, [sang Whitman addressing death]
> I bring thee a song that when thou must indeed come, come un-
> falteringly.[16]

Whitman, although he expressed at times the sentiment of internationalism, had no doubts about the doctrine of the mission of America. He was always a vigorous nationalist. Although he opposed slavery, he never relapsed into the narrow sectionalism of the abolitionist or the secessionist. Through all crises he held fast to the vision of the union of "These States." When in his thought he looked at America against a background of other nations, he saw his native land invested with a unique responsibility. Americans, as a race, were young. They were a vigorous people trekking westward across a wilderness continent. They were doers rather than thinkers. Their philosophy was expressed in action rather than in systems or ideas. The essence of American life was activism. The quietism of a Buddhist faith in Nirvana had no appeal to them. They solved the problems of living not by running away from life to the contemplation of the monastery, but rather by advancing upon life and grappling with the tasks which it set. With such generalizations Whitman described his American people, and with this hypothesis as a point of departure he described their destiny. Their mission was to use their strength and their energy to maintain the freedom of the individual. In "Pioneers! O Pioneers!" written before the war, he expressed the exuberant activism which pervaded the American democratic faith of that period:

> For we cannot tarry here,
> We must march . . . we must bear the brunt of danger,
> We the youthful sinewy races, all the rest on us depend.
> Pioneers! O Pioneers!
> All the past we leave behind
> We debouch upon a new and mightier world, varied world,
> Fresh and strong the world we seize, world of labor and the march,
> Pioneers! O Pioneers![17]

The war passed. The citizens of the victorious nation faced neighboring countries with a deepened and uncompromising nationalism. Whitman reflected the mood. "The time has arrived," he remarked, "when These States, in all their intercourse with powers, courts, or what not, shall preserve their own personality, with haughtiness and silence. . . . I hold it should be the glory and pride of America not to be like other lands, but different, after its own different spirit."[18] And the difference which would set off America from its neighbors was its mission to stand before the world as a witness for democracy. Whitman distilled this belief of the common people into deathless verse:

Sail, sail thy best ship of Democracy
    of Value is thy freight . . .
Thou holdest not the venture of thyself alone,
    nor of the Western continent alone . . .
With thee time voyages in trust, the antecedent
    nations sink or swim with thee,
Theirs, theirs as much as thine, the destination
    port triumphant.[19]

Chapter 12

THE RE-CREATION OF
THE AMERICAN UNION 1865-1917

Appomattox ended one of the two major wars of the nineteenth century. In the size and the power of armies and in the losses sustained, the American Civil War was comparable to the Napoleonic struggles in Europe. The Americans, however, concentrated into four years an amount of destruction and anguish which in the Old World was extended over more than a decade and a half. The intensity of the conflict was due to the unyielding will of the Southern people who began, in 1861, a fight for independence. They strove to set up a new nation which would differ from the old United States to about the degree in which Southern economy and social life differed from that of the North. The Confederacy might have surrendered with honor when Grant smashed Bragg's army at Lookout Mountain and Missionary Ridge in the autumn of 1863, for after this disaster the military outlook for the South was almost hopeless. But there was no thought of surrender on the part of the leaders or of the people. The war dragged on for a bloody seventeen months. The Confederacy did not die until its armies had been either dispersed or captured and until vast areas within its hoped-for boundaries had been laid waste. The Southern people gave battle for the right of self-determination to the limit of their strength.

Thirty-three years after Appomattox the United States mobilized a volunteer army in a war against Spain. Southerners enlisted under the national banner as readily as Northerners. Reconciliation between the sections was symbolized by the appointment of two ex-Confederate major generals to active command. By 1898 the sentiment of nationalism binding the American people together had triumphed over all rival emotions. Patriotism had taken on a common character from Maine to Georgia. The unity of 1898 presaged the even more complete unity of 1917.

The phenomenon of "Fighting Joe" Wheeler commanding New England Yankees in the Spanish-American War seems, in retrospect, even more remarkable when the Reconstruction era is recalled. In those years, by establishing Negro domination and carpetbag rule at the point of the bayonet, an angry victor humiliated a defeated people. Ex-Confederates in the late 1860's so resented the peace enforced by the central government that they organized a second rebellion under the name of the Ku Klux Klan. In spite of the fact that military organization was gone, Southerners found ways through the Klan and similar organizations to meet force with force. A neutral observer of the American scene as it existed in 1870 would doubtless have commented that war hysteria was still dominant in both sections and that the mood of hatred and the spirit of revenge were still powerful forces. Under the circumstances he might well have predicted that the Southerner would not give up the fight for independence in which he had spent his substance and his strength. If the observer were a European, he could have pointed in the Old World to many defeated groups among which the sentiment of nationalism persisted for generations under the yoke of the conqueror, and in which proscribed ideals manifested themselves in vigorous social action at the first favorable opportunity. Such a prophecy, as events turned out, would have been wide of the mark. Yet, in spite of the statesmanship of Grant and Lee, the one in tempering victory and the other in accepting defeat, the logic of the situation during Reconstruction would have supported the soundness of the forecast.

The dream of an independent Confederacy faded long before the end of the century, because the citizens of the South gave their loyalty once more to the United States of America. Loyalty is a voluntary action. Obedience can be coerced, but never loyalty. Before 1900 the vast majority of the Southern people had returned to the old loyalties. The change of mood in the South from that of Bloody Angle at Spotsylvania in 1864 to that of the A.E.F. in 1917 is one of the most important transformations in the history of the United States. It took place in scarcely more than thirty years, for Reconstruction did not end officially until the withdrawal of the troops from the South in 1877. The change illuminates some characteristics of American nationalism.

Before the break in 1861 powerful forces operated to hold the discordant North and South together. Of these the most important was a common language. The tenacity with which minorities, the world over, have clung to their native language is evidence of the prime importance of this aspect of culture for the sentiment of nationality. Language may be both a vehicle of communication and symbol of national ideals, as it becomes in Canada whenever majorities in the English-speaking provinces tamper with the use of French in the schools. After 1865 the common language facilitated reconciliation to an extent which cannot be measured. It was the vehicle for a literature which carried across the old dividing line of the war not only the ideas, but the moods and aspirations of the two sections. When Ireland strove for independence, Gaelic became the symbol of the national ideal. The Southerners had no language other than that which was common to the American people. It was a bond which made for friendship.

Before Sumter, also, a growing economic interdependence tied the restive sections together. After the fall of the Confederacy, Northern capital flowed into the South to develop mines and to build factories. On many boards of directors men from both sections sat side by side in the planning of private enterprise. In spite of an invading industrialism the South remained predominantly agricultural. New railroads and steamship lines carried Southern staple crops to markets within the United States and brought again Northern commodities to consumers in the old Confederacy. The Union after 1877 was established upon the solid foundation of mutual economic advantage.

Almost as soon as green had begun to conceal the scars of the battlefields, the humanitarian spirit began to soften the animosities of the war. Northern money went southward to found institutions which would provide new educational opportunities for the ex-slaves. After an early period characterized by mistakes of policy, these enterprises became adjusted to Southern conditions, and their managers brought them into conformity with the general policies of those ex-Confederates who were leading the section out of the war depression.

Before 1861 a common tradition had been a powerful bond between the sections. The nationwide drive to rescue Mount Vernon from the speculators suggested the importance of the national hero in holding the Union together. After Appomattox, however, the North and South had different traditions, personified by different heroes. Chancellorsville and Gettysburg had opposite meanings in Wisconsin and in Alabama. Wartime emotionalism persisted, moreover, in a hatred that was slow to die. Georgia and South Carolina did not forget Sherman's devastating march. And to the end of the century the names Libby and Andersonville brought bitter memories to the men of the North. The appeal in the North to the bloody shirt retarded, but did not prevent, reconciliation. The time has come after 1918 when the national tradition is again becoming a single conditioning force. Lee and Jackson have been lifted from the status of Confederate generals to that of national heroes. Arlington, the home of the commander of the Army of Virginia, has been transformed into a national shrine. And the fame of Lincoln has grown with the years in both North and South.

But neither language, economic interdependence, humanitarianism, nor the re-establishment of a common national tradition provides a satisfactory explanation for the phenomenon of the re-establishment of Southern loyalty to the Union. Inadequate also as an explanation is the fact that after 1877 the Southern commonwealths resumed in the management of national affairs the powers and responsibilities of sovereign states. Participation in the central government on the part of Southern communities had not prevented rupture in 1861. The chief factor which made reconciliation possible had to do with the race problem as it existed in the Southern states.

∽

Before 1850 Calhoun had insisted that the South and the South alone must decide upon the arrangements which should exist between the white and the colored people. Slavery was a discipline which, by enforcing order and getting work done, made it possible for the white man's civilization to flourish. Calhoun warned that upon the issue of white supremacy the South would not compromise. The war verified the accuracy of his foresight. The increase in the sense of insecurity in the South resulting from the growing opposition in the North to slavery finally so impaired the loyalty of the Southerner to the Union that he broke away and sought security in a nation of his own making. The most important post-Appomattox problem was to restore in Southern communities that sense of security with respect to the vital issue which they had enjoyed before 1820. This task was not accomplished by the national policies during the Reconstruction period.

The central political fact of Reconstruction was the assumption by the central government of the power to determine throughout the nation the legal frame which should govern the relations between the races. The freedman became the temporary ward of the United States. Racial equality in civil and in political rights was written into the Constitution by the Fourteenth and Fifteenth Amendments. So long as federal soldiers remained in the South to enforce the will of a determined United States, Southern intransigence was inevitable and Southern loyalty to the national Union difficult. The resolution of the difficulty began in 1877 with the withdrawal of the army.

Of equal if not greater importance than this event was the decision which the Supreme Court handed down on October 15, 1883, in the Civil Rights cases. The Court was considering the Civil Rights Act of March 1, 1875, the purpose of which had been to give force to the Fourteenth Amendment. That amendment had been formulated to enable the central government to protect the colored man. The act had made it a crime for any person to deny to all persons full and equal accommodation at inns, in public conveyances, or in places of public amusement. Mr. Justice Bradley for the Court declared that the Fourteenth Amendment did not invest Congress with power to legislate on subjects which are within the domain of the state or to create a code of municipal law. He denied that refusal to accommodate any citizen at an inn pinned upon him the badge of slavery. The essence of the decision, however, is not to be found in the general principles which it laid down but, rather, in the reality which it accomplished. By it the Court, in effect, turned over to local Southern communities the solution of the all-important race problem, subject to the limitation that chattel slavery should not be re-established. The Civil War had been fought, in the opinion of the South, over the question of where the control over the arrangements which governed the relations between the races should lie. In 1883, only eighteen years after the surrender of Lee, the Court accepted Calhoun's principle that the disposition of the race problem should be denied to the central government and be left to the local community. The decision, measured by its results, is one of the most important in the history of the national tribunal.

The decision was followed by the creation, already begun before the Court acted, of a substitute for slavery in maintaining the supremacy of the whites. Developing pragmatically and varying in different localities, the discipline had been evolved in its essentials by 1890. A variety of devices combined to make up the new control pattern. State laws and administrative usages kept Negroes from the polls and rendered them politically impotent in most areas of the old Confederacy. Economic disabilities added to political disadvantage in a section generally impoverished by war and defeat. The practice of share cropping as an organization of husbandry took the place of plantation slavery in regions that produced staple crops. As it worked out the system usually kept the "cropper" in economic dependency to the landowner or to the proprietor of the general store that supplied his needs throughout the year while he waited for the harvest. In the primarily agrarian postwar South, moreover, only a small minority of the population depended for their living on skilled trades. Lack of training, lack of opportunity to get training and custom in most communities hindered the Negro who had ambition to become a skilled worker. The Negro, under the blight of almost hopeless poverty, occupied the bottom level of the economic pyramid. A strict segregation of the races seemed to the ruling group the only solution for the social problems left in the wake of war and emancipation. Occasional and dramatic resort to lynch law by some whites impressed upon their colored neighbors the reality of subordination.

The discipline that subordinated the colored population of the South, together with the less burdensome but no less real caste system in the North, violated in principle the distinguishing doctrine of the old democratic faith, namely that of the free individual with its corollary, equality of opportunity. A specific legal problem arose. A case originating in Louisiana came up to the Supreme Court and led to a decision that remained the constitutional law of the United States until well into the twentieth century.

In 1890 the legislature of Louisiana enacted a statute that required railroads to provide "equal but separate accommodations for the white and colored races" and forbade all persons to use facilities other than those provided and assigned "on account of the race they belong to." A Negro plaintiff, convicted of attempting to defy the law, argued that the enactment violated the provision of the Fourteenth Amendment that requires the states to grant to all citizens equal protection of the laws. The opinion of the Supreme Court in Plessy v. Ferguson, 1896, upholding the law, mirrors the thought at that time of the dominant white group.

Said the Court: ". . . So far, then, as a conflict with the Fourteenth Amendment is concerned, the case reduces itself to the question whether the statute of Louisiana is a reasonable regulation, and with respect to this there must necessarily be a large discretion on the part of the legislature. In determining reasonableness it is at liberty to act with reference to the established usages, customs and traditions of the people, and with a view to the promotion of their comfort and the preservation of the public peace and good order. Gauged by this standard, we cannot say that a law which authorizes or even requires the separation of the two races in public conveyances is unreasonable or more obnoxious to the Fourteenth Amendment than the acts of Congress requiring separate schools for colored children in the District of Columbia, the constitutionality of which does not seem to have been questioned, or the corresponding acts of state legislatures. We consider the underlying fallacy of the plaintiff's argument to consist in the assumption that the enforced separation of the races stamps the colored race with a badge of inferiority. If this be so, it is not by reason of anything found in the act, but solely because the colored race chooses to put that construction upon it. . . ."[1]

The decision, in effect, confirmed that in the earlier Civil Rights cases. It established in federal law the principle that the regulation of the relations between the races should be considered a local problem and, for all practical purposes, should be left to the states. Such a settlement of what for Southern whites was a paramount issue enabled the forces of economic advantage, of common language, and of common cultural traditions to bring about in the South a vigorous sense of nationality.

Because the caste system that evolved after Appomattox denied the spirit of the doctrine of the free individual it required rationalization. Citizens of the South naturally took the lead after the end of Reconstruction in the task of developing social theories to apply to race problems. As before the war, Southern theorists commonly postulated a racial inequality springing from nature itself. To support this contention they pointed to the failure of the black race in Africa or elsewhere to achieve civilization unaided. Philip Alexander Bruce, a Virginia scholar, explained in the 1880's the point of view and disclosed the fears of the more thoughtful among the ex-Confederates. He assumed that the pre-Sumter institution of slavery had elevated the colored population of the United States to a cultural plane where a limited appreciation and understanding of civilization was possible. He feared that this progress would gradually be lost as a result of the alienation of the races in consequence of the problems arising out of the abolition of the old paternalistic servitude. The Southern Negro, Bruce thought in 1889, is destined to revert to the African original. "The return of the race to the original physical type," he remarked, "involves its intellectual reversion also. . . . Every circumstance surrounding the Negro in the present age seems to point directly to his further moral decadence. . . . The influences that are shaping the character of the younger generations appear to be such as must bring the blacks in time to a state of nature, so far as people inhabiting a country where a system of law and government prevails can fall into that state."[2] Bruce, in 1889, looked toward the future with alarm. He assumed that the Negroes would multiply more rapidly than the whites and that the race problem would grow progressively more difficult as the colored population took the road to Africa. He appealed to the North for understanding, sympathy, and aid.

Thomas Nelson Page, writing in 1904, saw a brighter future than Bruce. But the "principles" which went into the major premise of his argument were essentially those of his fellow Virginian. "One of these principles," said Page, "is the absolute and unchangeable superiority of the white race—a superiority—. . . not due to any mere adventitious circumstances, such as superior educational and other advantages during some centuries, but an inherent and essential superiority, based on superior intellect, virtue, and constancy . . . the white is the superior of every race."[3] Page urged, however, that justice and interest were united in the demand that the Southern white majority make every practicable effort to improve the lot of their colored neighbors. In particular the Negro should be given educational opportunities. "Light," said Page, "is safer than darkness . . . intelligence is better than stupidity . . . the South must educate all her population. She must do this, or she must fall behind the rest of the country."[4] Page would associate with the new discipline, subordinating the colored race, a new paternalism which would prevent segregation from producing the results which Bruce feared. Page expressed the temper and the outlook of the better elements in the post-Appomattox South.

The partial exclusion of the Negro from the promises of the American democratic faith, it should be added, in no way impaired the hold of that cluster of social beliefs upon American thought. From the days of Thomas Jefferson's Declaration of Independence, the race problem had required Americans to make an exception to the doctrine that "all men are created equal." Throughout the national history of the American people the fact of an enforced racial inequality had remained constant. But the discipline by which inequality of status was maintained had changed in form. The basic outline of the theory of inequality, however, also remained unaltered. The argument always began with a postulated natural inequality of ability between the races. From this major premise the steps in the argument developed after Appomattox followed inevitably. The individual colored man should be free, but not as free as the white man. The Negro could and should look forward to progress, particularly in the apprehension of the moral law, but he could not progress as far as the white man. Conversely the white man, in obedience to the moral law, must treat the segregated race with justice and humanity. It is our "plain duty . . ." said Page, "to do the best we can to act with justice and a broad charity and leave the consequence to God."[5]

The knowledge that through their state governments they had control of the relations between the races gave to the white majority of the South a sense of security. Once basic fears were allayed, old loyalties to the Republic came alive. As time brought healing to the wounds inflicted by the war, the "Lost Cause" gradually took the character of a noble and beautiful dream. But realistic Southerners by the end of the century were glad that the nation had not permanently broken apart.

~

The attitude of the colored minority toward subordination and the rationale supporting it grew, in part, out of the circumstances of the origin of that minority. Unlike any other immigrant group in the United States and also unlike most minorities in other nations or in the United States the American Negro had no cultural heritage of his own. His situation differed vastly from that of the Sudeten Germans in Czechoslovakia before Hitler broke the power of that nation. It differed from that of immigrant groups, such as the Norwegians or Italians, who brought their language and cultural heritage to their new home. The situation of the Negro differed also from that of the conquered American Indian who, as a member of a tribe, had behind him for support, as he faced the white man, an ancient and organized culture. What became the Negro minority began in the seventeenth century as isolated individuals, torn by violence from many tribes that differed in language and in culture.

These individuals were transported across the Atlantic and scattered widely along the eastern seaboard. Such dispersal brought to the unfortunate individuals complete loss of the old language and the culture which had provided the frame of reference for their lives. Only in the West Indies did enough slaves in some localities come from the same tribe to make possible the retention of some of the culture of the homeland. In what became the United States the Negro acquired, perforce, the language and such aspects of the white man's culture as the master permitted. Such an origin meant that developing American civilization was the only culture the Negro group as a minority ever had.

When slavery ended, the Negro of the South began to advance. He received significant help from schools, many of which were supported by funds from the North. Outstanding individuals appeared, as they had before 1861 beyond the boundaries of slavery. Perhaps the most important of the early leaders was Booker T. Washington, an ex-slave, who became the first head of Tuskegee Institute in Alabama. Recognizing the handicap of poverty and illiteracy, almost universal among the Southern Negroes, Washington urged them to accept segregation and to concentrate on acquiring the training that would make possible economic advance. Both halves of the Washington program suggest that American mores conditioned the attitudes of the Negro. The Negroes even reflected faintly the attitude toward color of the whites in the general, but not universal, tendency of the group to seek marriage unions with lighter rather than darker partners.

As the Negro advanced, he apprehended more clearly the nature and the significance for him of the American democratic faith. The doctrine of the free individual with its implications of equality of opportunity and equality before the law provided the leaders of the race with a satisfying goal. Before World War I, Booker T. Washington's slogan, "separate as the fingers and one as the hand," was being discarded. More and more the leaders urged upon whites and colored persons alike the full and universal translation into social realities of the principles of the democratic faith. The hope that such a goal might be achieved was a powerful factor supporting the loyalty of the minority to the nation.

At the same time and particularly after the Negro minority had made significant economic and cultural progress, the denial to the Negroes of the goal they sought began increasingly to create an uneasy conscience in the white majority. The nature of what Gunnar Myrdal after World War I called "the American dilemma" became increasingly clear to the citizens of the Republic, both white and colored. The growing awareness of this dilemma and the recognition of it as a peculiar American problem, like a difficulty a family must overcome within itself, furthered that sense of group consciousness out of which the sentiment of nationalism comes.

~

The restoration and the evolution of the sentiment of nationalism after the close of a bitter, fratricidal war is a major event in American history. It surpasses in importance even the industrial revolution that transformed American society between 1865 and 1917. As a result of these two synchronous developments a powerful and united nation existed on the North American continent in 1914. In that year opened an age of violence and revolution that was to bring disaster to Europe and a major threat to Western civilization. The existence at that time of a United States capable of playing a major rôle proved to be a determining factor in world history.

III

AFTER APPOMATTOX THE DEMOCRATIC FAITH IS MODIFIED AND DEVELOPED, AN ATTEMPT TO BRING IT INTO HARMONY WITH THE NEW NATURALISM OF DARWINIAN EVOLUTION AND TO MAKE IT USEFUL IN A SOCIETY UNDERGOING INDUSTRIAL REVOLUTION

Chapter 13

THE GOSPEL OF WEALTH
OF THE GILDED AGE

W HEN HIS WAR-TIME AMBASSADORSHIP in England came to an end, Charles Francis Adams returned to a new and strange America. He was astonished at some of the changes. "Most noticeable of these," he remarked in 1871, "is perhaps to be found in a greatly enlarged grasp of enterprise and increased facility of combination. The great operations of war, the handling of large masses of men, the influence of discipline, the lavish expenditure of unprecedented sums of money, the immense financial operations, the possibilities of effective cooperation were lessons not likely to be lost on men quick to receive and to apply all new ideas."[1] Adams recognized, however, that it was not the war alone that had brought in the new day.

A concatenation of events in the 1850's and 1860's initiated an industrial revolution in the United States. Previous to the fall of Sumter, states in the northeast quarter of the nation had been exploring their natural resources with scientific aid; during the same period the federal government had occasionally sent expeditions into wilderness areas to map the boundaries of mineral beds. The successors of Father Hennepin and Sieur La Salle and determined the extent and quality of the copper fields of Michigan; they had studied the more important eastern bituminous coal fields; and had brought to light the astounding wealth of iron ore which nature had thoughtfully placed so near the surface of the ground beside the shores of Lake Superior. Coal and iron are twin foundations of an industrial civilization. By the end of the Civil War, Americans noted that the nation possessed both minerals in what seemed unlimited amounts. It was possible for the ambitious entrepreneur of the mid-nineteenth century to visualize the manner in which coal and iron could be brought together. Since the beginning of their

151

national history, Americans had been a people scattered over a vast area. By constructing turnpikes, steamboats for lakes and rivers, and canals, they had partly solved their peculiar problems of great distances. But the railroad was the first development in transportation which offered the possibility of breaking down the semi-isolation of the sections and of transforming the nation into a single economic unit. Sufficient technical advance in railway construction had been made before Lincoln's inauguration to make possible the conquest of the Appalachians and the linking of the Upper Mississippi Valley to the Atlantic seaboard. The perfection of the air brake in 1868 marked the beginning of the modern railroad. Both railways and industry needed cheap steel and, in the 1850's, Bessemer in England and Kelly in America devised methods for making it. With the consolidation of Bessemer and Kelly interests in the United States in 1866, the age of steel and of the steam engine began. Almost at once bituminous coal surpassed water as the principal source of power for American factories. The preservation of the Union by war made possible the exploitation of the resources of America without the hampering conditions which would have attended the establishment of new international boundaries. The surrender of Lee meant that Americans could build their industrial civilization on a vaster scale than was possible in the nineteenth century for any other nation.

Before Grant's artillery had been hauled for the last time off Virginia battlefields, a number of American entrepreneurs had begun to demonstrate what free men could accomplish in such a country as the United States. The five years which succeeded the war, continued Adams bitterly, "have witnessed some of the most remarkable examples of organized lawlessness, under the forms of law, which mankind has yet had an opportunity to study. If individuals have, as a rule, quietly pursued their peaceful vocations, the same cannot be said of certain single men at the head of vast combinations of private wealth. This has been particularly the case as regards those controlling the rapidly developed railroad interests. These modern potentates have declared war, negotiated peace, reduced courts, legislatures, and sovereign States to an unqualified obedience to their will, disturbed trade, agitated the currency, imposed taxes, and, boldly setting both law and public opinion at defiance, have freely exercised many other attributes of sovereignty. . . . Single men have controlled hundreds of miles of railway, thousands of men, tens of millions of revenue, and hundreds of millions of capital. The strength implied in all this they wielded in practical independence of the control both of governments and of individuals; much as petty German despots might have governed their little principalities a century or two ago."[2]

Adams recorded only the beginning of the story; by the end of the century the machine age for America had come into being. Primitive technology had become developed technology. Small business had become big business. The old-time individual entrepreneur, who worked shoulder to shoulder with his help, had been replaced by the large corporation as the significant factor in industrial and commercial advance. And competition had been modified by the development of monopolistic tendencies. Americans, once divided on sectional lines, became increasingly conscious of a new grouping and tended to think of themselves as farmers, wage earners, or industrialists and business men. The immigrant stream across the north Atlantic swelled to the largest folk movement in modern history. Great urban centers appeared and sprawled without plan each year farther from their original centers. The frontier passed. The Old World suddenly became conscious that an industrial giant had appeared in North America and was squinting eastward and westward across the oceans to see what profits could be made abroad.

The preachers of the romantic democratic faith of pre-Sumter days were fond of pointing out that Providence had reserved America for the growth of civil liberty, and that, without the hampering restrictions of ecclesiastical or political autocracy or of a feudal aristocratic system, democracy had been able to raise its beacon in the New World. They might have added that Providence appeared to have scattered prodigious natural wealth throughout the area of the United States and dug on either side a moat of ocean width in order that the institution of industrial capitalism might have an opportunity to demonstrate the gifts it could bring to men. Never since it originated in the ancient world had that institution developed in so rich an environment with so few legal or political restrictions. In June, 1889, Andrew Carnegie, who had risen from the post of bobbin boy to become one of the greatest of the new luminaries in the American industrial sky, contributed to the *North American Review* what its editor declared to be "the finest article I have ever published in the *Review*."[3] The title of the piece was "Wealth."

The Carnegie essay was a formulation of a philosophy for the new era, a "Gospel of Wealth." It was not, however, the only philosophy of the period. Jay Gould, Jim Fiske, and Daniel Drew were among the prophets of the gospel of grab and hold. They represented what Thorstein Veblen later called the hawk influence of pecuniary competition. But all industrial capitalism was affected by this influence. Competition implied conflict, and conflict expressed itself in such stratagems as flank marches, surprise attacks, and even frontal assaults. The war of the market place was costly, with the result that the tendency toward the development of local peace areas, called "trusts," became almost irresistible. A later generation has called the decades which immediately followed Appomattox the age of the "robber barons." They were a dynamic company of chieftains recruited often from the ranks of the humble people. Some of them accumulated such power as no American had hitherto known. Their number included men who dreamed of building empires and who came near to transforming their visions into realities.

These new industrial Brobdingnags, who brought together capital, labor, and machines, were governed, particularly in the early phases of their activities, by what was expedient—for them. By 1900 most of these leaders had become convinced that what was expedient for them was best for the country. They had, moreover, no choice but to follow an ethics of expediency, if they would survive as individuals. The mores of a simpler agricultural and commercial era did not fit the conditions of an age characterized by the swift accumulation of industrial power. The new chieftains created not only new techniques of exploitation, of promotion, and of management, but also new customs and a new mental outlook.

Out of this turbulent, swiftly moving transition period came what Carnegie called the gospel of wealth. He apparently used the term to distinguish his formula from the discipline of economics which young John Bates Clark had called, a short time before, the science of wealth. But the king of steel had little to do with originating the gospel he preached; he merely formulated a philosophy as universal in the United States as faith in democracy.

The congeries of social beliefs which he called the gospel of wealth stemmed primarily from the *laissez-faire* attitude of the nineteenth century. The mercantilistic assumptions conditioning the thought of the Fathers of the Constitution had been reduced vastly in importance by the time Franklin Pierce came to the White

House. There was then no regulation of industry by the nation, save in the uncertain and shifting tariff policy, and almost no interference by the states. In pre-Sumter decades, when the small entrepreneur was the typical American industrialist, *laissez faire* was more a condition than a theory. Its important theoretical formulation did not come until big business had been subjected to assaults by both farmers and wage earners. The date, 1889, of Carnegie's essay is not without significance. It followed the revolt of the Grangers by more than a decade and a half. Twelve years before it appeared had occurred the railway strikes of the frightening summer of 1878. It was written three years after the Haymarket Riot in Chicago, the signal for a nation-wide crusade against anarchism. Its timing suggests that it was an apologia. In spite of the evidence to support this contention, the hypothesis does not seem to fit the facts. Carnegie formulated a folk philosophy which was not only being accepted, but was being acted upon by the farmers who joined the Grange and by the more able and ambitious laboring men who looked forward hopefully to individual advancement to the status of property owners. The steelmaster gave words to an economic philosophy which was dominant in the United States of the Gilded Age. It was an elaboration of the doctrine of the free individual of the American democratic faith and was a result of the discovery that this tenet had important utilities in the new industrial capitalism.

∽

The American gospel of wealth of the Gilded Age was erected upon a theory of property which had its most elaborate development in that Scottish common-sense philosophy dominating the intellectual atmosphere of most American colleges and universities in the decades immediately following Appomattox. This system of thought, in the opinion of its great American leaders, Presidents James McCosh of Princeton and Noah Porter of Yale, made it possible for Christianity to escape the pitfalls hidden within the idealism of Bishop Berkeley, of Immanuel Kant, and of Ralph Waldo Emerson and to come to grips with a real world of matter and men. The shadow of John Calvin lay across the formulas of common sense. "Each individual man," affirmed Noah Porter in 1884, ". . . has separate wants of body and spirit, to the supply of which he is impelled by original impulses of instinct and rational desire. . . . The supply of many of the wants of men implies the existence of property." Man's Creator, then, has laid upon him a duty to acquire property and to defend it, once it has come into his possession. The right of the individual to his property and the duty of the State to assist him in its defense is clear. Property rights derive from a higher law than that made by men. "Governments exist very largely—in the view of many, they exist solely—for the purpose of rendering this service [of defending rights in property]."[4] Porter would put the sanction of religion behind property rights. "God has bestowed upon us certain powers and gifts which no one is at liberty to take from us or to interfere with," affirmed James McCosh in 1892. "All attempts to deprive us of them is theft. Under the same head may be placed all purposes to deprive us of the right to earn property or to use it as we see fit."[5]

The corollary of the divine right of property was the acquisition of wealth by industry and thrift. This latter doctrine was not new. In America it ran back to seventeenth-century Puritanism. A godly man, said Cotton Mather, one Sabbath day in the early eighteenth century, must have two callings: his general calling and his personal calling. The first is, of course, "to serve the Lord Jesus Christ"; the second is "a certain *Particular Employment*, by which his Usefulness in his neighborhood is distinguished." "A Christian, at his *Two Callings*," Mather added, "is a man in a Boat, Rowing for Heaven; the House which our Heavenly Father hath intended for us. If he mind but one of his *Callings*, be it which it will, he pulls the *oar*, but on one side of the Boat, and it will make but a poor dispatch to the Shoar of Eternal Blessedness."[6] To be diligent in one's earthly calling was, then, a moral duty, a precept of that fundamental law basic to the theories of Calvinism and later of the democratic faith. To produce with energy but to consume sparingly and to the glory of God was the seventeenth-century Puritan doctrine sanctifying work and thrift. It was preached in the eighteenth century throughout the land by the Deist, Benjamin Franklin, creator of "Poor Richard." It was caught up by Francis Asbury and in the nineteenth century spread by his Methodist circuit riders throughout the continental interior. Its advice to the young man was: work and save, if you would win the game of life and honor the God who made you. "Work, for the Night is Coming" became a popular hymn of evangelical Protestantism.

When industrialism began after 1865 the creation of a new world, this Puritan code of worldly asceticism sprang into new importance. It had served well in a day when the wilderness was stubborn and when laborers were few. Then it had been a religious sanction behind inevitable frontier mores. But when Americans began the exploitation of the richest mineral resources of the world, the old doctrine began to have new uses. "By the proper use of wealth," wrote D. S. Gregory, author of a textbook on ethics used during the 1880's in many American colleges, "man may greatly elevate and extend his moral work. It is therefore his duty to seek to secure wealth for this high end, and to make a diligent use of what the Moral Governor may bestow upon him for the same end. . . . The Moral Governor has placed the power of acquisitiveness in man for a good and noble purpose. . . ."[7]

Better even than the formulation of the doctrine of property by the presidents of Princeton and of Yale, or even of Professor Gregory, was that of the head of Williams College. Mark Hopkins, like Emerson, was an old man when Lee surrendered. The great period of the two coincided. Both had last words after Appomattox. Hopkins carried forward into the new era the best tradition of evangelical Protestantism. He published in 1868 a treatise on ethics, entitled significantly, *The Law of Love and Love as Law*. The authentic voice of evangelicalism sounded through the book. Its very title suggests the change brought by romanticism during the Middle Period to American Christianity. The hardness of Calvinism had been softened. The old fear of God had relaxed. Love had been substituted for discipline. Hopkins set his theory of property against the background of a law of love. "The Right to Property," said the aging Hopkins in 1868, "reveals itself through an original desire. The affirmation of it is early and universally made, and becomes a controlling element in civil society. . . . Without this society could not exist. With no right to the product of his labor no man would make a tool, or a garment, or build a shelter, or raise a crop. There could be no industry and no progress. It will be found too, historically, that the general well-being and progress of society has been in proportion to the freedom of every man to gain property in all legitimate ways, and to security in its possession. . . . The acquisition of property is required by love, because it is a powerful means of benefiting others. . . . A selfish getting of property, though better than a selfish indolence or wastefulness, is not to be encouraged. . . . Industry, frugality, carefulness, as ministering to a cheerful giving, would then not only be purged from all taint of meanness, but would be ennobled."[8] The essentials of the Hopkins position were three: individualism, the sanctity of private property, and the duty of stewardship.

The post-Appomattox evangelist of the refurbished Puritan doctrine of property was a Baptist minister of Philadelphia, Russell H. Conwell, whose popular lecture, *Acres of Diamonds*, was said to have been repeated throughout the East and Middle West six thousand times. Such popularity was evidence that Conwell's gospel harmonized with the mood of the American middle class. "To secure wealth is an honorable ambition, and is one great test of a person's usefulness to others," said the preacher over and over again. "Money is power. Every good man and woman ought to strive for power, to do good with it when obtained. Tens of thousands of men and women get rich honestly. But they are often accused by an envious, lazy crowd of unsuccessful persons of being dishonest and oppressive. I say, Get rich, get rich! But get money honestly, or it will be a withering curse."[9] So was presented with forensic skill by Conwell the old doctrine of property and of stewardship. Its late nineteenth-century version ran as follows: If God calls a man to make money in his earthly calling, he holds the wealth he acquires as the steward of the Lord. "The good Lord gave me my money," said that faithful Baptist, John D. Rockefeller, to the first graduating class of the university which he had founded, "and how could I withhold it from the University of Chicago?"[10] In 1900 Bishop Lawrence of Massachusetts rounded out and perfected the modernized formula. To acquire material wealth is natural and necessary, he argued. "In the long run, it is only to the man of morality that wealth comes. We believe in the harmony of God's Universe. We know that it is only by working along His laws natural and spiritual that we can work with efficiency. Only by working along the lines of right thinking and right living can the secrets and wealth of nature be revealed. . . . Godliness is in league with riches. . . . Material prosperity is helping to make the national character sweeter, more joyous, more unselfish, more Christlike. That is my answer to the question as to the relation of material prosperity to morality."[11] Bishop Lawrence had transformed Cotton Mather's row boat into an ocean liner.

∾

Such was the Christian form of the late nineteenth-century gospel of wealth. Its secular counterpart differed from it only in the dropping of the supernaturalistic trappings. This version received its most cogent expression in the writings of Andrew Carnegie, who did not share the illiteracy of some of his contemporary industrial chieftains. He began his argument with an exposé of the fallacy of the "good old times" of simplicity and of equality. "In former days there was little difference between the dwelling, dress, food, and environment of the chief and those of his retainers." It was a time of "crude articles at high prices." Today a revolution has occurred, and the poor enjoy what formerly the rich could not afford. What were once luxuries have become necessities of life. Society has paid a price for the change in the rise of the great employer, the loss of contact between him and his men, the appearance of a graded class system, and the growth of ill will between the classes. "Human society loses homogeneity." The price is inevitable but not high for the beneficent results produced.

The foundations of modern capitalistic society are, according to the Carnegie theory, four: individualism, private property, the "Law of Accumulation of Wealth," and the "Law of Competition." These laws cause wealth to come to those who have the superior energy and ability to produce it. These four foundations "are the highest result of human experience, the soil in which society, so far, has produced the best fruit. Unequally or unjustly, perhaps, as these laws sometimes operate, and imperfect as they appear to the Idealist, they are, nevertheless, . . . the best and the most valuable of all that humanity has yet accomplished. . . . But whether the law [of competition] be benign or not, we must say of it . . . It is here; we cannot evade it; no substitutes for it have been found; and while the law may sometimes be hard on the individual, it is best for the race, because it ensures the survival of the fittest in every department. We accept and welcome, therefore, as conditions to which we must accommodate ourselves, great inequality of environment; the concentration of business, industrial and commercial, in the hands of the few; and the law of competition between these, as being not only beneficial, but essential to the future progress of the race."

To the socialist, Carnegie said: "Civilization took its start from the day when the capable, industrious workman said to his incompetent and lazy fellow, 'If thou dost not sow, thou shalt not reap,' and thus ended primitive communism by separating the drones from the bees." But Carnegie was aware of the thrust at capitalism contained in the question: How can the pursuit of individual selfishness result in the common good? Can altruism be substituted for acquisitiveness? Only by changing human nature itself, "a work of eons," said Carnegie. "This is not evolution," he added, "but revolution." The devastating character of this final thrust can be appreciated only when it is remembered that, at the moment, Darwinism held the central position in that climate of opinion in which American liberals and intellectuals lived.

"This, then," concluded the king of steel, "is held to be the duty of the man of Wealth: First, to set an example of modest, unostentatious living, shunning display or extravagance; to provide moderately for the legitimate wants of those dependent upon him; and after doing so to consider all surplus revenues which come to him simply as trust funds, which he is called upon to administer, and strictly bound as a matter of duty to administer in the manner which, in his judgment, is best calculated to produce the most beneficial results for the community—the man of wealth thus becoming the mere agent and trustee for his poorer brethren, bringing to their service his superior wisdom, experience, and ability to administer, doing for them better than they would or could do for themselves." In this principle "we have the true antidote for the temporary unequal distribution of wealth, the reconciliation of the rich and the poor—a reign of harmony, another ideal, differing, indeed, from that of the Communist in requiring only the further evolution of existing conditions, not the total overthrow of our civilization." As an end the pursuit of wealth is ignoble, "no idol more debasing than the worship of money," but as a means to larger social ends it is a glorious adventure. The old sneer at the man of trade is heard no more; the capitalist has become a prince. Such was Carnegie's dream of a capitalistic utopia. "Thus is the problem of Rich and Poor to be solved," he concluded. "The laws of accumulation will be left free; the laws of distribution free. Individualism will continue, but the millionaire will be but a trustee for the poor. . . . Such, in my opinion, is the true Gospel concerning Wealth, obedience to which is destined some day to solve the problem of the Rich and the Poor and to bring 'Peace on earth, among men goodwill.' "[12]

◇

The gospel of wealth perforce included an explanation of poverty, for in the Gilded Age the slum was as conspicuous as the millionaire. Both the Christian and the secular version of the formula developed against the background of blighted urban areas. The ecclesiastical preachers of the faith had their explanation. Poverty, taught the Porters and the Conwells, springs from laziness, lack of thrift, vice, and sometimes misfortune. This was the traditional explanation of the Puritan code of worldly asceticism. Poverty in the world, added the preachers, is as inevitable as sin and is largely the result of it. "The poor ye have with you always," said the Founder. To the poor man should be given aid and charity. His sins should be pointed out to him; he should be converted to the Christian faith and his feet set on the road called Strait.

The explanation of poverty by the secular prophets of the gospel of wealth did not differ fundamentally from that of the divines. Out of his Shakespeare, Carnegie clipped his answer to the many protesters complaining that success was hard in 1890:

> The fault, dear Brutus, is not in our stars,
> But in ourselves, that we are underlings.

He added: "Avenues greater in number, wider in extent, easier of access than ever before existed, stand open to the sober, frugal, energetic and able mechanic, to the scientifically educated youth, to the office boy and to the clerk—avenues through which they can reap greater successes than ever before within the reach of these classes in the history of the world. . . . The millionaires who are in active control started as poor boys, and were trained in that sternest but most efficient of all schools—poverty. . . . Congratulate poor young men upon being born to that ancient and honorable degree which renders it necessary that they should devote themselves to hard work."[13] Poverty, then, was viewed in terms of the individual, not of the mass. For the individual it was, or at least could be, a transient state. It was a blessing in disguise to the one who rose above it, but to him who did not, it was a symbol of shame, a sort of scarlet letter proclaiming that he was wanting in ability or character, or both.

The gospel of wealth was the intellectual concept of a generation that had stumbled upon easy money in a terrain well protected by nature from foreign brigands. It was the result produced when the individualism of a simpler agricultural and commercial civilization was carried over into a society luxuriating in all essential natural resources. But it was not the only result; this gospel of morality and of prosperity had its antithesis in the irresponsible philosophy of grab. The ill-fated gold corner of Fiske and Gould in 1867, the swindles of Crédit Mobilier, the wars between powerful bands of railroad buccaneers, the exploitation of the defenseless immigrant laborer, the sleight of hand which made valueless the bonds purchased with the savings of the small investor, the stubborn and

usually effective resistance of great corporations to social legislation in the states, and Mark Hanna's philosophy of "the public be
damned," were also ideological patterns produced by the same situation which gave rise to Carnegie's vision of a material paradise.
They were summed up in the philosophy of the greatest of Republican bosses, Matthew Stanley Quay. Asked, after he had elevated
himself to the Senate of the United States, why he did not work
for the people, he is said to have affirmed that he did. "I work for
the men the people work for." Jay Gould and Russell H. Conwell
represented the two extremes of individualism in an industrial age.
When Conwell's thesis, to use the dialectic of Hegel or of Marx,
was set against Gould's antithesis, the synthesis was Daniel Drew,
master fleecer of the lambs and founder of Drew Theological Seminary.

Was, then, the gospel of wealth merely a sham? It was called such
by the critics of the new American overlords, and they were able
to document their charges with distressing frequency. Had the gospel of wealth been nothing but hypocrisy, however, it could
scarcely have outlasted the century. It was, in fact, not merely the
philosophy of a few rich men but a faith which determined the
thinking of millions of citizens engaged in small enterprises. Its basic emphasis was upon the responsibility of the individual, confronting the hard uncertainty of life. The gospel of wealth explained the meaning of life with a metaphor that called life a testing
period in which those selected for distinction must unite character
with ability, and magnanimity with power. It was the philosophy
which lay behind the private charity for which the Americans of
the Gilded Age became justly famous. It was an effort to carry the
idealism and the moral code of Christianity and of the democratic
faith into a rapidly developing capitalism. The gospel of wealth
sought to harmonize competitive acquisitiveness with the fundamental moral law. Out of it came the unadvertised gift to the needy
family, the boys' club in a poorer section of the city, the private
university, the art gallery, and the great foundation. It was the first
effort to make a complete rationalization of capitalism, and it was
the capitalist's answer to his Marxist critics.

But American capitalism in the last three decades of the nineteenth century was not on the defensive. It was triumphant. The
depressions following the panics of 1873 and of 1893 had destroyed
many individuals, but they had raised no important doubts in the
American mind. In 1900 the sky was cloudless; the attacks of labor

in 1877, in 1886, and in 1894 had come to naught, and the Bryan crusade for inflation in 1896 had been turned back. The gospel of wealth was the core of a capitalistic philosophy for the individual and for society. It was a fighting faith. Through this faith the American business man said in effect:

We of the capitalistic persuasion put trust in the individual man. We make him a part, according to his particular skill, of a great and far-reaching industrial organization. We demote him when his ability fails, and discard him if we find a serious flaw of character. In our system there is nothing, save his own shortcomings, to prevent his rising from the bottom to the top. We have, then, a method, better than that of practical politics, for selecting the leaders of a democracy. By a process of pitiless testing we discover who are the strong and who are the weak. To the strong we give power in the form of the autocratic control of industry and of wealth with which the leader, who has thus risen by a process of natural selection, can and does do for the masses of the community what they could never do for themselves. We agree with Alexander Hamilton that the voice of the able few should be equal to, nay, greater than that of the mediocre many in the actual government of society. So we demand that the political State shall leave us alone. We have little faith in the State as a constructive agency and less in it as an efficient instrument. The politician is a slave to the whims of the masses, a master of favoritism for his own ends, and a waster of the public substance. We demand of the State protection of property. For this purpose we ask an adequate police, a sound banking system, a sound currency based on gold, and court decisions to nullify social legislation confiscatory in character. We demand a tariff to protect us against our foreign competitors and a navy to guard our commerce and our stakes in other lands. When the State has fulfilled these, its proper functions, we ask it to leave us alone. We point to the progress already achieved under *laissez faire*. We guarantee that, if our conditions are met, the sun of prosperity will fill the land with light and happiness.

This faith and philosophy became the most persuasive siren in American life. It filled the highways with farm boys trekking to the city. It drained the towns and countryside of Europe. It persuaded the educated young man that the greatest rewards of life were to be found in the business world. It taught the ambitious that power lies in wealth rather than in political office. It penetrated the workshop and paralyzed the effort of the labor leader undertak-

ing a crusade for justice to the working man. Who would choose
to be a labor leader when, in expanding and developing America,
he might become a captain of industry?

∽

Inevitably the philosophy produced a prescription for achieving
individual well-being. A corollary of the gospel of wealth was the
popular formula of success. The stream of success literature which
appeared after the Civil War became a flood by the end of the century. The patterns displayed in these writings suggest the intellectual climate in which the gospel of wealth flourished. "Young
men," said Horace Greeley, "I would have you believe that success
in life is within the reach of every one who will truly and nobly
seek it." L. U. Reavis made this sentiment of the New York *Tribune's* editor the theme of a little volume which he brought out in
1871 and called *Thoughts for the Young Men of America, or a Few
Practical Words of Advice to those Born in Poverty and Destined
to be Reared in Orphanage*. Success, taught Reavis, depends upon
a few simple rules: "Don't be Discouraged. Do the Best You Can.
Be Honest, and Truthful and Industrious. Do Your Duty, and Live
Right; Learn to Read, then Read all the Books and Newspapers
You Can and All Will Be Well After Awhile."[14] In a thousand variations of phrase this simple prescription for success was presented to
all Americans able to read the English language. It was as universal
as those other panaceas, "Castoria" and the compound of Lydia
Pinkham. It was acted out in the successes of that story-book
hero, Horatio Alger, and in the biographies for juveniles by
William Makepeace Thayer. In 1880 the latter paused to write
Tact, Push and Principle because a friend had written to the author: "The delusions of the times ought to be exposed, and young
men made to understand the *principle* wins, in the long run, instead
of luck or unscrupulous scheming."[15] Thayer completed his exposé
of the contemporary delusions in three hundred and fifty-four
pages and concluded: "It is quite evident from the foregoing that
religion requires the following very reasonable things of every
young man, namely: that he should make the most of himself possible; that he should watch and improve his opportunities; that he
should be industrious, upright, faithful, and prompt; that he should
tax his talents, whether one or ten, to the utmost; that he should
waste neither time nor money; that *duty*, and not pleasure or ease,
should be his watchword. And all this is precisely what we have
seen to be demanded of all young men in reliable shops and stores.

Religion uses all the just motives of worldly wisdom, and adds thereto those higher motives that immortality creates. Indeed, we might say that religion demands success."[16] In short, the theme song of the success broadcasters of post-Appomattox years was the old Puritan code of worldly asceticism. Possess the Puritan virtues and "failure is impossible. *Not* having them success is impossible."[17] "The top, in this little world," said another success philosopher, "is not so very high, and patient climbing will bring you to it ere you are aware."[18] The number and sales of the success books make clear that purveying the timeworn patent formula was a profitable business. Its Christian phrases are evidence of the importance of religion on the intellectual climate of the 1870's and 1880's.

In the next decade, however, a significant change occurred in the success literature. The God of the Puritans faded gradually from the pages of the success books and was replaced by a strange and worldly mysticism called New Thought. In the New Thought version of the success formula, the old virtues were still important, but new words and phrases appeared: "personal magnetism"; "mental control"; "the subtle thought waves, or thought vibrations, projected from the human mind"; the "Law of Attraction"; and the "Law of Success." Use "the subtle thought waves," advised the prophets of the New Faith, and sell the prospect a bill of goods. It was the origin of "high pressure salesmanship." "The currents of knowledge, of wealth, of success, are as certain and fixed as the tides of the sea," wrote Orison Swett Marden in 1894 in his first book, *Pushing to the Front*. The law of prosperity, he concluded in 1922, "is just as definite as the law of gravitation, just as unerring as the principles of mathematics. It is a mental law. Only by thinking abundance can you realize the abundant prosperous life that is your birthright."[19] Marden's publishers sold more than three million copies of his books. Though he never formally united with the cult of New Thought, his writings were filled with the ideas of the movement. The success philosophy was going naturalistic; by the development of a pseudopsychology it was becoming "scientific." This change in the pattern of the literature of success was evidence which suggested that Carnegie's naturalistic version of the larger gospel of wealth was triumphing over the supernaturalism of Hopkins and of Conwell.

∾

The supplanting of the phrases of religion by the catch words of New Thought in the jargon of the success literature suggests also a decline in the influence and prestige of Protestantism as the nineteenth century closed. Evidence to be brought out later makes clear that Christianity lost in the post-Appomattox decades its old authoritative position in American society. "Science" became the god of the new day. The developing technology which made possible the new industrialism was founded upon a workshop materialism; and empiricism guided the development of the new corporations. Before the Civil War, the Protestant churches had sought breathlessly to make their expansion keep pace with the swiftly moving frontier. After that disaster they were confronted by cities ballooning into monster population centers. Their task of adjustment was immediate and urgent.

For post-Civil War American Protestantism, the gospel of wealth became a formula which permitted the Church to make peace with popular materialism. The ancient tendency in the Christian religion to withdraw from the world, to stress the warfare between the spirit and the flesh, to think in terms of other-worldliness, was checked in rich America after the Civil War. In that age men emphasized the here and now. A people whose accumulation of wealth was rapidly increasing felt less need of the consolation of a belief in a life to come. Spirituality does not normally flourish in a materialistic age. Protestantism, always sensitive to shifts in the mores, made quick adjustment to the trend of the times. The Christian version of the gospel as preached by Bishop Lawrence and by Russell H. Conwell was, in effect, a Protestant stratagem to retain for itself a place in the new social order, to provide itself with a function, in short, to save itself as a significant social institution. Urban Protestantism cultivated the middle and upper classes who possessed the ultimate power in American society.

It is true that there were revolters within the churches. These will be considered in another place. It is also true that there was a sincere minority who strove to play the rôle of steward of the Lord to the full extent of their ability. Russell H. Conwell, the founder of Temple University, was one of these. But for American Protestantism as a whole, the gospel of wealth as presented by Conwell and by Lawrence was a sign of decadence. When a species in nature approaches the end of its course, it frequently tends to exaggerate the weapons or the armament which established its position. So, in time, the tusks of the sabre-toothed tiger grew too long, and those of the mastodon curved until they were no longer useful. As the end of the nineteenth century approached, American cities saw a spinescent Protestantism converting its substance into costly and extravagant edifices, material symbols of the ecclesiastical gospel of wealth. A similar phenomenon among the Catholics came later.

∽

The gospel of wealth of the Gilded Age, later dubbed "rugged individualism," grew out of changed social conditions which, in turn, had been brought about by the rise of industrial capitalism. The formulation of its doctrines depended heavily, in the early post-Appomattox years, upon current religious thinking. As the prestige of orthodox Protestantism declined because of the growing importance of science in popular thought, the formulas of the gospel of wealth were expressed more and more frequently in secular language. Yet, in spite of the shifts in phraseology, the essentials of the gospel of wealth remained virtually unchanged throughout the last third of the century.

The core of the pattern was the doctrine of the free individual with emphasis upon freedom of action in the economic sphere. The doctrine as it finally emerged was indebted to four different formulations of the philosophy of individualism. It derived, in the religious version of the gospel of wealth, from the Christian concept of the freedom of the individual as a moral agent. It contained the popular philosophy that life is a race in which the prizes should go to the swiftest of foot. In its economic implications the doctrine of the rugged individualists stemmed from the classical theories of Adam Smith and James Mill. This *laissez-faire* position was supported toward the end of the century, when the prestige of Darwinism was high, by the evolutionary concept of the struggle for existence. The persistent American philosophy of individualism never had greater intellectual support than in the last two decades of the nineteenth century.

The gospel of wealth was not a fully developed social philosophy. Yet it contained implications which caused it to range far in the field of social thought. Summary enumeration of these assists in achieving an understanding of the power of this pattern in popular American thinking.

The gospel of wealth implied that the government of society in that most important of all areas, the economic, should be in the hands of a natural aristocracy. This leadership should be chosen in the hard school of competition. The rugged individualists assumed that the competitive struggle of the market selects out the weak and the incompetent and puts in positions of power those individuals who are distinguished for initiative, vision, judgment, and organizing ability. The prophets of the gospel of wealth believed that the best interests of society are furthered by putting the government of the economic area of society into the hands of these natural leaders. This ideal, of course, became the fact. Industries became economic autocracies. Management was supreme within the boundaries of its particular economic domain. The sanction behind management was the possession of economic power.

The corollary to the doctrine of a natural leadership was the philosophy of the police function of the State. The State exists, taught Porter, McCosh, and Carnegie, to maintain order and to protect property. Its activities must be limited to these functions. In order to function as a policeman the State must possess power. Possession of authority, however, tends to the desire on the part of officials to increase their control. Such increase naturally leads to attempts on the part of the State to interfere with the arrangements of the economic government set up by the natural leaders within particular industrial bailiwicks. Under such circumstances the State may become malevolent. Individuals must protect themselves. For purposes of protection bills of rights were incorporated in the early state constitutions as well as in the instrument which established the federal government.

One of the chief reasons why the meddling State is dangerous to society, the argument continued, is to be found in the fact that the usages and institutions of political democracy do not put men of ability into positions of power. Politics lifts mediocrity into the saddle. The evil connotations of the words "politics" and "politician" were evidence of the popular judgment concerning the defects of realistic democracy. The gospel of wealth was a philosophy which functioned as a defense of economic government in the hands of what was supposed to be a natural aristocracy of ability against political government in the hands of mediocrity.

The prophets of the gospel of wealth assumed that the doctrine of stewardship established a proper and adequate control over the government of the economic leaders. Carnegie emphasized that stewardship would tie together a society which was dividing into classes. The more able, and hence the more wealthy, would dedicate their superior talents to the task of doing for the less able what they could not do for themselves. Through such a paternalistic pattern the class divisions would be overcome and the poor and the rich united.

The gospel of wealth inevitably implied a philosophy of poverty. Poverty should be for the individual a temporary status. With initiative, industry, and ability he should rise above it. For the masses who do not rise, poverty must be a badge of failure proclaiming that the individual is defective in capacity or morals or both. The philosophy emphasized individual responsibility. It implied that the democratic doctrine of the free individual has no meaning, if the individual citizen is not willing to buy his liberty at the price of responsibility.

The gospel of wealth assumed that the poor, the less fortunate in the competition of the market, would accept the leadership of the men who, rising to the top, became the industrial barons of the day. In making this assumption the proponents of the formula ignored two possibilities. The first was that those who failed in the economic struggle of the market might attempt to recoup their fortunes by an appeal to politics, that they might seek to win by political action what they had failed to get by economic action. The other possibility was that the underlings might raise up leaders out of their own number, acquire power by organization, and challenge the autocracy of industrial government. The last decade of the century saw both these possibilities become realities. Then the gospel of wealth became primarily a defense formula for the maintenance of the economic and social *status quo*.

Chapter 14

THE SCIENCE OF MAN

Noah Porter found in religion a sanction for the gospel of wealth. Andrew Carnegie, when he turned theorist, got on very well without an appeal to the supernatural. The shift marked a momentous change in American social thinking. To understand what was happening a word concerning the background is necessary.

American political thought of the Revolutionary period grew primarily out of eighteenth-century rationalism. It was founded on the theory of natural rights stemming from the natural law philosophy. Jefferson emphasized the supreme importance of reason. He pointed out the peculiar necessity of reason for the well-being of a self-governing republic. In short Jefferson's thought derived ultimately from Newton by way of Locke.

But the prestige of deism in America declined after the French Revolution. Evangelical Protestantism dominated the social thought of Trans-Appalachia and ultimately captured the Atlantic states of the cotton kingdom. Unitarianism developed in New England and was followed by the bold speculations of the transcendentalists. American social thought of the Middle Period was founded largely on religious postulates. Religion was the most powerful drive behind the humanitarian movements of the age. Even Fourierism, which in the French original emphasized nature, compromised with orthodoxy when it appeared in the United States. The old orthodoxy reached its apogee in the 1850's and in the Civil War.

Then came Darwinism. The great naturalist published the *Origin of Species* in 1859. Geology at the moment was rewriting the Genesis narrative of the origin and early history of the earth. The theologians were ruffled by the quiet humor of Louis Agassiz who had come from Switzerland to Harvard in the 1840's and who was wont to say to his classes: "Gentlemen, the world is older than we have been taught to think. Its age is as if one were gently to rub a silk handkerchief across Plymouth Rock once a year until it were reduced to a pebble." "I had suspected and silently decided that the Bible was wrong somehow," remarked William Lawrence, later Bishop of Massachusetts, after listening to Agassiz. "But if one yielded to science in the Biblical account of creation . . . where was one going to stop?"[1] The problem was serious. Orthodox Protestantism had staked its faith on the doctrine of a literally inspired scripture. It had steadfastly maintained that the highest knowledge is that which comes from revelation. The geologists ran a sap dangerously close to an old theological bastion.

Darwin had a significance for social thought similar to that of Newton for physical science. Darwin's doctrine of man placed him wholly within the organic realm, the product of an evolutionary sequence. As a consequence the hypothesis undermined the theological doctrine of special creation and its corollary that man had been created above the animals and a little below the angels. Darwinism brushed aside as myth the story of the fall of Adam and the idea of original sin as part of the fall. The Darwinian emphasis on continuity, on the emergence of one species from another was, in time, to stimulate archeology. To work out the genealogical tree of the human race scientists studied fossil man—Pithicanthropos, Neanderthal, Cro-Magnon. An even more revolutionary consequence had to do with the concept of the mind. Darwin's picture of evolution was that the earliest forms of life were so primitive as to possess nothing that could be called mind. Yet by imperceptible variations man evolved from these. Darwin rejected the theory that at any point in the evolutionary process Deity had interposed by creating mind. For the Darwinians, then, mind became, not a separate entity, but the functioning of a psychophysical process. The mind is the functioning of the brain and its associated nervous system. The old dichotomy of mind and matter disappeared and with it such theories as that of Emerson of a universal mind that he called the Over-Soul.

Preoccupation with the issues which produced the Civil War prevented an earlier general consideration of the philosophy of evolution. "Evolutionism and the scriptural account of the origin of man are irreconcilable," thundered Professor Duffield of Princeton's Calvinist theological seminary. "The Darwinian theory is in direct conflict with the teaching of the Apostle, 'All scripture is given by inspiration of God.' . . . If the development theory of the origin of man shall in a little while take its place—as doubtless it will —with other exploded scientific speculations, then they who accept it . . . will in the life to come have their portion with those who in this life 'know not God and obey not the gospel of his son.' "[2] The smell of brimstone drifted across the campus of Old Nassau.

But Darwinism did not pass. It did not even cloud with pessimism the thinking of those who accepted it, because it fitted into that optimistic nineteenth-century philosophy of progress. Darwin had traced the rise of biological species from simple protozoa to complex mammals. Could not a similar development be discovered in society? Was it not possible to have a "science of man"? Herbert Spencer in England had published in 1857 a little volume which he called, *Progress, its Law and Cause.* The possibility of the discovery of a law of progress dazzled more than one post-Appomattox social theorizer. The finding of such a law would make man in a peculiar sense the master of his fate. The first American to essay the task was a devout and steadfast Christian, Lewis Henry Morgan, lawyer, capitalist, and lifelong member of the Protestant Episcopal Church. The path he followed led through anthropology. When he had completed his task, he had put the sanction of science not only behind Carnegie's gospel of wealth, but also behind the whole American democratic faith.

～

The first of the social sciences in America to achieve an approximation to a naturalistic approach was anthropology. In this field of investigation Americans early assumed positions of world leadership. The existences of diverse Indian tribes on the frontier was a constant reminder to a few citizens of the United States that human society took other forms than those which they were pleased to call civilization. After the publication in 1776 of James Adair's book on the nations of the old Southwest, there appeared from time to time other descriptions of Indian societies. Albert Gallatin, when his duties as Jefferson's Secretary of the Treasury were over, became interested in the languages spoken in the forest. Schoolcraft, in the service of the United States, wrote in the second quarter of the nineteenth century several volumes of more or less desultory description of Indian societies and folklore. In 1851 Lewis Henry Morgan earnestly called to the attention of his fellow countrymen that vanishing natural resources of the New World and particularly of the United States which was made up of Indian cultures. He urged that this intellectual wealth be exploited by men of science before it was destroyed by the conquering advance of a more powerful race.

Morgan's appeal did not go unanswered. His pioneering work stimulated and guided an increasing group of investigators among whom Adolph Bandelier, John Wesley Powell, and Daniel G. Brinton were the most important. Morgan's study of the Iroquois antedated by twenty years Edwin Burnett Tyler's *Primitive Culture*, which marked the beginning of cultural anthropology in England. Morgan tried to observe the civilization of his United States against the backdrop of primitive cultures. The present purpose is not to summarize his anthropological theories, but rather to discover the guise which the American democratic faith assumed when viewed from the new perspective.

∿

In 1878, the year before Henry George published *Progress and Poverty* and while Lester Frank Ward was still writing *Dynamic Sociology*, Lewis Henry Morgan summed up his thought in an ambitious book entitled *Ancient Society*. A little later a Rochester postman brought him a letter from William Cullen Bryant of the New York *Evening Post* urging him to continue writing to earn "that immortality which no mere *belles lettres* writer can hope for in this changeful world."[3] Young Henry Adams, just resigning his professorship of history at Harvard, wrote the author that the book "must be the foundation of all future work in American historical science."[4] Herbert Spencer, soon to begin his sociology, sent a note commenting on the expected usefulness of the volume to him. Friedrich Engels was filled with enthusiasm. Back of the volume lay one of the strangest stories in American intellectual history. Its paradoxes suggest the conflicts and confusions of the mid-nineteenth century.

In 1840, the year Melville went whaling in the *Acushnet*, President Eliphalet Nott, presiding at the annual commencement of Union College in Schenectady, New York, sent young Morgan into the world with a bachelor of arts degree. Lewis hurried to his home near Aurora, New York, to march and sing in the Whig campaign for William Henry Harrison. When his favorite had won, Morgan turned to religious debate and to humanitarian crusading. He argued in a public address for the Mosaic account of creation and journeyed to Scipio, New York, to assail Demon Rum on that very street through which was carted, so it was said, more beer and whiskey than through any other village of the region. The cause of anti-slavery claimed him, and in its service he affected the pompous and sententious oratorical style in vogue in those years when windy young Americans worshipped at the shrine of Webster. He continued to follow conventional American patterns by reading law, in the hope of making the profession a stepping stone to political life or to business success. In the end he achieved both.

At Aurora, after his admission to the bar, he occupied his plentiful leisure in pursuing an interest which dated from his Union days. On the Schenectady campus he had lived in an environment of locked and bolted doors, through which from time to time serious young collegians passed by means of passwords and grips to secret rites and hooded mummeries; for Union College in the early nineteenth century was the fountainhead of that unique American culture trait, the Greek letter fraternity. Morgan at Aurora, not far from the site of the principal village of the Cayugas, organized a secret society that finally came to be called The New Confederacy of the Iroquois. Its objects were both intellectual and humanitarian, to preserve Indian lore and to protect a declining race. Financed by The New Confederacy, Morgan, the lawyer, forced the quashing of a fraudulent treaty by means of which a gang of sharpers had schemed to get possession of the better part of the Seneca reservation. The Indians, in gratitude, made the young attorney a member of the Hawk clan at the dance of the corn harvest in 1846. In 1851, the year of *Moby Dick*, Morgan, aided by an Iroquois named Ely Parker, brought out his first book, *League of Ho-de-no-sau-nee or Iroquois*. The volume is one of the classics of anthropological literature and, though the first scientific account of an Indian tribe, still remains one of the best comprehensive studies of the Iroquois.

After his *Iroquois*, Morgan turned from description of specific cultures to investigation of the process of social change; he was stimulated by an unexpected discovery he made when he paused on a business trip to Michigan to visit the Winnebagoes. Publishing some preliminary conclusions in 1871, he pushed on, pioneering, into the field of cultural evolution. His thinking was certainly influenced by that of Darwin and, perhaps, by that of August Comte and of Charles Fourier.

Darwin's evolutionary hypothesis nurtured in Morgan's mind the exciting hope that, by studying the varying cultures of the tribes of men from the primitive to the advanced stages, he could sketch in outline a science of man and discover the laws of progress. Brinton, Morgan's successor as dean of American anthropology, put the dream in words in 1895 on the occasion of his retirement from the presidency of the American Association for the Advancement of

Science. "Ignorant of his past, ignorant of his real needs, ignorant of himself, man has blundered and stumbled up the thorny path of progress for tens of thousands of years. Mighty states, millions of individuals, have been hurled to destruction in the perilous ascent, mistaking the way, pursuing false paths, following blind guides. Now anthropology steps in, the new Science of Man, offering . . . itself as man's trusty mentor and friend, ready to conduct him by sure steps upward and onward to the highest summit which his nature is capable of attaining; and who dares set a limit to that?"[5]

In his *Ancient Society* Morgan presented in 1878 what was in reality his formulation of the laws of progress. He was then in his sixty-first year and possessed of moderate wealth, the result of the success of a small railroad in whose management he shared. He had, moreover, interrupted his business activities and his practice of law long enough to serve several years in the legislature of New York State. Contact with politics had served to increase his youthful devotion to the ideals of democracy, and like his business associates, he frankly espoused the gospel of wealth.

Morgan, postulating the psychic unity of all men, proceeded to unfold the grand drama of the evolution of culture. He taught that the human race has advanced through three stages: savagery, barbarism, and civilization. The first ended with the invention of pottery and the second with that of the alphabet. The Iroquois were barbarians and the Eskimos, who had no pottery, were savages. Twentieth-century scholars have largely abandoned this Morgan classification, but it made a powerful impress on both the scientific and popular thought of the latter decades of the nineteenth century. Morgan affirmed that the basic institution, the family, had evolved from a postulated promiscuity through diverse intermediate stages to monogamy, which appeared when civilization was achieved. The origins of the State, he taught, are to be found in that early social unit called the *gens*, in which a group was bound together by an actual or assumed blood relationship. In ancient Greece, he pointed out, men first made the shift from the *gens* to the group united by territorial propinquity. The political unit, as a result, became a collection of neighbors instead of one of kinsmen. The change made possible the modern nation, larger and more powerful than any *gens* could be.

The most important aspect of the Morgan theory dealt with the institution of property. Presidents Porter and McCosh in the 1880's affirmed that the institution of private property was of divine origin. Morgan explained its genesis in naturalistic terms. He defined property as the representative of accumulated subsistence. The passion to possess property, he thought, began in human society at zero, developed at first slowly because men only slowly came to understand its importance, but, with the advance of civilization, finally became dominant over the human mind. The modern man, Morgan affirmed, lives in a property-getting age. New inventions, he believed, were the chief factors in educating mankind to the importance of property, for each succeeding stage in progress showed an increase in inventions and in the variety and amount of property which resulted therefrom. The bow and arrow was the precursor of the hunting stage, and the steam engine the forerunner of an industrial civilization. Technology, then, according to the Morgan theory, was the spearhead of economic advance and this, in turn, was the forerunner of all other social improvement. Alterations in property arrangements, Morgan observed, invariably brought changes in government and all other institutions of society.

When property first appeared in early savagery, it was held in common and this primitive communism was associated with a crude democracy. When property had become created in masses, and its influence and power began to be felt in society, Morgan continued, slavery came in; an institution violating all these democratic principles, but sustained by the selfish and delusive consideration that the person made a slave was a stranger in blood and a captive enemy. With property, also, came in gradually the principle of aristocracy, the striving for the creation of privileged classes. The element of property which has controlled society to a great extent during the comparatively short period of civilization, has given mankind despotism, imperialism, monarchy, privileged classes, and finally representative democracy. It has also made the career of civilized nations essentially a property-making career.[6] Karl Marx never made a more emphatic statement of the doctrine of economic determinism.

Morgan's Americanism outcropped in his reference to representative democracy. Despotism, imperialism, and monarchy were European culture patterns which had disappeared in the New World, he thought, in the American Revolution. The last vestige of a rigid class system had finally been destroyed in the United States with the defeat of the Southern planter and the destruction of Negro slavery. In America, property had finally produced representative democracy in a society where men moved from class to class in accordance with individual merit. At least such was the theory of the gospel of wealth. So Morgan put the American folk beliefs, the democratic faith, and the gospel of wealth at the top of his evolutionary sequence.

Morgan did not believe, however, that mankind had entered the last scene of the last act of the drama of human progress. He saw property become an unmanageable power and the human mind bewildered in the presence of its own creation. "A mere property career is not the final destiny of mankind," he remarked, "if progress is to be the law of the future as it has been of the past. . . . The dissolution of society bids fair to become the termination of a career of which property is the end and aim; because such a career contains the elements of self-destruction."[7] Here was the central idea of Marxism; the system of private property contains the seeds of social decay and economic developments will again, as they have in the past, usher in a new era.[8] When the intelligence of mankind rises to the height of the great question of the abstract rights of property, Morgan went on, including the relations of property to the State as well as the rights of persons to property, a modification of the present order of things may be expected. The nature of the coming changes it may be impossible to conceive; but it seems probable that democracy, once universal in a rudimentary form and repressed in many civilized states, is destined again to become universal and supreme. "Democracy in government, brotherhood in society, equality in rights and privileges, and universal education, foreshadow the next higher plane of society. . . . It will be a revival, in a higher form, of the liberty, equality and fraternity of the ancient gentes."[9] In these phrases Morgan restated in the language of naturalism the old American doctrine of democracy as the salvation of the world. For Morgan the fundamental law seemed likely to turn out, on further investigation, to be a natural law containing a law of progress. This latter law seemed to forecast the ultimate triumph of the democratic faith.

It should be noted that this next higher plane of ultimate democracy was to come as a result of the inexorable workings of a deterministic law of progress. It was this determinism that endeared Morgan to the Marxians. The phenomenon of a successful Yankee capitalist constructing a complete anthropological frame of reference for Marx's materialistic interpretation of history was almost enough to make Engels believe in the providence of God. When he finished reading *Ancient Society*, he promptly began a book which he called with characteristic German economy of phrase, *Der Ursprung der Familie, des Privateigenthums und des Staats, in Anschluss an Lewis H. Morgan's Forschungen*, 1884. "Not only does Morgan criticize civilization, the society of production for profit, the fundamental form of human society in a manner savouring of Fourier," commented the delighted Engels, "but he also speaks of a future reorganization of society in a manner that Karl Marx might have used."[10]

Morgan was a pioneer who ran an anthropological furrow where no plow had ever been before. To his age his theory was stimulating and enlightening. His idea of progress from savagery to barbarism and civilization entered into the fabric of the thought of the people where, as will be brought out later, it served important ends. In spite of his success, however, Morgan never permitted his philosophy to crystallize into dogmatism; to the end of his life, like a true scientist, he looked upon his conclusions as tentative. In the late 1870's Morgan visited yearly his younger anthropological friend and admirer, F. W. Putnam. "During one of these visits," wrote Putnam in 1895, "as I distinctly remember he stated that he was living a generation too early and got founded in his beliefs before he had the facts now in hand, but that it was too late to renew his work and do it all over with the knowledge of late discoveries and that I must take the matter up and show where he had made mistakes and also what of his would stand. He died December, 1881."[11] No American ever paid more eloquent homage to the ideals of science.

∽

Morgan, ranging over the cultures of the world, had discovered the American democratic faith as the end product of cultural evolution. The importance of this phenomenon would be slight if it were merely the peculiarity of an individual scholar. The same discovery was made by other anthropologists before the end of the century. Of these the most conspicuous was John Wesley Powell. When his ambitious intellectual undertakings are put beside those of Morgan, some characteristics of the *fin de siècle* climate of opinion are clarified. Powell had been wounded in the Civil War. In spite of disabilities arising from military service, he had, after Appomattox, pioneered in the exploration of the Grand Canyon. Held in by walls of mountainous height, he had voyaged down the muddy Colorado not knowing what falls or rapids might be concealed around the next bend. He had been the first white man to look up at these giant cliffs on which nature had lavished all the colors of the spectrum. His disappearance beneath the Colorado Plateau, his braving of the hazards of an unknown river, and his ultimate successful emergence below the Canyon became one of the great adventure stories of the 1860's. His explorations presented to a nationally conscious people a new natural wonder. Powell, the explorer, stirred the popular imagination.

He passed naturally into public life. The United States Geological Survey, established in 1879, owed much to his public activities, and for years he was its director. He became head of the United States Bureau of Ethnology, and in this capacity he sent exploring expeditions into every part of the United States which he thought would yield anthropological data. There was scarcely an American anthropologist of the period who was not indebted to him for aid, encouragement, or advice. He was probably the most widely known scientist of the 1890's. When he spoke, his words carried weight.

Powell was convinced, as the century drew to a close, that the age of religion had passed and with it the age of philosophy. He worshipped at the shrine of science. Science, he thought, had given to man the key which opened the gate upon the path of progress. The fogs of religious and philosophic illusion which still clouded the minds of men were, in Powell's opinion, the chief factors which were preventing science from enabling mankind to move forward even more rapidly. So Powell at the zenith of his career became the American high priest of the new positivism. He set out to dispel the mists of superstition and of fantasy and to bring his groping fellow countrymen out of the cloudbanks and into the clear, bright light of scientific knowledge. He wrote articles which were published in the leading scientific journals of the day. He put them together into books. His voice carried farther across the United States than that of any other American scientist. Josiah Willard Gibbs, the greatest scientific mind of the day, had not yet been discovered by Americans.

A few sentences suggest Powell's iconoclasm and his faith. What is philosophy, he asked, in a day when Josiah Royce and William James were famous names. It is the modern equivalent, he answered, of the folklore of the savage. "Both idealism and materialism are fallacious because they both attempt to reduce all the properties of bodies to one, and in so doing they transmute the realities of the world into magic and continue the superstitions of primeval culture."[12] Emerson had died in 1882, but the magic of his great faith still moved some Americans. "In the intoxication of illusion," said Powell in 1896, fourteen years after earth had closed the most important Concord grave, "facts seem cold and colorless, and the rapt dreamer imagines that he dwells in a realm above science— in a world which as he thinks absorbs truth as the ocean the shower and transforms it into a flood of philosophy." No man ever described more accurately the great transcendentalist. "Yet," Powell continued, "the simple and the true remain. The history of science is the discovery of the simple and the true; in its progress illusions are dispelled and certitudes remain."[13]

It is not the present purpose to review Powell's analysis of these certitudes of science. The immediate concern is a more limited task. Powell was convinced that he had demolished all of Emerson's kind. Now Emerson, among other rôles, had been the mid-nineteenth-century Isaiah of the American democratic faith. Did Powell, in destroying the philosopher, attack also his faith? When his writings are explored for the answer to this question, some unexpected findings come to light.

One of the most important tenets of the democratic faith was the belief in the unique origin and destiny of American liberty. Americans of the Middle Period were wont to give this doctrine a theistic setting. One is a little surprised, at first, to see emerging from Powell's iconoclasm the old doctrine tricked out in scientific garb. "The merit of Columbus," said Powell in 1899, "was his faith in science. . . . The new world was the trophy of science. . . . The discovery gave to science the hope that it might prevail against superstition. . . . The new world became the home of republics." Powell had already asserted, following Morgan, that "republicanism is the ultimate in social evolution." "The example of these republics," he continued, "has spread the egis of free institutions over much of western Europe, and the leaven of freedom works unrest for all monarchical governments of the world."[14] The preachers of 1850 had proclaimed the new world as specially reserved in the providence of God for development of liberty. Powell called the American world in a special sense the offspring of science and the arena where science won its greatest victories over superstition, thus speeding the evolution of men toward freedom. If Emerson's faith was folklore, Powell's almost identical beliefs fall into the same category.

An investigation of Powell's "certitudes" discloses that they are, in effect, a restatement in naturalistic terms of the old doctrine of the fundamental law. Powell's science emphasized absolutes as much as Emerson's religion. This fact was made particularly clear when he discussed the moral law. As an anthropologist he was aware that moral codes vary in different cultures. He pointed out that some aspects of the morality of other days would shock the modern mind. He could point to the tribal approval of the killing of new-born infants or of aged persons. He denied, however, that changes in morals implied that the moral law is an illusion. Its discovery is merely in the process of evolution. There is an eternal right and wrong. Duty, however, thought Powell, is not to be apprehended by blind conscience, but rather will be made clear by scientific knowledge of truth and of error. "The moral teachers of the times," he said, "are more and more eschewing the ancient doctrines of theoretical ethics and devoting their energy to practical ethics. Theories of faith are held in abeyance to theories of practice." He discarded the ethics founded upon the will of God believed in by such men as Mark Hopkins. He was approaching pragmatism, but he did not go all the way with William James. Powell lived in an absolutist Newtonian world. "It needs but a few generations to come and go," he went on, "before the new teaching of theory will be founded wholly on principles derived from practice. This will be the establishment of scientific ethics."[15] Science, in other words, will discover the laws of right and wrong as it has already brought to light those of matter and motion. Powell looked ahead to that happy day when science would pass beyond the frontier of mere description of human behavior into a phase in which it would be able to tell men how they should behave. The explorer of the Grand Canyon had his own dream of utopia.

The central doctrine of the democratic faith was that of the free individual. This was also the center of Powell's thought. "The annals of science," he remarked, "are the record of the discovery of individuals." And the utilization of scientific knowledge, he added, depends upon the initiative of individual inventors and individual men of enterprise.

∽

The objective of the present inquiry is to gain insights into the capacity to survive of the mid-nineteenth-century democratic faith. The evidence from the work of Morgan and Powell is suggestive. The democratic faith was a culture-religion. It grew up in a complementary relation to Protestant Christianity. Morgan and Powell helped to carry it over into the cult of science which was emerging at the end of the century. But they were not conscious of their effort. The old faith permeated the intellectual climate with a subtleness akin to that of the ether which physicists once postulated as the imponderable something filling all space. Morgan and Powell, honest investigators in pursuit of knowledge, both came out with the ideals of the democratic faith as the end product of social evolution. The phenomenon suggests the power of the faith to mold the thoughts of men who were unaware of the influences shaping their ideas.

Chapter 15

THE RELIGION OF HUMANITY

THE GOSPEL OF WEALTH was the result of an effort to implement the old democratic doctrine of the free individual in order to make it useful in a developing industrial capitalism. The new version of the philosophy of individualism, supported by Protestant theology or by Darwinian naturalism, became the ruling intellectual pattern of the period of economic transition which lay between 1865 and 1917. The gospel of wealth, however, did not go unchallenged. Criticism appeared immediately after Appomattox. The objectors challenged not only the doctrine of individual competition, but also both the religious and secular arguments which supported it.

The appearance of an aggressive humanism, a new religion of humanity, immediately after the end of the Civil War is one of the more significant events in the history of American democratic thought. The objective of the religion of humanity was to secure and to protect a larger human freedom and to make men understand that liberty implies responsibility. Like Morgan, the post-Appomattox humanists turned to science. When the anxieties of war relaxed, there was a sudden impact of Darwinism upon Christian orthodoxy. August Comte, who died in 1857, gave the world a positivist philosophy which affirmed that the theological stage in the progress of humankind had ended, as had also the succeeding stage of rationalistic philosophies. Mankind, thought Comte, had entered, in the nineteenth century, the age of science; in this new intellectual world man was destined to become the master of his own destiny. Comtean positivism affected American thought at the moment when Darwinism was challenging the old religious doctrines of the nature of man.

At the same time a revolution which grew out of the Civil War began to take form. The attitude of the common American citizen toward the central government began to change. Before 1861 the functions of the government were few. *Laissez faire* was a reality.

After the fall of Sumter the government was transformed by Lincoln and his advisers into a powerful instrument for saving the Union. The national government continued, after 1865, to loom large in American thought. Federal officials organized in the Freedmen's Bureau a vast and unprecedented welfare service for the new wards of the nation, and federal authority compelled ex-Confederates to accept political and social arrangements made in Washington. One of the chief problems of the post-Appomattox years, moreover, was the disposition of the unoccupied public domain, first crossed by a railway in 1866. The central government began, in a halting way, to turn to the sciences of geology and of mineralogy to aid in the exploration of the little-known wilderness for the disposition of which Washington was responsible. The creation of the U. S. G. S. had a double significance: it marked a first step in the realization of the ideal of the public service State (as opposed to a mere police State), and it was a pioneer public effort in America to put science to work at the task of the amelioration of human life. The U. S. G. S. was not, however, an isolated phenomenon. In these same post-Appomattox years a bureau of entomology took form in what was to become the United States Department of Agriculture. Pioneers in Connecticut, moreover, founded in 1875 the first agricultural experiment station in the United States. The new colleges of "agriculture and the mechanic arts" created by the Morrill Act of 1862 were also aiding in the task of making science the servant of man.

In such an age of pioneering, hope ran high. Science seemed to guarantee a rich and glorious future. Some events of the early post-Appomattox years suggested, however, that organized religion stood squarely across the path of scientific progress. When Ezra Cornell and Andrew D. White founded Cornell University in 1867, they established an institution which was to be free from all sectarian control. Their ideal was ahead of the times. To their astonishment they soon found themselves and their university the objects of a bitter clerical attack. This became so intense and so widespread that White was forced to fight back. In a lecture tour over the state he traced with vigor and effectiveness the history of the opposition of Christian theologians in Europe and in America to the advancement of science. He gathered his revised lectures together and published them in 1896 under the title, *The Warfare between Science and Theology in Christendom.* It was a devastating counter-thrust. White's two volumes mark the defeat in the United States of that old Protestant orthodoxy which insisted upon the use of a literally inspired Scripture as the highest source of human knowledge.

In the decade immediately following Lee's surrender appeared a movement which combined the various liberalisms of the age. To describe it some of its leaders used the phrase "religion of humanity." It was made up of militant young humanists who, after 1865, were convinced that organized Christianity had become in the United States the chief enemy of freedom. The prophets of the religion of humanity were not scientists, in the sense in which that term applies to Morgan and Powell. Yet the new liberals were devotees of science. They saw in it the hope of the world. For them science was a tool with which humanists could build a new society. But, for this task, they thought, more than science is required. They saw values in the old religion. Out of faith comes that inspiration which at its best causes the individual to spend his energies to the uttermost.

The new humanism was not the result of the teachings of any particular individual. It was not limited to a locality in the sense that transcendentalism centered in Concord. The post-Appomattox religion of humanity sprang up independently in different places on the Atlantic seaboard and in the Upper Mississippi Valley. It never became a sect. Its prophets were as individualistic as those of ancient Israel.

◇

In 1867 the talk in the Boston drawing rooms was of Longfellow's translation of the *Divine Comedy*, completed in that year. The Wednesday evening visits of James Russell Lowell and Charles Eliot Norton to the Longfellow home to listen critically to the reading of the proof had come to an end, and in the following year the poet sailed for England to receive the honors of Cambridge and of Oxford. On Memorial Day in 1867 Boston people went to their cemeteries to lay flowers on the fresh graves of their war dead. Inevitably they recalled their local hero, "that blue-eyed child of fortune," Colonel Robert Gould Shaw, who had died four years before while leading his Negro regiment in a hopeless charge on the Charleston front. For Boston, Shaw personified the ideals of the war days. The time was to come when James Russell Lowell would read on the Common a poem in his honor and William James pronounce an oration beside a memorial from the hand of St. Gaudens.

Shaw's spirit of high endeavor permeated the atmosphere of Boston's Horticultural Hall, filled with a large audience, on May 30,

1867. The aging Ralph Waldo Emerson was in the chair. Octavius Brooks Frothingham looked out from the platform over the earnest assembly and felt that a new age might be at hand. In the afternoon Frothingham's committee proposed a constitution. It was accepted. The Free Religious Association had come into being. Frothingham was chosen president of the new organization. He held the office until 1877, when he was succeeded by Felix Adler. Among the earlier vice-presidents associated with Frothingham were John T. Sargent, Ralph Waldo Emerson, and George William Curtis. The early boards of directors included the names of Frank T. Sanborn, Thomas Wentworth Higginson, Francis E. Abbot, and William Lloyd Garrison, the younger.

The Free Religious Association was an expression of idealism. Freedom and unity were its watchwords: freedom from bondage of sect and creed, from the provincialism even of Christianity itself; the unity of all the living world religions into a universal religion of humanity. The Association demanded an end of the intolerance of American Christianity toward new ideas—toward Darwinism and historical criticism of the Scriptures. It stood for freedom of thought and of inquiry. It urged an untrammeled search for the principles which should govern the new religion and enable it one day to unite the peoples of the world into a universal brotherhood. "The Dignity of Human Nature must be our watchword"; said Frothingham, "of human *nature*, not of human *character*. For human *nature* denotes the *capacities* of man, what he *ought* to be and *shall* be, not what he *is*. Human character expresses only the undeveloped condition of man, and is therefore not to be taken as a final stand. This doctrine does not belong to a sect or a church, but to all mankind. It assumes an entirely new conception of the basis of religious faith; it makes a new beginning; it starts a new system; it exactly reverses the ancient order of thought, and builds up from a completely original foundation."[1] Frothingham and his fellow prophets of the religion of humanity dreamed boldly of an ultimate world triumph of humanism.

Of the associates of Frothingham in the Free Religious Association, Francis Ellingwood Abbot was the most important. He had a professional philosophical training, and in 1867 Emerson had unsuccessfully supported him for the chair of philosophy at White's Cornell.

On January 1, 1870, Abbot, who had moved to Toledo, Ohio, published the first number of the *Index*, which for many years was the journalistic vehicle for the Free Religious Association. In number after number he repeated the basic "Fifty Affirmations," which expressed the creed, the program, and the goal of the new religion of humanity. Religion, proclaimed the *Index*, is the effort of man to perfect himself. Its root lies in universal human nature; because of this common root, historical religions are all one. Free Religion is emancipation from the outward law, and is voluntary obedience to the inward fundamental law. Its moving power is faith in man as a progressive being. Its objective is the perfection or complete development of man, the race serving the individual, and the individual the race. Its practical work is to humanize the world, to make the individual nobler here and now and "to convert the human race into a vast Co-operative Union devoted to universal ends."[2] The human mind, taught Abbot, is the ultimate seat of authority; there can be no progress without freedom of thought and expression. The practical program which will transform the hope of progress into a reality is the "continuous and universal education of man."[3] The religion of humanity, therefore, abandoned conventional Christian theism with its affirmation that God is working in the world. "Whether there shall be peace or war, rule or misrule, purity or corruption, justice or injustice," said Frothingham in 1872 in a volume which he entitled *The Religion of Humanity*, ". . . are questions that men must answer for themselves. There is no higher tribunal before which they can be carried; there is no super-human or extra-human will by which they can be dealt with. If things go well or ill rests with those who are commissioned to make them go."[4] He added that "essential human nature" is perfectly expressed as "the Messiah cradled in the bosom of every man."[5]

Frothingham longed for his old friend, Theodore Parker, to carry on the new movement. His desire, however, was tempered by a doubt as to whether Parker would have led it, for the religion of humanity had moved to the left of Parker's position. Frothingham, by the testimony of his cousin, Henry Adams, "scandalized Beacon Street by avowing skepticism that seemed to solve no old problems, and to raise many new ones."[6] But in spite of his skepticism the president of The Free Religious Association was a man of extraordinary spiritual power. Many of his contemporaries thought of him as a worthy successor to Parker. He had begun his active career before the war as a Unitarian clergyman. His thought had then been dominated by the transcendentalism of Emerson and of Carlyle. "It was balm and elixir to me," he wrote later in his autobiography. But the transcendental mood was too exalted and too mystical to last. Darwinism, moreover, had impaired Emerson's concept of an idyllic nature. "Absolute faith in that form of [transcendental] philosophy grew weak and passed away many years since," Frothingham went on, "and the assurance it gave was shaken; but the sunset flush continued a long time after the orb of day had disappeared and lighted up the earth. Gradually the splendor faded, to be succeeded by a softer and a more tranquil gleam, less stimulating but not less beautiful or glorious. The world looks larger under the light of stars."[7] The starlight of the post-Civil War years was the religion of humanity.

Its most important church was in New York City where Frothingham for years held services each Sunday in Lyric Hall on Sixth Avenue between Fortieth and Forty-first Streets. Here audiences numbering between six and nine hundred heard sermons with such titles as "Secular Religion" and "Reasonable Religion." "It had long ceased to be a Unitarian congregation. There were people of Catholic training, many of Protestant training, some of no religious training whatever, materialists, atheists, secularists, positivists—always thinking people, with their minds uppermost. It was a church of the unchurched."[8] The discourses were circulated widely in pamphlets and in the press. As Frothingham looked over the desk on Sunday morning, he saw among his supporters George Ripley, the journalist, Edmund Clarence Stedman, Calvert Vaux, the architect, Sanford R. Gifford, the painter, and C. P. Cranch, the poet. He preached until 1879, when his health failed. His later years were devoted to quiet writing in Boston. Before he died he paid tribute to the men who had formed his youthful thought in biographies of Theodore Parker and of Gerrit Smith, and in his *Transcendentalism of New England*. He died in 1895, three years after the passing of Whitman.

The radicalism of the Free Religious Association did not go unchallenged. It was assailed in the pulpits as a new form of infidelity. But the adversaries in the debate seldom met. In Boston, however, a forum appeared where conservatives and radicals could come together face to face. The Boston Radical Club assembled during the 1870's on the first Monday of every month, usually at the home of the Rev. John T. Sargent on Chestnut Street. Here on one occasion Thomas Wentworth Higginson and David A. Wasson led the assault of the liberals upon a well-fortified position held by Calvin and Harriet Beecher Stowe. On another occasion, one day in October,

1871, Charles Sumner, after he had written his fanaticism into the Fourteenth and Fifteenth Amendments, dropped in to discuss "The Function of the Heart in Religion," the title of the paper of the meeting.[9] John Fiske and Wendell Phillips also joined the melee on that day. At a November meeting the same year the aged Bronson Alcott came to hear the discussion of Julia Ward Howe's paper on "Moral Trigonometry." The author of the famous battle hymn was a conservative who had been pained by the destructive logic emanating from the trenches of the radicals. Determined to turn their own weapons upon them, Mrs. Howe wheeled her mathematical artillery into position and laid down upon her adversaries a withering barrage of moral sines and cosines. The appearance of such a paper suggests the growing popular authority of science. Each month the New York *Tribune* carried to its national clientele one or two columns of description and comment concerning the latest meeting of the Boston Club. Through these *Tribune* reports, therefore, and through the columns of the *Index* were disseminated the theological ideas of the new religion based on the dignity of human nature.

∽

The most picturesque and important prophet of the religion of humanity was not a member of the Free Religious Association nor a disputant in the Boston Radical Club but was an independent preacher of skepticism, Robert Green Ingersoll. Born on the frontier of western New York, he grew up on the prairie plains of the Upper Mississippi Valley. In this country, where the distant level horizon beckoned him to freedom, his father, a conscientious Calvinist minister, sought to confine the spirit of his son within the walls of the Genevan system. Young Ingersoll revolted against the prison. Denied an arts education because of family poverty, he turned to law. He had already made a reputation as a successful advocate when Lincoln called for volunteers in 1861. Without hesitation Ingersoll abandoned his practice and plunged into the great crusade. He helped to raise a regiment, and became its colonel. But military disaster in 1862 at the hands of General Bedford Forrest brought his service to an early end. He returned to his profession and, after 1865, became one of the most successful trial lawyers of the Gilded Age. His oratorical gifts took him into politics. His speech before the Republican Convention of 1876, in which he presented the name of "The Plumed Knight," James G. Blaine, made the speaker a national figure.

On that day it was made clear to the American people that Ingersoll possessed every gift needed by the American politician. He was friendly and generous. Though he served as attorney the new corporations, his primary interest was in the underdog. His wit was second only in his day to that of Mark Twain. In his speeches he could pass swiftly from effective ridicule to passages which lifted his audience to emotional heights. Political triumph and power beckoned him, but he renounced them. His mission in life became, not the aggrandizement of Robert Ingersoll, but rather the razing of those prison walls within which, as he thought, preachers and priests were attempting to confine the human spirit. The rebellion of his boyhood became the crusade of his lifetime. For the sake of humanity he accepted the rôle of the pariah of the Gilded Age.

Following the examples of Emerson and of Father Hecker, Ingersoll mounted the lecture platform. Here he discussed theology and biblical criticism. The people flocked to his discourses and paid willingly the admission fees he demanded. He twitted an enraged clergy with the fact that they did not dare to charge at the gate for their advice and admonitions. He poked fun at miracles. He approached the art of Clemens when he described the anxiety of Jonah in the belly of the whale. He became a theological roustabout. Good Calvinists condemned him to the hottest Hell, partly because his impeccable life gave them no opportunity for a scandal-mongering attack. His influence was prodigious. His voice carried across the Atlantic. The pious Gladstone once sought to crush this American unbeliever under the weight of a great name. A few intellectuals knew and followed Frothingham; a few more read in the *Tribune* the debates of the Boston Radical Club; but by 1880 there was scarcely a middle-class American from New England to the coast who did not know that the infidel, "Bob" Ingersoll, was the pulpit's dearest enemy.

The center of Robert Ingersoll's thought was the concept of the free individual; the foundation of his faith was a belief that the free man can save himself—and society—from the evils which, through all history, have beset the race. Ingersoll's basic postulate was that of a fundamental law, eternal and inexorable. But this is, he thought, no law of the God of orthodoxy; it is rather the law of nature, revealed in the field and in the laboratory to those men who observe carefully and reason logically. When Ingersoll's work was done, he had divorced, for himself and for many of his generation, the American democratic faith from Christianity and had restated it as a completely humanistic philosophy founded upon naturalistic assumptions.

What is nature? Nature, answered this itinerant evangelist of skepticism, is impersonal material and impersonal process. Nature is neither merciful nor cruel. Nature "produces man without purpose, and obliterates him without regret."[10] Having through the process of evolution produced man, nature has been lifted to a new plane. For through man, but man only, nature takes cognizance of the good, the true, and the beautiful.

What is man? Man, thought Ingersoll, is part and particle of nature. Man is the highest intelligence. Emerson's Over-Soul does not exist. Why, then, has man always believed in gods? Because, replied the lecturer, man is weak and ignorant. Both weakness and ignorance breed fear. From antiquity men have sought strength in the gods which they have created. Ingersoll's thought ran back to that Calvinistic God who was worshipped by that impecunious clergyman, his father. The son spent his life making war upon the image of a god who would condemn helpless human beings to the eternal anguish of the burning lake. "An honest God," he remarked, "is the noblest work of man." "Nearly every people," he went on, "has created a god, and the god has always resembled his creators. He hated and loved what they hated and loved, and he was invariably found on the side of those in power.[11] . . . Few nations have been so poor as to have but one god. Gods were made so easily, and the raw material cost so little, that generally, the god-market was fairly glutted and heaven crammed with these phantoms."[12] This was not cheap ridicule to get a laugh or to bring in gate receipts. Ingersoll was too good a lawyer to require the latter and too good a humorist to need to depend for effect upon blasphemy. He was in earnest. He well knew that he would pay, personally, for his witticisms. The price was high but he did not wince. To the good people of his generation he became a spiritual leper. By the devout he was more feared than Yellow Jack, because the fever destroyed only the body. Yet Ingersoll walked erect among his fellows. His was a war for freedom. The god of John Calvin was his enemy.

What are the fruits of this Christian religion as revealed by its history, he asked with bitterness. For answer, he pointed to the long record of opposition on the part of theologians to the advancement of learning. When religion was supreme in the Middle Ages, the progress of the race was impeded. Theological intolerance was finally brought to an end through heresy. "Heresy," said Ingersoll, "is the eternal dawn, the morning star, the glittering herald of the new day."[13]

If the gods are but phantoms upon whom shall men depend? To this question of anxious listeners Ingersoll replied: "If abuses are destroyed, man must destroy them. If slaves are freed, men must free them. If new truths are discovered, man must discover them. If the naked are clothed; if the hungry are fed; if justice is done; if labor is rewarded; if superstition is driven from the mind; if the defenceless are protected, and if the right finally triumphs, all must be the work of man."[14] How shall these good works be accomplished? We have at hand in this latter day to aid us, he answered, "Reason, Observation, and Experience—the Holy Trinity of Science."[15]

But Ingersoll did not content himself with vague philosophical notions. He was a practical man in a practical world. He was moved by the suffering which he beheld in that fateful summer of 1877 when thousands of the railroad workers of the nation, reduced to desperation by the hardships of the long depression following the Panic of 1873, preferred to strike rather than to accept another wage cut. Organized urban Protestantism was on the side of the employer. That courageous revolt of humane Christians who later advocated a Social Gospel had not yet come into being. Against such a background Ingersoll preached in Boston in 1878 a practical religion of humanity.

"The hours of labor should be shortened, . . ." he said. "What is the reasonable price for labor? I answer: Such a price as will enable the man to live; to have the comforts of life; to lay by a little something for his declining years, so that he can have his own home, his own fireside; so that he can preserve the feelings of man." And Ingersoll believed the ideal to be capable of attainment. Science, he thought, makes it possible for man to be a social engineer. "We invent," he went on. "We take advantage of the forces of nature; we enslave the winds and waves; we put shackles upon the unseen powers and chain the energy that wheels the world. These slaves should release from bondage all the children of men." Ingersoll's mood was militant. He spoke in a nation in which in 1877 the President had called out the army to put down uprisings among the workers but had made no effort to discover the nature of the ills from which they suffered. "I sympathize," he declared, "with every honest effort made by the children of labor to improve their condition. That is a poorly governed country in which those who do the most have the least. There is something wrong when men are obliged to beg for leave to toil. We are not yet a civilized people; when we are, pauperism and crime will vanish from our land."[16]

Ingersoll, like his American ancestors, believed in progress. He had his dream of the new society to be. It would be founded upon three cardinal principles. The golden age to come, he thought, will manifest a more equitable distribution of wealth. "We are doing what little we can," he remarked, "to hasten the coming of the day when society shall cease producing millionaires and mendicants —gorged indolence and famished industry."[17] In the new society, he went on, the useful shall be the honorable. The test of the good must be its utility to man. The indolence of conspicuous leisure is not good. Those who practice it will be covered with shame. And honest toil, no matter how lowly, will be held up to honor. Finally, in the new society, he concluded, the true will be the beautiful. Here was the foundation for a theory of aesthetics which implied that the test of beauty is utility and honesty. It was a shrewd thrust at the exaggerated ornamentation plastered over the surfaces of the romantic buildings with which Ingersoll's contemporaries symbolized the acquisition of new wealth.

Ingersoll was a prophet of human freedom. He defined liberty as escape from the thralldom of superstition and the oppression of intolerance. He defined it also as emancipation from the tyranny of poverty. He defined the good in terms of men rather than of gods. For him there was no value that was not a value for men. "We are laying," he said, "the foundations of the grand temple of the future—not the temple of all the gods, but of all the people— wherein, with appropriate rites, will be celebrated the religion of Humanity."[18]

On a March day in 1892 Robert Ingersoll stood beside the grave into which was lowered the body of his friend, Walt Whitman. A telegram had halted the lawyer's trip in Canada, and he had hurried to Camden to fulfil a promise to the poet. "Colonel Bob" spoke with feeling on that day, for the friendship between the two men had deepened with the years. "He was the poet of that divine democracy which gives equal rights to all the sons and daughters of men," said Ingersoll. "One of the greatest lines in our literature is his. . . . He said, speaking of an outcast: 'Not till the sun excludes you do I exclude you!' "[19]

Whitman, with Ingersoll, was also a disciple of the religion of humanity. With Frothingham, Whitman migrated from transcen-

dentalism to the new humanism. Whitman's faith, like that of Ingersoll, was born of war. Both knew what soldiering meant. Both
understood that, when men campaign together month after month,
when they face together the long grind of marches, the terror of
battles, and, perhaps, after the fight is over, find themselves in the
same hospital, they learn a mutual confidence and respect. Whitman called it "adhesiveness." And he thought "adhesiveness" a
force which binds disparate individuals into a social and spiritual
whole. There is no better expression of the mood of the religion of
humanity than that to be found in a few lines which Whitman left
among his unpublished manuscripts:

> I write not hymns
> I see the building of churches
> If I build God a church it shall be a church to men and women.
> If I write hymns they shall be all to men and women
> If I become a devotee, it shall be to men and women.[20]

∾

The religion of humanity was, in a sense, the reappearance of the
humanism and the faith in science and in reason of the eighteenth-
century Enlightenment. But the evolutionary hypothesis of Darwin and the positivism of August Comte had intervened between
President Ezra Stiles and Octavius Brooks Frothingham. Frothingham and Ingersoll borrowed from Comte the phrase "religion of
humanity"; but their creed was more a religious expression of
Comtean positivism than a phase of Comte's religion of humanity.
How much beyond the name the new humanism owed to the
French philosopher is difficult to say. In the early post-Appomattox years there appeared in the United States some associations organized to propagate the Comtean system. The Positivist Society
appeared in New York City in 1871. Soon after, two other organizations with the identical name, the Society of Humanity, came
into being and had brief careers. One of these, which met on Third
Avenue, was a radical group attended by Leon Trotsky,[21] among
others. A different expression of Comteanism was a volume entitled, *A Positivist Primer*, published in New York in 1871 over the
name, C. G. David. The author was David Goodman Croly, father
of a liberal son who, early in the twentieth century, founded *The
New Republic*. Seven years before he brought out the *Primer*,
Croly had written a pamphlet to suggest that the American race
problem might and should be solved by miscegenation, a word

which upon this occasion he contributed to the English language. He dedicated his *Positivist Primer* to "the only supreme being man can ever know, the great but imperfect god, Humanity, in whose image all other gods were made, and for whose service all other gods exist, and to whom all the children of men owe labor, love, and worship." He included in his exposition a brief statement of what he understood to be positivist beliefs: humanity is the supreme being; immortality exists, in objective and subjective forms, but not a conscious life of the mortal faculties; humanity should be paid service, love, and worship, the latter being reverence to the noble qualities in man; wealth should be devoted to humanity, not to individual luxury or aggrandizement; woman should be worshipped as the example of all that is good in humanity. (Worship of woman was one of the most striking features of Comte's bizarre religion of humanity.) But man should direct the practical details of life. Human conduct must be determined, not by rights, but by duties alone. These principles are valid or positive because they are proved by the discoveries of science.

The assessment of the influence of an idea or a system upon the thought-currents of a foreign nation can never be made with accuracy. So the problem of the relation of Comte to the American religion of humanity cannot be fully solved. That his contribution to the movement was important is evident. It is also clear that the religion of humanity was primarily an American movement arising out of native needs. One of these was the need for intellectual freedom. Pre-Sumter America had been dominantly rural, and most of the intellectual activity in American country life, both in the North and the South, had been carried on within the frame of evangelical Protestantism. The denominations, particularly the larger churches, had an influence in American civilization the extent of which is difficult for a twentieth-century generation to comprehend. The conservatism of organized religion and that of rural communities complemented one another. The vast influence of science upon American thought at the end of the century was due in part to the relative decline of rural communities and to the rise of the new city. The city was made possible by technological advance. So also was the industrialism which was transforming American civilization. The early prophets of the religion of humanity were men who sensed the importance of science as a creative instrument and who were, at the same time, aware of the hold which the old orthodoxy had on the minds of America. That Andrew D.

White had to fight for the principle of education free from religious control was evidence of the American temper of the 1870's.

The religion of humanity in its early anti-theological phase was an effort to implement the doctrine of the free individual by establishing intellectual liberty. It was also an attempt to discover the fundamental law in nature and in humankind without reference to a monarch deity, such as that of Calvinism. The prophets of the religion of humanity insisted that the individual apprehends this fundamental law through reason and reason alone. They rejected the mysticism of transcendentalism, together with the Christian doctrine of inspiration. They taught that the regeneration of individuals is the result of intelligence, rather than of the conversion emphasized by the evangelists. Before the war it had been a common American belief that Christianity and democracy would save the world. The prophets of the religion of humanity sought to separate the American democratic faith from the old orthodoxy of Protestantism.

Frothingham and Ingersoll, however, did not attempt to dissociate democracy from religion. They understood the driving force of religious faith. They did not seek to establish a cold and highly intellectualized humanism. They held aloft the noblest ideals of the race. They reminded their fellows that those ideals had been born in the minds of men and because of this fact were a just measure of the quality of human nature. Humankind, taught by Christianity through the centuries to think ill of themselves, had attributed these ideals to the gods. Men, taught Frothingham and Ingersoll, are rather themselves the gods, if they will but realize the nobility of which they are capable.

The path which led from the religion of humanity back to Emerson is clear. Emerson taught that the individual man holds in his hands the hammer of Thor. Emerson, however, put his faith in an intuition which transcended reason; Frothingham and Ingersoll returned to the faith in reason of the eighteenth century. But their god was no shadowy deistical Author of Nature. They sought their inspiration in that vision of human perfection which is the noblest product of human thought. The prophets of the religion of humanity, insisting as they did that men hold their destiny in their own hands, were attempting to supplant an outworn Christianity with the American democratic faith. They sought to make democracy, and democracy alone, the religion of the nation.

Chapter 16

THE RELIGION OF
HUMANITY AT WORK

DURING THE FIRST HALF of the nineteenth century the citizens of the Republic lived in a world of flux as the frontier hurried toward the Pacific and industrialism began the transformation of the northeastern states. After Appomattox the speed of social change accelerated. The last and most turbulent frontier came and went as settlers reclaimed the dry high plains from the wilderness. When the land available for human habitation had been occupied, Frederick Jackson Turner pointed out that an epoch in American history had come to an end, and that Americans were entering a new world. This world, of course, was that of the city. In the last four decades of the nineteenth century the gargantuan metropolis came into being where railroads converged upon a favorable harbor, upon a river junction, or upon a strategically located bit of lake shore.

Because of industrial exploitation, the natural wealth increased as a mountain reservoir rises when the snow melts on the uplands. But an ever-growing proportion of the husbanded water was sluiced off to irrigate the lands of the few. Giganticism appeared in industry, and the intimate personal relations of the small economic enterprise vanished. The distance between the worker and the owner-manager became great. There was no friendly path between the company house of the Pennsylvania coke-worker and the Fifth Avenue palace of Henry Clay Frick. It was equally as far from the railway office of Jay Gould to the farmstead served by the Erie. Social distances in the latter decades of the nineteenth century should be measured in terms of power; democratic equalitarianism disappeared as industrial and financial giants rose above the ranks of common men.

197

Europeans of the late nineteenth century who looked at the United States announced, with a sense of superiority, that Americans had surrendered to materialism. There was much evidence to support the contention. The materialism of the Gilded Age was sufficient to disturb that patriot, Samuel Clemens. The rise to power of the robber barons displayed a coarseness and brutality unequalled in American history. Seizing the machines which the engineers created, the new economic overlords used them as instruments for the amassing of private wealth. Many of them exploited the resources of the nation with almost no sense of social responsibility. In spite of their ruthlessness, moreover, they were the heroes of the last nineteenth-century generation. Foreign observers pointed to them as proof that a popular materialism had triumphed in the civilization of the western Republic. But such onlookers failed to observe among the common people certain movements caused, in part, by the very activities of the economic overlords, which expressed a vague but genuine humanistic idealism. Groping and only half articulate efforts to preserve the old ideal of the free individual stirred the American masses. The new humanism owed little to the theorists of the religion of humanity; yet as it expressed itself among the farmers and the wage earners it translated into social action the ideals of Octavius Brooks Frothingham and of Robert Ingersoll.

The factors which brought about the new humanism of the common people were two—insecurity for the individual and the increase in national wealth. After 1865 the problem of poverty shouldered its way as never before into American consciousness. Poverty was not new in American civilization. There had been plenty of rural poor as early as the seventeenth century. The standard of living of the Lincoln family spending a winter in an open-face camp on Pidgeon Creek in Indiana was not far above that of the forest-dwelling Indians. Nor was the urban poverty of the post-Appomattox years a new phenomenon. Since the times of Increase Mather's Boston the Atlantic Coast cities had fed their paupers. Mathew Carey and Theodore Parker, moreover, had pioneered before 1861 in rousing the social conscience of the citizens of the nation.

After 1865 the static hopelessness of the slum in the midst of increasing national wealth became a paradox which did not go undiscovered. The blighted areas of the cities increased in size and in population. Not many blocks from their tenements the poor could see that conspicuous leisure and conspicuous consumption to which

Thorstein Veblen pointed as the symbolic behavior designating an emerging economic aristocracy. In the 1870's American architecture broke out with a rash of jig-saw ornament. A mansard roof, topped with a cast iron railing, was the correct expression of elegance. The objective was ostentation. The overstuffed furniture emphasized ease. The Pullman car appeared on the railroad, not to bring to the United States the first-class compartment of Europe, for in the Western democracy all citizens traveled first class, but rather to enable those who could afford it to travel in greater comfort and privacy. In the brown decades it was not only poverty but also the visualization of the benefits of affluence which bred discontent. The tawdry display of the General Grant period created in the underling the desire to achieve a better life.

More important in causing the appearance of labor and agrarian movements was the factor of insecurity. The farmers, particularly those of the prairies and the plains, whose fields were far from the markets of the East and of Europe, discovered, after 1865, that they faced, beside the age-old hazards of nature, new ones which sprang from the arrangements of society. The price level began a general decline in 1865 which did not end until 1896. The husbandman who hauled his produce to the rural depot soon learned that the railroad which served him was also his master. And he found, moreover, that such railway magnates as Jay Gould were not benevolent despots but were, rather, overlords who were prepared to fleece him with fraudulent bond issues or to squeeze him with ruinous freight rates, as the exigencies of the accumulation of private wealth dictated. As time passed and the farmers of the frontier could not liquidate the mortgages on their holdings, they saw in the money lender a dangerous enemy. "Wall Street" became in the 1880's a name describing an ogre.

Insecurity brought anxiety also to the wage earner of the city and the mill town. To the periodic disasters inherent in the business cycle were added those hazards for the job-holder created by that stream of immigrants which debouched upon American shores and spread out, like a river flood, over the nation. At the same time evolution of technology threatened craftsmen with the obsolescence of their skills. The tempo of industrial change increased as the century drew to a close. Out of the flux of industry came opportunities as well as hazards. Many aggressive and able individuals escaped from the ranks of the wage earners and became employer-managers. Many of the economic overlords of the period had humble origins. But opportunity did not ameliorate the lot of those who either could not or did not take advantage of it. An American proletariat appeared. The homes of its members were to be found in the urban slums. For these dwellers in what Benjamin O. Flower called the "social cellar" the conditions of life were hard and its hazards at times overwhelming.

The inevitable human adjustment to danger, as old as man himself, is suggested by the herd of bison which draws together to face the wolves. Cooperation became the watchword among the farmers and workers alike. Men banded together for mutual help and protection. The phenomenon was not new in America. Cooperation among the farmers through the Grange was an evolutionary outgrowth of the barn-raising or house-raising bees of the frontier. The cooperation of trade unionism in the United States was a generation old when Sumter fell. Some of the prewar communistic societies, surviving after 1865, reminded Americans of the grandiose hopes of the Owenites and Fourierists. Cooperation was no new idea after 1865, but it achieved a new social significance. It took many forms and had many motives. Only the more important can be considered here.

The golden age of fraternal orders in the United States occurred in the years from 1865 to 1910 when Americans were moving from an old to a new civilization. In this period of transition the rapidity of social change increased for multitudes of individuals the sense and fact of insecurity. Fraternal orders offered a limited protection of their members in the form of insurance or mutual aid of other kinds. Some thirty-five hundred mutual assessment associations came into being between 1870 and 1910; of these probably three thousand failed. The average life of those which disappeared was fifteen years. Tens of thousands of Americans were identified with such cooperative enterprises. The rise of fraternal organizations cannot be explained wholly on the theory of economic determinism. Many of them were efforts to achieve a fuller life. The utilities of fraternalism, so great that secret societies go back in their origins to the undeveloped stages of human culture, need not be enumerated here. Suffice it to call attention to a few particular values emphasized among these organizations which proliferated between 1865 and the end of the century. Among the members of the colored race the development of secret orders suggested the importance of fraternity as compensation for a position of social inferiority. In his working hours the colored citizen might be an ash man or a domestic servant, but at night as a worshipful grand master his spirit was supported by sash and epaulets. Among immigrant groups fraternal orders assisted individuals to hold fast to their native culture and helped to satisfy the nostalgic longings of strangers in a foreign land. To the low-paid white collar class arising in the new cities secret societies offered escape from the drabness of a life chained to the routine of the counter. For the bank clerk or the bookkeeper the doors which swung only when the pass word was spoken opened upon a world of romance, a never-never land in which ideals became realities and men were brothers.

The ancient Masonic order had appeared in America in the eighteenth century. A few other societies had established themselves before 1861. After Appomattox, however, fraternities sprang up to serve the needs of every class and every group. There were burial societies and insurance enterprises. Some were promotion schemes to enrich their organizers. Most of them, however, sincerely aimed to satisfy deep human cravings. They were essentially religious organizations. Their number and success suggests that the traditional churches were not meeting adequately the needs of the new day. The faith upon which they were founded was usually neither Protestantism nor Catholicism, though the traditional doctrines of either might be accorded a formal deference. Theirs was the type of religion of which Francis E. Abbot spoke in the pages of the *Index* when he insisted that religion is nothing more than man's effort to perfect himself and that it springs from that element of universality in human nature making all peoples one. The post-Appomattox fraternalism expressed in social organizations the mood and the ideals of Abbot's religion of humanity. Of the organizations which appeared after 1865 the two most important for the present purposes were the Patrons of Husbandry and the Noble Order of the Knights of Labor.

∽

The Patrons of Husbandry, otherwise known as the Grange, was founded in 1867, and before many years took its place in thousands of rural hamlets beside the Church as a social institution of major importance. Its early growth was stimulated by the agrarian revolt against the railroad chicanery and domination. For a few years it assumed a quasi-political character while militant farmers developed within state governments devices for regulating the common carriers. The political phase, however, soon ended.

The appearance of the Patrons of Husbandry just after the close of the Civil War was significant of more than hostility to the railway barons. The words of a Grange song popular in the 1870's expressed more than was intended:

> The farmer's the chief of the nation,
> The oldest of nobles is he;
> How blest beyond others his station;
> From want and from envy how free;
> His patent was granted in Eden
> Long ages and ages ago;
> O, the farmer, the farmer forever,
> Three cheers for the plow, spade, and hoe.

The important thing about the verse is its date. It attempted to express the rural mood of Whittier's "Snowbound," published in 1866. Whittier's farmer suggested an age already passing, when the husbandman was the chief American type. Land gave to the small freeholder of the North and West the dignity which is born of independence. In the South land was the foundation of an aristocracy which had a lively sense of social responsibility and which led America in the cultivation of manners. A farmer, before 1861, might think of himself as a Northerner or a Southerner, but rarely as a member of a class. Times changed after 1865. The Southern planters were gone. Cities rose in the North with incredible swiftness. The urbanite of the last third of the nineteenth century was inclined to make a butt of his country cousin. To the would-be sophisticates of the new and raw urban communities the son of the old pioneer had become a bumpkin. The epithets "rube" and "hayseed" came into the American vernacular. The stage farmer with whiskers became a popular comedy character. Crevasses were opening in American society. The city stood over against the country. The city, moreover, became the seat of economic power. And the urban community was the scene of the most rapid advances in civilization. The countrymen followed, often belatedly, where the city led. As the century drew toward its close, the farmer had to contend with a sense of inferiority. At the same time, as the price level continued to drop and disaster overtook the husbandmen, particularly in the Mississippi Valley, anger flared up.

The early Grange and its song which proclaimed the farmer as the "oldest of nobles" and the "chief of the nation" should be viewed against such a background. The Patrons of Husbandry was not primarily an expression of organized revolt. It was, rather, an effort to achieve the good life. Its primary purpose was to add to the richness of living by means of a new institution in which persons of similar interests could enjoy the pleasures and benefits of fellowship. Its members met not only to discuss problems of interest to the husbandmen, but also to share in literary and musical programs, or merely to spend together a pleasant afternoon or evening. The rise of the Grange did not mean that evangelical Protestantism had disappeared from the countryside. The old orthodoxy lived on in rural America and retained a vigor which expressed itself, after 1918, in the revolt of the fundamentalists. But the weakness of Protestantism was its denominationalism. Denominations divided rural society into rival camps. The Grange, avoiding religious disputation, made for solidarity and brotherhood. In the Grange hall Methodists and Baptists could sit down together in peace.

∽

The Knights of Labor was the other significant manifestation of fraternalism after Appomattox. The organization came into being in the 1870's and grew swiftly in the following decade. Because its members were laborers and its meetings in its earlier years secret, it attracted, almost from the beginning of its career, nation-wide attention. It became the hobgoblin for the property-owning American middle class. Churchmen and business leaders assailed the Knights with such vigor that the order gave up its secrecy. But it continued to be essentially a fraternity.

The Knights attempted to organize labor into one big union. They made no distinctions among crafts. In the local assemblies, corresponding roughly to the chapters of fraternities, many trades were normally represented. Carpenters, textile workers, machinists, and unskilled workmen attended the periodic meetings held in the humble halls which were all the order could afford. Theoretically the organization was highly centralized. Terence Powderly, for years the leader of the Knights, exercised, according to the provisions of the constitution, great powers. Actually his leadership was weak and there was a large measure of local autonomy.

The history of the Knights is a narrative of confused policies and sometimes of contradictory objectives. In theory the organization opposed the use of strikes, yet the Knights carried on some spectacular conflicts. Powderly and his advisers strove to secure from state legislatures enactments which would benefit labor. All the social panaceas popular in the decades in which the Knights flourished became the subjects of hopeful discussion. In the propaganda issuing from the national headquarters and called "education" the members heard about cooperatives, Greenbackism, and the single tax. But the Knights had no political philosophy, no definite program. Powderly was no Marx. Powderly was the fumbling leader of an untutored army which aspired to a better life but had only vague ideas as to how it was to be achieved. Yet out of the confusion and futilities of the Knights emerged an ideal, the noblest in the history of American labor. The Knights beheld the vision of labor solidarity, of a brotherhood which would give meaning to the slogan of the order: "An injury to one is the concern of all." They hoped to achieve this brotherhood primarily through association with one another in a fraternal organization in which the humblest unskilled worker was as welcome as the high paid craftsman.

The grandiose nomenclature used by the order to support the dignity of the poor was no more naïve than the romantic architecture of the contemporary rich man's house, but it was more pathetic. There was little to relieve the drabness of life for the underlings in the days before the silver screen, the TV set, and the used car. In many a city block the corner saloon was not only the most important but the only place of entertainment for the man whose wages did not run to more than a few dollars a week. To such people the assemblies of the Knights offered a club. The ritual, which conformed to the familiar fraternal plan, brought a quantum of romance to bleak lives. The organization gave to its members a new sense of security. The Noble Order of the Knights of Labor was at bottom an effort on the part of the wage earners to achieve the good life, to live as men rather than as animals.

The "Labor movement of the 'eighties'," remarked Professor Norman Ware, the historian of the Knights, "was not a business but a religion, not a doctrinal religion like socialism, but a vague, primitive, embryonic sentiment, a religion in the making. The local assembly was something like a congregation living in times of persecution. The early Christians had their catacombs, and it is not irreverence that suggests that the Knights had their secret 'sanctuaries.' "[1]

The Knights crashed at the end of the 1880's after a sudden and spectacular rise. Many reasons contributed to the collapse. Their leaders were inept. They were badly organized for industrial combat. They were attacked by the propertied class as a conspiracy against society. After the Haymarket affair of 1886 the epithet "anarchist" was used against them. Important as were these reasons for failure, the principal cause was to be found in the fact that the Knights had undertaken an impossible task. The labor group to which the Knights hoped to bring solidarity was a potpourri of nationalities, speaking a babel of tongues, and divided by hostilities brought from the Old World. Labor had no common language, no homogeneous culture. The Russian immigrant disliked his Polish fellow worker. The French Canadian was suspicious of the Irishman. Among American workers in the early post-Appomattox decades the boundaries of social groupings followed national and religious lines. Men were Slavs first or Catholics first and wage earners second. The effort of the Knights to establish solidarity in such a group was a fantastic bit of Utopian idealism.

The skilled workers withdrew from the Noble Order and, under the leadership of Samuel Gompers, founded the American Federation of Labor. The new organization accepted Carnegie's gospel of wealth with one modification. Gompers demanded that the worker whose bargaining power was unequal to the strength of the new economic overlord be permitted that sense of dignity which springs from the knowledge that in the trade union he possesses an effective weapon with which to defend, if need be, his vital interests. In the doctrine of the closed shop the A. F. of L. challenged the absolutism of management in industry.

Gompers was not only the organizer but the spokesman of the trade union movement which gained strength in the last decade of the century. "The earth was intended for all mankind and not for a few," he remarked in 1896. "The true object of the labor movement is the seeking of a rational method by which these wrongs can be righted. It was born out of hunger for food at first, and then grew with the hunger for better homes, better lives and higher aspirations and ideals." "The object," he added in 1914, "is to attain complete social justice." The postulates of the labor movement, in the expressed philosophy of Gompers, were that the concentration of wealth and power into the hands of the few was a violation of the moral law and that the wrong should be corrected by returning to the individual workman the freedom which had been taken from him by the growth of the vast, impersonal, and autocratic corporation. He rejected paternalism either at the hands of management or of the State. "Doing for people what they can and ought to do for themselves is a dangerous experiment," he remarked in 1915. "In the last analysis the welfare of the workers depends upon their own initiative."[2]

The Gompers philosophy had parallels with that of Calhoun. The South Carolinian in proposing his theory of nullification argued that the Southern minority must be given an effective weapon with which to defend itself against the superior political power of the Northern majority. Gompers, in advocating the trade union and the closed shop demanded that the worker, impotent as an individual, be permitted a weapon with which to defend himself against the superior economic power of management. Both the labor leader and the Senator assumed that the doctrine of the free individual must atrophy if the individual is rendered incapable of self-defense. Calhoun, moreover, pointed out that, if the minority is prevented from protecting its vital interests when these are threatened, loyalty to the nation must inevitably suffer erosion. Gompers did not raise the point. His daily task was to meet the charge of his more reactionary adversaries that labor was un-American. He met these accusations not only with denials but with a homespun philosophy of humanism. Gompers saw in the labor movement the ideals of the religion of humanity at work in society. "The trade unions," he said in 1898, "are the legitimate outgrowth of modern societary and industrial conditions. . . . They were born of the necessity of the workers to protect and defend themselves from encroachment, injustice and wrong. . . . To protect the workers in their inalienable rights to a higher and better life; to protect them, not only as equals before the law, but also in their rights to the product of their labor; to protect their lives, their limbs, their health, their homes, their firesides, their liberties as men, as workers, and as citizens; to overcome and conquer prejudice and antagonism; to secure to them the right to life, and the opportunity to maintain that life; the right to be full sharers in the abundance which is the result of their brain and brawn, and the civilization of which they are the founders and the mainstay; to this the workers are entitled. . . . The attainment of these is the glorious mission of the trade unions."[3]

❧

Gompers was indebted for much of his social philosophy to a theory which was formulated in the United States even before the organization of the Knights of Labor. Ira Steward and George E. McNeill organized in Boston in 1869 the Eight-Hour League. Their effort was the outgrowth of an older short-hour movement which appeared in both Europe and America in the first half of the nineteenth century. Under the leadership of Steward and McNeill the Boston organization propounded a social theory which became the chief and the successful rival of Marxian socialism in the American labor movement of the last third of the century. "Poverty," said Steward in 1872, "is the great fact with which the labor movement deals."[4] For the solution of the problem of poverty he offered a seven-point program. Laborers should improve their condition and raise their status by their own efforts and should not depend upon the paternalism of the private humanitarian or the State. Shorter hours is the formula which will enable labor to improve its condition and to raise its status. The eight-hour day, without reduction of pay, will give the laborer leisure and, permitting him to leave his work without being exhausted, will enable him to become more civilized and to raise his standard of living. Shorter hours will give employment to more men. Reducing unemployment and raising the standard of living of the laboring masses will increase the home market for the products of industry. Shorter hours will cause more of the profits of industry to go into wages and less into dividends and will, therefore, tend to equalize the distribution of wealth. Ultimately this process will cause the wage system to disappear and labor will own and manage industry in the form of cooperatives.

What was the significance for the traditional democratic faith of the movements toward cooperation which stirred the farmer and the labor groups after Appomattox? They were the results of political freedom. Free men entered voluntary associations for purposes of fellowship and of mutual aid. Most of these cooperative enterprises were in the sense of social philosophy efforts to implement the doctrine of the free individual. They suggested that freedom does not imply the isolated man. Freedom is enhanced by cooperation. In the fraternal orders in particular appeared the implied philosophy that individual freedom is best expressed through and preserved by that principle of brotherhood so much emphasized by the prophets of the religion of humanity. The end of freedom was the achievement of the good life and the means to the end was self-improvement fostered by cooperation. Most of the cooperative enterprises were non-political. They were efforts to enhance the dignity of human nature by giving to the workers a sense of security born of the power to defend their vital interests. All these non-political cooperative efforts fitted into the pattern of the mid-nineteenth-century doctrine of the free individual. He should stand on his own feet. He should discipline himself. He should look forward to the time when the need for the external discipline of the State should be reduced to a minimum.

Chapter 17

THE EVOLUTION OF THE
PHILOSOPHY OF THE
GENERAL WELFARE STATE

In 1869, TWO YEARS AFTER Frothingham founded the
Free Religious Association, a young California journalist named
Henry George was in New York City attempting to establish a
telegraphic news service from the metropolis to the Pacific Coast.
In intervals between work he strolled about Manhattan fascinated
by the evidences of increasing wealth and developing culture. Cor-
nelius Vanderbilt, creator of the New York Central, rode about
town behind as fine a pair of horses as America afforded. Edwin
Booth had returned to the stage two years before after a voluntary
exile due to his brother Wilkes' disgrace. On February 3, 1869, the
great Hamlet opened Booth's Theatre on the corner of Sixth Avenue and Twenty-third Street, where night after night fashionable
society applauded sumptuous Shakespearean productions. The
young man from the coast was impressed by the brilliance of New
York. But he was more interested in the city's blighted areas.
Charles Dickens had once visited New York's Five Points and had
published a description which made that slum notorious in two continents. In this area only a minority of infants had the misfortune
to survive. Here youth decayed from what the inhabitants of the
Points called with a wry picturesqueness the "tenement house rot."
Vice and crime were normal ways of life in the Five Points and in
other less celebrated slums. New York was a city of contrasts where
Henry George faced the old riddle of civilization, the apparent
partnership between progress and poverty. One day the sensitive
young Californian, tramping the sidewalks, musing, saw suddenly
revealed before him the pattern of a noble life. Many years later he
told an intimate friend what happened. "Once, in daylight, and in

a city street," he said, "there came to me a thought, a vision, a call—give it what name you please. But every nerve quivered. And there and then I made a vow."[1] On that day Henry George dedicated himself to a search for the cause which without justice or mercy condemned little children to man-made hells. Dwight L. Moody would have called what happened to George a conversion. William James might appropriately have included the episode in his *Varieties of Religious Experience*. But, though George experienced conversion after the pattern of evangelical Protestantism, it was to a social rather than to a theological faith. The change was significant. It suggested that a new era was emerging which, in spite of its novelty, was keeping contact with American tradition.

Neither Henry George's mood nor his objective was new to the United States. For three decades before the Civil War that militant Unitarian friend of Emerson, Theodore Parker, had crusaded against the slum conditions of Boston. In the end his campaign to achieve righteousness had been deflected and had become a part of that larger movement to free the black man. Parker died on the eve of Sumter. But the battalions of freedom went on to triumph in the Emancipation Proclamation. The outcome of the Civil War bred a confident hope that humanitarian objectives could be realized with equal finality. Out of this humanitarianism grew a new version of the doctrine of the free individual. The gospel of wealth emphasized freedom from control by the political State. A new rationalism, born of the religion of humanity, established the concept of social planning and proposed the State as the best instrument available to free men in their efforts to destroy social evils and to further human welfare. Henry George was only one of a growing company of postwar Americans who saw in poverty a new slavery, which, like the old, destroyed the souls of men. On that day in New York City George saw a vision of a new Gettysburg and a new Appomattox.

To say that the philosophy of Henry George was the outgrowth of his own experience is to repeat what is true of all thinking men. Yet, perhaps in a peculiar way the events of his life conditioned his thought. He was born in Philadelphia in 1839, three years after Emerson published *Nature*. In his youth evangelical Protestantism reached its American apogee. But Henry George's devout father and mother worshipped after the manner of the Episcopal faith. Family poverty prevented an advanced education while family piety fixed in the boy's mind the accepted patterns of religious and moral ideas. In 1855 young George, sailing as foremast boy to Australia and to India, experienced a new freedom and gained a new perspective. When he returned, he found the home atmosphere too stuffy, and, partly as a consequence, sought his fortune in the California of the vigilante days. A sailor's training and the printer's trade were his only skills. The coarse materialism of the mining camp and the raw coast cities erased the marks of his childhood religious training and left him a young man's skepticism, disturbed, however, at times by nostalgia for the old faith.

He had little success at first on the California frontier; yet, when twenty-two and virtually penniless, he married a Catholic girl of eighteen. Ill fortune pursued him in spite of his desperate struggles to maintain his home. Having neither food in larder nor money in pocket when his second child arrived, he went into the street of his home town and begged five dollars from a stranger. George knew how it felt to be poor and hungry. Ultimately a moderate success came, but he never knew economic security until after *Progress and Poverty* became a best seller. Four experiences conditioned his thought: his early religious training, the frontier moods of materialism and of individual liberty, personal poverty, and his discovery in New York City of the social extremes possible in an industrial age. Though he cheerfully recognized his debt to English classical economists, his philosophy was essentially an American product.

It sprang primarily from the democratic faith. George never got outside the bounds of that humanistic thought-pattern and from it he derived those social beliefs that made him a crusader literally until the day of his death. But he neither knew nor followed Emerson. Henry George chose Thomas Jefferson for his patron saint; one of the Californian's most cherished books was Jefferson's compilation of the sayings of Jesus. George went back to the eighteenth-century Enlightenment for the foundations of this thought. The doctrines of democracy for him were those of the Declaration of Independence. He thought in terms of equality as well as of liberty. "In our time, as in times before," said George in 1879, "creep on the insidious forces that, producing inequality, destroy Liberty. On the horizon the clouds begin to lower. Liberty calls to us again. We must follow her further; we must trust her fully. Either we must accept her fully or she will not stay."[2] George's faith never failed. Twenty-eight years later, on the eve of his death, he repeated the democrat's creed: "I believe . . . that unto the common people, the honest democracy, the democracy that believes that all men are created equal, would bring a power that would revivify not merely this imperial city, not merely the State, not merely the country, but the world."[3] In one essential he departed from the democratic formula commonly accepted in the middle of the century; he did not see the hand of God in the course of American history. "It is blasphemy," declared George, "that attributes to the inscrutable decrees of Providence the sufferings and brutishness that come of poverty."[4] But Henry George's was no passive acceptance of the democratic faith; he sought to make it a power for righteousness in the land.

Progress and Poverty began with a religious experience in 1869 on the sidewalks of New York. As it took form in George's mind during the next ten California years, it led him to the discovery of God, not the God of the Methodist preachers he heard in California or of the Episcopalian rectors he knew in his childhood, but the Author of Nature of Thomas Jefferson and of the eighteenth-century Deists. For the philosophy of Henry George such a God was fundamental. In the beginning, George affirmed, the Author of Nature created the earth and man to live upon it and He endowed man with a natural right to use the earth. To buttress a position which was essentially his own, George fell back upon the authority of Herbert Spencer and pointed out that the Englishman had formulated the same idea in the first edition of *Social Statics*. Upon that natural rights major premise hung the entire philosophy of George. "It is not enough that men should vote; it is not enough that they should be theoretically equal before the law. They must have liberty to avail themselves of the opportunities and means of life; they must stand on equal terms with reference to the bounties of nature. Either this, or Liberty withdraws her light! Either this or darkness comes on, and the very forces that progress has evolved turn to powers that work destruction. This is the universal law."[5]

If George's vow to discover the cause of poverty followed the pattern of a religious conversion, his discovery a few months later of the answer to his question conformed to the pattern of religious revelation. He was riding alone on horseback through a California countryside where new land offices, erupting like pimples from the plain, proclaimed the disease known as a boom. Everywhere men were grabbing what they thought were the most promising spots, each hoping that his land would soon be found in the center of a large and flourishing city. George rode on to the hills from which he looked back across an expanse of virgin country at cattle grazing in the distance. To make conversation he asked a passing stranger the price of land in the vicinity. "I don't know exactly," was the answer, "but there is a man over there who will sell some land for a thousand dollars an acre." "Like a flash it came upon me," wrote George in later years, "that there was the reason of advancing poverty with advancing wealth. With the growth of population land grows in value, and the men who work it must pay more for the privilege. I turned back, amidst quiet thought, to the perception that then came to me and has been with me ever since."[6] Every man, thought George, has a God-given right to use the earth. "Our primary social adjustment [the private ownership of land] is a denial of justice. In allowing one man to own the land on which and from which other men live, we have made them his bondsmen in a degree which increases as material progress goes on. This is the subtle alchemy that in ways they do not realize is extracting from the masses in every civilized country the fruits of their weary toil . . . that is bringing political despotism out of political freedom, and must soon transmute democratic institutions into anarchy."[7] George's reference to anarchy was not mere rhetoric. The nation-wide labor wars of 1877 had for a few weeks thoroughly frightened the industrial East. German anarchists were appearing in America and were beginning to propagate their creed through pamphlet and press. Excitable persons began talking of possible social revolution. George published *Progress and Poverty* in 1879. After a discouraging start, it achieved a great popular success. By 1905 it was estimated that two million copies published in several languages had been sold. Henry George proposed a cure for American social ills which, avoiding both revolution and socialism, would conform to the tenets of the democratic faith. As a result wage earners and insecure small capitalists flocked to his standard. When anxious persons turned the pages of *Progress and Poverty*, they discovered that the author appeared to know his economic science. He spoke the language of Ricardo and of John Stuart Mill and gave life to their pale abstractions. He affirmed in phrases that all could understand that the social crisis which seemed to threaten the United States was the result of a failure to understand the nature of economic law.

Henry George hunted through the literature of classical economics for the theories and principles that might be useful to him. He rejected with the two Careys the Malthusian theory of population, but made Ricardo's law of rent the center of his economic discussion. Like William Graham Sumner and the other classical economists, Henry George was an ardent free trader. Turning to history, George argued that the reason for the failure of the ancient civilizations was the denial, through the permitting of private ownership in land, of the most basic of natural laws, namely, that all men must be as free to use the earth as they are to breathe the air. Given such freedom, the Malthusian doctrine breaks down because technological progress, George affirmed, will outrun population. George did not propose the complete nationalization of land but merely, as a practical measure, the appropriation by the State of the unearned increment in value which society itself brings about.

After the publication of *Progress and Poverty*, single tax clubs appeared in large numbers in England and America. By 1905 the pieces of *"Progress and Poverty* literature" from the pen of George alone were estimated by his son to have had a circulation of five million.

But the popularity of his social panacea is not the primary reason for the significance of Henry George. The implications of his doctrine rather than its formulation made 1879 an important milestone in the history of American social philosophy. George affirmed with Mathew and Henry Carey that, when economic laws are understood and obeyed, they lead to social justice. Malthus, calling in war and famine to correct overpopulation, declared by implication that ethics has no place in science. George assumed that science leads to meliorism; he believed that the natural laws which underlie society will, when fully understood, be found to coincide with those of morals. Discover natural law, obey it, he declared, and society will be on the road to Utopia. He was frank about his Utopianism. "But if, while there is yet time," he said, "we turn to justice and obey her, if we trust Liberty and follow her, the dangers that now threaten must disappear, the forces that now menace will turn to agencies of elevation . . . With want destroyed; with greed changed to noble passions; with the fraternity that is born of equality taking the place of jealousy and fear that now array men against each other; with mental power loosed by conditions that give to the humblest comfort and leisure; and who shall measure the heights to which civilization may soar? Words fail the thought! It is the Golden Age."[8] Man, therefore, has his destiny in his own hands. By using the State as an instrument for taking one specific economic action, namely the single tax, he can create a new and ethically superior society. Man can be a social creator, taught George. The State can be transformed from a necessary evil into a beneficent instrument. Economics can be made to evolve from a static into a dynamic science. And ethics must be the guide for both economic and legislative action. Henry George proposed a nine-teenth-century version of the eighteenth-century belief in the per-fectibility of man. Like Jefferson, he put his faith in reason and in democracy. For the determinism of Malthus and Ricardo he substituted a creative humanism.

The world has never known a prophet more sincere than Henry George. From 1869 to 1897 his life was one unremitting crusade. He plunged in the late '80's into political reform and made a spectacular, though unsuccessful, run for Mayor of New York. He was called again to political service in 1897 when he was asked to lead the fight against Tammany Hall a second time. No longer robust, he sought medical advice and was told by his physician that vigorous campaigning would probably prove fatal. "But I have got to die," he replied to the doctor. "How can I die better than serving humanity? Besides, so dying will do more for the cause than anything I am likely to be able to do in the rest of my life."[9] His wife, who had made his home a singularly happy one, supported his decision. "You should do your duty at whatever cost" was her reply to his question as to whether to accept the proposed nomination. Five days before the election he suffered a fatal stroke of apoplexy. A hundred thousand mourners filed past his bier in Grand Central Palace and an equal number failed to gain admittance. The funeral cortege that followed his body to the City Hall and across Brooklyn Bridge to Greenwood Cemetery was one of the most remarkable of American tributes to a private citizen. The acclaim did not end with the century. "Henry George," said John Dewey in 1933, "stands almost alone in our history as an example of a man who, without scholastic background, succeeded by sheer force of observation and thinking that were directed by human sympathy, and who left an indelible impress on not only his own generation and country but on the world and the future."[10]

Henry George was the evangelist of the new rationalism. An expanding and unregulated industrialism brought both good and evil to the American people. In the swiftly growing cities of the end of the century, populated by men and women drawn from the nations of the world, indifference, greed, and lack of knowledge of how to live in metropolitan centers compounded the evils of the time. George was a prophet who insisted that the evils were not necessary—an indigenous prophet whose basic ideas came out of the

American experience. Only in America could one man see in his lifetime the evolution from the empty frontier to the city slum. George, carrying forward the criticism of industrialism and urbanism that found early champions in Emerson, Thoreau, and Theodore Parker, powerfully furthered an indigenous movement for reform that achieved national importance in the Progressive Era.

∾

If George was the evangelist of the new rationalism, Lester Frank Ward was its philosopher. Ward was in his day one of the most learned men in America. He worked in natural as well as in social science. His volume, *Dynamic Sociology*, published in 1883 when *Progress and Poverty* was becoming a best seller, marks the beginning of American sociology. But in spite of his science, Ward's mood was that of Henry George. Ward was not content to limit his investigations to a cold and detached analysis of the conditions of human society. "I was an apostle of human progress," he wrote late in life, "and I believed that this could be greatly accelerated by society itself. I therefore wanted a progressive sociology."[11] Ingersoll and Frothingham believed that science could be made to take the place of supernaturalism as the foundation of a philosophy of meliorism. Ward showed how the task could be accomplished. He was the St. Augustine of the American cult of science. More than any other single individual, Ward formulated the basic pattern of the American concept of the planned society.

The boyhood experiences of Lester Frank Ward were similar to those of Ingersoll. Ward, a tenth child, was born in 1841 in Illinois whither his father had gone from New York State to work as a millwright on the locks of the Illinois and Michigan Canal. When the future scientist and sociologist was fourteen, the family jolted to Iowa in a "small covered wagon," living all the way on game which the guns of Lester and an older brother provided. "Roaming wildly over the boundless prairies of northern Iowa in the fifties, interested in every animal, bird, insect, and flower I saw, but not knowing what science was, scarcely having ever heard of zoology, ornithology, entomology, or botany, without a single book on any of those subjects, and not knowing a person in the world who could give me the slightest information with regard to them, what chance," asked Ward, "was there of my becoming a naturalist?"[12] Before his death in 1913, however, his contributions to biology, to geology, and to paleontology brought him an international reputation.

The death of his father ended the Iowa experience after two summers. Young Ward sought a job in the small manufacturing enterprise which an older brother was attempting to establish in Pennsylvania. He was already a student, avid for languages, studying Greek in his brother's shop and, at home, keeping a diary in French. Like Thoreau he taught school. The war came on. For a time he continued his teaching and his education, then he fell in love, married, and enlisted. Three wounds at Chancellorsville ended his campaigning and, in 1866, got him a government clerkship. For forty years he held minor posts at Washington. He published a large number of scientific articles, particularly in the field of paleo-botany. But the true story of his life is the narrative of his building of the edifice of his monistic philosophy. Henry George at the end of his life developed a martyr complex; Ward became in his own mind a deliverer, guiding the people into the land of Canaan. "I became a sort of Moses to them [the laboring classes] to lead them out of the wilderness of human thralldom."[13]

The early thought of Ward recapitulates the thinking and reflects the mood of the religion of humanity. The prairie boy had grown up in communities dominated by evangelical Protestantism. Young Ward attended many churches in Washington after the war. He and his wife, moreover, in the midst of formal studies and other reading went through much of the Old Testament. In 1869 they took up Tom Paine and Voltaire while, at the same time, skeptically attended spiritualist meetings. On September 12, Ward noted in his diary: "I went to the free religious meeting in the Council Chamber. They discussed Christianity, foeticide, and polygamy. I spoke."[14] On November 18 he helped to organize the National Liberal Reform League, an ambitious secret society which began with six members and died a few months later with four. Its objects, in the words of its charter, were "the dissemination of liberal sentiment; the opposition to all forms of superstition; the exposition of all fallacious moral and religious doctrines, and the establishment of the principles of mental, moral, and religious liberty, as embodied in the Declaration of Independence and the Constitution of the United States."[15] In a private memorandum Ward stated more explicitly the purpose of the organization. "Its members agree to leave one another in the undisputed enjoyment of all other tenets, doctrines, beliefs and isms, and unite upon the cardinal principles of hostility to the leading doctrinal teachings of the so-called Catholic and evangelical Protestant Churches, and of zeal for the triumph of reason and science over faith and theology."[16] Paine would have applauded the earnest young men who were seeking thus to re-establish in the national capital the spirit of the eighteenth-century Enlightenment. When the League was formed, Ward was working on the second chapter of his *Dynamic Sociology* which he called at the time *The Great Panacea*.

But work on this opus progressed slowly, for the corresponding secretary of the National Liberal Reform League became in January, 1870, the editor of the League's journal called *The Iconoclast*. "Science is the great Iconoclast," declared Ward in the second number. "Our civilization depends wholly upon the discovery and application of a few profound scientific and philosophical principles, thought out by a few great minds who hold the shallow babble of priests in utter contempt, and have no time to dabble in theology."[17] The indefatigable editor attacked the current assumption that morality depends upon Christianity and in the second number drove home a shrewd thrust by reprinting from Francis E. Abbot's *Index* an article on the religion of Lincoln by W. H. Herndon. The law partner pointed out that the Great Emancipator did not believe in miracles, the inspiration of the Scriptures, or the divinity of Jesus. He had, in fact, compelled Herndon in 1854 to "erase the name of God from a speech I was about to make." The article, as used by Abbot and Ward, is one of the earliest efforts to use the name of the dead Lincoln as a sanction for particular social and religious beliefs. *The Iconoclast* continued until the middle of 1871, emphasizing the "religious influence of science," disseminating the ideas of Herbert Spencer and the positivism of August Comte, but never referring to the latter's particular brand of the religion of humanity. The editorials were youthful and frequently shrill. There is no evidence that they made any impress on the thought of the day. The importance of the sheet is in the light it throws upon the development of the young philosopher and that of his fellow radicals in the first decade after the war.

Before Ward published his great book, he studied all the important European social philosophies. He was most influenced by Comte but parted company with the Frenchman in insisting that sociology must depend upon psychology rather than upon biology, as Comte affirmed. Ward was equally familiar with the work of the biologists, geneticists, and geologists. No other American social philosopher has set his thought in so well-developed a matrix of nature lore. Beside him in this field his intellectual enemy, William

Graham Sumner, was a sophomore. Nor did Ward use his cosmology, geological history, and biology merely for decorative effect; they were integral parts of his "monistic religion of humanity."

The ultimate in the cosmos, declared the author of *Dynamic Sociology*, speaking the language of classical physics, is matter and energy—pulsating, creative energy, transforming and retransforming matter. The stars in the heavens, the mountains, the trees in the forest, and the mind of man are but different manifestations of this basal energy. Nature is a unit. The movements of planets and of men are both part of a monistic system. Energy and matter, working through natural laws, produced life on the earth and then brought this life to its supreme manifestation in the human mind. Man, equipped with the ability to reason, can become a social engineer. Using his reason and his knowledge he can create a better society.

How can such progress be achieved? The essentials of the formula are simple. That basic energy which permeates the cosmos manifests itself among living forms in desires—for food, for reproduction, for security. These are the forces of nature which alone governed life on the earth until the advent of man. But nature is blind and natural processes are wasteful. Ward, the paleontologist, was impressed with the scores of false starts necessary in the Cenozoic Age before the modern mammals were finally evolved. As a biologist he noted the number of seeds and seedlings required to bring about a single forest tree. Natural forces, moreover, he emphasized, move in no definite direction; evolution goes backward as well as forward. Nevertheless, by this same hit-and-miss evolutionary process, nature had produced the mind of man, endowed with reason and foresight, and in so doing, had brought a new epoch to earth history.

What is the human mind? A function, answered Ward, of that part of his nervous system called the brain. Ward denied the old philosophical dichotomy between mind and matter; he denied the Emerson thesis of a "universal mind." He declared that the individual mind ceases to exist when the body dies.

Ward insisted that ideas rule the world of men. The function of the mind is, by using ideas, to put an end in human society to the wasteful economy of nature and to the blind operation of natural forces. By taking thought man can direct that energy expressed in human desires into socially beneficent channels. The mind can determine the goal to be achieved and the means by which it can be reached.

Before the dawn of science, however, Ward thought, human progress had still been largely the result of the operation of the blind forces of nature. In the beginning, Ward postulated, individual ape-men had struggled against one another in an animal world. With the dawn of mind they had been forced to cooperate to survive. After many centuries social organizations had finally produced the modern State. In such a world, war had been an instrument of progress, stimulating invention, and selecting out the weaker races. But the world had changed when Galileo and Newton had established the foundations of science. By the end of the nineteenth century the time had come for society to leave behind the Darwinian struggle for existence and to set itself to the task of creating a new order. The most urgent need, in Ward's opinion, was to discover the laws of thought. To know these would enhance the power of man more even than a knowledge of the laws of electricity. What social dynamos could be constructed when men understood the nature of thought and the controls which govern it!

Ward looked to experimental psychology to give man this new mastery over nature. But Ward's formula of progress did not end with a research program. "Intelligence, far more than necessity, is the mother of invention," he said in 1885, "and the influence of knowledge as a social factor, like that of wealth, is proportional to the extent of its distribution."[18] Knowledge had transformed one ignorant prairie farm boy into a world figure. Ward was convinced that the intellectual capacities of the common man were underrated and that universal education would not only augment the company of the intellectually elite who are the real leaders of the world but would make the average citizen more productive of ideas, more sympathetic toward social experimentation, and more willing to support intelligent legislation. Education was the foundation of progress. With Darwin and Lamarck, Ward believed in the inheritance of acquired characteristics. Knowledge could not, of course, be transmitted by the germ plasm; what was carried forward was the increased ability to acquire and to use it which resulted from education. For Ward, however, education was not mere child training; it was the search of the human mind for enlightenment; it implied investigation as well as the acquisition of knowledge.

Ward considered education a function of the State and, as a consequence, he urged the concept of the beneficent State. "This irrational distrust of government," he fumed, "not only makes it worse than it otherwise would be, but, so far as this is possible it tends to give it the character it is accused of possessing."[19] The shaft was aimed at William Graham Sumner and the other economic classicists. But Ward rejected Hegel's State worship along with Spencer's *laissez faire*. "There is one way of explaining the sterility of Hegel's philosophy of the state which does not convict him of mental imbecility," . . . he remarked. "This explanation is that he was an astute timeserver."[20] Ward urged, not that the State be set up as an object of worship, but that it be used as an instrument to regulate business, and to secure a more equitable distribution of wealth. He maintained, perhaps under the influence of Simon Patten, in 1889 that underconsumption was the great economic problem. "It is, therefore, useless to talk of increasing production except by the increase of the power to consume."[21] The State must deal with this problem. "There is no need of having any slums."[22] The State must find a solution for the problem of poverty. Malthus' law of population, he added, applies to the world of animals, as Darwin has proved, but not to the society of intelligent men as its formulator thought.

In 1906 Ward etched the portrait of the beneficent State of the future. Legislative bodies "will doubtless need to be maintained, and every new law should be finally adopted by a vote of such bodies, but more and more this will become a merely formal way of putting the final sanction of society on decisions that have been carefully worked out in what may be called the sociological laboratory. Legislation will consist in a series of exhaustive experiments on the part of true scientific sociologists and sociological inventors working on the problems of social physics from the practical point of view. It will undertake to solve not only questions of general interest to the State, . . . but questions of social improvement, the amelioration of the condition of all the people, the removal of whatever privations may still remain, and the adoption of means to the positive increase of the social welfare, in short the organization of human happiness."[23] In such a society democracy would become "sociocracy." Here was Ward's picture of the welfare state. Here was non-Marxist socialism resting on a foundation of democracy.

✧

Faithful single-taxers who read the issue of *The Standard*, the leading organ of their movement, published on August 31, 1889, found a comment by Henry George on a new novel which for more than a year had been the talk of literate Americans. Early in 1888, Edward Bellamy of Chicopee, Massachusetts, had scored a popular triumph with a romance which he called *Looking Backward*. George called it, somewhat unkindly, "a castle in the air with clouds for its foundation." William Dean Howells, on the contrary, liked his friend's book, and in 1898, after Bellamy's death, published in the *Atlantic* a eulogy of the famous Utopian.[24] Before the dean of American letters wrote his words of appreciation a flock of "Nationalist" clubs inspired by Bellamy's vision of the new society had come and gone. Bellamy attracted attention because he followed the new rationalism, frankly and enthusiastically, to its logical extreme. George would have the State take one all-important positive action; Ward would transform it into a laboratory for social experimentation; Bellamy proposed a total socialism.

Looking Backward is a romantic picture of American society in the distant year 2000 after Americans have had about a century to work out the implications of the "Great [but bloodless] Revolution" which Bellamy postulated as occurring in the 1890's. Americans in the year 2000 were, according to the Chicopee romancer, a healthy, happy people who lived in a mechanized world in which machinery not only lifted most of the heavy, wearisome tasks from the shoulders of men but added vastly to their enjoyment of the higher life. The State, directing all activities of production and of distribution, multiplied the national wealth by eliminating waste and so was able to guarantee security to every man, woman, and child. The secret of the change was the abolition of competition among individuals. All persons, from infants to the aged, received an equal income generous enough to provide for all the needs of life. The only inequality was in honors; titles and medals were awarded only to those who stood above their fellows in the service of all. The citizens of the Republic were organized as though they were an army. The youth were educated by the State until they reached the age of twenty-five. They then went for twenty years into labor battalions and with the aid of machines produced the goods upon which society depended. At forty-five, men and women retired to lives of freedom and of leisure. These elders chose from among their number the President and the Council who governed the nation.

Bellamy began his story with the intention merely of writing another book. He had chosen the profession of letters and he had to make a living. During the process of composition, however, he became unexpectedly a convert to his own dream. Through the lines which he gave to a character he confessed his conviction and his hope: "I described the physical felicity, mental enlightenment, and moral elevation which would then attend the lives of men. With fervency I spoke of that new world, blessed with plenty, purified by justice and sweetened by brotherly kindness, the world of which I had indeed dreamed, but which might so easily be made real." Bellamy, like George, believed in simple cures. Both men were convinced that society contained a single vital flaw, the discovery and correction of which would initiate the golden age. "The folly of men, not their hard-heartedness," said a character in Looking Backward, "was the great cause of the world's poverty. It was not the crime of man, nor of any class of men, that made the race so miserable, but a hideous, ghastly mistake, a colossal world-darkening blunder."25 This error was competition; its correction was the principle of brotherhood. "The principle of competition," added Bellamy, "is . . . the application of the brutal law of the survival of the strongest and the most cunning. The principle of the Brotherhood of Humanity is one of the eternal truths that govern the world's progress on lines which distinguish human nature from brute nature."26 "The primal principle of democracy," he went on, reflecting Rousseau, "is the worth and dignity of the individual. That dignity, consisting in the quality of human nature, is essentially the same in all individuals, and therefore equality is the vital principle of democracy. To this intrinsic and equal dignity of the individual all material conditions must be made subservient."27 The simple pattern of Bellamy's thought emerges. He believed that human nature is good, that brotherhood is the destiny of men, and that the positive State is a solution for the problem of the ills of society. "Let but the famine-stricken nation assume the function it had neglected," he pleaded, "and regulate for the common good the course of the life-giving stream [the production of goods flowing from the labor of men], and the earth would bloom like one garden, and none of its children lack any good thing."28

In September, 1888, twenty-seven enthusiastic Bostonians founded "The Boston Bellamy Club" to disseminate the doctrines of Looking Backward. Among the leaders were Thomas Wentworth Higginson of the Free Religious Association and the Reverend W. D. P. Bliss, a leader in the new social gospel movement in American Protestantism. The presence of the two was significant. Bellamy had proposed a socialist platform upon which both humanists and liberal Christians could stand. "Nationalist" clubs quickly appeared in many parts of the nation. In June, 1890, the *Nationalist*, the periodical of the movement, reported that it had knowledge of one hundred and twenty-seven clubs in twenty-seven states. The important centers were Boston, New York, and San Francisco. There were in addition clubs in Denver, Chicago, Minneapolis, and Philadelphia. In February, 1891, the *Nationalist* claimed one hundred and sixty-seven clubs of which several were in Canada. Thereafter the movement declined, swallowed up by that political crusade of the 1890's known as Populism. Before it passed, however, Bellamy's "Nationalism" had served as a temporary way station for several men on the road to other liberalisms. W. D. P. Bliss passed from nationalism into Christian socialism. Daniel de Leon, lecturer on international relations at Columbia, abandoned Bellamy for Marx.

As a popular movement, however, Bellamy's nationlism was a failure. It never achieved political importance. Its socialism made it an easy target. General Francis Amasa Walker, president of the Massachusetts Institute of Technology and a leader among orthodox American economists, attacked the Chicopee philosopher in the *Atlantic*. "I must deem any man very shallow in his observation of the facts of life and utterly lacking in the biological sense," concluded the General pontifically, "who fails to discern in competition the force to which it is mainly due that mankind have risen from stage to stage, in intellectual, moral, and physical power."[29] Robert Ingersoll also rejected Bellamyism, but for other reasons than those given by Walker. He saw in totalitarianism the defeat of the individual. "We are believers in individual independence," said "Colonel Bob" in 1892 when asked his opinion of Bellamy, "and will be, I hope, forever."[30]

Ingersoll's reply was too pat and Walker's verbal victory too easy. In Bellamy, for all his detailed picture of a new society, they did not face so much an accomplished theoretician as a man of faith. Bellamy's was not the faith taught in the churches but rather one that stemmed ultimately from Emerson's transcendentalism. It is easy to think of Bellamy, had he lived in Concord a generation earlier, as an enthusiastic charter member of Brook Farm. When a young man he wrote an essay which he entitled "The Religion of Solidarity" for the ideas of which he owed a debt to Emerson's "Nature." Young Bellamy recognized the importance of individual personality. But man as no more than a social atom seemed to him a petty thing. Moreover the picture of the individual as a wholly discrete entity was not true. In the center of each separate being dwells the impersonal universal soul, the Soul of Solidarity. The man who seeks may apprehend at least glimpses of the universal within him, the universal that binds all men together. Such an analysis of human nature made it possible for Bellamy to believe that his total socialism would work without resort to the discipline that was to characterize later actual totalitarian regimes.

Fraternal brotherhood has a perennial appeal. The insecurity which so many individuals experienced in the tough, cut-throat competition of the age of the robber barons made Bellamy's dream world seem to many wishful thinkers a possible haven where the weak could escape the penalties for weakness, the weary could find respite from the marketplace philosophy of dog eat dog and where the noble sentiment of brotherhood would replace the rule of "Devil take the hindmost." This religious character gave the Nationalist movement a momentary and limited success. Bellamy and the Nationalists added to the new and indigenous humanism of the end of the century a faith that the individual finds fulfillment in the group and that the fundamental law is that of brotherhood.

∽

The new humanism of the 1880's and 1890's was, like its eighteenth-century prototype, primarily an expression of discontent with the existing *status quo*. It appeared in the heyday of the older trusts when the small entrepreneurs of another era were in some industries in full retreat before the advance of big business. The farmers of the Upper Mississippi Valley, suffering from evils due in part to the exploitation of omnivorous and seemingly omnipotent railroads, were organizing in Granges, in Farmers' Alliances, and finally in the Populist party. The wage earners also were on the march. In the 1870's and the 1880's the Noble Order of the Knights of Labor was attempting the impossible task of establishing the ideal of solidarity within the ranks of the workers. Sporadic wars between labor and management caused Washington Gladden to express the fear that American society was flying apart, that within the United States centrifugal forces were overpowering centripetal forces. Gladden was apprehensive for another reason. In the swiftly growing cities, created by the new industrial era, social sinks had appeared in which humanity degenerated. The slum was not only a burden; it was a threat to American civilization. In such an American scene the new rationalists proposed a philosophy of hope.

They had little faith either in the creeds or the program of orthodox Christianity. They did not believe that the God of the

Christians either could or would bring social health and justice to America. If this were to be accomplished, it must be done by men. The new rationalists, moreover, felt that the disease had got beyond the simple therapy of Protestantism. The preachers taught that, if all men were converted to the true faith, society's problems would solve themselves. George, Ward, and Bellamy all demanded social solutions for social ills. They proposed to use the positive State as an instrument for bettering the unhappy lot of men.

Long before the new humanism appeared, Americans had drifted significantly far from the religious determinism of Calvinism. But, after 1865, as economists in America strove to lift their discipline to the level of a social science, determinism reappeared in economic theory. William Graham Sumner and Amasa Walker, following the great English classicists, warned that man interferes with economic laws at his peril. Karl Marx's "scientific" socialism also depended upon deterministic postulates. The humanists rejected both Sumner and Marx; these prophets of a better world repudiated determinism. They insisted that man can be the master of his fate, that his only reliance is reason, that the State is his instrument, and that the planned society is the solution for social ills.

They were all democrats. They were puritans who sought to cleanse the democratic faith of the "superstitions" of Christianity and of the pernicious doctrines of the gospel of wealth. The dispute between Ward and Carnegie centered on the doctrine of the free individual. The gospel of wealth retained the old pre-Sumter definition of freedom as absence of external authority. As man increases in virtue and knowledge, the fundamental laws of morals and of nature become increasingly effective in his life and the State relatively less necessary. The rationalists replied that the State should be made the servant rather than the master of its citizens. The planned use of this matchless instrument is the highest expression of human freedom. In brief, the prophets of the gospel of wealth insisted that collectivism and individualism are antithetical; the new humanists maintained that collectivism can be made the servant of individualism. Ward believed that ultimately social experimentation and intelligent social planning would produce laws so patently wise and just that they would be self-enforcing. When mankind achieves this high goal, he thought, the free individual will have come into his own.   ∽

The religion of humanity and the new rationalism were negative and positive aspects of the same late nineteenth-century humanism.

But this new humanism, although its disciples would have denied it, was, in fact, a parade of ancient beliefs tricked out in new costumes. Man, the creator, replaced God, the creator. The Holy Spirit became the spirit of humanity, the basis of natural religion. The aspiration of the religious heart and worship of divine perfection was discovered to be merely man's age-old effort to perfect himself. The mystic's feeling of the presence of God was, in the eyes of the new humanists, an old-fashioned way of describing the sentiment of human brotherhood. For the salvation of the soul by divine grace was substituted the concept of the liberation and expression of the basic goodness of human nature made possible by the increase of knowledge and the renovation of the environment. The ancient belief in the providence of God became the doctrine of progress by scientific advance. For the Christian technique of saving the individual by conversion was substituted the program of saving society by social inventions. The old Christian concept of a hell to be avoided beyond the grave was replaced by emphasis upon that degrading poverty to be avoided on the earth. The vision of paradise in another world became that of a golden age in the world we know.

∽

What was the significance for American social thought of this new humanism? It furnished the philosophy and much of the driving force of the crusade of the muckrakers which began in the last decade of the century. Let the cancers of society merely be exposed to the light, thought Henry Demarest Lloyd and the young Lincoln Steffens, and they will be cured, for human nature is basically good and will not tolerate corruption, when once it is brought to view. The new humanistic emphasis expressed itself in Christianity in the social gospel movement to be discussed in another chapter. The significance of the new humanism for pragmatism will also be considered later. Its greatest importance, however, was that it was the American substitute for Marxism. It was a native-born criticism of capitalism. In an age when Americans were building a new industrial civilization, the new humanism taught that man could create a better as well as a more productive society. It avoided Marx's suggestions of revolution and of the dictatorship of the proletariat. To Americans of the 1880's and 1890's this latter meant rule by the immigrant. The religion of humanity and the new rationalism were the counterpart in the United States of the contemporary European doctrines symbolized by the red flag.

Chapter 18

WILLIAM GRAHAM SUMNER, CRITIC OF THE POSITIVE STATE

IN 1872 A YOUNG CLERGYMAN named William Graham Sumner was called from his church at Morristown, New Jersey, to Yale by a faculty which was undecided whether to invite him to the chair of Greek or of political economy. Sumner was a lantern-jawed, gruff-voiced individual who seemed a little out of place in the pulpit. He welcomed the invitation. Though a brilliant classicist, he turned the scales in favor of that new and struggling discipline, political economy.

When he moved to New Haven, the new professor came home to a college he knew well. Here he had been graduated in 1863, when the Civil War was approaching the July climax of Vicksburg and Gettysburg. Without enlisting in the army or even waiting for commencement, he had sailed for Europe to continue his preparation for the ministry by studying Greek and Hebrew in Switzerland and metaphysics and biblical criticism in Germany. Sumner was all his life a fighter, but he decided in his student days, as he hired a substitute for military service, that he would strike his blows only in campaigns of his own choosing. His acceptance of the post at New Haven was evidence of his conviction that the church was destined to play a diminishing rôle in American life and that in the future the significant efforts for social improvement would be the work of scientists rather than of clerics.

Noah Porter had been elevated from the professorship of moral philosophy and metaphysics to the presidency of Yale in 1871. When, in the autumn of the following year, he welcomed Sumner to his first faculty meeting in the Old Brick Row, President Porter must have smiled with satisfaction at what appeared to be a perfect solution of the troublesome problem of getting a professor of political economy. The English economists, who led the world, were inclined to doctrines of doubtful theological soundness. John Stuart Mill was especially unorthodox. Infidelity, moreover, was raising a serpent's head in America where young men were crowding the public lectures of that persuasive lawyer, Colonel Robert Ingersoll. The little group of Congregational ministers who made up the Yale corporation were worried by the revolt of the prophets of a new religion of humanity against the old orthodoxy. Porter doubtless thought it a brilliant stroke to found Yale economics upon sound theology by entrusting it to a clergyman so well prepared for his ministerial profession. Sumner, moreover, was as thoroughly grounded in the classics as any professor on the faculty—a fact of no small significance in a day when the social sciences had little academic prestige. Every officer in the college was compelled to respect this new discipline of political economy when taught by a man who knew his Greek as well as the best of them.

But Sumner was a disappointment. He was soon heard by scandalized colleagues to say that the classics were overemphasized in American colleges. The new day, Sumner added, demanded less adherence to tradition, as represented by Latin and Greek, and more stress upon science. Such backsliding was disheartening, but it was of small importance compared with the next defection. In 1879, Porter, thoroughly aroused, summoned his professor of political economy to the presidential office and demanded that he abandon reading with his classes the works of the arch-infidel, Herbert Spencer. Behind Porter was a corporation clucking angrily at the discovery that they had hatched a duckling. The interview ended with the battle drawn, but Sumner was the ultimate victor in the campaign which followed.

❧

Political economy was a vague term in the 1870's. Sumner interpreted his function to be to study government as well as economics. His was a large intellectual domain, its size determined, in part, by the newness of the social sciences in the United States. Democracy, as well as capitalism, was inside the boundaries of his bailiwick. As time ran on, Sumner came to look upon democracy as not simply a system of government but as a way of life which could be only understood after the investigation of all social phenomena. He lived in an age of large intellectual undertakings. Students of society were striving to achieve vast monistic theories with which to explain human behavior. In England, Spencer was producing his *Synthetic Philosophy*. In America, Lewis Henry Morgan had presented a picture of societal evolution in his *Ancient Society* in 1878, and Lester Frank Ward was beginning the construction of those theories which he published in 1883 as *Dynamic Sociology*. In such a world the education of William Graham Sumner, like that of his other contemporary, Henry Adams, became a lifelong process. But the roads of Adams and Sumner early began to diverge. Both read Morgan and Spencer. Adams, at first, was inclined to accept the evolutionary approach to the study of society but later, under the influence of physics, gave it up. Sumner, however, had no doubts. He hung Darwin's picture over his desk, as a good Catholic puts the effigy of the Virgin in his chamber. But with all their differences Sumner, Adams, Morgan, and Ward were alike in one respect; with few signposts to guide them they were setting forth to discover the science of man, or as Sumner later called it, the science of society.

Sumner began with economics. When he surveyed economic literature which had been produced in the United States before 1872, he discovered that it was primarily a blend of theology and of English classical theory. Henry C. Carey, the first American economist, was, of course, an exception. His philosophy was strongly nationalistic. Patriotism motivated his attack upon the great English classicists who were, in his opinion, formulating theories intended to keep the United States in economic vassalage to Britain. But Carey was theologically orthodox, as was Robert E. Thompson, his disciple and professor of social science at the University of Pennsylvania. Thompson was a contemporary of Sumner's. His approach to his subject is suggested by his attempt to internationalize the old Puritan doctrine of the calling. "No one," said the Pennsylvania economist, "who believes in the continual government of the world by Divine Will, can doubt that the nations exist in consequence of that will. . . . Each state, like each man, has a vocation. Each nation is a chosen people. It has a peculiar part to play in the moral order of the world."[1] Thompson's use of theological presuppositions was not unique. Arthur Latham Perry of Williams College based his theory of rent on the proposition that "God is a giver and not a seller."[2] Americans attacked the Malthusian theory as atheistic in tendency and contrary to God's commandment to replenish the earth. Both protectionists and free traders supported their theories by assumptions concerning the divine will and design. Noah Porter must have felt that a sinister fate pursued him when, with a wealth of economists available who were theologically sound, he picked a clergyman who, soon after coming to Yale, quietly ushered Deity out of the economic back door. Sumner was not, however, a militant agnostic. "I have never discarded beliefs deliberately," he said in later life. "I left them in a drawer, and, after a while, when I opened it, there was nothing there at all."

Turning his back upon theological economics, Sumner at first allied himself with the English classicists and accepted their major positions. He delighted certain business barons among the Yale alumni by espousing *laissez faire*, then at its nineteenth-century apogee. But at the same time he irritated conservatives to the point of finally demanding his elimination from the faculty by making vigorous and continuous war upon the doctrine of protectionism, which, he thought, bred plutocracy. The protective tariff, taught Sumner, in agreement with the Manchester school, is contrary to sound policy and subversive of good morals. "At the port of entry the government lays a tax which it does not collect," he commented. "It says to the producer, 'I do not need to tax the consumer for myself, but I will hold him for you while you tax him.' "[3] Sumner advocated "sound money" in his first book *The History of American Currency*, published two years after he came to Yale. The classical laws of population, of supply and demand, and of rent all became part of his mental furnishings.

It was inevitable that a new and sincere searcher for economic truth in the 1870's should fall under the influence of the classical system. It had solidity and hardness and it fitted obviously with a multitude of facts. Except for its neatness and its perfection it had all the appearance of being a science, and it had no rival of importance in America. In 1872 some American physicists were teaching their students that the principal advances in the subject had already been made and that the task of the future would be to trace in detail the workings of the laws already discovered. John Stuart Mill was quite as smug. "Happily, there is nothing in the laws of Value which remains for the present or any future writer to clear up," he declared, "the theory of the subject is complete."[4] Late nineteenth-century science was inclined to dogmatism and Sumner, the young economist, became as dogmatic as Mill. He founded his thought on a Newtonian determinism.

But Sumner's chair included politics as well as economics. In the same early years in which he was reading Ricardo and Malthus he studied realistic American democracy by participating in it. November, 1876, found him in Louisiana in the midst of a political typhoon. The crisis of the disputed presidential election was on. Samuel J. Tilden, the Democratic candidate, needed but a single electoral vote to put him in the White House. Sumner was one of the representatives of the Democratic party among the group of "visiting statesmen" sent into Louisiana to watch the activities of a returning board which held in its hands the fate of the presidency. The political economist saw with disgust his Republican colleagues among the observers, among whom were John Sherman, James A. Garfield, Lew Wallace, and Matthew Stanley Quay, acquiesce in fraud and venality. Then the contested election went to the specially created Electoral Commission on which sat some of the most prominent statesmen of the day. There was not one among them but had heard of the old doctrine of the moral law. All were aware that the United States faced a crisis so grave as to give rise to talk of a new rebellion. Yet politics triumphed over morality. Sumner, observing the ways by which the Electoral Commission counted Rutherford B. Hayes into the presidency, learned a lesson in realistic democracy. He never forgot the implications of this new spirit of '76. If he had ever had any faith in the political State as an instrument for creating a better world, it evaporated during the episode which began at Baton Rouge and ended at Washington. Young Sumner returned to his office in the Brick Row to propose as a remedy for American political and social ills a modification of the Spencerian doctrine of *laissez faire* individualism. In 1884, the year after Lester Frank Ward brought out his *Dynamic Sociology*, Sumner published that pungent tract, *What Social Classes Owe to Each Other*. The book was a restatement in the American vernacular of the position of the great English classicists. But it was also the expression of a positive faith which had grown out of Sumner's own life experience.

His father had come as an immigrant from England. By hard labor, wise management, and frugal living the elder Sumner had accumulated a competence sufficient to give his son a college education. William Graham never forgot the philosophy of individualism which was the disciplining faith of his boyhood home. His father, fulfilling a parent's duty, gave him his chance. The responsibility for what he made of that chance, he thought, was his and his alone. Sumner never ceased to have contempt for that prodigal son who, after wasting his opportunities and his substance, came sniveling home for help. A man, thought Sumner, must take the consequences of his behavior. The place for the drunkard is the ditch; and a hungry belly is the proper reward for indolence. The initiative, industry, and self-discipline of individuals are, Sumner believed, the foundations of society. Venality and sentimentality were, in his opinion, ruling moods in the Gilded Age in which he lived. To such a generation Sumner declared that democracy can exist only among a hard-headed, self-reliant, and responsible citizenry. Young Sumner saw American democracy in the Gilded Age beset by two dangers. Self-seeking pressure groups were striving to control the political State in order to use it for the furthering of private profit. Rationalistic and delusive social philosophies, such as those of natural rights and of the general welfare State, were confusing and misleading the public mind. Sumner assailed both these enemies of democracy in crowded classrooms and through an amazing series of essays published in the more popular magazines. He became in the 1880's the American champion of *laissez faire*. Lester Frank Ward attacked him and Richard T. Ely, chief American protagonist of the German historical school of economics, led a revolt against him. Against these and many others, Sumner, borrowing a club from Darwin, fought back. His social philosophy ran as follows.

In the beginning was the dawn-man; and the man was with animals; and the man was animal. He was no special creation of God, made in the image of Deity but was, rather, a product of nature processes, a new form of life brought forth by the fecund earth and dropped into an environment already crowded. No banquet of nature, such as Henry George imagined, was spread before him. If he would have food he must fight for it. He lived in an economy of scarcity, and struggle was for him the price of life. Endowed neither with the fleetness of the antelope nor with the weapons of the carnivora, he found that, if he would survive, he must bridle his undisciplined impulses, accept limitations upon his individual freedom, and learn the hard lesson of cooperation with his fellows. This part of the argument was the Sumner criticism of those sentimental illusions about the brotherhood of man and the "spirit of humanity" which, in his opinion, befogged the thinking of such uplifters as Octavius Brooks Frothingham. Walt Whitman had said, as early as the 1850's, that society is held together by love. Its cement on the contrary, replied Sumner in the age of the robber barons, is antagonistic cooperation.

Civilization, Sumner added, has been produced by those ultimate drives, hunger, sex love, vanity, and ghost fear. These four horsemen of human nature by forcing primitive man to cooperate, enabled him to survive and finally to build a platform called civilization above nature and so make easier his struggle for existence. But no matter how high the platform or how advanced the civilization, man, Sumner insisted, cannot escape the necessity of adjustment to natural laws. Upon these society rests. The discovery of these is the first and last task of the scientist.

Against such a background the Sumner of the Gilded Age took up the doctrine of natural rights to life, liberty, and the pursuit of happiness upon which Jefferson had founded the democratic theory of the Declaration of Independence and which Associate Justice Stephen J. Field was in Sumner's day finding so useful in his construction of a dugout in constitutional law for the protecting of private property. From whom does man hold these natural rights, asked the Yale political economist? From God? Let the man born blind or a member of an inferior race beseech the Mercy Seat; silence is the answer he gets to his prayers. From nature? Nature lets the individual die with complete indifference. From nature there never was even a right to life; as for liberty and happiness, man wins them if he can.

Sumner found in the midst of American industrialism that a satisfactory philosophy of individualism does not follow from the major premise of mythical natural rights but rather from the postulates of discipline and of organization. "It was an easy way to attain the objects of our desire to put them into the list of the 'rights of man,' " said Sumner in 1887, "or to resolve that 'we are and of right ought to be' as we should like to be. . . . Liberty, . . ." he added, "is not a boon, it is a conquest, and if we ever get any more, it will be because we make it or win it. The struggle for it, moreover, must be aimed, not against each other, but against nature. When men quarrel with each other, as every war shows, they fall back under the dominion of nature. It is only when they unite in cooperative effort against nature that they win triumphs over her and ameliorate their condition on earth."[5]

From the doctrine of natural rights Sumner passed on to that of the positive, planning State. The State, he declared, is no Hegelian super-human entity; it is merely All-of-us. Its function is to guard liberty and to guarantee as far as possible that the individual shall have his chance. Its principal purpose is to maintain peace within the group, leaving economic life to evolve unhampered. The self-maintenance institutions of society are, as Marx and Morgan taught, basic. But they are controlled by natural laws with which the State interferes at its peril. The great danger in a democracy is that those citizens whose lack of capacity causes them to fare ill in the struggle for existence will attempt to use the State as an instrument to recoup their fortunes. Another peril, equally threatening, is the control of the State by and for the rich. Realistic politics in America, Sumner thought, had come to be little more than a scramble among interest groups. The more powerful the State is made, the greater will be the prize for those who control it, and the more intense the struggle of pressure groups. Sumner feared government in the hands of either the proletariat or the plutocrats. He urged the proponents of democracy to widen "the scope of the automatic organs of society which are nonpolitical, in order to see whether they will not prove capable, if trusted."[6] Louisiana had given him a glimpse of the potentialities of American politics. When Sumner remembered Boss Tweed and Mat Quay, he had difficulty in believing that the American government could ever be transformed into a wholly benevolent institution. To such social planners as Ward he said: It is a foolish and mischievous idea that a man should "sit down with a slate and pencil to plan out a new social world. . . . He is in the stream and is swept along with it. All his sciences and philosophy come to him out of it. Therefore the tide will not be changed by us."[7] Here spoke the determinist. Yet Sumner's life was a long crusade to improve democracy by urging the folly and danger of political efforts to create a social Utopia. His dream, like that of Thoreau, was of the independent, self-disciplined individual who stands on his own feet and is free to go against the facts of life with what wit and strength he possesses and who is rewarded according to his wisdom or folly, his enterprise or his neglect. But because all men share in frailty and folly and because each individual owes duties to his fellows commensurate with his rights, Sumner insisted that men should help one another when the chances of life turn out badly. This aid, however, should be a private and a personal stewardship. Sumner had many charities but even his closest friends knew little of them.

The early Sumner, then, was a crusader who believed that only the gospel of wealth formula would make democracy workable. He had, however, few illusions concerning the quality of government by the people. "A democratic republic," he remarked, "will never be neat, trim, and regular in its methods, or in the external appearance which it presents. A great many things are sure to be at loose ends, in a word, there is sure to be little discipline. There is a lounging air, a lack of formality. . . ."[8] No democracy, in other words, would ever look or act as did Bismarck's Germany which he knew so well from his student days. But Sumner preferred the democratic slattern to the autocratic strumpet.

∽

Time ran on. Sumner came under the influence of Julius Lippert and of Ludwik Gumplowicz, anthropologists of Germany and of Poland. Sumner moved into that field which he called the science of society. He eschewed the term sociology. That new discipline which Lester Frank Ward had helped to found was, in his opinion, the hunting ground of soft-headed ex-ministers, of professional up-lifters, in short, of all who saw Utopia beyond the next range of hills. With Lewis Henry Morgan, Sumner turned for his data to ethnology. He undertook prodigious labors. Each summer he mastered a new language so that no important description of primitive life might escape his net. He compared the cultures of the world. The fruit of this last phase of his thought was *Folkways*, published in 1906. In this volume he not only presented his concept of the mores but his appraisal of democracy in the light of his new knowledge.

In these *fin de siècle* years, when Sumner was ranging over the cultures of the earth, the world was changing. Sumner noted well the drift of events. In the United States a naval officer, Captain Alfred Mahan, published a book in 1890 which he entitled *The Influence of Sea Power on History*. Soon after a new navy put an end to American post-Appomattox impotence upon the oceans. In 1898 McKinley led the nation into war with Spain, a popular war—thanks to the yellow press. Two American fleets destroyed what was left of Spain's once proud empire. The United States emerged from the conflict with possessions scattered halfway round the globe. Again, as in 1848, the American citizen felt the mood of the conqueror.

Sumner, stirred as never before, protested against the new tendencies. He entitled his essay "The Conquest of the United States by Spain." Spain in the distant days of Charles V and of Philip II had pioneered in imperialism; so ran the Sumner argument. Mexico and Peru were the great prizes of the sixteenth century. Now for Spain the days of glory had passed, but the Republic of the West had stepped forth to do battle for the old imperialist faith. Even as Sumner wrote, soldiers of the North American democracy were beginning the bloody and costly "pacification" of the Philippine archipelago off the coast of China. American businessmen were already following the trails once blazed by Cortez and Pizarro to El Dorado. The techniques of the turn-of-the-century conquistadors were different from those of their sixteenth-century prototypes, but their spirit was the same. American imperialism, economic and political, had become a reality. The citizens of the United States had a new *Weltanschauung*.

Sumner observed the change with a sinking heart. Imperialism, he argued, requires armies and navies. It begets militarism. He pointed to Europe where conscript armies were increasing each year in numbers and in effectiveness. "It is militarism," said Sumner to triumphant Americans in 1898, "which is eating up all the products of science and art, defeating the energy of the population, and wasting its savings. It is militarism which forbids the people to give their attention to the problems of their own welfare, and to give their strength to the education and comfort of their children. It is militarism which is combating the grand efforts of science and art to ameliorate the struggle for existence. . . . Expansion and imperialism are at war with the best traditions, principles, and interests of the American people . . . expansion and imperialism are a grand onslaught on democracy."[9] President Theodore Roosevelt, however, assuming with enthusiasm the white man's burden, sniffed a few years later at such fears as those of Sumner and talked loudly of the importance of military power in maintaining the peace of the world.

After 1901, when Roosevelt was urging a more powerful navy, Sumner pondered the meaning of modern nationalism. He found enlightenment in his anthropological studies. "The sentiment of cohesion," he remarked in 1903, "internal comradeship, and devotion to the in-group, which carries with it a sense of superiority to any out-group and readiness to defend the interests of the in-group against the out-group, is technically known as ethnocentrism. It is really the sentiment of patriotism in all its philosophic fullness; that is, both in its rationality and in its extravagant exaggeration . . . Perhaps nine-tenths of all the names given by savage tribes to themselves mean 'Men,' 'The Only Men,' or 'Men of Men'; that is, We are men, the rest are something else. . . . This is the language of ethnocentrism; it may be read in the newspapers of any civilized

country today."[10] Ethnocentrism is but another word for nationalism. And Sumner saw nationalism threatening to become in the
twentieth century the enemy of democracy.

In 1903, when Sumner wrote his essay on "War," the Progressive
Era was getting underway in the United States. In spite of the
shocking disclosures of the muckrakers, hope ran high in America
that a better day was at hand. Side by side with imperialism there
developed a new democratic movement whose importance was
equal to that for which Andrew Jackson became the symbol. But
Sumner still saw America against a background of nationalistic
Europe. American Utopian dreams, he thought, concealed the hard
reality that competition among the nations of Europe was betray-
ing the individual into the hands of the leviathan State and by so
doing must sooner or later put an end to freedom and to democracy. "Never, from the day of barbarism down to our own time,"
said Sumner in the year before Edward VII of England completed
the creation of the Triple Entente, "has every man in a society
been a soldier until now; and the armaments of today are immensely more costly than ever before. There is only one limit possible to the war preparations of a modern European state; that is,
the last man and the last dollar it can control. What will come of
the mixture of sentimental social philosophy and warlike policy?
There is only one thing rationally to be expected, and that is a
frightful effusion of blood in revolution and war during the century
now opening."[11]

Compare Sumner and Melville on war. "It is the competition of
life, therefore, which makes war," said Sumner in 1903, "and that
is why war always has existed and always will."[12] Fifty-four years
earlier Melville had written in *Mardi:* "Evil is the chronic malady
of the universe. . . . And should . . . [the world] endure till mountain melt into mountain, and all the isles form one tableland; yet,
would it but expand the old battleplain."[13]

As Sumner looked out over the Western world in the opening
decade of the twentieth century he thought he saw a new era
emerging in which the ruling ideas would be socialism, imperialism,
and militarism. He looked upon each one of the three as the enemy
of the free individual. He was convinced that the core of each doctrine was the coercion of the individual by the State. A quarter of a
century had not passed after his death in 1910 before totalitarianism
built the three ideas into menacing power structures. Yet Sumner
was convinced that the drift of the times could not be stopped. Canute

could as easily sweep back the tide as a lonely, protesting democrat could check the march of Western civilization toward disaster. Yet, illogically, Sumner kept up and even intensified his fight for democracy. He had long since abandoned the political arena. His weapons were those of a scholar. His objective was enlightenment and insight. His conviction was that the forlorn and probably futile hope of democracy was that the men who profess it should understand what they are doing. He strove to see democracy against the background of the whole social scene.

∾

In 1906 Sumner published *Folkways*, an analysis of the importance of custom or channeled behavior in society. His essential argument was simple. Individual men, he affirmed, are governed ultimately, not by reason, but by those basic customs which Sumner called folkways or mores. These mores are not the creation of reason but take form over long periods of time as a result of the adjustments of the masses of society to their life conditions. Individual men are driven to such adjustments by basic physical and psychological needs. The dominant mores of a society are those ways of behaving which the group believes promotes its interests. Mores change because life conditions change. Mores sometimes make for progress and sometimes for retrogression; Sumner found many illustrations of harmful mores. Each individual is born into a complex of mores. From infancy the mores of his time and place exercise a coercive force upon him. Sumner's was an early statement of the doctrine of cultural determinism.

Folkways was a revolutionary book, though many years were to elapse before its significance began to be recognized. Its teachings ran counter to basic doctrines of the mid-nineteenth-century democratic faith. The first of these was the belief in a fundamental law of nature and of God, fixed and changeless, according to which not only the material universe but human society is governed. Democracy was thought of as the end product of social evolution. It was the way of life which guaranteed the individual liberty in the exercise of his natural rights and which made possible the most rapid progress in the realization in society of the fundamental moral law. The essence of this old democratic faith was its insistence upon the freedom of the individual and upon progress. The faith gave to men a sense of direction and to society a moral ideal, stable and dependable, toward which to advance. Expressions of this faith filled

American political and social discussion in the first decade of the twentieth century. In *Folkways* Sumner rejected this democratic faith with that same cold rationalism which had once led him to abandon his earlier Christian orthodoxy. He recognized that American democracy had two facets, romantic dreams and realistic behavior patterns. The romantic dreams were, for the most part, he thought, deductions from mythology. " 'Democracy,' " he said speaking of the United States, "is not treated as a parallel word to aristocracy, theocracy, autocracy, etc., but as a Power from some outside origin, which brings into human affairs an inspiration and energy of its own."[14] In such a sense "Democracy," thought Sumner, is a "phantasm." This romanticism protects it from realistic analysis and criticism. In the name of the phantasm, moreover, the ruling interests in the United States accomplish their private ends. Sumner pointed to the catchword, "American," as one of the most potent weapons which special interests fabricated from the materials of the democratic faith. "Who dare say he is not 'American'?" asked Sumner. "Who dare repudiate what is declared to be 'Americanism'? . . . If there is any document of Americanism, it is the Declaration of Independence. Those who have Americanism especially in charge have repudiated the doctrine that 'governments derive their just powers from the consent of the governed,' because it stood in the way of what they wanted to do. They denounce those who cling to the doctrine as un-American."[15]

Yet *Folkways* made a more far-reaching denial than that of the sanctity of the democratic dream. Its hypothesis of the mores collided with that absolutist ethics which was fundamental to mid-nineteenth-century thinking. Americans had assumed a fixed and eternal moral law to be the rock upon which society rests. Sumner marshalled proofs to demonstrate that ethical codes change from time to time and from place to place. "The mores," he said, "can make anything right and prevent the condemnation of anything."[16]

No break with nineteenth-century absolutism could be more complete. Chancellor Kent and Associate Justice Joseph Story had assumed that the basic principles of ethics are eternal. Their generation had looked upon civilization as progress toward a stable virtue in an orderly universe. When Sumner said that the mores can and do make any type of behavior seem right or wrong, he pictured mankind as adrift in an uncharted sea.

Sumner's one hope was science. He thought that science can pierce a little way the mystery which envelops human behavior.

His objective was to clarify in a small degree the insights of man. His research convinced him that the mores are produced, primarily, by behavior which is nonrational or, as Pareto later called it, non-logical. As a result Sumner rejected as fanciful such grandiose schemes of social engineering as those of Lester Frank Ward. The individual, taught Sumner, can do little to change the drift of the age in which he lives, for even the ethical code which he seeks to use as a measure for good and evil comes out of that age and of its mores. Sumner, with his colleagues in the natural sciences, was impressed with the reality and importance of determinism. But this conviction did not lead him into futilitarianism. Insignificant though it may be, the individual, he thought, can take effective action. He can propose variations in the mores which the masses may ultimately accept. Sumner saw only a narrow zone in which freedom of action in accordance with reason and intelligence is possible. In this zone, however, man has developed natural science as a tool of adjustment to the cosmic forces among which his life is cast. This remnant of freedom Sumner defended with all his strength against the encroachments of the all-devouring political State.

But, by 1906, Sumner thought that democracy was already a lost cause. He saw it as a moment in history whose passing was almost at hand. "In modern times," he said, "movable capital has been immensely developed and even fixed capital has been made mobile by the joint-stock device. It has disputed and largely defeated the social power of land property. . . . The effect of the creation of an immense stock of movable capital, of the opportunities in commerce and industry offered to men of talent, of the immense aid of science to industry, of the opening of new continents and the peopling of them by the poorest and worst in Europe, has been to produce modern mores. All our popular faiths, hopes, enjoyments, and powers are due to these great changes in the conditions of life. The new status makes us believe in all kinds of rosy doctrines about human welfare, and about the struggle for existence and the competition of life; it also gives us all our contempt for old-fashioned kings and nobles, creates democracies, and brings forth new social classes and gives them power. . . . When the earth is underpopulated and there is an economic demand for men, democracy is inevitable. That state of things cannot be permanent. Therefore democracy cannot last. It contains no absolute and 'eternal' truth."[17]

As the end of his life drew near, Sumner peered into the future from his own peculiar observation point. He saw democracy disappearing. What would take its place? He did not know and never tried to guess. In the darkness ahead he could see only the effort of politicians "by the application of social policy, to subject society to another set of arbitrary interferences, dictated by a new set of dogmatic prepossessions that would only be a continuation of old methods and errors."[18] He did not live to see his politicians become such realities as Mussolini, Stalin, or Hitler. He died before the "dogmatic prepossessions" of Aryanism and totalitarianism disturbed the peace of the world. He died, moreover, without regret. "I have lived through the best period of this country's history," he said to an intimate friend a few months before his final illness in 1910. "The next generations are going to see war and social calamities. I am glad I don't have to live on into them."[19]

The democratic faith of nineteenth-century America was primarily a formula for intellectual security. It taught the dependability of the fundamental law and the validity of the democratic ideal. Sumner, like Melville, declared that this supposed security is an illusion. "The only security," said the aging Sumner in 1905 to a group of young men who had just been initiated into the society of Sigma Xi, "is the constant practice of critical thinking. We ought never to accept fantastic notions of any kind; we ought to test all notions; we ought to pursue all propositions until we find out their connection with reality. That is the fashion of thinking which we call scientific in the deepest and broadest sense of the word."[20] In this speech, however, the old warrior inadvertently gave away his own private ethical absolutisms. He believed that freedom and honesty of thought, of investigation, and of expression are eternally good. Upon these and these alone man must depend for such security as he may succeed in winning in a shifting and terrifying world.

Chapter 19

ECONOMIC THEORY
AND THE POSITIVE STATE

AFTER THE SECOND INAUGURATION of McKinley in 1901, events gave a cumulative demonstration of the soundness of the observations of economist Arthur T. Hadley that monopoly and the concentration of economic power in the hands of the few were an inevitable development of the capitalist system. A series of episodes dramatized for the mass of Americans the existence of uncontrolled and politically irresponsible economic overlords. The first was the creation in 1901 of the vast United States Steel Corporation. Then followed, at irregular intervals, the Northern Securities case, and the legal assaults upon the Standard Oil and the Tobacco "trusts," all instituted by President Roosevelt. The Mann-Elkins Act and the Hepburn Act led to Congressional battles to establish curbs on the common carriers. Finally in 1913 the Pujo committee of the House of Representatives undertook an investigation of American business conditions. Its report affirmed the existence of a "money trust" and declared that there existed "a well-defined identity and community of interest between a few leaders of finance . . . held together through stock holdings, interlocking directorates, and other forms of domination over banks, trust companies, railroads, public service, and industrial corporations, and which has resulted in a vast and growing concentration of control of money and credit in the hands of comparatively few men."

The effect upon the public of these events was enhanced by the crusade of the muckrakers, earnest journalists and humanitarians who with sordid realism exposed to view not only the relations between business and politics, but those between big business, little business, and the consumer. The muckrakers told a sorry tale of meat prepared with scant regard for the public health, of the duping of a simple-minded public by the purveyors of spurious remedies, of the strangling of independent entrepreneurs by ruthless industrial giants, of the purchase of boards of aldermen and of state legislatures by transportation barons; in short, of the acquisition by a small group of business leaders of control over the political as well as the economic life of the American people. President-elect Woodrow Wilson in 1913 referred to an "invisible empire" which, behind a façade of democratic institutions, exercised the realities of power and dominated American life.

Wilson's phrase, "the invisible empire," was a politician's device to create a bogy with which to scare lethargic voters into supporting administration policies. The realist who analyzed and described the position of the economic overlord in American society in the first decade of the twentieth century was neither a muckraker nor a politician. Brooks Adams, Boston lawyer and grandson of John Quincy Adams, analyzed the social forces at work in early twentieth-century America with the hope of gaining some insight into coming events. He shared his brother Henry's skepticism of American political democracy. It was conditioned by industrial capitalism, and Adams thought that the outlook for that system was not promising.

Squinting his eye along the time line of American history Adams opined that the governing elite, "the industrial capitalist class," the class which William Dean Howells represented in Silas Lapham, reached its apogee during roughly the third quarter of the nineteenth century. In the fourth quarter restive voters began to attempt curbs in such measures as the Interstate Commerce Act and the Sherman Anti-Trust Act. The industrial governing class had, nevertheless, managed to retain supremacy to the year of grace, 1913, but whether it would be able to continue to hold its position was, thought Adams, a matter of doubt.

The weaknesses of the capitalist aristocracy in America were, in the opinion of Adams, several. Perhaps the most serious resulted from the method of its recruiting. "Modern capitalists appear to have been evolved under the stress of an environment which demanded excessive specialization in the direction of a genius adapted to money-making under highly complex industrial conditions. To this money-making attribute all else has been sacrificed, and the modern capitalist not only thinks in terms of money, but he thinks in terms of money more exclusively than the French aristocrat or lawyer before the French Revolution ever thought in terms of caste."[1]

Such extreme specialization had introduced into the social philosophy of the ruling class a dangerous principle. The capitalist leader "conceives sovereign powers to be for sale."[2] He buys, for example, national highways called railroads and manages them for his private profit. "He is not responsible for he is not a trustee of the public. If he be restrained by legislation, that legislation is in his eye an oppression and an outrage, to be annulled or eluded by any means which will not lead to the penitentiary. . . . Thus, of necessity, he precipitates a conflict, instead of establishing an adjustment. He is, therefore, in essence, a revolutionist without being aware of it."[3]

That ruling class which hopes to remain long in power must have some breadth in its social philosophy, but the capitalist overlord of America "is too specialized to comprehend a social relation . . . beyond the narrow circle of his private interests."[4] The chief defect of Silas Lapham's kind, thought Adams, is stupidity, a quality best illustrated by the business man's attitude toward the law. The man of great wealth, who depends for his power upon his money, is vulnerable and peculiarly dependent upon the law for his protection. The medieval knight, Adams pointed out, was not only a trained soldier; he monopolized the most effective instruments of offense and defense. The modern capitalist because he is no warrior must depend upon law enforcement not only for his protection but for his power. Enlightened self-interest, therefore, would appear to make him a leader inculcating tirelessly in the masses whom he rules the doctrine of respect for and obedience of the law. But the facts, thought the Boston attorney, are quite different. "In spite of his vulnerability, he is of all citizens the most lawless. He appears to assume that the law will always be enforced, when he has need of it, by some special personnel whose duty lies that way, while he may evade the law, when convenient, or bring it into contempt, with impunity. The capitalist seems incapable of feeling his responsibility, as a member of the governing class, in this respect, and that he is bound to uphold the law, no matter what the law may be, in order that others may do the like."[5]

The capitalist governing class covers up many of its refusals to obey the law and even deludes itself and the public by its control of the courts, particularly the Supreme Court of the United States. Under the American constitutional system the courts have become censors of legislation. "I find it difficult to believe," said lawyer Adams, "that capital, with its specialized views of what constitutes its advantages, its duties, and its responsibilities and stimulated by a bar moulded to meet its prejudices and requirements, will ever voluntarily assent to the consolidation of the United States to the point at which the interference of the courts with legislation might be eliminated; because, as I have pointed out, capital finds the judicial veto useful as a means of at least temporarily evading the law, while the bar, taken as a whole, quite honestly believes that the universe will obey the judicial decree. No delusion could be profounder and none, perhaps, more dangerous."[6]

Adams felt that the key to continued supremacy by the economic overlords lay in efficient national administration. Such efficiency was impaired not only by the judicial veto which might at any time wreck a legislative program, but was rendered difficult by the emphasis in a capitalist civilization upon specialization. "Apparently modern society, if it is to cohere, must have a high order of generalizing mind,—a mind which can grasp a multitude of complex relations—but this is a mind which can, at best, only be produced in small quantity and at high cost. Capital has preferred the specialized mind. . . . Capitalists have never insisted upon raising an educational standard save in science and mechanics, and the relative overstimulation of the scientific mind has now become an actual menace to order because of the inferiority of the administrative intelligence."[7]

Adams drove to his conclusion. Unless the capitalist rulers of America, he declared, develop immediately more ability in administration and more political sagacity than they have ever manifested, the disintegration which precedes revolution is inevitable. Evidences of that disintegration are, he warned, in fact, already apparent in a "universal contempt for law, incarnated in the capitalistic class itself,"[8] in the slough of urban politics, and, perhaps most important of all, in the dissolution of that primary and fundamental school of discipline, the home. Unless the capitalistic governors of America can make over their mentality and renovate their policy, Nature will settle our present perplexities "as simply and as drastically as she is apt to settle human perturbations."

Adams saw clearly that the central issue of American politics of the Progressive Era was the public control of economic power concentrated in the hands of a small ruling class. There was general agreement among liberals as to the danger of plutocracy. Adams proposed a lawyer's solution: the centralization of political power in the Federal government and the enforcement from Washington of that social discipline which unites a nation and without which, he thought, the Republic would in all probability fall a prey to foreign brigands.

Other remedies were proposed. In the Progressive Era a citizen's choice among the cures for the social ills of the time depended primarily upon which one of several economic philosophies satisfied his reason. Naturally the rising guild of economists acquired a peculiar importance in the stream of American democratic thought. In the opening decades of the twentieth century economic thinking marked out the main channels for the political ideas of the period.

～

Since the middle of the 1870's aggressive young economists, who had had the initiative to go abroad for study, had been returning to America with sheepskins in their valises which signified that they had won doctor's degrees in German universities. Some threescore of these were trained in that historical school of economics developed by German scholars who, following Friedrich List, found the classical system of England badly adapted to their national needs. When the stream of American students reached its flood, Imperial Germany, born at Versailles in 1871, was stirring with new life. The German people felt an *élan* which they had rarely known before. Bismarck, the Iron Chancellor who had created the Reich, effectively used the State as an instrument to solve both internal and external problems. Economists, such as Johannes Conrad at Halle, were public servants who dedicated their skill to the task of creating a new nation. The homing American students of the 1870's and 1880's were filled with enthusiasm and high resolves. Richard T. Ely, who returned in 1881, looked back upon his professors, Conrad, Knies, and Wagner, as humanitarians who "wanted to help bring about a better world in which to live."[9] Americans, he thought, should profit by the German example. Many of his returning fellow students agreed with him. There appeared among American economists a small but brilliant company of crusaders who were convinced that Bismarck's Imperial Reich had discovered the formula by which American democracy could be saved from the dangers which threatened it. The spirit of List was returning to the United States where, with aid from the two Careys, the founder of German national economics had first developed his theories.

In the emerging guild of economics in the United States the tradition of Adam Smith and David Ricardo had, after the Civil War, become dominant. Sumner's economic determinism was typical of

American acceptance of English classical theories. American classicists did not yield to the unorthodox youngsters returning from study in Germany without a fight. The conservatives were difficult to dislodge because in the early 1880's they held all the strategic positions. They occupied the chairs in the universities and influenced the theories of important organs of opinion. R. T. Ely, in 1935 at the celebration of the fiftieth anniversary of the American Economics Association, enumerated for the enlightenment of his younger colleagues the enemies of his militant youth. "Godkin and his associates who controlled the *Nation* perhaps come first," he said with feeling, "then Professor William Graham Sumner of Yale, David A. Wells, the amiable Perry of Williams College, and the belligerent Simon Newcomb of the Naval Observatory and of Johns Hopkins University."[10] Newcomb once in a review in the *Nation* dismissed one of Ely's first books with the comment that a man who entertained such views "was not fit to hold a position in an American university."[11] The Old Guard clung to a dogmatism comparable to that of the bishop who expounds the creed of a State religion. They had mistaken for science a philosophy which Thorstein Veblen later remarked was merely "a projection of the accepted ideal of conduct" of their age and culture.[12] "We rebels," Ely went on, "were fighting for our place in the sun. We wanted the right to exist scientifically and to express ourselves in writing and teaching."[13] The first fruit of their revolt was the American Economics Association.

In September, 1885, Simon Patten, Edwin R. A. Seligman, Edmund J. James, John Bates Clark, and R. T. Ely foregathered at Saratoga, New York, once the summer rendezvous of the slave-owning aristocracy of the South. In the company also were Andrew D. White, late minister to Germany and just then retiring as president of Cornell; Washington Gladden, pioneer in the crusade of the social gospel; and a young professor of political economy named Woodrow Wilson. "We, who had tasted the new and living economics which was taught in German universities," remarked Ely, "were depressed with the sterility of the old economics which was being taught in the American colleges. . . . Therefore we felt called upon to fight those who we believed stood in the way of intellectual expansion and of social growth. We were determined to inject new life into American economics."[14] The early autumn colors on the slopes of the surrounding foothills of the Adirondacks symbolized on this occasion more than the waning of the calendar year. The young Saratoga rebels were convinced that also for *homo economicus*, that amoral robot of classical economics, the sands of time were running out.

The revolters held long discussions. Some went further to the left than others. All, however, were anxious to found a society which all professional economists would join. They elected a *laissez-faire* conservative as the first president, but a committee which consisted of H. C. Adams, Washington Gladden, Alexander Johnson, J. B. Clark, and R. T. Ely drew up a liberal statement of principles. These ran, in part, as follows:

1. We regard the state as an agency whose positive assistance is one of the indispensable conditions of human progress. . . .

2. We believe that political economy is still in an early stage of development . . . and we look, not so much to speculation as to historical and statistical study of actual conditions of economic life for the satisfactory accomplishment of that study.

3. We hold that the conflict of labor and capital has brought into prominence a vast number of social problems, whose solution requires the united efforts, each in its own sphere, of the church, of the state, and of science. [This doctrine was announced just eight months before the detonation in Chicago's Haymarket Square of that dynamite bomb which produced the first American anarchist hunt.]

4. . . . . We believe in a progressive development of economic conditions, which must be met by a corresponding development of legislative policy.[15] [Two years later came the Interstate Commerce Act and in 1890 the Sherman Anti-Trust Law.]

Ely sought to make the *is* conform to the *ought*, to unite ethics and economics. "The ethical school of economists," he said, "aims . . . to direct in a certain definite manner, so far as may be, this economic, social growth of mankind. Economists who adhere to this school wish to ascertain the laws of progress and to show men how to use them."[16]

William Graham Sumner read Ely's "Essay on Ethics" and growled. His reply appeared a few months later under the title "The Absurd Effort to Make the World Over." He was the only one of the men of the older school who never joined Ely's association.

◞

A half century before Ely returned from Germany, Mathew Carey had advocated a protective tariff in order to create a complex and developed economic system in which opportunities would be multiplied for individuals. By 1885 the civilization of which Carey dreamed had become a fact. Behind tariff walls American capitalism had achieved the luxuriance of a tropical forest. But urban and rural poverty made it clear that the material and moral utopia for which Henry Carey had hoped had not come into being.

The Saratoga rebels faced courageously the evils of the new day. Theirs was the spirit of the religion of humanity. In economics they were convinced they possessed a science which would enable them to transform America into a brave new world. The Saratoga principles not only were a declaration of independence against the pessimism and determinism of classical economics but proclaimed the humanistic creed of a band of young scholars ready to tilt with fate. They sought to give meaning in the realm of economic law and enterprise to the democratic ideal of the free individual.

The Saratoga principles were generalities, requiring, if they were to be effective, more specific formulation. The Saratoga men were agreed as to ends. But the means by which these were to be achieved caused dispute. In the humanistic pattern which stemmed from Saratoga two somewhat discordant emphases appeared. One exalted individual enterprise, the other a planned economy. One would lean slightly, the other heavily, upon the State. One held fast to a modified gospel of wealth, the other boldly demanded collectivism. John Bates Clark was the leader of the first group and Simon Patten of the second.

～

Let us be loyal, urged Clark, to the principle of free competition in the open market, for only through such loyalty can we preserve our liberty under economic law.

Clark assumed that, in the long run, the individual who would serve himself must do so by serving others, by making for them the things they want and selling the product of his labor at a price commensurate with the satisfaction its possession will give the consumer. All producers become rivals in offering things desired and the prize goes to him who offers the best product at the lowest price. Since producers are also consumers they get the advantage which comes from rivalry in the field of production. Clark's vision of the beneficent potentialities of free competition in the open market dominated his life as completely as did that vision which came to Saul of Tarsus on the road to Damascus.

Clark's ideal community was not an earthly paradise to be attained at some distant future time but, instead, was an institution operating in the here and now. The market, or economic society, thought Clark, is like a mountain lake, fed by streams from the slopes and agitated by passing storms. There are times when its waves become the very symbol of change. But, let them rise as high as they will, the laws of hydrostatics are forever pulling them down from their white-crested defiance toward that equilibrium which transforms the surface into a mirror. The laws of hydrostatics are the analogue of those of economics. The lake which gives back, unblurred, the image of the trees along its shore is the open market in which competition is free. In it individual men, like the molecules of water, enjoy that harmony which is the product of equilibrium.

Such harmony never has been nor ever can be achieved in the world of men, thought Clark, for human society is dynamic, while the reflecting pool is static. The error of classical economics, he believed, lay in the fact that the great masters thought it possible to make the reflecting pool a reality. Into the lake flow streams which keep it in a process of change. Population increases and goods accumulate. New inventions and new forms of organization are devised. The wants of men grow. The lake becomes larger; it rises from level to level. But always, at each new level, the laws of hydrostatics pull its droplets toward that equilibrium which is never achieved. The market of reality is always in a state of greater or lesser agitation. It is ever enlarging, for into it the streams of change never cease to flow. But within the market (economic society) the principle of competition is always bringing the individuals who compose it toward that harmony in which prices conform to "standards of cost," wages to "the standard of the final productivity of labor," and interest to "the marginal product of capital." For each stage of such a dynamic society there is an ideal counterpart. In every stormy economic surface Clark saw the potential reflecting pool.

Reality for him was, therefore, both motion and rest, both the confused world of experience and the ordered world of the ideal. Clark affirmed that we inhabit a dependable cosmos in which there are eternal forces, for the discovery of which logic is as necessary as sense data. "There are certain principles which are equally valid in all times and places. They were true in the beginning of industry, are true now, and will remain so as long as men shall create and use wealth. They are not antiquated either by technical progress or social evolution."[17] For Clark the market of everyday experience was a compromise between the flux of human life and an ideal form, the theoretical open market. "There is at each period a standard shape and mode of action to which static laws acting by themselves would bring economic society. . . . The laws of equilibrium which produced the first static level would be identically the same as those which produced the second. . . . They make actual society hover forever about a changing standard shape."[18]

Clark's free man was, of course, none other than *homo economicus*. He was a producing and consuming machine, governed by pleasure and pain. A utility was that which gave him pleasure; the pain of effort was the price he paid for it. But Clark's economic man was not the automaton envisaged by Malthus. He was a democrat, politically free and morally responsible, with his destiny in his own hands. His duty was to make the fundamental economic law as well as eternal moral principles effective in society. For the discharge of both these obligations he needed the State, functioning in its ancient rôle as policeman.

To accept the Clark thesis concerning the importance of free competition in an open market was to pillory the monopolist as public enemy number one. "The very antithesis of competition is monopoly," declared the Columbia economist. "No description could exaggerate the evil which is in store for a society given hopelessly to a regime of private monopoly. . . . Monopoly checks progress in production and infuses into distribution an element of robbery. . . . Monopoly is not a mere bit of friction which interferes with the perfect working of economic laws. It is a definite perversion of the laws themselves. It is one thing to obstruct a force and another to supplant it and introduce a different one."[19] If monopoly should dominate the economic life of the twentieth century, warned Clark, the "dazzling visions of the future which technical gains have excited must be changed to an anticipation as dismal as anything ever suggested by the Political Economy of the classical days."[20]

John Bates Clark, of Amherst and Columbia, was a crusader. He called upon the righteous of his generation to go forth to war. The enemy was already within the gates. The private monopoly of the capitalist, he declared, makes possible the exploitation of the wage earner and of the consumer. The private monopoly of the selfish labor union permits the spoliation of the capitalist and of the consumer. Private monopoly has transformed the competition of the market from the honorable rivalry of men seeking profit through service into a jungle combat which must eventuate in organized social war. Monopoly has perverted, not discredited, the competitive system. It may be, Clark admitted, that state monopoly is useful and desirable. But general socialism, as Bellamy made clear, must inevitably replace individual liberty with coercion and, so, by paralyzing individual initiative, must put an end to progress. What to do? Call upon the State to discipline wrong-doers. Define and forbid the evil practices which make monopoly possible. Let the laws of men open the market and set us free again, for liberty flourishes under a government of laws, natural laws of economics, and withers under that of monopolists, economic dictators.

In the spring of 1914, a few months before the German armies violated the Belgian frontier, John Bates Clark crossed the campus of Stanford University and entered the principal lecture hall. About him on every hand were evidences of the capacity of the human spirit to rise above disaster. The destruction caused by the San Francisco earthquake was forgotten and the university, undaunted, faced the future. In such a setting Clark put forth the vision of an eastern warrior who had long since gone forth with spear and shield to fight for righteousness. "We may build a new earth," he said, "out of the difficult material we have to work with, and cause justice and kindness to rule in the very place where strife now holds sway. A New Jerusalem may actually arise out of the fierce contentions of the modern market. The wrath of men may praise God and his Kingdom may come, not in spite of, but by means of the contests of the economic sphere. . . . The reformer can point to his delectable mountains and trace a sure route over them, as they rise range on range and lose themselves in the distance. . . . Again and again barriers seemingly insurmountable will be passed. The impossibility of today will become the reality of tomorrow, and the dazzling vision of today will be the reality of the future and the starting-point for still grander achievements."[21] In such phrases Clark pictured the Utopia of individualism, created by free and responsible men who worked in harmony with economic law.

∽

Simon Patten spent the formative years of his life in the two most richly endowed regions of the world. The prairie plains of the United States not only possess a fertile, well-watered soil and a friendly climate but lie between rich reserves of coal and iron. Only one other area on the earth boasts such a combination of natural advantages, the central plain of Europe which stretches westward from Russia across Germany and Belgium to northern France. Patten as a child lived in a country where cornfields became forests in which the unwary farm boy might lose himself. As a youth he lived in Germany whose soil and mines supported one of the denser populations of the Western world. Patten believed that the chief error of the classical economists was their assumption of an economy of scarcity. The political economist from the black prairies of Illinois postulated an economy of abundance. "We no longer live in an age of deficit and pain," he said in 1907 when he was a professor at the University of Pennsylvania, "but rather in an age of surplus and pleasure when all things are possible if we will but keep our eyes turned towards the future and strip our intelligences for their tasks."[22]

Patten admitted that the theory of scarcity had once been sound. It had been invalidated, however, he thought, by the rise of science. Equipped with knowledge, and made efficient by scientific techniques, modern man, believed Patten, can make nature yield a surplus. Science has solved the problem of production.

But Patten, looking about him in the United States, beheld want and suffering, not only in the blighted areas of the cities but even in the countryside of his own Illinois. He saw the paradox of poverty in the midst of plenty. He explained it by pointing to the asymmetrical economic development which was the product of the policy of *laissez faire* and by the wastefulness which resulted from the practice of competition. American conditions, he thought, refuted the contention of his friend, John Bates Clark, that the open market provides the proper and sufficient control for the economic forces which operate within an industrial civilization. Patten believed that the ills which beset democratic America and, in particular, the want which destroyed the liberty of millions of its citizens were the inevitable products of the faulty ideals of the gospel of wealth. They were the rank fruit of uncontrolled individualism.

Patten also believed in the power of ideals in human life. "Ideals are telic," said Patten in 1911, using a word which Ward had coined, "and must point out the means by which the end is reached. . . . Every clear ideal must meet this test. Without means of attainment and measures of results an ideal becomes meaningless. The real idealist is a pragmatist and an economist. He demands measurable results and reaches them by means made available by economic efficiency. Only in this way is social progress possible."[23] In Patten's mind a vision took form of a society founded upon an economy of abundance in which mankind would find a richer and a fuller life.

He considered this ideal the driving force within what he called, in a paraphrase of Ward, dynamic economics. For the means to make real this social dream his thought ran back to Germany. He recalled that careful management by the German people which stood in such painful contrast to the careless wastefulness of Americans. Johannes Conrad had taught him while at Halle how government can manage the use or consumption of wealth in such a way as to control and even to increase production. Patten was one of the first American economists to point out the economic disaster which threatened when the masses lose purchasing power. The logic of the Philadelphia economist drove toward economic nationalism. He approved of protectionism as a device of management. He looked to statistics as the sources of the information upon which policy must be based. He asserted the importance of efficiency both in private and in public business. But, again like Ward, though an advocate of a planned economy he proposed no specific pattern for national autarchy. He contented himself with the affirmation that Americans must turn from competition to cooperation, from the chaos of individualism to an efficient, pragmatic, planned economy, in other words, from Ricardo to List.

∽

Contemporary with Clark and Patten was that strange figure who disturbed the complacency of early twentieth-century intellectuals, Thorstein Veblen. He had studied with Sumner but had been influenced by Sumner's later anthropology rather than his earlier economics. Like Patten, Veblen saw America from the viewpoint of the rich Upper Mississippi Valley where he had been born of immigrant parents.

As Veblen looked at the realities of the business scene in the first decades of the twentieth century, he saw American economic life confused by a collision between two forces. Modern scientific civilization had produced, he thought, engineers, to use the term in a broad sense, whose energies were devoted to the making of goods. They were the creators of the machines of the new industrialism; they were the production managers of the integrated industries of the twentieth century. They controlled productive power which had never been put to full use and which was capable of bringing about within the United States a material revolution. But their hands were tied. They were not masters but servants. They took their orders from captains of finance whose ultimate object was not the making of goods but of money.

Nor did Veblen intend his analysis entirely as a criticism of individuals. He sought to describe the economic system which through a process of evolution had come into being in the United States. It was, he said, a pecuniary economy, its central driving force the profit motive. The analogy to the struggle for profits was war, thought Veblen. In business competition could be seen the stratagems, the maneuvers, the surprise attacks, and the frontal assaults which are the essence of military campaigns. Profit seeking stimulated predatory tendencies. The ethics of the market place tended toward those of the hawk. No one need be blamed that this was true; predation inheres in a pecuniary economy. The eighteenth-century pirate had reappeared as the twentieth-century trust. The result slows up production.

The essential characteristic of the pecuniary economy of the America of his day, thought Veblen, was the price system. And the essence of this was the business cycle, that dreary and terrifying alternation of prosperity and depression. When the masters of capital had overproduced and could no longer make money, they suspended production—they stayed the hand of the engineer. So Veblen came to what he conceived to be the basic antagonism within American capitalism, namely the opposition between the making of goods and the making of money. But he had no clear-cut solution for the dilemma which he observed. He was no Marxist. He spoke vaguely in his later books of some engineer-managed economic order which would replace the price system. These suggestions the later Technocrats translated into specific proposals. But Veblen contented himself with criticism. As events turned out, Veblen was a precursor of the institutional economics so important to the New Deal period.

Chapter 20

THE SOCIAL GOSPEL AND
THE SALVATION OF SOCIETY

In 1872 when the railroad kings were the economic lords of America, the Reverend Jesse H. Jones, a Congregational minister in North Abington, Massachusetts, felt that the time had come to bring to fruition a plan that had been forming in his mind since he had read John Ruskin's *The Crown of Wild Olive*, published in America in 1866. The Slade professor of the fine arts at Oxford, having turned from the reform of art to that of society, was preaching a curious economic and social philosophy which he called communism. Jones aspired to the rôle of the Ruskin of America, although his proposed program differed much from that of the Englishman. It had, in fact, more in common with the platforms of the ill-fated Fourierist communities which rose and fell in the 1840's.

Jones felt that the Christian Church should minister to the industrial wage earner and to the railway worker as much as to the employer. In Boston in 1872 Jones founded the Christian Labor Union, using the local assembly of the new Knights of Labor as his model. The purpose of the organization was the education of the workers and the support of labor reforms. All the members of the little band which Jones gathered about himself were ardent supporters of Steward's Eight-Hour Movement. One of these, a Catholic and a former judge in New Orleans, had once fallen under the spell of Fourierism and still meditated colonization schemes. To carry its message to America the Christian Labor Union established a monthly journal, hopefully named *Equity*, and appointed Jones its editor.

Under the influence of the cooperative movement developing in Great Britain and in the United States, *Equity* proclaimed the desirability of cooperative banks, workshops, and stores. Boldly espousing the cause of socialism, it proposed the public ownership of machinery, of mediums of exchange and transfer, and of the products of industry prior to their final distribution. In 1873 the failure of Jay Cooke and Company threw American business into panic. When the Erie Railroad men went on strike in the next year, *Equity*, going thoroughly Marxist, proclaimed the walkout to be the "first gun of the new revolution."

The revolution did not materialize, but the depression continued. In December, 1875, *Equity* suspended for want of funds. The last number contained the valedictory message of Jones, a document of some significance for those who would discover the mood of American Protestantism in the administration of President Grant. The editor had hoped for "a calm, deep, reverent, thorough discussion of the labor problem from the Christian standpoint." He had met with silence. "Except what two or three personal friends may have said, and a letter from a Negro minister in Arkansas, there has never come from a Christian brother one word of cheer. On the contrary, by silence or otherwise, the whole effort has been disapproved; and the editor, like Paul, is counted a 'pestilent fellow' whom all would heartily rejoice to see silenced." If Jesse H. Jones hoped that, also like Paul, he would ultimately be canonized by a repentant church, he was doomed to further disappointment. Nevertheless, American Protestantism or, more accurately, some of its leaders did ultimately repent. Through a new social gospel these prophets made a determined effort at the turn of the century to transform the churches of America into agencies for the amelioration of the unhappy lot of the House of Want.

∽

When Jones advocated socialism, he put himself beyond the pale of respectability. Socialism was the object of almost universal American criticism in the 1870's and the 1880's. Not that American leaders understood it very well. The chief citizens of the United States during these early post-Appomattox decades were inclined to group under the same generic term, "socialism," such diverse expressions of discontent as labor unions and the communistic anarchism of Johann Most. Henry Ward Beecher was unintentionally accurate in describing the American state of mind when he spoke of socialism as drifting in from the eastern ocean like a Newfoundland fog. Although during these years there was little knowledge of the niceties of the Marxian dialectic, there was a widespread conviction that socialism was bad. In spite of the fact that the Socialist Labor Party of the 1870's was insignificant in numbers and strength, the socialist movement was already becoming a bugaboo. Even that young liberal economist, Richard T. Ely, who pioneered in the effort to make Americans intelligent with respect to socialist theory, raised the alarm. Just back from his studies in Germany, he published in the *Christian Union* in 1884 a series of articles under the title, *Recent American Socialism*. They attracted wide attention and provided material for pulpit polemics against the foreign menace. "What we have to fear," concluded Ely, although he did not consider the threat immediate, "is large loss of life, estrangement of classes, incalculable destruction of property and a shock to the social body which will be a serious check to our economic growth for years to come."[1]

American Protestantism found itself after 1865 in a position of increasing difficulty. Its traditional doctrines were being eroded by science and by historical criticism. Radical proponents of the new religion of humanity were proposing their faith as a substitute for what they called an anachronistic Christianity. These humanists even charged that the Calvinist conception of God as an avenging Deity who punished some of his children forever in the burning lake was a relic of barbarism and a menace to good morals. Protestant ministers, particularly those in the new cities, found it increasingly hard to answer the questions: What should the pulpit preach; what should the churches do in a troubled world? The rank and file held fast to the old orthodoxy and contented themselves with the doctrine of stewardship of the gospel of wealth. A small but increasing minority began the development of what they called "a new theology."

Theodore Thornton Munger, a Congregationalist minister in New Haven, Connecticut, took the lead in the new movement. His volume, *The Freedom of the Faith*, published in 1883, expressed the mood and presented the ideas of the progressives. "The New Theology," said Munger, "accepts the phrase, 'a religion of humanity,' but it holds that it is more than an adjustment of the facts of humanity, and more than a reduction of the forces of humanity to harmony." Munger went along with science. He accepted evolution as the probable method of physical creation. He welcomed the new view of the Scriptures made possible by historical criticism. But he held fast to theism. He insisted that "the main relations of humanity are to God and that these relations constitute a theology, a science of God."[2] Nor did Munger avoid the issue between individualism and socialism. He stood fast on the old doctrine of the free and account-able individual. "Every man," he said, "must live a life of his own, build himself up into a full personality, and give an account of him-self to God; but [the new theology]," he added, ". . . also recog-nizes the blurred truth that man's life lies in his relations; that it is a derived and shared life; that it is carried on and perfected under laws of heredity and of the family and of the nation; that while he is 'himself alone' he is also a son, a parent, a citizen, and an insepa-rable part of the human race; that in origin and character and destiny he cannot be regarded as standing in a sharp and utter individu-ality."[3] Between the poles of individualism and socialism Munger worked from the traditional Protestant position toward middle ground. The new theology became a leaven which finally, through the social gospel movement, transformed American Protestantism.

～

In the year following the demise of Jesse H. Jones's *Equity* the Congregational Publishing Society brought out a disturbing little volume entitled *Being a Christian*. It has been called the first book of the social gospel movement. Its author, a young minister in Spring-field, Massachusetts, had recently resigned from the editorial staff of that great religious journal, the *Independent*, because he disap-proved of its policy of accepting what he considered dubious adver-tisements. In the centennial year of American independence this religious rebel declared that Christian discipleship is not the result of any ritual observance, the acceptance of any body of dogmas, or even any emotional mystical experience. He who would be a fol-lower of the Nazarene, declared Washington Gladden, needs but to accept as the ruling axiom of ethical conduct the command that a man shall love his neighbor as himself.

Gladden had grown up on a farm near Owego, New York, and had attended the Williams College of Mark Hopkins. As a senior he had written "The Mountains," which had been accepted as the alma mater song. Great as was his debt to Hopkins it was small com-pared to his obligation to Horace Bushnell. Bushnell had progressed from a local pastoral fame in Hartford, Connecticut, in the 1830's to an international reputation in the 1860's. He sought to humanize Calvinism. Before Mark Hopkins he had emphasized the law of love. Bushnell had pointed out to his young friend Gladden the humanity of the Founder of Christianity. The older clergyman emphasized that the crucifixion was not an event intended primarily for the con-venience of later theologians seeking to establish the justice of God, but was rather the martyrdom of a man filled with the divine spirit who, in going to his death for what he believed, set an example in self-sacrifice for all the world. When, after 1865, conservative doctors of divinity opened fire on Bushnell, young Gladden hurried to his defense.

Putting, like Munger, the teachings of Bushnell to work in his own life, Washington Gladden gradually evolved during the 1870's most of the fundamentals of the social gospel. In the same decade Octavius Brooks Frothingham was formulating the basic concepts of the American religion of humanity; Ingersoll was rising to the climax of his campaign of ridicule and vituperation against the old orthodoxy; and Lester F. Ward was completing his magnum opus, *Dynamic Sociology*. The last three dismissed theism as outmoded by science. Unlike them Gladden held fast to the faith. He welcomed science and scholarship as the partners of religion. Evolution offered a new picture of the process of creation. Historical criticism, thought Gladden, was the friend rather than the enemy of the Scriptures. The passing of the doctrine of literal inspiration lifted from his clerical shoulders the burden of defending against the jibes of Ingersoll the literal historicity of such famous sea tales as that of Jonah and the whale. Gladden became a crusader for the new liberalism.

In 1882 he was called to Columbus, Ohio, where he remained as pastor and pastor emeritus until his death thirty-six years later. In the Ohio capital he plunged with the vigor of a Peter Cartwright into that most pressing problem, the relation between employers and employees. Gladden was at the same time courageous and conciliatory. He spoke his mind boldly. He became a man of action who, because of his honesty and common sense, won the confidence and respect of both capitalists and laborers. In 1885 when the entrepreneur class of the industrial East was watching the rise of the Knights of Labor with growing anger and fear, Gladden told the employers that labor had a right to organize and to strike. At the same time he reminded his ministerial colleagues that their churches were following rather than leading American social movements. He pointed to the widening gulf between the man at the mahogany desk and his brother working in the machine shop. Gladden asked whether "there shall be a caste system recognized and established in our churches; so that the rich shall meet by themselves in the grand churches, and the poor in the mission chapels; and that there shall be no sympathy between the two classes, but only alms, with a certain haughty condescension on the one side, and a qualified mendicancy, with envious resentment, on the other."[4]

Gladden's answer in 1885 to the question, what to do about the problem of labor, was typical of his middle-of-the-road liberalism. He rejected complete communism or socialism on the ground that such a society must produce weak and flabby individuals. Only by requiring a man to stand on his own feet, to take his hard knocks without running to some political substitute for mother's knee, and to develop initiative and prudence could characters of strength and resiliency be created. In his adherence to this traditional American emphasis upon the individual, Gladden was as uncompromising as W. G. Sumner or as William James. Gladden dismissed contemptuously the notion masquerading as socialism in the 1880's that private property is robbery. He proposed the cooperative as the only hope of labor to achieve economic independence and security. He advocated in addition a limited State socialism in the form of the public ownership of utilities. This moderate stand, however, was enough to brand him as a radical in 1887, when conservatives mobilized without success to prevent the surrender of the Federal government to the demand of the farmers that the railroads be regulated.

Ten years passed after the establishment of the Interstate Commerce Commission. Washington Gladden, surveying the American scene, felt grave forebodings. Big business, defended by the constitutional philosophy of Stephen J. Field and David Brewer, was increasing its hold on American resources and its power in American politics. The battalions of labor, badly disorganized by the collapse of the Knights following the anarchist trials in Chicago in 1886, were rallying again about the standard of that ambitious cigarmaker, Samuel Gompers. Industrial war had blazed up at Homestead, Pennsylvania, in 1892 and at Chicago in 1894. The only solution of the labor problem which President Cleveland or the Federal courts could offer was the coercion expressed in the labor injunction and in the army. Gladden became convinced that in American civilization the forces making for disruption were gaining the ascendency over those making for cohesion. Class war was no longer a possibility; it was a reality. "We are driving," he declared in 1899, "toward chaos."[5]

Gladden sought desperately for a principle or a formula which would stop the break-up of a great civilization. He proclaimed in the last hours of the nineteenth century the need of a new sense of the community. He agreed with Royce, though he did not mention the philosopher, that the individual can only be saved by the community. What is the uniting principle which holds a people together? asked Gladden. Is it the State? It should be, he answered, thinking of the American democratic faith. Then, with that political realism which is one of the oldest of American characteristics, he rejected the hypothesis. The State is not the bond of unity; it is the cockpit of strife. The national capital is the battleground for endless wars among special interests. The State has already fallen largely under the control of the employer class; only conflict can restore it to the people. Is, then, Gladden continued, the Christian Church the institution which will overcome the forces making for disintegration? It would be, he maintained, if it were true to the ideals of its Founder. But look at it. Note its sects and denominations divided by petty rivalries and demoralized by corrosive jealousies. Note its tendency to take "a class view of all social questions; to regard the grievances of the laboring poor as wholly imaginary and their complaints and uprisings as evidences of depravity; to take sides, rather positively, with the employing class."[6] Let the Christian Church establish unity within itself before it attempts the pacification of society. Let its ministers catch the vision of social justice before they attempt to lead the people in the ways of right living. Gladden did not consider the regeneration of the Church a hopeless prospect. He was a vigorous, pioneering crusader for Church unity. But he recognized that he had not yet found the principle which would check the disintegration of American society.

Individualism unmodified, affirmed Gladden, creates a society which is like a pile of sand. It has no coherence and falls apart at the least disturbance. Socialism, he added, creates a society which is like a liquid solution. The individual element loses its identity and is swallowed up by the mass. Gladden found the mean between the two extremes in the formula of the "socialized individual." He went beyond the doctrine of stewardship in the gospel of wealth. True to his Christian faith, he maintained that the ideal of unity requires a belief in God. Science, he pointed out, is atomistic; it emphasizes specialization and discloses the many in the cosmos. Only God is one, and man must seek unity through Him. The only teaching which has a chance of saving society is the doctrine of the fatherhood of God and the brotherhood of man. This formula provided him with a unifying principle. The humanists who affirmed merely the latter half missed, thought Gladden, the central truth. But so far as they went, they were right. "What men call 'natural law,' by which they mean the law of greed and strife . . . is not a natural law," declared the Columbus preacher; "it is unnatural; it is a crime against nature; the law of brotherhood is the only natural law. The law of nature is the law of sympathy, of fellowship, of mutual help and service. It is only when a man owns the bond that binds him to his kind that he has any chance of becoming an individual."[7] Gladden furthered the doctrine of the fundamental law as an item of Christian faith.

Gladden balanced his preaching of the good with blows against specific evils. In the early 1890's he assailed the potent American Protective Association for its attacks upon Catholic citizens. In 1905 he exploded a bomb which jarred American Protestantism from coast to coast. In a paper entitled, "Shall Ill-Gotten Gains be Sought for Christian Purposes?" he asked the American Board of Commissioners for Foreign Missions, to its vast discomfort, to explain why its solicitation of a gift of a hundred thousand "tainted" dollars from the head of what was reputed to be the most predatory of American trusts did not make the Church a partner with plunderers? In the melee which followed, the Protestant clergy demonstrated that the art of obscurantism was not dead. As for Gladden, his work was done. The scarred veteran of a score of battles died on that fateful second of July, 1918, when French and American machine guns turned back the advance of the gray columns along the road to Paris.

&

Two years after Washington Gladden published *On Being a Christian* an earnest young man named William Dwight Porter Bliss graduated from Amherst. In the summer between his junior and his senior years he had watched with astonishment and dismay the railroad strikes of 1877 which culminated in the battle of the Pittsburgh roundhouse. Years before, his parents had gone as missionaries to Turkey to carry the Christian civilization of America to the heathen. Bliss had been born in Constantinople and had spent his boyhood in that great city linking the East and the West. The summer of 1877 made clear to this young American, who was just discovering his homeland, that he who would go in search of heathendom need not look outside the boundaries of the United States. Bliss became a missionary to America from Constantinople and from Robert College.

He studied theology at the Hartford Theological Seminary and on the side mastered Henry George's *Progress and Poverty*. When the Fabian Society was organized in England in 1883, partly as a result of George's British lecture tour, Bliss read English socialism in the Fabian tracts. In 1886 he found himself in charge of St. George's Episcopal Church in the factory town of Lee, Massachusetts. The young minister to the wage earners promptly joined the Knights of Labor and became the master workman of a local assembly. His work among the Knights brought Bliss into contact with George McNeill, veteran leader of the Eight-Hour Movement. Rarely have two men influenced one another more profoundly. McNeill indoctrinated the pastor with the Eight-Hour philosophy of progress and together the two discussed innumerable plans for the betterment of labor. In 1890 Bliss resigned the Boston pastorate to which he had been promoted in order that he might establish in South Boston what he called the Mission of the Carpenter. Before many months the mission became a church for working people. Here among other activities, an organization called the Brotherhood of the Carpenter held weekly meetings for the discussion of labor problems. Bliss's senior warden was George McNeill, whom the minister had rescued from the agnosticism into which he had been driven as a young man by the preachers of the gospel of wealth. The Church of the Carpenter was a perfect expression in institutional form of the ideal of the social gospel movement.

Meanwhile Bliss had been pushing the battle for social justice on other fronts. In 1887 with Bishop F. D. Huntington of New York he had founded the (Episcopal) Church Association for the Advancement of the Interests of Labor, popularly known as CAIL. Its basic principle was that new doctrine of solidarity expressed in the formula, the fatherhood of God and the brotherhood of man. The association declared that God is the sole possessor of the earth, that man is only the steward of His bounties, and that the end of life is labor, when labor is defined as the exercise of body, mind, and spirit for the broadening and elevating of human kind. The duty to labor is universal, thought Bliss, and the quality of a man's work, rather than riches or birth, should be the standard of social worth. The most important plank of the CAIL platform was the conclusion that the chief of man's God-given rights is the right to work. CAIL was a success in the sense that it soon secured a large and influential membership from among the clergy of the Church. Bishops, rectors, and laymen cooperated in its effort to achieve social justice by pleading the cause of labor before the employer, by furthering the passage of industrial legislation, and by establishing a Council of Conciliation and Mediation to function in labor disputes. CAIL was one of the most important early fruits of the social gospel movement.

In the year of the founding of CAIL, Edward Bellamy published *Looking Backward*. Bliss read it with such enthusiasm that, in 1889, he became a charter member of the first Nationalist club to be organized in Boston. But even as he signed his name to the first roll of members Bellamy's message of humanism seemed to him a diluted broth. Recognizing the power which sometimes lies in a name, Bliss hunted up the Reverend Francis Bellamy, an obscure cousin of the novelist who had suddenly become a celebrity. The two called the organizing meeting of the Society of Christian Socialists within a few months after the establishment of the Nationalist club. A journal called the *Dawn*, with Bliss as editor, promptly appeared. So Bliss, early in his career, passed beyond the middle-of-the-road positions of Munger and of Gladden to the affirmation that socialism expresses the true meaning of the formula of the brotherhood of man under the fatherhood of God.

The East was even colder to Christian Socialism that it was to Bellamyism; in the Upper Mississippi Valley Bliss's organization became a Christian tail to the Bellamy kite. For a brief space the Christian Socialists boasted a state organization of local clubs in Illinois and in Kansas. But Populism satisfied the intellectual and emotional demands of the western farmers without requiring agrarian individualists to subscribe to an unfamiliar doctrine of solidarity. Neither Christian Socialism nor Bellamyism ever got into the grass roots. Bliss, on an organization tour, stopped in Iowa to inspect two experiments in religious communism at Icaria and Amana. At the latter the Boston reformer was impressed with the economic success of the twenty-four hundred pious Germans who owned some twenty-five thousand acres and capital valued at one million dollars. Bliss came back to Boston pondering a scheme to establish a Union Farm, an up-to-date Brook Farm where clergymen, who were Christian Socialists, might live in common and devote a part of each day to manual labor. Unfortunately the divines did not share Bliss's enthusiasm for manual labor; there never was a Union Farm. Bliss himself soon gave up the plan of reforming society through the example of experimental communities and returned to his former advocacy of the complete program of socialism.

Meanwhile *Dawn* had met the same fate as Jesse H. Jones's *Equity*. The undiscouraged Bliss in his campaign for solidarity tried a new stratagem. The Fabian Society by the end of its first decade had made an important place for itself in English thought. In February, 1895, Bliss took the lead in founding The American Fabian Society. Similar beginnings were made almost simultaneously in California and Washington under the influence of Lawrence Grunland. The inevitable journal, this time called *The American Fabian*, appeared, and Bliss was again the editor. Contributing editors were Edward Bellamy and Henry Demarest Lloyd. Fabianism, however, went the way of Christian Socialism. Yet Bliss refused to give up the fight.

The publishing firm of Funk and Wagnalls asked him to undertake the editorship of a proposed *Encyclopaedia of Social Reform*. In 1897 he brought out a monumental compendium of information running to more than fourteen hundred pages. It was a pioneering enterprise. The resources of American scholarship were still limited; critical standards were not well developed in the American intellectual climate. Bliss called to his aid as contributors or revisers of articles some of the best men of the times. His list included John R. Commons, William A. Dunning, Franklin H. Giddings, Arthur T. Hadley, Graham Taylor, David A. Wells, and Carroll D. Wright. The *Encyclopaedia* was an important event in the battle for humanitarian reform in that it brought to lieutenants on widely separated fronts information concerning the progress of the campaign. It was Bliss's greatest achievement. One of the longest and best of its articles was from his pen and had to do with Christian Socialism in Europe and America. Although his organization had died, Bliss was determined to preserve its ideals against the time when the Christian Church should discover that its true function was no longer to sanctify the philosophy of individualistic capitalism, but was to take the lead toward a cooperative commonwealth.

The American variety of Christian Socialism, according to Bliss in the *Encyclopaedia*, had a program for the individual, for the State, and for the Church. It demanded of the individual that he recognize the principle of brotherhood and that he sacrifice time, money, and, if necessary, position for his conviction. It also required of him participation in humanitarian enterprise and called upon him to join those labor organizations striving for social justice. The program for the State demanded a reform of politics. The rule of the boss must be destroyed. Democracy must be made real by the adoption of the initiative and referendum, proportional representation, and the granting of suffrage to women. The Eight-Hour Movement must be furthered that men may have more time to labor in the home, the library, and the church. Municipal socialism must be developed until cities own their utilities; give work to their unemployed; and provide parks, baths, and even publicly owned tenements for their people. State socialism must be advanced until the nation owns and manages its railways, telegraph lines, and express services. In business the principle of competition must be replaced by that of cooperation. Finally by a land tax whose rate would increase at periodic intervals the nation should recover for its people the ownership of its soil and its natural resources and restore to its citizens their God-given right to live upon the earth and to enjoy its bounties. In its program for the Church, Christian Socialism demanded that denominations repudiate the selfishness of capitalism and that they found their teaching on the principle of social solidarity.

Henry George, rather than Karl Marx, was the patron saint of this socialism. Its essence was gradualism rather than revolution, brotherhood in a classless society rather than class war. Unlike the religion of humanity it did not hope to achieve the golden day through the efforts of man alone. It frankly accepted theism. "We hold," said Bliss, "that God is the source and guide of all human progress."[8] In spite of its obvious debt to the Sermon on the Mount, it did not, however, win American Protestantism.

∾

In the autumn of 1893, while W. D. P. Bliss mourned the failure of his Society of Christian Socialists and while other Americans lamented the inability of the Cleveland administration to check the most formidable depression for twenty years, the quiet campus of Iowa College, later Grinnell, was stirred by the advent of a new professor. The Reverend George D. Herron of the First Congregational Church of Burlington, Iowa, had been called to fill the new chair of Applied Christianity which had been endowed for him by one of his Burlington parishioners, Mrs. E. D. Rand. Herron was born in Indiana of working-class origin and was brought up in an intensely religious home. After a short term at a Wisconsin academy he became in 1883 a boy preacher at twenty-one. He cultivated the Lord's vineyard in the Middle West in obscurity until at a Minnesota conference of Congregational ministers he read a paper, "The

Message of Jesus to Men of Wealth." Herron charged that the most pernicious type of American pauperism was that of the rich who lived at the expense of society without giving adequate return. The fame of the young radical of the Upper Mississippi Valley ballooned with that of the Populist movement and soon took him, with the aid of Mrs. Rand, to his academic post. Mrs. Rand moved to Grinnell, and the grateful college made her daughter, Carrie, dean of women. For the next seven years Herron was the most prominent and probably, with the exception of Ohio's Washington Gladden, the most influential preacher in the Middle West.

There was no subtle dialectic in the thought of this philosopher of the corn belt. When he began his lectures to Grinnell undergraduates at the age of thirty-one, he announced that he was proud of the fact that he had no opinions; he possessed only "beliefs and convictions." These he set forth with finality in pungent addresses and in little books which enjoyed some enthusiastic reviews. One platform invitation led to another, for Herron was an effective speaker. He lectured at colleges and divinity schools; he talked before church congregations, and he spoke to popular audiences. His tours took him from the Atlantic to the Pacific. Everywhere he aroused controversy; everywhere he made enemies among the supporters of the established order. In San Francisco he was the center of a storm from which he emerged in triumph. In the decade of the Populist crusade he was the ecclesiastical counterpart of William Jennings Bryan. Herron stumped the country for the Kingdom of God.

His message was simple. For the law of selfishness which governs capitalism, men must substitute the law of love set forth in the Sermon on the Mount. Capitalism must be replaced by socialism. (In 1900 Herron joined the Socialist party.) The doctrine of the brotherhood of men "is the most revolutionary expression ever uttered, and the seed of mighty revolutions now on their way."[9] It is, thought Herron, a doctrine of equalitarianism which destroys the distinctions between the rich and the poor, the cultured and uncultivated. The Church must give up the flesh pots and must accept the cross of sacrifice. "I would save the Church," he said with that impressive solemnity which captured his audiences, "from the false position of existing and working for its own glory and religious aggrandizement."[10] Herron's power was almost hypnotic. He equalled even the great Moody's ability to command the spirits of men. His gospel of the redemption of society through the sacrifices of individuals was the antithesis of the gospel of wealth. Russell H. Conwell urged his hearers to get rich; George D. Herron demanded that they spend themselves to the uttermost. He pointed to the single tax movement, he pointed to Bellamyism and above all to Populism as evidence that God was, even then, working in the world. Deity was bringing about a revolution. The Kingdom was at hand. Let not the children of men falter in this hour of crisis and of triumph. In that Kingdom the law of love would not only improve the lot of the poor farmer and the pinched wage earner, it would put the unlearned man on a footing of equality with his educated brother. Herron roused such a storm of protest from the economic and ecclesiastical lords of America as to give President Gates of Grinnell an opportunity to become one of the heroes in the perennial battle for academic freedom.

From childhood Herron, completely devoid of humor, cherished the belief that he was destined to play a messianic rôle in the redemption of the world. He was, in the words of William Allen White, "one of God's pedestal dwellers, always moving about in bronze and marble."[11] He was as sure of himself as Joseph Smith; like the Mormon prophet he became neglectful after a time of certain ancient social standards and customs which he felt had been outgrown. As the end of the century approached, he began to speak of marriage as, like capitalism, a coercive institution. An earthquake shook Grinnell in 1901 when, two months after Herron's wife had obtained an uncontested divorce, the prophet of the cross married Carrie Rand. The Congregational ministers of the district unfrocked their colleague who, they thought, was taking the law of love somewhat too literally. The influence and prestige of Herron plummeted from the skies.

Yet Herron's work was not done. His gospel of sacrifice produced two concrete results, Charles M. Sheldon's *In His Steps* and the Christian Commonwealth Community of Georgia. The former Grinnell professor became an exile in Europe. From across the Atlantic he struck a blow for liberalism in America when he brought about the investment of the bulk of his mother-in-law's fortune in the founding of the Rand School of Social Science in New York City.

Before 1914 Herron's Italian villa attracted attention as a rendezvous for interesting intellectuals from many countries. After 1917 the aging prophet became again a crusader and strove with some of his former energy to bring to the liberals of war-torn Europe an understanding of the democratic idealism of Woodrow Wilson.

∼

"The world is ruled by ideas," said Herron in 1893. "Every few centuries God drops a great idea into the soul of man."[12] The Grinnell instructor believed that his constantly repeated gospel of the redemption of society by sacrifice was such a divinely implanted idea. This formula dropped into the soul of the Reverend Charles M. Sheldon, a Congregational minister at Topeka, Kansas, the center of a New England Puritanism transplanted to the plains. The fruit was a novel entitled *In His Steps,* first published in 1898. An amazing sale totalling more than fifteen million copies admitted this book to the select company of great American tracts. T. S. Arthur's *Ten Nights in a Bar Room,* Harriet Beecher Stowe's *Uncle Tom's Cabin,* and Sheldon's *In His Steps* are supreme in this literary field. Sheldon remained true to the philosophy of his book when he used its small royalties to further social progress.

Sheldon in his story proposed as the solution for social ills that each individual, rich or poor, when faced with a decision, should pause to ask himself the question: "What would Jesus do?" In such a way the ethics of the Sermon on the Mount, of Gethsemane, and of Calvary would be made regnant in American life. The novelist described in simple and effective language the revolution which occurred in the lives of the parishioners of his hero, Henry Maxwell, after they had taken the pledge to ask themselves the question at every personal crisis during a trial year. When the success of Maxwell's experiment was becoming a triumph at the end of the twelvemonth period, the young minister found himself facing the critical question in an unexpected way. So also was his ecclesiastical superior, a cultivated and humane bishop, who had supported the clergyman in his crusade. Independently the two men reached the same answer, namely that each must give up his success, abandon the comfort and security of his professional post, and devote his life and substance without reservation in new fields to the amelioration of the lot of the underprivileged masses. The two established a social settlement in Chicago where the bishop and the minister sought to give concrete meaning to the brotherhood of man.

In his concluding chapter Sheldon described a public meeting at the settlement in which the topic of discussion was the social efficacy of the question. In the midst of the discussion a man rose and told of his long-continued and futile efforts to obtain work after he had lost his job as a result of the introduction of new machinery. His small reserve had disappeared and his family was suffering. He asked Henry Maxwell what, in such a situation, Jesus would do. The novelist used this situation as a device to permit him to consider the answers of the single taxer and of the socialist who arose to make reply to the jobless questioner. The author rejected both. The answer of the Topeka philosopher to the unemployed man was that, when the Kingdom of God shall have been realized on earth, the law of that Kingdom which is sacrifice and the bearing of one an-other's burdens will be triumphant. In such a world no man can lack for work. Sheldon repudiated the Christian Socialism of Bliss; he added to Gladden's concept of the socialized individual the Herron doctrine of social redemption through individual sacrifice. The concluding sentence of the book epitomizes the romantic senti-ment and the utopianism which gave it a place next to the Bible as the most widely read religious book in America in the first decade of the twentieth century. "And with a hope that walks hand in hand with faith and love, Henry Maxwell, disciple of Jesus, laid him down to sleep, and dreamed of the regeneration of Christendom and saw in his dream a church of Jesus 'without spot or wrinkle or any such thing,' following Him all the way, walking obediently in His steps."

∽

Two years before Charles M. Sheldon produced his romance Ralph Albertson founded on a wornout cotton plantation twelve miles east of Columbus, Georgia, the Christian Commonwealth Colony, whose purpose was to obey the teachings of Jesus "in all matters of life, labor, and the use of property." At Oberlin Theo-logical Seminary and later as the Congregational pastor of a work-ing men's parish in Springfield, Ohio, Albertson had been influenced by the thought of Henry George, of Edward Bellamy, of Wash-ington Gladden, and of George D. Herron, who addressed Albert-son's Springfield congregation during the panic of 1893. Tolstoy, extreme Christian pacifist and humanitarian, also profoundly in-fluenced the Springfield pastor. During the Pullman strike of 1894 Albertson saw class war at first hand. He witnessed the uncontrolled and often purposeless destruction wrought by the mob, the stern use of force by Grover Cleveland's soldiers, in hand to hand strug-gles on the streets and in the railroad yards. On every side he saw idealism, save that perhaps of Eugene V. Debs, degenerate into ha-tred. Albertson became convinced that the Pullman war was the natural and inevitable result of an economic system with a central principle of competitive profit-seeking. He decided that in the desert of materialism which was called the United States he would create an oasis of self-forgetting brotherhood.

On the day before that happy Thanksgiving Day in 1896 when every eastern industrialist returned thanks for the defeat of William Jennings Bryan, Albertson and the first contingent of the Christian Commonwealth Colony arrived at the Georgia plantation. A second group of families, who had traveled from Lincoln, Nebraska, reached Commonwealth on the day before Christmas. A third party ended a three months' trip by prairie schooner from Nebraska on August 27, 1897. Those rigors and uncertainties of life on the Great Plains which had brought about the Populist revolt reinforced the appeal of Albertson's experiment in Christian brotherhood.

The colony applied the principles of diversified agriculture to its thousand acres. It built a simple cotton mill and manufactured coarse towels for sale in the open market. In a printing shop was published a monthly journal *The Social Gospel*. This journalistic venture soon became one of the main supports of the colony. The magazine dealt with all phases of Christianity and devoted only a small fraction of its space to the colony. George D. Herron was a contributing editor and Charles M. Sheldon a friendly supporter. The social arrangements of the colony conformed to the American mores. Each family had a cottage of its own or had rooms in the old plantation house. Eating was done in the common dining hall or in the family quarters as desired. Labor was managed by a time chart which recorded the contribution of each individual. There were no rewards. Puritan asceticism was conspicuously absent; the colony encouraged such play as its poverty would permit.

The property arrangements were complete communism. The management of the colony was an equally complete democracy. Albertson refused election as president in order to set an example in humility. The central principle of the enterprise was that of the open door. The man who asked admission was taken into the fold no matter what his past had been or what his abilities were. As a member of the colony he enjoyed equal political and economic status with the rest. No tramp was refused admittance nor was he expelled when he became a parasite. Jane Addams, visiting Commonwealth, inquired if the open door policy did not cause an influx into the colony from the neighboring poor house. She was told that such a migration had occurred the winter before, but that the colony fare of corn meal and cowpeas had caused the paupers to retreat to their former abode where bacon was supplied occasionally. The poverty of the colony, said Jane Addams, was "so biting that the only ones willing to face it were those sustained by a conviction of its righteousness."[13] "We have all lived for months and months," said the *Social Gospel* in January, 1900, "on less than three cents each meal to divide with the world's destitute ones." "We cannot indulge in luxuries," added Albertson, "until we have honestly preferred God's poor above ourselves, nor even hold or use life's necessities in any selfish way."[14] The ideal of the colonists, by their own confession, was St. Francis of Assisi. Greatest among the many outside friends of the colony was Count Tolstoy. "I feel concerned," he wrote to an American correspondent, "about all that goes on at the Christian Commonwealth. I read all their journals with deep interest and never cease to rejoice at the firmness of their views and the beautiful expression of their thoughts."[15] Well might the great Russian be concerned. Here on a Georgia plantation the Christian law of love as the sole governing code was being put to the practical test.

Three blows in quick succession destroyed the Commonwealth in 1899. A heavy freeze in February so damaged the crops and fruit trees as to jeopardize the food supply. A small cabal of renegade members, admitted by the open door policy, sought by false charges to throw the colony into bankruptcy in order to secure a share of its property. Two of the more obstreperous trouble makers were taken into custody by the sheriff. In court the colony easily won a victory which was at the same time a disastrous defeat. In calling the sheriff the colonists had abandoned, in spite of the protests of Albertson, their basic principle of non-resistance. They had appealed from the law of love to that of physical force. Their faith was shaken and their morale lowered. Dissension appeared. In the midst of the trouble typhoid fever swept the colony. The epidemic ended the enterprise. A voluntary petition of bankruptcy was filed and the court, after all accounts were settled, distributed eight dollars and fifty cents to each family. "The experiment," remarked Jane Addams, "portrayed both the weakness and the strange august dignity of the Tolstoy position."[16]

～

"Revolutions," said George D. Herron in 1893, "even in their wildest forms, are the impulses of God moving in tides of fire through the life of men."[17] This theistic faith was the core of the thought of the man who in the first two decades of the twentieth century lifted the social gospel above the romanticism of Sheldon and the dogmatism of the Grinnell prophet to intellectual dignity. Walter Rauschenbusch had passed middle life when he published, in 1907, his first important book, *Christianity and the Social Crisis*. For many years before writing this essay he had been quietly teaching Church history at the Rochester Theological Seminary, lost apparently in the half-forgotten controversies of vanished generations. The habitat of his thought was antiquity, the Middle Ages, and the Reformation. But he saw the intellectual battles of other days through the eyes of that young minister to the poor of the West Side of New York City he once had been. Of this New York period he remarked that he could never forget "the procession of men out of work, out of clothes, out of shoes, and out of hope. They wore down our threshold and they wore away our hearts."[18] Gradually for Rauschenbusch at Rochester the dark materials of Church history began to take on a new significance and its episodes to fall into a sequence which illuminated the problems of the present and threw forward a light which disclosed the possibilities of the future. He abandoned the task of the historian for the rôle of the prophet. A prophet, he remarked by way of definition in 1917, is a man who has "a religious conviction that God is against oppression and [is] on the side of the weak."[19]

The social gospel movement had made progress before Rauschenbusch wrote *Christianity and the Social Crisis*. The new theology of Munger, the work of Gladden, and the idealism of Bliss and of Sheldon had borne fruit in an increased social consciousness on the part of the churches. In 1908 the establishment of the Federal Council of Churches was a partial fulfillment of Gladden's dream of unity. The Council's vigorous declaration of support for the rights of labor was a triumph for the social gospelers. Other results were the institutional churches, modeled on social settlements, which had appeared in almost every great American city. In the more liberal and more important theological seminaries the study of contemporary society had taken its place beside that of Hebrew antiquity. A vigorous and intellectually sophisticated literature sprang up from coast to coast as educated young clergymen added their voices to the "demand that social justice be defined in Christian terms." A secular progressivism was in the air as the twentieth century opened. "Progress" was the word which disclosed the

character of the intellectual climate of the period of the first Roosevelt. And to millions of Americans "Progress" was synonymous
with "reform." The rising demand for a march forward in America convinced Rauschenbusch that God was again at work in the
world. The church historian became fired with the hope that, after
nineteen hundred years of human travail, the "great day for which
the ages waited" was about to dawn.[20] He conceived his task to be
the renovation of a theology which had dominated Christian
thought for more than a millennium. It was an ambitious program.
The hand of tradition is nowhere heavier than when it is laid on
theology. But the quiet church historian did not overestimate his
strength. He became, before the end of the first quarter of the
twentieth century, a world figure in Christendom. His was the only
American plea for a social gospel that was heard across the Atlantic.

Rauschenbusch began his work in 1907 with the volume, *Christianity and the Social Crisis*. Five years later he wrote a second discussion of contemporary social problems under the title, *Christianizing the Social Order*. In 1917, a few weeks after the United States
entered the World War, he delivered a series of lectures at the
Yale Divinity School collected in a volume called *A Theology for
the Social Gospel*. These three books established the position of
Rauschenbusch and of the social gospel in the intellectual world.

The Rauschenbusch philosophy, like those of Henry George and
of Lester Frank Ward, began with criticism of the existing order
and ended with a positive program. In the days when the muckrakers were at their apogee, Rauschenbusch pointed to industrial
capitalism as the primary cause of the evils besetting American society. The institution was bad, thought the Rochester theologian,
rather than the men who lived and worked within it, iniquitous as
some of these had been proved to be. The fact that men were not
worse after a prolonged experience with capitalism was proof of a
tough goodness in the human heart. Rauschenbusch borrowed from
the liberals of his age four much used arrows for discharge against
the capitalist dragon. He demanded the end of competition, which
he called the law of tooth and nail. "Competition as a principle," he
declared in 1912, "is a denial of fraternity."[21] But the competition
among small enterprises was giving way to the monopoly of giant
corporations, nation-wide in scope and dictatorial in policy. "In
business," he said, "the autocratic principle is still in full possession,
unshaken and unterrified, with its flag flying from every battlement.
Business is the last entrenchment of autocracy, and wherever de-

mocracy is being beaten back, the sally is made from that citadel."[22] He borrowed his third arrow from agrarian Populism which was reappearing in developed form as the Progressive movement. Under capitalism, he charged, the middleman has become the controlling figure. Rauschenbusch repeated the familiar catalogue of the middleman's sins, adulteration of foods, short weights, spurious advertising, and irresponsible selfishness. Finally and fourthly the Rochester critic assailed the profit motive. In a simple economy, profit is a legitimate reward for labor, but where profit is traceable to some kind of monopoly privilege, "it is tribute collected by power from the helpless." Twentieth-century industrial capitalism had become in Rauschenbusch's opinion "a mammonistic organization with which Christianity can never be content."[23] "If we can trust the Bible," he added in 1917, "God is against capitalism, its methods, spirit and results."[24]

From big business Rauschenbusch turned his attention to the churches of the United States. He saw them against a background of nearly two thousand years of ecclesiastical history. He became convinced that they were failing in the charge committed to them. "The common mind of the Christian Church in America," he declared, "has not begun to arrive at any solid convictions or any permanent basis of action. The conscience of Christendom is halting and groping, perplexed by contradicting voices, still poorly informed on essential questions, justly reluctant to part with the treasured maxims of the past, and yet conscious of the imperious call of the future."[25] To his fellow Christians Rauschenbusch proposed two ideals, one a picture of the better society and the other a statement of a new theology.

The new society must substitute the moral law for that of the jungle. "Christianizing the social order means bringing it into harmony with the ethical convictions which we identify with Christ. . . . The fundamental step is the establishment of social justice by the abolition of unjust privilege."[26] The just society, thought the Rochester theologian, implies cooperation and approximate equality among its members, collective property rights, and, of course, democracy. "A condition in which one-fourth of the race holds all the opportunities of livelihood in its arbitrary control, and the other three-fourths are without property, without access to the earth, and without an assured means of even working for a living, is neither American nor Christian. Property is a means of grace, and a good job is another."[27] But property, to serve men effectively, must be socialized. He did not suggest the complete communism of the Christian Commonwealth. He demanded rather the nationalization of those economic resources upon which society rests, minerals, forests, and water power. He would also, following Henry George, take away from the private owner the unearned increment to the value of his land. In short the Rauschenbusch picture of the new society differed little in mundane details from that of the revisionist socialists. He looked to labor to bring in, but not by war, the glad tomorrow. Labor, he declared, "is the most modern of all classes, the product of today, the creator of tomorrow, the banner bearer of destiny."[28]

How is the new day to be achieved? The Rauschenbusch answer to this question is his contribution to Christian theology. Mankind, he postulated, is possessed of a vast reserve of latent moral energy, the release of which is the chief human problem. The solution was discovered and announced in antiquity by no less a person than the Carpenter-Teacher of Palestine, who neither founded a Church nor desired that one be established. He spoke only of founding a kingdom. He called it the Kingdom of God. He thought in terms of a kingdom on earth. "The Kingdom of God," said Rauschenbusch the theist, "is not a concept nor an ideal merely, but an historical force. It is a vital and organizing energy now at work in humanity. Its capacity to save the social order depends on its pervasive presence within the social organism."[29] If the ideal of the Kingdom was announced so long ago, why has it been ineffective for these near-two thousand years? The blame, thought Rauschenbusch, lies with the theologians and the ecclesiastics. The Christian Church was organized in the Roman world and quickly developed interests peculiar to itself. The theologians, speculating about the meaning of the phrase, Kingdom of God, began to limit its implications. St. Augustine completed the devolution of a great ideal when he identified the Kingdom of God with the Catholic Church. Although the Protestant rebels enlarged the concept, they never re-established it in its original all-inclusive sense. The time had now come, thought Rauschenbusch, when Christians must forget the peculiar interests of their little churches and must join in a nation-wide, even a world-wide, effort to bring about the amelioration of society. For nearly two thousand years that divine force which is the Kingdom of God has been impeded, taught Rauschenbusch, by the limitations and inadequacies of man's conception of this Kingdom as an ideal. Rauschenbusch tore away the theological wrappings concealing what he thought to be the truth and disclosed to his fellow Christians in its original purity the ideal of the Founder of the faith.

As Rauschenbusch spoke in New Haven in 1917 the war in Europe was entering its third summer and the President of the United States was beginning the mobilization of the nation's manpower. Rauschenbusch did not think the war a holy crusade. He was no sentimentalist when he maintained that the fundamental law of society is that of love, or in Paul's phrase, of "charity." The Kingdom of Evil, declared Rauschenbusch, is a present-day fact. Capitalism with its greed and its ruthless and cruel competition is one of its manifestations and the war spirit which causes a people to seek by violence to impose its will upon its neighbor is another. The Kingdom of Evil is populated no longer by the phantom devils so dear to the hearts of the older theologians but by visible and tangible enemies of mankind: the monopolist who exploits the common people, and the imperialist who trades a thousand lives for a square mile of land. The greatest of all world wars is that between the Kingdom of God and the Kingdom of Evil. Where the battle lines of this conflict are drawn up, there must the Christian prophet be in the thick of the fight. His objective must be justice for all men on this earth. His weapon must be intelligence whose cutting edge is religious conviction. His tactics must be that loyalty which quails before no sacrifice. The Kingdom of God is expressed in cooperation rather than competition, in altruism rather than egoism, in human solidarity rather than strife. God is the bond which unites all men of whatever creed, nation, or race. Only by His aid can men hope for freedom, peace, and justice.

What was the significance of the new theology of Rauschenbusch for that American democratic faith which in its origin was under such heavy debt to an older Protestantism? Rauschenbusch believed that the Kingdom of God would be the complete expression of the democratic ideal. "Some, apparently, would be willing to think of God as less than omnipotent and omniscient," he remarked, "if only he were working hard with us for the Kingdom which is the only true Democracy."[30] The internal enemies of democracy were in his opinion the captains of industry and of commerce who set themselves against industrial democracy in any form. "They have aligned themselves," he asserted, "with all the absolutist kings who resented the demand for a parliament or a douma as an interference with God-given rights, and yielded to compulsion as slowly and ungraciously as they could." "We can at least refrain," he

added, "from perpetuating and increasing the handicap of the fee-
bler by such enormous inequalities of property as now we have. . . .
They are the institutionalized denial of the fundamental truths of
our religion, and Democracy is the archangel whom God has sent
to set his blazing foot on these icebergs of human pride and melt
them down."[31]

Rauschenbusch reasserted the doctrine of the fundamental law,
the basic tenet of the old democratic faith. "Since the first century," he maintained, "the divine Logos has taught us the universality of Law and we must apply it to the development of the Kingdom of God."[32] "Suppose," he added in explanation of the nature of
this law, "we had a God who embodied the doctrine of the survival
of the fit, the rule of the strong, and the suppression of the weak,
how would that have affected the character of Western civilization? How much chance would there have been for democracy?
Instead of that, love has been written into the character of God
and into the ethical duty of man; not only common love, but self-
sacrificing love."[33] Only in a society governed by this law can individuals be free. To the traditional doctrine of the mission of America to bear witness to democracy before the world Rauschenbusch
gave a new turn. The social gospel with its mission of establishing
the Kingdom of God on earth, he asserted, "is the religious reaction
to the historic advent of democracy. It seeks to put the democratic
spirit, which the Church inherited from Jesus and the prophets,
once more in control of the institutions and teachings of the
Church. . . . It seeks . . . to create a more sensitive and more modern conscience. It calls on us for the faith of the old prophets who
believed in the salvation of the nations."[34]

∽

The American democratic faith, as it emerged in the Middle Period, was under a heavy debt to Protestantism. Emerson and Thoreau tried to purge the democratic pattern of the theological survivals it contained. The prophets of the religion of humanity after
1865, discarding Christianity, attempted, in effect, to make democracy a national religion. The gospel of wealth, that economic amplification of the doctrine of the free individual, was sanctified by
Protestantism. Rauschenbusch contemptuously threw out of the
window the gospel of wealth. He considered Noah Porter's sancti-
fication of private property a perversion of Christianity. Of Carnegie's effort to support economic individualism by means of the Dar-

winian hypothesis Rauschenbusch declared that Darwinism, with its theory of the struggle for existence, denies every democratic hope.

The essence of democracy is cooperation among free men of good will. For Rauschenbusch cooperation implied a socialistic approach to the problems of society. Good will, he thought, stems from that charity of which Paul once spoke to his friends in Corinth. The Christian socialism of the social gospel owed nothing to the materialistic dialectic or the class struggle of Marx. It was the Christian counterpart of that humanism which, in America, began with the Enlightenment, modified evangelical Protestantism, was the core of transcendentalism, became militant in the religion of humanity and late nineteenth-century neo-rationalism, and which found its supreme expression in the democratic faith. When Rauschenbusch contemplated in his imagination that Kingdom of God destined, one day, to become an earthly reality, he saw that it was nothing else than the democratic dream come true.

Chapter 21

THE GOSPEL OF WEALTH
AND CONSTITUTIONAL LAW

THAT THEOLOGY OF PROPERTY which Presidents Mc-
Cosh and Porter elaborated and which Carnegie called the gospel
of wealth contained an internal conflict which became increasingly
evident as Appomattox receded. When Conwell and Rockefeller
united in urging young men to aspire to that success which was
symbolized by riches and to that power to do good which wealth
brings, they had little to say to the man who, in spite of his best
efforts, failed to achieve the mahogany desk. It was clear, however,
that they expected the man who failed, as well as his neighbor who
succeeded, to acquiesce in the system which they supported. So
long as opportunities for individual initiative were plentiful in the
early stages of the exploitation of vast natural wealth, the mutter-
ings of underlings could be and were ignored. But in the 1870's and
1880's wealth was magnifying the few, while poverty, widespread
and increasing, was abroad in the land. The masters of capital were
acquiring power such as Americans had never before possessed.
In such a scene the prophets of the gospel of wealth urged the individual to be discontented with his lot, in the sense of trying to
escape from poverty, and at the same time to accept his fate if he
failed to win a competence in the struggle of the market. The rugged individualists urged the citizen to strive to increase his well-
being so long as he acted only in the economic realm. But they
insisted that he must not attempt to better his lot by political activities. He must accept such position as he achieved in a competitive system, and, if that position happened to be poverty and insecurity, he must not attempt either to change the system or to seek
aid through politics.

The social philosophy of the gospel of wealth required of the
masses a self-denial which was quite out of harmony with Ameri-

can tradition. As early as the depression following the Revolutionary War the debtor farmers of the back country had used their political power in the legislatures of many states to secure legislation to improve their condition. In later years the poor men of the North and West supported that demand for free land which eventuated in the Homestead Act of 1862. Struggling manufacturers as early as 1816 had asked of Congress and had secured a protective tariff. Of all the Utopian dreams which had flourished in American history none was more fanciful than the idea that the citizens of the Republic could be persuaded to refrain from politics when they believed that political activity could further their private interests.

After Appomattox such maneuvering became almost immediately important. Privately owned railroads, with little or often no sense of social responsibility, imposed what transportation rates they would upon the shippers. The injustice and extortion abounding in the 1870's led to the Granger revolt which, in a few states of the Upper Mississippi Valley, broke temporarily the control of the railway kings over the legislatures. In industrial areas wage earners sought shorter hours and improved conditions of health and safety. The official policy of the Knights of Labor was to better the lot of the working man through reforms largely to be commanded by the states. The Grangers, the Knights, and the Populists were all part of an American political tradition older than the federal Constitution.

As the century drew to a close, conflicts among economic groups increased in intensity. As the power of the financial magnates and of the industrial barons grew with the drift toward monopoly, rebellion spread among farmers, laborers, and even the small entrepreneurs. The storm was brewing which caused Washington Gladden to fear for American institutions.

∽

In 1895 an aged associate justice of the Supreme Court rose in what had been the old Senate Chamber to read a concurring opinion. In it he described the contemporary scene in forceful language. The case had to do with the income tax which Congress had written into the Wilson-Gorman tariff of 1894. The law was in obvious opposition to the taxation clauses of the Constitution. Its framers hoped, however, that the Supreme Court would approve the measure as it had done a similar act passed during the emergency of the Civil War. When Stephen J. Field set forth his individual reasons for agreeing with the Court's nullification of the income tax, he pointed to the specter of a civil war of another kind. The questions raised by the case, he said in that rhetoric of which he had long been master, "go down to the very foundation of the government. If the provisions of the Constitution can be set aside by an act of Congress, where is the course of usurpation to end? The present assault upon capital is but the beginning. It will be but the stepping-stone to others, larger and more sweeping, till our political contests will become a war against the rich; a war constantly growing in intensity and bitterness."[1]

Field, who has been called a doctrinaire, was also a realist. He had long recognized the potential power of numbers in a representative democracy. He sensed the vulnerability of the small minority who possessed vast accumulations of capital. He sought to defend these men of property, not because he was himself rich, for he was not, but because he believed in that upstanding individualism, controlled by a sense of stewardship, which was the social creed of the gospel of wealth. The principal weapon for such defense was the Constitution of the United States interpreted by the courts. The judicial tribunal, when need should arise, must be set against the usurping legislature. Only by such balance could the rights of the minority be protected against the tyranny of the majority and those fundamental principles upon which orderly and progressive society depends be preserved. Field had advocated this point of view since 1873. But he could not remember the time when the beliefs of the gospel of wealth had not governed his thought.

Son of a Congregational minister, Stephen J. Field spent his early boyhood in the Connecticut village of Haddam, where trim, white houses grouped about a central green were symbols of New England ideals of order and restraint. For two adolescent years he lived in Smyrna with an older sister and her husband, Josiah Brewer, a missionary to the Greeks. Returning to America, young Field graduated from Williams College in 1838, taking with him, besides his diploma, a generous measure of the absolutist moral philosophy of Mark Hopkins. Field read law in the days when Story and Kent dominated American thinking in jurisprudence and became a partner in the New York office of his older brother, David Dudley Field. There he acted as assistant in the formulation of those codes of civil and criminal procedure which David in 1850 laid before the legislature of New York State. The younger Field, however, was not present when this occurred, for he had joined, the year before, the gold rush of the "Forty-Niners."

California in 1849, where mining camps formed and dissolved like rafts of river driftwood, was a synonym of anarchy. In the gold fields the ultimate law was lynch law, and government was often a capricious mob. Into such a scene Field, determined and ambitious, brought the ideal of a government of law. With pockets empty he appeared in 1849 at Marysville, a town some two or three days old beside the Sacramento River, and purchased on paper a promising block of city lots. Getting himself elected *alcalde*, he pointed out to certain prospering fellow townsmen who ran gambling places the importance of police protection for their business. Winning their agreement, he levied a tax of five dollars a table, and, with this municipal income hired a police force. He sought to transform Marysville into a California Haddam. He never ceased to be proud of his results. "Whilst there was a large number of residents there of high character and culture who would have done honor to any city," he reminisced in 1877, "there were also unfortunately many desperate persons, gamblers, blacklegs, thieves and cutthroats; yet the place was as orderly as a New England village. There were no disturbances at night, no riots, and no lynching. It was the model town of the whole country for peacefulness and respect for law."[2]

Giving over his duties as *alcalde* after a few months to William R. Turner, a newly appointed state judge, Field contended successfully in 1850 for a seat in the legislature. Here he continued his war against frontier anarchy by drafting the civil and criminal practice act of the new state, using for his model the codes on which he had worked in his brother's office in New York. He modified, however, his brother's handwork, because he recognized that the English common law had little relevance for the problems of California miners. He doubted, moreover, whether sufficient firsthand knowledge could be found in the personnel of any legislature to make possible intelligent and appropriate legislation for the mines. As a consequence the Field codes provided that the justice courts in mining matters should recognize the customs of the locality. By so doing he set in motion a process which finally wrote the pragmatic arrangements of the mining camps into decisions of the Supreme Court of the United States. But Field was not a legal pragmatist. He was an absolutist. "The law is a science," he declared in 1858 after he became a member of the California Supreme Court, "whose leading principles are settled. They are not to be opened for discussion upon the elevation to the bench of every new judge, however subtle his intellect, or profound his learning, or logical his reasoning. Upon their stability men rest their property, make their contracts, assert their rights, and claim protection. It is true that the law is founded upon reason, but by this is meant that it is the result of the general intelligence, learning, and experience of mankind, through a long succession of years, and not the individual reasoning of one or several judges. . . . We should not blindly adhere to precedents, nor should we more blindly abandon them as guides."[3] Recognizing flux in the affairs of individuals and of communities, Field sought the security of changeless and eternal principles. In this respect his point of view was that of Story and of Kent —a blend of absolutism and empiricism—absolutism as to the fundamental law, empiricism in the application of changeless principles to changing situations.

Field in California was no armchair legal theorist. Twice he faced lynching mobs to plead for the accused, and, what was more important, for respect of law. He was willing to take personal risks for his beliefs.

Bad as were the mobs of the mining towns, the California courts were little better in the first turbulent days of the gold rush. When that hot-tempered Texan, Judge William R. Turner, in defiance of a specific provision of the law, overruled Attorney Field, who was trying a case before him, the resulting courtroom scene began a dispute during the course of which the belligerent New Englander was heavily fined, imprisoned, and twice disbarred by his judicial superior. At the advice of a member of the State Supreme Court, Field acquired the art of shooting from the hip—he was probably the only justice in the United States Supreme Court who ever possessed that useful accomplishment. He so perfected his marksmanship that two challengers to duels withdrew before the appointed hour. To that philosophy of a government of laws which he had brought from the East he added, perforce, the frontier ideal that the individual must be able and willing to take care of himself. Field, however, sought to hasten the time when the toting of guns would be abolished, but he never gave up his conviction that the individual should stand on his own feet and ask favors of no one.

True to the code of individualism, Field took his chances in the world of business with the zest of the typical American entrepreneur. He made a small fortune out of the unearned increment in the value of the lots he purchased at Marysville thirty years before his fellow Californian, Henry George, declared such land speculation to be the unpardonable social sin. The speculator, however, promptly lost his money in fines imposed by the vindictive Turner, in an expensive political campaign, and, some said, in the barroom pastime of gambling. While heavily in debt and paying interest on some loans at the rate of ten per cent a month, he secured, as a member of the legislature, the passage of a bankruptcy act generous in its protection of the property of debtors. Returning to private life, he refused to take advantage of the law which he had written and discharged meticulously his obligations out of the income from his practice. He refused to ask even for a compromise on interest, though the current rates declined vastly before his debts were discharged. His action was a costly demonstration of his personal devotion to the principle of the sanctity of contracts. Although he gave up the opportunity to acquire riches by going on the California bench, he admired such men of wealth as Collis P. Huntington and Leland Stanford. He considered these railway magnates to be among the most important builders of civilization on the coast.

Field believed that the individual should be free to use his talents as he thought best, to accumulate what property he could, and to manage it as he saw fit. For Field the aggressive and successful man was the creator of prosperity and so the benefactor of the community. Such a man should aid the weak and the less able; Field never forgot either. In short, the personal philosophy of Stephen J. Field was an exact replica of the gospel of wealth, a complete acceptance of the attitudes of individualistic capitalism. In Field's thought, Carnegie's code for the individual was blended with the American political belief in a government of law. Field derived his faith and his ideals from the quiet customs of Haddam; from the Calvinism of its pastor, his father; from the philosophy of Mark Hopkins; from his own study of the common law; and from his experience with life on the California frontier. When President Lincoln called Field to a seat on the Supreme Court, the California justice brought with him a personal code and system of beliefs about society that were sharply defined in his thought and were fixed in his character.

After Appomattox, Field at Washington watched with growing apprehension the waxing power of Congress. He saw President Johnson humbled by a vindictive and powerful political clique. In the McCardle case he became aware at first hand of the power of this same dominant legislative majority. After the Supreme

Court had heard arguments which involved the constitutionality of the reconstruction policy of the Radical Republicans, Congress, controlled by the men whose policies were under debate, removed the case from the jurisdiction of the Court. The prestige of that tribunal suffered, as a consequence, serious diminution. Field's subsequent record suggests that he never forgot this humiliating episode. It taught him the revolutionary potentialities of uncontrolled legislative majorities. In frontier California he had argued that the legislature must be restrained by the electorate. In Washington during the reconstruction era his faith in so simple a democratic procedure declined. In 1873 he boldly declared his conviction that legislatures, state or national, which threatened the rights of men must be restrained by the courts.

The occasion which caused Field to announce his formula was an episode in Louisiana which led to the Slaughter House cases, first series. The carpetbag legislature of that reconstructed state, by setting up a monopoly whose ostensible purpose was the protection of health, had deprived many honest butchers of the right to carry on their business. They chose to plead their cause an Alabama attorney, John A. Campbell, who had resigned from the Supreme Court when his state seceded from the Union. Campbell, the disfranchised ex-Confederate, abandoned the traditional Southern demand for states' rights and urged the cause of nationalism. He took his stand under that recent lean-to which the Radical Republicans had added to the constitutional structure of the United States, the Fourteenth Amendment, hated throughout the South because it contained the harsh reconstruction policy of the vindictive conqueror. That part of the Amendment which forbade the states to deprive any "person of life, liberty or property without due process of law," Campbell argued, established a law of citizenship "as broad as the law of freedom" and "brought the federal government into immediate contact with every person and gave to every citizen a claim upon its protecting power."[4] The Alabama attorney, pleading for the injured butchers, declared that the Amendment "was designed to afford a permanent and powerful guarantee" to those natural rights of men, "life, liberty, property, protection, privilege and immunity."[5] Campbell lost his case, but he persuaded Mr. Justice Field. The ex-*alcalde* of Marysville proclaimed in a powerful dissent that those natural rights of men to life, liberty, and the pursuit of happiness which had been enumerated in the Declaration had been written into the

Constitution by the Fourteenth Amendment. They are, declared Field, inalienable rights bestowed upon man by his Creator. Until 1868 the law had recognized but had not conferred them. When the Fourteenth Amendment was ratified in that year, natural and inalienable rights became a specific part of the constitutional law of the United States.

The majority on the Court, however, rejected the argument of Attorney Campbell's brief and of Field's dissent on the ground that both threatened to destroy the federal character of the American government. If the United States were to consider the natural rights of every citizen to be included among his constitutional "privileges and immunities" as Campbell and Field desired, the states would become mere shadows. The decision came at a time when the bayonets of blue-coated soldiers supported the legal but unaccepted state governments throughout the former Confederacy.

When the Slaughter House cases came back to the Supreme Court in 1883, with tables reversed as a result of a new Louisiana law which abolished the slaughtering monopoly, the Court again decided that the act of the legislature must prevail. Field concurred in the decision, but he did not agree with the reasoning which supported it. He repeated the arguments of his now ten-year-old dissent and maintained that the original law which the Court now allowed to die had never been constitutional. These two Field opinions were contributions of great importance to the unfolding of the constitutional law of the United States.

A scanning of the literature of the age discloses a figure outside the ranks of law men who perhaps played a part in that fateful battle of theories which did not end until a formula had been produced by which the Supreme Court could, at will, nullify the acts of state legislatures for the purpose of protecting such property as it would.

In 1862 Mark Hopkins, president of Field's alma mater, journeyed to Boston to deliver a series of lectures before the Lowell Institute. In book form they met with sufficient favor to warrant a second edition in 1867. One strand of Hopkinsian thought seems to acquire significance when read in the light of Field's constitutional theory. "Inalienable rights," said the president of Williams College, "are those of which a man cannot divest himself by contract; which he may not, under any circumstances, lawfully demit; but he may forfeit them by crime, and be wrongfully deprived of them by others." "All inalienable rights," Hopkins went on, "may be included in those of life and liberty. . . ." That is right, concluded the lecturer, which a man must do that he may attain the end for which God made him (Cotton Mather's doctrine of the two callings of men). Rights, therefore, must be based on the relation of those things to which we have a right to the attainment of our own end or that of others. "[Governments] have too often been instruments of oppression. . . . But in the light of our discussion government has no right *to be*, except as it is necessary to secure the ends of the individual in his social capacity; and it must, therefore, be bound *so to be* as to secure these ends in the best manner. This is the whole principle, and only the full application of it is needed to make governmental and social movements on the earth correspond in their order and beauty to the movements of the heavens."[6] "As in our intercourse with our fellow men," said Field in 1883 in his famous concurring opinion, "certain principles of morality are assumed to exist without which society would be impossible, so certain inherent rights lie at the foundation of all action and upon a recognition of them alone can free institutions be maintained. These inherent rights have never been more happily expressed than in the Declaration of Independence, that new evangel of liberty to the people. . . . Among these inalienable rights, as proclaimed in that great document, is the right of men to pursue their happiness, by which is meant the right to pursue any lawful business or vocation, in any manner not inconsistent with the equal rights of others, which may increase their prosperity or develop their faculties, so as to give them their highest enjoyment."[7] Or, Field might have added, which would enable the individual to "attain the end for which God made him." "Government," said Hopkins, "has no right *to be*, except as it is necessary to secure the ends of the individual in his social capacity."[8] "The Fourteenth Amendment," said Field in 1885, ". . . undoubtedly intended not only that there should be no arbitrary deprivation of life or liberty, or arbitrary spoliation of property, but that equal protection and security should be given to all under like circumstances in the enjoyment of their personal and civil rights; that all persons should be equally entitled to pursue their happiness and acquire and enjoy property; that they should have like access to the courts of the country for the protection of their persons and property, the prevention and redress of wrongs, and the enforcement of contracts. . . ."[9]

The foundation of the thought of Field and Hopkins was a belief in the doctrine of the free individual. Both men sought to defend individual freedom by an appeal to the doctrine of the fundamental law. For the president of Williams this was the law of God; for the Associate Justice it was Jefferson's natural law. Both Hopkins and Field assumed and affirmed that human freedom derives from that cosmic constitutionalism which keeps the universe in order and which makes human society possible. Men, in striving for liberty, therefore, are not seeking to achieve the new; they are holding fast to a birthright as ancient as the human race.

The story of the aftermath of the Field dissent is one of the most familiar in American constitutional history. In the late 1880's the majority of the Court began following the intellectual trail that Field had blazed and which, during more than a decade of waiting, he had not allowed to grow up to brush. Long before the end of the century he had triumphed.

Field had advanced the argument that the natural rights of man to life, liberty, and the pursuit of happiness had been incorporated in the Constitution by that clause of the Fourteenth Amendment which guaranteed the "privileges and immunities" of citizens. These rights, declared Field, comprised the meaning which the vague words were intended to carry. The majority of the Court rejected the argument on the ground that such an interpretation of the Fourteenth Amendment would destroy the federal nature of the American government. When the Court swung to the Field position, the formula used was "due process of Law." The phrase appeared in the Fifth as well as the Fourteenth Amendments. One was a restriction upon the power of the nation and the other upon the power of the states. The Court did not define "due process." It merely said, when specific laws impaired the rights of men as understood in the traditional American philosophy of individualism, they were unconstitutional because they took property from the individual without "due process of Law." When corporations were defined as persons for legal purposes, the formula which enabled the Court, particularly after 1900, to write the gospel of wealth into constitutional law was complete. It has commonly been said that the Court, in nullifying state legislation under the Fourteenth Amendment, followed the theory of *laissez faire*. The contention, of course, is true. But the implications of the phrase borrowed from the economists are too narrow. The arguments of Field made clear that his purpose was to measure legislation against the principles of individualism which crystallized in the decades which followed Appomattox into that philosophy called the gospel of wealth.

State legislatures, in the control of angry majorities, reminded Field uncomfortably of mobs he had once known and faced in California mining towns. He became apprehensive in the 1870's and the 1880's of the specter of the malevolent State. Thoreau, the Concord pencil-maker, opposed to such a State in the 1840's a conscience enabling him to know and directing him to obey that higher law which he believed to be above the State. Thoreau would not resign his conscience to the legislator. He would not accept the principle of majority rule, for, as he once remarked, any man, more right than his neighbors, already constitutes a majority of one. Field believed in the higher law, but he rejected Thoreau's anarchistic philosophy of civil disobedience. Field put his trust in the courts. Judges, he thought, must serve as the conscience of society. He maintained that it is their function, when occasion demands, to measure the acts of men or of governments, not only by the principles set forth in the Constitution, but by those natural and inalienable rights which the Fifth and the Fourteenth Amendments wrote into that instrument. If the courts should abdicate to the changeful legislature, the results would be caprice and tyranny. The Supreme Court, thought Field, must abandon the policy of self-denial and must stand forth boldly as the guardian of order and the guarantor of security.

Associate Justice Miller summed up the Field philosophy in a vigorous opinion in 1875. "It must be conceded," he said, "that there are rights in every free government beyond the control of the state. A government which recognized no such rights, but held the lives, the liberty, and the property of its citizens subject at all times to the absolute disposition and unlimited control of even the most democratic depository of power, is, after all, but a despotism of the many—of the majority, but none the less a despotism. The theory of our governments, state and national, is opposed to the deposit of unlimited power anywhere."[10]

Great as was the victory of that group of justices who forged "due process" into an instrument by which the social philosophy of the gospel of wealth could be written into constitutional law, their triumph was not complete. While "due process" was being shaped, the same Court was hammering out the antithetical doctrine of "police power" of the states. In its origin this doctrine was one of the judicial results of the political upsurge of the Middle Period called

Jacksonian democracy. "Police power" was in its earliest forms an expression of the concepts that in the American system the people rule and that in the matter of regulation of private property, the most important exercise of people's power is in the states. After Appomattox the phrase became an increasingly important formula in the hands of the justices of the Supreme Court. Its value lay in the fact that it had all the indefiniteness of the powers reserved to the states at the time of the ratification of the Constitution. By the first decade of the twentieth century the Supreme Court was in a position to reject any piece of social legislation enacted in a state, under the theory that it deprived persons of property without due process of law, or to sustain the act on the ground that it was a proper exercise of the police power of the commonwealth. When the Court used "due process," it normally decided the case according to the philosophy of the gospel of wealth; when the justices fell back upon "police power," they determined the dispute before them in terms of that emerging philosophy of the positive State which was the contribution to American political thinking of the social philosophers of the religion of humanity, of the advocates of the social gospel, of the Populists, and, after 1901, of those forward-looking citizens who called themselves "progressives."

By the end of the nineteenth century the Supreme Court had become the institutional expression of the social conscience of the American people. But in so functioning it found itself in a difficulty similar to that of the physicists after Einstein had upset some of the assumptions of the Newtonians. For several years the laboratory investigator, as one of them remarked, used Newton's concept of ether on Mondays, Wednesdays, and Fridays and got on equally well without it on Tuesdays, Thursdays, and Saturdays. The Supreme Court in balancing "due process" against "police power," *laissez faire* individualism against the positive State, reflected the conflict in American social thought which began in the 1870's and became increasingly sharp as the turn of the century approached.

❧

During the same years in which Supreme Court justices were shaping "due process" into a curb for fractious legislatures, the federal courts were also formulating the doctrine of freedom of contract for use against labor unions. This doctrine was also a derivative of the gospel of wealth. It was the logical outgrowth of the old doctrine of the free individual. Freedom of contract was fixed in

American mores in that Middle Period which was dominated by the farmer and the small entrepreneur. Citizens of the Republic were free to make contracts to buy, to sell, or to perform services for another. The post-Appomattox legal doctrine of freedom of contract was a potent distillation from the broad social concept of pre-war years.

Field did not formulate it. But he aided in its creation, first, by emphasizing the doctrine of natural and inalienable rights and, second, by inserting into the literature of judicial opinion a telling quotation from Adam Smith. The many references in later court decisions in inferior courts to these Smith sentences suggest the importance of this action of the Justice from California. "It has been well said," declared Field in 1883, referring to Smith, "that 'the property which every man has is his own labor; as it is the original foundation of all other property, so it is the most sacred and inviolable. The patrimony of the poor man lies in the strength and dexterity of his own hand, and to hinder his employing his strength and dexterity in what manner he thinks proper, without injury to his neighbor, is a plain violation of this most sacred property.' "[11]

The growth of the concept of freedom of contract began in 1877 at a time when the findings in the Massachusetts case, Commonwealth v. Hunt, in 1842, were commonly regarded as established in labor law. That decision, written by Chief Justice Shaw, dismissed the theory of natural rights, as well as the English doctrine of that special unlawfulness peculiar to labor unions, and affirmed that whatever one person may lawfully do, any number may lawfully undertake, even if the result is to maintain a closed shop.[12] The initial step in the abandonment of the Shaw position was the direct result of the first American nation-wide labor crisis which produced in the summer of 1877 a wave of apprehension, the like of which industrial America had not known since that July in 1863 when Lee marched into Pennsylvania.

Four years of corroding depression following the financial panic of 1873 had brought thousands of Americans to the brink of starvation. The announcement in July, 1877, by the principal railroads of another ten per cent wage cut lighted a conflagration which, like a forest fire before the wind, roared from New York to Kansas and from Michigan to Texas. The railway workers were badly organized and had had little experience with strikes. Their action was unpremeditated. In those July days of 1877 middle-class Americans, nervously picking up the morning paper from their doorsteps, read under melodramatic headlines of the seizing of rolling stock by strikers and the occupation of terminals by mobs. From Pittsburgh came dispatches setting forth that the local militia, called out to maintain order, had fraternized with the strikers and that reserves from the eastern part of Pennsylvania had been driven by an infuriated populace into the roundhouse in the railway yards from whence they had sent out calls for help. The retreat to the roundhouse was called by a Pittsburgh paper the Lexington of the social revolution. A few days later the story ended with the news that the blue uniform of the regular army had appeared in Pittsburgh, sent by President Hayes at the request of the Governor. The nation breathed easier. As detachments of the regular army unsheathed their bayonets in other communities, middle-class Americans relaxed. Their anxiety gave way to anger against the labor leaders.

Walter Q. Gresham, a former officer in the Civil War, was judge of the United States District Court at Indianapolis when the railway men of the Hoosier state went out. For several months before the strike he had been busy with the petitions in bankruptcy of railroads that were casualties of ruthless competition or victims of the brigandage of inner rings. When strikers, accompanied by a nondescript mob, seized the Indianapolis railway station, Judge Gresham, sniffing again the smoke of battle, called a mass meeting of substantial citizens in his courtroom. Leaning over his judge's desk, he told an audience, largely made up of fellow veterans of the Civil War, that the authorities of the city and the state were supine and that society was disintegrating if it had not already dissolved. Like Muhlenberg, the fighting parson of the Revolution, Gresham from the desk of authority called for volunteers. He promptly organized two military companies and put an ex-general in command of each. When the Governor of Indiana declined his proffered assistance, Gresham remembered that he was a federal judge. By the simplest of syllogisms he assumed authority to direct the activities of the companies for the achievement of his own purposes. The federal court, he argued, was responsible for the management of the railroads in receivership in order that justice might be done to debtor and creditors. Whoever balked the court in the performance of its duty of management was guilty of an obstruction of the administration of justice. Strikers who refused to permit trains to run were balking management and were, therefore, obstructing justice. They were clearly in contempt of court. Summoning the federal marshal, Spooner, Gresham ordered him to use the new military companies as a legal *posse*. Since the volunteers had neither arms nor ammunition, because the Governor of the state would have nothing to do with them, Spooner advanced alone to the railway station, where he proclaimed in a loud voice to the assembled crowd that they were in contempt of court. Thereupon the supposed revolutionists, acting strangely out of character, permitted the trains of the bankrupt railroads to move. The leaders of the strikers were, nevertheless, arrested and jailed.

Meanwhile, federal troops arrived at the urgent request of Gresham, and at the head of these Marshal Spooner advanced boldly to Terre Haute and to Vincennes. Crossing the frontiers of the Gresham syllogism, Spooner moved a train of the Vandalia road whose president, despite the embarrassment of a solvent company, had appealed to the federal authorities for aid. Force ultimately broke the strike and sent the cowed railway men scurrying to their old bosses to beg for reinstatement in their jobs. Then Judge Gresham brought into court his prisoners charged with contempt.

To guarantee impartiality he invited to preside at the trial Justice Thomas Drummond of the United States Circuit Court, an official notable for character and independence. Drummond, after hearing the evidence and the arguments of attorneys, found the defendants guilty and imposed sharp sentences. Since the case was one in contempt, there was no jury and no appeal. Drummond suspended his argument from a major premise which reaffirmed the right of every man to freedom in the making of contracts. No man, he emphasized, can claim a right to any rate of pay since wages depend upon the law of supply and demand. Nor can a striker lawfully prevent a laborer from working at wages he is willing to accept. A strike of railway men, he added, is a threat to society because of the importance of transportation for the life of the community. Ignoring such reasoning as that of Justice Shaw in Commonwealth *v.* Hunt, Judge Drummond routed the strikers by insisting upon their rights. It was the solution of a rationalist whose premise was individualism. From the proposition that the welfare of society depends upon free competition among individuals, it follows logically that, if a labor union prevents by any means a man from making a contract to perform work, it deprives him of one of his natural and inalienable rights.

During the great strike of 1877 Gresham and Drummond forged a double-edged weapon. Gresham inaugurated the use of the injunction in labor disputes and Drummond wrote into the record that doctrine of freedom of contract which made the injunction effective in almost any labor crisis. In 1894 the Supreme Court completed the work which the judges from Indiana and Kentucky had begun.

Panic and depression in 1893 again overtook the American people. In 1894, when suffering was acute, a wage cut announced by the Pullman Palace Car Company was the signal for a strike. Labor leaders had learned much since the primitive days of 1877. In Chicago were the headquarters of the young but well-organized American Railway Union headed by a fighting idealist named Eugene V. Debs. Supporting the old principle of the Knights of Labor that an injury to one is the concern of all, the railway men of Chicago inaugurated a sympathetic strike which spread quickly as far west as the Rockies. A nation still in the horse and wagon stage of highway transportation faced the threat of economic paralysis. When locomotive fires were dumped in the Chicago yards and strings of loaded box cars idled on the sidings, federal officials in Chicago again took the initiative. Ignoring that stubborn states'-rights Democrat, Governor John P. Altgeld, they appealed to President Cleveland for troops to quiet disorders that were interrupting the mails and were menacing property. On July 2 the federal court issued an injunction which commanded Debs and "all other persons whomsoever" to refrain from interfering with the carrying of the mails or with interstate commerce and "from compelling or inducing, or attempting to compel or induce, by threats, intimidation, persuasion, force, or violence any of the employees of the said railroads to refuse to perform any of their duties as employees of the said railroads in connection with interstate business."[13] The little word, "persuasion," was freighted with an ominous implication, for it meant that the court enjoined any and all private citizens from attempting to persuade a railroad employee to exercise his right to terminate his contract with his employer. So Field's God-given inalienable right of liberty was suspended for the duration of the war. On the following day, despite the protest of Altgeld, a detachment of federal soldiers proceeded to the zone of disturbance. Debs, arraigned for conspiracy in restraint of trade and for contempt of court, later testified that the injunction broke the strike.

In October, 1894, Justice David J. Brewer rose in the old Senate chamber to deliver the opinion of the United States Supreme Court in the matter of the Debs appeal. Not far from him sat his uncle,

Justice Stephen Field, who as a boy had journeyed to Smyrna with Brewer's missionary father. As the Associate Justice read his long and heavily documented opinion he doubtless felt that he was making an important contribution to that structure of constitutional theory which Field had begun in his Slaughter House dissent. To Field's doctrine of inalienable individual rights, and to his theory that the courts must be aggressive in maintaining order and guaranteeing security, Brewer added the doctrine of national power. "The entire strength of the nation," said the Justice, "may be used to enforce in any part of the land the full and free exercise of all national powers and the security of all rights entrusted by the Constitution to its care. The strong arm of the National Government may be put forth to brush away all obstructions to the freedom of interstate commerce or the transportation of the mails. If the emergency arises, the army of the Nation, and all its militia, are at the service of the Nation to compel obedience to its laws. . . . The right to use force does not exclude the right to appeal to the courts for a judicial determination and for the exercise of all their powers of prevention. Indeed it is more to the praise than to the blame of the government, that, instead of determining for itself questions of right and wrong on the part of these petitioners and their associates and enforcing that determination by the club of the policeman and the bayonet of the soldier, it submitted all those questions to the peaceful determination of judicial tribunals, and invoked their consideration and judgment as to the measure of its rights and powers and the correlative obligations of those against whom it made complaint."[14] The labor injunction had been upheld. Four years before the denial of the Debs appeal Mr. Justice Miller for the Supreme Court had declared significantly: "There is a peace of the United States." The ultimate defense, then, of the gospel of wealth was to call upon the state acting in the rôle of policeman.

∽

It was the appeal of the ideal of the independent and upstanding individual as much as the desire to protect corporate property which caused Field and his colleagues at the end of the century to essay the task of fixing the gospel of wealth in American constitutional law. Such a generalization as the foregoing cannot, of course, be proved. It is suspended from the assumption that the justices of the Court were men of sincerity who were unwilling that the Court should shirk its responsibility in an age when American society was, to an extraordinary degree, in flux. Most of the justices in 1900, moreover, were men past middle life.

The vigorous early expressions of the gospel of wealth had conditioned their thinking in the formative years of their lives. To these men Henry George was the purveyor of a quack remedy and Edward Bellamy no more than a romancer. Lester Frank Ward's philosophy of a planned economy was buried under a rubble heap of ponderous phrases and of technical words which the public never accepted. Field's colleagues saw in the extreme collectivism of what was preached in America as Marxian socialism the antithesis of the traditional American ideal of individualism. The Christian socialists spoke with little authority partly because the prestige of Protestantism had declined. Philosophies of collectivism were forming in America but only in a very restricted area in social legislation were they given concrete expression before 1917.

Under such circumstances it was natural for such a man as Field, whose career had been molded in the pattern of individualism to seek to defend the faith by which he lived. His significance lies in the fact that he was the first justice to sense the dangers which the new age presented to the old faith. When, in the 1880's, his colleagues began also to share his apprehension, they rallied to his side. Then occurred that most extraordinary of episodes in American constitutional history. The Supreme Court abandoned its ancient policy of self-restraint. It transformed the old due-process clause into an instrument with which it built the individualism of the gospel of wealth into a constitutional law of the nation. It called a corporation a person so that no property would go unprotected. It created in the doctrine of the freedom of contract a weapon with which to meet the challenge of organized labor to the absolute authority of the employer within his shop. Yet it also developed the doctrine of the police power of the states and used this as the formula with which to approve such collective social legislation as commended itself to the justices.

There was criticism, even among the justices themselves, of the abandonment of the old policy of judicial self-restraint. Before the century ended representatives of labor and of the farmers challenged the aggrandizement of judicial power. But the trend was not halted and, so far as the federal courts were concerned, no restrictions were set up.

The mood of that early majority of the Supreme Court which started that tribunal on the road toward supremacy but which used the new power sparingly is suggested by the argument of Associate Justice Brewer. Brewer believed in a fundamental law which derived from God. For him the ultimate task of the judge was to find that eternal law which expressed right and justice. "There is nothing in the power of the judiciary," said Brewer in an address before the New York Bar Association in 1893, "detracting in the least from the idea of government of and by the people. The courts hold neither purse nor sword; they cannot corrupt nor arbitrarily control. They make no laws. They establish no policy, they never enter into the domain of public action. They do not govern. Their functions in relation to the State are limited to seeing that popular action does not trespass upon right and justice as it exists in written constitutions and natural laws. So it is that the utmost power of the courts and judges works no interference with true liberty, no trespass on the fullest and highest development of government of and by the people; it only means security to personal rights—the inalienable rights, life, liberty, and the pursuit of happiness; it simply nails the Declaration of Independence, like Luther's theses against the indulgences upon the doors of the Wittenberg church of human rights and dares the anarchist, the socialist, and every other assassin of liberty to blot out a single word."[15]

Mr. Justice Brewer's eloquent periods present a perfect statement of that legal faith in a fundamental law which still dominated at the end of the century his profession and the bench. He believed that the courts, by the use of logic, could and did, in piling precedent on precedent, establish on the fixed foundations of eternal principles the actual law which governed men. In so doing the judges gave social reality to that old American ideal of a government of laws and not of men. But his reference to "socialists," "anarchists," and other "assassins of liberty" is significant. It suggests that he identified the fundamental law with the economic and social order of which he was a part. Brewer's faith recalls Melville's phrase: "Each generation thinks its own eternal."

IV

AMERICAN DEMOCRATIC THOUGHT IS CONDITIONED
BY THE COMING OF A NEW INTELLECTUAL AGE

VI

Chapter 22

JOSIAH ROYCE REINTERPRETS DEMOCRACY AND CHRISTIANITY

In the first decade of the twentieth century when the deterministic philosophy of William Graham Sumner was crystallizing into *Folkways*, Josiah Royce walked quietly each day across the Harvard Yard to his office to pursue further that ethical investigation which resulted in 1908 in a little book, *The Philosophy of Loyalty*. It contained a reasoned rejection of the pessimistic outlook. It provided new philosophic foundations for the American democratic faith. Royce saw that that faith, in spite of the hopeful conclusions of Morgan and of Powell, was threatened. Its enemy was Darwinism. Sumner was an illustration of the social thinker who, too much persuaded by the evolutionary doctrine, saw in man only an intelligent animal engaged in a struggle for existence, and democracy with all that it implied as to the freedom and the development of the individual moving toward extinction. Royce did not believe that democracy was about to die. Those creeds which Sumner called phantasms Royce made the cornerstones of his philosophical edifice. To a materialistic and money-mad generation he proclaimed again the importance of ideals. "We want not less talk about evolution," he said, as he stood at the threshold of a long professional career, "but more study of human life and destiny, of the nature of men's thought, and the true goal of men's actions. Send us the thinker who can show us just what in life is most worthy of our toil, just what makes man's destiny more than poor and comic, just what is the ideal that we ought to serve; let such a thinker point out to us plainly that ideal, and then say, in a voice that we must hear, 'Work, work for that; it is the highest'—then such a thinker will have saved our age from one-sidedness, and have given it eternal significance."[1] In such phrases Royce announced his own aspirations. He hoped to be that thinker. He spent his life in an effort to gain a further insight into that truth which is eternal, and so to bring a stabilizing force into that United States whose citizens he saw worshiping at the foot of Sinai the golden calf of novelty. "An entirely false interpretation of the doctrine of evolution," Royce remarked near the end of his life as progressivism was becoming a crusade, "has led some people to imagine that in any department of our lives, novelty as such must mean true progress toward the goal. Hence you constantly hear of the New Education, the New Psychology, the New Thought, the New Humanity. . . . As a fact, what you and I really most need and desire is not the new, nor yet the old. It is the eternal."[2]

Royce's aspiration and his philosophy had its origin in a mining camp on the California frontier. Josiah Royce's parents as a young couple with their two-year-old daughter had jolted across the plains in a prairie schooner in the summer of 1849 and had narrowly escaped death in the Carson desert when they lost the trail. On that occasion a burning bush brought to Sarah Eleanor Royce, tramping alone ahead of the wandering party, a mystical experience which gave her not only peace but strength to encourage her despairing husband. Josiah was born in 1855 in a camp called Grass Valley on the western slope of the Sierras. He grew up a spindling youngster with a head too large for his body and a shyness which made a lonely boyhood. Since Grass Valley had no educational facilities, Mrs. Royce, with a Puritan's faithfulness to the obligations of parenthood, carried on a school in her own home. Her disciplined mind and positive character were the first great influence in the life of her son. In a disordered and changeful society she knew the peace of the God of the burning bush. She sought to rear the boy in the Christian faith that had made her journey to California a hegira and that gave her poise and dignity in the raw camp beside the Mother Lode. When Josiah, as an adolescent, went to the academy in San Francisco, whither the family had moved, his thought had already begun to set in such a fashion as to make idealism the only possible answer to the questions which his mature years brought him. But the religion of the son was not the Protestantism of his mother. "I was born a non-conformist," remarked this child of the frontier. He early recognized that his mother's faith belonged to the past and that the future called for a new religious formulation. He agreed with most of the denials of those other young radicals, Frothingham,

Ingersoll, and Ward, whose life work, like his, began as sectional conflict came to an end. But Royce was not content with their religion of humanity. He pushed on beyond humanity in a search for the Absolute.

Graduating with distinction from the University of California in 1875, two years after paralysis had ended Whitman's active career, he received through the aid of a patron a year of philosophical and literary study in Germany. When in 1876 Daniel Coit Gilman exchanged his presidential office at Berkeley for that of the new Johns Hopkins University, he offered young Royce one of the first twenty fellowships for study at the Baltimore institution. In the summer of 1877, when the battle of the Pittsburgh roundhouse frightened American conservatives, the Johns Hopkins graduate student made a pilgrimage to Cambridge, Massachusetts, to seek the advice of William James, an adventurer in ideas, whose work seemed as much to forecast a new era as did the rebellion of the railway workers. James urged Royce to cast in his lot with philosophy, but reminded him that the America of Jim Fisk and Boss Tweed, of P. T. Barnum and Dwight L. Moody was no Athenian academy. Royce, in the spirit of his pioneering parents, took the risk of becoming a philosopher in the Gilded Age. In the following spring he shipped off to Noah Porter at Yale a thesis entitled "Of the Interdependence of the Principles of Knowledge." Porter approved the effort, perhaps because he found some consolation in the discovery of one young American who was not following William Graham Sumner's path to a Spencerian perdition. With his doctor's degree Royce returned to Berkeley to become a member of the department of English literature. But his Harvard friend did not forget him in his frontier isolation. In 1884, two years after the death of Emerson, James engineered a temporary call to Harvard which in 1886 President Eliot made permanent. Royce at Harvard, sensing the confusions and contradictions of a dawning epoch, devoted himself to the task of bringing coherence to the tangled strands of American thought.

∽

Royce, like a good frontiersman, began his thinking with the individual. As a boy in California he had known communities whose histories were shorter than the life of a man. California had in fact, he thought, "been a notable theatre for the display of political and financial, and, on occasion, of intellectual individuality of decidedly extraordinary types."[3] It has produced Collis P. Huntington and Leland Stanford, James Lick and Denis Kearney, Henry George and Stephen J. Field. It is, Royce added, "the strong individual type of man that in a great democracy is always necessary. It is just this type that, as some of us fear, the conditions of our larger democracy in more eastern regions tend far too much to eliminate."[4] Henry George, the prophet of San Francisco, preached that men must be free to live on and to use the land with which God endowed them. Stephen J. Field, ex-*alcalde* of Marysville, proclaimed the inalienable natural rights of men to life, liberty, and the pursuit of happiness. Josiah Royce, the third of this remarkable California trio, insisted that the problems of social life, of philosophy, and of religion are, at bottom, the problems of the individual. Unless men be free, thought Royce, human life loses its significance. "The world is of importance," he remarked in 1881, "only because of the conscious life in it."[5]

Among Royce's boyhood recollections of the squalid little mining camp in which he first saw the light were some of the products of uncontrolled individual freedom—nature scarred by unsightly diggings, saloon brawls, vigilante committees establishing order with rope and gun. In 1886, three years after Ward published his *Dynamic Sociology*, Royce in a history of California emphasized the evolution of an Angel's Camp from the chaos of unrestrained individualism to a measure of disciplined order. He pointed out the inevitability of the transition. What was its meaning for the democratic doctrine of the free individual? Daniel Boone, who had once fled from Kentucky when society had closed in about him, had built a lonely cabin in the bison country far up the Missouri River. For this frontiersman freedom meant limitless open country, immediate and continuous contact with nature, and the absence of man-made regulations. Royce had been reared in similar freedom in Grass Valley. But he early abandoned it. The path he followed took him from the mining town to the seaport, San Francisco, and thence to old German villages where human life ran in grooves that had been a thousand years in forming. In Germany he came to understand that neither solitude nor mere absence of law makes men free. What was the freedom of the Kentucky hunter to that of his contemporary, Goethe? Individualism, concluded Royce, thrives only in communities.

Communities of men require laws which limit freedom, and the larger the community, the more numerous the ordinances required for the government of its members. Royce, in facing the problem of reconciling liberty and authority, carried the question from the level of political theory to its ultimate philosophical implications. Royce was the first American thinker to front squarely the apparent contradiction between the first and the second doctrine of the democratic faith, between the postulate of a fundamental law and that of the free individual. For Royce, as for Emerson and Thoreau, the fundamental law was inherent in the structure of the universe. It is, thought Royce, the underlying constitution of nature and of human society. It is the changeless and eternal will of God, a manifestation of the Absolute. In such a universe how can man be free? Why is he not a slave whose apparent freedom is but a fantasy?

Royce turned to the question, What is man, posed by Melville's Father Mapple. Melville had answered: Man is mystery. Royce asserted that man is will. Royce did not attempt to avoid, as did Emerson, the problem of evil in the world. He did not call it, with the Concord transcendentalist, the absence of the good. Nor did he seek to cover up the determinism implicit not only in science but in his own concept of the changeless Absolute. This determinism was the foundation of the pessimism not only of Sumner, but of his great contemporary, Samuel Clemens. Young Royce, at the outset of his intellectual career, explored pessimism to its uttermost frontiers.

"Leaving all else out of account," he said, "this one great fact of suffering would be enough to make us doubt the worth of life. Contemplate a battlefield the first night after the struggle, contemplate here a vast company the equal of the population of a great town, writhing in agony, their groans sounding at a great distance like the roar of the ocean, their pain uneased for many hours, even death, so lavish of his favors all day, now refusing to comfort; contemplate this and then remember that as this pain is to the agony of the world, so is an electric spark drawn from the back of a kitten to the devastating lightning of many great storms; and now estimate if you can the worth of all but a few exceptional human lives. . . . Briefly and imperfectly I state the case for pessimism, not even touching the economical and social argument, drawn from a more special consideration of the conditions of human life. Such then, is our individual human life. What shall we call it and whereunto shall it be likened? A vapor vanishing in the sun? No, that is not insignificant enough. A wave, broken on the beach? No, that is not unhappy enough. A soap bubble bursting into thin air? No, even that has rainbow hues. What then? Nothing but itself. Call it human life. You could not find a comparison more thoroughly condemning it."[6]

This outburst was not mere rhetoric. It voiced one of Royce's deepest convictions, namely, if man is no more than an intelligent animal, if the end of his life is merely to keep alive, then he is indeed a wave broken on the shore, a bubble bursting in the air. For Royce, however, pessimism was the beginning rather than the end of the argument, since the pessimist can describe only the life devoted to self and he proves conclusively that such a life is worthless. But the unselfish life, the life of devotion, of sacrifice, and of contemplation, in short, the higher life in the Ideal, is beyond the pessimist's criticism. The practical significance of pessimism, thought Royce, is in its disclosure of the inadequacy of the naturalistic philosophy which stems from Darwinism that man is but an intelligent animal. As a consequence, pessimism itself sets the philosopher and the moralist the task of discovering the ideals which men should follow and the goal toward which the race should strive.

The scientist thinks only in terms of the world made known by sense perceptions. Royce assumed another world, that of the Ideal. The individual lives in both at the same time. In this second, this invisible world, he is free. But his freedom is achieved, paradoxically, because he is a member of a community. Upstanding independence, thought Melville, in harmony with the attitude of Americans of the Middle Period, is the core of individualism. Melville's opinion was that of the frontiersman and of that other nineteenth-century company of individualists whose fishing boats and whose merchant and whaling ships were found on every sea. The ideal of the democratic faith was that every man should have his fair chance to make himself an Ahab or a Boone. Long before Royce returned from Germany, however, the American whaler and deep sea merchantman had virtually disappeared, and by the time the philosopher went to Harvard the vacant land of the frontier had been appropriated. The specialization and the organization of corporate industry had been substituted for the independence of the hunter and of the sea captain. No longer could the normal man take pride in being his own boss; he was a hired man, and his boss also was usually a hired man. Royce sought to preserve the ideal of individualism in a world in which the individual was an atom in a complex and closely knit society. Royce believed that the individual should seek to find in the community a freedom which neither the frontier nor the sea could offer, the freedom of an Emerson or a Whitman.

◇

An episode in Cuba at the very end of the nineteenth century, although Royce never used it in his published work, illustrates his individualistic philosophy. Aided by a small and devoted group of doctors, nurses, and enlisted men, Walter Reed battled and finally overcame yellow fever. All risked their lives, and one of the company, Dr. Jesse Lazear, was killed by the dread disease. This group was a community in the Roycean sense. A society, thought Royce, may be but an aggregation of individuals who are perhaps competing or contending with one another. A community is united. The little company fighting yellow fever were united by loyalty, not to one another, although that was not lacking, but to a common cause. This cause gave significance to their lives. Moreover, they chose their loyalty voluntarily; no one compelled them to brave the mysterious Yellow Jack. The choice was a demonstration of the freedom of each. Yet, once they had chosen their cause, it held them in an iron discipline; it forced Lazear to give up his life. Was Walter Reed's individuality impaired by merging his personality with those of others in the yellow fever community in Cuba? Was his integrity impeached by the surrender of his will to the tyranny of the cause he served? His countrymen did not think so. The man they honored was the man who had been brought out, perhaps created, by that cause and that community to which he gave himself. He was saved by the community, saved from mediocrity, from insignificance, from being merely an intelligent animal. Reed in his life had solved the problem of harmonizing freedom and authority. From beginning to end, Reed, Lazear, and the rest remained free individuals re-dedicating themselves each hour to the common cause and freely accepting the discipline which their task imposed.

The episode suggests the outline of Royce's philosophy of loyalty which he developed in its final form after the twentieth century had opened. Loyalty lifts the individual above the meaningless service of self and gives him citizenship in the realm of the Ideal. Since loyalty is always a free act, and its object always a disciplinary force, liberty and authority become partners, not adversaries. The loyal citizen, working through the institution of democracy to achieve the common good, finds the coercion of the State unnecessary, for the cause disciplines him more effectively than the State ever could.

Loyalty, thought Royce, will save the individual caught in modern mechanized civilization. Royce saw in standardization the chief danger threatening American democracy. Because of the ease of communication among distant places, he said in 1902 at the University of Iowa, "because of the spread of popular education, and because of the consolidation and of the centralization of industries and of social authorities, we tend all over the nation . . . to read the same daily news, to share the same general ideas, to submit to the same overmastering social forces, to live in the same external fashions, to discourage individuality, and to approach a dead level of harassed mediocrity."[7] He proposed a modernized "provincialism" as an antidote to the poison of standardization. Frederick Jackson Turner saw the rambling American Republic divided into competing and sometimes antagonistic sections. Royce had little interest in Turner's sectionalism. His term, "provincialism," had quite a different connotation. "For my present purpose," he said, "a county, a state, or even a large section of the country, such as New England, might constitute a province. For me, then, a province shall mean any one part of a national domain, which is, geographically and socially, sufficiently unified to have a true consciousness of its own unity, to feel a pride in its own ideals and customs, and to possess a sense of its distinction from other parts of the country."[8] Let the individual citizen cherish such provincialism, urged Royce. Let him be loyal to his province. Give "him faith in the dignity of his province, . . . make his ideal of that community lofty, . . . and you have given him a power to counteract the leveling tendencies of modern civilization."[9] True provincialism will prevent, thought Royce, that mob spirit, that mass stampede to which every society is susceptible but which is the negation of the democratic ideal of government by discussion. "A nation composed of many millions of people," said Royce a third of a century before the emergence of the Nazis in Germany, "may fall rapidly under the hypnotic influence of a few leaders, of a few fatal phrases."[10] The mob spirit destroys that uniqueness which gives the individual his value and his significance. The province, by saving the individual, saves the nation and its civilization.

Royce formulated in his theory of the province and of loyalty an ideal which would give direction to American democracy and significance to American life. To a generation disturbed by the on-rush of industrialism and confused by the immigrant invasion, he declared: Loyalty sums up the ideals of the American democratic faith and points to the way by which men may bring order out of modern chaos and substitute justice and charity for the law of the jungle that operates in the market place. Loyalty shows you how to solve the problem of making collectivism serve the ends of individualism.

◇

If Whitman translated a democratic faith which he found at the crossroads and on the street corners of America into verse, Josiah Royce sought to lift it to the status of a true religion. He pre-sented, in fact, to his generation a religion of loyalty and of the Great Community. He frankly admitted as much. It was his solu-tion of the problem of what to do about that decline in the prestige of Christianity which resulted from the refusal of a scientifically minded age to accept the old theology.

In spite of his student years in Germany, Royce rejected Hegel's doctrine that the individual must be swallowed up by the State. Royce declared the individual must save himself by losing himself in a community of loyal men. Royce was, in the final analysis, a national thinker who conceived his task to be the resolution of the apparent contradictions of American democracy and the explora-tion of the limits and implications of its idealism. The starting points of his thought were two postulates: the existence of eternal prin-ciples of truth and of morality, and the reality and importance of the ideal of the free individual. His conclusion was that loyalty, a voluntary act, makes it possible for the individual to obey the eternal fundamental law without being a slave.

Royce recognized that the democratic faith, as he found it, was a cluster of ideals and of value judgments. As such they were proper grist for the philosopher's mill. His principal contributions to the faith are found in his affirmation that voluntary cooperation must be the foundation of the perfected State. The discipline of the dic-tator leads to moral death; that of loyalty to a cause which tran-scends the self is the essence of that humanity which distinguishes man from the beast.

Royce, one of the most learned men of his day, was convinced that ideals correspond with reality; the apprehension of these is beyond the capacity of the explorer who uses merely the tools of science. Royce denied that ideals are phantasms clouding the thought of men. He affirmed, in effect, that the ideals of the democratic faith, when fully understood, are the end toward which history moves. To deny the validity of these, he thought, is to deprive human nature of its dignity and human life of its meaning.

~

Royce did not overlook a weakness in his philosophy of loyalty. He recognized that men serving causes with devotion might, because of their very loyalties, find themselves antagonists, even enemies facing one another across a shell-torn no-man's-land. Such a situation developed in fact after August, 1914. Did the World War invalidate the theory? Royce thought not. It merely demonstrated again the undeveloped ethical state of the world. So long as men remain ethically immature, conflicts in causes are bound to arise. But even in such a state there is one universal and all-inclusive cause, namely loyalty to the principle of loyalty. Royce replied vigorously to those who jeered at the idea as a meaningless absurdity. Assume, he said in effect, that your enemy is as loyal to his cause as you are to yours. Respect his loyalty as the highest manifestation of ethical conduct. Such respect is loyalty to the principle of loyalty. If two enemies are thus loyal to loyalty, they are already well advanced toward the reasonable ending of their dispute and the establishment of a stable peace. Only on such a foundation is a community of nations possible.

As soon as the World War broke out, Royce turned his thought to the solution of the problem of how a society of contending nations can be transformed into a community of nations. He had no faith in a political league. He sought rather to develop invisible ties similar to those which brought the self-governing dominions to the aid of Britain in August, 1914. He entitled his last book, which was on the press when he died, in 1916, *The Hope of the Great Community*. If such a world-wide community should ever come into being, it would be the result, he thought, of an hierarchy of loyalties—loyalty to family, to province, to nation, to the world-wide human race. "For my part," he said to his race-conscious fellow countrymen in 1908, "I am a member of the human race, and this is a race which is, as a whole, considerably lower than the angels, so that the whole of it very badly needs race-elevation. In this need of my race I personally and very deeply share."[11] "Let this spirit of loyalty to loyalty become universal, and then wars will cease; for then the nations, without indeed lapsing into any merely international mass, will so respect each the loyalty of the others that aggression will come to seem inhuman."[12] The central point of the Royce proposal was that only if mankind makes ethics (the fundamental law) supreme, can the world hope to be freed from the scourge of war. Men have from the beginning of history used ethical principles (the moral law of the ancient Hebrews and the natural law of the Greeks) to discipline naked power to humane ends. Ethics have no meaning outside a community of persons. The hope of the Great Community was Royce's answer to the contention of Melville and of Sumner that wars will continue to be fought as long as there are men to fight. Josiah Royce's philosophy of loyalty was, in essence, a formula for voluntary cooperation. He recognized that such cooperation is the core of the democratic system. Lester Frank Ward felt that reason is sufficient to persuade men of the utility of such cooperation. Royce would add to intelligence religious motivations. For Royce the philosophy of loyalty was, in reality, a religion of loyalty, a religion that expresses itself in the will of persons to transcend their own selfish desires in an effort to achieve the general good. In this act of will the individual finds his true freedom.

∽

The factor which differentiated Royce and Ward was the effort of the philosopher to re-establish the foundations of a religion that would be more than humanism. The philosophy of loyalty was, in fact, a by-product of a system to the creation of which he devoted his life. The central objective of all his philosophizing was to prove the existence and discover the nature of the Absolute, or what his church-going neighbors called God. When his work was done, Royce's Absolute had many similarities to Emerson's Over-Soul. Because God is in man, Emerson thought human nature divine. For Royce, in his last days, the Absolute was the completion of the Great Community. The Great Community, it will be recalled, is that world-wide company of the loyal men and women who live in the realm of the Ideal. Their lives are short. No one of them ever attains all his objectives, ever completes all the good work he has started. Above them and in them, completing their lives and supplementing their work is the Absolute, changeless and eternal. Emerson sometimes spoke of the Over-Soul as a universal Mind of which the mind of a man is a part. Royce's Absolute was more than universal Mind; He was universal Will including the minds and wills of living men and, at the same time, supplementing and completing them. He was, therefore, a single entity and also a community. The Absolute was the personification of the Great Community.

The present study is not concerned with the epistemology or the metaphysics which lay behind Royce's concept of the Absolute and which were elaborated in his most important books, *Sources of Religious Insight, The World and the Individual,* and *The Problem of Christianity.* He hoped to substitute for the discredited Christian orthodoxy of his mother's generation a philosophy, constructed by the most rigorous logic, which would include all science and which would arm men effectively for the age-old struggle against evil. He sensed the religious quality of the democratic faith. If that faith, he thought, were chained to a decaying orthodoxy, it would die. If men, such as Ward, thought to save it by depending wholly upon reason, they also were bound to fail. Royce founded his democratic faith upon the changeless and eternal Absolute Will.

In 1916, as the German armies rested after the carnage before Verdun, Royce died. Save for the war he might have become another Emerson, inspiring a generation of youth with a new idealism. But, unfortunately for the fame of Royce, the young men who returned to America from St. Mihiel and the Argonne were already citizens of a new and harsh world. They were in no mood to pay heed to a kindly and cloistered philosopher who talked about loyalty to loyalty.

But times change. If Americans of the 1920's were disillusioned, their sons and daughters of the 1940's and 1950's were anxious and confused. In spite of the triumph of science the mid-century generation recognized more clearly than had their predecessors its limitations as a foundation for a philosophy of life. Prestige returned to religion and reached new heights. Royce, who had contributed much to the development of Christian thought, was re-discovered and became again important.[13]

Chapter 23

THE SIGNIFICANCE OF THE FRONTIER AND OF THE LAW OF ENTROPY

OF ALL THE SOCIAL DISCIPLINES which brought forth professional guilds in the decades following Appomattox that of history was most directly and intimately concerned with the democratic faith. Such documents as the Declaration of Independence and the Constitution were part of the grist of its mill. The national heroes and triumphs, together with the Republic's villains and defeats, were material for historical lectures, professional papers, and monographs. The earlier historians of the American people devoted themselves for the most part to what might be called the biography of the American State. They traced the rise of the United States from its humble origins in the colonies, through its successful revolution, to and beyond the sectional conflict of the 1860's.

One of the first and greatest of these national historians was George Bancroft. For him history was a large canvas and the story of the rise of the Republic a noble narrative. With a conscience sensitive to the requirements of his task, Bancroft accumulated and analyzed the vast quantities of raw material out of which his story grew. He composed most of his great work in the Middle Period when the democratic faith took form. He did not discover that faith. It pervaded the intellectual climate in which he lived. It was of the essence of his thought. At times it lifted his narrative into stirring rhetoric. In 1858 he described the Declaration of Independence. "This immortal state paper," wrote Bancroft, "was 'the genuine effusion of the soul of the country at that time,' the revelation of its mind, when in its youth, its enthusiasm, its sublime confronting of danger, it rose to the highest creative powers of which man is capable. . . . As it was put forth in the name of the ascendant people of that time, it was sure to make the circuit of the world, passing everywhere through the despotic countries of Europe; and the astonished nations, as they read that all men are created equal, started out of their lethargy, like those who have been exiles from childhood, when they suddenly hear the dimly remembered accents of their mother tongue."[1]

Bancroft, like Emerson, lived on into the postwar epoch. In these later years Emerson's star was setting, but Bancroft's remained a national luminary. Two Presidents honored him with the post of Minister to Germany. The pattern of his thought remained unchanged. He delivered before both Houses of Congress on February 12, 1866, a memorial address on Abraham Lincoln, the frame of reference of which was the prewar democratic faith. "In the fullness of time," said Bancroft, "a republic rose in the wilderness of America. Thousands of years had passed away before this child of the ages could be born. From whatever there was of good in the systems of the former centuries she drew her nourishment; the wrecks of the past were her warnings. . . . The fame of this only daughter of freedom went out into all the lands of the earth; from her the human race drew hope."[2] In 1874 Bancroft returned from Germany and eight years later concluded his magnum opus with two volumes which he called *The History of the Formation of the Constitution of the United States*. His narrative ended with the first inauguration of Washington. He used, as the backdrop of his scene, a picture of the Old World on the brink of revolution. What a contrast, he thought, between that world and the New! Bancroft concluded his history with powerful sentences. "In America," he said, "a new people had risen up without king, or princes, or nobles. . . . By meditation and friendly councils they had prepared a constitution which, in the union of freedom with strength and order, excelled every one known before. . . . In the happy morning of their existence as one of the powers of the world, they had chosen justice for their guide; and while they proceeded on their way with a well-founded confidence and joy, all the friends of mankind invoked success on their unexampled endeavor to govern states and territories of imperial extent as one federal republic."[3]

Bancroft was an incurable romantic. It is significant that his romanticism survived not only the war but also that era of political debauchery which disgraced the Grant administration. The same was true of Whitman's romanticism. The explanation of the apparent paradox is to be found in the fact that the democratic faith functioned at a different level from the plane of realistic democracy. Corruption in politics merely meant to Bancroft a falling away from the ideals of an old faith; it did not impair the validity of those ideals. Bancroft, the historian, was an important factor in carrying the democratic formulas of the mid-nineteenth-century America into the postwar system.

～

But, in these years, a self-conscious and professionalized history was rising in the United States. Chairs were multiplying in the universities. A guild was forming which looked for inspiration and guidance to the historical scholars of Europe. Scientific history made its appearance in the meticulous and exhaustive criticism of historical sources. Romanticism gave way to realism and rhetoric subsided into the dull monotones of the monographic style. Yet this period of transition was an exciting one in the history of American historical writing. The pioneers of scientific history were the explorers of a new world. They began the search for those forces which lie concealed within the flow of events. They peered behind the annals of politics to discover the surge of economic movements. The new historians, moreover, were disciplined to a code of honor. They pursued truth. They disdained to make history the servant of any particular cause. They looked upon themselves as a band of free scholars whose task was to deepen the perspective for living actors in on-going social scenes. When the new historians contemplated the mass of popular writing about American history, they found the narrative poverty-stricken in useful interpretation and encumbered with a burden of mythology. The romantic period in American letters had helped to fix many legends in American folk history. The new guild members considered it part of their obligation to truth to attack favorite old stories concerning John Smith or George Washington. Nor did they permit to escape such later tales as those which clustered about Marcus Whitman. The new historians appearing in the United States were, on the whole, men of high hope. They were convinced of the utility for civilization of the discovery of historical reality and causation. Their scholarship was too sophisticated for them ever to look upon history as a science of predictive value. But they were universally convinced that progress is associated with enlightenment and, consequently, that the illumination of a dark or obscure past makes for that advance in thought which is the first aspect of advance in civilization.

The new historians emerged in an age when in the United States evolving industrialism was drifting toward monopoly capitalism. But they moved in an intellectual climate still dominated by that cluster of ideals which Whitman called the democratic faith. Lewis Henry Morgan had sought to demonstrate in 1878 that these ideals are the end toward which social evolution has moved and is moving. What is the testimony of the historians who were his contemporaries as to the place of the democratic faith in the American intellectual firmament? Does the record demonstrate that the historians attacked also the mythology of romantic democracy when they went about smashing lesser icons on the walls of the national temple? Space prevents the examination of the material necessary for a complete answer to the question. Two historians, Frederick Jackson Turner and Henry Adams, have been chosen to illustrate trends in the thinking of American historians at the end of the century about the democratic faith.

∽

Turner graduated from the University of Wisconsin in 1884 when Bancroft was bringing out his final "Author's Revision." A year later the new historians organized the American Historical Association. It was a period of high hopes in the intellectual world of the United States. Not only history but other social disciplines were rising. Young Turner did not at once decide to cast his lot with scholarship. He spent a year as a journalist in Madison, a year which gave him a broader understanding of the civilization of the Old Northwest. He returned to the university to fill a tutorship in oratory and rhetoric and to begin the study of history with William Francis Allen. Allen's chief interest was Rome, but his thought ranged widely in the historical field. He contributed much to the solution of Turner's later problem of discovering the relationship between the history of a frontier community beside the Great Lakes and the vast narrative of the movements in Western civilization. At Allen's suggestion Turner read Heeren, the historian of Göttingen who had influenced Bancroft. In the work of the German scholar Turner found reinforcement for his own ideas of the importance for historical interpretation of economic and social changes. Turner's teaching moved from rhetoric and oratory to history. He won his master's degree in 1888 with a thesis which had to do with the fur trade in Wisconsin.

Turner spent the next year at Johns Hopkins where he studied with that young radical, Richard T. Ely, who had only recently participated in a successful revolt within the guild of American economics against the dominance of English classical theory. Turner also took work with Woodrow Wilson, and a warm sympathy united the two men. Events were to prove that the thought of these two concerning the American democratic faith was cast in the same mold.[4] Herbert B. Adams supervised at Johns Hopkins Turner's doctor's thesis, which was an enlargement of his fur trade study. In his work with Adams the young Westerner collided with a theory of history which he ultimately largely rejected. It was sometimes called the "germ theory" to make it fit with the thought of an age whose intellectuals were inclined to look upon society as an organism. It was, in reality, a theory of the evolution and the migration of culture. Adams belonged to an important group among the new historians who saw the history of their native land as an evolution out of the history of Europe. In attempting to trace in the Old World the roots of American democratic institutions they went back through time as far as Magna Charta. Under the influence of Darwin's hypothesis, they made history look something like an evolutionary sequence. Adams required the discreetly skeptical Turner to begin his study of frontier trading posts with Phoenicia and Rome.

The significance for ideas concerning American democracy of this new historical approach was obvious. One of the most frequently repeated concepts in the rhetoric of the Middle Period was that of the uniqueness of the American democratic contribution to the world. Bancroft, in his history, had presented America as an innovator to whom the Old World looked with hope. The history, which emphasized the migration of culture across the Atlantic, impaired a popular belief. Historical realism was eroding romanticism in the American tradition.

Turner was a realist, but his realism had a different setting from that of Adams. This setting was a growing American interest in the frontier and a developing American sentiment of nationalism.[5] Since the time of James Fenimore Cooper a considerable company of Americans had been discovering the frontier as a limitless source of raw material for literary and scientific creation. Bret Harte published "The Luck of Roaring Camp" in 1868 and "Outcasts of Poker Flat" in 1869. Josiah Royce turned out his study of frontier California in 1885. Hamlin Garland, like Turner a son of Wisconsin, published in 1891 under the title, *Main Traveled Roads*, his realistic stories of the farm life of the Upper Mississippi Valley.

Cooper and Harte used the frontier material for purposes of romance. Cooper, however, critic of democracy, found on the frontier the perfect democrat, Leatherstocking, who personified the ideals of the democratic faith.[6] Royce, philosopher and prophet of idealism, who spent his life in an effort to reconcile liberty with authority, was conditioned by his frontier upbringing. His study of the evolution of California mining camps from chaos to order contributed much to his later solution of his problem.[7] Garland was a humanitarian, interested in ameliorating the lot of the poor. He exposed frontier poverty. The historians were late among American intellectuals in the discovery of the possibilities which lay in frontier material. An impressive body of frontier literature was already in existence when the young historian from Wisconsin read his paper at Chicago in 1893.

The frontier was an aspect of the civilization of the United States which helped to make it unique. There were, to be sure, frontiers in Canada, in Hispanic America, in South Africa, and in Australia. Citizens of the United States, however, were but little aware of these. Traditionally the thought of Americans turned toward Europe. The existence of a frontier in the American sense was what distinguished the United States from European nations. Under such circumstances it was inevitable that the frontier should be emphasized in expressions of American nationalism. After Appomattox, literary nativism became important in the writings of Mark Twain, son of Trans-Appalachia and a sojourner for a time on the California frontier. From 1869, when he brought out *Innocents Abroad*, to 1889 when he contributed to American letters *A Connecticut Yankee at King Arthur's Court*, Clemens ridiculed the institutions of Europe, directing his jibes particularly against those nondemocratic elements in European culture, monarchs and aristocracies. He was the culmination of a movement which began with Emerson's intellectual declaration of independence. In 1885 Josiah Strong, clergyman, in an imperialistic volume called *Our Country*, which was widely distributed in Protestant circles, emphasized the West as the heart of the Republic and the repository of its peculiar civilization. In 1891 developing American nationalism expressed itself in Captain Mahan's first book on the influence of seapower. Turner rowed with the current of this new nationalism. He was a frank nationalist. American history, he remarked in 1889 in a review of Theodore Roosevelt's *Winning of the West*, "needs a connected and unified account of the progress of civilization across the continent. Aside from the scientific importance of such a work, it would contribute to awakening a real national selfconsciousness and patriotism."[8]

Turner returned to Wisconsin to become a colleague of Allen in the department of history. His devotion to the ideals of scholarship had a religious character and flavor. "The man who enters the temple of history," he remarked in 1891, "must respond devoutly to that invocation of the church, *Sursum corda,* lift up your hearts."[9] In his thought he wrestled with the problem of reconciling Herbert Adams' theory of the migration of culture with his own conviction of the uniqueness of America or, more specifically, of the American democratic way of life. He was too honest and too skillful a historian to reject completely the Adams position. Yet he felt it inadequate and even misleading. He became convinced that the old, when transplanted in the American environment, became a genuine new. By 1891 he had achieved his solution.

Turner's explanation for the uniqueness of American democracy was the existence of the frontier. For this young adventurer in history, the frontier was neither a place nor a state of mind. It was an evolution. From the first seventeenth-century settlements to near the end of the nineteenth century American society had always been starting afresh in new wilderness areas and in each new place had developed swiftly from simplicity to complexity. "What the Mediterranean Sea was to the Greeks, breaking the bond of custom, offering new experiences, calling out new institutions and activities," said Turner in 1891, "that the ever-retreating Great West has been to the eastern United States directly, and to the nations of Europe more remotely."[10] "The most important effect of the frontier," said Turner in his famous paper at Chicago in 1893, "has been the promotion of democracy here and in Europe."[11] "American democracy," he reiterated in 1914 in much quoted phrases, "was born of no theorist's dream; it was not carried in the *Susan Constant* to Virginia nor in the *Mayflower* to Plymouth. It came out of the American forest, and it gained strength each time it touched a new frontier."[12] Democracy, therefore, had a unique origin in America.

Turner believed, with Josiah Royce, in the efficacy of ideals. He was convinced that Leatherstocking and his successor, the cabin-farmer, gave to America its distinctive and its noblest ideals. What were these? They were first of all that of the free individual. Turner, speaking of the pioneer, emphasized "the fierce love of freedom, the strength that came from hewing out a home, making a school and a church and creating a higher future for his family." The West, added the historian, "gave us Abraham Lincoln, whose gaunt frontier form and gnarled, massive hand told of the conflict with the forest, whose grasp of the ax-handle of the pioneer was no firmer than his grasp of the helm of the ship of state as it breasted the seas of the Civil War." "Democracy," concluded Turner, "became almost the religion of the pioneer. He held with passionate devotion to the idea that he was building under freedom a new society, based on self-government, and for the welfare of the average man."[13]

Did Turner think that America had a unique destiny in the world? His answer was emphatic. "Western democracy," he said in 1903, "through the whole of its earlier period tended to the production of a society of which the most distinctive fact was the freedom of the individual to rise under conditions of social mobility, and whose ambition was the liberty and well-being of the masses. This conception has vitalized all American democracy, and has brought it into sharp contrasts with the democracies of history, and with those modern efforts of Europe to create an artificial democratic order by legislation. The problem of the United States is not to create democracy, but to conserve democratic institutions and ideals."[14] "Other nations have been rich and powerful," he added in 1910, "but the United States has believed that it had an original contribution to make to the history of society by the production of a self-determining, self-restrained, intelligent democracy. It is in the Middle West that society has formed on lines least like Europe. It is here, if anywhere, that American democracy will make its stand against the tendency to adjust to a European type."[15]

Edward Channing of Harvard, according to a tradition among his students, was wont, when inaugurating a new seminar, to open a drawer and, taking out a pamphlet, to remark of his colleague: "Here, gentlemen, is where Turner got his ideas from."[16] Channing then returned the pamphlet mysteriously to the drawer. If the students had taken the trouble, they could have found on the shelves of Widener a hundred such pamphlets and in addition more than a score of books. And they need not have gone outside the literature of the Middle Period. For the basic ideas of Turner were the doctrines of the American democratic faith. He expressed them all. His idealism was the outgrowth of a faith in the existence of a fundamental moral law. He believed in progress. He developed in detail the doctrine of the free individual. He insisted upon the unique origin and the unique destiny of American democracy. To the commonly accepted pattern of the Middle Period he suggested a few variations. In keeping with the mood of his age, he abandoned the theistic interpretations of the origin of American democracy and substituted for it the naturalistic explanation that it was a product of the American forest. Whitman had expressed a similar idea in "Pioneers, O Pioneers." Turner abandoned the old millennial democratic hope of pre-Sumter days that democracy would one day conquer the world, for he spoke of the conservation of democracy and of its stand against the European type. Such an interpretation of Turner does not detract from his stature. Whitman transformed the democratic faith into magnificent verse; Turner into immortal history.

When Turner's writings are used as source material, they suggest the importance of the democratic faith for American thought as the twentieth century opened. To the support of the doctrine of the free individual and of the unique origin and destiny of American democracy Turner marshaled impressive evidence from economic and social history. He traced the emergence of social beliefs from social scenes. He translated an old faith into the new idiom of scientific history. He overemphasized, to be sure, the importance of the frontier; a study of Emerson would have given him new insights. But his overemphasis was his strength. His thesis stirred not only national but sectional pride. It was, in fact, an expression of that loyalty to one's province which Josiah Royce urged as the only sound foundation of nationalism.[17] Before his death Turner had become a prophet among historians. Since his passing his fame has mounted. Detractors have appeared, but they have found the students of the master fierce contenders. The emotionalism of the battle suggests that more than a scientific hypothesis is at stake. The controversy over the Turner thesis affects tenaciously held social beliefs. One suspects that the fame of Turner will not decline until the American democratic faith has waned.

∽

The career of Henry Adams was the transmutation into an individual life of the allegory of Melville's *Mardi*, a literal journey about the earth in search of a philosophy of life, or, as Adams called it, of history. One catches glimpses of him in the second half of the nineteenth century in many corners of the earth like a trim clipper discharging and taking on cargo in the ports of the world—at Harvard in the fifties listening to Agassiz lecture and reading in the

study of James Russell Lowell; at London in the 1860's acting as
secretary to his ambassador father, Charles Francis Adams, reading
de Tocqueville, Darwin, and Comte and talking to the geologist,
Lyle; back at Harvard in the 1870's teaching medieval history;
dining out in Washington in the 1880's and writing his great history
of the administrations of Thomas Jefferson and James Madison;
traveling to Japan, and thence to the South Sea Islands, following
the trail which Melville had blazed in Tahiti. In 1893 Henry Adams
published his *Omoo* privately under the title, *Memoirs of Marau
Taaroa, Last Queen of Tahiti*. The summer of 1895 found him in
Normandy with the Cabot Lodges discovering the twelfth century
in Mont-Saint-Michel. These aré but the more important ports in
which he dropped anchor, and they all contributed to that rich experience which was his life. But for the most part they had only an
indirect connection with that other journey famous as "the education of Henry Adams."

It began with de Tocqueville and the democratic faith. "I pass my
intervals from official work," Adams wrote from London in 1863,
"in studying de Tocqueville and John Stuart Mill, the two high
priests of our faith. . . . I have learned to think de Tocqueville my
model, and I study his life and works as the Gospel of my private
religion. The great principle of democracy is still capable of reward-
ing a conscientious servant."[18] From the enthusiastic French democrat Adams passed naturally and with enthusiasm to Darwin. While
still a secretary in London, young Adams came under the spell of
that exuberant nineteenth-century optimism which found in the
evolutionary hypothesis nature's law of progress. "Natural Selection led back to Natural Evolution, and at last to Natural Uniformity. This was a vast stride. Unbroken Evolution under uniform
conditions pleased every one—except curates and bishops; it was
the very best substitute for religion; a safe, conservative, practical,
thoroughly Common-Law deity."[19]

Darwinism, however, was but a new lantern in a corner of an
old universe. Galileo, Newton, Descartes, and Francis Bacon had
spread on the canvas of seventeenth- and eighteenth-century thought
the picture of nature as a cosmic machine, composed of a complex
of lesser machines, all fitted together with infinite nicety and turned
by the belt of immutable law. It was the creation of mathematics,
physics, and chemistry; Darwin brought biology, hitherto little advanced beyond taxonomy, within its circumference. That strange
Frenchman, August Comte, added sociology, Morgan ethnology,

and Karl Marx the discovery that history, also, is a product of the cosmic machine. By the middle of the nineteenth century it seemed to men that the walls of the cathedral of knowledge were practically complete. What remained to be done was to add some tiles to the roof, a buttress here and there, and to carve a few more saints above the doors. In such a universe Henry Adams grew to maturity. "By rights, . . . Adams should also have been a Marxist, but some narrow trait of the New England nature seemed to blight socialism, and he tried in vain to make himself a convert. He did the next best thing; he became a Comteist, within the limits of evolution."[20]

Comte, borrowing from Turgot and Saint-Simon, had restated in the first volume of his *Cours de philosophie positive*, published in Paris in 1830, the postulate that human knowledge evolves in accordance with a law of three stages. Man, from the time he emerged as a thinking animal, was puzzled and terrified by the mysteries about him. He attempted to explain the observed facts of nature by theological formulae, at first a Bushman's fetishism and finally the Christian's monotheism. This theological period was very long. Dissatisfied, man passed in the seventeenth and eighteenth centuries to a metaphysical explanation of nature; depending upon reason, he constructed generalizations about natural laws and natural rights. The third stage, which Comte believed to be at hand in his day, was that of science. In this "positive" phase the eighteenth-century search for essences or absolutes was replaced by attempts to elucidate the relationships among phenomena. Positivism in the middle of the nineteenth century both shocked and scared the clergy, for it relegated them and their ecclesiastical institutions to the category of anachronisms. Comte added to their discomfort with his concept of the necessary hierarchy of sciences, a pyramidal structure erected upon the laws of nature and logic in a certain order: mathematics, astronomy, physics, chemistry, biology, sociology. By a long hard path man had climbed upward until, in sociology, he had reached the desired peak, had become master of his own destiny and could create his own Beulah Land. When John Stuart Mill, eager disciple of positivism, read the later volumes of the *Cours* he found to his disgust that Comte's Beulah Land was a strange, half Catholic country. Like Mill, Henry Adams became a positivist but rejected the Comtean religion.

In the late 1860's Henry Adams returned from England to an America strangely transformed by the war and sought an opportunity to carry on the family tradition of public service. He journeyed to Washington with the vague dream of putting science to work in public affairs. He was pleased at the elevation to the presidency of that taciturn soldier who had organized the victory over rebellion and had then treated his adversary as a gentleman should. Young Adams felt that the chief need of America, disorganized by civil strife and poisoned by Reconstruction, was discipline and organization. These two are, by the by, the essence of science. Adams felt that under the soldier's leadership science would have its opportunity; with its aid Americans would march toward national greatness. Then one day in 1869 he read in the press the names of Grant's proposed Cabinet, a handful of cheap politicians, a wealthy merchant, and, for window dressing, one or two figures of national stature. Adams felt ashamed, not of Grant, but of himself for misinterpreting so completely the American scene. He took one look at realistic American democracy and decided that he must plan his life afresh.

This first-hand view of American realistic democracy shattered Adams' romantic democratic faith which he had known as a boy before the war. A similar experience had no such effect on Adams' contemporary, Whitman. Through the horrors of war, the hatreds of Reconstruction, and the exposure of filth in the Grant administration Whitman held fast to his faith. For him it was the source of life-giving hope. Adams abandoned hope. His brother, Brooks, has described what happened to Henry when he heard the announcement of Grant's Cabinet. "He blushed for himself because he had dreamed it to be possible that a democratic republic could develop the intellectual energy to raise itself to that advanced level of intelligence which had been accepted as a moral certainty by Washington, by his own grandfather, and most of his grandfather's contemporaries of the eighteenth century, and whose dreams and ideas he had, as he describes, unconsciously inherited. He understood at length, as his ancestor had learned, that mankind does not advance by his own unaided efforts, and competition, toward perfection. He does not automatically realize unity or even progress. On the contrary, he reflects the diversity of nature. It is the contrast between the ideal of the kingdom of heaven, peace and obedience; and the diversity of competition, or in other words, of war. Democracy is an infinite mass of conflicting minds and of conflicting interests which by the persistent action of such solvent as the modern competitive industrial system, becomes resolved into what is, in substance, a vapor, which loses in collective intellectual energy in proportion to the perfection of its expansion."[21]

The following summer found Adams in Europe astonished, almost equally, at the sudden war which brought the German Empire into being and at an invitation from Charles W. Eliot, Harvard's new president, to join his staff as an assistant professor of medieval history. Adams accepted reluctantly, having at the time little interest in the Middle Ages. What was worse, he had no theory, such as Darwin's evolutionary hypothesis, to give medieval society meaning for the modern world. O. C. Marsh could show to an enthusiastic Huxley how the five-toed eohippus of the Eocene became the one-toed horse of the Pliocene but Henry Adams, in 1870, saw no relation (although he did later) between the Virgin in her medieval Gothic cathedral and the noisy locomotive which took him from New York to Cambridge to begin his professorship. But he had an inquiring mind, singularly free, for his generation in America, from theological and social superstitions. He set to work to treat history as a social science and not, as George Bancroft was still doing, as a Te Deum of the democratic faith. Adams, seeking freedom for exploration, introduced to Harvard the method of the seminar. As the years passed, a sense of futility grew upon him; he felt that the burrowings of his class in medieval law and feudal practices were a waste of time for himself and his students. To the regret of his associates he abandoned his post in 1877 and returned to Washington in the same year in which a disillusioned Sumner, home from Baton Rouge, began his crusade to purify democracy.

Adams chose to write the history of the first two decades of the nineteenth century when the romantic dream was beginning to form in the American mind. He was disillusioned concerning democracy, though he soon discovered that he had a disturbing fondness for the shade of Albert Gallatin. Still a Comteist, Adams began to hope that the application of the methods of science to the historical materials left by the generation of Thomas Jefferson would throw some light upon the pressing question as to whither American democracy was tending in the 1880's. In 1891, as Whitman and Melville died, Adams published the final volume of his *History of the United States, 1801–1817*. It was promptly and justly acclaimed the finest product of the new scientific history to be produced in America. Here was an honest re-creation of a vanished age, a thorough study of realistic politics as manifested in domestic policy and

diplomatic maneuver. Within Adams' volumes the historical superstitions of romantic democracy found no place. His was a work
of thorough-going naturalism, an inspiration and a guide to that
small but increasing company of American scholars who were seeking, through the application of science to history, to penetrate to
the inner realities of that baffling complex called American life. But
Adams was dissatisfied when he surveyed the handsome volumes
standing, like soldiers, in mass formation on his book shelf as though
about to march upon the final citadel where Ignorance held captive the secret of social progress. He reached the conclusion that
his campaign had failed, and, what is more important, that conventional narrative history would never capture that all-important
strong point. He could find no meaning in the sequence of historical events, in the fact that Madison succeeded Jefferson in the presidential office and that Monroe succeeded Madison. He was, moreover, beginning to suspect the futility of the optimism of his fellow
historians who, following Comte as he had done, were trying to
discover the factors which had aided or impeded democratic advance in order to speed the evolution of the American democratic
state. Since 1869 in Adams' mind the conviction had been growing
that democracy is the process of degradation. As to the reason
for this downward trend he was not yet, in 1891, quite clear, but
he was convinced that history in the large sense of Lewis H. Morgan held the answer.

If the education of Henry Adams began with the addition of
Darwinian evolution to a Newtonian universe, it ended with the disruption of that simple mechanistic philosophy at the close of the nineteenth century by the discovery of radium. Between these two outstanding intellectual events in Adams' life was a third, the realization
of the import of the second law of thermodynamics, the law of entropy. "There is a universal tendency to the dissipation of mechanical energy," Adams noted, ". . . any restoration of mechanical
energy . . . is impossible; . . . within a finite time . . . the earth
must . . . be unfit for the habitation of man."[22] Evolution seemed
to lead upward from the protozoa to man; entropy to lead downward from heat to coldness, from life to death. In the end Adams
chose as the theme of his philosophical symphony the concept that
the solar system, as the sun cools, is driving toward the ultimate
chaos of the "heat-death." This was the antithesis of that philosophy of progress which was of the essence of the mid-nineteenth-
century democratic faith.

Does the record of history throw any light on the nearness or remoteness of that time when men shall literally be frozen from the earth and history itself shall end? Adams thought it did. As a young man he saw coal become a source of power surpassing all others. He watched a developing technology create an industrial civilization. For his contemporaries the mills and the railroads were the material evidence of progress; for Adams they symbolized an increasing dissipation of energy. In the nineties he stepped for a few months out of a noisy and hurrying machine age into the quiet of a primitive culture. In Tahiti he caught a glimpse of what the world was like before civilization began, and later at Mont-Saint-Michel he saw what the Christian world had been before science had created industrialism. He returned to America from France to write the saga of man's defeat at the hands of progress.

What is man? Melville had said he is a mystery; Adams called him a force. As a spider in its web lures its prey, so man, thought Adams, attracts other natural forces. But for thousands of years, after man emerged from the womb of nature, he acquired but little force outside his own body, only a club, a boat, a bow and arrow, fire, and a few domestic animals; Adams had seen in the South Seas such a culture in operation. He noted that religion was important among the Polynesians and that its ceremonies and formulas were efforts to tap occult sources of energy. For thousands of years before and after the dawn of conscious history, Adams thought, mankind conserved the small amount of energy at its disposal and sought additional power through religion. Then, about 1600, Galileo and Newton introduced the idea of mechanical causation, an event of transcendent importance because it brought to an end the first period in the history of thought. Thought, Adams believed, is as much energy as electricity; before 1600 religious thought was the principal force outside the human body operating in human society.

The work of Galileo and Newton in laying the foundations of science ushered in the mechanical age, the period of the water wheel, the steam engine, and the labor-saving machine. For the first time in history coal beds became important, and streams were used for other purposes than navigation or water supply. Man suddenly found himself possessed of mighty forces. He had scarcely adjusted himself to the new order when, about 1900, thought passed into a third phase as the mechanical age gave way to that of electricity with the dynamo as the symbol of the new order. But the age of electricity was hardly begun when the discovery of radium made clear that still another, the ethereal age, was but a few years off. "An immense volume of force had detached itself from the unknown universe of energy, while still vaster reservoirs, supposed to be infinite, steadily revealed themselves, attracting mankind with more compulsive force than all the Pontic Seas of Gods or Gold that ever existed."[23] Was this cosmic stirring a sign of that dissipation of energy which would end in chaos and death? Adams was inclined to think so.

The puzzling aspect of history to Adams was the immense duration of the religious period and the increasing brevity of the succeeding three periods. Obviously the explanation must be sought outside man himself, for during the entire length of the historical time line the physical equipment of man and his power of logical thought had remained practically a constant. The laws of physics suggested the obvious solution of the problem. If man is a force capturing other forces, he is also a captive. In this concept may be found Adams' substitute for the democratic doctrine of the free individual. "The sum of force attracts," said Adams, "the feeble atom or molecule called man is attracted; he suffers education or growth; he is the sum of the forces that attract him; his body and his thought are alike their product; the movement of force controls the progress of his mind, since he can know nothing but the motions which impinge on his senses, whose sum makes education."[24] Man, then, is part of nature's deterministic scheme, a pawn in a cosmic chess game. "No one is likely to suggest a theory that man's convenience had been consulted by Nature at any time, or that Nature had consulted the convenience of any of her creations. . . . In every age man has bitterly and justly complained that Nature hurried and hustled him, for inertia almost invariably ended in tragedy."[25] Clearly, as the mechanical age gave way to the electrical and that to the ethereal, Nature was hurrying and hustling man as never before; Nature was expending unprecedented energy on the earth. "At the rate of progress since 1800, every American who lived into the year 2000 would know how to control unlimited power. . . . To him the nineteenth century would stand on the same plane with the fourth—equally childlike—and he would only wonder how both of them, knowing so little, and so weak in force, should have done so much."[26]

Adams had sufficient training in mathematics to suspect that, when he found acceleration in nature, he might find its expression in a formula; he tested the hypothesis that energy has flowed into the earth in accordance with the law of inverse squares. He found that the mechanical period lasted three hundred years. The square of that number is ninety thousand, the approximate duration in years of the religious period; Homo sapiens emerged in the glacial age and ninety thousand years ago was as good a guess as any for the appearance of men in the Pleistocene. The square root of three hundred is approximately seventeen and a half; the electrical age, therefore, would end about 1918. By adding four more years, the square root of seventeen, Adams forecast that man would reach the limit of thought as a force about 1922. To explain his point he used the comet as a figure of speech. "The simplest figure, at first, is that of a perfect comet—say that of 1843—which drops from space, in a straight line, at the regular acceleration of speed, directly into the sun, and after wheeling sharply about it, in heat that ought to dissipate any known substance, turns back unharmed, in defiance of law, by the path on which it came."[27] The long straight line of the comet's path was the religious period; the three short periods after 1600 were the curve through which it swung past the blazing sun in a field of energy unbelievably intense. But Adams turned to other figures. If this energy pouring on the earth behaved like an explosive, a new equilibrium would soon be established; if it behaved like a vegetable, "it must rapidly reach the limit of growth; and even if it acted like the earlier creations of energy—the saurians and sharks— it must already have reached its expansion."[28] By any analogy an end of some sort had come.

He was persuaded of the plausibility of this conclusion by a phenomenon which followed the disappearance of the religious period. That long phase had seen polytheism slowly give way to monotheism; multiplicity had been replaced by unity. In twelfth-century France, Adams found a culture which was the product of unity. In *Mont-Saint-Michel and Chartres* he painted a medieval scene in which the lines of perspective converged on a single point where stood the image of the Virgin in whom the world of the Middle Ages was united. Above its economic and political institutions stood the Cross before which knelt the ecclesiastics, the statesmen, the warriors, the men of affairs, and the artists: the painters, sculptors, glass-makers, wood-carvers, and builders. The cathedral at Chartres expressed that sense of order and of security which springs from unity. The religion of the Virgin was like a levee beside some super-Mississippi protecting a beautiful medieval landscape from a rising flood of natural energy. In the seventeenth century Galileo and Newton breached the dike and let in the river. The twentieth, thought Adams, would see the flood reach its crest. Already in 1910 he noted the swirl of the new forces, symbolized by the motor car, the telephone, and the improved artillery of the military parades which passed from time to time beneath the towers of Notre Dame in Paris. Adams thought that, although the old cathedral was as beautiful as ever, it was but a relic of a distant golden day when all men bowed down before the Everlasting One. The unity of medieval life was gone, replaced by the multiplicity of modern life. Was multiplicity perhaps the anteroom of chaos, the chaos of the heat-death, when history would cease to have any meaning? Adams did not know. But he was sure that the flood of energy would remake society.

Since that day when Newton formulated the laws of motion, energy in an accelerating stream had been pouring upon the earth from seemingly inexhaustible reservoirs. It was both benevolent and malevolent; constructive and destructive. It had enabled men to elevate their standards of living to hitherto undreamed-of heights; and it threatened to disrupt society. The most potent agency in the education of twentieth-century men, thought Adams on the threshold of the century, would be the bomb, doubling in effectiveness and in numbers every ten years. Prayers to God to bring to pass the brotherhood of man would be, he thought, of as little use in the twentieth century as the rain dances in the kivas of the Pueblo Indians. "Power leaped from every atom, . . ." said Adams of the scene about him in his old age. "Man could no longer hold it off. Forces grasped his wrists and flung him about as though he had hold of a live wire; . . . fire-arms ravaged society, until an earthquake became almost a nervous relaxation."[29]

The democratic faith of the Middle Period had been a philosophy of unity. It had suggested the picture of a dependable cosmos in which free men, governed by the fundamental law, climbed haltingly yet persistently toward higher plateaus of virtue and of civilization. The faith created a sense of spiritual security. One suspects that the aging Adams longed to be again comforted and inspired by it. His secret desire seemed to be to recapture that unity which the Middle Ages knew. But he saw energy pouring at an accelerating rate upon the earth, abolishing the customs and disrupting the organizations of men. Power was the keyword of the twentieth century.

Adams, as a philosopher, was neither optimistic nor pessimistic. He contented himself with propounding a hypothesis concerning social change. He felt that another ten years would bring its verification or rejection. Meanwhile he had no scheme to suggest to the new American, no fault to find, no complaint to make. To Adams in 1904 the "next great influx of new forces seemed near at hand, and its style of education promised to be violently coercive. The movement from unity into multiplicity, between 1200 and 1900, was unbroken in sequence, and rapid in acceleration. Prolonged one generation longer, it would require a new social mind."[30] The prophecy was shrewd. The democratic faith, thought Adams agreeing with Sumner, is doomed. Before that single generation passed the world became familiar, not with one, but with several new social minds— the return to handicrafts and the policy of passive resistance of Gandhi, the fascism of Mussolini, the national socialism of Hitler, and the communism of Russia and China.

Chapter 24

A NEW SCIENCE
AND A NEW PHILOSOPHY

For Americans as, in fact, for Europeans a major shift of thought set off the twentieth century from the nineteenth. Developments in science stood at the center of change. The shift compared in magnitude with that earlier revolution marked by the emergence of science itself in the seventeenth century.

A particular view of the cosmos governed work in the natural sciences and conditioned social thinking in the eighteenth and nineteenth centuries. Descartes and Newton had painted for men a portrait of the universe as, in the words of David Hume, "one great machine, subdivided into an infinite number of lesser machines . . . adjusted to each other with an accuracy that ravishes into admiration all men who have ever contemplated them . . ."—a deterministic universe of relentless cause and effect, a universe that could be represented by a model. This view of nature etched by natural science provided a background for social thinking in the eighteenth and nineteenth centuries. The description of a mechanistic nature suggested by natural science had its counterpart in the picture proposed by the classical theorists of an economy as, like a bridge, a balance of stresses and strains, an equilibrium of pulls and thrusts. Classical economic theory continued beyond John Bates Clark into the twentieth century. The determinism of the Newtonian cosmos also had its reflection in the determinism of what Karl Marx called scientific socialism.

In 1887 Charles Peirce bought a house and tract of land in what he called the wildest county in the northern states. Son of a Harvard mathematician, he had grown up in Cambridge where he became a friend of the young William James. Peirce had taught for a time at Johns Hopkins. Moving his library and his family to the new home near Milford, Pennsylvania, he now devoted himself wholly to research and writing on philosophy and logic. The clangor of advancing industrialism was remote from the Peirce habitation. But into his study came the ideas circulating at the time in the world of thought. In particular, Darwinism impressed him as a most important new insight into nature and he fitted evolution into his own thinking. Peirce, however, was a mathematician and logician rather than biologist. He directed his attention primarily to the mechanistic and deterministic cosmos as the physicists of the day understood it. A doubt crept into his mind that the accepted picture of the universe expressed the whole truth. His investigations led him to the conclusion that the concept of a perfectly articulated machine universe represented an unproved and, in fact, unprovable hypothesis. Peirce thought of himself as a working scientist. Beginning with the molecular hypothesis of chemistry, he saw in this position an entry for the calculus of probabilities. He noted that chance is primary. Chance was explicit in the fresh, free, and unlimited multiplicity of life. In the year in which he made his home in Pennsylvania he recognized "an element of indeterminacy, spontaneity, and absolute chance in nature."[1] How else, Peirce added, could the scientist account for the emergence of novelty from exact law.

Peirce did not himself change the course of thought in physics. The scientists of the end of the century seem to have been for the most part unaware of him. Yet this lonely mathematical theorist who lived out his latter years in poverty and neglect was one of the first of that time to sense that, to use a later phrase of Sir James Jeans, the cosmic machine has some wobbling joints. In the early twentieth century the penetration of the atom following upon the accidental discovery of radioactivity not only opened new and seemingly limitless vistas but cast doubts on what had long been accepted in the world of physics as eternal verities. That clear distinction of classical physics between matter and energy dissolved as, in time, the men of the laboratory learned to transform the one into the other. The most dramatic break with the past occurred in 1905 when Albert Einstein published his Special Theory of Relativity in which he made clear the inadequacy for certain scientific problems of the Newtonian concepts of absolute space and absolute time. Quantum mechanics completed the destruction of the old scientific absolutes. Abandoning the strict determinism of the nineteenth century, the twentieth century worked with what Peirce had called the "calculus of probabilities."

Peirce did not live to see this new age far advanced. He died in 1914. But he had been one of the first to glimpse the new horizons. Before the nineteenth century ended he had communicated something of his vision to his old friend, William James. And for American social thought the primary contribution of Peirce was the assertion that the meaning of any truth is to be found in its consequences.

∽

William James was convalescing in France in 1901 when his friend Royce sent him a copy of the latter's two-volume study, *The World and the Individual*. James read it completely, delighted to find his associate pulling his philosophy together into a coherent system and expressing his thoughts with such grace and effectiveness. It was Royce's most important book. "It makes youthful anew," James wrote to a friend and student of Royce, "the paradox of philosophy—so trivial and so ponderous at once. The book leaves a total effect on you like a picture—a summary impression of charm and grace as light as a breath; yet to bring forth that light nothing less than Royce's enormous organic temperament and technical equipment, and preliminary attempts, were required. The book consolidates an impression which I have never before got except by glimpses, that Royce's system is through and through to be classed as a light production. It is a charming, romantic sketch; and it is only by handling it after the manner of a sketch, keeping it within sketch technique, that R. can make it very impressive."[2] The Roycean system was indubitably a light production in contrast with the work of William James, into whose winnowing basket went every important idea current at the end of the century. James was the antithesis of Hamlet. James faced intellectual issues with the zest of a mountain climber; he was not content until he had reached the outlook to be gained by a clear-cut decision. He made his most important choice when he drew back from Royce's sophisticated collectivism to a primitive individualism which was reminiscent of the American frontier of an earlier period.

But William James was no frontiersman. The son of a poet and essayist, he was reared in the East and in Europe. Ralph Barton Perry has brought to life the forgotten and somewhat pathetic figure of the elder Henry James. William's childhood background was his father's preoccupation with Swedenborgianism; his attacks upon the pantheism of his friend, Ralph Waldo Emerson; and his ardent advocacy of the Utopian socialism of Charles Fourier. Royce

was born into a crude mining society, James into the elite. His father
had a genius for friendship, and young William sat at table with
many of the choicest spirits of the nineteenth century. Royce was
shy and compensated for his isolation by philosophizing about the
community. The personality of William James had warmth and
resonance, with the result that his friends were as numerous as those
of his father. In this respect he resembled his student, Theodore
Roosevelt. The younger man, however, used his gifts to make sympathetic and understanding contacts with men of all classes and in
all walks of life: cowboys, labor leaders, pugilists, intellectuals, financial magnates, political bosses. James never escaped from the
elite. He looked at life through the spectacles of a class that was
proud of its energy and of its successes and that was satisfied, on the
whole, with the *status quo*. James never wholly escaped from the
gospel of wealth. If he later decried "the bitch goddess success," he
might have remembered that he was born into the upper class and,
with his younger brother, Henry, inherited a considerable substance.

William James, moreover, was the personification of the best in
post-Appomattox nationalism. Cosmopolitan though he was by
training and as a result of the fortunes of his adult life, he was essentially American. He was fond of Europe, where antiquity enriched the present and where society was ordered and mature. Yet
he wrote from France in 1901, when his Gifford lectures at the
University of Edinburgh and a prolonged illness had kept him
abroad for nearly two years: "I long to steep myself in America
again and let the broken rootlets make new adhesions to the native
soil. A man coquetting with too many countries is as bad as a biga-
mist, and loses his soul altogether."[3] He liked America because of the
greenness and plasticity of its culture, a trait not without importance
for his philosophy. He felt that the corruptions of American plutocracy were less offensive than the venalities of Europe. Above all, he
loved the woods beside the tiny lake nestling at the foot of Cho-
corua in the White Mountains. Here he retired at the end of a busy
academic year at Cambridge to contemplate with aversion, as he
threaded the despairing worm upon his hook, the philosopher's
trivial and ponderous task.

William James was twenty-three when Lee surrendered. He had
followed neither Grant nor Sherman. Like his contemporaries, William Graham Sumner and Henry Adams, he was innocent of war.
Demobilized veterans, such as Robert Ingersoll and Lester Frank
Ward, looked down upon his type. Unmindful, James pursued his

scientific education and in 1872 began teaching as instructor of physiology at Harvard. In the same year young Sumner was called from his pastorate at Morristown to the chair of political economy at Yale. Both men, in spite of their failure to enlist in the crusade of the 1860's, were fighters, and both, as the twentieth century opened, wrote distinguished essays on war.

It was inevitable that the majority of Americans in the post-Appomattox generation of William James should believe in the efficacy of individual effort to bring about material and social change. The tide of industrialism was sweeping over America as the bore roars up the Bay of Fundy. As new cities rose and new industrial empires came into being, it was difficult not to believe with Henry Demarest Lloyd that man is the creator of society. All current popular American faiths, the gospel of wealth, the religion of humanity, emphasized the creative rôle of the active individual. James went with his age.

$\sim$

In 1878, when William James was thirty-six, Lewis Henry Morgan expounded in *Ancient Society* what he took to be the law of progress. James in the same year contracted with Henry Holt and Company to write a book, which appeared twelve years later, *Principles of Psychology*. The volume was one of the most important of James's many attacks upon the type of philosophy giving rise to such concepts as that of Morgan. A law of progress that really existed would have done violence to every conviction that James held dear. It implied a cosmic orderliness and a determinism which left no rôle for the individual save that of an automaton. What would be the use of striving to advance, if the cosmos has stacked the cards of history in favor of progress? What is the moral advantage to the individual of struggling to do what the forces of nature are compelling him to do? Were Americans, freed after many years from Calvinistic foreordination, to become slaves to scientific determinism? The danger, thought James, lurked in the growing prestige of Darwinism. The hypothesis of the great naturalist seemed to imply an automatic and irresistible advance through the geologic ages. Morgan was one of the first to attempt to discover whether social progress is analogous to biological change. James dissented. He strove to find for the individual a philosophic world in which he would be important because of his uniqueness rather than because of his similarities to his fellows.

Recalling the conviction of Peirce that the neat and finished

Newtonian cosmos was an unverified and unverifiable hypothesis, James struck out into what he looked upon as a chancy universe, a universe in which hazard is pre-eminent because certitude does not exist. The older thinkers had insisted that beneath the flux men observe and experience on the surface of nature and society lies a central harmony of laws and principles fixed through all time. In American social thinking of the nineteenth century men had expressed this idea in the doctrine of the fundamental law. The nineteenth-century man looked upon the function of intelligence as penetration beneath the surface of change to the foundation of what had always been and always would be true. For James at the end of the nineteenth century the time had come to abandon these old and comforting formulas for intellectual security. The disconcerting fact he beheld was the fact of chance and spontaneity reaching to the very core of reality. There is no abiding peace at the center of the flux of life. All is flux. Looking about him James saw a plastic universe, emerging, evolving, growing, decaying. Not even God, thought James, knows how it will come out.

Such a view of reality provided the background for the Jamesian concept of the creative individual. If Henry Adams thought of the individual as a unit of force, James looked upon him as a center of spontaneity. The individual person, always a unique being, in his own way and by his own actions makes the universe different from what it was before he appeared. Perhaps the novelties he effects seem minuscule when looked at in the perspective of the far-ranging universe that science has discovered. Even so, that fact does not destroy the principle of spontaneity and creativeness.

James saw pragmatism as the method of creation by men. He preferred, however, the term radical empiricism. What was this empiricism that James called radical? The test of the truth of an idea is not to be discovered by logic after the manner of the rationalist philosophers but by setting the idea to work and discovering its consequences. Action transcends contemplation; experiment supplants syllogism. Truth is not an essence that inheres in an idea. Truth may or may not happen to an idea. Truth is relative, not absolute. An idea may be true today in one set of circumstances and false tomorrow when circumstances change.

A chancy universe requires man, the creator, to be tough-minded. He must live with change. He must accept hazard as a primary condition of life. But he does not live out his days alone. The transcendentalism that James had heard discussed in his home when he was a boy tinged his thought. If James rejected the old absolutisms of religion along with those of science, he also rejected the idea that creative man moves alone in a purely naturalistic universe, a universe from which all trace of God has vanished.

∿

Like the young men of his generation James began his thinking with an acceptance of the validity of science in its proper realm. Being trained as a scientist, he had, however, fewer illusions than some of his contemporaries concerning the extent of the usefulness of science to man. He was aware that, when science is taken as a mistress, she can become as mean a hussy as religion. He rejected the dogmas, the indexes, and the assumptions of superiority of both science and religion.

James dismissed all religious beliefs which he found colliding with the verities of science, and he agreed with Melville that science is only a lightship illuminating a particular reef and intensifying the enveloping darkness. The darkness, thought Melville, is Mystery. God is past finding out. The individual must build his life on ignorance and live it out without hope of security. Royce took issue with Melville. Logic will pierce the Mystery, he declared. So armed, Royce plunged into the ring of darkness and, after a time, returned with the Absolute. See, he said in effect, there is no darkness. What was darkness was the Absolute and, now that we begin to know Him, that which was blackness is becoming a great light. William James looked long and sympathetically at Royce's Absolute, for he was a sincere admirer of his California friend. But, much as he wished to believe that Royce was right, James found the same old wall of night at the limit of the lightship's rays. He concluded, therefore, that Royce's Absolute was merely a large piece of phosphorescence mistaken by his colleague for the sun.

Yet James was as deeply interested as Royce or Melville in the mystery beyond the limits of knowledge. James pointed out that no human being can live merely by the light of knowledge. Every day, nay, every hour, the individual is compelled to make decisions, the favorable outcome of which he cannot be assured in advance. Faith, thought James, is the willingness to take risks when the issue is not sure. One of the elementary facts of life, James taught, is the necessity to believe—the necessity, for example, of the businessman to believe in the probity of his partner when he cannot possibly know what thoughts of treachery his associate may harbor in his heart. James added that faith in the honesty of a partner tends to create that honesty. Faith has a creative function in the life of the world. Without faith human knowledge would be a dwarfed and puny thing. Suppose, for example, that the revolutionary leaders of 1776 had not had faith that they could make good their declaration of independence. There would have been no United States and no knowledge of the possibilities of achievement of the Americans as a politically free people. The faith of 1776 was a risk; the event, independence, was not assured; the faith helped in an essential way to bring about the event. The validity of the faith depended, therefore, upon the results which it produced. By such logic James pointed out the importance of the will to believe.

James was predisposed by personality and upbringing to religious faith. Emerson's Over-Soul had from childhood been part of his mental furnishings. As James contemplated the ring of darkness at the limit of the lightship's rays, he was convinced that faith would enable the individual to explore the shrouded regions. He had a lively interest in all types of religious experience. He was indefatigable in his search for the "facts" of what happened in the conversion of a Methodist, in the experience of a Quaker who listened to the inner voice, or in the revelations of prophets such as Joseph Smith. James, it should be remembered, was a psychologist in a day when introspection was the chief research tool of that discipline. Through trained introspection the scientist, thought James, could make contact with and experience directly the realities within himself. James, unfortunately, never had a mystical experience like that of Sarah Eleanor Royce in the Carson desert. He was compelled to study the experiences of other men. He observed that in case after case prayer seemed to raise the level of energy within an individual, to increase, in the phrase of the engineer, his electric potential. Whence comes this energy? From the outside, thought James, from the darkness which encircles the lightship. It flows from out there into the individual's higher or idealistic self which is constantly striving to maintain the mastery over his lower or animal self. What is the power line which brings it in? The psychologists, declared James, in recent years have made the important discovery of the subconscious self. In the phenomenon of prayer or of mystical experience the subconscious self, beginning with the Me, extends into the darkness and makes contact with a More. In fact, like the transmission line, the subconscious is always there, a channel for impulses from the More to the Me. Faith in the existence of the

More enables a man to test his importance for human life. Refusal to believe does not disprove the existence of the More but merely closes the door to possible knowledge of the utmost importance to mankind. James believed that his intellectual confreres, dazzled by science, were fast closing that door. He put his back against it to hold it open.

The argument just outlined was set forth in 1902 in *The Varieties of Religious Experience*. It had a great success. Disheartened Protestants, seeking something to replace the discredited dogmas of the old orthodoxy, welcomed James with enthusiasm. He transformed what threatened to become a rout into an advance. The social gospelers, in particular, looked upon him as the defender of their cause. Did he not say that faith is justified in the works it produces? But the skeptics, such as Justice Oliver Wendell Holmes, remained skeptics even in spite of the massed evidence of the *Varieties*. They feared that James, in the eagerness of his search for the "facts" in the phenomena of the spiritualistic séance and of table-tapping in the dark, was sometimes gullible. He swallowed, they thought, too many tall tales from the frontier which lies between this world and the next.

James, undaunted by the skeptic's criticism, pushed forward. His More, or God, was unlike Emerson's Over-Soul. James was quite willing to accept more gods than one. He felt, in fact, that evolution might as reasonably produce a new god as bring forth that peculiar mammalian form called man. Yet he was unwilling to agree with Emerson, or Royce, that God pervades everything as did the ether of classical physics. In short, James rejected absolutism in all its forms. He complained that the absolutist assumes that a single unifying principle lies at the center of the universe, calls it God or the Author of Nature or the Over-Soul or the Absolute, and then assumes that everything we know or think or believe derives ultimately from this single source. All we know of the universe, affirmed James, is that it is plural, that it is made up of many separate and particular things, and that it is best described by "the social analogy; plurality of individuals, with relations partly external, partly intimate, like and un-like, different in origin, in aim, yet keeping house together, interfering, coalescing, compromising, finding new purposes to arise, getting gradually into more stable habits, winning order, weeding out."[4] It is a plastic universe in which creation is constantly going on. It is not developing toward some predetermined end; not even God knows how it will come out. God or the More is one of its particular and separate parts. Faith affirms and the evidence available suggests that He is striving to achieve the good. The fact that there is still plenty of evil suggests that God is not omnipotent. He is finite. He will help men and men can help Him in the struggle to achieve the good. Using faith as a tool, James had entered the darkness beyond the limit of the lightship's rays and emerged later with his hypothesis of a finite God striving in a pluralistic universe.

᭞

What, then, is progress? It is not the working out of predetermined and automatic natural laws. Morgan's law of progress, thought James, is an illusion. It destroys the significance of the individual by making him a pawn in Nature's chess game. The individual human being is a player in the game. He inhabits a universe in which creation is not finished and for which not even all the blueprints are drawn up. He is in his small way a creator. His uniqueness is his most important quality. In such fashion James tossed on the rubbish heap all the absolutisms of the nineteenth century: deism, transcendentalism, orthodox Christianity, and classical physics. He lifted into philosophy the well-nigh universal belief of the common men of America that man can effect material and social changes, that he can create, and that he is, in fact, creating a new civilization. This belief had produced among some of the disciples of the religion of humanity dreams of Utopia: Henry George's golden age, Lester F. Ward's sociocracy, and Edward Bellamy's great romance. William James did not go so far. He had too much respect for the toughness of evil to hope that it would ever be abolished, at least by men. Having made God finite, James was unwilling to fall into the absurdity of making man omnipotent. Man, like God, thought James, can accomplish only a limited good.

How does man effect progress? James' answer was pragmatism or, as he preferred to call it, radical empiricism. It contained two cardinal principles, the pragmatic method and the pragmatic theory of the truth. The first interprets ideas or concepts in terms of their results. Set an idea to work in the actual world, affirmed James, and study its consequences for experience and practice. This is the method of the scientist who tests his hypothesis in the laboratory. If the results satisfy, the idea is true. It should be remembered that the idea helped to create the truth which the laboratory test verified. Without the hypothesis, there could have been no verification, just as without the faith of the rebels of 1776 there could have been no

United States of America. Without free and creative minds there could be neither hypothesis nor faith. "Mind *engenders* truth *upon* reality," said James in 1907 in reply to his critics. "Our minds are not here simply to copy a reality that is already complete. They are here to complete it, to add to its importance by their own remodeling of it, to decant its contents over, so to speak, into a more significant shape. In point of fact, the *use* of most of our thinking is to help us to *change* the world. . . . Thus we seem set free to use our theoretical as well as our practical faculties . . . to get the world into a better shape, and all with a good conscience. The only restriction is that the world resists some lines of attack on our part and opens herself to others, so that we must go with the grain of her willingness, to play fairly. Hence the *sursum corda* of pragmatism's message."[5]

The attack upon James (and upon his fellow pragmatists, John Dewey and F. C. S. Schiller) was led by theologians and philosophers who were unwilling to exchange the stability and the security of the old absolutisms for the hazards and uncertainties of pragmatism. The scientists made no protest, for already the discovery of radium had wrecked the absolutism of classical physics. As for common men, in 1903 they beheld faith and hypothesis put to the pragmatic test at Kitty Hawk, North Carolina, with the result that a new reality appeared to the world: man, the conqueror of the air.

᷍

Everyday Americans were prepared to accept the Jamesian pragmatic thesis even if they did not always understand the epistemological implications of the principle. Activism dominated American culture, as Father Hecker so well understood when he sought to minimize the importance of medieval quietism in American Catholicism. By demanding that ideas be set to work, James made activism the foundation of his thought. Individualism was the essence of American democracy and pluralism of the political ideas that governed the federated Republic. *E pluribus unum* was stamped on every silver dollar. The United States had extended its boundaries to include an area almost as large as Europe; it had advanced from comparative poverty to immense national wealth; it had risen from the international impotence of the Jay Treaty of 1795 to a position among the great powers. Under such circumstances Americans, including William James, could be pardoned for believing in progress. James formulated in terms of a sophisticated philosophy the essential ideas and convictions of his countrymen. He became the philosopher of a buoyant, vigorous, and undefeated Americanism. When William James made the creative individual the center of his philosophy, he pushed his canoe into the main current of American thought. When he urged in America the importance of activism, he sought with his paddle to give the Mississippi a push toward the sea.

But James' thought suggests frailty as well as robustness. Americans, when they contemplated Nature's ultimate victory over the individual, turned usually to Christianity for assurance of the friendliness of the cosmos. They disliked Calvin's avenging God and fiery hell and, by the middle of the nineteenth century, they had practically got rid of both. The hymns of evangelical Protestantism emphasized the safety "in the arms of Jesus," the strength of the "rock in a weary land," and the guidance of a "kindly light." The dispensing of comfort was one of the most important of their pastor's duties.

William James also sought security in religion. His private bogy was that same second law of thermodynamics with which Henry Adams was preoccupied. "This world," James admitted sadly, "may indeed, as science assures us, some day burn up or freeze."[6] When the human race is no more, what will become of the values and the standards of the pragmatic philosophy? The essence of James' pragmatism was humanism. Ideas to assist in the creation of truth must satisfy men. What knowledge and philosophy we have, he thought, is based on human experience. When mankind is frozen off the earth, the philosophies and values of humanism must vanish. The prospect of the ultimate heat-death was upsetting to William James. He hurried to his finite God for help and comfort. "God's existence," said James, "is the guarantee of an ideal order that shall be permanently preserved. . . . [If the world freeze,] the old ideals are sure to be brought elsewhere to fruition, so that where God is, tragedy is only provisional and partial, and shipwreck and dissolution are not the absolutely final things."[7] The phrase "ideal order that shall be permanently preserved" suggests that James, who seemed to have thrown over the doctrine of the fundamental law, in the end came back to a version of it—a unique version in keeping with James' emphasis on the unique individual.

∽

So James used the pragmatic argument to support religious faith. Only against the background of his ideas of the relation between God and man can we glimpse the full meaning of his idea of personality, the personality of the free, creative individual. James published in 1899 an essay entitled "On a Certain Blindness in Human Beings." The "blindness" he referred to is the inability of each human being to understand the inwardness of other lives. Each separate life, James insisted, has to itself a private warmth and glow and self-justification beyond the reach of other human beings looking at the person from the outside. To achieve even an approximation of an understanding of another's inner life requires an imaginative sympathy that projects itself deep into another being but can never completely plumb the depths. The effort ends at the margin of mystery. For this reason, James thought, tolerance of others is, at bottom, humility before something that lies beyond one's power to grasp. "The practical consequence of such a philosophy," James remarked, "is the well-known democratic respect for individuality." Here emerged the Jamesian version of the old doctrine of the free individual.

From such a theory of personality came James' emphasis that the total value of human life in the world lies in its inexhaustible variety, in a richness that no single mind can comprehend, in the fact that this human totality is a reservoir of spontaneity that balks the imagination. Ralph Barton Perry, friend and biographer of William James and one of the most discerning among the students of his thought, has summed up the Harvard philosopher's contribution to the doctrine of the free individual. "So we are brought back," said Perry, "to the individual man and to that strange blend of attributes which gives him what nobility he has: his sense of his own limitations and almost insuperable resistance, coupled with fidelity to the good as he sees it, and with a willingness to risk failure whose magnitude corresponds to the greatness of the undertaking. . . . James was not the enemy of mediation, gentleness, and the finer arts [as some of the critics of pragmatism have implied]; of all places in the world James would have felt most out of place in the market place. He was the enemy of authority and dogma, of fatalism, of despair, and escapism, of stagnation, of inhumanity, and of the oppressive weight of established things. He was the friend of collective hope in a changing world—of hope based on the concerted efforts of responsible individuals."[8]

Americans were prepared to accept Jamesian pragmatism. It urged activism in a society whose culture was charged with activism. By demanding that ideas be put to work and judged by their results James put his philosophy in an American tradition of empiricism as old as the Constitution—which the Founding Fathers looked upon as an experiment. His portrait of the autonomous and creative individual suggested the Declaration of Independence, the frontier, the independent farmer in whom Thomas Jefferson put his trust, and the central doctrine of the American democratic faith, that of the free and responsible man and citizen. Pragmatism was the first indigenous American philosophy.

∽

One day in 1891 William James received a letter of appreciation of his *Principles of Psychology*, his first important book, published the year before. "I don't know that I told you," the letter read, "that I have had a class going through your psychology this year and how much we have all enjoyed it. I'm sure you would be greatly gratified if you could see what a stimulus to mental freedom, as well as what a purveyor of methods and materials, your book has been to us."[9] The letter came from a young man named John Dewey who, as he wrote, was a member of the faculty of the University of Michigan.

Dewey had been born in 1859 in the shadow of Vermont's Green Mountains. As a boy he knew the rural civilization that had dominated America before the Civil War. As a youth he had watched the swift and accelerating change of the American industrial revolution that spanned the years between the Civil War and World War I. In the midst of this evolution Dewey had won his Ph.D. in 1884 at the new Johns Hopkins University, at the time perhaps the most intellectually exciting place in the United States. When, as a young man, he wrote the letter in 1891, neither he nor James could foresee that the enthusiastic writer was destined to become in the early decades of the twentieth century America's most influential philosopher and most significant teacher of pragmatism. Year after year he turned out notices, articles, and books until the corpus of his work grew to be immense. He became the prophet who gave a new philosophy and with it a new momentum to American education. As the schoolman's philosopher he made his greatest impress on his generation.

Like James, John Dewey accepted the dictum of Peirce that ideas can only be understood by what they do. But after taking off from that starting place the paths of James and Dewey diverged. James called his position "radical empiricism"; Dewey spoke of his as "instrumentalism." Intelligence, he once remarked, is man's sole means and guide to a satisfying future. James emphasized the individual and stands in the tradition of Emerson and Thoreau as a philosopher of individualism. Dewey, moving with and reinforcing a shift in American thought as the twentieth century opened, emphasized social activity and the manner in which social change can be brought about. James, like Thoreau, was more interested in well-being than in well-doing, trusting to intuition as a revelation of reality. He never lost his awareness of the mystery and believed pragmatism to be a method whereby the values of the old supernaturalism could be preserved. Dewey, satisfied with the world of nature disclosed by science, thought of instrumentalism as a method by which man through intelligence can change reality. James believed in God; Dewey's pragmatism was a method for eliminating concepts of a supernatural deity.

John Dewey, moving in the early twentieth century into a position of leadership, was a contemporary of Theodore Roosevelt, Thomas A. Edison, and the young Henry Ford. Dewey was not only at home in a bustling America that was impressed by visible and practical results; he stressed the importance of the method that gets such results. He saw this as the method of science in which theory or hunch is put to the experimental test and the results observed. Dewey insisted that the role of intelligence is not primarily to understand reality but rather to change reality to make it more to man's liking. He saw the school as an instrument for remaking society.

Dewey was a humanist and moralist who thought in terms of practical and attainable goals. For Dewey the thing in all life most worthy of devotion is the process by which the goal is achieved, the vision of the ideal made real. He was quite willing to call this process God and so define deity in purely naturalistic terms. Dewey insisted that every devoted act to add to the sum of knowledge or to improve the lot of men is a religious act. But also, like Emerson, Dewey insisted that, when the dream has come true, nothing permanent has been achieved. The new situation has its imperfections. It is always incomplete. The very success of the achievement of goals creates the need for new goals and new efforts to reach them. The life of society is a process of constant change. No good is fixed but is only a stepping stone to a good further on.

Looking out over industrial America growing so swiftly in the capacity to produce goods and services, John Dewey felt that American ideas concerning liberty and individualism had lagged dangerously behind the forces and demands of social change. He believed that the citizens of the Republic had failed to understand that in an industrialized society the liberation of individual capacity as an end requires the use of organized social effort as a means, that the attainment of effective individuality is a community project, not merely a personal achievement or prerogative. At the same time Josiah Royce was saying that we are saved by the community. Also at the same time socialist thinking was appearing, particularly in the theoretical writings of Daniel De Leon.

If pragmatism, the first indigenous American philosophy, became a pervasive influence in American thought in the twentieth century, it did not go uncriticized by Americans. Morris Cohen was one of the most cogent and friendly critics of Dewey and the school that accepted his leadership. Cohen's position, as well as that of Dewey, illustrates an aspect of American thinking in the swiftly moving twentieth century.

"When Dewey and his disciples insist that philosophy must serve human weal and welfare," said Cohen in an essay on American thought left unfinished at his death in 1947, "they assert something which no one can or wishes to dispute. . . . But the significant question really is, wherein does human weal consist? When they exclude from human welfare the philosophy which is naught but a distant vision and can serve only as a consolation, or intellectual pastime, they seem to me to be falling into a most grievous error. For not only do consolations and pastimes—the essence of religion and art—most directly minister to human welfare bringing us relief from anguish and offering us positive joy, but no human work could long prosper without them . . . the humblest human wisdom has always recognized the dullness of naught but work. . . . They are also misled by the phrase 'making the world a better place to live in,' which suggests mastery of the environment rather than our own desires. But as long as human desire outruns human capacity . . . the way to happiness must include not only the mastery of nature but the mastery of ourselves. . . . No philosophy that lacks a cosmic outlook can hope to do full justice to the specifically human problem. . . . In seeing human fate as part of a great cosmic drama, men arise above their petty limitations and learn to look upon their passions and achievements with a measure of aloofness which is essential to any vision that can be called philosophic and to any civilization that can be called liberal."[10]

In spite of criticism, however, Dewey's instrumentalism became and continued the most influential American philosophy in the first half of the twentieth century. His emphasis on action rather than logic, on immediate practicality rather than theory, on the search for new solutions rather than the holding fast to old standards all fitted the mood and temper of a people who were moving, without fully realizing what was happening, into their century of power.

Chapter 25

THE FREE INDIVIDUAL
IN THE PROGRESSIVE ERA

In the summer of 1897 Henry James acquired Lamb House at Rye, England, a weathered, red-brick, Georgian house that was to serve as his "little downward burrow" and "tight anchorage" for the rest of his days. So Henry James permanently abandoned the United States at the very time his brother, William, was beginning to make momentous contributions to American thought. But Henry James, the artist, found England not only a greater stimulus for his particular genius but a point of vantage from which to view America, which in his heart he never truly gave up.

Henry James' England gives perspective on William James' America. Henry's life at Lamb House covers almost exactly the years known as the Edwardian Era in English history, an epoch marked by brilliance and pride. London was the financial capital of the world. At Westminster Englishmen made decisions that affected the lives of people over much of the world. The wealth of the greatest empire on earth flowed into the island kingdom, supporting a mode of life that a later English generation, after two catastrophic wars, can only recover in the imagination through histories or through novels such as those that James wrote at Lamb House. The Edwardian period was the climax of an order that had begun with Victoria. When Henry James died in 1916, the age had already ended for England.

Americans have come to call the years of their history between the turn of the century and 1917 the Progressive Era. It was also a time of climax, when most Americans assumed that the dawn would always be rosy and that progress would continue indefinitely into the future. After 1914 Britain's relative position in the world declined. By contrast the Progressive Era, in which the United States assumed the status of a power of the first rank, stands as a prelude to a century in which the nation accumulated such power as no nation-state had ever possessed. Henry James died after the recession in the tide of Britain's fortunes had begun. William James passed in 1910 when the upsurge of American power was only beginning to gather momentum.

President-elect Wilson in 1913 coined the phrase "The New Freedom" to describe a cluster of political ideas. Alfred Kazin, writing in 1942, set a discussion of the 1920's under the title "The Great Liberation." Certainly in that decade American society changed ~~iftly~~. A struggle for the rights of women that began at Seneca ~~York~~, in 1848, ended in the triumph of suffrage in 1920. ~~opportunity~~, however, represented only half of the eman- ~~tion~~. Women entered upon careers and participated in sports to ~~extent~~ never dreamed of by their nineteenth-century grand- mothers. Costume changed to meet the requirements of the new activities. New fashions appeared in ideas as well as dress. Theories that originated with Dr. Sigmund Freud of Vienna became current in the popular literature of the decade. Attitudes inherited from a more conservative epoch underwent transformation as American novels, in the phrase of Wilbur Cross, "struck sex o'clock." Kazin's phrase fits the decade of the 1920's well. But it applies also to earlier years. Freud lectured in the United States before World War I broke out in Europe. State after state adopted woman suffrage in the Progressive Era. The ferment of change that reached its maximum activity in the 1920's was working in the times of Theodore Roosevelt and Woodrow Wilson.

The Great Liberation was, in fact, under way at the turn of the century. Natural science broke out of the confines of Newtonian physics and scientists began to explore the new and mysterious cosmos of the atom and of Einstein's curved space. The pragmatism of William James and the instrumentalism of John Dewey brought to the discourse of social ideas a new freedom from old assumptions and antique absolutes. The early pragmatists urged their generation to throw off the slavery of Newtonian determinism and to adventure with bold experiments into uncharted spaces. Woodrow Wilson, though not himself by philosophy a pragmatist, expressed perfectly the mood of the political era that ended in 1917 and that of The Great Liberation which extended beyond the close of the war. "Progress!" he exclaimed in 1913. "Did you ever reflect that that word is almost a new one? The modern idea is to leave the past and to press on to something new." The Progressive Era saw only the beginnings of The Great Liberation. Henry James, looking out from Edwardian England, never understood the emerging America that his brother helped significantly to create.

The conditions of the Progressive Era, wholly aside from the shift and developments in scientific thought, suggest the virtual inevitability of the emergence of such a philosophy as pragmatism, elaborating the assumption that change is the essence of reality. No less than five developments came to a kind of climax in those years. The American industrial revolution that got under way in the 1850's with the development of a method for making cheap steel by 1914 had transformed American civilization. At that time in terms of volume of production of manufactured goods the United States led the world. An urban revolution accompanied the rise of industrialism as Americans moved from their scattered farms to work indoors in factories, stores, and offices. At the same time an immigrant flood, limited by only one major restriction, and representing the greatest migration in history, transformed the ethnic character of the American population before the outbreak of war in Europe virtually dried up the stream. The war with Spain in 1898 and the acquisition of possessions scattered half way round the globe dramatically gave the Republic that had so long lived largely to itself the status of a great power in the society of nations. Finally that emergence of true universities, in progress since the middle of the nineteenth century, had produced not only a large number of centers of learning but a few that ranked with the best in the world. These five revolutions coming synchronously to maturity in the first three decades of the twentieth century made that period a vibrant and dynamic era.

A subtle and profoundly significant change in the outlook of the early twentieth-century Americans came when awareness of the importance and the possibilities of science broadened out from the laboratories to the worker in the factory and the family in the home. Bacteriology, founded as a science by Pasteur in France, had been introduced into the United States in the decades following the Civil War. Leaders of public health, equipped with the new scientific knowledge, responded to the challenge of the new city with increasing effectiveness. The dramatic conquest of two of the most dreaded scourges of earlier history, diphtheria and yellow fever, highlighted the picture of an advance against disease on a broad front. Medical research and public health practices achieved concrete results in lengthening the individual expectancy of life. As a result of this triumph the conviction began to take form in the mind of the common man that science could protect him, even add to his life.

At the same time developing science made possible a new technology founded on the dynamo, new metal alloys, and the internal combustion engine. Then, in 1903, the Wright brothers, achieving man's age-old dream of escaping from the earth into the air, expanded almost without bounds the thought and imaginations of men. Scarcely a decade had passed after Kitty Hawk before Henry Ford, initiator of mass production, had made available to the common man the new freedom of the motor car. The prestige of science grew with the swift advance of technology.

Inevitably American civilization became increasingly secularized. Men conditioned to looking upon science as an agency for lengthening and enlarging their lives listened with increasing approval to the naturalism that John Dewey propounded. The experiments of the laboratory provided the background for the pragmatic approach to social institutions and problems. Quite naturally in a society undergoing swift, multiple, and profound changes a philosophy appeared in pragmatism which declared that change is synonymous with reality, that there is no central abiding peace beneath the flux of things.

∽

In this Progressive Era of growth and mounting complexity the old American doctrine of the free individual came under new scrutiny. Tradition brought into the age the ideas both social and political that had grown in America out of the affirmation in the Declaration of Independence of the inalienable rights of the individual to life, liberty, and the pursuit of happiness. These had long since found expression in universal manhood suffrage and in that open class system that distinguished American society from that of Europe. The gospel of wealth, the late nineteenth-century elaboration of the Puritan doctrine of work and stewardship, carried on past the turn of the century to shape the outlook of men in all walks of life. But already in Edward Bellamy and Henry Demarest Lloyd critics had appeared to challenge the desirability of competition in the market place. In addition theories of collectivism new to America identified the individual with his economic or social group and saw his destiny as determined by that of the group. William James found in his radical empiricism a new philosophy for an old individualism. John Dewey used his instrumentalism to buttress the new collectivism. Americans in the Progressive Era discussed freely the whole spectrum of social theory from individualism to collectivism.

Henry Adams sensed and pointed out a central fact of the period. The growth of science and the accompanying advance of technology made the raw energy of nature available to men at an accelerating rate. This energy, channeled to social ends through ever more complex machines, stimulated the growth in size and complexity of economic enterprise. Peter Drucker, a quarter of a century after Adams, suggested that enterprise is the most important autonomous organization to emerge since the appearance of the nation-state. By the time of the Progressive Era corporations representing large concentrations of economic power had become a factor of great importance in the economy. In these, after 1900, beside the traditional pattern of owner-manager appeared increasingly the new management of professionals that Frederick W. Taylor had shown to be necessary and whom he had done so much to train.

Before the entry of the United States into World War I, Henry Ford—who developed the mass production of the assembly line—had emerged as the most spectacular innovator among the industrialists of the time. Ruling the company he built up, he became the supreme example of the older owner-manager type of direction of enterprise. His creation of the ubiquitous Model T made his name a household word. Inevitably he became in the latter years of the Progressive Era an American symbol. In a long tradition that included, among others, Robert Fulton, Cyrus McCormick, and Alexander Graham Bell, the originator of the Model T came to symbolize the creative individual, the person who through imagination, knowledge, and will had made a new thing and put it to work in society.

The Ford symbol expressed several ideas. The creator and director of enterprise provided evidence to support an American belief as old as the eighteenth century that man by the use of reason can change his environment. The symbol gave expression to the Horatio Alger theory and ideal of the free individual together with its implication of an open class structure in which a man wins his status through his own efforts and accomplishments. The bicycle mechanic had become one of the greatest of the captains of industry. The theory of the free individual expressed in the Ford symbol dominated American thought of the time as it related to economic and social life. Its counterpart in the political sphere was the concept of the free and responsible voter who not only shared in a small way through his ballot in the decisions of government but who might aspire to the office of president. But, even as it appeared, the Ford symbol was rejected by a minority of citizens.

Collectivism provided the rival philosophy. Before the beginning of the Progressive Era, Bellamy, avoiding the use of the word socialism, had popularized in *Looking Backward* the idea of a collectivist society. One of the Bellamy nationalist clubs provided a temporary resting place for Daniel De Leon on his way into fully developed socialism.

De Leon, son of a Jewish surgeon in the Dutch colonial army, had been born on the island of Curaçao. From a gymnasium in Amsterdam he came to New York where Columbia University awarded him an LL.B. in 1878. He left the law to lecture for six years in Colombia on Latin-American diplomacy at a time when interest in Pan Americanism was growing. De Leon supported that pioneer prophet of American progressivism, Henry George, when the author of *Progress and Poverty* ran for mayor of New York City in 1886. Two years later the man from Curaçao joined the Knights of Labor when that organization was already in decline. Then after a brief identification with the Bellamy nationalist movement he became a member of the Socialist Labor Party, a small organization supporting Marxism that had been founded by some German intellectuals who had migrated to the United States. De Leon immediately became editor of *The People,* the journal of the organization, and the dominant figure in the party. De Leon in the columns of his paper attacked the trade unions of the American Federation of Labor, an organization rising to replace the dying Knights. Convinced that the American labor movement must become socialist, De Leon called leaders such as Gompers labor fakirs because they limited their objectives to mere improvement of the job within the free enterprise system.

De Leon was not content merely to parrot a Marxism imported from Europe. He was a thinker sufficiently original to impress the later revolutionary, Lenin, who read his writings some time after the Bolshevik Revolution of 1917. For all his debt to Marx, however, De Leon departed sufficiently from the master to give his socialism an indigenous American quality. It became the official doctrine of the Socialist Labor Party and later of the I. W. W. which De Leon, together with William D. Haywood and Eugene V. Debs, helped to found in 1905. Later both De Leon and Debs withdrew when the "direct actionists," with their doctrine of sabo-tage and violence, won control of the Wobblies. But the De Leon social philosophy, in spite of his repeated failures as a leader, re-mained the most important expression of collectivist thought in the Progressive Era. Like the contemporary Fabianism of Edwardian England the De Leon theory advocated a socialism adapted to the peculiarities of the national culture.

The immigrant from Curaçao insisted that the laborer could only be effective as a working member of a group. He must organ-ize for action on two fronts, the economic and the political. In the economic sector he must abandon the craft union limited to skilled workers in favor of all-inclusive industrial unions. In the political sector the working man must build up a political party not for the purpose of controlling the state but rather for destroying it. The De Leon plan called for the staging of mass strikes by indus-trial unions for the double purpose of forcing immediate conces-sions and of solidifying the organizations through combat. Mean-while labor's political party must build up its membership until it could command the votes to win the presidency and the Congress. The labor movement, De Leon insisted, must carry on political ac-tion, for to abandon politics would throw the industrial union back on "methods of barbarism—brute force exclusively." The revolu-tion of violence was not part of the De Leon plan. But in this scheme political socialism would not deal with reform. De Leon saw the party merely as an instrument to win power. When the party had won the presidency and the Congress, the President would resign and the Congress adjourn *sine die*. Then the network of industrial unions would become the ruling power of the socialist state. The syndicalist ideas of the De Leon theory emerged clearly in the un-derstanding that the states would be abolished and the basic units of the nation would be the industries managed by the industrial unions.

Here was revolution carried out by the ballot box, government abolished by legislation. De Leon's theory paralleled that of Marx and Engels in the declaration that ultimate government would be, to use the words of Engels, the "administration of things." The dif-ference between the American and the Europeans lay in the De Leon assumption that the administration of things or control of the economy would occur before class differences had been wiped out. In De Leon's schemata the state would not be the instrument by which a dictatorship of the proletariat could crush the bourgeoisie.

The unions would accomplish this task. The state would not wither away, as in Marxist theory; it would be abolished.

The Socialist Party of America, founded in 1901, represented a rejection by the larger number of American radicals outside the ranks of the I. W. W. of both De Leon's theories and his leadership. Nominally Marxist, the party adhered to the Second International. It was a polyglot group that included in William E. Walling, an advocate of the technique of revolution by force, and a number of gradualists similar to the British socialists. Theory did not particularly interest the members of the party. Debs, the perennial candidate for president, was primarily an evangelist of a humanitarian socialist gospel that emphasized the greed of the rich and the sufferings of the poor. All leaders of the party, however, agreed with De Leon in continuous opposition to the "pure and simple" trade unionism that was the policy of the stubborn Gompers. American socialism reached its political crest in 1912 when Debs polled some 900,000 votes in an election in which the principal contenders were Wilson, Theodore Roosevelt, and William Howard Taft.

Perspective on the difficulties faced by the organizers of American socialism and, at the same time, on the strength of the tradition of the free individual may be had in the reading of comments by visiting Europeans to the United States during the Progressive Era. In 1906 H. G. Wells, English Fabian, came for a firsthand look before publishing *The Future in America.* Wells described the "thwarted hopes" and "deepening discontent" of the American working man that resulted from the "huge accumulations of property in a few hands that is now in progress."[1] Even more significant was the comment published in the same year by Werner Sombart, distinguished German economist and socialist. Sombart remarked that "the United States is the one country in which the . . . Marxian theory of evolution has been most minutely fulfilled; in the accumulation of capital it has reached the stage . . . immediately preceding the Götterdämmerung of the capitalist world." Yet Sombart found that the American worker was "on the whole not *dissatisfied* with the existing conditions; on the contrary his view of the world . . . is most rosily optimistic. . . . [He] is not in any way antagonistic to the *capitalistic economic system* as such. . . . Indeed . . . he enters into it with all his heart: I believe he loves it." Sombart's thought was conditioned by the class system that Europe had inherited from the Middle Ages, a system that distinguished the gentleman from the common man and in which differences in manners, speech, and dress normally distinguished the two classes. To his surprise the German found that "every American from the newsboy up is possessed with . . . a yearning . . . to attain the top by climbing over others. . . . Since all are seeking success . . . everyone is forced into the struggle to beat every other individual; and a steeple chase begins . . . that differs from all other races in that the goal is not fixed but constantly moves ever further away from the runners." He added "that there is no socialism among the American laboring class, and that those who are called socialists are really only a handful of bankrupt Germans with no following."[2] In 1902 the Mosely Industrial Commission, made up of representatives of British industry, studied American industrialism for more than two months. One of this group commented on what seemed to him important differences between the New World and the Old. He saw the European employer as concerned primarily with keeping the worker in his place, while the American manager was interested in getting the most out of his employee and had no compunctions about treating him like a self-respecting human being. Another member of the group found the suggestion box a peculiarly American institution. "This is a matter," he remarked for English ears, "which would not be tolerated in most factories in England, as the management would think the employee was getting too large for his place if he suggested improvement . . . and would in all probability discharge him."[3]

The foregoing comments on the American industrial scene by European observers coming to the United States soon after the turn of the century help to explain why collectivism either as proposed by Marx or by De Leon found determined advocates among relatively few American workers in the Progressive Era. However, Robert W. Smuts, who has examined thoroughly the writings of European observers, has pointed out that these commentators—because of their own backgrounds—give a distorted emphasis to American characteristics that seemed to them to depart from the European pattern. "Struck by the relative classlessness of America," Smuts remarked, "they tended to ignore the fact that even in America economic power was concentrated in a few hands. In this sense America had a class hierarchy as much as any country in Europe. . . . Class conflict in America, therefore, remained very largely a paradox to Europeans. They perceived it was a struggle for the benefits of free enterprise capitalism rather than an attempt to destroy it. But they failed to see that it was even more a struggle for power, with capital intent on preserving absolute control, and the unions on gaining for the worker a voice in the establishment of all the conditions of his work. The underlying issue was the traditional American right of each man to determine for himself the basic terms of his life."⁴ The union, in spite of the paradox involved in its powerful discipline and its frequent autocratic leadership, had become a primary instrument for maintaining, in the economic sphere, the doctrine of the free individual.

∽

The Progressive Era gets the name by which it has come to be known from a political movement that appeared around the turn of the century and grew in the number of its adherents until by the beginning of the first Wilson administration it included a substantial majority of the American electorate. It stands out in the history of the Republic as the first effective effort of the American people to deal with the problems that grew out of unregulated industrialism. In the end the most important and potentially revolutionary achievement of the progressive crusade was the constitutional amendment that made possible the graduated income tax.

In progressivism all the thought trends of the foregoing decades found expression. It could not have been otherwise. Progressivism was a mass movement which united diverse elements in American society. It transcended the agrarianism and the sectionalism of the Populists and the humanitarianism of such urban reformers as Jacob Riis and Jane Addams. It was a crusade in which farmers, wage earners, and small businessmen all marched shoulder to shoulder. In a democratic United States the philosophy of such a movement could not be expressed in neat and logical formulas. Progressivism was a potpourri of social theories and beliefs.

It was frankly humanistic. The progressive leaders took for granted the power and the dignity of man. Their central thought was the welfare of human beings. They believed that man, by using his intellect, can remake society, that he can become the creator of a world organized for man's advantage. Many liberals appealed to the supernatural. The social gospel was the religious phase of the progressive movement. But the social gospel, itself, was the result of the capture of American Protestantism by humanism. The humanistic origins of the Progressive Era may be found in the eighteenth-century Enlightenment. The immediate precursor of progressivism was the religion of humanity.

Society, thought the Progressives, constantly undergoes evolution. But they looked upon society only as an aggregation of individuals. It has no meaning outside the individuals who compose it. It has no soul. There was no Hegelian concept of the State in American thinking. The collectivistic tendencies of the Progressives stemmed for the most part from the doctrine of the free and autonomous individual. No American urged that it is the duty of the individual to worship the State or his destiny to submerge himself in mystical union with the group. The Progressives, following the American tradition, assumed that creation is the work of individuals rather than of the State.

The optimistic doctrine of man upon which Progressivism was founded was evidence of how far the American people had traveled from Calvin's tenet of human depravity. Calvin had taught that human beings, inherently corrupt, can only be saved by the grace of God. Progressivism was a conscious effort of the first American generation of the twentieth century to save itself. Yet Calvinism was not wholly denied. The Progressives assumed—they were compelled to assume if they were to believe in progress—that the free individual will exercise his creative power in accordance with moral principles. They looked upon man as a progressive being in whom intelligence and virtue are slowly gaining the ascendancy over animal impulses. "I believe, as I believe in nothing else," remarked Woodrow Wilson in 1913, "in the average integrity and the average intelligence of the American people. . . . This great American people is at bottom just, virtuous, and hopeful; the roots of its being are in the soil of what is lovely, pure, and of good report."[5] Wilson assumed in short that mankind is ultimately governed by a fundamental moral law.

The practical consequence of this optimistic doctrine of man was an unshakable confidence in the democratic process. Wilson epitomized the political problem of the Progressive Era when he pointed out that the monopolist had created an "invisible empire . . . above the forms of democracy."[6] A minority had usurped control of the nation. The task of the reformer was to return their government to the people. The most publicized of the reforms of the Progressive Era sought to remedy defects in the working of political democracy. The purpose behind the direct primaries was to break the control of the party boss (and of the monopolist for whom he worked) over the selection of candidates for office. The objective of the initiative and the referendum was to make possible an appeal from a corrupt legislature to a virtuous electorate. The constitutional amendment which provided for the direct election of senators was intended to drive the Matt Quays and the Mark Hannas from the more important of the two houses of Congress. Because the Progressives believed that the American people are "at bottom just, virtuous, and hopeful," their proposed cure for the ills of democracy was more democracy.

This confidence in the common people had an important consequence. If the Progressive trusted the "average man" as a voter to use his ballot with intelligence and under the guidance of moral principles, why not trust him as a businessman to carry on his vocation in the same way? The answer is, of course, that the Progressives did have such confidence. They accepted American competitive capitalism. "This development of our Commonwealth," said R. T. Ely after the first World War but speaking of the ideals and achievements of the Progressives, "is a method of saving our present economic civilization, and for improving our economic order, while still retaining its essentials in private property and private contract."[7] John Bates Clark devoted himself to arguing the case of competition on the one hand against monopoly and on the other against socialism. Louis Brandeis did the same. "Business," declared President-elect Wilson in 1913, "we have got to untrammel, abolishing tariff favors, and railroad discrimination, and credit denials, and all forms of unjust handicaps against the little man." "America was created," he added, "in order that every man should have the same chance as every other man to exercise mastery over his own fortunes."[8] Wilson as President sought to release the creative energies of the American people by re-establishing economic freedom.

The Progressives, therefore, accepted the individualism of the gospel of wealth. They approved its basic formula that life is a race in which the economic prizes go, of right, to the fleetest. Implicit in Progressive thought was that doctrine of responsibility which declared that the individual must take the consequences for his deficiencies and his failures. The Progressives thought also in terms of the doctrine of stewardship as it expressed itself in private charity. Theirs was an age in which the American public was being trained to give as never before. The money which supported health and character-building agencies came from private individuals. Philanthropists supported independent schools, colleges, and universities. The first great foundations appeared.

Yet the Progressives initiated in the United States criticism of the doctrine of stewardship. They pointed out that the gospel of wealth had been used to further selfish ends. While the monopolist sanctimoniously repeated the creed of equality of opportunity, he ruled his industry as an autocrat. Maintaining, moreover, that he was the creator of American prosperity, the industrial baron undertook to become the guardian of the people, doing for them, as he said, what they could not do for themselves. By 1900 the economic overlords had developed the Hamiltonian formula of rule by the wiser few into the ideal of guidance of the State by the bigger business men. Wilson set his face against this trend in American thinking. "Benevolence or Justice?" asked Wilson after he had denounced the activities and purposes of the "invisible empire." "I don't care how benevolent the master is going to be," he answered, "I will not live under a master."[9] Wilson attacked what he considered a perverted doctrine of stewardship by reaffirming in its Jeffersonian purity that individualism which was the core not only of the gospel of wealth but of the democratic faith. The strategy was old. When in the history of any religion did reformers not claim to be returning to the ancient truth upon which the faith was founded?

At the same time that Wilson was seeking to purify the gospel of wealth he was advocating the positive State. He urged, with John Bates Clark, that competition be freed in order that American economic life might be regulated by the automatic forces of the open market and at the same time, following Lester Frank Ward, he worked effectively toward the establishment of governmental planning. Realistic democracy is a middle-of-the-road process. Americans have tended to avoid doctrinaire extremes. The Progressive movement combining both of those antagonistic formulas, the gospel of wealth and the theory of the positive State, was conforming to the traditional American practice of compromise.

The Progressives looked upon the State as having a dual rôle, that of policeman and that of planner. As policeman its function was ultimately to enforce the fundamental law. Theodore Roosevelt, with his penchant for simplification, divided trusts into two categories, good and bad. He attempted to stop the practices of the wrongdoers. But the Progressives also beheld afar off the vision of a planned society.

There were many social planners among the Progressives. Herbert Croly, founder and editor of the *New Republic*, was one of the most earnest. He thought that his fellow countrymen had pursued too long a policy of drift, believing that "somehow and sometime something better will happen to good Americans than has happened to men in any other country."[10] Croly did not abandon this simple faith merely because it was absurd. It contained, he thought, the essence of an American ideal, the vision of a better future. "The way to realize a purpose," said the later editor of the *New Republic*, turning schoolmaster to his generation, "is not to leave it to chance. . . . The problem belongs to American national democracy, and its solution must be attempted chiefly by means of official national action."[11] The positive State must be substituted for *laissez faire;* the ideal of the public interest must transcend that of private interest; purposive planning must replace drift.

Theodore Roosevelt, apt pupil of Croly, developed in 1912 the idea of the positive state into what he called the "New Nationalism." The emergence of the United States in 1898 as a world power of the first order of magnitude provided part of the background for the Roosevelt philosophy. The nation-state is, first of all, a power structure. Croly's book and Roosevelt's New Nationalism represent the first important attempts by Americans to explore theoretically and practically the possibilities of state power in the domestic scene. Later observers have pointed out that the New Nationalism contained the germ of the corporate state. Power always contains the possibilities of both good and evil. Though the political leaders of the Progressive Era pioneered in new uses of state power, statism in the evil sense did not arise. The traditional doctrines of the free individual and the fundamental law disciplined the power of the State to humanistic ends.

The social planners of the Progressive Era turned for their philosophy to pragmatism. They put their faith in science. A re-reading of the books and speeches of the Progressive Era makes clear the influence of pragmatism upon the thinking of those who proudly attached to themselves the designation *liberal*. "Change we must have," said R. T. Ely, "the only question is, what will be the nature of the change? Growth can be guided and directed by intelligence, or by what Professor Lester F. Ward in his *Dynamic Sociology* called teleological action."[12] "Social teleology," explained Albion W. Small of the University of Chicago, "in so far as it is scientifically observable, seems to admit of neither a single nor an unchanging standard. There is no absolute social good any more than there is absolute social value. . . . There is no social teleology, there are social teleologies."[13] "This is a world of experiment and change,"

wrote Charles E. Merriam, "a world in which constant readjustments are being made in the future even more rapidly than in the
past, as man's control over the forces of nature, including human
nature, expands and develops and reaches points hitherto unat-
tained."[14] "The planning department of the democratic state," said
Herbert Croly, "is created for action. . . . It plans as far ahead as
conditions permit or dictate. It changes its plans as often as conditions demand. It seeks above all to test its own plans, so as to discover whether they will accomplish the desired result."[15] In declara-
tions such as the foregoing the Progressives called in pragmatism to
answer the question how planning should be conducted in the positive state. The answer was empiricism. That plan is good which
works. Progressivism was an aspect of the rising cult of science.

Man, warned Croly, must not become the slave of science, "Democracy," he insisted, "can never permit science to determine its
fundamental purpose, because the integrity of that purpose depends
finally upon a consecration of the will. . . . During the early
history of civilization political and economic power rested frankly
on the exercise of force. . . . Little by little, however, the human
race began to accumulate a fund of social virtue. . . ."[16] The words
suggest that Croly was smuggling ethical absolutism in through the
back hall of his philosophical edifice to give support to a brave
façade of pragmatism. From Theodore Roosevelt to Woodrow
Wilson, the greater and lesser profits of Progressivism seldom wan-
dered far in their thinking from the theory of an absolute and eternal world order. Wilson, although as President he established the
most important administrative agencies which made possible the
pragmatic approach to national planning, lived in a world of eternal
values in which progress is a journey toward moral perfection and
ultimate reality is to be found in the kingdom of the ideal. "We are
going to climb the slow road," said the President-elect in 1913, "until it reaches some upland where the air is fresher, where the whole
talk of mere politicians is stilled, where men can look in each other's
faces and see that there is nothing to conceal; and whence looking
back over the road, we shall see at last that we have fulfilled our
promise to mankind. We had said to the world, 'America was created to break every kind of monopoly, and to set men free, upon a
footing of equality' and now we have proved that we meant it."[17]
Wilson saw the vision of that day when the mission of America
should be fulfilled in the triumph of what Emerson called "Moral
sentiment" in the affairs of men. The pragmatism and the science

worship of the Progressive Faith were veneers laid on ethical beliefs which in American history were as old as Puritanism. Because the disciples of Progressivism assumed that the new power put in the hands of men by science would be controlled by ethical principle they were optimistic. "We think of the future, not of the past," said Wilson, "as the more glorious time in comparison with which the present is nothing."

Chapter 26

THE "MISSION OF AMERICA" IN THE PROGRESSIVE ERA

THE PROGRESSIVE ERA was a period of internal ferment sandwiched between two external events of transcendent importance for the United States. In 1898 the Western Republic, by driving the last of the officials of a decadent Spain from the New World, raised itself to a first-rank power. Americans conquered an empire. They disciplined strange races living on distant islands. There were many citizens whose thoughts continued after 1898 to run in the old grooves and who wondered how it was possible to reconcile the doctrine of the free individual with that of imposed imperialistic control. But the *Zeitgeist* was shifting. Americans enjoyed the mood of the conqueror. They accepted imperialism in 1900. They reached into their pockets for money with which to build new battleships. The digging of an Isthmian canal became the symbol of national efficiency and energy. American dollars planted in the rich soil of the lands bordering the Caribbean Sea produced harvests of sugar and bananas. The State Department at Washington began to talk about the solemn duty of instructing in manners those small and sometimes unwashed nations to the southward whose political upbringing had left much to be desired. Then, just as Americans were getting used to their new rôle, the nations of Europe fell to fighting one another. The guns on the western front opened fire just as the crusade for domestic democratic reform of the American Progressives was reaching its climax in the Wilson administration. Finally in 1917, the Progressive Era closed, when bugles warned the citizens that for Americans a new day was dawning.

During the Progressive Era citizens of the United States probed the meaning of that third tenet of the traditional democratic faith, the doctrine of the mission of America. Their minds ran outward as never before in the history of the nation. The churches, at the turn of the century, were beginning to realize an old dream of a vast and effective missionary enterprise. In American colleges student volunteers hopefully repeated the slogan, "the evangelization of the world in this generation." After 1898 other students went out as teachers to the Philippines and to Puerto Rico. Both materialists and idealists took roads that led outward from America to adventures in distant lands. The citizens of the Republic built colleges and oil tanks in Asia. Of the many who contributed to the discussion of the duty and destiny of the United States four have been chosen here to illustrate the drift of American thought: a clergyman, a sailor, a politician, and an educator.

∾

Josiah Strong was a restless and gifted young Congregationalist who, after graduation in 1869 from Western Reserve and some study in the Lane Theological Seminary, became a sky pilot in that boisterous Wyoming town known as Cheyenne. It was the age of the long drive from Texas to Montana. For two years the young preacher waged war upon the saloons, the gamblers, and the fancy ladies of the cowboys' rendezvous to which he had come. His success led to an invitation to Reserve to serve as chaplain and as instructor in theology. From here he went, after three years, to a pastorate in Sandusky. But his energy was too great to be confined within the limits of a single community. He accepted in 1881 the office of secretary of the Congregational Home Missionary Society. His ability brought him the commission to write for the missionary society a tract which would lay before the intelligent and propertied classes of the Gilded Age the case for home missions. The result was an amazing book published in 1885 and entitled *Our Country*. It at once lifted its author from local to national fame. Religious organizations distributed thousands of copies. It was translated into European and into Oriental languages. The approbation is significant and suggests that Strong had caught some important post-Appomattox moods of American evangelical Protestantism.

Strong was an early social-gospeler. There was a suggestion of Populism in his warnings of the dangers of the concentration of wealth in the United States. He reflected the mood of Gladden when he expressed sympathy for the hard lot of labor and urged the Church to realize its social responsibilities. But he was no radical. He listed the perils which beset American civilization—immigration, Romanism, Mormonism, intemperance, socialism, and mammonism. Bad as were conditions in the East, he maintained, they were worse in Trans-Mississippia. If America and the world were to be saved, the godless West must be brought within the Kingdom. And, if America should fail, the world would be lost. The book was a sensation. As men and women read it, they saw themselves as actors in a fateful and swiftly passing moment in which the destinies of the planet hung in the balance.

The central formula of *Our Country* was summed up by Austin Phelps, D.D., in the paragraph with which he concluded his lauda-tory introduction to the volume. "Success in the work of the World's conversion," said Phelps, "has, with rare exceptions, fol-lowed the lines of human growth and prospective greatness. . . . The principles of such a strategic wisdom should lead us to look on these United States as first and foremost the chosen seat of enterprise for the World's conversion. Forecasting the future of Christianity, as statesmen forecast the destiny of nations, we must believe that it will be what the future of this country is to be. As America goes, so goes the world in all that is vital to its moral welfare."[1] Strong's book is merely an elaboration of this doctrine of mission.

The Strong thesis was that the United States, controlling a vast area and possessing immense natural resources, is destined to become the dominant nation of the world. Such a future is not assured pri-marily because of the material good fortune of the American people but rather because they are of Anglo-Saxon stock. The former Re-serve chaplain saw the population of the United States increasing to a density comparable to that of Europe. He talked in terms of a national population of a thousand millions. Following consciously the reasoning of Emerson, he argued that immigration, in spite of dangers which he enumerated, was increasing American virility by bringing new elements into the American stock. Sooner or later the United States must take the leadership in the globe-encircling com-munity of English-speaking peoples. Strong quoted with approval a remark attributed to Benjamin Franklin about England in which the author of the French alliance spoke of that "pretty island which, compared to America, is but a stepping-stone in a brook scarce enough of it above water to keep one's shoes dry."[2] "It is manifest," Strong declared, "that the Anglo-Saxon holds in his hands the des-tinies of mankind, and it is evident," he added, "that the United States is to become the home of this race, the principal seat of his power, the great center of his influence."[3]

Strong peered into the future and saw the vision of a magnificent expansion. "Long before the thousand millions are here, the mighty centrifugal tendency, inherent in this [Anglo-Saxon] stock and strengthened in the United States, will assert itself. Then this race of unequaled energy, with all the majesty of numbers and the might of wealth behind it—the representative, let us hope, of the largest liberty, the purest Christianity, the highest civilization—having developed peculiarly aggressive traits calculated to impress its institutions upon mankind, will spread itself over the earth. If I read not amiss, this powerful race will move down upon Mexico, down upon Central and South America, out upon the islands of the sea, over upon Africa and beyond."[4] Before its triumphant advance upon its God-given mission inferior races must give way, even as the American Indians had fallen back before the westward-trekking pioneers. "It would seem," said Strong, "as if these inferior tribes were only precursors of a superior race, voices in the wilderness crying: 'Prepare ye the way of the Lord!' "[5]

But Strong's was not wholly a gospel of *Machtpolitik*. The historic success and the ultimate destiny of the Anglo-Saxon were, in his opinion, both dependent upon the fact that this race was the carrier of two great ideas, namely, "civil liberty" and "spiritual Christianity." "Does it not look," asked Strong, "as if God were not only preparing in our Anglo-Saxon civilization the die with which to stamp the peoples of the earth, but as if he were also massing behind that die the mighty power with which to press it?"[6]

Before the Civil War the usual statement of the doctrine of mission was that the United States should be a witness for democratic principles before the world. Strong consciously emphasized a Darwinian struggle for existence among nations and races and confidently expected the survival of the fitter Anglo-Saxons. This shift of emphasis occurred more than a decade before the United States acquired a single island possession. The enthusiastic acceptance of Strong by American evangelical Christianity seems to suggest that it was passing beyond nationalism to imperialism.

As the century drew to a close, Strong's influence in Protestant circles increased. He became a leading religious journalist. In magazines and in a stream of books he championed the social gospel and became one of the most prominent of the leaders of the growing Protestant group who believed it possible to achieve the Kingdom of God on earth. In spite of the development of his thought, however, the pattern of his nationalism remained fixed. In a book, called *Expansion*, which he published in 1900, he rejoiced that America had assumed the white man's burden. It "is our duty," he declared, as Funston's men fought the Moros in Mindanao, "to establish and maintain order in the Philippines." But our aim must be the well-being of the Filipinos. "We must accept this new responsibility as a trust for civilization."[7] "It is time," he concluded, "to dismiss 'the craven fear of being great,' to recognize the place in the world which God has given us and to accept the responsibilities which it devolves upon us in behalf of Christian civilization."[8]

As the opening years of the twentieth century ran on, Strong saw bayonets glinting in Europe as nations moved toward 1914. But his faith and his optimism remained unshakable. He still believed in 1913 that the Kingdom was not far off. "Knowledge and benevolence," he remarked, "are all that are needed to make men efficient co-labourers with God in building the Holy City on the earth."[9] In this year he announced a volume which he did not live to write. Its theme was to be that "America is the great laboratory of the world, where these problems which concern all peoples are farthest advanced and will soonest reach a crisis; and that we have some special facilities for solving them."[10] Strong died in 1916 just before his fellow countrymen embarked upon the great crusade to save the world for democracy.

The Strong thesis is worth analysis. It was an expression of ethnocentrism. It asserted the superiority of American ways and ideals. Strong, figuratively, thanked God that Americans were not as other people. It was, of course, a post-Appomattox expression of manifest destiny. Perhaps its most significant aspect was its emphasis upon race—upon the God-given superiority of the American Anglo-Saxon and his divine mission to dominate the civilization of the world.

This idea was not new in the American thought stream. In May, 1846, Thomas Hart Benton of Missouri had announced a similar belief in the Senate of the United States. "Since the dispersion of man upon the earth," said the Senator on the eve of the war with Mexico, "I know of no human event, past or present, which promises a greater, and more beneficent change upon the earth than the arrival of the van of the Caucasian race [the "Celtic-Anglo-Saxon" division] upon the border of the sea which washes the shore of eastern Asia. . . . The van of the Caucasian race now top the Rocky Mountains, and spread down to the shores of the Pacific. In a few years a great population will grow up there, luminous with the accumulated lights of European and American civilization. . . .

Civilization, or extinction, has been the fate of all people who have found themselves in the track of the advancing Whites, and civilization, always the preference of the Whites, has been pressed as an object, while extinction has followed as a consequence of its resistance. . . . The apparition of the van of the Caucasian race rising upon them [the Yellow race] in the east after having left them on the west, and after having completed the circum-navigation of the globe, must wake up and reanimate the torpid body of Asia. . . . The moral and intellectual superiority of the White race will do the rest: and thus the youngest people, and the newest land, will become the reviver and the regenerator of the oldest."[11]

Strong, at the end of the century, brought Benton up to date. The ex-missionary to Cheyenne believed the establishment, under the leadership of the United States, of the world supremacy of the Anglo-Saxon to be the necessary prelude to the appearance on earth of the Kingdom of God. Such ethnocentrism was not limited at the beginning of the twentieth century to the United States. There were in many important European countries patriots as naïve as Strong. The conviction of the superiority of the ways of the in-group to those of the out-group appears to be an inherent quality of nationalism. The doctrine of mission is a rationalization which provides a philosophical justification for national—and racial—pride. Strong wrote first in 1885 just before the tide of immigration from southern Europe began to swell to important proportions. Because of the relative homogeneity of the older American population he was able to make his nationalism a blend of national and racial arrogance. He spoke for what was, in world outlook, a smug and self-righteous generation.

∽

Alfred Thayer Mahan was a product, though not a typical one, of nineteenth-century America. He conformed to the intellectual climate of the middle decades in his attachment to orthodox Christianity and in his acceptance of the social beliefs of the gospel of wealth. He differed from the majority of his generation in his military background. His father was a professor at West Point. The son graduated from the Naval Academy in 1859. At the very beginning of his professional career, he was swept into the humanitarian crusade of 1861. Religion, individualism, humanitarianism, and a sense of duty were the foundations of the sailor's thought.

Mahan, after 1865, belonged to a relatively diminishing company of sea-going Americans. Mahan's duties after the Civil War took him on far journeys about the world. He learned to know the important ports of South America, Africa, Asia, and Europe. He had the luck, moreover, to be in Paris during the last days of the Empire and in Rome when the temporal power of the Papacy came to an end. He had, as a result of professional duty and of good fortune, such a world view as was to be found in post-Appomattox America only among the students who had returned from graduate study abroad.

Called upon, in 1885, to prepare a course of lectures in naval history at the newly established War College at Newport, Rhode Island, Mahan set to work to distill from his sources a philosophy which he hoped would be useful to naval officers and perhaps to the national government. He published his lectures in 1890 under the title, *The Influence of Sea Power upon History, 1660–1783*. It promptly became one of the most celebrated books of the nineteenth century and its author a world figure.

It was not accidental that the acclaim accorded Mahan was more immediate and was greater in Europe than in the United States. The book was important because of its significance for the world scene into which it dropped. The times were characterized by a rapidly intensifying nationalism. The mid-nineteenth-century unification of Italy and of Germany had brought to the European galaxy of powers new political entities. A swiftly developing industrialism was increasing the striking power of armies and of navies. When anxious nations faced one another across fortified frontiers, the sentiment of nationalism inevitably became intensified. Mahan's book has often been considered important because of its preaching of the doctrine of naval power. Its significance runs, however, far beyond the subject of battleships. Mahan gave clear and logical expression to a realistic philosophy of nationalism. He transformed blurred ideas which were universally held into sharply etched concepts. Because he was a citizen of the United States, far removed from the European struggle for power, the acceptance of his ideas in any European nation was not impeded by that very national rivalry which was his theme. A British comment by G. S. Clarke in 1898 illustrates the reception abroad of Mahan's volumes. "Speaking as an outsider," said Clarke, "Captain Mahan wielded a force which could not have been exerted by any British writer, even if his equal had appeared among us, and others besides myself felt a thankfulness that the stirring message had come from across the

Atlantic. It is not correct to say that the lesson was entirely new. The idea that sea power exercised a peculiar sway over the destinies of nations had been dimly understood as far back as the time of Thucydides. . . . But no one had ever been able to explain in what maritime strength consisted, to trace its action with unerring hand through the long pages of history, to unravel the tangled threads of causation and show forth the controlling influence of naval operations over land campaigns. No one had ever built up a philosophy of the sea."[12]

In his first book on sea power Mahan announced postulates which he never abandoned though in his later years his thinking went far beyond navies. The first of these fundamental concepts was that the essence of international rivalry is a struggle for power. The second was that, because the oceans are the most important international highways, control of the sea has a peculiar importance for national power. From these premises his argument developed logically. A nation must be thought of in terms of a fort. Its boundaries are its exterior walls; its population is its garrison. The location of any given nation-fort with respect to the sea and, in particular, to important sea-lanes is a factor of primary significance in the analysis of its strength. But there are other factors scarcely less vital. How long is the nation's coastline and what are its characteristics with respect to access to the sea and to the hinterland? What is the character of the garrison? Is it large enough to man the defenses in an emergency? Does it have that economic organization and technical skill necessary to provide the materials of war? Does it have a merchant marine and men trained to the sea? Without these a navy loses half its strength. Can the nation-fort concentrate on sea power or does its location compel it to divide its resources between land and sea armament? Finally, does the garrison have a political organization sufficiently developed to enforce that cooperation and discipline without which no fortress can be defended? These were searching questions. They clarified the thinking of many a befuddled politician.

Mahan's triumphs in Europe were sometimes embarrassing. On one occasion, when he visited England on a cruise in line of duty, the British government showed him honors which were not extended to his commanding admiral. The fact that he was at sea at all was a reflection of the attitude of the lords of the American navy who, after the publication of his second volume on sea power, told the scribbler that it "was not the business of a naval officer to write books" and packed him off to the routine of the deck. Mahan retired in 1896.

Two years later the Spanish-American War brought him back to active duty as member of the board of strategy which directed the successful naval operations of that decisive conflict. The American people came out of that war more naval-minded than they had been since the famous ship-duels of the War of 1812. The inevitable corollary of the new interest in battleships was an increase among his own countrymen of the influence of Mahan. President McKinley sent him in 1899 to the Hague as American delegate to this first peace conference. The publicity surrounding this duty tended to associate Mahan in the popular American mind with arbitration and peace as well as with force and war. The retired admiral became an elder statesman. For this rôle he implemented and perfected his philosophy of nationalism.

One of the ideas most discussed among Americans at the turn of the century was that of the brotherhood of man. It had been advanced by the prophets of the religion of humanity and their humanistic successors. About 1900 it was a central tenet of the rapidly rising social gospel movement. Extremists, appearing in the late 1890's, were demanding compulsory arbitration among nations as the best method by which to transform the ideal of brotherhood into a social reality. Against such a background the kindly and conscientious Mahan developed his philosophy of the relation of force to nationalism. The proponents of compulsory arbitration hoped to elevate international law to the power and efficacy of domestic law. As the latter had put an end to duels and to local feuds of violence, it was hoped that the former would be able to terminate the resort of nations to the arbitrament of arms. The advocates of peaceful arbitration had behind them a humanitarian tradition more than a century old, and one which had been strengthened by victory over slavery in 1865 and by the liberation of the oppressed Cubans in 1898. The American of 1900 tended to see war as the savage antithesis of humanitarianism and looked upon its eradication as the next great objective in world progress. In such an intellectual climate Mahan undertook to counsel his fellow countrymen with respect to the rôle of force in international affairs.

His approach to his subject was as American as Conwell's "Acres of Diamonds." Mahan's argument grew naturally out of those foundations of his thought, Protestant orthodoxy and the gospel of wealth. The pattern of his philosophy was identical with that of the American democratic faith. He did not repudiate the postulates set forth in *The Influence of Sea Power*. He merely included with them another which had always been implicit in his thinking. This new principle which appeared in his post-1898 essays was that old and familiar doctrine that above the laws of men there exists a fundamental law of nature and of morality. "There is unquestionably a higher Law than law," said Mahan in 1899, "concerning obedience to which no other than the man himself, or the State, can give account to Him that shall judge. . . . The responsibility of the State to its own conscience remains unimpeached and independent."[13] The fundamental law, which is the ultimate governor of the individual, rules also in the society of nations. It is apprehended by the conscience of the individual and by the collective conscience of the State. In either case effectiveness of conscience implies liberty of action. The "divine right of conscience," remarked Mahan, "will, among Americans, receive rare challenge."[14] Mahan pointed to the history of his country to illustrate his next contention that, when conflict arises between moral law and positive law the latter must give way. The destruction of slavery illustrated the point. From the general principles of moral freedom and moral responsibility for both individuals and States Mahan passed naturally to the conclusion that, while arbitration is possible and desirable to settle disputes in which no moral principle is involved, any plan for compulsory arbitration must be discarded because it may force a nation to compromise on matters in which conscience is involved. To compromise with a moral principle is, in effect, to deny the principle. For a nation to agree in advance to arbitrate all questions of ethics would, therefore, be to cast loose from the fundamental moral law. The "evils of war," said Mahan, "are less than the moral evil of compliance with wrong."[15] "The great danger of undiscriminating advocacy of Arbitration, which threatens even the cause which it seeks to maintain, is that it may lead men to tamper with equity, to compromise with unrighteousness, soothing their conscience with the belief that war is so entirely wrong that beside it no tolerated evil is wrong. Witness Armenia and witness Crete. War has been avoided; but what of the national consciences that beheld such iniquity and withheld the hand?"[16]

This excursion into the absolutist morality of the American democratic faith did not cause Mahan to forget that he had earlier described the morally free political State as a nation-fortress, an individual unit in a competitive society of nations. In his later years he devoted himself to the solution of the problem of reconciling ethical absolutism with the international fact of virtually unregulated national power. Pacifism was growing in the United States in the first decade of the twentieth century. The enemies of war became more insistent in their demand that the rule of international law be substituted for that of force in the affairs of the society of nations. Suggestions for a League to Enforce Peace were heard. Americans of influence supported the peace movement. With their objectives Mahan sympathized, but he refused to approve the means proposed. He published his final conclusions in 1912, that famous year when the Progressive tide was at flood. He had long since abandoned the activities of a naval officer for the quiet of a simple home on the south shore of Long Island. At Quogue he lived beside the Atlantic, the history of which he had written and had helped to make. He was an old man whose life was running out, as the undertow slips seaward after the wave has broken. But he was not through. He completed in 1912 a philosophy which was the result of the thought of a lifetime.

The pacifists who crusade against war and who would substitute law for force forgot, in the opinion of Mahan, that man-made law is merely regulated force. Effective international law requires logically an adequate international police force. For so long as evil exists in the world, force will be necessary to meet it. Mahan opposed the idea of an international police on the ground that it would bring about the decay of nationalism particularly in Western civilization in which nationalism is most developed. The "principle of independent nationality . . ." remarked Mahan, "has played . . . a great and beneficent part in the history of European civilization for the past four hundred years."[17] Mahan saw the decline of nationalism as retrogression and warned that it would reduce the ability of Western peoples to deal successfully with the more numerous but less advanced non-European races.

Rejecting the rigidity of formal, man-made law as expressed in the concept of compulsory arbitration Mahan introduced into his argument the concept of the equilibrium of natural forces in the society of nations. "The trouble with law," he said, "is that, being artificial and often of long date, it frequently is inapplicable to a present dispute; that is, its decision is incompatible with existing conditions, although it may rest on grounds legally unimpeachable. The settlement, therefore, is insecure, its foundations are not solid; whereas in the long run the play of natural forces reaches an ad-

justment corresponding to the fundamental facts of the case."[18] He
had in mind the legality of Spanish sovereignty in Cuba in 1898.
If international law had been strictly interpreted, the United States
would have had no ground for intervention. But, in this case, the
law was permitting a sovereignty to survive which did not conform
to the realities of the world at the end of the nineteenth century.
Spanish rule had been established when Spain was strong; but the
successors of Ferdinand and Isabella had permitted the kingdom to
become weak. The disappearance of Spanish sovereignty in Cuba
in 1898 was merely the expression of a new equilibrium of natural forces.

Mahan sought to harmonize the concept of equilibrium of natural
forces with the doctrine of natural rights and of the moral law. He
used the American Monroe Doctrine as an illustration. "The point
I wish to make . . . ," he declared, "is that the Monroe Doctrine is
a moral question, based upon considerations substantially just, one
of natural right, of policy, not of legal right; that a legal standing
for it cannot be established by a general code of law, though it
may be specific treaty agreements; and that in these respects it does
not stand alone, but is reproduced where similar conditions obtain,
though not necessarily with equal imperativeness. It is the reflex, as
against distant outsiders, of the instinctive impulse toward self-
preservation, and as such represents natural right—which is moral
right—as opposed to legal. In international affairs this is home rule
versus centralization, the latter of which is the goal of unlimited
arbitration."[19] "National power," Mahan continued, "is surely a
legitimate factor in international settlements; for it is the outcome
of national efficiency, and efficiency is entitled to assert its fair
position and chance of exercise in world affairs. It should not be
restricted unduly by mere legal tenures dependent for their existing
legality upon a prior occupancy; which occupancy often represents
an efficiency once existent but long since passed away. The colonial
empire of Spain, unimpaired a bare century ago, now wholly disappeared, is a familiar instance."[20]

Mahan saw whither his logic was leading. He frankly asked himself whether his reasoning was merely a less bald way of affirming
that might makes right. He denied that it does and to prove his case
he returned to his original ethical frame of reference. Might is evidence of efficiency and efficiency is, in part, the result of moral
power expressing itself in organization and in discipline. Might is
but "the indication of qualities which should, as they assuredly will,

make their way to the top in the relations of states. . . . Such qualities, capabilities, not only confer rights, but entail duties, none the less real because not reducible to legal definition such as the interference . . . of the United States alone, backed by the silent arms of Great Britain, in Cuba in 1898. The competition of such national efficiencies makes for the soundness and equity of the whole international community. It is only when the might of some one state, or ruler, the symbol of its efficiency, becomes uncondi- tioned by opposition, through the exhaustion or recreancy of other nations, that the national efficiency, not meeting competition, tends to abuse and decay like all uncontrolled power. Rome and Carthage, Louis XIV, Napoleon, are familiar instances."[21]

Mahan's argument had to Americans a familiar ring. It was, in fact, an application to the society of nations of that dominant *laissez-faire* doctrine of the gospel of wealth. The gospel of wealth was an enlargement of the doctrine of the free individual of the older democratic thinking. Mahan's concept of the natural but ever shifting balance of power was an amplification of his earlier concept of the necessary moral freedom of the State. Mahan thought of the State in terms similar to those in which the advocate of *laissez-faire* individualism considered the entrepreneur. As the individual should stand on his own feet receiving the rewards of his industry, his efficiency, and his virtue and paying the penalties for his vices and his stupidities, so should the State. Mahan's doctrine of the natural balance of forces among competing nations was the international counterpart of John Bates Clark's theory of free competition in the open market. Clark maintained that, if competition remained free, the market, through the operation of natural law, would regu- late economic life. Mahan insisted that natural law would, in the long run, balance and harmonize the forces which were operating in the society of nations. But Mahan insisted that the doctrine of stewardship must be extended to nations. The rights which a nation, like an individual, derives from strength must be balanced by com- mensurate duties toward the weak. These obligations must not be turned over to a Super-State. His argument was the same as that advanced by the believers in the gospel of wealth. The paternalistic State, argued the prophet of *laissez faire*, inevitably impairs that moral fiber of the individual upon which civilization rests. The Super-State, thought Mahan, would impair the principle of nation- alism upon which modern civilization is founded. The doctrine of stewardship, therefore, brings free nations under the control of the fundamental and absolute moral law. With this contention Mahan concluded his systematic philosophy of nationalism. His doctrine of a higher law which governs the relations of nations was of vast importance in American thought in 1917.

∽

Through Theodore Roosevelt, Mahan became a factor of importance in American history. But another man also helped to shape the ideas of the first Roosevelt—the brilliant and eccentric younger brother of Henry Adams. Brooks Adams published in England in 1895 and in the United States in 1896 a philosophy of history constructed, like Mahan's theory of sea power, out of a long historical sweep. He called his book *The Law of Civilization and Decay*. Charles A. Beard in 1943 wrote an introduction for a reprinting. Adams' theory grew in part out of Darwinism. Adams was also influenced by the economic determinism of Marx. The logic of the Adams theory led him to the conclusion in the 1890's, when a far-ranging depression demoralized the Western world, that the center of economic power (and hence of real power) was continuing its earlier westward course and was now beginning to move from Britain to America. To seize that leadership an ailing world so badly needed the United States must, Adams thought, begin building an empire.

Brooks Adams saw much of his brother-in-law, Henry Cabot Lodge. Into the ken of the two emerged in the 1890's a third Harvard man, young Theodore Roosevelt. Brooks Adams, foreseeing an important career for the rising T. R., began plying him with advice even before he became Assistant Secretary of the Navy, a post he resigned to become lieutenant colonel of the Rough Riders. "The whole world, as I look at the future and the present," wrote Adams to Roosevelt while memory of the depression was still fresh, "seems to me to be rotting. The one hope for us, the one chance to escape our slavery [to economic malaise] even for a year, is war, war which will bring down the British empire. . . . I have watched your career with deep interest. You may remember just a year ago in Washington I told you to sell. You may understand me better now. You are an adventurer and you have one thing to sell—your sword. . . . Capital will not employ you if you have a conscience, a heart, patriotism, honesty, or self-respect. Clive and Nelson had the luck to live when they could fight, and believe in themselves and their country. Wall Street is a hard master. It only wants men it can buy and own."

When Roosevelt became "His Accidency," President of the United States, in 1901, Adams wrote: "Thou hast it now: King, Cawdor, Glamis. The world can give no more. You hold a place greater than Trajan's for you are the embodyment [*sic*] of a power not only vaster than the power of the [Roman] empire, but vaster than men have ever known. . . . You will always stand as the President who began the contest for supremacy of America against the eastern continent."[22] In the following years Brooks Adams and A. T. Mahan were much at the White House.

∽

Roosevelt came to the presidential office after the United States had acquired an empire but before it had completed the pacification of the Philippines. He approved the imperialistic outthrust of the United States. He looked upon it as a manifestation of national strength and a good omen for the future. "Nations that expand and nations that do not expand may both ultimately go down," he wrote in 1900, two years after he had returned from San Juan Hill, "but the one leaves heirs and a glorious memory, and the other leaves neither."[23] Roosevelt was determined that his United States should bequeath glory to posterity. In that campaign year of 1900 when Americans accepted imperialism and elevated the lieutenant colonel of the Rough Riders to the vice-presidency, his mind ran back to Rome. "It is only the warlike power of a civilized people," he remarked, "that can give peace to the world."[24]

The Roosevelt philosophy of nationalism, like the theories of Strong, Mahan, and Brooks Adams, began with Darwinism. Roosevelt made the struggle for existence among nations the starting point of his thought. He lived in an age whose thinking was dominated by that evolutionary anthropology which Lewis H. Morgan had done so much to establish. Roosevelt accepted the picture of the evolution of mankind from savagery through barbarism to civilization. He expressed the idea simply, for Roosevelt's was no subtle intellect. The peoples of the world, he taught, may be divided into two classes, the civilized and the backward. The former, as for example, the United States, have made significant advance along the road of progress; the latter, typified in 1900 by the tribes of the Philippine archipelago, are straggling in the rear. The civilized peoples, thought Roosevelt, have a moral duty to assist evolution by helping to uplift the retarded peoples. "The responsibility of America for the moral well-being of the people of Africa is manifest," he said in 1909 upon the celebration by the Methodist Episcopal Church of the African Diamond Jubilee. "Our wealth and our power have given us a place of influence among the nations of the world. But world-wide influence and power mean more than dollars or social, intellectual, or industrial supremacy. They involve a responsibility for the moral welfare of others which cannot be evaded."[25] "Of course," he added with characteristic complacency, "the best that can happen to any people that has not already a high civilization of its own is to assimilate and profit by American or European ideas, the ideas of civilization and Christianity, without submitting to alien control; but such control, in spite of all its defects, is in a very large number of cases the prerequisite condition to the moral and material advance of the peoples who dwell in the darker corners of the earth."[26] Roosevelt's was a doctrine of international stewardship. He had no doubts as to whether he was his brother's keeper.

But civilized peoples also, thought Roosevelt, may be divided into two classes: those who are virile and progressive, and those who have become slothful, weak, and degenerate. Americans, of course, he numbered among the virile and progressive. Had they not created a mighty nation where once a wilderness had been? But Roosevelt was fearful that their very success might be the cause of their undoing. Riches, he thought, might transform a nation of lean pioneers into one of flabby coupon-clippers. To combat degeneracy Roosevelt preached in books and speeches and illustrated in his behavior the doctrine of the strenuous life. "I preach to you, then, my countrymen, that our country calls not for a life of ease but for a life of strenuous endeavor. The twentieth century looms large before us with the fate of many nations. If we stand idly by, if we seek merely swollen ease and ignoble peace, if we shrink from the hard contests . . . then the bolder and stronger peoples will pass us by, and win for themselves the domination of the world."[27] Roosevelt was the most effective preacher of his day. He surpassed even the mighty Bryan. "We are a great people," he shouted. "We gird up our loins as a nation, with the stern purpose to play our part manfully in winning the ultimate triumph; and therefore we turn scornfully aside from the paths of mere ease and idleness, and with unfaltering steps tread the rough road of endeavor, smiting down the wrong and battling for the right, as Greatheart smote and battled in Bunyan's immortal story."[28]

As President, Roosevelt put his philosophy into action. Under his leadership, as commander in chief, the pacification of the Philippine tribes was completed and the work of training the people of the archipelago in self-government was begun. He proclaimed in 1904 the freedom of Cuba, subject to the limitations of the Platt Amendment. Establishing a financial protectorate in the Dominican Republic, he announced the Roosevelt corollary to the Monroe Doctrine, by which pronouncement the United States assumed the rôle and responsibilities of international policeman in the Caribbean region. By a deft maneuver he abolished the sovereignty of Colombia in the isthmus of Panama and set up what amounted to a puppet state. He not only strengthened the navy but he sent it around the world for the purpose not only of showing to neighboring nations that the United States possessed a fighting force but of reminding the admirals that the proper place for a fleet is the ocean and not the harbor. And he was honestly convinced that every one of these acts conformed to the moral law.

Like Mahan, Roosevelt believed in fighting for the right. "In 1861," he said, "Abraham Lincoln and his associates scorned the advice and importunity of the peace people. . . . They plunged the country into the most terrible struggle the world had seen since the close of the Napoleonic wars; and thereby they perpetuated the Union and abolished slavery and rendered inestimable services to mankind . . . when the choice lay between righteousness and peace they chose righteousness. . . ." Like Mahan, Roosevelt insisted that an absolute moral law governs the society of nations. "We hold," he said in 1911, "that the same law of righteousness should obtain between nation and nation as between man and man."[29]

His philosophy of nationalism was constructed out of the doctrines of the democratic faith. He had faith in a fundamental law and in progress toward a better world. He believed in freedom for the responsible nation as in that for the self-governed individual. He had a lively sense of the mission of America. "We must bear in mind," he said at Christiania, Norway, in 1910 when he received the Nobel Peace prize, "that the great end in view is righteousness, justice as between man and man, nation and nation, the chance to lead our lives on a somewhat higher level, with a broader spirit of brotherly love for one another. Peace is generally good in itself, but it is never the highest good unless it comes as the handmaid of righteousness; and it becomes a very evil thing if it serves merely as a mask for cowardice and sloth, or as an instrument to further the ends of despotism or anarchy."[30]

∽

The San Francisco press announced on May 2, 1898, that Admiral Dewey had destroyed the Spanish fleet which stood guard at Manila Bay. A wave of excitement and enthusiasm spread over the city which topped the hills beside the Golden Gate. In the evening an audience which had gathered at Metropolitan Hall to hear the president of Stanford University discuss an educational subject cheered when he announced that he had changed the title of his address. On the evening of May 2, David Starr Jordan spoke on the subject "Lest We Forget." The Stanford president was an impressive figure in 1898. He was tall and heavy-built. He was one of the most distinguished and the most earnest men on the Coast. His moral convictions had been formed in his youth by that transplanted nineteenth-century Puritanism of the Upper Mississippi Valley.

On the night of May 2, while crowds on the streets outside the hall cheered for Dewey, Jordan pointed out that the victory might lead the United States into a grave blunder. He urged, since the enemy ships had been conquered, that the American fleet be withdrawn from the islands. To stay was, in his opinion, to jeopardize American democracy. A people who believe in government by the consent of the governed, he warned, cannot with safety impose permanently their will upon alien tribes. If we were to hold the Philippines, he added "we should be committing the folly and crime which has always lain at the foundation of empire, and which is the cause of its ultimate disintegration everywhere."[31] From that address until the entry of the United States into the World War the Stanford president was the most important American pacifist.

Yet the basic assumptions of President Jordan did not differ in essential detail from those of A. T. Mahan or of Theodore Roosevelt. Jordan was a biologist. Darwinism provided the frame for his thought. "The claim is sometimes made on an assumed basis of science," he remarked, "that all races of men are biologically equal, and that the differences of capacity which appear are due to opportunity and to education. But opportunity has come to no race as a gift. . . . The progress of each race has depended upon its own inherent qualities."[32] Inequality of progress, therefore, argued biological inequality. Jordan, with his generation, had no doubts concerning the superiority of the white race.

With Mahan and Roosevelt, the Stanford president also accepted the current faith in a fundamental moral law. He believed in the doctrine of stewardship not only as it applied to individuals but to the relations of advanced to backward nations. He approved and advocated missionary activity. But the effort to assist undeveloped people to achieve the better life must, he thought, be the work of individuals, not of governments. "Individual men," he remarked, "may struggle as they will against heathenism. A government must recognize religions as they are."[33] Jordan held up to ridicule that new maxim which after Manila he suggested should be put on the ensign of the Republic: "The free can conquer but to save."

Such uplift of other races as any government would bring about must, thought the Stanford leader, be accomplished by peaceful means. To use force is to break the moral law. For the fundamental law which underlies all human society guarantees autonomy to inferior as well as to advanced peoples. If the Anglo-Saxon "has a destiny incompatible with morality," said Jordan, "and which cannot be carried out in peace, if he is bound by no pledges and must ride rough shod over the rights and wills of weaker peoples, the sooner he is exterminated the better for the world."[34]

During that first decade of the twentieth century when Mahan was perfecting his formula for the use of force in the defense of righteousness, Jordan was attacking war on the ground that it turned the direction of evolution downward. War, he urged, destroys those citizens of a nation who are physically and mentally fittest. The inferior survivors re-populate the earth. The deterioration produced by war caused the Roman Empire to crash and plunged Europe into the Dark Ages. Jordan's was a persuasive argument. It had a vogue. But the pacifism of the Stanford president did not prevail.

◇

More significant than the varying conclusions of Strong, Mahan, Roosevelt, and Jordan is the identity of their postulates. Each one saw in the rivalry among races and nations a potential jungle struggle and each affirmed that such a conflict must be abated by the establishment of the moral law as the foundation for international relations. The generation for which Mahan and Jordan spoke walked in the shadow of John Calvin. The ethics of pragmatic expediency might prevail upon such an occasion as that in which Roosevelt grabbed the Canal Zone. But the plea of expediency was not effective as a justification. Roosevelt felt it necessary to take high moral ground when he spoke of the refusal of Colombia to accept a just price for the right of transit. Americans assumed that the affairs of nations must be governed by the same moral code as that which provides the standards for intercourse among individual men. Some of the consequences of this assumption became increasingly clear after August 2, 1914.

Chapter 27

THE GREAT CRUSADE AND AFTER

W ORLD WAR I DIVIDES TWO EPOCHS. Before 1914 a century had unrolled whose prevailing peace had been only seldom interrupted. Its wars, though some were significant, were brief and limited in the area involved. It was the last great age of empire-building by European nations, and the time of Europe's pre-eminence in the world. The glories of England's Victorian and Edwardian Ages were matched in different ways by the Germans and the French on the Continent. In 1914 an age of violence and revolution opened. The 1914–1918 War, to use a British name, with its long stalemate of the trenches, destroyed the flower of the young manhood of the great nations that had contributed so much to the building of Western civilization. After the guns had been silenced, Europeans moved swiftly to new and even greater disasters.

For Americans what was long called the Great War marked a major turning point in their history. The century of immunity from involvement in the combats on the eastern continent had ended. The old sense of security against which Americans for a hundred years had developed their institutions and their democratic philosophy had been shaken, to disappear completely with the fall of France in 1940 and Pearl Harbor in 1941. Perhaps most important of all, the events that led up to the first war had called into question that philosophy of freedom and of a fundamental law that for earlier generations had reinforced the belief in progress and the hope of a better future. World War I presented the American democratic faith with its first great challenge.

∽

The American press on Sunday, August 2, 1914, announced that the Giants were holding a precarious lead over their Chicago rivals in the National League and that the Athletics were, for the time being, masters in the rival association of ball clubs. "Paris is preparing startling new styles," exclaimed *The New York Times*. "Velvet hats are the last word in fashion." On the theatrical page of the great daily the producer announced the four hundred and thirty-eighth performance of *Potash and Perlmutter*, the Jewish comedy hit. In an interview in the *Times* Richard C. Cabot, M.D., of Boston, in the public eye because of his new book, *What Men Live By*, advocated the therapeutic value of prayer. The prisoners of Sing Sing had been so well behaved that on this day they were being permitted to run the institution. Talk issuing from Oyster Bay, where Theodore Roosevelt was in political retirement, hinted of a possible reunion in 1916 between Bull Moosers and the defeated Republicans. The Senate was at work upon a proposed new instrument for federal regulation of big industry. Business was jittery, according to the financial page of the *Times*, not as a result of congressional threats but because of the war scare in Europe which had been steadily growing worse as the week progressed. But the day of rumors had passed. The first six pages of the *Times* were given over to the news that Germany had declared war on Russia and that the armies of every important nation of Europe were on the march.

Americans could hardly believe the dispatches. To intelligent men it seemed fantastic that the great powers of Europe should fall to fighting among themselves. The world had become topsy-turvy. In spite of the existence of conscript armies and of a naval race between England and Germany, the average American businessman assumed that the entangling bonds of international trade and industry had made wars among the great powers impossible. The leading editorial of the *Times* on August 2 suggests what were probably nearly universal American first thoughts on that disturbing Sunday morning. It was written before the news of the invasion of Belgium or of the British decision to fight. After assailing war because of the material losses which must result, the *Times* concluded: "The moral loss is greatest of all, for the friends of peace have counted upon the highly civilized nations like England, France, with the United States, to discountenance war, to make wars impossible. It will be a terrible backsliding. . . . They [the powers of Europe] have reverted to the condition of savage tribes roaming the forests and falling upon each other in a fury of blood and carnage to achieve the ambitious designs of chieftains clad in skins and drunk with mead." The philosophy behind the *Times* editorial had now acquired a venerable antiquity in American thought. It was that old theory of social change which affirmed that the advance from savagery to civilization had been at least in part the result of a more perfect apprehension of the underlying moral law. Against the background of this belief in progress the war among the nations of Europe could appear in no other light than as a reversion to the condition of savagery. Progress was being replaced by retrogression.

Twenty-eight months after the first divisions of the Imperial Reich goose-stepped across the Belgian border, President Wilson in one of the most powerful addresses in American political history called upon the Congress to declare war upon the German government. It was done after less than four days of debate. Not long thereafter, on May 18, 1917, the legislative branch passed a conscription act. On June 5 the people of the United States witnessed an amazing spectacle as more than nine million, five hundred thousand men presented themselves to the draft boards of their communities and placed their names on the rolls from which the national army was to be selected. There were scattered cries of opposition, but the voices of the objectors were feeble and futile. In September the drafted men assembled at their local railway stations and quietly entrained for cantonments scattered throughout the United States.

The question asked here is not: why did the President decide to deliver his fateful war message, but rather why did the young men of America quietly assemble on their home-town station platforms during those September days of 1917 to begin the journey which for so many of them ended under a white cross in France? In the Revolution and in the Civil War governments had felt it necessary to offer material bounties to volunteers. The federal draft of 1862 had practically failed. Its successor in 1863, more skillfully drawn, had achieved a measure of success in spite of the fact that it produced riots which terrorized for days the city of New York. Although Confederate draft laws secured better results than those of the federal government, they never achieved the success of the Selective Service Act of 1917. The draft laws of the Civil War, moreover, were passed to meet pressing emergencies. The invader was already on Southern soil when the Confederate Congress first took action. The enactments sponsored by the Lincoln administration came after the very existence of the nation had been threatened by the success of Confederate arms. In 1917 no enemy soldier had obtained a foothold in the United States and few Americans believed that the integrity of the nation was immediately imperiled. The problem of the explanation of the acceptance of the draft is made more difficult when it is recalled that no American man in 1917 believed war to be merely a summer adventure as their grandfathers in both North and South seem to have done in 1861. The conscripted Americans who assembled at the railway stations of the nation in September, 1917, knew something of the realities of war. Twelve months before, they had followed day by day in the press that great battle of Verdun which began on February 21 and ended on November 2. The carnage before Fort Douaumont and Fort Vaux marked the climax of one of the bloodiest campaigns in modern history. The vocabularies of the newly drafted Americans contained the significant words: machine gun, barrage, and gas. Few recruits had not at one time or another constructed for themselves a mental picture of a trench filled with dying and dead men. They understood that trenches were the goal of the journey upon which they were embarking. In spite of all these considerations the Provost-Marshal General reported with enthusiasm and truth: "At the station sometimes the whole town would be assembled to cheer the parting moments of 'the boys.' "[1]

～

For thirty-two months from August, 1914, to April, 1917, war in Europe haunted the thought of the American citizen. The battles of the eastern and western fronts stole the headlines. The United States was the happy hunting ground of the propagandist. In this struggle to win the sympathies of Americans the Entente nations achieved an outstanding victory. The masses sympathized with France and England and hoped they would win. The Lafayette Escadrille, made up of young Americans who volunteered to fight for the Allied cause, forecast the drift of American thought.

The propaganda which emanated from London and Paris emphasized with endless repetition two points. The Entente fought for right and justice, for liberty and democracy. The Central Powers believed in autocracy. They were dominated by militarism. For them might was right. They had started the war. Atrocities were the inevitable offspring of the blood-lust of the Hun. Stories passed through American communities by word of mouth. Some were fixed in print. Lord Bryce, whom Americans trusted, lent the great weight of his name to a report on Belgian atrocities.

What the atrocity propaganda actually achieved cannot be measured. The American generation to whom it was directed had few defenses against it, for these citizens of the isolated Republic were unsophisticated with respect to the ways of war. They knew and understood the propaganda of political parties. But they were not trained to look upon war as the normal expression of national rivalries in Europe. The American belief in progress had fathered the conviction that war among civilized powers was an anachronism. Because Americans tended to believe that Germany started the conflict they were prepared to accept even the wildest tales of rapine and torture. Atrocity propaganda was undoubtedly from the point of view of the Allies a useful stratagem.

It was made effective by what might be called bad showmanship on the part of the Germans in their conduct of the war. Their first blunder, from the point of view of winning the sympathy of the American people, was the invasion of neutral Belgium and its corollary, the doctrine of a "scrap of paper." The act in American opinion violated in several particulars the fundamental moral law. A strong power without provocation pounced upon and virtually destroyed a weaker neighbor. The Germans pleaded necessity for their violation of the treaty by which they had guaranteed Belgian neutrality. A treaty is a contract and the contract is the foundation of economic and social relationships in American democratic society. Hereditary status still played a part in determining European social arrangements, but in the United States status had passed with the destruction of slavery. To deny that contracts are sacred obligations was to deny the ruling philosophy of America. Important as was the breach, even more significant for American thought was its purported justification on the ground that necessity made the treaty a scrap of paper. The implications of Bethmann-Hollweg's much exploited phrase were several. Behind the event and its justification appeared to many Americans to lie the assumption that a nation must make its decisions wholly upon the basis of what it considers to be its interests. Its activities cannot be restrained by any supposed moral law. A nation must, in fact, be a law unto itself. If the national interest can be advanced by the violation of treaties, then violation is the intelligent and realistic policy. Behind the assumption that a nation must be governed wholly by its interests appeared to lurk not only the denial of the existence of a moral order to which men and nations must yield obedience but the affirmation that men must seek new definitions of right and wrong, if, perchance, those words had any values worth preserving. The German doctrine, as expressed in action, seemed to great numbers of Americans to make law the will of the strong.

The invasion of Belgium came at a time when the moral law was being much emphasized in American thought. Both Alfred Mahan and David Starr Jordan made it the foundation of their differing philosophies concerning international behavior. It provided the background of the appeals of the Progressive crusaders who were seeking to overcome the evils of capitalism and of political corruption. In such an age, when hope in a new and better day ran high, the invasion of Belgium seemed to be a denial of morality and a reversion toward some new dark age. Propaganda of incomparable effectiveness in the United States was the appeal to American humanitarian sentiments in the effort to bring relief to the dispossessed and suffering Belgian people.

A second example of bad German showmanship so far as America was concerned, was the manner in which the Central Powers used the submarine. It is an axiom of war that tactics are determined by the nature of the weapon used. Tactics have changed because weapons have changed. Studied realistically, the new submarine appeared to be primarily an instrument of ambush. Its only defense lay in concealment. Because of the naval inferiority of Germany, the submarine could only be used with the hope of decisive results against enemy commerce. Since the primary object of war is to win, the realistic policy was to attempt to bring England to terms by destroying enough of her merchant ships to cut off her food supply. Because of the effectiveness of small cannon against submersibles, it was inexpedient to attempt to save passengers or crews. When the British charged inhumanity, the obvious German answer was to point to the horrors of the slow starvation of women and children brought about in Germany by Jellicoe's blockade. Many Americans, in fact, were incensed at this British blockade, both because it affected their purses and because it impaired the prestige of the United States. As a people, Americans were outraged by the warfare of the submarines.

The historian can only speculate as to why the Americans of 1915 chose to ignore the frightfulness of the British blockade and to be enraged at that of the submarine. Yet such was the case, and President Wilson, in demanding that Germany put an end to *Lusitania* episodes, spoke for a people thoroughly aroused. Perhaps the explanation is to be found in the fact that naval blockades were permitted by international law, although the British warships did not comply with the detailed requirements of the law. The blockade had long been recognized as a way of fighting; the federal government had used a blockade against the Confederacy. More important was the fact that fundamental to American thinking about the submarine was the assumption that even in war the moral law forbids certain types of behavior to the combatants. Water supplies must not be poisoned, and women and children must not be put to the sword. If, unfortunately, civilization in its advance toward a higher moral level had not yet progressed beyond the necessity of an occasional war, conflict must be made as humane as possible. The action of the Germans suggested that the code of war was a phantasm and that custom can make anything right and anything wrong. The difference between such a view and that of an absolutist ethics was irreconcilable.

A third event which disturbed the citizen of the United States was the rise of German military power. Americans viewed with increasing apprehension the possibility of German triumph in Europe. The blow to American business, heavily involved in the war trade, would be tremendous. The possibility of a German attack upon American coast cities was seriously discussed. By force President Wilson established protectorates over Haiti and the Dominican Republic in 1915 and 1916, partly to prevent any European power from obtaining possession of strategic harbors as bases for launching attacks against American commerce. Most important of all, Americans believed that the German government had flouted the principles of morality and that a German victory would enthrone in the world the philosophy of force and of expediency. Without knowing it the people of the United States had come to a turning point in their history.

The rise of German military power served to intensify the sentiment of nationalism among the people of the United States. Wars tend to make nations appear before the world almost as personal entities. Anthropomorphic stereotypes are created. As the German arms won success after success, the stereotype which for Americans symbolized the Reich took the form of a colossus, bold, ruthless, and efficient. Americans became intensely aware of themselves as a national group, living in a turbulent and dangerous world.

Other events determined the emotions of Americans and the drift of their thought. Of these the crucial one was the announcement on January 31, 1917, by the Imperial German government that, beginning on the following day, all shipment within the designated war zone about the British Isles would be sunk. It seemed to American citizens, not only that Germany had applied the philosophy of a scrap of paper to an agreement with the United States, but also was definitely challenging the right of Americans to use the high seas in pursuit of their legitimate interests. The single concession in the German note which permitted one American ship to enter and to leave Falmouth each week on designated days, if the hull were marked with three vertical red and white stripes each one meter wide, seemed to Americans to add insult to injury. Across the continent on that fateful January 31 angry protests rose in section after section as the sun moved westward. On the following morning the Boston *Evening Transcript* called the roll of the nation's press for the information of its readers. *The Express-Advertiser* of Portland, Maine, declared: "The hour for temporizing is past." The New York *Globe* added: "If war comes it will be a holy and righteous one—a war on war, a war for peace, a war for a better world." The Cleveland *Plain Dealer* editorialized: "Germany challenges civilization." The Louisville *Courier-Journal* demanded immediate war. The Chicago *Herald* called the German note a "masterpiece of cynicism and savage irony." The St. Louis *Republican* said: "The German note is a bold declaration that, for Germany, might will in future make right on the sea." The Memphis *Commercial Appeal* proclaimed: "If to maintain our rights means war, so let it be." The Sioux Falls, S. D., *Press* believed it to be "inconceivable that the United States should give such tacit approval of lawlessness as would be implied in acceptance of the German conditions." The *Journal* of Albuquerque, New Mexico, regarded the severance of diplomatic relations as inevitable. The Ogden, Utah, *Standard* considered the announced German policy "a reverting to the barbarous—to the poisoning of wells in warfare." Almost alone from San Francisco came a warning to the American people to move slowly. America should do nothing, said the *Chronicle*, "until she is specifically injured." "Germany," said the Denver *Post*, "is rushing to her doom. There is no plan in the universe that permits a nation to succeed by such methods as these." To the clamor rising throughout the nation the *Transcript* on February 1 added its voice: "From the quixotic adventure of imposing upon the Old World a 'peace without victory,' we are brought up with a sharp turn by the imperative necessity of defending American honour, American rights, American lives, and

American property–against a war without quarter with which Germany has threatened, not the New World only, but the whole world. . . ."

The German declaration of the renewed submarine blockade threatened American investments, challenged American social beliefs, and impinged upon American national pride. The universal implication in the American editorials of protest was that the military colossus of Europe had reached that point in a career of madness in which German leaders were telling Americans what they might and might not do. After this piece of bad maneuvering on the part of the rulers of the Imperial Reich, it would have been difficult to have prevented the American mass movement in support of an immediate declaration of war.

The fact was, however, that in February, 1917, the United States was not prepared to make war upon such a power as Germany. In April, when President Wilson delivered his fateful message to Congress, responsible leaders in England were thoroughly frightened by the effectiveness of the new submarine campaign. Russia was going through revolution, and the future of that nation was doubtful. Had Wilson been Machiavelli, he would have divested himself of sentiment and would have attempted an estimate of the situation confronting the American nation. In the light of a philosophy of expediency the war still would have appeared to be merely another in that wearisome succession of conflicts among the armed tribes of Europe. The Entente appeal to morality would have seemed to be little more than an effort to support the morale of their own people and to draw neutrals into their war against the central powers. If the United States should make war upon Germany, the American government would be compelled to depend upon the Allied nations to hold the enemy for many months while the unprepared Republic was creating and training an army. If the Germans should break through the western front and force France or England out of the war, the American people would find themselves in the position of having lost a war before they had gotten into action. The actual momentary break through the Allied lines by the German army in the spring of 1918 suggests the gamble which President Wilson took in asking Congress to declare war. The reconstruction of the mental processes of the Chief Executive preceding his decision is not the present problem. It is sufficient to note here that Wilson decided to declare war first and to make adequate preparations for it afterward; the people of the United States supported the President's action.

∽

The first task of the administration, after the President had reached his decision in the privacy of his own thought, was to formulate a theory as to why the United States should go to war. As American culture requires judges to support their decisions by a formal appeal to reason in the opinions handed down from the bench, so it required of the President in 1917 a similar appeal to logic to show why the decision for war was inevitable. Wilson presented his logical construction at the same time that he announced his decision to Congress in the famous message of April 2. He repeated his thesis again and again during the succeeding months in addresses as powerful as any ever delivered by an American chief executive. The Wilsonian formula had the simplicity of a Doric column. It stated that two philosophies had arisen in the world: one a doctrine of force and expediency, and the other a faith in moral principles and in the efficacy of the cooperation of men of good will. On the one hand was irresponsible autocracy exploiting whom it would and threatening the world; and on the other was responsible democracy expressing the idealism and the will of the people and now or never the hope of the world. Autocracy had forced the war upon democracy. "This is a war of high principle," declared the President in his message to Congress in December, 1917, "debased by no selfish ambition of conquest or spoliation. . . . We know, and all the world knows, that we have been forced into it to save the very institutions we live under from corruption and destruction."[2] Wilson rose to his greatest heights in his creation of a philosophical context for American participation in the World War. He lifted war propaganda from the level of the goblin story of the Belgian babe with hands and feet cut off to that of a call to his fellow countrymen in the twentieth century to take up the old search for the Holy Grail. In his demand that the world be made safe for democracy he assumed the rôle of prophet of the American democratic faith. He reminded the people of its great doctrines: the doctrine of the moral order, the philosophy of progress, the doctrine of the free individual, and the doctrine of the mission of America to carry democracy to the world. He called upon his people to fight not simply to maintain the rights and the honor of the nation but to achieve a world victory for the national democratic religion.

Abstractions are, however, as religious leaders have known for centuries, notoriously ineffective in moving masses of men. Abstractions must be translated into concrete symbols. Before April 2, 1917, the negative symbol of the military colossus of Europe had taken fairly definite form. The images suggested by the phrases "Hun" and "blond beast," used by the Allies, were familiar in most American households. After the American declaration of war it became the duty of the Creel Committee to sharpen the representation of the enemy as a bogy and to bring the developed symbol into direct relation with the democratic faith. As a consequence Guy Stanton Ford, in an official *Red, White and Blue* pamphlet, presented the monster of the twentieth century against a background of smoking villages and shattered cathedrals. "Before them," he said, speaking of the German war leaders, "is the war god to whom they have offered up their reason and their humanity; behind them the misshapen image they have made of the German people, leering with bloodstained visage over the ruins of civilization."[3] In another *Red, White and Blue* pamphlet, edited by Dana C. Munro, George C. Sellery, and August C. Krey, were reproduced with elaborate documentation most, but not all, of the Belgian atrocity stories. In this pamphlet the blond beast reeled through a career of arson and pillage, of the defiling of holy places and the destruction of altars, of wanton butchery, and of rapine. It was the *Red, White and Blue* pamphlet entitled *Conquest and Kultur*, however, which proclaimed the philosophical significance of a German victory and in particular what its effect would be upon the democratic faith of America. With vast diligence Wallace Notestein and Elmer E. Stoll combed the writings produced in Germany for the social philosophy lying behind German behavior since the beginning of the war. The result of their labors was one of the most powerful propagandist documents ever scattered among the American people. By a collection of hundreds of quotations, effectively arranged, it sought to show how German thought challenged at every point the democratic faith; in particular it demonstrated that the Germans would substitute for the doctrine of the moral law, the source of the ideal of universal peace, a frank philosophy of force and of expediency from which inevitably stems the glorification of war. "History must always be in flux; war, therefore, must be taken as part of the divinely appointed order."[4] " 'World power or downfall!' will be our rallying cry. Keeping this idea before us, we must prepare for war with the confident intention of conquering and with the iron resolve to persevere to the end, come what may."[5] "Ye shall love peace as a means to new wars, and the short peace better than the long. I do not advise you to work, but to fight. I do not advise you to compromise and to make peace, but to conquer. . . . Let your labor be fighting and your peace victory. You say that a good peace hallows even war. I tell you that a good war hallows every cause."[6] "War is the noblest and holiest expression of human activity. War is beautiful."[7] "It seems to us who are filled with the spirit of militarism that war is a holy thing, the holiest thing on earth."[8] "Must Kultur rear its domes over mountains of corpses, oceans of tears, and the death rattle of the conquered? Yes, it must. . . . The might of the conqueror is the highest law before which the conquered must bow."[9] The words, deeds, and appearance of this symbolic monster of the twentieth century were harmonious. The symbol made clear the creature against whom Americans were fighting.

Inevitably a positive symbol of the embattled American took form. Before April 2, 1917, it had been difficult for the citizen of the United States to romanticize any of the Allied nations save Belgium. After that date it became necessary for Americans to dramatize and romanticize themselves. In the creation of the vision of the crusader for righteousness President Wilson took the lead, but the symbolism sprang up spontaneously among the people. It was a folk product. It steadied the fighting mood and strengthened the will to win. On June 14, 1917, in his most important address since April 2, Wilson called upon his people to sacrifice. "For us there is but one choice. We have made it. Woe be to the man or group of men that seeks to stand in our way in this day of high resolution. . . . Once more we make good with our lives and fortunes the great faith to which we were born, and a new glory shall shine in the face of the people."[10] The crusader, according to the conventional religious symbol, has a shining countenance. In September the first detachments of the National Army entrained for their cantonments and to them the President addressed a message. "The eyes of all the world will be upon you," he wrote on September 3, "because you are in some special sense the soldiers of freedom. . . . Let us set for ourselves a standard so high that it will be a glory to live up to it, and then let us live up to it and add a new laurel to the crown of America."[11] Months later columns of soldiers swung in easy rhythm through the entrance gates of the cantonments and turned onto the highways leading to the transports. This was the tensest moment on the home front. "The lads that go now," wrote a Californian, as he bade farewell to the young men from the Coast states, ". . . go, God's own avengers of the unspeakable suffering of the people of Belgium, Northern France, Poland, Serbia, Rumania, and Armenia. As they march, unseen in the clear air above them are the spirits of the American mothers and babies that perished in the roaring sea, murdered in the *Lusitania*. They go to cleanse the earth of the men who began by violating treaties and have progressed by violating the common promptings of humanity which have been held sacred by the red Indians of America and the black tribes of Africa. They are the armed guards of American honor, of the covenants of Almighty God. . . . Good-bye, boys, acquit yourselves like men."[12] A chaplain of the First Division stood one evening in the following summer on the edge of a wheatfield near Soissons. "And everywhere I looked," he said later, "the trampled wheat was dotted by recumbent figures. . . . They might have been wearied troops that had thrown themselves down to sleep. They slept, indeed, the sleep no earthly reveille could disturb. I wish you could have seen that silent company under the summer twilight. It was not gruesome then, and it was not all tragedy. There lay the best of America, not dead nor sleeping, but alive so long as we will it to live. For America, if it is anything lasting, means what they showed—free, unswerving loyalty to an ideal."[13] The symbol was complete; although individual crusaders were dead, they yet lived in the cause which never dies.

This American rationalization of the participation of the United States in the World War took unconsciously the form of a morality play. It was the story of a hero provoked by a villain to mortal combat. It was evident to the dullest mind that the actors were symbolic figures and that the conflict was none else than the age-old struggle between good and evil. When the drama took form, the issue had not been settled. Unless Americans were to repudiate their belief in progress, the ultimate triumph of good was inevitable. Implicit in it was the vision of that happy day when the foot of the hero would be upon the breast of the villain and when the conqueror would declare that, henceforth, goodness and mercy would reign among the sons of men.

It was a soul-stirring play. In it the century-old democratic faith found its perfect expression. The vision was the creation of a people suffering the acute anxieties of insecurity. The drama maintained morale on the home front. It helped to lessen the heartaches in a million homes. It assisted in persuading the men and women of America to applaud that denial of faith in liberty which filled the federal penitentiaries with political prisoners. The drama helped the home-town man, ignorant of the realities of war, to acquiesce in the throwing of thousands of inexperienced and half-trained boys from the later drafts into the carnage of the Argonne.

❧

The drama of the morality play of American propaganda had less utility in the army. The mood of exaltation began to fade for that recruit, Private Jones, on the first morning which he spent peeling potatoes for the company mess. Once in the army, Americans adjusted themselves to the new routine and forgot heroics. They sang that belligerent song, "Over There," not because each had a fixed determination to "get the Kaiser," but because it helped to while away dull and weary hours. Another song, however, "Oh, How I Hate to Get Up in the Morning," came from the heart. It expressed perfectly the restiveness of the average American citizen under the mechanized discipline of the military forces and his anticipation of the liberty to come when he should be mustered out.

As American divisions arrived in France, American doughboys found themselves plunged into intensive training from which, after drill, they escaped into a world few had dreamed of when they had first entrained for camp at the home-town station. An American intelligence officer from G. H. Q. observed a French city one evening in September, 1918, and noted in his diary: "Place full of newcomers, trying to dry up France in one evening. Also full of tarts, with Yanks falling *en masse*." "Interesting life, this, but sordid," he added the next day. "Behind scenes and see wheels work. . . . Not as romantic as tired businessman gets them in fiction. No secrets, and one long process of disillusionment. As D—— says: 'Only through daily contemplation of one's own impeccable virtue one escapes abyss of cynicism.' "[14] War is a realistic business. It is not a gentleman's game. When a soldier at the front found himself personally confronted with a live and active enemy equipped with rifle, bayonet, and hand grenade, abstract principles of morality gave way to expediency. The alternatives were to kill or to be killed. There was valor, honor, and sacrifice at the front, but, in the army, devotion to an ideal shrank from the grandiose proportions of the dream of saving the world for democracy to keeping alignment in an advance, to doing a dangerous job when called upon, and to giving a hand to a soldier in trouble.

President Wilson, the personification of the crusading spirit of the twentieth century, had a final hour of triumph. When the guns were stilled, he went to Europe to assist in making peace. He journeyed in Europe from one tumultuous throng to another. His faith in democracy was refreshed when he heard in strange tongues the cheers of the common people. In the Old World in city after city he spoke of that kingdom of the ideal not made with hands where the harried spirits of men may find peace and life. "From the first," said he, "the thought of the people of the United States turned toward something more than winning this war. It turned to the establishment of the eternal principles of right and justice. . . . There is a great tide running in the hearts of men. . . . Men have never been so conscious of their brotherhood. . . . And it will be our high privilege . . . not only to apply the moral judgment of the world to the particular settlements which we shall attempt, but also to organize the moral force of the world to preserve those settlements, to steady the forces of mankind, and to make the right and the justice to which great nations like our own have devoted themselves, the predominant and controlling force in the world."[15]

૨

One day in December, 1918, President Wilson stood before Pershing's men and addressed the soldiers who had gone through the Second Marne, Belleau Wood, St. Mihiel, and the Argonne. It was one of the more poignant moments in American history. The orator and his audience lived in different worlds. Wilson spoke of the impending Peace Conference as the end of an epoch. America, he thought, stood on the threshold of a new world. He was right; but the new world was not one which he anticipated. The soldiers whom he addressed had already had a foretaste of the disillusionment to come. The harvest of war is memories. As Pershing's men on that chill December day in France listened to Wilsonian periods describing the dream world to be, some of them recalled those occasions when, detailed on grave-digging duty, they had buried the victims of modern savagery. They were not so sure that Paradise was to be born of Hell.

૨

In those days of triumph in Europe the President in all probability did not recall a particular hour of anguished indecision in April,

1917. It came after he had tried long and hard to keep the nation out of war. But the German leaders had called his hand by proclaiming unrestricted submarine warfare. German U-boats had sunk three American merchantmen. A wave of anger was sweeping over the country. In the loneliness of supreme executive office the President had to make the fateful decision. He needed to talk to some one. On April 1, 1917, he sent for Frank Cobb, editor of the New York *World*.

Cobb later described a most remarkable conversation. "He [Wilson] said he couldn't see any alternative, that he had tried every way he knew to avoid war. . . . Then he began to talk about the consequences for the United States. He had no illusions about the fashion in which we were likely to fight the war. . . . 'Once lead this people into war,' he said, 'and they'll forget there ever was such a thing as tolerance. To fight you must be brutal and ruthless, and the spirit of ruthless brutality will enter into the very fibre of our national life, infecting Congress, the courts, the policeman on the beat, the man in the street.' " "[Wilson] thought," Cobb continued, "the Constitution would not survive it; that free speech and the right of free assembly would go. He said a nation couldn't put its strength into a war and keep its head level; it had never been done. 'If there is any alternative, for God's sake, let's take it,' he exclaimed."[16]

The event proved the accuracy of the President's apprehensions. On June 15, 1917, the first Espionage Act became law. It was a normal wartime measure built in part out of the experience of the Civil War. The act made it a crime to make false statements with intent to interfere with the military success of the United States, to promote discontent or mutiny among the armed forces or to obstruct recruiting or the draft. In the crisis and peril of war the common danger compels some curtailment of the liberties of citizens.

In the autumn of 1917 the Bolsheviks in Russia toppled the liberal Kerensky government and opened a new chapter in world history. On May 16, 1918, the President signed far-reaching additions to the Espionage Act. These made it a crime to disparage the sale of war bonds and to express contempt for the government of the United States, the Constitution, the flag, or the uniform of the armed forces. The enlarged Espionage Act expressed the temper and the will of the American people. As the war developed into what was looked upon as a crusade for democracy and for righteousness, an aroused public turned on those who failed to conform to the general attitude and behavior.

Public opinion supported harsh governmental measures against those who refused for conscience's sake to bear arms. The declaration of war in April, 1917, had confronted the members of the Socialist Party with a cruel dilemma. They had to choose between loyalty to the nation and to the ideal of that solidarity of workers over the world proclaimed by the Second International. The party lost heavily in membership. Those who stood fast on the party line that the war was a capitalist-made conflict suffered much from governmental police action. Debs, a party leader of almost three decades' standing, made a speech in Ohio in 1918 that was sharply critical of American economic leaders and of the repressive measures of the government. Convicted under the Espionage Act, the court sentenced him to ten years in prison. The penalty seemed just to multitudes of parents whose sons had been maimed or killed on the battlefields of France. In all, the government prosecuted some 1500 persons. Some sentences ran to fifteen years. The I. W. W., for some years before the war under the leadership of "direct actionists," faced the most hostile public opinion and the most severe governmental repression. When the war ended, the Wobblies had ceased to exist as an organization of national importance.

Immediately after the war came the brief "Red scare," brought about, in part, by unsolved bomb outrages in different parts of the nation. In part it was a carryover of wartime emotionalism. During a period of great tension, five Socialist representatives elected to the New York State legislature were excluded from that body and Victor Berger, Socialist representative from Wisconsin, was twice excluded from the House of Representatives. The Attorney General of the United States, A. Mitchell Palmer, rounded up and caused to be deported two hundred forty-nine radical aliens. Applauding Americans dubbed the ship that carried the deportees away from our shores the "Soviet Ark." A jury in Massachusetts, after a trial in which the radical opinions of the defendants were emphasized, convicted Nicola Sacco and Bartolomeo Vanzetti of the murder of a paymaster in South Braintree, though no evidence conclusively connected the men with the shooting.

∽

For Europe World War I, with its four-year stalemate of trench warfare and the degeneration of military strategy into that of mere attrition, was a catastrophe that came near to wiping out the manhood of a generation. For America the war lasted eighteen months. War losses, though heavy, did not comprise its principal impact from the conflict. This impact was on the thinking and the outlook of the citizens of the Republic. A peaceful people of the Progressive Era, swiftly building up great productive power and making a beginning in the regulation of industrialism, saw with incredulity Europe collapse in 1914 into barbarism. Before Sarejevo most Americans, on the few occasions they thought about such problems, assumed that the advance of civilization had made such an atavism impossible. Then, when the United States joined the conflict, the war vastly stimulated among Americans the sentiment of nationalism. It took the form of national pride when General Pershing, in 1918, faced the most determined efforts of the British and French leaders to establish the policy of incorporating the American reinforcement into their own sadly depleted forces. The mighty and independent army that assembled in its own sector on the Western Front and that fought the bloody Meuse-Argonne campaign symbolized the spirit and the power of the nation at war. Nationalism also took the form of a development of the old doctrine of the mission of America to meet the conditions of the twentieth century. The mission was expressed in the phrases, "the war to end war" and "the war to make the world safe for democracy." Nationalism also had a less lovely aspect. The great American majority that worked and sacrificed willingly to bring about the victory dealt harshly, even after the enemy had surrendered, with many who preached dissident ideas. For the time being nationalism set bounds to the doctrine of the free individual. President Wilson's forebodings in the dark hour when he poured out his thoughts to Editor Cobb were not all realized but some of them came true.

But, most important of all, the war marked the end of an epoch. In 1914 for Europe and in 1917 for the United States an age of violence and revolution began. From that time forward the American democratic faith must carry on in an unstable and strife-plagued world.

V

THE AMERICAN DEMOCRATIC FAITH SURVIVES IN
A TIME OF REVOLUTION AND VIOLENCE

Chapter 28

THE FUNDAMENTAL LAW AND
THE GREAT LIBERATION, 1918-1941

On April 13, 1943, there occured an event in the national capital that had larger implications than appeared on the surface. The President laid aside for an hour the task of directing the war effort of a nation engaged in a new and global struggle and drove to a marble memorial standing beside the Potomac. It housed a statue of Thomas Jefferson. On the walls were graven words of Jefferson that spoke a warm humanism and faith in the reason of free men. "We hold these truths." The phrases that followed affirmed natural rights, man's endowment from the Author of Nature, and declared liberty and reason to be the only sound foundation on which to set a nation. The President, dedicating the memorial, commented that, at the moment, Americans fought for the ideas and ideals suggested by the phrases. On this, as on many other occasions, he reminded his fellow countrymen of the reality of their democratic faith, a faith that the principles of liberty and humanity do not find the boundaries of their validity at the border of the American jurisdiction but that they have relevance for men everywhere. In the nineteenth century men commonly spoke of these principles of liberty and humanity as a fundamental law undergirding the good society.

One would expect a ceremony on that day, for April 13, 1943, was the two-hundredth anniversary of Jefferson's birth. But the affair was more than perfunctory. The creation of the Jefferson Memorial was more than an isolated event. It demonstrated again, as the dedication of the Lincoln Memorial had done before, a national need and desire for symbols that both citizens and strangers can understand. Americans, having no living monarch to personify the nation and the ideals on which it rests, have found compensating and unifying symbols in the memories of the great men of earlier days. The importance of the dedication of the Jefferson Memorial in 1943 lay in the fact that it was part of a development that had begun some years before and was to go on after the event. For a century the name of Jefferson, political leader, had been bracketed in American tradition with that of his great political opponent, Alexander Hamilton. Then, in the mid-twentieth century, the name of Jefferson had begun to move away from that of Hamilton. A Jeffersonian literature had grown significantly in volume and quality. The effigy of Jefferson and a representation of Monticello had appeared on opposite sides of the ubiquitous five-cent piece. A project had been announced and the funds provided to gather together, to edit, and to publish every item of Jeffersonian writing. These events, when combined, signified a reappraisal of the Virginia planter. The times provided a background. Mid-twentieth-century Americans had unexpectedly found themselves facing the challenge of allied totalitarianisms while still half incredulous that such a phenomenon could really be. Under such circumstances they elevated the status of the author of the Declaration of Independence in the galaxy of American heroes and gave to the memory of Jefferson a place in the highest stratum of symbols beside that of Washington and Lincoln.

∽

But we outrun our story. Citizens of the Republic who had paid attention to the drift of American thought in the first third of the twentieth century could be pardoned some astonishment at that resurgence in the 1940's of some of the ideas of the eighteenth-century Enlightenment suggested by the new stature of Jefferson. If any notions semed to the sophisticated men of the early twentieth century to belong in the museum of curious and outmoded doctrines, it was the belief in natural rights that Jefferson had written into the Declaration of Independence and the larger concept of the immutable fundamental law of which it was a part. The Great Liberation was then under way.

The physicists had won emancipation from the mechanistic and deterministic Newtonian model of the cosmos, an imprisonment that had led some mid-nineteenth-century members of the guild to assert that the major discoveries of physics had been made and that the remaining tasks were those of refining existing knowledge. The discovery of radioactivity, followed by the penetration of the atom, not only opened new and apparently limitless vistas but cast doubt upon what had long seemed eternal verities. That clear distinction of classical physics between matter and energy dissolved as the men of the laboratory learned to transform the one into the other. Perhaps energy was the ultimate reality of nature. But the physicists, true to their positivistic approach, recorded only what they could observe and verify and left ultimate reality to the philosophers. In 1927 Werner Heisenberg announced the Principle of Uncertainty, a principle that affirmed that it is impossible to determine at the same time the position and the velocity of an electron. Quantum physics finally demolished the two pillars of the old science, causality and determinism. The laws of science came to be phrased in terms of probability, an evolution that recalls the pioneer insights of Peirce. Looking back from the second quarter of the twentieth century, the mechanistic cosmos of Descartes and Newton seemed quaint, a proper cosmology for a horse and buggy civilization. In the larger understanding of a new age it had become a particular case whose validity was limited. The new physics provided the backdrop for the drama of twentieth-century society. As Europeans in the early eighteenth century had struggled to understand Newton's mathematics, so Europeans and Americans in the early twentieth century tried to comprehend Einstein's discovery of relativity. Dramatic success in the physical sciences with an almost immediate impact through technology on society, spurred the efforts of the scholars who worked in the rapidly evolving social sciences.

Morton G. White has told part of the story of the shift in American social thinking in a volume he subtitled *The Revolt Against Formalism*. In this he dealt with four selected social thinkers: a historian, a philosopher, an economist, and a lawman. A full narrative of what was happening in the history of ideas would, of necessity, recount momentous changes in natural science and important developments in practically all the social disciplines. A revolution of the first order of importance was under way.

In this great shift the relation between the two major aspects of the movement, the natural and the social sciences, is not clear. Of the men of the time Henry Adams most conspicuously attempted to relate natural science to social thought. Charles Peirce united the two aspects in his pioneer suggestion of pragmatism. But beyond this achievement Peirce had relatively little influence on the thought of his own day. Not until long after his death did he find his place in the history of thought in America. The theory of evolution in the life sciences conditioned the thought of Peirce, James, and Dewey. An over-all look at the battlefield where the forces of scholarship were advancing against the intrenchments of ignorance suggests that the evolutionary hypothesis, spawning a diverse progeny of the species social Darwinism, played the rôle of the front line division that maintains contact with armies on both right and left. Social Darwinism mediated between the physical and the social sciences. These two, pushing forward together, achieved in the first third of the twentieth century the Great Liberation.

Certainly Darwinism shaped the thought of the late nineteenth-century determinist William Graham Sumner. In 1887, the year in which Peirce moved to his Pennsylvania home, Sumner held up to scorn nothing less than the central self-evident truth of the Declaration of Independence, the doctrine of natural rights. Sumner pointed to the emergence of humankind from the mammalian world through the evolutionary process. The grim and bloody picture of nature did not suggest to Sumner that man, unique among mammals, had a natural right to life. In the competition of nature with other living forms man survived if he could. As for the supposed natural rights to liberty and to the pursuit of happiness, they seemed to Sumner worse than illusions, rather invitations to individuals to avoid by wishful thinking the hard realities of existence. The facts are, thought Sumner, that man must fight and must work to win whatever freedom he enjoys. And the measure of that freedom will be small indeed. Sumner saw the individual as a chip floating on the river of social life, moved, like other human chips, by a current that he could not control. The New Haven sociologist summed up this aspect of his philosophy in the title of his essay "The Absurd Effort to Make the World Over." Sumner stood mid-way between a world that was passing and one that was emerging. He had not escaped from the old determinism, but he had won emancipation from one of the absolutes that had provided the underpinning for eighteenth-and nineteenth-century social thought.

William James went far beyond the New Haven Darwinist. The seed that Peirce had planted in his mind grew into pragmatism. Denying the rigidities of a cosmos created after the pattern of an engineer's blueprint, James insisted that the guiding plan of creation is unfinished, that flux is the ultimate reality. Truth is not fixed and eternal; truth resides in the event, in the outcome that follows action. As for man, he is a potential and actual creator in a plastic universe whose destiny is to accept the hazards inherent in the eternal flux of things and to act on faith, the prosperous outcome of which is not certified in advance.

As the twentieth century got under way the revolt against old absolutisms gathered momentum. Thorstein Veblen turned his artillery on classical economics. He ridiculed it as a neat and deterministic philosophy built up about the mechanical economic man whose responses were supposed to be controlled by a meter that registered pleasure and pain. Basing his thought on the psychology of instincts of his day, Veblen maintained that *homo economicus* never existed.

∽

A lawman, Oliver Wendell Holmes, noticed with disapproval the uses which the Supreme Court, guided by Justices Field and Brewer, had made of the concept of the natural law. As a young man he had been a member of the informal metaphysical club in Cambridge to which Peirce and James had belonged. Holmes thought the idea of a natural law absurd but that the widespread belief in it called for explanation. "There is in all men," the Justice remarked in 1918, "a demand for the superlative, so much so that the poor devil who has no other way of reaching it attains it by getting drunk." "It seems to me," he added, "that this demand is at the bottom of the philosopher's effort to prove that truth is absolute and of the jurist's search for criteria which he collects under the head of natural law. . . . The jurists who believe in natural law seem to me to be in that naïve state of mind that accepts what has been familiar and accepted by them and their neighbors as something that must be accepted by men everywhere."[1] The Holmes comment did not voice the full objection to judicial efforts to weave the thread of natural law into the pattern of judicial interpretation. Many others among the lawmen of the first half of the twentieth century demurred, but none more cogently than Judge Charles E. Clark of the United States Circuit Court of Appeals. "If people are not in command of their own government," said Clark in 1942, "but are actually subordinate to some yet more remote sovereign who upholds and justifies unsanitary conditions, long hours of labor and general defiance of social welfare as a freedom required by some vague constitutional command or higher law of nature, then we are nearer either anarchy or the rule of the autocratic few than we are democracy."[2]

What followed from the Holmes skepticism concerning natural law was suggested by Jerome Frank, later to become a judge of the

United States Circuit Court of Appeals. "He [Holmes]," said Frank, "has himself abandoned, once and for all, the phantasy of a perfect, consistent, legal uniformity and has never tried to perpetuate the pretense that there is or can be one. . . . As a consequence whatever clear vision of legal realities we have attained in this country in the past twenty-five years is in large measure due to him. . . . Holmes almost alone among the lawyers adopts that skeptical attitude upon which modern science has builded, that modern skepticism which looks upon thought as instrumental and acknowledges the transient and relative nature of all human thought-contrivances. Holmes has been telling us for fifty years that, in effect, the Golden Rule is that there is no Golden Rule."[3] With these words Frank concluded his book, *Law and the Modern Mind*, 1930, one of the most important and influential statements of that position among lawmen known in the 1920's and 1930's as legal realism.

Legal realism illustrates in a special way the temper of the Great Liberation. Its effort to abandon the old, its vision of new horizons, above all its acceptance of science as the road to truth reflected the new mode. Law is one of the most ancient of social disciplines. Tradition has always exerted a powerful influence as law has changed to keep abreast of movement in society. Law, moreover, stands at the center of the most obvious and most important institutions of social control. Legal realism did not represent a general movement among twentieth-century lawmen. It was the work of a minority most of whom were legal scholars in law schools. These men took note of the phenomenon that set off the twentieth century from its predecessors, namely, the advance on a wide front of the social sciences—economics, sociology, anthropology, social psychology, political science. The legal realists, without batting an eye, undertook to transform a discipline as old as Hammurabi into a twentieth-century science. The phrase, "science of law," became a catchword.

Writers on jurisprudence in the nineteenth century had subsumed the life values that provided the ultimate norms for human behavior under the general phrase "fundamental law" or, more commonly, "moral law." They looked upon the positive law as it existed in constitutions and statutes as attempts to create specific norms for concrete social situations, norms that were always conditioned by the fundamental law beneath them. The legal realists broke with this tradition. Nineteenth-century textbooks in jurisprudence reminded Thurman Arnold, one of the most vocal of the group in the 1930's, of treatises in theology. The realists looked upon written constitutions and the positive laws that issued from the legislatures as instruments of social engineering.

The Yale Law School, the most important center of legal realism, called Edward S. Robinson, a psychologist, to its faculty, an appointment that suggested the hope that a science of law could both use and duplicate the achievements of the natural sciences. Robinson's book, *Law and the Lawyers*, 1935, suggests some attitudes of this company of path-breakers in legal thinking. "Modern man," said Robinson, "has learned that in his mastery of his physical surroundings and of his body his success has been in direct proportion to his factual knowledge." "Today," Robinson went on, "men watch with apprehension their own increasing mastery over physical nature. They have the uneasy feeling that they are producing the machines that must sooner or later be used by themselves to destroy themselves. They grow morally earnest about the situation and write articles for the magazines. But too rarely do they bring to bear upon this great problem that intellectual integrity, that frankness and cool perspective of nature which has built the machines of war and which is man's only hope in the control of himself. Solemn men who go about the world preaching that there is something more to be relied on than facts, that there is something more necessary to human life than intellectual honesty, are doing what they can to prevent the world from catching up with science."[4]

Here the positivist spoke. What facts did the legal realists turn up? Most realists found the final expression of law to lie in the behavior of officials, especially the decision made by the judge in the particular case. Much publicized were their further discoveries that social prejudices or cherished economic theories too frequently caused a judge to decide a case before him as he did. Thurman Arnold noted further that, after making his decision on the basis of his predelictions, the judge writes an opinion which traces what purports to be the inevitable logic that led from legal precepts and precedents to the decision—a ritualistic performance, thought Arnold, required by a public determined to believe that the law is certain. The realists pointed to the fact that for the litigants in the case the judge's decision constitutes the law, a datum that led to the further frequent assertion that the judge makes the law. These ideas of the legal realists jarred old assumptions and ruffled ancient dignities. They were intended to do just that; legal realism was, in part, a political crusade. The realists kept up a continuous drum fire at that majority of Supreme Court justices that denied the new powers sought by the federal government in the early days of the New Deal. The recalcitrant majority, said the legal realists, wrote the economic and political theories of a vanishing age into their decisions and, by so doing, retarded the creation of a governmental structure adequate to the needs of a dynamic era.

The realists combined an interest in scientific theory with that in immediate practical application, much as the eighteenth-century scientists had done. "Lawyers are social engineers," said Robinson. Arnold agreed and emphasized in his *Symbols of Government* the importance of the fact-minded leader to guide a public that still lived by myths. In seeking facts that would establish a science of law the realists directed their inquiries (after the manner of scientists) to the *is* in legal institutions and behavior. They insisted that the *ought* has no place in science. They needed only facts. "The notion is gaining common circulation," said Robinson, speaking for psychology as well as for legal realism, "that we might do well to transfer to our social problems that type of fidelity to fact which in other realms has been so profitable. But such a transfer is a serious matter. . . . The entire outlook of the philosophy needs to be changed. Such a venerable distinction as that between moral and natural causes will have to be uprooted. It will be necessary to realize that the coolest calculation of the criminal is as much a natural phenomenon as is the convulsion of an epileptic. It will be necessary to set aside the question as to who is deserving of our hatred and of substituting the question as to what, as a matter of fact, can be done to increase our control over human behaviour."[5]

Roscoe Pound, dean of the Harvard Law School, objected. He spoke for the old tradition that had come down from the eighteenth and the nineteenth centuries and that still persisted in the era of the New Freedom. He insisted that jurisprudence must consider "not merely how judges decide but how they ought to decide to give effect to the purposes of the legal order, not only how the legal order takes place but how it should go forward. The question of ought turning ultimately on the theory of values is the most difficult one in jurisprudence."[6] Morris R. Cohen, legal philosopher, added his criticism to that of Pound by pointing out to the realists a dilemma they ignored. If law is to be a form of social engineering, said Cohen, "ideas of the desirable social aim in the law are indispensable. And, if we do not subject these ideals to critical study, we continue to use them in traditional and superstitious ways."[7] In other words moral ideas, if they are to be adequate to our complex age, must be criticized as rigorously and as intelligently as legal and social institutions.

To the realists the dichotomy of is and ought, emphasized by Pound and Cohen, reflected the type of thinking of an age that these intellectual pioneers had left behind. For the realists social process, as John Dewey insisted throughout the entire period, was the central reality and the accumulation of knowledge the highest value. Knowledge, spreading out the widening circle of its illumination, would enable men to advance with ever surer footing up the mountain trail of progress. "Men laughed at the germ theory of disease," Robinson reminded his contemporaries in 1935, "but they have accepted the less credible story of vitamins without a murmur except that of interest." "This constant growth in man's control over nature," he continued, "has been called *Progress* and progress has become the central motif of our culture. In such an atmosphere it would have been impossible not to recognise that legal science [as practiced in the past and even by a majority in our day] has imposed a constant drag upon the adventurous spirit of the times." No better description of the outlook and the mood of the Great Liberation could be found.

∽

Lincoln Steffens returned to the United States in the late 1920's after an extended stay abroad. He felt the drive and rush of life west of the Atlantic. America had changed since he wrote near the beginning of the century those pieces he called *The Shame of the Cities.* The new spirit of the place, as he sensed it, stirred him. "Mr. Owen D. Young told me one day," wrote Steffens, "something about the General Electric Company's big experimental plant where chemists, physicists,—all sorts of scientific researchers—were gathered to carry on, partly for the company, but partly for science and themselves, their intensive specialized work. All that, he said, went to show that big business was absorbing science, the scientific attitude and the scientific method. Cocksureness, unconscious ignorance, were giving away to experiment. . . . About that time E. A. Filene came along, reporting that he had heard a vice-president of General Motors . . . say: 'We don't think any more in business. Oh, we may have our opinions. . . . We may think up a theory, but we don't act on our theories any more. We send our theory or our need into the laboratory and so have it tried out. If it doesn't work, we change the theory, scrap it. But if a theory, modified, works, we make it into an engine or a car and put it out for trial on the market, but—even then it's only a sort of working hypothesis. We go on monkeying with that and other theories and hunches to improve the car on trial.' " Here was pragmatism at work in an area to which it was perfectly suited.

Steffens felt the movement of the age. His imagination ran ahead. "This is revolutionary," he continued. "If this spirit had got out of science laboratories into business in a business country, it would seal the doom of our old Greek-Christian culture. It would spill over into politics, economics, life. No more thinking, no more right thinking; no more believing or logical reasoning from premises to conclusions. . . . Wondering would supplant convictions; insight, inspiration; experience would blow up argument; and as for our conclusions, they would not be uplifted into principles and creeds but tried out as working cars or working hypotheses. . . . A new, the new culture was sweeping down over us. . . ."[8] Here was the exuberance of the Great Liberation—the affirmations and denials of an age possessed of new and swiftly increasing power.

Steffens might have used other evidence to support his prophecy of the passing of our "Greek-Christian culture." Observers, both inside and outside the churches, noted that in the latter half of the 1920's the prestige of religion had dropped to a low point. The anti-intellectualism of the fundamentalist crusade, the humiliation of the Scopes trial—publicized around the world—and the shallowness of the thinking of modernism disclosed by the schism in Protestantism all combined to bring down the prestige of the old faith that had been so important in the planting of the English colonies. There were many who were prepared to believe that a "new culture was sweeping down over us."

❧

Morris Cohen categorized some of the legal realists as functionalists. He referred in particular to Karl Llewellyn of the Columbia Law School, one of the ablest of the group, and one who preferred the term *functionalism* to that of *legal realism*. The term *functionalism* was for the 1920's and 1930's one of those words that throws open a window on the mind of a period. Functionalism appeared as a central concept of the new institutional economics that grew in large part out of the work of Veblen and other rebels against the mechanical theories and the natural laws of nineteenth-century economics. A functionalist school arose in anthropology. It had significance of the first importance for any history of ideas about the fundamental law.

Functional anthropology followed the rejection of a cluster of ideas that began to form in the eighteenth century. The men of the Enlightenment had learned to think in terms of the concept of civilization, civilization created by man and capable of being improved by man when he learned to understand the laws of human nature. The early nineteenth-century August Comte marked out in his system of positivism the stages in the evolution of thought through which mankind has passed on the road to the present age of science. Ethnologists and anthropologists of the later nineteenth century, influenced by Comte, used materials drawn from subliterate as well as historic cultures to trace the line of societal evolution from savagery through barbarism to the present imperfect civilization. The urge to reform as well as the belief in progress spurred the efforts of these searchers in the science of man. They combed through the customs and institutions of the societies existing in their day for survivals come down from earlier cultural stages, survivals that had once been useful but which now burdened men striving to move forward to a better life. If such survivals could be identified and exposed to view, the men of today could intelligently undertake their elimination. From the enlightenment philosophers to the evolutionary anthropologists the assumption persisted that man, who creates society, can only achieve progress if he understands the laws of cultural growth, laws that have equal relevance for all men everywhere.

The functional anthropologists of the Great Liberation shook themselves free from this old monistic theory of linear evolution. As they journeyed here and there over the earth to study at first hand peoples whose life-ways differed greatly from the civilization of the West, they saw the cultures of the Samoans, the Navajos, or the Trobriand Islanders as discrete entities, each a functioning cultural whole. The investigator in the field ceased to look for survivals of some earlier stage in cultural evolution but, instead, tried to find the meaning of a custom or an institution for the culture in which it functioned. The new departure represented a revolutionary change in outlook. For evolutionary monism the anthropologist of the new day substituted pluralism. He saw each culture, whether it existed on an island in the Pacific, in the rain forest of the Amazon valley, or on the high plateau of Tibet, as a legitimate expression of the potentialities of human nature. Each culture stood as an aesthetic configuration to be studied in terms of its own *Gestalt* and to be judged in terms of its own standards. Every culture had standards by which to define the good life, just as each had its own particular religious beliefs and practices. The anthropologist of the Great Liberation, carrying the democratic principle of tolerance beyond the national borders, insisted, at least for the investigator, on a higher tolerance toward life-ways that were different and strange. To condemn a tribe in the New Solomons in terms of standards accepted by twentieth-century Americans would not only be irrelevant but would be a manifestation of ethnocentrism. Implicit in the principle of higher tolerance was the romantic idea of peaceful co-existence among the diverse cultures of the world. Ruth Benedict, whose *Patterns of Culture* went into a paper-backed edition, was perhaps the most influential writer in carrying the new outlook to the non-professional public.

The significance of the functionalist school of anthropology for the concept of a fundamental law of universal import is obvious. Cultural relativity meant ethical relativity. Moral codes belonged to the tribe and were the outgrowth of the life experience of the tribe. Out of acceptance of this position anthropological field workers, it must be added, gained an objectivity that made possible the accumulation of new knowledge of great significance. Out of this knowledge came some of the most important insights into the life of man in society that the twentieth century achieved. But the old idea of a fundamental law of universal validity faded from sight.

The period of the Great Liberation of the earlier decades of the twentieth century, when considered in all its aspects and when judged by its achievements, is one of the most remarkable in American intellectual history. It is to be compared only with that revolutionary and constitution-making age that ran from 1765 to the end of the eighteenth century. Liberation from many nineteenth-century thought-ways gave a certain *elán* to rebels against an older formalism. New knowledge won in the social sciences made new creativity possible. Creativity was needed, for in the midst of the period the vastly complex economic order fell into chaos. And chaos brought on crisis. To their credit it should be said that the American generation of the Great Liberation, faced with social disaster, effected successful governmental solutions that avoided those extremes of fascism, on the one hand, and communism, on the other, to be found in the political arrangements of contemporary Europeans. The New Deal was a kind of middle way, blending tradition and novelty.

To round out the picture of this revolutionary intellectual age one must see the social scientists and social theorists as actors reading their lines before a backdrop that natural scientists were diligently repainting. These natural scientists left some of the areas of their canvas blank. In other areas they drew patterns that defied understanding in terms of old-fashioned common sense. Still other portions displayed with startling clarity emerging forms that simultaneously evoked both hope and terror. The whole panorama of the new backdrop bore little resemblance to the trim and orderly Newtonian picture of the cosmos that previous generations had used as a background for their social thinking.

∽

Over against the successes of the men of the Great Liberation should be set what may justly be called some failures. If these men had demonstrated, as no previous American generation had done, that knowledge is power, and, if its leaders had used newly won power to create a vastly dynamic civilization, there were some who failed to realize, at first, that power, in itself, is amoral. Power may be made to serve either beneficent or evil ends.

Oliver Wendell Holmes, however, never lost sight of the rôle of force in societal affairs. No one in pre-Pearl Harbor America developed the power implications of cultural relativism in more uncompromising terms than did the acknowledged patron saint of legal realism. Darwinism conditioned his thought. He disclosed his views privately to his British friend, Pollock. "I loathe war . . . ," said Holmes in 1920 when the memories of World War I were still fresh, "but I do think that man at present is a predatory animal. I think that the sacredness of human life is a purely municipal ideal of no validity outside the jurisdiction. I believe that force, mitigated so far as may be by good manners, is the *ultima ratio* and between two groups that want to make inconsistent kinds of world I see no remedy except force. . . . It seems to me that every society rests on the death of men."[9]

As the long truce that began in 1918 extended into the 1930's a trend appeared in one of the most recent of the social disciplines, political science, that sought to focus thinking and research on the fact of power. These men looked upon the nation-state as, at bottom, a power structure. Influenced, in part, by the European-born theory of geopolitics but more by the drift of international events, some of those who specialized in international relations moved toward the conviction that ultimate reality in the international scene is to be found in the unending power struggle among the greater nation-states. For these political scientists the thesis of the power struggle as the ultimate reality in international affairs illumined swiftly moving and increasingly ominous events. It seemed to make prediction possible. More than one of these political scientists warned of the approach of World War II. Finally, after war actually came, Nicholas Spykman, one of the ablest of the group, phrased succinctly and clearly an idea that had been evolving for some two decades. "War in the twentieth century," said Spykman, "is total war, the combination and integration of military, political, economic, and ideological tactics. Contrary to popular opinion, total war was not the invention of the Germans but the result of a long process of historical development. . . . The result is that the distinction between the war time and the peace time forms of the power struggle have now been effaced completely. No state can think any longer of preparation for national defense merely in terms of future conflict. The struggle is waged continuously. Total war is permanent war."[10] Here was a hard realism, stated by Spykman in its extreme form, that was also part of the intellectual revolution of the Great Liberation. If events should prove the Spykman analysis to express the whole truth, the old dream of the brotherhood of man, at the very core of the nineteenth-century idea of the fundamental law, must become no more than the happy fancy of a child's fairy tale.

◇

The war with Nazi Germany was underway at Spykman's untimely death. Americans, looking eastward across the Atlantic, saw as never before in their history the face of naked power. In the 1930's they had watched the Nazi state deny intellectual freedom, regiment the youth, and carry on the long pogrom against the Jews. Then the Nazi terror broke out of the national borders to overwhelm neighboring states. It was this terror, more than the seemingly more remote Communist terror that brought suddenly to the test in the United States some of the ideas of the Great Liberation. If cultural relativists stood fast in the position they had taken concerning moral values, they would have to admit before 1941 that it was both irrelevant and impertinent for Americans to judge Nazi behavior by American standards. One of the founders of the functionalist school in anthropology, Bronislaw Malinowski, recognized this fact, abandoned the position, and spend his last years developing a cultural theory that would disclose the evil in the Nazi methods.

As for the legal realists, there were some among their fellow lawyers who refused to forget the aphorism that the judge makes the law. Pound of Harvard had more than once pointed out that the clear meaning of such a statement was that the official makes the law. In 1945 Robert Jackson attacked the realists in a paper that dealt with the nature of law. "Of course there is a school of cynics," said the Justice, "in the law schools, at the bar, and on the bench who will disagree and many thoughtless people will see no reason why courts, just like other agencies, should not be weapons of policy. It is a current philosophy, with adherents and practitioners in this country, that law is anything that can muster the votes to put in legislation, or directive or decision and backed with a policeman's club. Law to those of this school has no foundation in nature, no necessary harmony with the higher principles of right and wrong. They hold that authority is all that makes law and that power is all that is necessary for authority. It is charitable to assume that such advocates of power as the sole source of law do not recognize the identity of their incipient authoritarianism with that which has reached its awful climax in Europe."[11] Mr. Justice Jackson's attack was extreme and a bit unfair. The legal realists had been liberals who looked upon themselves with justification as champions of the cause of a better life for all men. They had brushed away many cobwebs from the windows of law schools and judicial chambers. Jerome Frank, after World War II, rose to the defense of Holmes. Holmes, who fought through four years of the Civil War and who devoted a long life to public service, was perhaps the greatest of the humanistic thinkers of the twentieth century. If he made skepticism the center of his thought, it was a skepticism founded on humility. Holmes did not pretend to know the meaning of the universe. He insisted that truth can only be had through "free trade" in ideas. "I . . . define truth," he once remarked, "as the system of my limitations and leave absolute truth for those who are better equipped. With absolute truth I leave absolute ideals of conduct equally to one side."[12] He approached the good life with the conviction that all easily formulated ethical maxims must meet the test of experience. "Man is born a predestined idealist," Holmes said at another time, "for he is born to act. . . . To act is to affirm the worth of an end, and to persist in affirming the worth of an end is to make an ideal."[13] Frank spoke for all the legal realists, himself included, when he rejected as "ridiculous" the "charge that the pragmatists, including Holmes and his followers, have cold-shouldered morals and noble ideals."[14]

Yet in the exuberance of the Great Liberation the relativists in the law had taken positions that brought forth the criticisms of Roscoe Pound and Morris Cohen. The brutalities and finally the threat to the American people of Nazi totalitarianism, as Justice Jackson intimated, disclosed in a time of crisis some weaknesses to counterbalance the strengths of the new legal realism. Had Justice Jackson, before making his criticism, read the law reviews with greater care, he would have discovered that Llewellyn, one of the most prominent of the realists, had, five years before, reached the conclusion that the old doctrine of the fundamental law not only did but should persist to condition with its ideals and standards the creative thought of the time. His statement is one of the most extraordinary affirmations of the pioneering scholars. "The goal of the law is justice," said Llewellyn in 1940 after Poland and Holland had fallen before the Luftwaffe and the panzer divisions of the Third Reich, "and judges like other officials, are not free to be arbitrary. . . . For Pound the heart and core of jurisprudence is what the heart and core of jurisprudence ought to be to any scholar: to wit, right guidance to the judge—or the legislator—or to the administrator. And I for one am ready to do open penance for any part I may have played in giving occasion for the feeling that modern jurisprudes or any of them have ever lost sight of this."[15]

It was in such a time and in such an atmosphere that Americans lifted the memory of Thomas Jefferson to a place in their galaxy of heroes beside that of Washington and Lincoln.

THE DOCTRINE OF THE FREE INDIVIDUAL IN THE MIDDLE PERIOD OF THE TWENTIETH CENTURY

The emergence of the Jefferson symbol in the 1930's and 1940's involved a paradox. The author of the Declaration of Independence had been the most important American philosopher following the social thought of the Enlightenment. Into that famous document Jefferson had written by implication a theory that portrayed society as made up of an aggregate of discrete individuals, the individual standing in polar relation to society. Out of this Enlightenment view had grown the doctrine of the free individual, as understood in the early nineteenth century. The free individual was a social atom. In the simple agricultural-commercial society of the time freedom was both symbolized and confirmed by the achievement of universal manhood suffrage. But when the Jefferson Memorial was built beside the Potomac, American society was vastly more complex. Both theory and practice had changed. The revival of Jeffersonianism suggested a determination on the part of Americans to hold fast to the essence of the Enlightenment doctrine.

∽

Changes in the social scene preceded shifts in social theory. The America of the first half of the nineteenth century was a country in which most of the population lived in small communities where people knew their neighbors and usually their family histories. Aside from a few small cities, the United States was a land of villages and of scattered farmsteads. The pattern of the isolated farmstead, so different from the European peasant village and the early New England town, had been fixed in American life by the land survey act that originated with the Congress of the Confederation. In spite of the mobility of the population expressed in the westward movement families tended to remain in the same neighborhood. A child normally grew up as a member of an extended family that comprised, beside the immediate circle of the household, a considerable company of grandparents, uncles, aunts, and cousins. Such a family brought to the individual a measure of security that was both psychological and, at times, material. The variety and popularity of the home songs of the mid-nineteenth century reflected the importance of the family in the culture of the time. In this society the individual man worked alone. He managed a family-size farm or, in the South, a plantation. In the village he kept a blacksmith shop or a store or practiced the profession of doctor or lawyer. The minister, whose congregation gathered on Sunday in one of the several village churches, was the center of the most important social group outside the family. Everywhere outside the largest cities contacts were personal and associations face to face. This was the community that Royce knew as a child in California and which he made the center of his philosophy.

The industrial and urban revolutions of the second half of the century brought important alterations. In the economy the corporation supplanted the individual enterpriser as the most important unit. The new type of enterprise was a social structure whose cooperative life was disciplined by regulations analogous to the laws of the state. It was also a power structure capable of action to achieve its purposes. The significance of enterprise for social theory lay in the fact that it was a group of persons organized to carry on manufacturing or commerce. As American industrialism evolved, two groups—management and labor—crystallized within enterprise and stood in polar relation to one another. In agriculture the family-size farm continued the normal unit outside the cattle country. In the latter half of the century groups began to form in farming communities. The Grange, after a brief period of political importance in the 1870's, continued as primarily an organization to further social intercourse and self-improvement among its members. The recommendations of the Country Life Commission appointed by President Theodore Roosevelt in 1907 led to a widespread development among American farmers of cooperatives organized on Rochdale principles. In the second decade of the twentieth century the farm bureaus came into existence. By the 1920's farmers had achieved a new national organization in addition to the Grange in the American Farm Bureau Federation. The counterpart in industry and commerce of the farmers' organizations could be found in manufacturers' associations, chambers of commerce, and labor unions. In economic life various kinds of groups had achieved primary importance. The individual played his rôle as a member of one or more of these.

The urban revolution of the years between the Civil War and World War I brought similar changes. As Americans left the farms and small towns to adventure in the burgeoning cities, they abandoned such face-to-face association with neighbors as that provided by small communities. A majority also left behind much of the security offered by the extended family. In the metropolis the nuclear family of husband, wife and one, two, or three children became the primary institution. This fact, together with the impersonality of the great city, tended to increase the isolation of the individual. This characteristic of the rising city lay behind the proliferation after the Civil War of fraternal organizations, mystic brotherhoods that helped to restore for their members a sense of self-importance bruised by the anonymity of life amid great crowds. Neighborhood gangs appeared among children and adolescents. Because much of the population of the cities came from the immigrant flood, nationality organizations such as the German *Turnerbund* came into being. In his social life the individual found his rôle or rôles as a member of one or more groups.

In politics the theory of the importance of the individual voter persisted through the Progressive Era. The atomistic theory which the Enlightenment had applied to political life continued in the period of the progressives in efforts to develop direct democracy by such devices as the initiative, referendum, and recall. When put to the test, however, in the changed social scene, these reforms failed to achieve the hoped-for results. Instead, the political triumph of the determined and indefatigable Anti-Saloon League in writing the Eighteenth Amendment into the Constitution pointed out the importance of the group, the pressure group, as a technique by which citizens might achieve the ends they sought. The free individual as a member of such a group became possessed of a power he never enjoyed as a political atom in the earlier form of democratic society.

∽

Inevitably a changed social scene led to changed social thinking. The social sciences, developing swiftly in the invigorating atmosphere of the Great Liberation, speeded the evolution of social theory appropriate to the new day.

Lester Frank Ward held fast to the idea of the atomistic individual but also emphasized the group as expressed in the state. First among American theorists, he advanced, though in dim outline, the concept of the welfare state. Edward Bellamy's Utopia founded on the machine carried the idea further, even to the substitution of cooperation for the competition traditional in economic life. De Leon and the Marxists after the turn of the century pressed for a fully developed socialist society.

Sumner, contemporary of Ward and De Leon, rejected the ideas of both. Yet his researches, which produced the important concept of the mores, led him to deflate the importance of the individual. Sumner faced the basic questions: Should the individual be considered an autonomous unit capable of shaping his environment, as James and Dewey insisted he could, or should he be looked upon as the creation of the society of which he was a part? Sumner answered the latter question in the affirmative. The mores, Sumner thought, provide the continuum that holds the successive generations to a steady and uninterrupted course. The mores carry the institutions and establish the values by which men live. In such an affirmation Sumner came near to saying that the mores, the societal environment, make the man. The individual through his behavior can achieve only a minute variation in a particular mos. Veblen, student of Sumner, carried the position to its extreme. He virtually denied the existence of the individual because, he insisted, society creates the man. What knowledge a man acquires in his life is a social product accumulated by social action through the generations. Society gives the individual not only the skills he learns to use but even the habits that provide the configuration of his way of living. The achievements of the great entrepreneurs such as Henry Ford, Veblen thought, are, in reality, the achievements of society. As a consequence no man has a just claim to special reward. The anthropologists, studying subliterate peoples, developed such ideas as those of Sumner and Veblen about human behavior into the concept of culture. Man, they said, is unique among all living forms in that he creates culture. In the 1920's and 1930's, as the idea of cultural relativism emerged, the anthropologists discovered that culture conditions, perhaps determines, the behavior of the individual.

Sumner and Veblen followed the eighteenth century in setting the individual in polar relation to society. Meanwhile, other students of society, dissatisfied with the sweeping generalizations of these two investigators, sought a new approach. They observed that the individual from the beginning to the end of his life lives as a member of a succession and variety of groups—the family, the peer groups of childhood and adolescence, the school, the cluster of friends, the fellow members of a church, the associates in occupation. This line of investigation revealed the group as the mediator between the individual and society. The social scientists found the essence of group life in the interactions between the individuals who compose it. Within the group the individual experiences both acceptance and rejection. From it he receives intimations of the outlook and the values of society. To the collective experience of the group he contributes from his own center of life. These reciprocal influences between individual and group comprise the essential nature of the social process.

The individual lives as a member of many and diverse groups in each of which he has a rôle that differs from his rôle in other associations. So the members of a particular group see a side of an individual personality that non-members never observe. In this fact the psychologists and sociologists who worked together in the development of social theory found a partial explanation for the phenomenon that William James had noted, the impossibility for any person fully to comprehend another personality. Personality is a reality with many facets. Observation and analysis of the society about them had led the sociologists and the psychologists to transform the Lockean idea of the individual as a social atom into the concept of the person who is a part of the give and take of the social process that centers in the group. By the end of the 1920's the evolution of social theory had left behind the simple doctrine of the free individual of the eighteenth and nineteenth centuries. The study of the social process through which the infant and child is taught the ways of his culture marked out boundaries to individual freedom. Investigation did not support the extreme position of Sumner that the mores make the man; rather it disclosed the vast complexity of personality and prepared the way for research that still continues.

∾

At the same time that the sociologists pushed forward their analysis of the group the psychologists were assimilating into their investigations the insights of Sigmund Freud and of the behaviorists whose work began with Pavlov. Freud's theory of the unconscious was part of that major shift in thought that intervened between the nineteenth and the twentieth centuries. So also was the emergence of behaviorist psychology. These two dvelopments compelled a radical revision of ideas held about human nature and personality that prevailed in the time of Emerson. The two made their first impact upon American social thought in the time of the Great Liberation.

That these new insights had implications for democratic theory did not escape some social thinkers in that phase of American intellectual history. The philosophy of democracy rests on the postulate that the individual voter arrives at his decision as to how to cast his ballot by a process of reasoning. Democracy assumes, as its point of departure, free discussion and uncoerced decision. The behaviorists described the actions of men as responses to particular stimuli. Freud discovered that some decisions are made in the unconscious and that the function of reason is to defend them when they emerge into consciousness.

The popular impact of the two schools of psychology was most apparent in the fiction of the 1920's and 1930's. But here and there individual critics of democracy appeared from various callings and used these systems (or one of them) to support their points of view. A tendency became important in the 1920's among such critics to divide society into two classes, the few (the elite) and the many. "The vast majority of men," said H. L. Mencken, journalist and prophet with a large following, ". . . cannot take in new ideas, and they cannot get rid of old fears. They lack logical sense; they are unable to reason from a set of facts before them, free from emotional distraction. But they also lack something even more fundamental: they are incompetent to take in the bald facts themselves."[1] The history of man, according to Ralph Adams Cram, one of the most famous of American architects in the first quarter of the twentieth century, is "the history of the eternal conflict between quantitative and qualitative standards."[2] The artist inveighed against the tyranny of a majority that never rose above mediocrity. Some men, Cram continued, those of character and intelligence, are "competent to see clearly, capable of thinking constructively, and with a will to lead capably."[3] "The great mass of men have always been of the Neolithic type."[4]

Thurman Arnold, legal realist in the period of the Great Liberation maintained that institutions, like individuals, have personalities. As the psychiatrist sees the individual, Arnold maintained, not as one person but as a "whole set of characters" each called forth by a different stimulus, so the societal institution has many rôles, some of them conflicting. If an individual needs faith and ideals, a government or an economic system needs creeds such as law, economics, theology, or a democratic faith. But these creeds "must be false in order to function effectively" because they "must express contradictory ideals and must authoritatively suppress any facts which interfere with those ideals."[5] The most stubborn of the false creeds, thought Arnold, was that of "an abstract man . . . who had the ability to understand sound principles and the free will to follow them." "All this folklore persisted," he added, "in a time when the theory of free will, sin, and repentance was disappearing from thinking about the individual's troubles. Psychiatrists and psychologists no longer explained individual conduct on the basis of a free will choice between good and evil. . . . By 1937 people had lost interest in theoretical ethical principles for maladjusted individuals. The term 'sinner' had gone from all sophisticated psychology." Arnold, in discarding the old doctrines of the free individual and the fundamental law, put his faith in the hypothesis of mechanistic behaviorism. Arnold insisted that the fact-minded leader, who understood the realities that had been discovered by psychology and anthropology, must lead the common man who still lived by emotion and myth.

Even as it appeared, the social theory based on the few and the many was being discovered by the research of the social sciences to be an over-simplification. The new understanding of the rôle of the group tended to discredit it. Americans grew skeptical, moreover, when in the 1930's they discovered the postulate of the elite and the masses to be a cornerstone of the philosophy of totalitarian dictatorship developed to support both the Nazi and the Communist tyrannies. These dictatorships, the skepticism of the traditional democratic faith of such men as Mencken and Cram, and the laborious efforts of the social scientists to discover the relation between the individual and society, all together provided a background for thinking when economic disaster caused Americans to take a new and hard look at their institutions and their values.

∾

The depression which began in the United States with the stock market crash of 1929 was a European as well as an American phenomenon. Europeans moved to extremes that Americans never duplicated. The successful Marxist war-time revolution in Russia had brought forth the phenomenon of Communist totalitarianism. The malaise that followed the close of World War I led first to the totalitarianism of the Fascists in Italy and then to its Nazi counterpart in Germany. In all three countries Europeans turned the state into a leviathan that swallowed up the individual and his rights. This European scene provided part of the context for the development of social ideas in America during the 1930's.

A later generation finds it almost impossible to reconstruct in the imagination the suffering, the anxiety and, at times, the despair that the depression brought to Americans. The record of millions unemployed sets forth only the basic facts. Three statements from contemporary observers and actors, culled from a vast literature of description and exhortation, assist persons of a later age to recover something of the mood of the times. Ex-president Herbert Hoover in 1935 described the world scene as seen by a man who held fast stubbornly to the American tradition of the free individual. When he spoke in San Diego, on September 17, Constitution Day, he was the rejected leader, reviled by millions of his fellow countrymen. The day of his acceptance and honor was yet to come. "In the hurricane of revolutions which has swept the world since the Great War," said Hoover, "men struggling with the wretchedness and poverty of that great catastrophe and the complications of the machine age, are in despair surrendering their freedom for false promises of economic security. Whether it be Fascist Italy, Nazi Germany, Communist Russia, or their lesser followers, the result is the same. Every day they repudiate every principle of the Bill of Rights. . . . Here is a form of servitude, of slavery—a slipping backward toward the Middle Ages. Whatever these governments are, they have one common denominator—the citizen has no assured rights. He is submerged in the State."[7]

George S. Counts looked out over America with the eyes of a man who was convinced that the old economic order had failed and that the nation must find salvation in a new collectivism. Counts, a member of the faculty of Teachers College in New York, was a disciple of John Dewey, believing with him that ideas—in particular when set to work in the schools—could become the instruments for remaking society. Counts, along with many of his contemporaries, visited the U.S.S.R. to see at first hand the experiment in progress in that country. In a book that followed, called *The Soviet Challenge to America*, Counts, though himself never a Communist, presented the challenge as that of social planning in contrast to the chaos and drift of individual enterprise. Then in 1932, while Hoover was still in the White House, Counts published a pamphlet entitled *Dare the School Build a New Social Order?* "Consider the present condition of the nation," he said. ". . . Here is a society that manifests the most extraordinary contradictions: a mastery over the forces of nature, surpassing the wildest dreams of antiquity, is accompanied by extreme material insecurity; dire poverty walks hand in hand with the most extravagant living the world has ever known; an abundance of goods of all kinds is coupled with privation, misery, and even starvation; an excess of production is seriously offered as the underlying cause of severe physical suffering; breakfastless children march to school past bankrupt shops laden with rich foods gathered from the ends of the earth; strong men by the million walk the streets in a futile search for employment and with exhaustion of hope enter the ranks of the damned; great captains of industry close factories without warning and dismiss the workmen by whose labors they have amassed huge fortunes through the years; automatic machinery increasingly displaces men and threatens society with a growing contingent of permanently unemployed; . . . the wages paid the workers are too meager to enable them to buy back the goods they produce; . . . federal aid to the unemployed is opposed on the ground that it would pauperize the masses when the favored members of society have always lived on a dole . . . an ideal of rugged individualism, evolved in a simple pioneering and agrarian order at a time when free land existed in abundance, is used to justify a system which exploits pitilessly and without thought of the morrow the natural and human resources of the nation and of the world."[8] So spoke the Socialist.

The third observer selected was a social scientist, a member of the faculty of the University of Wisconsin. Kimball Young, familiar with the new theory of society of the sociologists, looked at Americans caught in the depression to see what their behavior would demonstrate concerning American civilization. "Yet in spite of critical times for the capitalistic order and for its associated political democracy," said Young in 1934, "in spite of the disappearance of many of the features of the earlier *laissez faire*, it is amazing how the ideology of individualism hangs on in our non-material culture as well as in business. For the masses, in this country at least, there still remain among other beliefs the following. (1) Faith in the individual's capacity to rise in the social scale. The open class system remains an incentive to personal ambition. (2) The faith in popular education reflects this in another way. . . . (3) Speaking of Americans, most amazing of all is the toleration by the masses of their recent sufferings, based doubtless upon their deep-seated faith in the fundamental correctness of the present economic and political system. The slight amount of violence through several years of intense economic hardship is considerable evidence of the continued strength in the foundations of the established order."[9]

In the actions taken to pull the nation out of the slough of depression Americans avoided extreme measures. They turned to the political state, in particular as it was represented by the national government, as an instrument with which to deal with the calamities of the time. In this action they followed a course that Lester Frank Ward had urged a half century before, and they built on experience with national power gained in the Progressive Era and in World War I.

What was the significance of the New Deal for the doctrine of the free individual? In the temporary relief measures it established the principle and precedent that in times of general disaster the State must come to the aid of distressed individuals. It developed through the instrumentality of the state systems of social insurance to provide unemployment benefits and old age pensions, social security measures designed to strengthen the independence of individuals. President Franklin D. Roosevelt spelled out the philosophy of this New Deal implementation of the doctrine of the free individual. "The Republic," said the President, "had its beginning, and grew to its present strength, under the protection of certain inalienable political rights—among them the right of free speech, free press, free worship, trial by jury, freedom from unreasonable searches and seizures. They were our rights to life and liberty. As our nation has grown in size and stature, however—as our industrial economy expanded—these political rights proved inadequate to assure us equality in the pursuit of happiness. We have come to a clear realization of the fact that true individual freedom cannot exist without economic security and independence. 'Necessitous men are not free men.' People who are hungry and out of a job are the stuff of which dictatorships are made. In our day these economic truths have become accepted as self evident. We have accepted, so to speak, a second Bill of Rights, under which a new basis of security and prosperity can be established for all, regardless of station, race or creed."[10]

In making this summary of philosophy the President was aware that the New Deal also had supported at the same time an old and a new theory having to do with the free individual. Thomas Jefferson had seen in the independent farmer, master of a family-size farm, the bulwark of democracy. In moving to support agriculture the New Deal took two specific measures designed to give preference to the small farm as against the large corporate farm. A top limit was put on benefits going to any one farm enterprise. An attempt to exempt the Central Valley Reclamation Project from the established limitation of farms in irrigated areas to one hundred sixty acres was beaten down. In the New Deal agricultural policy the Jeffersonian theory of individualism prevailed. The independence of the individual farmer was supported. At the same time the Wagner Act took account of twentieth-century thinking concerning the group. In giving legal protection to collective bargaining the act vastly strengthened the labor union. As a consequence of firm legal support American labor developed the most powerful unions in the world. Through these the worker won an important voice in decisions concerning the basic conditions of his life. The new unions that grew up after the Wagner Act were, for the most part, industrial unions. De Leon, at the beginning of the century, had seen the industrial union as a power structure that would be able to replace the state. American Communists after World War I looked upon the industrial union as one of the most powerful potential weapons for effecting the revolution. When in the New Deal period the industrial union achieved great size and strength, labor, accepting the American economic order, used its power to improve the lot of the worker within the system. But the system was no longer the unregulated industrialism of the turn of the twentieth century. The powers of the national government had been magnified to enable it to deal with the great economic power structures that had arisen in the United States. The free enterprise system survived the depression but had been modified to enable Americans to overcome weaknesses that disaster had brought to light. As for the old doctrine of the free individual, in the new policy with respect to the unions he was given the means to fight his own battles, and in the matter of the support of farm prices and of social security the maintenance of individual freedom was made a national community project—collective action supporting individual liberty.

❧

To give reality to what President Roosevelt called "the second Bill of Rights" Americans in the 1930's moved far along that road toward big government that had its origin in the Progressive Era. At the same time the exigencies of international life in an age of war and revolution reinforced, as armaments mounted, the trend toward big government. The first Bill of Rights had been the product of suspicion of government. Eighteenth-century Americans had refused to put their full trust even in government originating with the people and controlled by representatives of the people. They had, as a consequence, written the Bill of Rights into the Constitution and by so doing had, figuratively speaking, fenced off an area of freedom about each individual that government was forbidden to enter and to violate. Now in the twentieth century, as big government appeared, the disparity of power between the individual and the giant state became increasingly evident. The situation bore directly on the doctrine of the free individual.

Even before the depression the Supreme Court, warned by some tyrannies practiced amid the emotionalism of the Red Scare, had moved to establish more firmly the freedoms guaranteed by the Bill of Rights. In 1925 in Gitlow v. New York the Court assimilated the four freedoms protected by the First Amendment—freedom of religion, speech, the press and of assembly but not others—in the due process clause of the Fourteenth Amendment. As this amendment established limitations on the powers of the states the action of the Court provided the means for protecting the individual against tyranny at the hands of state officials. Then, during the 1930's, the Court adopted an unprecedented policy in dealing with civil rights cases. Hitherto the judges had assumed an act of Congress or a state legislature to be constitutional until proved by the individual litigant or defendant to be in violation of the Constitution. After the shift in policy in civil rights cases, if an act appeared on its face to deny freedom of religion, speech, of the press, or of assembly, the Court presumed it to be unconstitutional. The burden of proof was thus shifted to the federal or the state government as the case might be. The Court further required that government, state or national, meet a rigorous standard in proving constitutionality. To justify such an act the government must prove the existence of a "clear and present danger" to the public safety. The phrase was that of Justice Holmes, an untiring champion as a member of the Court of the principle of seeking truth through "free trade in ideas." In many cases that dealt with oppression practiced on individuals and with disadvantages inflicted upon minorities (in particular the Negro) the Court defended civil rights and gave concrete meaning to the generalizations of the Bill of Rights. By setting apart the four liberties it had designated them as of more fundamental importance than any other part of the Constitution. By such policies the Court before World War II helped to redress the balance between the individual and big government and between the individual and an oppressive majority. The justices accepted and implemented the doctrine of the free individual.

∽

Again times changed. In World War II the United States and its allies destroyed the totalitarian regimes that had appeared in Italy, Germany, and Japan. In terms of international power, however, the outcome of the war was as much a victory for the Soviet Union as for the American Republic. Soon after V-J Day a cold war developed between the Free World and the Communist Bloc. The new crisis in world affairs put again to the test in the United States the doctrine of the free individual. The situation posed the question of how much individual liberty must be sacrificed in order to maintain the security of the nation.

The post-World War II problem grew directly out of a new technique of carrying on the international power struggle, a technique that originated with and was perfected by the Communist rulers of Russia. The tactic was that of infiltration, both open and secret, by Communist agents of government institutions and of private organizations. It had its analogy in the guerrilla warfare carried on by men out of uniform in the conflicts of earlier ages. The growth in importance of groups, in particular free associations, in the complex civilization of the twentieth century added to the vulnerability of the United States to the tactic of infiltration. The disclosure of the spying activities of Fuchs, the Rosenbergs, and others gave warning of the dangerous nature of the threat.

In the Taft-Hartley Act the federal government, taking account of the disastrous possibilities of the political strike, moved to curb Communist power in labor unions. The Supreme Court, taking judicial notice of the direction of the Communist Party in the United States from Moscow, sustained the constitutionality of the provisions in the act concerning communism. In the meantime in most unions the members and leadership, aware of the fact that the right of freedom of association necessarily carried with it responsibility for the actions of the organization, drove the Communists from positions of authority.

In 1951 the Supreme Court upheld the conviction under the Smith Act of 1940 of the leaders of the Communist Party in the United States. The Court ruled that the activities of these leaders, actually under the discipline of a foreign power, constituted a conspiracy to overthrow the government and that, in view of the inflamed international situation, this conspiracy must be considered a "present and immediate danger" to the public safety. Justice Frankfurter in a concurring opinion discussed certain implications of the decision for the relation between the national security and the doctrine of the freedom of the individual. "The right to exert all governmental powers in aid of maintaining our institutions and resisting their physical overthrow," said Frankfurter, "does not include intolerance of opinions and speech that cannot do harm although opposed and perhaps alien to the dominant, traditional opinion. The treatment of minorities, especially their legal position, is among the most searching tests of the level of civilization attained by a society. . . . No matter how clear we may be that the defendants now before us are preparing to overthrow the government at the propitious moment, it is self-delusion to think we can punish them for this advocacy without adding to the risks run by loyal citizens who honestly believe in some of the reforms these defendants advance. It is a sobering fact that in sustaining the conviction before us we can hardly escape restriction on the interchange of ideas. We must not overlook the value of that interchange. Freedom of expression is the well-spring of our civilization —the civilization we seek to maintain and further by recognizing the right of Congress to put some limitations upon expression. Such are the paradoxes of life."[11]

Justice William O. Douglas dissented from the decision of the majority of the Court in the case of the top-level Communists, basing his refusal to concur on his estimate of the situation at the time. "In days of trouble and confusion [the depression of the 1930's] when breadlines were long, when the unemployed walked the streets, when people were starving, the advocates of a short cut by revolution might have had a chance to gain adherents. But today there are no such conditions. The country is not in despair; the people know Soviet communism; the doctrine of Soviet revolution is exposed in all its ugliness and the American people want none of it. How it can be said that there is a clear and present danger that this advocacy will succeed is, therefore, a mystery. Some nations less resilient than the United States, where illiteracy is high and where democratic traditions are only budding, might have to take drastic steps and jail these men for merely speaking their creed. But in America they are miserable merchants of unwanted ideas; their wares remain unsold." The Douglas view did not prevail, either with the Court or with the people in general. Later, second-level leaders of the Communist Party in the United States faced trial and went to jail.

In the early 1950's fears roused by the manifest aggressions of the Soviet Union and by the rise of a militant Communist dictatorship in China were intensified by the continuing war in Korea. The truce of 1953 did in itself only a little to quiet apprehensions on the part of the general public. The specter of atomic war lurked behind every important move in the international scene by the Communist powers. In such a time of anxiety the crusade against Communists within the United States grew in intensity. The executive branch adopted procedures for discovering security risks in public employ. Investigating committees of Congress summoned and questioned witnesses in an effort to discover possible Communist infiltration into schools, colleges, and universities, into Protestant churches, into Hollywood, into editorial sanctums, into industry engaged in production for defense, and into government itself, including the armed forces. In the conduct of some of these investigations the committees disregarded those rights of witnesses that since the beginning of the nation had been conserved and guarded by the courts. The tensions of the time provided a background for a blaze of publicity for committee activities through press, radio, and television unequalled in our history. Inevitably publicity so great extended beyond the national boundaries. To many observers in other lands the United States seemed to be pursuing Communists at home using methods that seemed to deny the democratic process.

In the latter months of 1954 Senator Arthur V. Watkins and his associates in the United States Senate stemmed the emotional tide and prepared the way for the effective mobilization of the moral sense of the nation. Joseph N. Welch, special counsel for the United States in an inquiry arising from a controversy between Senator Joseph R. McCarthy and the Secretary of the Army, reflected after that climactic event on the affair in which he had participated. "It seems to me," he said to a group of lawmen in Chicago, "that we are measuring our reactions in this country certainly by our emotions and not by logic or reason. . . . The two principal emotions now in evidence in this country in the area where I was acting are fear and hate, and fear and hate when fanned to white heat are frightening to me, and anyone who fans these emotions to a white heat, I think, may be doing this country a disservice. . . . It is not necessary for us to live in a steady atmosphere of fright and terror. It is not necessary for us to hate as much as it seems to me we do. I have always thought hatred a bad diet, and I must say that I think a steady and prolonged diet of fear and hate might well destroy us. . . . It seems to me that in this lovely land of ours there is no problem we cannot solve, no menace we cannot meet, nor is it in any sense necessary that we either surrender or impair our beautiful freedoms." Times of tension sometimes produce new words or phrases. That of the middle years of the twentieth century brought forth a significant coinage: "Fifth Amendment Communist" and "anti-anti-Communist."

Defenders of the old freedoms who appeared in important numbers during the period of tension focused on three points. They attacked the principle of guilt by association. They insisted that in the case of a person suspected of subversion association is not conclusive, that justice required that specific acts be proved before the defendant could be condemned and penalties enforced against him. They also in pursuance of the second aim reminded their fellow citizens, to use the words of Edwin M. Griswold, dean of the Harvard Law School, that one "of the functions of government based on long experience, is at times to protect the citizen against the government. This function has been performed, to some extent, by the Fifth Amendment, although not always perfectly, and not always without some loss to legitimate government interests. While protecting the citizen against the government, the Fifth Amendment has been a firm reminder of the importance of the individual."[13]

The third point emphasized by the defenders of the old liberties had to do with security. Genuine dangers, both internal and external, intensified the search for security. Faced by a determined and powerful adversary, the United States combined military preparedness with diplomacy in the building of defenses not only for the nation but for the free world. As armaments evolved in variety and grew in destructiveness, and as the armed forces increased in size and striking power, military critics of more grandiose schemes pointed out that the goal of absolute security is an illusion, that security in a dangerous world must, of necessity, be a relative matter. The defenders of the old liberties pointed out that the same principle applied within the nation to security against infiltration. They insisted that in the domestic scene also the dream of absolute security is an illusion. "What we have to do [in a chancy world]," remarked George F. Kennan, a former ambassador to Russia, "is not to secure a total absence of danger but to balance peril against peril and to find the tolerable degree of each . . . a ruthless, reckless insistence on attempting to stamp out everything that could conceivably constitute a reflection of improper foreign influence in our national life, regardless of the actual damage it is doing or the cost of eliminating it, in terms of other American values, is the one thing I can think of that could reduce us all to a point where the very independence we are seeking to defend would be meaningless, for we would be doing things to ourselves as vicious and tyrannical as any that might be brought to us from outside."[14] Mr. Kennan added: "The first criterion of a healthy spirit is the ability to walk cheerfully and sensibly amid the uncertainties of existence, to recognize as natural the inevitable precariousness of the human condition, to accept this without being disoriented by it, and to live effectively and usefully in its shadow." The defenders of the old freedoms applied the foregoing principles concerning security to policies having to do with immigration and with the security code of the federal government and to the activities of Congressional investigating committees.

The decade of the 1950's saw a nation-wide struggle between citizens over the proper method for dealing with the dangers posed by the Communist tactic of infiltration. After the Korean truce and the later perceptible relaxation of international tension the defenders of the old liberties made progress against those who advocated extreme measures in the effort to eradicate subversion. It was clear to those who observed the times that Americans in the school of adversity were learning how to preserve freedom in the midst of danger.

⌒

Justice Frankfurter in his concurring opinion spoke of minorities. From the beginning of the Republic the affirmation in the Declaration of Independence of the individual's inalienable right to life, liberty, and the pursuit of happiness has goaded Americans to take notice of the disadvantages they have imposed upon minorities among them. In the middle of the twentieth century the efforts to bring about the abolition in law and in custom of discriminations of all kinds against minorities were the most marked in the history of the nation. They offered evidence of the continuing vitality of the old doctrine of the free individual. The fact that considerations of justice and fair play sanctioned the attempts to put an end to the disabilities of weaker groups suggested the continuing importance of the concept of the fundamental law.

Chapter 30

NATIONALISM, SYMBOLS, AND THE MISSION OF AMERICA

IF EFFORTS TO ACHIEVE national security achieved pre-eminence in the middle of the twentieth century, it should be remembered that a sense of the need for security was not new to the men and women of the 1950's. For the people of the United States the age of wars and revolutions began in 1917 when they mobilized a great army to fight in Europe. That war stimulated a sentiment of nationalism that remained a factor of primary importance in American history from that time forward.

Nationalism in 1924 virtually closed the borders to immigrants who, before 1914, had entered sometimes at the rate of a million a year. The methods chosen for restrictive nationalism took on some of the coloration of the race theories that stemmed from the nineteenth-century Frenchman Gobineau. National strength was by some advocates of restriction identified with a supposed purity of race. A perverted nationalism powered the racial prejudices and the barbarities of the Ku Klux Klan of the 1920's. Nationalism, conditioned by the disillusionment that Americans experienced after World War I and reinforced by the seeming security provided by oceans on east and west, revived traditional isolationism. The United States refused to enter the League of Nations or to make any commitments that might involve the country in the politics of Europe. Americans in the 1920's did not fear any particular nation but they feared war. Assuming that Europe, home of nations that for centuries had engaged in intermittent conflicts, was the breeding ground of war, Americans determined to remain aloof from that danger area. Never again should American young men become involved in those old tribal contentions. A minority of citizens opposed the policy of isolation, but their voices did not prevail. Only in 1941, after the Japanese had sunk or wrecked much of the Pacific fleet at Pearl Harbor, did Americans find unity in a war for survival.

The "long truce" that intervened between the two world wars was a time of contrasts, of progress and deterioration, and of uncertainties. Swift technological advance speeded the growth of industrial power and added to the terror of armaments. The depression, for the time being, turned economic advance into retrogression. The postwar generation tried to live with prohibition and became increasingly anxious when the underworld in the great cities developed open gang warfare for the wealth to be had in the illicit liquor traffic. Fundamentalism rose to challenge the modernism of urban Protestantism and to write the anti-evolution statute of Tennessee. The interwar years saw swift advance in the natural and the social sciences as scholars broke away from the absolutisms of the nineteenth century. It was a time of questioning of the fundamental law, of relativism, of a new realism in the view of the international scene as primarily a power struggle between the great nation-states. In the 1930's young men of military age began to question the nobility of joining the armed forces merely to further an age-old and meaningless struggle for power. Cynicism sometimes described the patriot as the dupe of the propaganda that proclaimed the righteousness of the national cause. In this cynicism was one side of the pacifism that characterized the interwar years. Another side was manifested by the determination of sincere Protestants never again to lend the support of religion, as had been done in World War I, to a barbarous and monstrous institution and practice. Pacifism, demands for preparedness, isolationism, arguments for collective security, ethical relativism and self-sacrificing idealism all intermingled in the 1930's, making that decade in thinking about international affairs a confused and irresolute time.

In these years between the wars new symbols of nationalism achieved importance. They were an important aspect of the thought of the time, but the interpretation of their significance presents difficulties and must always be uncertain.

∽

The need for symbols to give concrete expression to nationalism and to national ideals has already been considered and the evolution of symbols in the first half of the nineteenth century described. In the transition years from 1865 to 1917, when the American people emerged from a simple agrarian and commercial civilization into a dynamic industrial age, the old symbols, especially the Declaration of Independence and the memory of Washington, continued to be important. But, after the turn of the century new symbols began to evolve beside the old. They came to full development after 1917. As is the case with all symbols, different individuals or groups used them to support diverse ends. In this very fact, however, lay part of their importance.

The emergence of the Jefferson symbol in the 1930's and 1940's has been pointed out. It followed in time the appearance of two others. The first of these was the Constitution.

Before the Civil War, when North and South debated violently the interpretation of the Constitution, that great document could hardly achieve symbolic status for the whole nation. Such a development could only take place after the Union had been restored in spirit as well as in law. The extraordinary unanimity of Americans in World War I demonstrated that the old division had passed into history.

Americans as belligerents looked upon that war as a struggle against the principle of arbitrary power, described as "militarism." They thought of their own system as a "government of laws and not of men." They noted that the Founding Fathers had set forth the principles of free government, now challenged by military autocracy, in the Constitution. Before the year 1917 had ended one commentator referred to the Constitution as the "Ark of the Covenant."

During the 1920's when citizens—save the farmers—enjoyed prosperity, Americans watched the Russian Bolsheviks liquidate capitalism in that country. Americans observed the rise of Lenin's dictatorship followed, after his death, by that of Stalin. They noted throughout the decade the continuous use of force by the Communists, developing at times into the extremes of a blood purge. In the same years citizens of the Republic saw Mussolini, at the head of his black shirts, destroy parliamentary government in Italy and organize a Fascist dictatorship in Rome. Such events helped to cause the disillusionment of those Americans who had hoped and believed that victory in World War I would make the world safe for democracy.

In these years the Constitution came to stand out as a symbol that distinguished American principles and practices from those developing in parts of Europe. James M. Beck, prominent publicist of the times, published in 1924 *The Constitution of the United*

States. It ran through seven editions. "The great purpose of the Constitution," said Beck, "is to assert these eternal verities of liberty and justice. . . . A constitution, therefore, is something more than a scheme of government; it is the definite expression of a higher law." Calvin Coolidge, then President of the United States, wrote a foreword for the Beck essay. "The Constitution of the United States," said the President, "is the final refuge of every right that is enjoyed by any American citizen. So long as it is observed those rights will be secure. Whenever it falls into disrespect or disrepute, the end of orderly organized government as we have known it for more than a hundred and twenty-five years will be at hand. The Constitution represents a government of law. There is only one other form of authority and that is a government of force. Americans must take their choice between these two. One signifies justice and liberty; the other tyranny and oppression. To live under the American Constitution is the greatest privilege that was ever accorded to the human race."[1]

Inevitably the Supreme Court, the final interpreter of constitutional law, became associated with the Constitution as a symbol. Also, inevitably, the legal realists of the New Freedom attacked what seemed to be a popular determination to venerate the Court and the Constitution as symbols. In the early days of the New Deal a majority of the Court resolutely held fast to old constitutional interpretations and thwarted the New Dealers in their efforts to change the relations between government and the economy. Supporters of the *status quo* found the Constitution as symbol a useful weapon with which to advance their cause. Thurman Arnold, one of the most prominent of the legal realists, analyzed what he looked upon as the folklore of the time. "Ideals of law," he remarked, "arise from the hearts of the people, not from the refinements of intellectuals."[2] Law is a reservoir of symbols that have great emotional values for the people. Law, as folklore, serves the deep-seated needs of the "masses who want to believe [the myth] that government is moral, rational, and symmetrical."[3] "It was this faith in a higher law," Arnold added, "which made the Supreme Court the greatest unifying symbol in the American government. . . . To find peace men denounced government by men, and sought relief by reciting principles. The fundamental assumption of the folklore about government during the great depression was that principles could be more trusted than organizations."[4]

President Roosevelt's proposal in 1937 to reform a Supreme

Court that had nullified many basic New Deal measures brought a demonstration of the power of the symbol that comprehended the Court and the Constitution. His suggestion to add new judges raised a political hurricane in the country. The Judiciary Committee of the Senate, responding to public pressure, brought in a report adverse to the proposal. "Let us, of the 75th Congress," said the *Report*," declare that we would rather have an independent court, a court that will dare to announce its honest opinion in what it believes to be the defense of the liberties of the people, than a court that, out of fear or sense of obligation to the appointing power, or factional passion, approves any measure we may enact. We are not the judges of the judges. We are not above the Constitution. . . . We declare for the continuance and perpetuation of government and rule by law, as distinguished from government and rule by men and in this we are but reasserting the principles basic to the Constitution of the United States. . . ."[5]

In the years between the two world wars the Constitution as symbol grew in power as the European social religions of communism and of fascism waxed in importance. This rôle of the Constitution continued after World War II. The Constitution creating a republic was written in 1787 to provide an American alternative to monarchy. It remained in the middle decades of the twentieth century the American alternative to European dictatorships. The Founding Fathers who met at Philadelphia sought to make the individual secure against extension to the United States of the Old World system of hereditary aristocracy; their twentieth-century descendants hoped to defend the individual against the coercion and the regimentation of totalitarian mass movements. In the twentieth century the Constitution had become a symbol equal in emotional power to those about which the peoples of Europe have rallied; the British crown, the fasces, the swastika, the hammer and sickle.

∽

The Lincoln symbol rose with that of the Constitution. It is true that the memory of the war President had been venerated from the day of his martyrdom. But to a generation many of whose members had seen him or known him personally he remained an intimate and very human hero. To them he was a man of humor who, whenever possible, made a story carry his point. In the nineteenth century collections of Lincoln stories, authentic and apochryphal, grew in size. Emerson, in a eulogy of Lincoln some time after the

excitement of his death had passed, remarked that if it had not
been for the printing press, Lincoln "would have become mytho-
logical in a very few years."[6]

It is strange that the mystical Emerson should have so misjudged
the temper of the scientific age into which he had come in his declining years. He thought that telegraphs and newspapers, that
books of history and biography, that scientific historical criticism
and doctrines of evolution had put an end to such folk mythology
as had transformed Odin into a god. Doubtless most of Emerson's
contemporaries agreed with such a conclusion. Yet twentieth-century generations, who never saw Lincoln in the flesh, who thought
they were scientific, and who were sure they were sophisticated,
elevated the dead Lincoln to the status of a demigod.

The evidence is on every hand. It consists primarily of the use
of Lincoln's words as an argument for the validity of a position or
the soundness of a principle. The implication always is that, if
Lincoln so believed, the matter is closed. No one can guess the
number of times since 1900 references have been made to Lincoln,
the authority, in the political and social literature of the nation.
His name has been called upon to support causes as widely different
as those of Calvin Coolidge and Earl Browder.

American poets have been more explicit in their homage to the
shade of Lincoln. Edwin Markham published in 1901 his *Lincoln,
the Man of the People*. It was the last great poem which, in the
tradition of Emerson's memorial address, presented the war President as a product of the culture of the young Republic. Nine years
later Edwin Arlington Robinson's "The Master" suggested the
shift toward apotheosis.

> For he to whom we had applied
> Our shopman's test of age and worth,
> Was elemental when he died,
> As he was ancient at his birth:
> The saddest among kings of earth,
> Bowed with a galling crown
> Met rancor with a cryptic mirth,
> Laconic—and Olympian.

During the dark days of World War I, when liberty and democracy seemed at stake, Vachel Lindsay wrote "Abraham Lincoln
Walks at Midnight." Its theme was the return of the troubled spirit
of Lincoln to his old home where

On the well-worn stones
He walks until the dawn-stars burn away.

*   *   *

He cannot rest until a spirit-dawn
Shall come;—the shining hope of Europe free;
The league of sober folk, the Worker's Earth,
Bringing long peace to Cornland, Alp and Sea.

It breaks his heart that kings must murder still,
That all his hours of travail here for me
Seem yet in vain. And who will bring white peace
That he may sleep upon his hill again?

Lindsay's poem inspired Oswald Villard's *Nation* to comment editorially on "The Poetical Cult of Lincoln." "Our poets," said the editorial writer, "have a folk-hero who to the common folk-virtues of shrewdness and kindness adds essential wit and eloquence and loftiness of soul. Perhaps the disposition just now to purge him of all rankness and make him out a saint and a mystic may not last forever, but obviously it is a step in his poetical history analogous to those steps which ennobled Charlemagne and Arthur and canonized Joan of Arc."[7]

The *Nation's* staff writer obviously thought that the celebration of folk-heroes was a part of the license allowed to poets. Even as he wrote, however, John Drinkwater, an Englishman, finished his play, *Abraham Lincoln*. It opened in New York in 1919 and achieved a triumph. In 1920 the playwright published a little book, *Lincoln, The World Emancipator*. It began: "Lincoln, the world emancipator. It is a significant phrase, having surely an air of reality for those who know the story of the man. . . . Intimately of the world, yet unsoiled by it; vividly in contact with every emotion of his fellows and aware always of the practical design of their lives; always lonely, brooding apart from all, yet alienated from none—Abraham Lincoln, pioneer, citizen, country lawyer, astute politician, and incorruptible statesman, stands readily enough in the alert imagination as a new symbol of generative power. Already, half a century after his death, the mind of man perceives in this single-hearted champion of a moral idea a figure to whom all sorrows and ambitions may be brought, a touchstone by which every ideal of conduct may be tried, a witness for the encouragement of the forlornest hope."[8]

Drinkwater's religious implications are unmistakable. How much he meant by his words is obscure. They probably should not be taken literally. Their significance, however, lies in the fact that they were not looked upon as funny. His, however, was not the only rhetoric concerning Lincoln to use the language of worship. In February, 1931, in the midst of a gaunt and despairing winter when dark rumors of revolution were whispered about, Dr. John Wesley Hill lifted his hands in supplication. "Oh, Lincoln," he prayed, "Arise! Stand forth that we may gaze upon thy furrowed face. Look upon us; pity us; speak to us as thou didst at Gettysburg; stretch forth thy hand; point the way of destiny and duty that America may be thy living monument down to the end of time. Oh, Lincoln, come down from thy summit of bronze and march!"[9]

The opening weeks of 1937 saw shadows deepen in America as news of calamities and of strife filled the press. Vast floods brought destruction and death to New England and the Ohio Valley. Industrial war raged in the automobile and the steel industries. Abroad England sought to repair the damage caused by the constitutional crisis ending in the abdication of Edward VIII. Franco shelled the defenses of Madrid and seemed about to enter the city. Mussolini, conqueror of Ethiopia, in imitation of the Caesars, prepared a triumphal tour to Tripoli and to Libya to proclaim Italy a Moslem power. Hitler, standing on January 30 before a wildly cheering Reichstag, repudiated the Treaty of Versailles and brought an epoch of European history to an end. On February 12, 1937 a sonnet led the New York *Herald Tribune's* "Conning Tower" and was signed by the initials G.A. The poet used Whitman's title, "O Captain, My Captain!"

> Lincoln, thou shouldst be living at this hour,
> Son of the soil, brother of poverty,
> Those hard sharers of great destiny;
> Exemplar of humility in power,
> Walking alone to meet thy waiting fate
> Whose shadow was reflected on thy brow,
> Lincoln, thy people invoke thy spirit now—
> Preserve, protect, defend our sovereign state!
> Lover of justice and the common good,
> Despiser of lies, from thy yonder solitude
> Consider the land of thine and freedom's birth—
> Cry out: It shall not perish from the earth!
> Engrave upon our hearts that holy vow.
> Spirit of Lincoln, thy country needs thee now.

A cult has a ritual. Ritual is the expression of reverence through symbolic and repeated behavior patterns. The Lincoln ritual is performed each year on February 12. On that day or on the nearest possible day the press and the popular magazines publish again the familiar stories and portraits. Editorial writers discuss Lincoln once more and often seek to judge current happenings against the eternal verities which guided his life. Children in the public schools pronounce the Gettysburg oration or the Second Inaugural.

Inevitably unbelievers appeared. Unbelief in myths and long accepted doctrines characterized the period of the Great Liberation. The Lincoln symbol emerged and came to maturity in that dynamic and troubled time. In 1931, the year after Jerome Frank's *Law and the Modern Mind*, Edgar Lee Masters published *Lincoln, the Man*. It was a hostile study, done in the debunking spirit that flourished among biographers in the 1920's. The intensity and the character of the opposition to the book suggests the hold of the symbol on the American people. The editors of *The Literary Digest* compiled comments on the Masters effort. Among them were the following: "It is far too late in the day for any small confectioner of acidulated anti-social epigrams to attempt the destruction of the fame of Abraham Lincoln." "Lincoln belongs to the ages; Edgar Lee Masters, in this instance, to but a fleeting and nasty moment." "We are thus reminded now that we must revere Lincoln with greater sanctity. This latest abuse will accomplish good if it wakens all of us, as it should, to our duty to give expression to our love of Lincoln by applying to our lives the ideals of human service which governed his career and assure for him immortality."[10]

A cult requires a sanctuary. That of Lincoln has three—the birthplace in Kentucky, the grave in Illinois, and the great Memorial at Washington. Of these the last is the most important. Analysis reveals significant characteristics. It is a Greek temple. Within it is a graven image. Daniel Chester French's figure is a romanticized Lincoln. Three devices enhance the religious atmosphere; on the walls in bronze are the words of the hero; a light falls from the ceiling upon his forehead; and above the brooding figure is an inscription. It reads: "In this temple as in the hearts of the people for whom he saved the Union the memory of Abraham Lincoln is enshrined forever." Hubert Work, Secretary of the Interior, called the Memorial in 1926 holy ground. In such temples and with similar inscriptions the citizens of ancient Greece placed statues of

Apollo. By so little is the twentieth century after Christ separated from the fifth before His coming.

In the years between the wars the Lincoln symbol, reverence for the memory of the man who had saved the Union, connoted more than nationalism. Remembrance of a leader who remained humble, wise, and steadfast in time of crisis had a special appeal to Americans whose lives were cast in an age of arrogant totalitarianisms. The phenomenon of Lincoln, Woodrow Wilson once remarked, makes it possible to believe in democracy. In 1939, the year in which Hitler signed a friendship pact with Stalin and sent his planes and armies across the Polish border, Robert Sherwood's drama, *Abe Lincoln in Illinois*, played to packed houses month after month. On December 3 of that year Sherwood reviewed in the *New York Times Book Review* Carl Sandburg's *Abraham Lincoln: The War Years*. "He starts *The War Years*, "wrote Sherwood, "with the usual appreciative Foreword surveying his source material . . . but he reveals the odd nature of his essential research when he says, 'Taking my guitar and a program of songs and readings and traveling from coast to coast a dozen times in the last twenty years, in a wide variety of audiences I have met sons and daughters of many of the leading players in the terrific drama of the Eighteen Sixties.' From these sons and daughters he obtained old letters and pictures and clippings and reminiscences and rumors which led him to upper shelves in remote libraries. Thus his 'program of songs' (like Homer's) brought him into the very spirit of the people, the same people of whom—and by whom, and for whom—was Abraham Lincoln."

∽

At a time when liberal democracy in Europe was retreating before totalitarian mass movements anxious citizens of the United States saw the mission of their nation to be to hold fast to a traditional faith. A literature appeared and grew quickly in volume that undertook to re-examine the origins and the nature of the principles on which liberal government in the United States rests. The writers of this literature rediscovered Jefferson and set him in his new place in American tradition.

Then came another literature of counterattack directed against the philosophies that supported the European totalitarianisms. Horace Kallen, Walter Lippmann, Ralph Barton Perry, and William Allen White stood out among those who fought in the battle of ideas for the principle of freedom and the belief in the dignity of man. In 1940 Perry published *And Shall Not Perish from the Earth*. It was the year in which France fell. Perry concluded his book with a call to a people still irresolute, still clinging to isolationism, to fulfill their mission. "To believe in democracy for ourselves," he said, "and at the same time to remain neutral in our hearts and wills, as between democracies and their avowed enemies, is nonsense. To believe in democracy for ourselves, and at the same time to be indifferent to its fate elsewhere is absurd. . . . If in the name of freedom or tolerance or democracy, we cultivate detachment, indifference, suspended judgement, localism, relativism, or passivity on these very issues themselves, we shall end by becoming disloyal to them in our hearts. If democracy be the great and good thing that we believe it to be, we should expect its cost to be high."[11] Next the page of dedication at the beginning of the book Perry in the accepted American tradition placed by themselves some words of Lincoln spoken on December 1, 1862. "Fellow-citizens, we cannot escape history. . . . No personal significance or insignificance can spare one or another of us. The fiery trial through which we pass will light us down, in honor or dishonor, to the latest generation. . . . We shall nobly save or meanly lose the last, best hope of earth."

◇

American hesitations and uncertainties in the years when Hitler was getting under way his effort to dominate Europe contrast strangely with the course of action forced upon the United States by World War II and the international conditions that followed it. The outcome of that conflict had brought victory to American democracy but it had, at the same time, brought triumph to Russian communism. The men who looked out from the Kremlin upon the world saw the traditional adversaries of Russia, Germany, and Japan eliminated for the time being from the power struggle among the nations. In their place a power vacuum had appeared. At the same time defeated France was trying to recover from a long occupation. The war had inflicted wounds on Britain that only time and great effort could heal. Russia, too, had been wounded. The masters of the Soviet state, moreover, did not possess at first the atom bomb that had appeared so suddenly and decisively in 1945. Yet, in spite of disadvantages, the international situation, by the standards of any period of modern Russian history, was favorable to the Soviet

Union. The time for an enlargement of the area of Soviet power had come. Moscow established control over a group of European satellite states.

In the United States, untouched by the destructive acts of any invader, the war effort had magnified its productive capacity. In 1945 the nation stood possessed of power surpassing that of any state in history. This power, together with the momentary weakness of its war-time allies, forced upon America the leadership of the free world. Events had made the nation the final bastion of freedom. After the war no citizen could fail to understand the responsibilities that came with leadership. Then it was that the old concept of the mission of America to further the cause of democratic liberty in the world, that had originated as part of a romantic democratic faith in the early nineteenth century, became, perforce, in an age of violence and revolution, the mainspring of a realistic policy in international affairs.

Chapter 31

THE FUNDAMENTAL LAW
AFTER HIROSHIMA

Nature provides a background in a peculiar sense for the history of the American people. Until the end of the nineteenth century Americans had a frontier where men and women lived and worked in immediate contact with the forces and moods of untamed nature. The forests, the plains, the mountains put their stamp on those who dared to face the hazards and the hardships of the wilderness. Then in the age of the American industrial and urban revolution nature seemed to be subdued to discipline. The great majority of Americans came to live and work in the artificial environment of the city, leaving behind the nature of field and forest with which earlier generations had struggled. In the middle of the twentieth century Americans found themselves again, and unexpectedly, forced to deal with primitive nature face to face. But it was a nature their forefathers never knew. That revolution in science that began with Gibbs and Maxwell had in 1945 enabled man to unleash the energy that keeps the stars blazing in the sky. Thereafter man must live as best he might in the midst of elemental force.

Like the men of the frontier, their descendants in the mid-twentieth century found nature kind and cruel, offering hope and threatening disaster, as nature threatened the lonely cattleman on the plains, when he faced the sudden, icy blizzard and did not know whether he and his horse could reach the safety of the ranch house. The forces unleased by mid-twentieth-century scientists lent a helping hand to the biological investigator seeking to track down the cause of a disease. They offered the promise of power to turn the wheels of industry. A beneficent nature, offering hope and giving life. John Hersey in 1946 described the reverse face of this new aspect of nature that men had come upon within the atom. "A tremendous flash of light cut across the sky," Hersey wrote.

"Mr. Tanimoto had a distinct recollection that it traveled from east to west, from the city toward the hills. Both he and Mr. Matsuo reacted in terror—and both had time to react [for they were 3,500 yards from the center of the explosion.] Mr. Matsuo dashed up the front steps into the house and dived among the bed rolls and buried himself there. Mr. Tanimoto took four or five steps and threw himself between two big rocks in the garden. . . . He felt a sudden pressure, and then splinters and pieces of board and fragments of tile fell on him."[1] The record reads that the United States pioneered in the creation and use of the most destructive weapon man had ever known or dreamed of.

Mr. Hersey etched a picture of nature in the mid-twentieth century, terrifying and offering hope. The men of the time moved along a one-way street. They had harnessed the power of the sun and could not let it go. For good or ill they must live with this new energy. There could be no turning back.

The age dealt with the problem of power as every preceding age had done. But the order of magnitude of power set off the post-Hiroshima world from its predecessors. Presently giant nation-states, armed with the H-bomb, faced one another across a line marked by armed guards. The cold war that developed after V-J Day seemed to offer a melancholy verification of the analysis of international politics offered by Nicholas Spykman in 1941. Total war—said Spykman—a phenomenon of the twentieth century, is perpetual war. The thoughts of the world focused on power.

◇

Doubtless it was inevitable that it should be so. Power is of the essence of life. Henry Adams spoke with accuracy, though not the whole truth, when he categorized the individual man as a unit of power. When the single man emerges, as did Hitler and Stalin, wielding the compounded power of the organized nation-state, one aspect of the portrait of man in society comes into view. ". . . Power, like energy," remarked Bertrand Russell in 1938, "must be regarded as continuously passing from any one of its forms into another, and it should be the business of social science to seek the laws of such transformation."[2] The students of international relations have come nearest to obeying the Russell injunction. Accepting in large part the Spykman analysis, they have attempted diligently to analyze the power potentials of the nations, from their expression in the speed of the latest jet fighter to the still-unused reserves of strategic materials, from the effectiveness of broadcasts beamed across critical borders to that of the H-bomb. If fear stimulates the inquiry, hope also urges it on.

The cold war that dragged through the middle decades of our century illustrates, however, not new but old methods of dealing with power to keep it under control. Through the centuries men have tried to neutralize power by means of countervailing power. Since the modern nation-states first appeared in Europe the concept of an international balance of power has provided the cornerstone on which foreign offices have sought to rest their diplomatic uprights and cross beams. Nor has the concept and understanding of the realities of power been limited to international affairs. The Founders of our Republic established a cunningly devised system of checks and balances among the branches of the national government. Democracy distributes power, through the suffrage, among all adult citizens.

But dependence upon the use of countervailing power is only one of two traditional ways that men have used in their continuing struggle to tame power. The Hebrew prophets declared the Lord of Hosts to be a moral god. The Greeks formulated the idea of natural law. The moral code of ancient Israel and the Greek vision of justice embedded in nature and in the hearts of men became instruments in Western tradition by means of which men sought to subjugate power and to discipline it to humane ends. Outside Western tradition the effort to constrain power by means of moral ideals and principles runs as far back in time as Buddha and Confucius.

Perhaps it was true, as some of the most thoughtful in the middle years of the century insisted, that the magnification of power had shattered the old world order. Perhaps that generation in the West had lost, as Walter Lippmann affirmed it had, what he called "the tradition of civility." To find some clues as to whether these gloomy allegations were warranted is the purpose of the present inquiry.

～

Perhaps it is inevitable in the mid-twentieth century that the physicists who first released in society the energy of the atom should be among the most sensitive of their generation to the necessity for the understanding that, in the end, only the moral convictions held by men can tame power. Hans Bethe, one of the creators of the original atom bomb, gave public voice to this ancient wisdom when, in April, 1950, he spoke of the moral implications of the then publicly proposed hydrogen bomb. "Whoever wishes to use the hydrogen bomb in our conflict with Russia," he said, "either as a threat or in actual warfare, is adhering to the old fallacy that the end justifies the means. The fallacy is the more obvious because our conflict with Russia is mainly about means. It is the *means* that Russia is using, both in dealing with their own citizens and with other nations that we abhor; with their professed aim of providing a decent standard of living for all, we have little quarrel. Therefore I believe we would invalidate our cause if we were to use in our fight, means that can only be termed mass slaughter. . . . We believe in peace based on mutual trust. Shall we achieve it by using hydrogen bombs? Shall we convince the Russians of the value of the individual by killing millions of them? If we fight a war and win it with H-bombs, what history will remember is *not* the ideals we were fighting for but the method we used to accomplish them. These methods will be compared to the warfare of Ghengis Khan who ruthlessly killed every last inhabitant of Persia."[3] Brave words. Robert Oppenheimer at about the same time had similar questionings. Five years later C. P. Snow, British physicist and novelist, found moral questioning still continuing. "The bomb," he said, "has staggered scientists with a moral shock from which the best and most sensitive will not easily recover. Up to 1945 the climate of science was optimistic. Now that unquestioning optimism has drained away from most of the scientists I know. Technology is successful they feel. As for science, they do not go in for facile despair, but there is a weight on their brows."[4]

When Oppenheimer, in a position of governmental responsibility, expressed moral hesitation, he laid himself open to the charge of being subversive. Withdrawal of security clearance from Oppenheimer suggested the tragic conflicts and confusions of the times. The crash program for the H-bomb went forward because the principle of countervailing power required that the United States not fall behind in the grim atomic race. Yet, as the years ran on, Americans remained deaf to the urging of the few who advocated a preventive war. Standards born of an ancient, humane tradition kept the multiplying bombs silent in their hiding places.

Then came the tests at Eniwetok in the spring of 1954, verifying before the world the accuracy of Bethe's forecast of a possible future. Sir Winston Churchill spoke of a "balance of terror" that seemed to be superseding the traditional balance of power. "It is to the universality of potential destruction," he added, suggesting a supreme moral paradox, "that we may look with hope and even confidence."[5] Only the years could certify to the soundness of Churchill's hopeful conclusions. Moreover, because inspection of the nuclear potential of a nation had become impossible, mankind "will have to live from now on," said Eugene Rabinowitch, editor of the *Bulletin of the Atomic Scientists*, "with unlimited and unchecked stockpiles of atomic and thermonuclear explosives, piling up first in the United States and the Soviet Union, then in Great Britain, and later in other countries as well."[6] In such a world, shrunken in size, where nations, crowded together, jostled one another, men inevitably cast about for means to control power. Perhaps Churchill's phrase, "balance of terror," did not fully describe the realities of the day. Perhaps all peoples whose governments controlled nuclear weapons were inclined to shrink back from Bethe's panorama of mass slaughter. Perhaps there are elementary standards of behavior universally held. Perhaps something like a fundamental law operates in the hearts of men and could blunt the edge of the crisis in the twentieth century. Perhaps this idea, held by some, was merely a fantasy of wishful thinking.

Different men reacted in diverse ways to such suggestions, depending on their beliefs and their estimates of the situation in the world. On July 8, 1955, nine distinguished scientists from both sides of the Iron Curtain stated their position in a message sent to the heads of all governments possessing nuclear weapons. Bertrand Russell headed the group. Albert Einstein signed the appeal just before his death. Two other scientists from the United States supported the statement. It read: "In view of the fact that in any future world war nuclear weapons will certainly be employed, and that such weapons threaten the continued existence of mankind, we urge the Governments of the world to realize, and to acknowledge publicly, that their purposes cannot be furthered by a world war, and we urge them, consequently, to find peaceful means for the settlement of all matters of dispute between them."

The warning and the appeal of the scientists made clear that the existence of nuclear weapons provided in the mid-twentieth century a new support for an old view of mankind. Christianity, from its beginning, had insisted, in its ideal of the brotherhood of man, that mankind is a single entity. The Nazis and other extreme nationalists in the 1930's had maintained that nations comprise the only realities and that the concept of man is a meaningless generalization. "The accompanying statement," said Bertrand Russell in an explanatory memorandum, ". . . makes it clear that neither side can hope for

victory in such a [nuclear] war and that there is a very real danger
of the extermination of the human race by dust and rain from
radioactive clouds. . . . To abolish war will demand distasteful
limitations of national sovereignty. But what perhaps impedes
understanding of the situation more than anything else is that the
term 'mankind' feels vague and abstract. People scarcely realize in
imagination that the danger is to themselves and their children and
their grandchildren, and not only to a dimly apprehended humanity.
. . . If the issues between East and West are to be decided in any
manner that can give any possible satisfaction to anybody, whether
Communist or anti-Communist, whether Asian, European or American, whether white or black, then these issues must not be decided
by war. We wish this to be understood both in the East and
the West."[7]

In the opinion of the nine scientists who lent their names to the
message, scientific knowledge had, by implication, come full circle.
Science began in the efforts of men to subdue a hard and frequently
terrifying nature so that they might survive. By the middle of the
twentieth century science had accumulated and put into the hands
of men such a body of knowledge that the instruments it had
brought into being threatened not the tribe or the nation but mankind with extermination.

Other scientists published their disagreement with some of the
extreme conclusions of the Russell group. An international congress
of nuclear scientists from both sides of the Iron Curtain in 1955
stimulated vast and reasonable hopes for the future beneficent use
of atomic energy. Moreover, interchange of knowledge among
members of the congress began a return to the basic principle on
which scientific endeavor rests. But in spite of new hopes the fact
remained that destructive power beyond the capacity of the imagination to comprehend had come into existence and must be held
in control.

∽

An operation in a different power struggle, and one within the
nation, throws some light on tendencies in twentieth-century
thought. On December 16, 1954, the Committee of the House of
Representatives, of which H. Carroll Reece was chairman, handed
up to the House a report four hundred thirty-two pages in length
of its investigation of tax-exempt foundations. Apparently its
authors thought of it as a bomb. Like the explosion at Eniwetok
some nine months earlier it had a fall-out. "Throughout the text of

this report," the scribe of the Committee said, "the names of certain individuals appear in a distinctive kind of type. This was to identify them as having been cited by the Attorney General of the United States or by various governmental agencies for associations or affiliations of a questionable character." There followed a list of eighty-two names of citizens of the United States that included some of the most distinguished men working in the field of social thought. These were the fishermen who chanced to be within the Committee's radioactive zone.

Possessed of authority derived from the vast power vested by the Constitution in the House of Representatives, the Committee initiated hearings and terminated them in mid-course. On the basis of testimony presented and of individual excursions of its staff into the massive literature of the social sciences the majority of the Committee (or what passed for one) loosed, among other activities, an attack upon the methods and attitudes that have achieved importance in the period of the Great Liberation before World War II. Labeling as empiricism the techniques of gathering facts and making inductions from them without regard to preconceived theories, the Committee questioned the desirability of support for undertakings of such a character. "This Committee wishes to make it clear," the Report read, "that it has not attacked, and does not attack, empiricism. To do so would be an absurdity. . . . It seems to this committee that there is a strong tendency on the part of many social scientists whose research is favored by the major foundations toward the concept that there are no absolutes, that everything is indeterminate, that no standards of conduct, morals, ethics and government are deemed inviolate, that everything, including basic moral law is subject to change, and that it is the part of the social scientist to take no principle for granted in social or juridicial reasoning, however fundamental it may heretofore have been deemed to be under our Judeo-Christian moral system." The report continued under the rubric, "Moral Relativity": "It is the privilege of any individual to doubt our existing moral codes. Where social scientists presume, however, to approach solutions of human problems, or problems of human relationships, upon the major premise that there is doubt concerning the validity of our basic moral precepts, they run counter to what the public is convinced is its own interests. Consequently this Committee sees no justification for the use of the public funds which foundation capital and income represent to finance research with such an approach."

The majority of the Committee took their stand on their interpretation of the old concept of the fundamental law. The Report made clear that its authors considered a belief in the Judeo-Christian moral system to be widespread among the American public—sufficiently widespread so that it could be forged by the Committee into a weapon of sufficient potency to compel Congress to take steps to limit the freedom of the foundations. The majority's attack on relativity and its implied insistence on the unchanging nature of the moral code, when viewed in the context of the entire report, suggested an ominous tendency to use what Thoreau called the higher laws as means for forcing investigators of man and society by the withdrawal of foundation support to conform to thought patterns approved by the Committee.

The minority, opposing the report, appealed to the same fundamental law as did the majority. "Each step in the proceedings of this committee," said the dissenters, accusing the majority of flouting basic ethics in their methods and practices, "placed an ugly stain on the majestic record of the House of Representatives and the great tradition of the American people. The minority membership . . . feeling that fundamental American principles were under attack in the committee diligently attending its meetings. . . . The majority report should, in all fairness, state at least the following: . . . The proceedings were grossly unfair and prejudiced, . . . The record which was constructed by the staff is not reliable. . . . The proceedings and the rendition of the report are both tragic events. The minority members are filled with a sense of deep sorrow in the contemplation of the monstrous nature of both."

The significance of the Reece report for the present inquiry lies in the assumption, by both parties to a bitter controversy, of the potency in mid-twentieth-century America of an appeal to a higher or fundamental law. The failure of the report to evoke after its publication reverberations of consequence suggests that it was the minority that sensed more accurately the mind and temper of the public. Among this public, in fact, influences of growing strength operated reaffirming and strengthening old beliefs.

⌒

The story of one such influence in America began in 1878 when the scholarly ascetic, Cardinal Pecci, was named Pope Leo XIII. Within a year after his election Pope Leo published the encyclical,

"Aeterni Patris," in which he urged all scholars, ignoring the subtleties of the "scholastic doctors" of a former age, to return in the original of the writings of Thomas Aquinas. The document is the manifesto of Neo-Thomism. To further the design to bring back to the modern world the influence of the great medieval Dominican, Leo established and endowed chairs of Thomistic philosophy at the University of Louvain and at the Dominican Collegio Angelico in Rome. To fill the chair at Louvain the Pope chose a young Belgian priest, Joseph Désire Mercier, destined to become the famous Cardinal Mercier of World War I. Almost without exception the leading names in American Thomism in the twentieth century have been scholars trained by the Dominicans or in the Institut Superieur de Mercier at Louvain. From one or the other of these institutions came, among others, Jacques Maritain, Walter J. Farrell, and Fulton J. Sheen.

Neo-Thomism came to the United States as an important force in the period between the two world wars. In 1930 C. G. Haines published in Harvard University's series, *Studies in Jurisprudence*, a volume he entitled, *The Revival of Natural Law Concepts*. Neo-Thomism had influence beyond Roman Catholic circles, but scholars and churchmen of that faith were its principal protagonists. "Of late," remarked Sidney Hook in 1938, "many signs point to a militant reassertion of Catholic philosophy in American culture. Whether this movement is directly connected with the growing interest—and rôle—of the church in the political scene is difficult to say. But it throws a revealing light upon the character of the appeal which Neo-Thomism makes to restless minds in search of a center."[8] The movement continued during and after World War II.

At the center of Neo-Thomism stands the old doctrine of natural law, not in the form it took in the philosophy of Plato but with the theological underpinning given it in the Middle Ages. In 1943 the then-Monsignor Fulton J. Sheen noted some specific items covered by the concept in its Neo-Thomist version. "Divorce and voluntary sterility," he said, "are not wrong because the Church says they are wrong. The Church says they are wrong because they are violations of the natural law which binds all men."[9] In 1949 Dean C. E. Manion of the Notre Dame College of Law attempted a precise definition of just what is meant by natural law in the philosophy of St. Thomas. "The natural law," said the dean, "is man's understanding through his reason of the eternal law of God. It presumes the existence of a creator of man's nature as a human being, and it presumes man's ability through his unaided reason to know what he ought to do in relation to his fellow men."[10]

Four years later the editors of *Commonweal* invited Reinhold Niebuhr to discuss in the pages of that journal Protestant positions with respect to the dilemmas and the conflicts of the mid-twentieth-century world. In his essay Niebuhr commented on the Thomist doctrine of the natural law. "The absence of genuine exchange of thought between Catholic and Protestant thinkers," he said, "is particularly fruitful of misunderstanding on the question of Natural Law. I would like myself to persuade Catholic friends that our failure to accept Natural Law theories does not mean that we are committed to moral relativism, or even 'nihilism.' I would like to prove the honesty of our convictions that the 'moral law,' which our Lord summarized in the double love commandment is not to be equated with a 'Natural Law' that is drawn from Stoic and Aristotelian conceptions."[11]

A mid-twentieth-century resurgence of Protestantism that surpassed any similar phenomenon in the nation's history provided a background for the Niebuhr declaration. Ministers over the land preached the old message to congregations that crowded the churches. Radio and television supplemented the pulpit. American Christians organized the National Council of Churches in order that they might cooperate with their brethren overseas through the World Council of Churches in the task of making the principles of Christian morality effective in the life of the nations.

The Catholic and Protestant positions differed in important details of content in their descriptions of the fundamental law, but both agreed in their insistence upon the existence and the discoverability of principles and ideals for individual and social behavior universally valid in space and time. Implicit in both positions was the conviction that such principles and norms, together with the faith out of which they grow, comprise man's ultimate resource for taming power to humane ends.

The evidence from religious thought of continued and growing emphasis in American thought on the idea of fundamental principles of right and justice beneath society is clear. Investigators in the social sciences, however, laboriously accumulating data and drawing what inferences their material seemed to warrant, reached less positive conclusions.   ∽

Anthropologists of the mid-twentieth century, with some warrant, considered the concept of cultural relativity to be a major accomplishment of their science. This theory persistently reminded the investigator in the field that he must park, so far as possible, his baggage of values derived from his own culture outside the tribal area he had entered and try to see the culture he had come to study only through the eyes of the people who carried it. Such discipline, when applied to research, made possible that accumulation of knowledge about the cultures of the world that lies behind those important insights with which anthropology has enriched twentieth-century thought.

In 1947 the American Anthropological Association attempted to give the theory of cultural relativity practical application in a new world situation. In that year Melville Herskovits prepared for the executive committee of the Association a "statement on Human Rights" that was submitted to the Commission on Human Rights of the United Nations. Herskovits, taking the familiar position of the anthropologists of the period of the Great Liberation, pointed out that every people regards its own values as "eternal verities" because they have been taught to regard them as such. If a twentieth-century person is to avoid ethnocentric judgments, Herskovits continued in effect, he must suspend judgment altogether and try to act and regard other culture systems as if they were of equal validity with his own. Herskovits, however, added one qualification. In instances where political systems deny citizens the right of participation in their government or seek or conquer weaker peoples "underlying cultural values may be called on to bring the peoples of such states to a realization of the consequences of the acts of their governments, and thus enforce a brake upon discrimination and conquest." Herskovits did not explain where the underlying cultural values reside or by whom they would be enforced; but he clearly opened a breach in the doctrinal front of ethical relativism.

After 1947 the flow through the crack increased. In 1952 the Werner-Gren Foundation for Anthropological Research celebrated the completion of its first decade with an inventory of the discipline undertaken through papers read at an International Symposium on Anthropology. At this congress David Bidney squarely and forcefully raised the question of cultural relativism. "The doctrine of cultural relativism," said Bidney, "is apparently regarded as one of the major achievements of contemporary ethnology by many American anthropologists, although there have been some notable exceptions, such as Cooper, Hallowell (1952), Kluckhohn (1949), and Mean (1950), and there have been indications of a growing appreciation of humanistic values." Bidney singled out Malinowski for special comment. "I know of no better example in contemporary anthropology," the commentator remarked referring to Malinowski, "of the disparity of ethnological theory and practice under critical conditions. In the end, Malinowski [under pressure of a powerful inner urge to find a basis for criticism of Nazi totalitarianism], too, was prepared to justify the very ideals of a democratic society for which his scientific theory failed to account." In a paper distinguished for its careful and sympathetic analysis of the work of others Bidney stated his own conclusions. "My general impression is that cultural relativists are so concerned to safeguard cultural differences that they fail to appreciate the polar requirement of a common core of objective values. There can be no mutual respect for differences where there is no community of values also."[12]

Even before Bidney wrote, Kluckhohn, with funds provided by a foundation, had initiated a study by anthropologists of values in selected cultures. The enterprise suggested an interest of growing importance in an age of magnified power. More important, perhaps, than this particular study, is the fact that anthropologists, as their science unfolded and their perspective broadened, ceased looking at diverse cultures as static entities but rather viewed them as dynamic systems that could be studied in terms of their achievements and stage of advance. The concept of evolution returned to the science, but not the single-line evolution of the latter half of the nineteenth century. This dynamic view of cultures brought into focus tendencies of culture patterns, such as science and industrialism, to spread widely across cultural boundaries. The idea of evolving cultures emphasized the possibility of cultural advance or retrogression depending upon the response of the peoples bearing the cultures to changing experience. Against such a background the idea of cultural relativity has taken on new meanings and the possibility of the discovery of universal values has been recognized.

◡

Had the anthropologists taken a careful look at the necessities of their science, the necessities for science in general, they would have come upon a system of values that can be spelled out and can provide a standard by which diverse evolving cultures can be measured. The steps in the argument are as clear as tracks in new snow.

The urge to know lies at the center of life. Knowledge is the product of the dynamism of life. Knowledge is also the underpinning of a culture or civilization. The civilization evolves as knowledge increases. The difference in the body of knowledge available for use in the affairs of life suggests the chief reason for the differences that distinguish the society living on Manhattan in the days of the coach and four and in that of the motor car and the jet plane. The process by which the darkness of the unknown is transformed into the light of new knowledge is an orderly process in the same sense that a chemical reaction is an orderly process. The method is this: The investigator, whether he be a Newton or an obscure young man working in the corner of a laboratory, must have freedom—freedom to pursue truth wherever the evidence leads. If he finds that some one has erected across the trail he is following the sign *Restricted area—Keep out* he must ignore it. Freedom is fundamental. But freedom is not all. The investigator must report what he finds accurately and faithfully. If he falsifies his results, if he warps them to a party line, he makes no addition to knowledge; he merely wastes his time. And that of other men, for the acquisition of knowledge is a social process and those who seek new knowledge must depend upon one another. The investigator stands on the shoulders of those who have gone before him and works in collaboration with his contemporaries. The whole process is made possible by mutual trust, which is the harvest of integrity.

The diligent application of reason to the problems the scientist has in hand brings the new knowledge that, in turn, brings social change. But to be effective, reason must be disciplined by an ethical code, the code of freedom, honor, mutual aid, and the complete subordination of the individual will to the cause of truth. These are the laws of creative life—universal laws, valid in every time and in all places, iron laws that admit of no compromise. One recalls the unhappy demise of the Piltdown Man after an exciting career in the museums and the textbooks. "To many commentators," observed Ernest Nagel in 1954, "the ideals realized in the enterprise of science are also the ideals which are indispensable to the successful operation of any society of free men. Many thinkers, like John Dewey in America, have based their hopes for the future of mankind upon the extension of the habits of scientific intelligence to every stratum of communal life and to every form of communal organization." Nagel did not share the incorrigible optimism of Dewey but he held fast to the same faith. "It may indeed be the case," said the author of *Sovereign Reason,* "that the temper of mind essential to the exercise of such intelligence has no immediate social future. But the cultivation of that intellectual temper is a fundamental consideration for every liberal civilization. By making manifest the nature of scientific reason and the grounds for continued confidence in it, contemporary philosophy of science has been a servant of men's noblest and most relevant ideals."[13]

∽

The importance of science in modern civilization misled Dewey into a too-easy optimism concerning the possibility of extending the laws that govern the acquisition of new knowledge into all aspects of society. Bacon's old truism should have reminded him that knowledge is power. Power is, in itself, amoral, to be put to good or evil purposes by the man or the group who possesses it. We have considered some aspects of power as it exists in the modern world in the form of atomic energy. Some scientists in the years that followed World War II considered the possible social consequences of another kind of power, that which arises out of the knowledge of the springs and the mechanisms of human behavior. Their speculations had a bearing on the question whether and in how far Americans in the years following the surrender of Japan accepted the old idea of a fundamental law valid for all men.

Henry Thoreau built his solitary cabin at Walden Pond in the mid-nineteenth century and found in it a vantage point from which a dedicated individualist could judge society in terms of the higher laws as understood in his day and by him. A century later B. F. Skinner, a psychologist, created an imaginary Walden Two wherein he might entertain himself by following to their logical conclusions some of the implications that inhere in the body of knowledge about behavior that psychologists have amassed. In Skinner's story a beneficent social engineer created Walden Two at mythical Canton and made it an enclave of peace and order, peopled by brave, healthy, and happy men and women. It was the dream of Brook Farm come true save that the social engineer who knew his psychology had replaced the naïve Concord company of Utopians who believed in their transcendentalism. The pleasant tale recounted the journey, presumably in 1948, of "the Professor," a psychologist, with a small and varied company, to Walden Two and their astonished observations of life in that earthly paradise. On the way back home Castle, the philosopher in the band, began to speculate as to whether Walden Two might not forecast some larger possibilities for the future. " '. . . Behavioural engineering,' he was saying. 'If you really had a technology which could manipulate human behaviour, you could raise some puzzling questions. But isn't that wishful thinking?' " Perhaps "the Professor," to whom the question was addressed, had been reading George Orwell's *Animal Farm*, published two years before *Walden Two* appeared in the bookshops. He set down some of the meditations called forth by Castle's query. "The evidence, I thought, seemed clear enough. . . . I could imagine a potent technology composed of principles already used by politicians, educators, priests, advertisers, and psychologists. The techniques of controlling human behaviour were obvious enough. The trouble was, they were in the hands of the wrong people—or of feeble repair men."[14] Edward S. Robinson in the days of the Great Liberation had assumed that the techniques would be in the hands of the right men.

The year after *Walden Two* appeared Orwell published *1984*, a carefully analyzed description of that inverted Utopia in which Big Brother, by combining a knowledge of psychology with a technology shaped to his purpose, manipulated for his own ends the people of Oceania. Orwell's book gave mid-twentieth-century Americans pause.

Four years passed. Then B. F. Skinner continued, in a monograph entitled *Science and Human Behaviour*, the ruminations stirred by Castle's question. The year was 1953. "There are certain rules of thumb," said Skinner, "according to which human behaviour has long been controlled which make up a species of pre-scientific craft. The scientific study of behaviour has reached the point where it is supplying additional techniques. . . . We have no guarantee that the power thus generated will be used for what now appear to be the best interests of mankind." Perhaps through the author's mind floated the image of the Nazi overlords and their manipulation of the German masses or perhaps the similar phenomenon in Communist Russia. "Are we to continue to develop a science of human behaviour," Skinner went on, "without regard to the use which will be made of it? If not, to whom is the control which it generates to be delegated? This is not only a puzzling question, it is a frightening one; for there is good reason to fear those who are most apt to seize control." Skinner continued, seeking an answer to Castle's question, "Much has been said recently of the need to return to 'moral law' in deliberations concerning human affairs. But the question *Whose*

moral law? frequently proved embarrassing. Faced with the problem of finding a moral law, acceptable to the peoples of the world,
we become more acutely aware of the shortcomings of the principles
proposed by any group or agency. The possibility of promoting
such principles either through education or military conquest
is not promising." Skinner turned to science; can science provide a dependable version of the fundamental law? Perhaps. "If a
science of behaviour," he commented, "can discover those conditions of life which make for the ultimate strength of men, it may
provide a set of 'moral values' which, because they are independent
of the history and culture of any one group, may generally be accepted." For Skinner, skepticism remained. The concluding sentence of his book called only for stoic acceptance of hard realities.
"We can console ourselves," he said, "with the reflection that
science is, after all, a cumulative progress of knowledge which is
due to man alone, and that the highest human dignity may be to accept the facts of human behaviour, regardless of their implications."[15]

On May 17, 1954, less than a year after the publication of Skinner's book, the Supreme Court of the United States used its vast
authority to change certain hard realities within the nation. On that
day the court struck down legal racial segregation in the schools.
The unanimous opinion made no overt reference to ethics or to a
moral code. The justices outlawed segregation on the purely legal
ground that it denied the colored child "that equal protection of the
laws guaranteed by the Fourteenth Amendment." To prove the fact
of unequal treatment the Court noted the findings of several specific
psychological studies. These had demonstrated that the inevitable
consequence of segregation backed by law is a numbing sense of
inferiority on the part of the colored child. "Whatever may have
been the extent of psychological knowledge at the time of Plessy v.
Fergusson [1898]," the Court added, "this finding is amply supported by modern authority. Any language in Plessy v. Fergusson
contrary to this finding is rejected."[16] The carefully constructed
legal phrases of the opinion concealed from no one the fact that the
justices looked upon the question before them as a moral issue. Here
was power disciplined by moral ideals, moral ideals that had been
clarified and fortified by knowledge gained by behavioral science.
    The decision, moreover, had relevance for Skinner's question,
"*Whose* moral law?" One suspects that the justices, though they

were dealing with a parochial issue, did not consider themselves to be interpreting and applying a merely parochial moral law limited to the culture of the United States. If they thought of the moral law as having a general, even universal, validity, such a conviction must have been reinforced by the reception accorded their decision. It is true that a senator from Georgia immediately took the stance of cultural relativity. "Ways must be found," said Mr. Russell, "to check the tendency of the court to disregard the Constitution and the precedents of able and unbiased judges [and] to decide cases solely on the basis of the personal predelictions of some of its members as to political, economic and social questions."[17] But the larger history was different. The immediate acclaim of the press and leaders of practically the whole non-Communist world, together with the delay of the reluctant and chagrined Soviet overlords in announcing the decision to their people, posed in a peculiarly significant way the question *"Whose* moral law?" Perhaps the Court had announced a principle accepted by peoples the world over as an aspect of a fundamental law underlying all societies.

〜

In 1949 Erich Fromm, a psychoanalyst, made the comment of a physician on the question of whether behavioral science had or could discover what Skinner later called "those conditions of life which make for the ultimate strength of men." Fromm's ideas, elaborated in two books, also provided evidence of the state of mid-twentieth-century American thinking concerning the fundamental law. Fromm pointed out that the analyst deals with individuals, not societies. He mentioned two possible aims of psychotherapy. On the one hand the doctor may have adjustment as the aim of analytic cure, adjustment meaning a person's ability to act like the majority of the people in his culture. Fromm seemed to have less interest in this approach. "In the second view," said the psychoanalyst, "the aim of therapy is not adjustment but optimal development of a person's potentialities and the realization of his individuality." "Here the psychoanalyst," said Fromm, "is not an adjustment counsellor, but, to use Plato's expression, the 'physician of the soul.'" "This view," Fromm went on, "is based on the premise that there are immutable laws inherent in human nature and human functioning which operate in any given culture. These laws cannot be violated without serious damage to the personality. If someone violates his moral and intellectual integrity, he weakens or even paralyses his whole personality. He is unhappy and suffers. . . . The problem of mental health cannot be separated from the basic human problem, that of achieving the aims of human life: independence, integrity, and the ability to love." Fromm did not think the insight he was describing stemmed wholly from modern depth psychology. Behind it lay an impressive body of ancient wisdom. "In trying," he said, "to give a picture of the human attitude underlying the thinking of Lao-tse, Buddha, the Prophets, Socrates, Jesus, Spinoza, and the philosophers of the Enlightenment, one is struck by the fact that in spite of significant differences there is a core of ideas common to all of these teachings." The analyst did not attempt to arrive at a complete and precise formulation. The "following," he said, "is an approximate description of this common core: man must strive to recognize the truth and can be fully human only to the extent to which he succeeds in this task. He must be independent and free, an end in himself and not a means to any other's purposes. He must relate himself to his fellow men lovingly. If he has no love, he is an empty shell even if his were all the power, wealth, and intelligence. Man must know the difference between good and evil, he must learn to listen to the voice of his conscience and to be able to follow it."[18]

$\sim$

More than half a century had passed since Charles Peirce had pointed out to his generation the reality of chance, and, by so doing, had helped to prepare the way for the Great Liberation. Peirce was a pioneer in that revolution of thought and that new understanding of an infinitely complex cosmos that made possible the immensely creative twentieth century—a century in which creativity had so magnified the power available to men. After Hiroshima, however, knowledge of the uses to which power had been put, and might again be put, chastened the exuberance of the earlier years of the century. In a time when people moved with what caution they could manage among hidden dumps of nuclear weapons and in the midst of actual or potential areas of totalitarian slavery, the thoughts of more and more Americans, in spite of the continued skepticism of some, tended to run to a re-emphasis on the old doctrine of the fundamental law. Back of this tendency seemed to be the belief that this doctrine provides the one ultimate hope for defending the individual against the leviathan state and for meeting and curing the twentieth-century disease of totalitarian terror created out of the power that comes from the knowledge of how men behave and from the possession of and the ability to use the energy of the blazing stars.

As they looked out into the cosmos whose realities Gibbs, Maxwell, and Einstein had been among the first to glimpse, a cosmos in which Americans had again come face to face with the elemental forces of nature, some recalled the lines of a poet of the pioneers of the Great Plains, Wilson Clough.

> For this is the land of the few against the unpersonal much,
>   and the consciousness of holding on;
> Of silent spaces, of stoic horizons, and the knowledge of
>   the newness of coming. . . .

REFERENCES

CHAPTER 1

1. Unpublished manuscript in possession of Lucy Mayo-Smith Phillips.

CHAPTER 2

1. Ralph Waldo Emerson, *Complete Works of Ralph Waldo Emerson* (Centenary ed. 1904), VII, 27.
2. Quoted in Warfel, Gabriel, and Williams, *The American Mind*, 1937, 436.
3. Vernon Parrington, *Main Currents of American Thought*, 1927, II, iv, v.
4. Clinton Rossiter, *Seedtime of the Republic*, ch. 13.
5. Johnson and Graham's Lessee v. William M'Intosh, Wheaton, 543, 572.
6. Joseph Story, *Miscellaneous Writings*, 1835, 74.
7. William Ellery Channing, *Works* (11th ed.), II, 1.
8. Emerson, *Works* (Centenary ed.), I, 113–114.
9. Joseph Story, *Commentaries on the Constitution of the United States*, 1873, II, 606.
10. James Kent, *An Address*, 1836, 6.
11. Joseph Story, *Commentaries on Equity Jurisprudence*, 1836, 33–34.
12. Joseph Story, *An Address*, 1829, 30.
13. Ralph Waldo Emerson, *Works* (Centenary ed.), XI, 236.
14. William C. Jarvis, *Republican*, 1820, 56.
15. Frederick Grimke, *Nature and the Tendency of Free Institutions*, 1856, I.
16. Ralph Waldo Emerson, *Works* (Centenary ed.), 215–216.
17. James Fenimore Cooper, *The Deerslayer* (Everyman's ed. 1922), 8–9.
18. Leonard Bacon, "The Nation," a hymn, 1833.
19. Samuel Kirkland Lothrop, *Oration*, delivered in Boston, July 4, 1866.
20. Quoted by L. H. Butterfield, "July 4, 1826," *American Heritage*, June, 1955.
21. George Robertson, *Oration*, 1843.
22. John G. Nicholay and John Hay, *Complete Works of Abraham Lincoln*, 1905, VI, 156–158.

CHAPTER 3

1. Louis Agassiz, *Essays on Classification*, 1857, 135.
2. Helmut Richard Niebuhr, *The Kingdom of God*, 1937, 19.
3. *Ibid.*, 22.
4. *Ibid.*, 25.
5. Lyman Abbott, *Henry Ward Beecher*, 1903, 434–435.
6. S. J. Case, *The Millennial Hope*, 1918, 181.
7. *The Kingdom of God*, 142.
8. Joseph Emerson, *Lectures on the Millennium*, 1818, 120.
9. Seth Williston, *Millennial Discourses*, 1849, viii.

10. *Book of Commandments* (ed. of 1884), 44–45, ch. XXXVII, verses 9, 11, 14, 15, 26, 27, 30, 31.
11. *Lectures*, v.
12. Mark Hopkins, *Essays and Discourses*, 1847, 442–443.
13. George Robertson, *Oration*, 1843, 31.
14. Anonymous, *Treatise on the Millennium*, 1838, 32.

CHAPTER 4

1. Bliss Perry, *Heart of Emerson's Journals*, 207.
2. R. W. Emerson, "Nature," *Emerson's Complete Works* (Riverside ed., 1883), I, 10.
3. R. W. Emerson, "Self-Reliance," *Complete Works* (Riverside ed., 1883), 11, 51.
4. Perry, 152.
5. R. W. Emerson, "Over-Soul," *Complete Works*, II, 253.
6. R. W. Emerson, "Nature," *op. cit.*, I, 15–16.
7. R. W. Emerson, "Over-Soul," *op. cit.*, II, 253.
8. Quoted by Stuart P. Sherman in *Essays and Poems of Emerson with an Introduction by Stuart P. Sherman*, 1921, xxxiv.
9. *Ibid.*, xxxii.
10. Bliss Perry, *Heart of Emerson's Journals*, 156–157.
11. *Ibid.*, 238.
12. *Ibid.*, 263.
13. Henry David Thoreau, *Writings of Thoreau* (New Riverside ed., 1893), X, 38.
14. All foregoing quotations from "Civil Disobedience," *Writings of Thoreau* (New Riverside ed., 1893), Vol. X.
15. Perry, 238.
16. R. W. Emerson, "Self-Reliance," *Complete Works*, II, 47.

CHAPTER 5

1. W. G. Brownlow, *Americanism Contrasted with Foreignism, Romanism and Bogus Democracy, in the Light of History, Reason, and Scripture*, 1856, 9–10.
2. Orestes Brownson, *Essays and Reviews*, 1852, 381.
3. Quoted in Daniel Sargent, *Four Independents*, 1935, 202.
4. *Essays and Reviews*, 1852, 370.
5. *Ibid.*, 352.
6. *Ibid.*, 372–381.
7. *Americanism*, 96–97.
8. Orestes Brownson, *The American Republic*, 1866, xiv.
9. Quoted in Elliott, *Life of Father Hecker*, 1894, 91.
10. *Ibid.*, 82.
11. *Ibid.*, 83.
12. *Ibid.*, 84.
13. *Ibid.*, 93.
14. *Ibid.*, 155.
15. *Ibid.*, 140.
16. *Ibid.*, 89.
17. *Ibid.*, 176.
18. *Ibid.*, 89.
19. Isaac Thomas Hecker, *The Church and the Age*, 1887, 80.
20. *Ibid.*, 80.
21. *Ibid.*, 82.
22. Elliott, 90.
23. *Ibid.*, ix–x. For an excellent study of Hecker see Vincent F. Holden, C. P. S., *The Early Years of Thomas Hecker* (1819-1844), Washington, 1939.

Chapter 6

1. Quoted in R. M. Weaver, *Herman Melville, Mariner and Mystic*, 1921, 147–148.
2. *Ibid.*, 149.
3. *Ibid.*, 250.
4. *Mardi* (Constable ed., 1922), II, 244–245.
5. *Ibid.*, II, 240–242.
6. For a discussion of Melville's symbolism see Charles Feidleson, Jr., *Symbolism and American Literature*, Chicago, 1953.
7. Nathalia Wright, *Melville's Use of the Bible*, Durham, 1949, 186.
8. *Pierre* (Constable ed., 1922), 199.
9. *Mardi*, II, 375.

Chapter 7

1. Mathew Carey, *The Olive Branch or Facts on Both Sides, Federal and Democratic*, 1814, 20.
2. *Ibid.*, 11–12.
3. *Ibid.*, 3.
4. K. W. Rowe, *Mathew Carey, a Study in American Economic Development*, 1933, 120. This is the best study of Carey.
5. Mathew Carey, *Address Delivered before the Philadelphia Society for Promoting Agriculture at its Meeting on the Twentieth of July, 1824*, 1824, 55.
6. Mathew Carey, *An Appeal to the Wealthy of the Land*, 1833, 4.
7. September 20, 1839.
8. Henry Carey, *Principles of Social Science*, 1859, III, 265.
9. *Ibid.*, III, 228–229.
10. *Ibid.*, III, 229.
11. A. D. H. Caplam, *Henry Charles Carey, A Study in American Economic Thought*, 1931, 63.

Chapter 8

1. Grace Elizabeth King, *Mount Vernon on the Potomac, History of the Mount Vernon Ladies' Association of the Union*, 1929, 19–20. Quoted with the permission of The Macmillan Company.
2. *The Charleston Courier*, July 4, 1843.

Chapter 9

1. John C. Calhoun, *A Disquisition on Government, and a Discourse on the Constitution of the United States*, 1852 ed., 5.
2. R. K. Cralle, ed., *The Works of Calhoun*, 1867, III, 445.
3. George Fitzhugh, *Cannibals All*, 1857, 116.
4. Cralle, *Works*, IV, 417–418.
5. *Disquisition*, 7.
6. *Ibid.*, 12.
7. Cralle, *Works*, IV, 420.
8. *Ibid.*, 416, 420.
9. *Disquisition*, 48–49.

Chapter 10

1. James D. Richardson, *Messages and Papers of the Presidents*, VI, 7.
2. Pamphlet published at Augusta, Ga., 1868, in the Sterling Library, Yale University.

3. Horace Bushnell, pamphlet published Hartford, Connecticut, in the Sterling Library, Yale University.
4. Address before the General Assembly of the State of Georgia; February 22, 1866; Milledgeville, Ga., 1866, pamphlet in the Sterling Library, Yale University
5. Address before the General Assembly, 1866, pamphlet in Sterling Library, Yale University.
6. Jefferson Davis, speech in the Senate, Jan. 10, 1861, pamphlet in Sterling Library, Yale University.
7. Dunbar Rowland, ed., *Jefferson Davis: Constitutionalist, his Letters and Speeches*, 1923, V, 50.
8. *Ibid.*, V, 104.
9. Gustavus A. Henry, speech in Confederate Senate, Nov. 29, 1864, pamphlet in Sterling Library, Yale University.
10. Richardson, *Messages and Papers*, VI, 10.
11. For a study of the editorial opinion of northern newspapers see *The Course of Northern Sentiment from Secession to Civil War*, by Howard C. Perkins, an unpublished thesis in the Sterling Library, Yale University.

CHAPTER 11

1. For further illustrations see Cleveland Rodgers and John Black, eds., *The Gathering of the Forces*, 1920, I, 3–27.
2. C. J. Furness, ed., *Walt Whitman's Workshop*, 1928, 94–95. Quoted with the permission of the Harvard University Press.
3. *Ibid.*, 95.
4. *Ibid.*, 109.
5. *Ibid.*, 84.
6. "For You O Democracy," *Leaves of Grass*, 1891–1892, 99.
7. Walt Whitman, *Complete Prose Works*, 1892, 35.
8. "Year that Trembled and Reel'd Beneath Me," *Leaves of Grass*, 1891–1892, 241.
9. *Ibid.*, 78.
10. Furness, 57.
11. *Ibid.*, 57–58.
12. Whitman, *Complete Prose Works*, 1892, 336–337.
13. Furness, 55.
14. *Ibid.*, 56.
15. *Ibid.*, 127–128.
16. Henry Seidel Canby emphasizes this poem as manifesting a deepening of Whitman's thought. See R. E. Spiller and others, eds., *Literary History of the United States*, 1948, I, 489.
17. "Pioneers! O Pioneers!" *Leaves of Grass*, 1891–1892, 183.
18. Furness, 55.
19. "As a Strong Bird on Pinions Free," Commencement Poem, Dartmouth College, June 26, 1872.

CHAPTER 12

1. U.S., 163, 537 ff.
2. Philip A. Bruce, *The Plantation Negro as a Freeman*, 1889, 243–246. Quoted with the permission of G. P. Putnam's Sons.
3. Thomas Nelson Page, *The Southerner's Problem*, 1904, 292–293. Quoted with the permission of Charles Scribner's Sons.
4. *Ibid.*, 298.
5. *Ibid.*, 298.

CHAPTER 13

1. *North American Review*, April, 1871, CXII, 243.
2. *Ibid.*, April, 1871, CXII, 244.
3. Quoted in B. J. Hendrick, *The Life of Andrew Carnegie*, 1932, I, 330. Quoted with the permission of Doubleday, Doran & Company.
4. Noah Porter, *Elements of Moral Science*, 1885, 362, 368.
5. James McCosh, *Our Moral Nature*, 1892, 40.
6. Cotton Mather, *Two Brief Discourses, one directing a Christian in his General Calling; another directing him in his Personal Calling*, 1701, 37–38.
7. Daniel Seely Gregory, *Christian Ethics*, 1875, 224.
8. Mark Hopkins, *The Law of Love and Love as Law*, 1868, 182–183.
9. Russell H. Conwell, *Acres of Diamonds*, 1890, 19. Quoted with the permission of Harper & Brothers.
10. Quoted in John T. Flynn, *God's Gold*, 306. Quoted with the permission of Harcourt, Brace & Company.
11. *World's Work*, I, 286–290.
12. *North American Review*, June, 1889, CXLVIII, 656, 661, 660, 664.
13. Andrew Carnegie, *The Empire of Business*, 1902, 18, 109, 122. Quoted with the permission of The Carnegie Foundation.
14. L. U. Reavis, "Thoughts for the Young Men of America, etc.," enlarged ed., 1873, 11–12.
15. William Makepeace Thayer, *Tact, Push and Principle*, 1881, 8.
16. *Ibid.*, 354.
17. H. L. Reade, *Success in Business, or Money and How to Make It*, 1875, 66.
18. J. G. Holland, *Every-Day Topics*, 1876, 112.
19. Orison Swett Marden, *Prosperity, How to Attract It*, 1922, 4–5. For an excellent study of the American success cult see A. Whitney Griswold, unpublished thesis, Sterling Library, Yale University.

CHAPTER 14

1. William Lawrence, *Fifty Years*, 1923, 13–14. Quoted with the permission of Houghton Mifflin Company.
2. Andrew D. White, *A History of the Warfare of Science with Theology in Christendom* (1925 ed.) I, 79–80.
3. B. J. Stern, *Lewis Henry Morgan*, 1931, 189.
4. *Ibid.*, 190.
5. *Popular Science Monthly*, 1895, XLVIII, 72.
6. Lewis Henry Morgan, *Ancient Society*, 551–552.
7. *Ibid.*, 552.
8. *Ibid.*, 552.
9. *Ibid.*, 552.
10. Friedrich Engels, *Origin of the Family*, etc., Trans. 1902, 26.
11. Stern, *op. cit.*, 195.
12. *American Anthropologist*, n.s., II, 31 (Jan. 1900).
13. *Science*, n.s., III, 271 (1896).
14. *American Anthropologist*, n.s., I, 724–725 (1899).
15. *Ibid.*, n.s., I, 744 (1899).

CHAPTER 15

1. Octavius B. Frothingham, *Recollections and Impressions*, 1891, 285. Quoted with the permission of G. P. Putnam's Sons.
2. *The Index*, vol. 1, No. 1 (Jan., 1870).
3. *Ibid.*
4. Octavius B. Frothingham, *The Religion of Humanity*, 1872, 171.

5. *Ibid.*, 109.
6. Henry Adams, *Education of Henry Adams*, 1918, 35. Quoted with the permission of Houghton Mifflin Company.
7. *Recollections and Impressions*, 137.
8. *Ibid.*, 128.
9. New York *Tribune*, Oct. 30, 1871.
10. Robert G. Ingersoll (*Works*, Dresden ed., 1900) I, 59–60.
11. *Ibid.*, I, 7.
12. *Ibid.*, I, 10.
13. *Ibid.*, I, 250.
14. *Ibid.*, I, 59.
15. *Ibid.*, I, 86.
16. Robert G. Ingersoll, *Hard Times and the Way Out*, Oct. 20, 1878, 21, 22, 23.
17. *Works, op. cit.*, I, 89.
18. *Ibid.*, 89.
19. *Ibid.*, XII, 474.
20. C. J. Furness, ed., *Walt Whitman's Workshop*, 1928, 43.
21. Woodbridge Riley, "La Philosophie Française en Amérique, II. Le Positivisme," *Revue Philosophique de France et de l'Etranger* (May–June, 1919).
   For the beginnings of the American career of Positivism see Richmond L. Hawkins, *Positivism in the United States (1853–1861)*, 1938. The author points out that Comte's ideas were brought to America primarily through John Stuart Mill and, after 1853, through Harriet Martineau's translation of Comte's works, first published in that year. The chief American apostle of Comte's strange "religion of humanity" was a British immigrant named Henry Edger who came to America in 1851. After changing location several times Edger finally made his home in the Long Island village called Modern Times, a community founded in 1851 by Josiah Warren and Stephen Pearl Andrews and dedicated to the principle of the "sovereignty of the individual." The anarchism of Modern Times, boldly rejecting both the institution of the State and that of marriage, had no relation to that of Henry Thoreau. Edger passed from Warren's anarchism to Comte's religion and carried on an extensive correspondence with the philosopher. After Modern Times failed as a community about 1857, Edger continued to live in the village, re-named Brentwood. He sought diligently to propagate the faith but gathered to his company only ten converts, among whom were his wife and three of his children. About 1880 the disappointed Edger abandoned the United States to spend his declining years in France, the land of his hero.

CHAPTER 16

1. Norman Ware, *The Labor Movement in the United States*, 1860–1895, xvi. Quoted with the permission of Appleton-Century-Crofts, Inc.
2. Samuel Gompers, *Labor and the Common Welfare*, 1919, 16, 22, 150. Quoted with the permission of E. P. Dutton & Company.
3. *Ibid.*, 6–9.
4. W. D. P. Bliss, *Encyclopedia of Social Reform*, 1897, 1233.

CHAPTER 17

1. Henry George, Jr., *The Life of Henry George*, 1900, 193.
2. *Progress and Poverty*, in Henry George, *Works* (1898–1901), II, 545.
3. G. R. Geiger, *The Philosophy of Henry George*, 1933, 75.
4. *Works*, II, 546.
5. *Ibid.*, II, 545.
6. Geiger, 76.

7. *Works*, II, 546–547.
8. *Ibid.*, 549.
9. Geiger, 76.
10. *Ibid.*, ix.
11. Lester Frank Ward, *Glimpses of the Cosmos*, 1913, III, 172. Quoted with the permission of G. P. Putnam's Sons.
12. B. J. Stern, ed., *Young Ward's Diary*, 1935, ix–x. Quoted with the permission of G. P. Putnam's Sons.
13. *Glimpses of the Cosmos*, III, 231.
14. Stern, 304.
15. *Ibid.*, 314.
16. *Ibid.*, 314.
17. *Iconoclast*, August, 1870.
18. *Glimpses of the Cosmos*, IV, 11.
19. *Ibid.*, IV, 67.
20. *Ibid.*, V, 131.
21. *Ibid.*, IV, 165.
22. *Applied Sociology*, 1906, 313.
23. *Ibid.*, 339.
24. *Atlantic Monthly*, LXXXII, 253.
25. Edward Bellamy, *Looking Backward*, 1888, 328.
26. *Nationalist*, I, 18.
27. *Equality*, III, 26.
28. *Looking Backward*, XXVIII, 328.
29. *Atlantic Monthly*, 1890, LXV, 262.
30. *Ingersoll's Works*, VIII, 500.

CHAPTER 18

1. *Fortnightly Review*, XXVIII, n.s., 502.
2. *Ibid.*, 497.
3. Quoted in Harris E. Starr, *William Graham Sumner*, 1925, 236.
4. Quoted in Thorstein Veblen, *The Place of Science in Modern Civilization*, 1919, 65.
5. A. G. Keller and Maurice Davie, eds., *Essays of William Graham Sumner*, 1934, I, 301. Quoted with the permission of the Yale University Press.
6. *Ibid.*, II, 235.
7. *Ibid.*, I, 105–106.
8. *Ibid.*, II, 231.
9. William Graham Sumner, *The Conquest of the United States by Spain*, 1899, 24–25.
10. Keller and Davie, eds., *Selected Essays of William Graham Sumner*, 1924, 317–318. Quoted with the permission of the Yale University Press.
11. *Ibid.*, 333.
12. *Ibid.*, 316.
13. *Mardi* (Constable ed., 1922), II, 244–245.
14. *Folkways*, 1906, 176. Quoted with the permission of Ginn & Company.
15. *Ibid.*, 177.
16. *Ibid.*, 521.
17. *Ibid.*, 162–163, 194.
18. *Ibid.*, 98.
19. A. G. Keller, *Reminiscences of William Graham Sumner*, 1933, 109.
20. W. G. Sumner, *Earth Hunger and Other Essays*, 1914, 23–24.

Chapter 19

1. Brooks Adams, *Theory of Social Revolutions*, 1913, 208.
2. *Ibid.*, 209.
3. *Ibid.*, 210.
4. *Ibid.*, 210.
5. *Ibid.*, 212–213.
6. *Ibid.*, 219.
7. *Ibid.*, 217–218.
8. *Ibid.*, 227.
9. *American Economic Review, Sup.* March, 1936, 143.
10. *Ibid.*, 143.
11. *Ibid.*, 146.
12. Thorstein Veblen, *The Place of Science in Modern Thought*, 1919, 65.
13. *American Economic Review, op. cit.*, 145.
14. Richard T. Ely, *The Ground Under Our Feet*, 1938, 132. Quoted with the permission of The Macmillan Company.
15. *American Economic Review, op. cit.*, 144.
16. R. T. Ely, *Social Aspects of Christianity*, 1889, 122.
17. John Bates Clark, *Essentials of Economic Theory*, 1907, 555.
18. *Ibid.*, 556–557.
19. *Ibid.*, 374, 375, 559.
20. *Ibid.*, 375.
21. John Bates Clark, *Social Justice without Socialism*, 1914, 47–49.
22. Simon Patten, *The New Basis of Civilization*, 1907, Introduction.
23. *The Survey*, June 3, 1911, XXVI, 388.

Chapter 20

1. See Johns Hopkins University, *Studies in Historical and Political Science*, April, 1885, 293–294. The articles were reprinted in the *Studies*.
2. Theodore T. Munger, *The Freedom of the Faith*, 1883, 27–28.
3. *Ibid.*, 23.
4. Washington Gladden, *Working People and their Employers*, 1885, 188.
5. Washington Gladden, *Social Facts and Forces*, 1899, 198. Quoted with the permission of G. P. Putnam's Sons.
6. *Ibid.*, 212.
7. *Ibid.*, 220.
8. W. D. P. Bliss, *Encyclopaedia of Social Reform*, 1897, 258.
9. George D. Herron, *The Christian Society*, 1894, 128.
10. *Ibid.*, 8.
11. M. P. Briggs, *George D. Herron and the European Settlement*, 1932, 10.
12. George D. Herron, *The New Redemption*, 1893, 12.
13. Jane Addams, *Twenty Years in Hull House*, 1910, 278–279.
14. Ralph Albertson, *Social Incarnation* (Commonwealth, Ga.), 1899, 8.
15. *Social Gospel*, October, 1899.
16. *Twenty Years in Hull House*, 277.
17. George D. Herron, *The New Redemption*, 1893, 15.
18. Ray Stannard Baker, *The Social Unrest*, 1910, 268.
19. Walter Rauschenbusch, *A Theology for the Social Gospel*, 1917, 276.
20. *Ibid.*, 422.
21. Walter Rauschenbusch, *Christianizing the Social Order*, 1912, 179.
22. *Ibid.*, 195.
23. *Ibid.*, 313.
24. *A Theology of the Social Gospel*, 1917, 184.

25. *Christianity and the Social Crisis*, xii–xiii.
26. *Christianizing the Social Order*, 1912, 337.
27. *Ibid.*, 350.
28. *Ibid.*, 449.
29. *A Theology of the Social Gospel*, 165.
30. *Ibid.*, 179–180.
31. *Christianizing the Social Order*, 364.
32. *A Theology of the Social Gospel*, 225.
33. *Ibid.*, 271.
34. *A Theology of the Social Gospel*, 4–6.

CHAPTER 21

1. *Polloc* v. *Farmer's Loan and Trust Co.*, 157 U.S. 607 (1894).
2. Stephen J. Field, *Reminiscences*, 1893, 37.
3. *Ex Parte Newman*, 9 California 526.
4. Conyers Read, ed., *The Constitution Reconsidered*, 1938, 173–174. For a full discussion of the development of the doctrine of due process, see Walton Hamilton, *The Path of Due Process of Law* in above volume, 1938.
5. *Ibid.*, 173.
6. Mark Hopkins, *Lectures on Moral Science*, 1867, 258–259, 266.
7. *Butchers' Union Co.* v. *Crescent City Co.*, 111 U.S. 746, 756 (1883).
8. *Lectures on Moral Science*, 1867, 266.
9. *Barbeir* v. *Connolly*, 113 U.S. 27, 31 (1885).
10. *Loan Association* v. *Topeka*, 20 Wall. 655, 663 (1875); quoted in *University of California Publications*, Social Sciences, 1932, I, 415.
11. *Butchers' Union Co.* v. *Crescent City Co.*, 111 U.S. 746, 756 (1883).
12. Walter Nelles, "Commonwealth *v.* Hunt," *Columbia Law Review*, 1932, XXXII, 1151.
13. Leon Whipple, *The Story of Civil Liberty in the United States*, 1927, 252.
14. 158 U.S. 582–583.
15. New York Bar Association, *Proceedings*, 1893, 46.

CHAPTER 22

1. Josiah Royce, *Fugitive Essays*, 1920, 303.
2. Josiah Royce, *Race Questions and other American Problems*, 1908, 160, 162.
3. *Ibid.*, 215.
4. *Ibid.*, 218.
5. *Fugitive Essays*, 303.
6. *Ibid.*, 152.
7. *Race Questions*, 74.
8. *Ibid.*, 61.
9. *Ibid.*, 79.
10. *Ibid.*, 95.
11. *Ibid.*, 53.
12. *Ibid.*, 251–252.
13. See Bibliography.

CHAPTER 23

1. George Bancroft, *History of the United States*, Author's last revision, 1884, IV, 450.
2. George Bancroft, *Memorial Address*, 1866, 4, 6.
3. *History of the United States*, 1884, VI, 474.

4. See page 247.
5. For nationalism, see Chapter 8.
6. See page 21.
7. See pages 305–306.
8. Fulmer Mood, ed., *The Early Writings of Frederick Jackson Turner*, 1938, 23. Quoted with the permission of the University of Wisconsin Press.
9. *Ibid.*, 67.
10. *Ibid.*, 83.
11. Frederick J. Turner, *The Frontier in American History*, 1920, 30. Quoted with the permission of Henry Holt & Company.
12. *Ibid.*, 293.
13. *Ibid.*, 267, 268, 275.
14. *Ibid.*, 266.
15. *Ibid.*, 281–282.
16. Mood, *Early Writings*, 3.
17. See page 310.
18. W. C. Ford, ed., *A Cycle of Adams Letters*, 1920, I, 281–282.
19. Henry Adams, *The Education of Henry Adams*, 1918, 225. Quoted with the permission of Houghton Mifflin Company.
20. *Ibid.*, 225.
21. Brooks Adams, *Degradation of the Democratic Dogma*, 1919, 108–109.
22. *Ibid.*, 141. For the best discussion of Adams' philosophy see William Jordy, *Henry Adams, Scientific Historian*, 1952.
23. *The Education of Henry Adams*, 495.
24. *Ibid.*, 474.
25. *Ibid.*, 493.
26. *Ibid.*, 496–497.
27. *Ibid.*, 489.
28. *Ibid.*, 496.
29. *Ibid.*, 494–495.
30. *Ibid.*, 498.

CHAPTER 24

1. Charles Peirce, *Collected Works*, VI, 13.
2. R. B. Perry, *The Thought and Character of William James*, 1935, I, 812. Quoted with the permission of Little, Brown & Company.
3. *Ibid.*, II, 316.
4. *Ibid.*, II, 442.
5. *The New York Times*, November 3, 1907, Part V, 8.
6. William James, *Varieties of Religious Experience*, 1902, 517. Quoted with the permission of Longmans, Green & Company.
7. *Ibid.*, 517.
8. Ralph Barton Perry, *Characteristically American*, 1949, 86, 92.
9. Perry, *Thought and Character of William James*, II, 517.
10. Morris R. Cohen, *American Thought*, 1954, 296–297. Quoted with the permission of The Free Press.

CHAPTER 25

1. H. G. Wells, *The Future in America*, 1906, 105–107.
2. Quoted in Robert W. Smuts, *European Impressions of the American Worker*, 1953, 2, 13, 29.

3. Mosely Industrial Commission to the United States, Oct.–Dec., 1902, *Reports of Delegates*, Manchester, 1903, 9, 190–191.
4. Smuts, *European Impressions*, 27–28.
5. Woodrow Wilson, *The New Freedom*, 1913, 64, 89. Quoted with the permission of Doubleday, Doran & Company.
6. *Ibid.*, 35.
7. Richard T. Ely, *Hard Times—the Way Out*, 1931, 93.
8. *The New Freedom*, 207, 292.
9. *Ibid.*, 207.
10. Herbert Croly, *The Promise of American Life*, 1909, 3.
11. *Ibid.*, 24.
12. Richard T. Ely, *An Introduction to Political Economy*, 1889, 100–101.
13. "Notes and Abstracts," *American Journal of Sociology*, January, 1903.
14. Charles E. Merriam, *New Aspects of Politics*, 1925, 158.
15. Herbert Croly, *Progressive Democracy*, 1914, 370–371. Quoted with permission of The Macmillan Company.
16. *Ibid.*, 404, 409.
17. *The New Freedom*, 42.

CHAPTER 26

1. Josiah Strong, *Our Country*, 1885, vii.
2. *Ibid.*, 166.
3. *Ibid.*, 179.
4. *Ibid.*, 175.
5. *Ibid.*, 176.
6. *Ibid.*, 165.
7. Josiah Strong, *Expansion*, 1900, 295.
8. *Ibid.*, 302.
9. Josiah Strong, *Our World*, 1913, 82.
10. *Ibid.*, ix.
11. Quoted in H. R. Warfel, R. H. Gabriel, and S. T. Williams, *The American Mind*, 1937, 478–479.
12. *The Nineteenth Century*, February, 1898.
13. *North American Review*, October, 1899.
14. *Ibid.*
15. *Ibid.*
16. *Ibid.*
17. Alfred T. Mahan, *Armaments and Arbitration*, 1912, 1. Quoted with the permission of Harper & Brothers.
18. *Ibid.*, 12.
19. *Ibid.*, 82–83.
20. *Ibid.*, 84–85.
21. *Ibid.*, 85–86.
22. The Adams letters to Roosevelt are quoted in A. E. Beringause, *Brooks Adams*, N.Y., 1955, 204, 208–209.
23. Theodore Roosevelt, *Works*, Memorial ed., 1925, XV, 291. Quoted with the permission of Charles Scribner's Sons.
24. *Ibid.*, 291.
25. *Works*, XVIII, 353.
26. *Ibid.*, 344.
27. Theodore Roosevelt, *The Strenuous Life*, 1900, 20. Quoted with the permission of Appleton-Century-Crofts, Inc.
28. *Works*, XV, 341.
29. *Works*, XVIII, 417.
30. *Ibid.*, 411.
31. David Starr Jordan, *The Days of a Man*, I, 616.

32. David Starr Jordan, *War and Bread*, 1915, 32.
33. David Starr Jordan, *Imperial Democracy*, 1899, 87.
34. *Ibid.*, 92.

CHAPTER 27

1. Provost-Marshal General, *Second Report*, 1917, 237.
2. Richardson, *Messages and Papers of the Presidents*, XVII, 8405.
3. Wallace Notestein and Elmer E. Stoll, eds. *Conquest and Kultur*, 1917, 5.
4. *Ibid.*, 44, from Treitschke's *Politics*, 1916.
5. *Ibid.*, 19, from von Bernhardi, 1911.
6. *Ibid.*, 34, from Nietzsche.
7. *Ibid.*, 35, from editorial in *Jung-Deutschland*, October, 1913.
8. *Ibid.*, 36, from Werner Sombart, 1915.
9. *Ibid.*, 37, from Karl A. Kuhn, 1914.
10. Woodrow Wilson, *Messages and Papers*, 1917, 24, I, 74–75.
11. Richardson, *Messages and Papers of the Presidents*, XVI, 8352.
12. William Wood and Ralph H. Gabriel, *In Defense of Liberty*, 1928, 267.
13. Henry R. Miller, *The First Division*, 1920, v-vii.
14. Anonymous, *Wine, Women, and War*, 1926, 203–204.
15. Woodrow Wilson, *International Ideals*, 1919, 2, 24.
16. Quoted in Ray Stannard Baker, *Woodrow Wilson: Life and Letters*, VI, 490, 506–507.

CHAPTER 28

1. Oliver Wendell Holmes, *Harvard Law Review*, 1918, XXXII, 40 ff.
2. Charles Clark, "The Function of Law in Democratic Society," *University of Chicago Law Review*, 1942, 393.
3. Quoted with the permission of Brentano's.
4. Edward Robinson, *Law and the Lawyers*, 1935, I, 7.
5. *Ibid.*, 3, 22.
6. Roscoe Pound, "Jurisprudence," *Encyclopaedia of the Social Sciences*, VIII, 485.
7. Morris Cohen, *American Thought*, 1954, 176. Quoted with the permission of The Free Press, Glencoe, Ill.
8. *The Autobiography of Lincoln Steffens*, 851–852.
9. *Holmes-Pollock Letters*, II, 36, 41. Quoted with the permission of the Harvard University Press.
10. Nicholas Spykman, *American Strategy in World Politics*, 1942, 38, 40.
11. Quoted in Brown, "The Vitality of International Law," *American Journal of International Law*, April, 1945, 533.
12. Oliver Wendell Holmes, *Collected Legal Papers*, 304–305.
13. *Justice Oliver Wendell Holmes, His Book Notices and Uncollected Letters and Papers*, 1936, 143.
14. Jerome Frank, "A Conflict with Oblivion: Some Observations on the Founders of Legal Pragmatism," *Rutgers Law Review*, IX, 450.
15. K. W. Llewellyn, "On Reading and Using the Newer Jurisprudence," *Columbia Law Review*, 1940, XL, 603.

CHAPTER 29

1. H. L. Mencken, *Notes on Democracy*, 1926, 101.
2. Ralph Adams Cram, *Sins of the Fathers*, 45.
3. Ralph Adams Cram, *End of Democracy*, 6–7.
4. Ralph Adams Cram, *Convictions and Controversies*, 192.
5. Thurman Arnold, *Folklore of Capitalism*, 1937, 356–357. Quoted with the permission of the Yale University Press.
5. *Ibid.*, 5, 69.

7. Herbert Hoover, *Addresses Upon the American Road*, 1938, 59–60. Quoted with the permission of Charles Scribner's Sons.
8. George S. Counts, *Dare the School Build a New Social Order?*, 1932, 32–34. Quoted with the permission of The John Day Co.
9. Kimball Young, *An Introduction to Sociology*, 1934, 581. Quoted with the permission of the American Book Co.
10. January 12, 1944.
11. Dennis et al *v.* U. S., 1951, 34 U. S. 494, 95 L.E.D., 1137, 71 S. Ct. 857.
12. Quoted in Erwin N. Griswold, *The Fifth Amendment Today*, Cambridge, 1955, 74–75. Quoted with the permission of the Harvard University Press.
13. *Ibid.*, 75–76.
14. *Ibid.*, 72–73.

CHAPTER 30

1. James M. Beck, *The Constitution of the United States*, 1924, 1925 ed., v, vi, ix, xi.
2. Thurman Arnold, *Symbols of Government*, 1935, 225. Quoted with the permission of the Yale University Press.
3. *Ibid.*, 238.
4. Thurman Arnold, *Folklore of Capitalism*, 1937, 63–64, 68. Quoted with the permission of the Yale University Press.
5. *Adverse Report of the Committee on the Judiciary on a Bill to Reorganize the Judicial Branch of the Government*, Overbrook Press, Stanford, 1937, 17–36.
6. R. P. Basler, *The Lincoln Legend*, 1935, 307.
7. May 17, 1919.
8. John Drinkwater, *Lincoln, the World Emancipator*, 1920, 3–4.
9. *National Republic*, February, 1931.
10. February 28, 1931.
11. Ralph Barton Perry, *And Shall Not Perish from the Earth*, 1940, 153–154.

CHAPTER 31

1. John Hersey, "Hiroshima," *New Yorker*, XXII, No. 29, Aug. 31, 1946.
2. Bertrand Russell, *Power*, 1938, 13–14. Quoted with the permission of W. W. Norton & Co., Inc.
3. *Bulletin of the Atomic Scientists*, April, 1950, 102.
4. *The New York Times Book Review*, January 30, 1955, 29.
5. Quoted by Richard H. Rovere, *New Yorker*, January 29, 1955, 74.
6. *Ibid.*
7. Quoted in *The New York Times*, July 9, 1955.
8. Sidney Hook, "The Baptism of Aristotle and Marx," *The Nation*, April 9, 1938, 415.
9. Fulton J. Sheen, *Philosophies at War*, 1943, 130. Quoted with permission of Charles Scribner's Sons.
10. Quoted in *The New York Times*, December 10, 1949.
11. Reinhold Niebuhr, "A Protestant Looks at Catholics," in *Catholicism in America*, 1954, 32. Quoted with the permission of Harcourt, Brace and Co.
12. Krober and others, *Anthropology Today*, 1953, 694–695.
13. Ernest Nagel, *Sovereign Reason*, 1954, 306, 308.
14. B. F. Skinner, *Walden Two*, 1948, 256. Quoted with the permission of The Macmillan Co.
15. B. F. Skinner, *Science and Human Behaviour*, 1953, 347–348, 445, 449. Quoted with the permission of The Macmillan Co.
16. Quoted in *The New York Times*, May 18, 1954.
17. *Ibid.*
18. Erich Fromm, *Psychoanalysis and Religion*, 1950, 74, 76. Quoted with the permission of the Yale University Press.

BIBLIOGRAPHY

THE GREAT AND RAPIDLY GROWING literature dealing with ideas and their history in America cannot be described or even listed in a bibliography of appropriate length for the present volume. The following bibliography is intended for readers who may wish to push further in certain areas or subjects or who desire to explore points of view that differ from those expressed in the present work.

GENERAL

The pioneer study is V. L. Parrington, *Main Currents in American Thought*, 3 vols. (N.Y., 1927). Brilliant and provocative, American history interpreted with a Jeffersonian bias. The third volume (dealing with the post-Civil War period) is a collection of chapters and fragments left when Parrington died. Oscar Cargill, *Intellectual America* (N.Y., 1941), emphasizes literature and the migrations of ideas from Europe. Alfred Kazin, *On Native Grounds* (N.Y., 1942), contains a critical account of the American literature in the 20th century. Charles A. and Mary R. Beard, *The American Spirit* (N.Y., 1942), traces American intellectual history by means of single theme, the idea of civilization, and expresses a challenging humanistic "world view." Merle Curti, *The Growth of American Thought* (N.Y., 1943), covers the entire chronological story and relates ideas to the social matrix in which they function—an indispensable work. Van Wyck Brooks, *Makers and Finders: a History of the Writers in America, 1800–1915* (N.Y., 1936–1952). A major work in many volumes that deals with greater and lesser writers and with the intellectual climates of which they were a part. H. S. Commager, *The American Mind* (New Haven, 1950), opens with an interpretive chapter on the final decades of the nineteenth century and deals with all important aspects of thought in the twentieth. R. C. Spiller and others, *Literary History of the United States*, 3 vols. (N.Y., 1948). A cooperative history with chapters on individual writers and particular periods. Volume III contains complete bibliographies of writers. M. G. White, *Social Thought in America*

(N.Y., 1949), describes the revolt against nineteenth-century absolutisms in the early twentieth century as expressed in the work of Veblen, Holmes, Dewey, and C. A. Beard. R. D. Mosier, *The American Temper* (Berkeley, 1952), interprets American thought in terms of successive patterns (Puritanism, Enlightenment, Romanticism, and Pragmatism). L. B. Wright, *Culture on the Moving Frontier* (Bloomington, 1955), describes the agencies (churches, schools, textbooks, libraries, etc.) that subdued the tendencies toward barbarism on successive frontiers. Harvey Wish, *Society and Thought in America*, 2 vols. (N.Y., 1950–1952), contains parallel narratives of social and intellectual history. M. R. Cohen, *American Thought* (Glencoe, Ill., 1954). A posthumous collection of essays and fragments from the pen of a perceptive philosopher; assembled and edited by F. S. Cohen.

AMERICAN SOCIETY GENERAL

R. H. Gabriel, ed., *The Pageant of America*, 15 vols. 1926–1929. A series of topical volumes emphasizing pictures which are tied together and interpreted with extensive text. A. M. Schlesinger and D. R. Fox, eds., *A History of American Life*, 13 vols. (N.Y., 1927–1948). A series of period volumes each presenting a conspectus of the social and intellectual life of the time. R. H. Gabriel, ed., *The Library of Congress Series in American Civilization* (Cambridge, 1951; 19 volumes projected, 5 published). A series of topical volumes dealing with different aspects of American society in the twentieth century.

SELECTED SPECIALIZED STUDIES

W. J. Cash, *The Mind of the South* (N.Y., 1941). The impact of slavery on the thought of the South. Clement Eaton, *Freedom of Thought in the Old South* (Durham, 1940). The development in the ante-bellum South of an intellectual blockade against undesired ideas. H. N. Smith, *Virgin Land* (Cambridge, 1950). A new and important interpretation of the American frontier. Oscar Handlin, *The Uprooted* (Boston, 1951). A study of immigrants. R. Hofstadter, *Social Darwinism in American Thought, 1860–1915* (Philadelphia, 1944). An account of a basic change in thought in the period. Stow Persons, ed., *Evolutionary Thought in America* (New Haven, 1950). A group of studies on the wide ranging influence of Darwinism. D. Riesman and others, *The Lonely Crowd* (New Haven, 1950; abridged, N.Y., 1953). A study of changing American character in the twentieth century. D. M. Potter, *People in Plenty* (Chicago, 1954). An important study of the national character and a new interpretation of the frontier. E. W. Knight, *Fifty Years of American Education, 1900–1950* (N.Y., 1952). A widely ranging history covering topics from grammar to graduate school. J. L. Kandell, *The New Era in Education* (Boston, 1955). Educational problems and issues in an age of totalitarianism. F. O. Matthiessen,

American Renaissance (N.Y., 1941). An interpretation of the classical period in American literature with emphasis on aesthetic considerations. Charles Feidelson, Jr., *Symbolism and American Literature* (Chicago, 1953). An original and important interpretation of the classical and modern periods.

ECONOMIC THOUGHT

A. A. Berle, Jr. and Y. C. Means, *The Modern Corporation and Private Property* (1932). A study of the corporation in the 1920's. A. A. Berle, Jr., *The 20th Century Capitalist Revolution* (N.Y., 1954). A description and appraisal of the corporation in mid-century. P. Drucker, *The Concept of the Corporation* (N.Y., 1946). An analysis of the corporation as a social institution. S. B. Clough, *The American Way* (N.Y., 1953). A description of the American economic system prepared first for foreign readers. R. W. Davenport, *U.S.A. Permanent Revolution* (N.Y., 1951). A *Fortune* study of change and stability. Joseph Dorfman, *The Economic Mind in America*, 3 vols. (N.Y., 1946–1949). A thorough study of the period from 1606 to 1918. F. R. Dulles, *Labor in America* (N.Y., 1949). A study of the rise and importance of the modern labor movement. Siegfried Giedion, *Mechanization Takes Command* (N.Y., 1948). An analysis of mechanization in modern American industry. Norbert Wiener, *The Human Use of Human Beings*, rev. ed. (Garden City, 1954). A provocative analysis of the potentialities of cybernetics for society. J. G. Wylie, *The Self-made Man in America* (New Brunswick, 1954), a study of an American "myth."

POLITICAL THOUGHT

C. A. Beard, *The Republic* (N.Y., 1943). An inquiry in the form of a conversation into the nature of the Federal Republic. D. W. Brogan, *Politics in America* (N.Y., 1954). A survey, historical and analytical, by an informed Britisher of American political institutions and practices. E. S. Corwin, *The Constitution and What it Means Today*, 11th ed. (Princeton, 1954). A standard work of the place of the Constitution in American life. K. W. Deutch, *Nationalism and Social Communication* (N.Y., 1953). An interpretative analysis of nationalism as a social phenomenon. C. M. Destler, *American Radicalism, 1865–1901* (New London, 1946). A history of indigenous radicalism. H. H. Quint, *The Forging of American Socialism* (Columbia, S.C., 1953). Early Marxism in the U.S. D. D. Egbert and Stow Persons, eds., *Socialism and American Life* (Princeton, 1954). A useful collection of essays. Richard Hofstadter, *The American Political Tradition* (N.Y., 1948). Emphasizes the thought of leaders from Jefferson to F. D. Roosevelt. Louis Hartz, *The Liberal Tradition in America* (N.Y., 1955). A history of political theory in America in terms of Locke. A. M. Schlesinger, Jr.,

The Age of Jackson (1945). Emphasizes the liberal uprising in the East. A. M. Schlesinger, Jr., *The Vital Center* (Boston, 1949), a statement of liberal philosophy to meet post-World War II conditions. F. A. von Hayek, *The Road to Serfdom* (Chicago, 1944), discusses the dangers of the intrusion of the state into business. P. R. E. Viereck, *Conservatism Revisited: the Revolt Against Revolt* (N.Y., 1949). A lively discussion of conservatism. Clinton Rossiter, *Conservatism in America* (N.Y., 1955). A history of conservative thought from John Adams to the mid-twentieth century. Walter Lippmann, *The Public Philosophy* (Boston, 1955), an analysis of the decline of democracy in Western civilization and a proposed remedy. B. F. Wright, *American Interpretations of Natural Law* (1931). A study of natural law in the courts. W. O. Douglas, *An Almanac of Liberty* (Garden City, 1954), a selection of episodes, actions, and opinions emphasizing the defense of liberty. Elmer Davis, *But We Were Born Free* (Indianapolis, 1954). One of the most effective attacks on "McCarthyism."

RELIGIOUS THOUGHT

Catholicism in America (N.Y., 1954). Reprint of a series of articles from *Commonweal* by Catholics, one Jew, and one Protestant. K. S. Latourette, *The Great Century*, A.D. *1800*–A.D. *1914* (N.Y., 1941). A comprehensive history of Christianity in the U.S. A. P. Stokes, *Church and State in the United States*, 3 vols. (N.Y., 1950). A comprehensive and thorough study by a former canon of the Washington cathedral. A. C. McGiffert, *The Rise of Modern Religious Ideas* (N.Y., 1915). A work of basic importance. F. H. Foster, *The Modern Movement in American Theology* (N.Y., 1939). Important for the understanding of Modernism. C. H. Hopkins, *The Rise of the Social Gospel, 1865–1918* (New Haven, 1940). Primarily a history of ideas. W. S. Hudson, *The Great Tradition in the American Churches* (N.Y., 1953). A history of American Protestantism in terms of the principle of voluntary association. H. F. May, *Protestant Churches in Industrial America* (N.Y., 1949). A social history of the impact of industrialism and urbanism on the churches. Abbé Felix Klein, *Americanism: a Phantom Heresy* (Aquin Book Shop, Atchison, Kan., 1951). An account of the controversy by a French Catholic who opposed the criticisms in France of "Americanism." H. R. Niebuhr, *The Social Sources of American Denominationalism* (1929). Important for the social origins of several denominations. George Hammar, *Christian Realism in Contemporary American Theology* (Uppsala, Sweden, 1940). A study by a Swedish scholar of the positions of Reinhold Niebuhr, W. M. Horton, and H. P. Van Dusen. H. R. Niebuhr, *Christ and Culture* (N.Y., 1951), an important statement of aspects of mid-century Protestant thought. H. W. Schneider, *Religion in 20th Century*

America (Cambridge, 1952), a comprehensive study of organized religion.

PHILOSOPHICAL THOUGHT

P. R. Anderson and H. M. Fisch, *Philosophy in America* (N.Y., 1939). A useful survey. W. H. Werkmeister, *A History of Philosophical Ideas in America* (N.Y., 1949). An important critical history. P. P. Wiener, *Evolution and the Founders of Pragmatism* (Cambridge, 1949). A study of backgrounds.

SELECTED REFERENCES FOR PARTICULAR WRITERS

EMERSON

E. W. Emerson, ed. *The Complete Works of Ralph Waldo Emerson,* 12 vols. (Boston, 1903–1904). C. C. Bigelow, ed., *Uncollected Writings; Essays, Addresses, Poems, Reviews and Letters by Ralph Waldo Emerson* (N.Y., 1912). E. W. Emerson and W. E. Forbes, eds., *The Journals of Ralph Waldo Emerson,* 10 vols. (Boston, 1909–1914). R. L. Rusk, *The Life of Ralph Waldo Emerson* (N.Y., 1949). The standard biography. H. D. Gray, *Emerson: A Statement of New England Transcendentalism as Expressed in the Philosophy of its Chief Exponent* (Stanford, 1917). A leading study of Emerson as philosopher and critic.

THOREAU

H. G. D. Blake, ed., *Thoreau's Complete Works,* 5 vols. (Boston, 1929). H. S. Canby, *Thoreau* (Boston, 1939). A full-length biography that emphasizes Thoreau, the writer. J. W. Krutch, *Thoreau* (N.Y., 1948). A biography that emphasizes Thoreau's attitudes toward nature.

MELVILLE

R. M. Weaver, ed., *The Works of Herman Melville,* 16 vols. (London, 1922–1924). W. E. Sedgwick, *Herman Melville: The Tragedy of Mind* (Cambridge, 1944). A full-length biography. J. Leyda, *The Melville Log: A Documentary Life of Herman Melville, 1819–1891* (N.Y., 1951). Authoritative. N. Wright, *Melville's Use of the Bible* (Durham, 1949). A study of a neglected aspect of Melville's thought.

CALHOUN

R. K. Cralle, ed., *John C. Calhoun Works,* 6 vols. (N.Y., 1853–1855). C. M. Wiltse, *John C. Calhoun,* 3 vols. (Indianapolis, 1944–1951). The best biography.

LINCOLN

J. C. Nicholoy and J. Hay, *Abraham Lincoln, Complete Works,* 12 vols. (N.Y., 1905). C. Sandburg, *Abraham Lincoln: The Prairie Years,*

2 vols. (N.Y., 1926). *Abraham Lincoln, the War Years*, 4 vols. (N.Y., 1939). A vivid and detailed biography. J. G. Randall, *Lincoln, the President: Springfield to Gettysburg*, 2 vols. (N.Y., 1945). Continued as *Lincoln the Liberal Statesman* (N.Y., 1947). A biography founded on considerable hitherto unused material.

HENRY GEORGE

The Complete Works of Henry George, 10 vols. (Garden City, 1906–1911). C. A. Barker, *Henry George* (N.Y., 1955). A thorough study of George's life and thought.

BELLAMY

A. E. Morgan, *Edward Bellamy* (N.Y., 1944). A documented biography. A. E. Morgan, *The Philosophy of Edward Bellamy* (N.Y., 1945). Excerpts from Bellamy's writings and analysis of his social thought.

WARD

S. Chugerman, *Lester F. Ward, The American Aristotle* (Durham, 1939). The best study of Ward.

PEIRCE

P. P. Wiener and F. H. Young, eds., *Studies in the Philosophy of Charles Saunders Peirce* (Cambridge, 1952). T. A. Goudge, *The Thought of C. S. Peirce*, (Toronto, 1950). One of the best expositions of Peirce.

WILLIAM JAMES

R. B. Perry, *The Thought and Character of William James*, 2 vols. (Boston, 1935). Still the best study of James. H. M. Kallen, ed., *The Philosophy of William James: Drawn from his own Works*, (N.Y., 1925).

ROYCE

J. E. Smith, *Royce's Social Infinite* (N.Y., 1950). An interpretation of the development of Royce's thought which relates it to Christian theology. J. H. Cotton, *Royce of the Human Self* (Cambridge, 1954). A critical study of Royce's theory of the individual.

HOLMES

M. Lerner, ed., *The Mind and Faith of Justice Holmes* (Boston, 1943). Selections from his writings.

DEWEY

S. Hook, ed., John Dewey, *Philosopher of Science and Freedom: a Symposium* (N.Y., 1950). A collection of appraisals of Dewey. N. J. Fleckenstein, *A Critique of John Dewey's Theory of Nature and the*

Knowledge of Reality in the Light of the Principles of Thomism (Washington, D.C., 1954). M. C. Baker, *Foundations of John Dewey's Educational Theory* (N.Y., 1955). Essentials of Dewey's educational philosophy.

BROOKS ADAMS

A. F. Beringause, *Brooks Adams, a Biography* (N.Y., 1955). A thorough study.

HENRY ADAMS

W. H. Jordy, *Henry Adams: Scientific Historian* (New Haven, 1952). Best analysis of Henry Adams.

VEBLEN

Joseph Dorfman, *Thorstein Veblen and his America* (N.Y., 1934). Strong on Veblen's times. Louis Schneider, *The Freudian Psychology and Veblen's Social Theory* (N.Y., 1948).

INDEX